D1569941

Fetching the Old Southwest

Fetching the Old Southwest

Humorous Writing from Longstreet to Twain

James H. Justus

University of Missouri Press
Columbia and London

Copyright © 2004 by
The Curators of the University of Missouri
University of Missouri Press, Columbia, Missouri 65201
Printed and bound in the United States of America
All rights reserved
5 4 3 2 1   08 07 06 05 04

Library of Congress Cataloging-in-Publication Data

Justus, James H.
    Fetching the Old Southwest : humorous writing from Longstreet to Twain / James H. Justus.
        p.   cm.
    Includes index.
    ISBN 0-8262-1544-0 (alk. paper)
    1.   American wit and humor—Southwest, Old—History and criticism. 2.   Humorous stories, American—Southwest, Old—History and criticism. 3.   Longstreet, Augustus Baldwin, 1790–1870—Criticism and interpretation. 4.   American wit and humor—19th century—History and criticism. 5.   American literature—Southwest, Old—History and criticism. 6.   Twain, Mark, 1835–1910—Criticism and interpretation. 7.   Southwest, Old—Intellectual life. 8.   Popular culture—Southwest, Old. 9.   Southwest, Old—In literature.   I. Title.
    PS437.J87 2004
    641.5976—dc22

                                                                                        2004016547

♾ This paper meets the requirements of the
American National Standard for Permanence of Paper
for Printed Library Materials, Z39.48, 1984.

Designer: Jennifer Cropp
Typesetter: Crane Composition, Inc.
Printer and binder: Thomson-Shore, Inc.
Typefaces: Palatino, Caflisch Script, and Berkeley Book

For my sister
Jane Brookshire
and in memory of
Elizabeth Huff Justus (1904–2001)

Contents

Acknowledgments

In the several years I have been working on this project I have accrued many debts, beginning with my former students in three graduate seminars who, though they may have begun our sessions as skeptics, ended them by reading the humorous texts with fresh eyes, good ears, and workable methodologies. It is altogether appropriate that for a literature whose status has always depended upon the complex circuit between oral and written discourse, I should have been the fruitful beneficiary of both the freewheeling discussions of and imaginative essays on Big Bears, stomp-and-gouge fights, frontier parlor etiquette, disturbers of the peace, hunting protocols, confidence artistry, and the dynamics of yarn-spinning. I am particularly indebted to Keith Newlin, Charles Johanningsmeier, Edward Watts, and Sheila O'Brien.

Over the years specific individuals have contributed to the way I have read both the humorous texts and the primary forms, published and otherwise, contemporary with them. For their examples and suggestions I thank Ben Harris McClary, J. A. Leo Lemay, William Bedford Clark, Hershel Parker, Mary Ann Wimsatt, M. Thomas Inge, Jerome Loving, James Perkins, M. Jimmie Killingsworth, and George Brown Leach. I am especially grateful for the personal generosity and scrupulous scholarship of my late partner and colleague, Wallace E. Williams. This book has benefited enormously from the rigorous readings of an earlier draft by my Indiana University colleague Terence Martin and readers for the University of Missouri Press. Their suggestions and those of the press's director, Beverly Jarrett, have helped to make *Fetching the Old Southwest* more accurate and more shapely. I could not have asked for a more attentive editor than Gary Kass, whose searching queries did what all good critics do—sent me back to the texts. When I have failed, ignoring Captain Suggs's advice to make every edge cut, it has been my own fault.

My research has been facilitated by the tireless energies of the professional staff of the Indiana University Libraries and of the university's Lilly Library. My special thanks go to Anya Peterson Royce for her encouragement as former dean of faculties and to the Graduate School and its divisions at Indiana University for two sabbatical leaves. I am grateful to Barbara A. Johnson for her editorial acumen and to Dean Mendenhall and Andrew Hoover, who tried to make the computer and its mysteries less intimidating to me.

As I hope the following pages will show, my work has been measurably strengthened by the testimony of countless diarists, correspondents, and keepers of daybooks to be found in many collections of personal and family papers that have been preserved by caring hands. This body of writing from both the literate middle class and the semiliterate yeomanry is a rich documentary record housed in many libraries. I am especially indebted to the personnel of several institutions who were unfailingly generous in giving me access to their magnificent collections, and who often suggested relevant documents that I had known nothing about: University of Memphis, University of Georgia, Emory University, Georgia Historical Society, Alabama Department of Archives and History, University of Alabama, Louisiana State University, Mississippi Department of Archives and History, University of Mississippi, University of Southern Mississippi, and Samford University.

I wish also to thank the American Association for State and Local History for a grant-in-aid for research for necessary travel. Finally, my thanks go to Curtis E. White for his companionship and cheerful patience in transporting me and my notebooks all across the lower South at a crucial stage in the project.

Abbreviations

I have noted directly in the text page references for quotations from the humorous sketches. Secondary references and additional commentary are found in the footnotes. For bibliography, see Edward J. Piacentino's compilation "Humor of the Old South: A Comprehensive Bibliography," in *The Humor of the Old South*, ed. M. Thomas Inge and Edward J. Piacentino (Lexington: University Press of Kentucky, 2001), 263–309. Abbreviations of the most frequently cited works are as follows:

AS   *Life and Public Services of an Army Straggler*, by Kittrell J. Warren (1865; reprint, ed. Floyd C. Watkins, Athens: University of Georgia Press, 1961)

Cohen   *Humor of the Old Southwest*, ed. Hennig Cohen and William B. Dillingham, 3rd ed. (Athens: University of Georgia Press, 1994)

CP   *Major Jones's Chronicles of Pineville: Embracing Sketches of Georgia Scenes, Incidents, and Characters*, by William Tappan Thompson (Philadelphia: T. B. Peterson, 1845).

DC   *A Narrative of the Life of David Crockett of the State of Tennessee by David Crockett* (1834; reprint, ed. James A. Shackford and Stanley J. Folmsbee, Knoxville: University of Tennessee Press, 1973)

FT   *The Flush Times of Alabama and Mississippi: A Series of Sketches*, by Joseph Glover Baldwin (1853; reprint, ed. James H. Justus, Baton Rouge: Louisiana State University Press, 1987)

GS   *Augustus Baldwin Longstreet's* Georgia Scenes *Completed: A Scholarly Text*, ed. David Rachels (Athens: University of Georgia Press, 1998)

HET *The Humor of H. E. Taliaferro*, ed. Raymond C. Craig (Knoxville: University of Tennessee Press, 1987)

HJ *Ham Jones, Ante-Bellum Southern Humorist: An Anthology*, ed. Willene Hendrick and George Hendrick (Hamden, CT: Archon, 1990)

HT *High Times and Hard Times: Sketches and Tales by George Washington Harris*, ed. M. Thomas Inge (Nashville: Vanderbilt University Press, 1967)

MJC *Major Jones's Courtship: Detailed, with Other Scenes, Incidents, and Adventures, in a Series of Letters by Himself*, by William Tappan Thompson (1843; revised and augmented in 1872; reprint, Atlanta: Cherokee Publishing, 1973)

MJS *Major Jones's Sketches of Travel, Comprising the Scenes, Incidents, and Adventures in His Tour from Georgia to Canada*, by William Tappan Thompson (Philadelphia: Carey & Hart, 1848)

MW *Mississippi Writings*, by Mark Twain (New York: Library of America, 1982)

Oehl. *Old Southwest Humor from the* St. Louis Reveille, *1844–1850*, ed. Fritz Oehlschlaeger (Columbia: University of Missouri Press, 1990)

PPW *Polly Peablossom's Wedding; and Other Tales*, ed. T. A. Burke (Philadelphia: T. B. Peterson, 1851).

PW *Cavorting on the Devil's Fork: The Pete Whetstone Letters of C. F. M. Noland*, ed. Leonard Williams (Memphis, TN: Memphis State University Press, 1979)

RT *Rowdy Tales from Early Alabama: The Humor of John Gorman Barr*, ed. G. Ward Hubbs (University: University of Alabama Press, 1981).

SD *Odd Leaves from the Life of a Louisiana Swamp Doctor*, by Henry Clay Lewis, ed. Edwin T. Arnold (1850; reprint, Baton Rouge: Louisiana State University Press, 1997)

SL *Sut Lovingood. Yarns Spun by a "Nat'ral Born Durn'd Fool.["] Warped and Wove for Public Wear*, by George Washington Harris (New York: Dick & Fitzgerald, 1867)

SS *Adventures of Captain Simon Suggs, Late of the Tallapoosa Volunteers; Together with "Taking the Census" and Other Alabama Sketches*, by Johnson Jones Hooper, ed. Johanna Nicol Shields (Tuscaloosa: University of Alabama Press, 1993)

SSL *Streaks of Squatter Life, and Far-West Scenes*, by John S. Robb (1847; reprint, ed. John Francis McDermott, Delmar, NY: Scholars' Facsimiles & Reprints, 1978)

TBT   *A New Collection of Thomas Bangs Thorpe's Sketches of the Old Southwest,* ed. David C. Estes (Baton Rouge: Louisiana State University Press, 1989)

TM   *Theatrical Management in the West and South for Thirty Years,* by Solomon F. Smith (1868; reprint, New York: Benjamin Blom, 1968)

Fetching the Old Southwest +≡❧

Introduction

The South-West, embracing an extensive and highly interesting portion of the United States, is completely *caviare* to the multitude.

—Edgar Allan Poe

i.

The reputation of the actual southern backwoods is itself a history-rich narrative of long standing, but the transformation of that literal geography by a wondrous and often lying imagination has always been a better one. The colonial origins of this better story should never be underestimated; the most telling literary record, however, is the one collectively produced by amateur writers from the 1830s to the Civil War. James Atkins Shackford tells the story of this enterprise in three impeccable sentences:

> Two of the very earliest products of this new literacy were David Crockett's *Autobiography,* by a real backwoodsman himself; and Augustus Longstreet's *Georgia Scenes,* by a literary man making use of those materials for his own literary purposes. It developed through a long line of humorists, and finally culminated in Mark Twain. The original strain at last petered out as the primitive conditions of life out of which it had grown disappeared.[1]

1. James Atkins Shackford, "David Crockett, the Legend and the Symbol," in *The Frontier Humorists: Critical Views,* ed. M. Thomas Inge (Hamden, CT: Archon, 1975), 209.

The economy of that summary would seem to obviate the necessity for any long-winded rehashing in books about southern humor, including this one. Yet redundancy, which happens to be a conspicuous feature in the humorous sketches, has never discouraged academics, including this one.

When colleagues in better-known academic fields have expressed their curiosity about "Southwest humor," they have usually assumed that my decades-long fascination with the subject was a geographical departure from my work in southern literature. When on rare occasions I have confessed to inquiring strangers on air flights that I was engaged in writing a book on humor of the Old Southwest, I have appreciated their interest: "I know a few cowboy yarns" and "Do you include Hispanic jokes?" and, once, "My sister is married to an oil company guy in Houston, and he specializes in stories about drunk cattlemen." Like most of the antebellum humorists (and like most academics who are drawn to them), I have always been receptive to storytellers. Cutting to the bone is an intuitive gesture for these strangers, one that shares a quality of the kind of ephemeral newspaper prose that lies at the center of my interest: the assumption that jokes must have goats and that ordinary life is a negotiation of rival claims and needs. The (present) Southwest is a rich geography of masculine competition that the scribes of the (historic) Old Southwest would have understood.

Buffs of certain popular forms like to think that their favorites—detective fiction, science fiction, international spy thrillers—are snobbishly neglected by critical elitists (though that is clearly not an issue wherever "cultural studies" have taken the field); but, as I have elsewhere argued, critical attention to antebellum southern newspaper humor has never gone wanting, beginning with its flourishing in the 1830s and 1840s.[2] As numerous bibliographies show, the commentary has been with us almost as long as the humor itself. That commentary, however, has most often followed the preference of the antebellum authors themselves for short forms: the brief notice, the essay, the scholarly article, the critical sketch of a single subject, chapters in books on larger topics. *Fetching the Old Southwest: Humorous Writing from Longstreet to Twain* originated several years ago as an attempt at a comprehensive account of this significant writing in one book-length study. Whatever virtue can be claimed for the treatment of authors I have included, even this long volume neglects many

2. James H. Justus, introduction to *The Humor of the Old South*, ed. M. Thomas Inge and Edward J. Piacentino (Lexington: University Press of Kentucky, 2001), 1.

sketches of important pseudonymous scribes and even some interesting writers who wrote under their real names. As the project gradually evolved into a cultural study of the era that gave birth to this writing, I kept before me three working assumptions:

1. Though the writing from the Old Southwest is more varied in genre than is customarily assumed, in both bulk and interest its humor is the most important.

2. Though there are significant differences in topics, techniques, and purposes among the dozens of writers who contributed to this movement, certain features are so configured that we can make some generalizations about their common created world.

3. Despite the imaginative latitude, conceptual intensity, and stylistic exaggeration of the writing, the humorists' created world is a reliable index to the social and cultural actualities of the lower South in the thirty-odd years before the Civil War.

Of these assumptions, the third has proved to be troublesome. For many years both literary and social historians believed that this writing, however funny it may be, was valuable as a resource—that is, as primary documents in social history. Specifically, two of the best collections of lawyers-turned-authors, Augustus B. Longstreet's *Georgia Scenes* (1835) and Joseph G. Baldwin's *Flush Times of Alabama and Mississippi* (1853), figured in some historiographical circles as trustworthy texts for telling us what we should know about the antebellum South. Unlike, say, the plantation novel, whose idealized romantic trappings made even regional historians uncomfortable, the protorealistic spirit of these "amateur" sketches invited readers to see their depiction of rawboned society as a truer reflection of the lower South before war made it into a nation.

The argument was persuasive. As so many of the writers claimed at the time, the humor depicts the customs, manners, habits, amusements, and speech of the settlers and transients whose life in the backwater South and West contrasted notably with civilization in the North and East. The desire to record a way of life before it disappeared seemed often to be the chief motive for the professionals who became authors. That motive was articulated explicitly by William T. Porter, the editor of the *Spirit of the Times,* the New York weekly that did so much to popularize the ungenteel prose from the South and West. His two anthologies in 1845 and 1854 were, in effect, efforts at an informal social history. There is no reason to suppose, however, that such justifications, either in the original pieces or in Porter's shrewd compilations, were anything more than expedient rationales for a body of writing whose subject matter and the vernacular styles for rendering it seemed to depart so radically from conventional standards of literary art.

ii.

George Catlin, the nineteenth-century artist who made Native Americans his signature western icon, once lamented: "Few people even know the true definition of the term 'West'; and where is its location?—phantom-like it flies before us as we travel." The term still fluctuates, as Edwin Fussell noted, between what we think of as *location* and its more relative meaning as *direction*.[3]

For one of the humorist authors, Richard Smith Elliott, "the West" in antebellum days meant "the country between the Mississippi and the Alleghenies." For a Hudson Valley writer like James Kirke Paulding, "west" was nearer than far: he wrote an admirer in 1837 that he would feel rooted in "the Soil of my Country" only when he could gain the respect of the "Great West," the "depository" of all the "genuine characteristicks of Americans." The recipient of this letter lived in Cincinnati.[4] Elsewhere, Paulding described the Mississippi River—yet farther west than Cincinnati—as the great artery "of the immense region that extends from nobody knows whence, to the Lord knows where." Two historians have reminded us that the federal bureaucracy in the late eighteenth century "had only the haziest knowledge of this portion of the nation's frontier." As late as 1844, in a history designed for schoolchildren, Lambert Lilly identified the "Western States" as those "states and territories which make up a large part of the Valley of the Mississippi River."[5] Even before the Civil War, which tended to settle some ambiguities, it was somewhat easier to designate "South"—it comprised all those states allowing slavery. Yet in the early years of tumultuous settlement, the lower southern states and territories were, alternately and interchangeably, South and West, or (with neat practicality) the South-West. Regional location phrases

3. Edwin Fussell, *Frontier: American Literature and the American West* (Princeton, NJ: Princeton University Press, 1965), 3–4, 141.

4. Richard Smith Elliott, *Notes Taken in Sixty Years* (St. Louis, 1883), 113; *The Letters of James Kirke Paulding*, ed. Ralph M. Aderman (Madison: University of Wisconsin Press, 1962), 190.

5. James Kirke Paulding, *Letters from the South by a Northern Man* (1817; rev. ed., New York, 1835), 1:154; Thomas D. Clark and John D. W. Guice, *The Old Southwest, 1795–1830: Frontiers in Conflict* (Norman: University of Oklahoma Press, 1996), 1; Lambert Lilly, *The History of the Western States* (Boston, 1844), 9.

such as "at the South" and "at the West" commonly referred to the same geography, and in the minds of those who migrated to the region after the War of 1812, the conjunction of South and West was both a literal and metaphorical condition. A wag once remarked that it was called the Southwest because it was south and west of Boston, thereby fixing the spiritual and cultural divide between civilization and promise. In the "cartography of the mind," writes one historian, "South and West enticed and menaced in similar ways."[6] That similarity was the imaginative premise behind the reports of almost every foreign visitor to the United States.

Geographers complain of regionalists who expend too much energy "trying to put boundaries that do not exist around areas that do not matter."[7] But the Old Southwest did have boundaries—give or take a state or two—and it was an area that would matter a great deal for what Flannery O'Connor called "nashnul" interests. Although the Old Southwest technically centered on the territory of the future states of Alabama and Mississippi ("the Creek-dominated region of Georgia west of the Ocmulgee River and the area south of the Tennessee River"), the "almost accidental development of a distinctive regional economy and society" transcended official designations.[8] Latitude in terminology was never troubling to earlier observers of the "new country" as they cheerfully described the topography, climate, and wildlife in Alabama, Mississippi, Louisiana, Kentucky, Tennessee, and, later, Arkansas and Texas. Except for Kentucky, these were still the states categorized as the Southwest in the federal census of 1850.[9]

For the purposes of this book, I have chosen to be as inclusive as logic allows in the matter of relevant geography. Where writing from contiguous areas has seemed pertinent, I have risked becoming the expedient imperialist by annexing North Carolina and Missouri to my cultural map of the Old Southwest. By the same token, although some scholars prefer *southern frontier humor* or *humor of the Old South* as more accurate designations for the region's most characteristic writing, I have chosen to retain

6. Lewis O. Saum, *The Popular Mood of Pre–Civil War America* (Westport, CT: Greenwood, 1980), 220.

7. George H. T. Kimble, "The Inadequacy of the Regional Concept," in *London Essays in Geography*, ed. Lawrence D. Stamp and Sidney W. Woolridge (London: Longmans, Green, 1951), 159.

8. Clark and Guice, *Old Southwest*, ix.

9. Gilbert Imlay, *A Topographical Description of the Western Territory of North America*, 3rd ed. (1797; reprint, New York: A. M. Kelley, 1969), 524; Frederick Jackson Turner, *The United States 1830–1850: The Nation and Its Sections* (1935; reprint, Gloucester, MA: Peter Smith, 1958), 32–33.

the older form, which acknowledges that most of this writing appeared after the frontier line had moved farther west and which dissolves most traces of the Confederate genteel that mythmakers once promoted for anything southern. For most of the twentieth century the amusing newspaper sketches that flourished in American journalism from the 1830s to the Civil War were called humor of "the Old Southwest."

From the very beginning, Judge Longstreet knew that the example and authority of Savannah and Augusta never quite encompassed Georgia's rawer settlements. As Leo Lemay has demonstrated, the prototypes of this ephemeral writing can be found in Virginia and Maryland in both their colonial period and in the early Republic.[10] Even South Carolina was fertile ground for producers (and consumers) of the humor we designate *southwestern*, in part because even seaboard states contained wide, uneven swatches of scenery and population that the newspaper authors favored. Although in *Fetching the Old Southwest* I have occasionally become a squatter in expanded geography, I have tried to exercise restraint by not becoming a settler there.

As late as 1860, William Henry Milburn was describing the development of the Mississippi Valley in terms that later frontier historians would find pertinent. Western character, concluded the clergyman, inclined to "close scuffling and grappling, a sort of knock-down attitude visible through all the moods" of its "representative" members.[11] By the time he wrote, Milburn's description was not merely the result of experience in the scuffling new country: it was built upon the voluminous volumes of other authors, foreign and domestic, who with scant variation had been evaluating the manners, customs, speech patterns, and values of the Southwest for a half-century. It also reflected the less solemn accounts of the humorists who, beginning in the early 1830s, had entertained thousands of readers. Paulding's depository of "genuine characteristicks" was a rich if ambiguous miscellany to be found in Sartartia as well as Cincinnati— and in Devil's Fork, Tuscaloosa, Fisher's River, Hardscrabble, Cockerell's Bend, and Eufalia, sites that bore little resemblance to those that migrating sons had abandoned in South Carolina and Virginia.

With the benefit of hindsight, we might guess that many patrician Virginians found the new country hard going because it was more western

10. J. A. Leo Lemay, "The Origins of the Humor of the Old South," in *The Humor of the Old South*, ed. M. Thomas Inge and Edward J. Piacentino, 13–21 (Lexington: University Press of Kentucky, 2001).

11. William Henry Milburn, *The Pioneers, Preachers, and People of the Mississippi Valley* (New York, 1860), 355.

than southern. It prefigured social and cultural patterns that Americans after about 1870 came to regard as western: unlettered vitality; stubborn individualism (both grim and comic varieties); a bent toward risk-taking; boom-and-bust towns; casual violence and summary justice; civil behavior only partly socialized by eastern conventions; the prominence of eccentrics and scofflaws; cattle-raising and herding as a major occupation; and an uneasy accommodation to a Native American presence. Only its richer ethnic mix made the Far West substantially different from the largely Anglo Southwest. What became familiar moments in the later "western"—saloon fights, shoot-outs in dusty streets, lonely ranchers vulnerable to Indian raids, life in military garrisons—have their prequels in the humorous writing of the Old Southwest: stomp-and-gouge fights, country boys ripe for conning, hunters and rivermen ripe for challenge, and village matrons and know-it-alls busily civilizing their neighbors.

There is yet another aspect of how the southwestern frontier and its aftermath anticipated that of the Far West. If such popular forms as the dime novel, the Hollywood film, and television serials have forever inscribed "the western" as a genre that tends to amalgamate and foreshorten a vast geography and a half-century into scenes, situations, and characters of about 1870, so too the popular humor of a generation earlier depicts the people and places of the newly resettled Indian lands of the Mississippi Valley with scarcely a hint of historical development or discriminating locales. Except for Baldwin's *Flush Times,* with its raucous etiology of a country "just setting up," the humor unfolds as a kind of *found condition.* There is an assumption that a backcountry exists, one of forests and clearings, scantily populated by squatters, hunters, trappers, and eccentric loners; yet the authors' interest is customarily focused on crossroads, hamlets, and villages like Rackinsack, whose often transient population behaves like most residents in older, conventional towns, interacting for business and pleasure with undisguised self-interest. Although backwoods roarers are bellicose enough to trumpet their *particular* sites as the best on earth (not just Arkansas, but the Devil's Fork on the Little Red River; not just Mississippi, but the Yazoo hills), their garrulous identifications with place are so rhetorically perfunctory that one booster's favored spot is indistinguishable from another's. They *all* live in the most fertile region, where unsurpassingly rich soil raises up prodigal harvests of corn, cotton, buxom girls, and fearless fighters. Moreover, the authors themselves are remarkably indifferent to the individualizing of a geography that their subjects call home.

Georgia Scenes (1835) inspired imitation in a spirit of rivalry appropriate to the general tenor of its time and place. That spirit led amateur writers to anchor their reports in a supposedly tangible topography. A favorite maneuver was to suggest uniqueness of place in titles that were state-specific: *Mississippi Scenes* (1851); *Kups of Kauphy: A Georgia Book in Warp and Woof* (1853); *The Flush Times of Alabama and Mississippi* (1853); *Fisher's River (North Carolina) Scenes and Characters* (1859); *Odd Leaves from the Life of a Louisiana Swamp Doctor* (1850). But except for Henry Clay Lewis's bizarre, Poe-esque scene-painting of Louisiana swamp country, the humorous sketches in these books only indifferently depict specific cultural customs or the geographical peculiarities of distinct locales. Longstreet's Georgia is intended to represent the raw and morally unenlightened counties west of Augusta and Savannah; Baldwin's Alabama and Mississippi are geographically uniform; Joseph B. Cobb's Mississippi could be any of the states below the Ohio River and north of Louisiana. Almost from the first, the correspondents sent in their dispatches dutifully datelined Tuscaloosa; Greeneville, East Tennessee; Baton Rouge; Hawkins County, Kentucky; Little Rock—as if the geography mattered. But like many of the backwoods figures that the sketches celebrated, the woods and villages in which their verbal and physical exploits are set all look, sound, and feel the same. Moreover, practical jokes, embarrassing episodes, and adventures in the wild are narratively no different in 1855 from what they were in 1835. In the reading experience, it is almost as if settlement had always been a completed process.[12]

For most of the humorists, landscape is human geography, and the space meriting their attention, despite demographic history, has already filled up: there are too many people (especially lawyers), and raw nature seems strangely circumscribed. Trails, rivers, and canebrakes are as domestically shaped as cabins, stables, and churches. Landscape—nature unshaped by the human hand—is crowded with frolics, courtings, quiltings, faro games, oyster suppers, camp meetings. One curious effect of this discursive density is not that the backcountry has suddenly taken on liveliness and diversity (the advantages of towns), but that the mythic backwoods, stripped of their natural definition and function, have been replaced by glut and disorder, the price that boom times exact for more

---

12. Until 1850 the individual states of the lower South inspired in their residents a remarkably thin affirmation of affection and loyalty, sharing traits found in modern urban areas. See Kenneth M. Stampp, *The Imperiled Union* (New York: Oxford, 1980), 255, 265; Frank E. Vandiver, "The Confederacy and the American Tradition," *Journal of Southern History* 28 (1962): 280–81; Michael O'Brien, "The Lineaments of Antebellum Southern Romanticism," *Journal of American Studies* 20 (1986): 174–76.

sequenced development. In an atmosphere of frenetic social and economic competition, place is not special—it is simply where such jockeying occurs. For the humorists who have left us this picture, attitudes toward their necessary settings are ready-made, casual, conventionalized.

For all their thinness in geographical particulars and their casual reliance upon character types, the sketches of the humorous authors enjoy the merit of many other kinds of effective writing: the sense of having been generated out of an actual place by authoritative observers. The writers who aspired to make oral storytelling the nub of their verbal art began with the clear understanding that what they wanted to do was not simply to tell jokes—a staple way of killing time then as now.

iii.

What is the difference between a humorous anecdote and a joke? Both are informed by the local circumstances of their telling, and the success of both depends upon the narrating skills of a performer, one who is conditioned by an immediate audience that may inspire variations in detail and emphasis from performance to performance. Replicability is the single formal requirement of each. The joke is, as it were, an abstract of a humorous narrative in which the agents are not characters but generic types—"a doctor," "an old maid," "a rabbi and a priest," or even "this man"—who wait for their summons in some imaginary greenroom and who then interact in a pre-scripted situation justified only by the verbal wit of Anonymous. The most notable feature of the joke is its minimalism, its deliberate skeletal form, as if its creator were too bored to bother with the enriching substantiveness that would individualize the participants or setting; the creator is dominated by ends, not means, defined mostly by eschatological desire. The oral narrative may also be shaped only to realize its "point," but not necessarily so. The teller of the anecdote relishes means as well as ends: the significant detail, but also the sheerly ornamental, the trivial, the redundant, the red herring. The oral narrator gives names to his characters and distinctive tags to their voices, their clothes, their obsessions.

Garden-variety editors of antebellum newspapers, those who made no pretense of doubling as humorous correspondents, routinely made up their columns with "fillers"—oral jokes reduced to a couple of sentences: in effect, abstracts of abstracts. (The form raggedly survives in the pages of the *Old Farmer's Almanac* and *Grit,* but many fillers in nineteenth-century newspapers are so stripped down that they resemble arcane residual texts from a forgotten culture, baffling and vexing, and inviting the kind of investigative gloss that would require a subsidiary text three times their length.) The humorists were observers of a culture that their readers might regard as alien—indeed, they shared this view even as some of them participated in the life of that culture, and that stance allowed them, even at their most patronizing, to report on the doings and sayings of real men and women. Although a few anecdotes, even of the more gifted authors, are damagingly abbreviated (sometimes comprising only a single paragraph), all of them were composed as something other than filler. Verbal byplay, give-and-take action, audience response, authorial intervention: the usual components of the humorous anecdote are compositionally predictable, but the specific articulations—the relative space devoted to detail, the complexity of motive and action, the orthographical precision—show the writers grappling with the means for rendering what they actually saw, heard, and experienced.

Fillers, the verbal version of jokes, came from no place. In his immodest effort to represent "human nature," Anonymous had to answer to no actual human nature. The humorists' anecdotes began as a kind of peephole into a culture that was actual even if it was strange and marginal in the eyes of its readers; they ended as windows on a culture temporally and spatially circumscribed by a majority culture whose development depended upon patterns of orderly process. The humorous sketches worked because, I suspect, their chief subjects seemed resistant to a national agenda; the authors' business was to profile those characters irrelevant to the principles of coherent progress: oddities, eccentrics, specialized specimens—characters, not "human nature." Fillers were the voice of society at large; the humorous sketches were conceived as the collective voice of the American backwash imitated in print.

In their waning years, my two elderly aunts in East Tennessee lived side by side on the same street, intimate neighbors as well as loving sisters. Judith, the elder, though she had presided over the burial of three husbands, honored the memory of her third, a preacher, by recalling his jokes for the presumable enjoyment of others. She was a splendid raconteur, equally comfortable with the generic jokes her last husband preferred and those stories she remembered from family lore of more than a half-century before, as well as anecdotes of friends and relatives of more recent vintage. Hattie, whose singular trait was a refusal to lie, even to indulge in the mild "white" kind customarily told in the unpremeditated aura of social intercourse, enjoyed hearing stories of real people—those she knew or knew of—caught in embarrassing situations. She liked stories of actual local life, even gossip that contained names, dates, and figures, and was impatient with Judith's recital of *mere jokes*. If she came into the room at the end of one of her sister's performances for visitors, she invariably wanted to know what she had missed—"Who did that?" or "Where was this?"—and upon being assured it was "just a joke," she let her body communicate her response: a perceptible snort, a slight shake of the head, a dismissive hand gesture, sometimes an audible *oh* that was at once an expression of disappointment and a deflationary critique. (Once when an up-to-date cousin repeated one of the jokes of Irvin S. Cobb, Hattie mumbled that she didn't know any Cobbs.) As a storyteller, Judith was liberal and capacious, an eager exploiter of narratives both found and made. As a critic, Hattie knew what she liked: circumstantial tales, fat and filled-out, shapeless perhaps, but meaningful because they were, at least in their origins, true. Jokes could be dismissed because they were nothing but fabrications, made-up stories without significance since they dealt with human beings in the abstract—generics who had even less reality for Hattie than did people from North Carolina.

Although she didn't care for jokes, Hattie always appreciated her sister's storytelling techniques, and when family anecdotes were the occasion, Judith could be expected to deliver the enjoyment that Hattie always expected of real stories. The sources may have been true enough, but what most mattered was the storytelling moment and the artful structuring of the stories, with special attention to pacing, details (often repeated for emphasis), and climax. Judith's knowledge of Mark Twain was spotty, but she knew all about his principle of the "snapper."

It is doubtful that my aunts ever heard of the antebellum antecedents of Twain, but the characters who populated their narrative world would not have been alien to them. Unlettered, even illiterate figures drawn from what is now designated as "southern plain folk" shamble, stalk, and strut their way through the humorous sketches, fictive ancestors of the actual people familiar to southerners for most of the twentieth century. Despite historians' efforts to clarify and discriminate, the spectrum of plain folk was (and is) wider than the popular image would have it. *Poor white*, alas, is still the shorthand most comfortable for Americans.

Over the past two decades or so we have grown smugly self-congratulatory in developing a more "humane" view of the traditional objects of our laughter: African Americans, Irish cops, Jewish mothers, mothers-in-law, gay men. "Consciousness raising," writes one authority, "is in fact, the name we give to the gradual elimination of permissible targets of mockery."[13] In the 1980s a distinguished critic of American literature, lecturing on *Huckleberry Finn*, remarked in passing that the southern redneck was the only definable group remaining in our society unprotected by political correctness. As far as I can determine, that observation still holds. Poor white southerners (and some not so poor) are the only coherent group for whom others' scorn can be candidly ventilated through jokes and epithets without fear of censure.

Though always a substantial presence, marginalized whites in the South, a region itself marginalized for so many years of the republic, have survived this attitude along with poverty and bad health care. Indeed, they have endured (it might be argued) by the strength of others' scorn and without much interest in assuming protective coloring, those means that other minorities rely on so matter-of-factly: name changing, passing, imitation (of tonier tastes in cuisines, clothes, house furnishings), voice coaching, putting down roots elsewhere, learning to shop like Fitzgerald's Nicole rather than Rosemary. Over time, their aggressive integrity in being poor white—their stubborn refusal to sacrifice their amusements, their tastes, their religion, their speech—has in fact resulted in some cultural victories, notably the absorption into the national consciousness of such disparate phenomena as country music, fundamentalist religion, stock-car racing, Wal-Mart, and the militia movement. We may feel safe in denigrating the common white southerner, but it has been difficult to ignore him. The historical course of the poor white's relations with his economic and social betters has ranged unevenly, from the exasperation of William Byrd with the colonial lubbers to the bemused tolerance of the southwestern humorists for antebellum yeomen.[14] It has compassed fear and loathing, political opportunism, and humanitarian outreach during twentieth-century depression and war. During the literary flourishing we call the Southern Renascence, varieties of the type have been given impressive readings by Faulkner, Warren, Welty, and O'Connor; they have been rendered by such diverse techniques as reductive realism (T. S. Stribling), comic grotesquerie (Erskine Caldwell), and redemptory meditation (James Agee). In short, the southern poor white has not suffered literary neglect.

The aim of the present study is not to focus on how this figure prospers among the Longstreet generation of authors, though in fact he comes to

13. Marcel Gutwirth, *Laughing Matter: An Essay on the Comic* (Ithaca, NY: Cornell University Press, 1993), 62.

14. William Byrd, *Histories of the Dividing Line betwixt Virginia and North Carolina*, ed. William K. Boyd and Percy G. Adams (New York: Dover, 1967), 91–92.

us in that writing as more varied, sympathetic, and complex than we might have any reason to expect from "gifted amateurs." While he sometimes sports the typal tag of *cracker* (*redneck* became the favorite successor term), he is not always poor, and he shows more characterological depth than many later avatars. Though the Old Scots term for a boastful fellow is appropriate for much of this writing, *cracker* by the 1830s had become so generalized that the authors found few occasions to use it. Writing from the Old Southwest is dominated by sturdy figures in the margins who rarely share their creators' embrace of the modern, but it is more comprehensive in scope than we might expect. In the interaction of the well-spoken (literates, if not always gentlemen) with the *only*-spoken (quasi-literates) lies a larger cultural scene of accommodation that, in part, accounts for the vigor and enterprise of southern antebellum life before it was found wanting by revisionists.

In *Fetching the Old Southwest* I have used *cracker* only when the context requires it (as in my discussion of John S. Robb's lengthy definition) and tried to avoid *poor white*, primarily because its continued popularity among armchair sociologists belittles more than it describes, and secondarily because the humorists themselves tended not to think of their subjects in this categorical way. One of their rationales for writing was to document "originals," "characters," individuals who stood out as remarkable specimens among the mass. (Even the Whiggiest authors only rarely used the smirky catch-all term "the democracy," commonly found in planters' correspondence and some travelers' accounts.) For my own convenience, and at the risk of imprecision, my generalization of choice is usually *yeoman*.[15] This stalwart archaism, itself blurred in association, is more neutral than any of the pejoratives on hand; it also has the virtue of inclusiveness of the wide range of backcountry types as the humorists and their contemporaries portrayed them. When the context is the convergence of educated narrators and backwoods storytellers, I have used *vernacular* to apply to both speaker and his speech.

15. Definitions of *yeomen, plain folk, common people, poor whites,* and even *planters* remain awkwardly elusive; see David M. Potter, "Depletion and Renewal in Southern History," in *Perspectives on the South: Agenda for Research,* ed. Edgar T. Thompson (Durham, NC: Duke University Press, 1967), 84. For a summary of arguments over terminology, see Randolph B. Campbell, "Planters and Plain Folk: The Social Structure of the Antebellum South," in *Interpreting Southern History: Historiographical Essays in Honor of Sanford W. Higginbotham,* ed. John B. Boles and Evelyn T. Nolen, 48–77 (Baton Rouge: Louisiana State University Press, 1987).

Henry James had Rudyard Kipling in mind when he praised the freshness of an art that took as its subject "the vulgar majority, the coarse, receding edges of the social perspective," but that majority was not only
the favored subject of the antebellum humorists; it also demanded of its
practitioners a corresponding style.[16] From the beginning, these sketches,
even when the best ones had been gathered into hardcover collections by
publishers in Philadelphia and New York, were unequivocally "vulgar"
fare. The bumptiousness we often associate with this writing comes primarily, of course, from "vernacular speakers," not the educated authorial
stand-ins. One of the striking traits of southwestern humor is the persistent, scrubby coarseness it aggressively projects as an impudent alternative discourse to respectable literature. It professes to be the bad boy among
the Sunday schoolers, opposed to the decorous, the elegant, the genteel.
It claims for itself the earthy path of unrestraint, as if life comes not from
civilized seemliness but from gross, unfettered extravagance spoken and
acted in concert to undercut a style based on taste and grace. It shouts, it
calls attention to itself, it celebrates lingual outlawry even as it honors the
disdained and rough margins of American society.

Yet, as we might expect from a body of writing that noisily pushes its
difference, the truth is considerably less brazen. It sometimes tries too
hard to be the mode of the rebel, so much so that its rhetorical flamboyance puts the lie to the fiction that this is writing that is *real* or *sincere* or
natural. Plain-folk vernacular, then as now, only rarely can bear the heavy
sheen of artifice that the humorists love to employ. There is perhaps no
more composed writing in the nineteenth century than the humorous
sketches. Their aesthetic calculation, even when the frail talent that sets
pen to paper dooms many of them to mediocrity, occasionally rivals the
fastidiousness of a Henry James. At the same time, the sketches are a riot
of conventions. As discourse, they come down to us as a compendium of
available materials—not merely the pool of character types and comic
situations, but also the linguistic means for putting them to work: figures
and tropes drawn promiscuously from both the eighteenth and nineteenth
centuries, verbal echoes, quotations, and allusions bounded neither by
geography nor historical era.

More than canonical writing of its time, humorous discourse uses the
derivative and secondhand to suggest the original and unique. It is a
commonplace with theorists of language that every text from the outset

16. Henry James, "Rudyard Kipling," in *Literary Criticism* (New York: Library of
America, 1984), 1:1127.

exists under the jurisdiction of prior discourses with their own, often alien, networks of associations; but the humorous texts seem particularly prone to other systems of citation and quotation. The radical professions of difference that they shout are mostly bluster to disguise the voracious ingestion of hints, whispers, and sotto voce inspiration from their generic and stylistic precursors. Jonathan Culler has called intertextuality "the general discursive space that makes a text intelligible."[17] The humorous authors' anxiety that their whole enterprise (much less the separate forays) might not be intelligible led to intensive and often self-conscious reliance upon that general discursive space, which they filled up with the distractions of propriety and the tried-and-true. That so many of these newspaper sketches are rereadable, that they manage to come down to us with point and pithiness, is one measure of the authors' frequent success in casting their work as *fresh.*

Both the humorists' self-consciousness and the heavy legacy of literary convention, as I have suggested, decisively remove these sketches from the category of "documents" in any modern historiographical sense. Yet, as I hope will be clear in the pages that follow, if these "amateur" pieces of writing do not faithfully reflect their cultural milieu, they are assuredly refractions of it—distortions, as it were, in a cracked mirror. From A. B. Longstreet to G. W. Harris and Kittrell Warren, the world depicted in this writing is run by dissemblers, frauds, jokers, swindlers, and sharpers who perform through the arts of flattery, impersonation, and sleight-of-hand. That ethical uniformity is made possible by *artifice.* The testimony of ordinary literates (planter families, teachers, businessmen, preachers) may also be skewed, but it is a more accurate reflection of daily life in the settlement period than the humorous texts. If it is social history that we want, the more reliable sources are apt to be the contemporaneous private genres: diaries, daybooks, correspondence.

The cultural context of this writing includes on-the-spot impressions not merely of ordinary (and not-so-ordinary) literate observers, but also of those men and women who, like the humorists, were driven to itemize scenes, record behavior, and digest what they saw and heard as generalizations (some of them from great moral conviction). Travelers to the southwestern interior are not always reliable witnesses, but their fascination and (more commonly) their discomfort are often memorable threads in the tapestry. Amateur historians, protosociologists, gazetteer writers,

17. Jonathan Culler, *The Pursuit of Signs: Semiotics, Literature, Deconstruction* (Ithaca, NY: Cornell University Press, 1981), 12; see also 104, 106.

and compilers of emigrants' guides contributed their own special takes on what the Old Southwest was like. So too the memoirists, who in the vastly changed world after Appomattox looked back to what seemed a more innocent time and place. If none of these collateral texts by themselves can supply an accurate picture of the conditions of authorship among the humorists, their pooled perspectives give important clues to the creative dispositions of the authors who mined the matter of the Old Southwest.

In its own way, the humor of this region is as artful a distortion of *the way things were* as plantation romance. The Longstreet generation of authors may have been writers of the left hand, but their productions, as we now know, are imaginative constructs—distillations of people and events observed and reconstructions of dialect and speech mannerisms overheard. Like any other art, the newspaper sketches were made, not found. They are not source materials, but a literary legacy in their own right.

Part I

Mythmakers and Revisionists

Chapter 1

The Myth of the Ruined Homeland

In Dixie's fall,
We sinned all.

—Bill Arp

i.

The mythic image of the Old South is by now almost too familiar for an author to ask readers to patiently endure yet one more summary. It has been memorable *because* it is mythic: a place of "deference, paternalism, stability, and peace," where slaves were content and refused freedom when offered it, masters were caring, "and yeomen were nonexistent."[1] From the end of the Civil War to World War I, the history of the South shrank—or, rather, it was apotheosized—into a mythic moment, almost outside time, in which striving and mobility were sweaty phases irrelevant to the blossoming of a cavalier nation. What historians now refer to as the Lost Cause movement began with Confederate survivors intent on reviving wartime reputations and ensuring their memory, and the impetus came from former general Jubal Early, whose Southern

---

1. Leslie J. Gordon, " 'Let the People See the Old Life as It Was': LaSalle Corbell Pickett and the Myth of the Lost Cause," in *The Myth of the Lost Cause and Civil War History,* ed. Gary W. Gallagher and Alan T. Nolan (Bloomington: Indiana University Press, 2000), 173–74.

Historical Society would be a major vehicle for rewriting the military record. The result was a spooky historical construct, an "alternate reality" of creative nostalgia hammered out with a (literal) vengeance.[2]

The primary purpose of southern revisionists was to make secession a heroic act so that the former Confederates might salvage honor from military defeat and thereby obscure the self-destructive decisions of their political leaders. The mission enlisted the help of the military distaff, notably Mrs. Jefferson Davis, her daughter Winnie ("the Daughter of the Confederacy"), and LaSalle Corbell Pickett ("the Child-Bride of the Confederacy"). The popular spirit of national reconciliation did not deter the activists from their concerted efforts to remake their history along mythic lines. In sanctifying Robert E. Lee and some (but not all) of his generals, it was not unusual for them to invoke the legendary names of Saladin, Bruce, Rupert—and King Arthur—to memorialize the South's fallen warriors. Schoolchildren saved pennies to finance statues and shrines that began appearing in public spaces, and an ideology of sacrifice became the chief theme of memorial associations, veterans' organizations, and commissions charged with staging ceremonies on battle anniversaries.[3] Southern writing generally in the late nineteenth century resembled, in the words of one historian, the appeal of the defense counsel "after an adverse judgment." With the failure of the South to establish itself as a nation, its apologists "tried through eloquence to achieve what had been lost forever on the battlefield."[4]

It was the civilian corps of the Lost Cause revisionists that achieved the most spectacular success. The apotheosis of the Confederate military led seamlessly to the lifting up of the special people it had defended. Southern

2. David W. Blight, " 'For Something beyond the Battlefield': Frederick Douglass and the Struggle for the Memory of the Civil War," in *Memory and American History*, ed. David Thelen (Bloomington: Indiana University Press, 1989), 34–38. Scholarship on the movement is extensive, including the Gallagher and Nolan collection; Thomas L. Connelly and Barbara L. Bellows, *God and General Longstreet: The Lost Cause and the Southern Mind* (Baton Rouge: Louisiana State University Press, 1982); Gaines Foster, *Ghosts of the Confederacy: Defeat, the Lost Cause, and the Emergence of the New South, 1865 to 1913* (New York: Oxford, 1987); Charles Reagan Wilson, *Baptized in Blood: The Religion of the Lost Cause, 1865–1920* (Athens: University of Georgia Press, 1980); and Rollin G. Osterweis, *The Myth of the Lost Cause, 1865–1920* (Hamden, CT: Archon, 1973).

3. Antoinette G. van Zelm, "Virginia Women as Public Citizens: Emancipation Day Celebrations and Lost Cause Commemorations, 1863–1890," in *Negotiating Boundaries of Southern Womanhood: Dealing with the Powers That Be*, ed. Janet L Coryell and others (Columbia: University of Missouri Press, 2000), 81–86.

4. Robert A. Ferguson, *Law and Letters in American Culture* (Cambridge, MA: Harvard University Press, 1984), 293.

academics, politicians, clergymen, poets, and patriotic women's groups worked tirelessly in projecting the image of a superior antebellum society led by wise men who, after separating themselves from an oppressive union, conducted a war for honor not unlike that of an Arthurian tournament. As Michael O'Brien reminds us, and as most historians affirm, before 1860 southern nationalism was more a hypothesis than a fact.[5] Compensating for that political incohesiveness (and the real subject of the postbellum mythmakers) was a nebulous abstraction: *southern culture.* It incorporated the old republican spirit of independence and manly resistance to "tyranny," the principle of states' rights, and miscellaneous communal virtues signified by the catchphrase "sacred way of life." What the southern states most importantly had shared as a nation, however, had the least bearing on their reimagined history. In their own grand Reconstruction, slavery became well-nigh irrelevant.[6]

Nothing unified the old Confederacy like defeat. Robert Penn Warren put it best. Only "at the moment when Lee handed Grant his sword was the Confederacy born," he wrote; "in the moment of death the Confederacy entered upon its immortality."[7] If the antebellum North had been about enterprise, ideas, piety, and commerce, the South had been about leisure, feeling, family, and agriculture. Society in the North had been atomistic and competitive, while in the South it had been clannish and cooperative. In the polarized mind-set of revisionists, the only genuine culture that the United States had enjoyed in its brief history flourished below the Mason–Dixon line, and it had been crushed by barbarous moderns under the aegis of finance capitalism. The grand claim that the Old South had achieved this rare civilization is typified by a speech in 1883 by Dabney H. Maury, who told a veterans' reunion that "no higher civilization" had "ever existed on earth" than the nation the old soldiers

5. Michael O'Brien, "The Lineaments of Antebellum Southern Romanticism," *Journal of American Studies* 20 (1986): 176; Avery O. Craven, *The Growth of Southern Nationalism, 1848–1861* (Baton Rouge: Louisiana State University Press, 1953), 6–7, 11. Shared defeats in the war "did more to produce a southern nationalism . . . than southern nationalism did to produce the war," writes David Potter in *The Impending Crisis, 1848–1861* (New York: Harper and Row, 1976), 469.

6. Kenneth M. Stampp, *The Imperiled Union* (New York: Oxford, 1980), 255, 265; Grady McWhiney, *Southerners and Other Americans* (New York: Basic Books, 1973), 3–4.

7. Robert Penn Warren, *The Legacy of the Civil War: Meditations on the Centennial* (New York: Random House, 1961), 15. Fred Hobson sets the moment some years earlier: the 1850s debates, when "the South became a nation of the spirit envisioning itself a nation in fact." *Tell about the South: The Southern Rage to Explain* (Baton Rouge: Louisiana State University Press, 1983), 24.

had fought to preserve. Moreover, it was destroyed *because* of its honor, purity, and cultured graces by "money-seeking Puritan invaders."[8] And if regional envy lurked behind the wrecking of the homeland, some partisans made sure the Puritan invaders knew what they had maliciously ruined.

Even while organizing exclusionary genealogical societies and chapters of the United Daughters of the Confederacy, the managers of the new southern heritage encouraged a popular audience both North and South for the historical fiction of Mary Johnston and the fictional history of Thomas Nelson Page. For the mythmakers the end point was always the same whatever genre they chose—to promote the "nationalistic organicism" of the failed Confederacy. That "nation" began as individual states rather inorganically being cobbled together, but, after defeat, it was unified by a single ideology: that "the Old South was a great, if doomed civilization and white southerners a kind of benightedly chosen people."[9] The immediate impetus for recasting its history into what has been called "a pseudopast"[10] may have been the symbolic sacrifice at Appomattox, but the strength of its deep inscription came largely from the dedication of female survivors. Mothers and daughters, who during the war had established canteens and sewing circles, secured precious hospital supplies, and maintained sickrooms, after the war prodded local and national governments to set aside civic places for memorial buildings and statues and such sacred spaces as Confederate museums and the Lee mausoleum at Washington College. Even more lasting was their founding of Memorial Day. Like their male counterparts, but with more affective immediacy, the female survivors made the centerpiece of their efforts the glory of the cause that had been lost, not the ideologically ambiguous stretch of early settlement in the lower South.[11]

If affirming an ideal social order gave the Old South "formidable power in its postbellum afterlife,"[12] that power peaked as late as the 1930s—a half-century after the cultural revisionists had begun their work. Stark

8. Quoted in Lloyd A. Hunter, "The Immortal Confederacy: Another Look at Lost Cause Religion," in Gallagher and Nolan, *Myth of the Lost Cause,* 206.

9. Jefferson Humphries, "On the Inevitability of Theory in Southern Literary Study," *Yale Journal of Criticism* 3 (1989): 187. See also Stephen A. Smith, *Myth, Media, and the Southern Mind* (Fayetteville: University of Arkansas Press, 1985), esp. 12–25.

10. Patrick Gerster and Nicholas Cords, "The Northern Origins of Southern Mythology," *Journal of Southern History* 43 (1977): 572.

11. Valeria Gennaro Lerda, "Southern Landscapes and Civic Improvement: Women's Clubs in the Progressive Era," in *Southern Landscapes,* ed. Tony Badger, Walter Edgar, and Jan Nordby Gretlund (Tübingen: Stauffenburg Verlag, 1996), 75–79.

12. David Moltke-Hansen, "Between Plantation and Frontier: The South of William Gilmore Simms," in *William Gilmore Simms and the American Frontier,* ed. John Caldwell Guilds and Caroline Collins (Athens: University of Georgia Press, 1997), 17.

Young's novel *So Red the Rose* (1934), a document of exacerbated filiopiety that only a transplanted Mississippian in New York City could ventilate with such gravity, is a kind of synopsis of what it meant to be a southern aristocrat. It encompasses the requisite architecture and landscape, genealogically proud ancestry, impeccable courtly manners, speeches about freedom and personal rights, and scenes of action with all the energy of *tableaux vivant*. It is difficult today to account for the popularity of Young's novel except as transregional wish fulfillment, but two years later, Margaret Mitchell's *Gone with the Wind* (1936) was even more successful in sweeping up voracious readers. Less stately than *So Red the Rose*, its hearty narrative survives even its clunky prose; but most of all it invests the Myth of the Ruined Homeland with a gritty activism that puts in the shade all prior exercises in mournful resignation for a lost way of life.

The popular conflation of Mitchell's novel with the David O. Selznick film three years later has obscured the author's urgency to bypass much of the sentimental misrepresentation of a monolithic, aristocratic South. Her north Georgia is firmly a frontier region whose society, as one critic has observed, is closer to the spirit of A. B. Longstreet and Davy Crockett than to Thomas Nelson Page. Atlanta and its environs are vividly contrasted to the hierarchies of values in Charleston and Savannah; its society is aggressively fluid and heterogeneous, allowing even the ignorant (and Catholic) Gerald O'Hara to achieve wealth and power. If O'Hara is the typical interior planter in Georgia (as Mitchell apparently intended), he is little different from Thomas Sutpen, whom Faulkner created at the same time to represent the antebellum milieu in Mississippi. Like Faulkner's in *Absalom, Absalom!* (1936), Mitchell's backcountry is a society ruled by "ambition, ruthlessness, amorality, selfishness, and disregard of the commonweal."[13] The Tara template and that of Sutpen's Hundred are more reliable in harmonizing the romantic planter image with its actual antebellum model than any that can be found in the works of the Lost Cause publicists. Prototypes in the lower South were more like O'Hara and Sutpen than those evoked in the docent patter still to be heard when it's Pilgrimage time in Natchez.

In his retelling of Sutpen's story—Faulkner's version of striving and mobility in the Old Southwest—to his Harvard roommate, Quentin Compson repeats some of the "bombastic phrases" that the parvenu thought

---

13. Darden A. Pyron, "The Inner War of Southern History," *Southern Studies* 20 (1981): 6–9. See also the essays in Pyron's edited volume, *Recasting: "Gone With the Wind" in American Culture* (Miami: University Presses of Florida, 1983), esp. Louis D. Rubin Jr.'s "Scarlett O'Hara and the Two Quentin Compsons."

appropriate to a planter society that was already busy throwing off its origins. Unlike his roommate, Quentin is temperamentally at home with the quaintly stilted style as he echoes what he knows of Sutpen's motive for correcting early "mistakes": "he repudiated that first wife and that child when he discovered that they would not be adjunctive to the forwarding of the design."[14] Though his creator does not, Sutpen overvalues an elite society he sees as already achieved, blind to the fact that his own struggle in the Mississippi hinterland exposes its fragility. *Absalom, Absalom!* invests heavily in the formative frontier phases of the lower South, in effect complementing, not contradicting, the similar rawness of interior Georgia in *Gone with the Wind.* Both authors reinstate a social history that the custodians of the Ruined Homeland found convenient to forget.

The retrospective Old South that the mythmakers created was an amalgam of history, memory, and wish fulfillment. It was a land, in W. J. Cash's famous description, hanging "poised, somewhere between earth and sky, colossal, shining, and incomparably lovely—a Cloud-Cuckoo-Land." Robert Penn Warren's less acerbic term, "City of the Soul," captures the poignant mix of mourning and longing in the reimagined South.[15] The core premise behind southern nostalgia was, in the words of Lewis Simpson, "a stable antebellum civilization centered in the harmonious pastoral plantation and the beneficent institution of chattel slavery."[16] Planter culture became not merely the compelling referent for all postbellum texts, but the masterplot, an ur-fiction whose mythic structure and narrative texture would become codified in the writings of local-colorists, essayists, poets, and professional historians (some of them national as well as regional). What is made most of is *place,* not merely as the nation ruined by the invader, but as determinant and shaper of souls. After Appomattox, place is what is left.

Making the most of a diminished thing, authoring in the late nineteenth century plunders memory, reattributing value to tangible icons recovered out of such literal excavations as a rusty saber, tattered colors, a letter from Andersonville prison, a memorial wreath of hair, a charred brick. Authoring becomes an act of transubstantiation: not satisfied with memorial deeds of homage (as in dedication of statues or a succession of

14. William Faulkner, *Absalom, Absalom!* in *Novels 1936–1940* (New York: Library of America, 1990), 216.

15. W. J. Cash, *The Mind of the South* (1941; reprint, New York: Knopf, 1954), 133–34; Warren, *Legacy,* 14.

16. Lewis P. Simpson, *The Fable of the Southern Writer* (Baton Rouge: Louisiana State University Press, 1994), 77; see also Smith, *Myth, Media, and the Southern Mind,* 12–18.

Decoration Days), the southern imagination transforms the actual residue into a burnished scene in which the original features are heightened, idealized in a dream of pastoral harmony and slow-motion procession outside time. The authoring enterprise, inscribed in dozens of volumes of personal histories, novels, and short stories, posits the same story.

Unlike contemporary sketches of the newspaper humorists who capture differentiation in their culture, most of the memoirs of antebellum figures who live into the 1880s offer a cultural totality: the purging memory works to erase contradictions and subversions. "Consensus," argues one theorist, "is a form of death at the group level."[17] Especially in the rich, repetitive narratives of survivors both male and female, regional identity effaces individuality in such a way that storytelling, for all its multiple hands, becomes a single story with a single protagonist: southern narrative itself. Consider the implications in the language of those who took up the task of trying to preserve the qualities of the "old civilization" when the society itself had disappeared—in the words of one speaker, "how to relight the old fires upon the new altars." The Episcopal bishop of Alabama confessed in his 1887 book: "I have a special fear that our young people, as they recede farther and farther from our times, will gather their views of the recent past from partisan histories rather than from sacredly preserved traditions."[18]

The most conspicuous casualty of the energetic custodians of the Myth of the Ruined Homeland was the lower South's frontier history. The dogged actuality of the migration and settlement periods shows up as mere foreshadowings in the masterplot, reduced to vague chronology so that the cultured planter might take his central position undistracted.[19] In an astute gesture of substitution, a sleekly abbreviated pre-South became more satisfying than the actual turbulent past. The revisionists looked back and discovered Virginia as the cradle of all southern values and in that backward glance found a sustaining source of patrician comfort. Virginia was the linchpin both in the region's myth of origins (southerners as cavaliers) and its myth of achievement (the South as the only real

17. Dean MacCannell, *The Tourist: A New Theory of the Leisure Class* (New York: Schocken Books, 1976), 25.

18. Richard Hooker Wilmer, *The Recent Past from a Southern Standpoint: Reminiscences of a Grandfather* (New York, 1887), 14; see also John B. Gordon and Charles C. Jones, Jr., *The Old South: Addresses Delivered before the Confederate Survivors' Association in Augusta, Georgia* (Augusta, 1887), 13.

19. The planter as "landed gentleman rather than as exploiter of soil and labor" is the mythic figure that caught the popular imagination, according to Rowland Berthoff, *An Unsettled People: Social Order and Disorder in American History* (New York: Harper & Row, 1971), 287.

civilization to develop in the American states).[20] The apologists would have sensed (perhaps retrospectively) the rightness of the decision of wartime leaders to move the Confederate capital from Montgomery to Richmond. Though perhaps in defiance of both logic and logistics, the act was at least symbolically appropriate. When at last the great war came, the southern imagination was ready to elide the awkward old backwoods, merging it happily with the Old Dominion's rich colonial and republican history. In this sleight-of-mind, the Old Southwest was Virginia Redux.

The humorists preside, we might say, over the prehistory that a Lost Cause sensibility effectively eliminated from the record. Even before the death of some of them, their versions of a time and place were, for highminded reasons, being silently expunged from official communal memory. It was not that Longstreet and his followers were too crude or racy— even propagandizing mythmakers still cherished such yarns—but that the time and place the humorists re-created was not conducive to the filiopiety in which the Old South masterplot was draped. In Cash's view the settler, even the "surplus talent" from Virginia, did not march into the Old Southwest trailing clouds of patrician glory. Those who eventually grew into the elite were the most promising of "the strong, the pushing, the ambitious" among "the old coon-hunting population of the backcountry." The frontier, Cash concluded, "was their predestined inheritance." This revision of the revisionists has always nettled modern southerners, even those without an agenda. It is always hard to take seriously the courtly ceremonies at the big house when the success of its residents is attributed "to cunning, to hoggery and callousness, to brutal unscrupulousness and downright scoundrelism." Academics can never be as stylistically overheated as this Carolina newspaperman, but the evidence of historians in fact supports much of the substance of Cash's analysis. The Myth of the Ruined Homeland made retrospective aristocrats out of the planters, the "natural flower of the backcountry grown prosperous."[21]

While young patricians set the tone for arrogant swaggering, lounging,

---

20. Ritchie Devon Watson, Jr., traces the "mythic shift in the antebellum Southwest" from yeoman to cavalier in his introduction to *Yeoman versus Cavalier: The Old Southwest's Fictional Road to Rebellion* (Baton Rouge: Louisiana State University Press, 1993). The classic study of the revisionists' myth of origins is William R. Taylor, *Cavalier and Yankee: The Old South and American National Character* (New York: George Braziller, 1961).

21. Cash, *Mind of the South*, 28, 32–33. For generally balanced assessments see the eleven essays gathered in *W. J. Cash and the Minds of the South*, ed. Paul D. Escott (Baton Rouge: Louisiana State University Press, 1992).

smoking, drinking, and "talking horse," their yeoman counterparts insisted on their own unrestricted liberty, which foreign visitors often interpreted as surly impertinence. One traveler warned other Europeans when in the interior not to treat with contempt those people performing menial jobs. "Let no one . . . indulge himself in abusing the waiter or hostler at an inn," for no citizen could imagine that any honorable situation should "subject him to insult." Even Timothy Flint, the tolerant native, foresaw how the dislike of subordination and deference in "forward and plunging young men" of all stripes would pose a problem for responsible leadership in the Southwest.[22] At least one Englishman, visiting on the eve of the Civil War, professed to see little difference between quality and commonality among southerners, who were still living in a condition "not much elevated from that of the original backwoodsman." Admitting that his views had been shaped by yarns about "passions ungoverned" and the habitual use of "pistols, knives, and poniards, in barrooms and gambling saloons," William Howard Russell nevertheless concluded that the people generally "have all the air and manners of settlers."[23]

Despite their often carping insensitivity, travelers in the Southwest are an invaluable source of the frontierlike quality of mind and behavior of its residents. As in most other respects, Tocqueville was the most perceptive. In the loose democracy of the lower states, he observed, the most opulent citizens fraternized with poorer ones because what they held in common was a drive for self-betterment.[24] Valuable as travel reports may be, however, the humor of the Old Southwest remains the most significant literary product of the settlement process and, as such, the most valuable corrective to the romantic sensibility of the postbellum revisionists. Quite apart from its intrinsic literary merit—and there is quite a bit of it—this writing offers a sociological window on the ragtag democracy of the lower South before its makeover as an elite, genteel culture. Even the most casual reader of this humor cannot fail to note that a recurring narrative situation consists of the direct and frequent interaction of literate (or merely ambitious) go-aheaders with the quasi-literate squatters,

22. John Bradbury, *Travels in the Interior of America in the Years 1809, 1810, and 1811,* in *Early Western Travels, 1748–1846,* ed. Reuben Gold Thwaites (Cleveland: Arthur H. Clark, 1904–1907), 5:304–5; Timothy Flint, *A Condensed Geography and History of the Western States or the Mississippi Valley* (1828; reprint, ed. Bernard Rosenthal, Gainesville, FL: Scholars' Facsimiles & Reprints, 1970), 1:449–50.

23. William Howard Russell, *My Diary North and South* (Boston, 1863), 300–301.

24. Alexis de Tocqueville, *Democracy in America* (1835; trans. George Lawrence, New York: Harper & Row, 1966), 576, 456.

yeoman farmers, and backcountry loners who were never "adjunctive" to the enterprise of bringing the region under orderly and civilized sway. The process that generated this writing was as prolonged and uneven as the frontier line itself.

An important aspect of the humor is the authors' awareness of how fleeting, how volatile and changing, their milieu actually was. Many of the sketches are genial memorials to a time and place that had already receded even as it was being evoked. The burden of Longstreet's *Georgia Scenes*, many of Thomas Bangs Thorpe's Mississippi Valley sketches, all of Baldwin's *Flush Times*, some of Sol Smith's *Theatrical Management*, and a number of Joseph Field's pieces implicitly summon up a spirit of former times, and some are explicitly fashioned as retrospective and contrastive. As moderns, the authors subscribed to the general ideology of mainstream intellectuals and statesmen—namely, that one of the continuing missions of Americans, to settle the continent for Americans, was unfinished, but that some geography previously out of bounds to a white presence had already passed under the progressive control of an ordered and orderly society.[25] Most of the humorous sketches in fact celebrate that partial achievement even as they reenact the raw contingencies, the awkwardnesses, the violent and crass manners left over from a prior time.

The rambunctious Lincoln County stage that one of Longstreet's narrators makes the focus of *Georgia Scenes* is different from and earlier than the vaster, more chaotic areas of Alabama and Mississippi that Baldwin chose eighteen years later as the setting for *Flush Times*. Both books, however, are retrospective accounts, recalled and embroidered from the satisfying viewpoint of a present that represents both gain and loss. The gain is settlement itself: the steady growth of a society boasting law, manners, and civilized conduct as an extension of the values of older, more settled regions. But wisps of nostalgia rise from the otherwise self-satisfied tone of both *Georgia Scenes* and *Flush Times*. What is sensed as lost is the freshness of the original confrontation, the uneasy yet fruitful accommodation of literate leadership (whose ultimate triumph in frontier competition is

25. But perhaps not as briskly as Longstreet pretends at the end of "The Fight." In 1855, twenty years after the "darker" counties had supposedly emerged into the light, one correspondent in Savannah wrote waggishly as if the civilizing process was continuing: "I hear the back woods of Georgia is becoming quite civilized, by means of Ice cream Parties, quite a novel idea to the Country People, to hear of Ice creams & Water Ices." James H. Johnson to James Waring, August 14, 1855, Waring Family Correspondence, Georgia Historical Society, Savannah.

never in doubt) with often recalcitrant but virile men indifferent to the civilizing institutions necessary for a just and coherent culture.

By 1835, Georgia, at least in Longstreet's view, is practically free of embarrassing frontier growth pains; by 1853, Alabama and Mississippi have settled into the social and economic patterns that will confirm their role in a (probable) prosperous future. If Longstreet self-consciously murmurs his thanks that all of Georgia is now Christian, law-abiding, and respectable, he also betrays his relish of its prior rawness, its primitive individualism, in the lingual vigor and pungent detail that spur his imagination when he returns to a more honest republican past. Baldwin is more candid about his sense of loss—he makes himself one of the expedient adventurers who found it possible to have it both ways—and he is more frankly actuated by the shift from chaotic to orderly society. Having witnessed the coming of respectability, he packs his bags and moves to California to immerse himself once again in another Flush Times.

If the postwar romancers chose as their given a cultural condition already achieved and lost, that condition required a sense of repose and habit, the better to stress the South's wanton destruction by a soulless enemy. As we have noted, such autobiographers and memoirists make little distinction between their individual histories and social history— the abiding image is that of the Ruined Homeland. In most of the antebellum years, however, at least in the Old Southwest, there was not yet a homeland to be ruined—only a tentative space hovering between wilderness and settlement. Only in the late 1850s did certain southerners realize that they had forged a society almost at the same instant it was threatened with extinction. Before that, individuals wrote not of a condition achieved but about the circumstances of achieving. In the forty years before the Civil War the lure of newly opened lands, not new nationhood, was a chief preoccupation for migrating settlers, who saw their lives changed by opportunities seized (and sometimes lost).

Some of the pioneers who after Reconstruction began to depict their personal experiences during the formative years acknowledge, in defiance of official mythmaking, the coarse-grained textures of their achieving. These accounts, often dictated to daughters or nieces whose typed transcripts were preserved in family trunks or deposited in county libraries, sometimes appeared as contributions to old-timers' columns in local newspapers. One clergyman's memoirs recount struggle recast in serenity and matter-of-factness. One entire phase of his life is reported in a single sentence. After opening a blacksmith shop in a Mississippi settlement that lacked a hardware store, he writes, "I accumulated wealth rapidly, and soon ranked with the rich people of the community."[26] Most accounts, however, are detailed chronicles of hardship (clearing new land, building crude cabins, suffering illnesses and family deaths, making only a subsistence living) written from a present of survival and respectability. Struggle is seen as the mark of simpler, primitive times—a *then* to be cherished in a modern *now* of easier times (easier, but often of diminished character). Yet even these grittier success stories are often forged as romances of migration and heroic tales of regional destiny. The kinetic energy of the settlers' efforts—risk-taking, scouting trips to scope out better land, negotiating disputed land claims—often overlays a kind of tribal creation story. In one case, a granddaughter makes the latent explicit. In her introduction to Col. James Saunders's memoirs, Elizabeth S. Stubbs draws attention to the author's "stirring recital" as an Alabama "warrior-emigrant": "Old Virginia lies behind him. The Indian vanishes with the smoke-wreath of his rifle's breath. He builds his wilderness castle, *a log cabin,* and so the life of a great State begins, and Alabama looms out of territorial chaos."[27] Such documents appear in the archives of every state in the lower South, reminders of a yeoman-flavored stage that was practically erased in the masterplot of Lost Cause writing.

As early as 1836, Alexander Porter, a prosperous Louisiana planter, was already a success story. His self-interpreted life is remarkable neither in its details nor in its governing themes. Its generic American quality is struck by the balancing of home past and home future: Porter leaves home in order to better himself where opportunities await. Home past is the site of values where ambitious young men learn the "lessons of freedom and independence." Home future is the arena of testing in which those lessons must be practiced in such a way that the young will not prove themselves "unworthy." Yet, as one episode makes clear, self-interest is an important part of home values. Porter's decision to leave Nashville in 1809 carries the blessing (and practical advice) of Andrew Jackson himself: "[L]et all you say and all you do look to your advantage in the future." Porter's scene of leave-taking is familiar: the young man bidding adieu to friends, boarding a flatboat to go among strangers "in the hope of bettering" his fortune. The home that is left behind may well be the "spot consecrated" by affection, but it is the home that lies before him

---

26. F. D. Srygley, *Seventy Years in Dixie* (Nashville, 1893), 267.
27. Elizabeth S. Stubbs, introduction to *Early Settlers of Alabama,* by Col. James Edmonds Saunders (New Orleans, 1899).

that must be wrested from a world of strangers whose own self-interest will not easily coincide with his own.[28]

Unexceptional as it is, Porter's story is tonally and qualitatively different from the life writing of a generation later. It plays on mythmaking that centers on the pioneer, the articulate variant of the yeoman farmer, the Jeffersonian shaper of American values. For the memoirists who experienced the Civil War, this compelling symbol of rural democracy capable of generating success stories virtually disappeared. It was replaced by the figure of the planter who, having once presided over his acres and his slaves, suffers from a predatory commercial society and is left to mourn the ruins of a briefly achieved civilization. In the earlier texts, the expanding frontier of the Old Southwest is wrought by independent, competitive, modest farmers; in the later, the settlement stage is miraculously telescoped into a coherent, stable civilization guided by beneficent planter-aristocrats who seem never to have known the frontier.

ii.

For a full generation after the war of 1812 in the territories and states that would become the Cotton South, the typical southern planter, as we now know, was neither genteel nor dominant. John Quincy Adams told Tocqueville that the new states south and west of Massachusetts were being settled by "adventurers" from all over the Union whose greatest passion was for making money.[29] The spirit of avid exploitation and ordinary greed, however, was not created by rivermen, hunters, and confidence men—however violent and mean their lives may have been—but by planter scions, land dealers, professionals, and silky entrepreneurs of dubious ethics. Early on, many of them would have been embarrassed to call themselves aristocrats. A few might also have been embarrassed at a later generation's rehabilitative efforts to transform their serviceable houses into the resplendent iconic homes without which the myth of southern aristocracy was merely a cultural and spiritual abstraction. Antebellum planters by all accounts were a careless lot when it came to making their homes the centerpieces they should have been in a story of material success. One diarist in the Low Country commented that there

28. Wendell Holmes Stephenson, *Alexander Porter: Whig Planter of Old Louisiana* (Baton Rouge: Louisiana State University Press, 1934), 10–11.

29. George Wilson Pierson, *Tocqueville in America* (Baltimore: Johns Hopkins University Press, 1996), 419, 672.

was "hardly a house not even the very best which has not air holes in all directions."[30] Actress Fanny Kemble, resident as well as visitor, was unhappy with the domestic disorder of even South Carolina plantations ("gates broken, the fences carelessly put up," farm implements "sluttishly scattered about a littered yard, where the pigs seemed to preside by undisputed right; house-windows broken, and stuffed with paper or clothes").[31]

Farther west, the view was no more pleasing. A New England schoolteacher in the 1840s wrote of her dismay with Georgia plantations, "where the master's residence had not a pane of glass in the windows, nor a door between the apartments." A New York mercantile clerk noted that the houses of the more prosperous planters around Macon were mostly shells, one floor "layed and no partitions," although blankets sometimes were put up "to divide the rooms at night"; and since there were no upper floors to obstruct the vision, "you can lay in bed and take observations in the heavens." During his stay in Alabama, Philip Gosse complained of poorly constructed houses of even wealthy and respectable planters, often windowless and with walls "full of crevices." He too could lie in bed at night watching the sky. The sun, he wrote, through "uneven boards" without lathing or papering, "plays at bo-peep, and the wind and rain also."[32]

Aside from Mark Twain's "House Beautiful" chapter in *Life on the Mississippi,* perhaps no account of the antebellum mansion repudiates the mythic image with such thoroughness as Frederick Law Olmsted's, the result of a three-month tour of planters' homes "between the Mississippi and the Upper James River." The landscape architect, even in the waning years of strident peace, was stunned by the discrepancy between what he was told he could expect in houses "where they 'sot up for travellers and had things'" and the uncomfortable reality of the actual experience. His report, in terms of what Terence Martin has called a rhetoric of negation, is a "catalog of lament" for what Olmsted did *not* find:

30. Mary Grace Cooper Diary, (SPR 259), Alabama Department of Archives and History, Montgomery.

31. *Journal of Frances Anne [Kemble] Butler* (Philadelphia, 1835), 134. After two years on the American stage, the English actress married Georgia planter Pierce Butler, whom she left in 1846. Her *Journal of a Residence on a Georgian Plantation* was written during her marriage but not published until 1863, when it was intended to influence the British against the slaveholding South.

32. Schoolteacher quoted in James C. Bonner, *A History of Georgia Agriculture, 1732–1860* (Athens: University of Georgia Press, 1964), 177; A. T. Havens Journal, 1842–1843, Hargrett Rare Book and Manuscript Library, University of Georgia Libraries,

no gardens, no flowers, no fruit, no tea, no cream, no sugar, no bread (for corn pone—let me assert, in parenthesis, though possibly as tastes differ, a very good thing of its kind for ostriches—is not bread) . . . , no curtains, no lifting windows (three times out of four absolutely no windows), no couch . . . , no hay, no straw, no oats . . . , no discretion, no care, no honesty . . . , no stable, but a log-pen. . . . I did not [see] a thermometer, nor a book of Shakespeare, nor a piano-forte or sheet of music; nor . . . reading-lamp, nor an engraving or copy of any kind, of a work of art of the slightest merit.[33]

Olmsted is quick to point out that he is not describing the houses of "poor whites" but the residences of cotton planters. Being forced to sleep "in a room with others, in a bed which stank, supplied with but one sheet, if with any" was no longer the affront it had once been; but this easterner's bar of expectation was higher than most. His wanting list eerily anticipates that of H. L. Mencken, in tone and substance, more than a half-century later in "The Sahara of the Bozart" (1920).[34]

Although the word *aristocracy* doesn't fall as effortlessly from the lips of heritage-obsessed southerners as it did a generation ago, the grand evocation of "a lost way of life" on countless home tours in the lower South continues to exact from visitors a tacit acknowledgment of a condition formerly invoked as Old South Aristocracy. That it was always an Old World term applied metaphorically to new world conditions (inaccurate even for the families on the Chesapeake Bay) did not keep *aristocracy* from casual use throughout nineteenth-century society. Jefferson's coinage, *natural aristocracy,* and Emerson's use of the same term as a character trait that elevated the individual beyond egoism, was transformed by the late 1850s into a sheerly material referent with the success in the South of what Daniel R. Hundley scathingly called "Cotton Snobs": vulgar,

---

University of Georgia, Athens; Philip Henry Gosse, *Letters from Alabama: Chiefly Relating to Natural History* (London, 1859), 153–57.

33. Frederick Law Olmsted, *The Cotton Kingdom: A Traveller's Observations on Cotton and Slavery in the American Slave States, 1853–1861* (1861; reprint, ed. Arthur M. Schlesinger, New York: Da Capo Press, 1996), 519–20. In *Parables of Possibility: The American Need for Beginnings* (New York: Columbia University Press, 1995), Terence Martin argues that a rhetoric of negation has always been a "protean mode of discourse" in American culture, both high and low: "celebratory negatives" served to define the new nation against Old World patterns by proclaiming what it was not, what it did not have.

34. Olmsted, *Cotton Kingdom,* 520. For the complex relationship of Mencken and the South, see Fred Hobson, *Serpent in Eden: H. L. Mencken and the South* (Chapel Hill: University of North Carolina Press, 1974).

flashy, and uneducated parodies of eighteenth-century tidewater planters.[35] Even the patrician-inflected migration of South Carolinians from Sumter into the newly opened lands to the west could not disguise a general rage for the financial main chance.

As we now know, those who flocked into the former Indian lands were not merely a few ambitious elites from Virginia and South Carolina, but a democratic miscellany of poor farmers, professionals, mechanics, apprentices, shopkeepers, laborers skilled and unskilled, gamblers, curiosity seekers, and "adventurers"—categories, moreover, that were never exclusive among themselves nor safe from incursions from the genuine elite. What they all had in common was the promise of improving their lot. Apologists among later antebellum whites found it ideologically useful to deemphasize or even ignore social distinctions. Racial unity was more crucial in verbal battles with the North than economic and class differences. Especially just before the outbreak of hostilities, major regional interests would not have been served by planter pretentiousness toward poorer and slaveless whites whose support would soon be sought in the impending conflict.

In one important sense, however, the southern apologists were accurate in their depiction of white society. What political success the Old South enjoyed by the 1850s it owed in part to the porousness of class lines that began of necessity in the settlement period. In most of the lower South the disproportionate influence of wealthy planters was a fact of political life, yet power could never be taken for granted. Political equanimity was insured by elective office (in turnouts and rotation common enough to forestall the development of an oligarchy), and men of modest social rank often enough filled governorships and seats in the state assemblies.[36]

In the language of ideology, a dominant center always governs its own margins. Although the price of such governance may be mutual "contamination," center and margin in the antebellum era were so essentially

35. Daniel R. Hundley, *Social Relations in Our Southern States* (1860; reprint, ed. William J. Cooper, Jr., Baton Rouge: Louisiana State University Press, 1979), 170. An allied term, *natural gentleman,* was conceived as a middle type in the tension between culture and nature; the American yeoman, writes Stowe Persons, combined "the best moral and social qualities of both." *The Decline of American Gentility* (New York: Columbia University Press, 1973), 65–67.

36. William J. Cooper, Jr., *Liberty and Slavery: Southern Politics to 1860* (New York: Knopf, 1983), 446–47; Ralph A. Wooster, *The People in Power: Courthouse and Statehouse in the Lower South, 1850–1860* (Knoxville: University of Tennessee Press, 1969), 112, 116. See also Steven Hahn, *The Roots of Southern Populism: Yeoman Farmers and the Transformation of the Georgia Upcountry, 1850–1890* (New York: Oxford, 1983), 96.

constituted that the term seems inapplicable. Even the conventional (and consensual) social assignment of power to the wealthy planter never altered the general consonance between poorer whites and their better-heeled governors, either in biological stock or in worldview. James Oakes argues persuasively that "physical movement, upward mobility, and social fluidity" were the crucial sources of a southern worldview. Differences in social rank were obvious, but in practical public life, pretentious assertion of place or exercise of power among the transplanted elite was no more common than deference among the lower ranks.[37]

Though they may often have been grudging, accommodation and assimilation were practical modes of social interaction. Public gatherings attracted the entire spectrum. Militia musters, court days, camp meetings, events organized around important visitors, and especially political canvassing were all species of theater deliberately designed to accommodate all ranks of men (and often women). On such occasions as shooting contests, organized games, and political stumping, deference was never noticeable even in the crowds clamoring to hear visiting dignitaries. Hamilton Pierson described the guests at the wedding of a state legislator's daughter as a "thoroughly promiscuous crowd" of "all ages and all grades of people that the region produced," and, he added, "all seemed equally to enjoy the gathering, as they were free to do in their own way."[38] Although ranks in the militia corresponded roughly to customary distinctions in everyday life, on both training days and during call-ups to battle (with the British or the Creeks), officers and privates congregated together after drills and sorties, swapping stories and drinking from the same jugs.[39] What passed as the "quality" in the 1830s and 1840s—planters, professionals, and some businessmen—depended for their well-being on

37. James Oakes, *The Ruling Race: A History of American Slaveholders* (New York: Knopf, 1982), 67–68. See also Carl N. Degler, *Place over Time: The Continuity of Southern Distinctiveness* (Baton Rouge: Louisiana State University Press, 1977), 92–93; and Bertram Wyatt-Brown, "Community, Class, and Snopesian Crime: Local Justice in the Old South," in *Class, Conflict, and Consensus: Antebellum Southern Community Studies,* ed. Orville Vernon Burton and Robert C. McMath, Jr. (Westport, CT: Greenwood, 1982), 189–91.

38. Hamilton W. Pierson, *In the Brush; or, Old-Time Social, Political, and Religious Life in the Southwest* (New York, 1881), 100.

39. William C. Davis, *A Way through the Wilderness: The Natchez Trace and the Civilization of the Southern Frontier* (1995; reprint, Baton Rouge: Louisiana State University Press, 1996), 310. Rich contexts are available in the essays in *Inside the Natchez Trace Collection: New Sources for Southern History,* ed. Katherine J. Adams and Lewis L. Gould (Baton Rouge: Louisiana State University Press, 1999). See also Bertram Wyatt-Brown, "The Antebellum South as a 'Culture of Courage,' " *Southern Studies* 20 (1981): 213–46.

the goodwill, cooperation, and needs of what in private they might call "the democracy." For their part, while they were always alert to haughtiness in their educated betters, most clients, customers, patients, employees, guides, and artisans were innocent of any egalitarian enthusiasm.

That such accommodation across lines of class and vocation worked more often than not is attested by daybooks of semiliterates. In their primary function, these practical documents are relentlessly precise—about work schedules, weather, crop yields, seed prices, costs of farm implements, and, frequently, notations about personal health and treatments of ordinary diseases and ailments. Although overseers, plain farmers, and (occasionally) sharecroppers rarely hesitated to interlard their factual entries with expression of feelings, such matters are clearly regarded as a bit wasteful of time and paper. Some entries are so laconic that they only hint at important ongoing stories: relationships with neighbors, friends, and fellow church members; kinship responsibilities; and sexual liaisons. Even in such abbreviated form they have the virtue of simplicity in contrast to the discursive indulgence that usually marks their counterparts from the offices of planters. Only rarely do these literate yeomen show frustration arising from business relationships with planters better off than they. And despite an ingrained prudery (which lends a kind of arch coyness to their language), they record instances of social interaction with as much candor as the better-educated keepers of daybooks.

The case of an Alabama overseer near Montgomery is instructive. John G. Traylor engaged to be overseer for a Mr. Rives on New Year's, 1834, an agreement he renewed over the next several years, bettering the terms for himself each time. At the end of 1839 he listed the six crops of cotton he made for Rives in numbers of bales (from 66 in 1834 to 230 in 1839). In 1841 he wrote in his daybook: "I bought 170 Akers of land from Mr John Garet an got rites for it." In 1842 he went to a sale in Montgomery and "bout 5 negros." By the time Traylor ended his diary in 1847 he had become a successful small planter. We have no reason to suppose that his pattern was unique. His entries betray none of the inherited snobbery of larger planters, some of whom were well-off when they migrated, and considerable pride in his own industry as well as cheerful optimism. At the beginning of 1835, his entry was brief: "this is the commencement of 1835—go a hed steam boat—." A year later the entry was similar: "Set in with Mr. Rives for another year an gets $400 go a head." On December 27, 1838: "Dave Tidwell ben a corting. This is Chrismus times heds up."[40]

40. John G. Traylor Diary (SPR 302), Alabama Department of Archives and History, Montgomery.

iii.

Oakes asserts that class lines were so permeable that it is futile now to try to "locate clearly delineated boundaries between slaveholders and non-slaveholders," much less to trace distinctions between small slave-holders and larger.[41] The record of marriage patterns shows that class distinctions mattered little when white southern males chose their mates. For females, money mattered over family name in the South, as it did everywhere else. A gossipy letter from a Mississippi woman in 1846 suggests that respectability was a condition more earned than inherited. The correspondent approved of the recent marriage of a Miss Cheatham; her wealthy husband, despite the "circumstance of his being a self-made man," would now allow the fortunate lady "to indulge every whim or caprice."[42]

There was some obvious grandstanding in the democratic sentiment of Thomas Cobb of Georgia when he boasted that in the South all white men were the same: "The poorest meets the richest as an equal; sits at his table with him; salutes him as a neighbor; meets him in every public assembly and stands on the same social platform."[43] But it was not all political posturing. We know that southerners, regardless of class and station, were much alike in background, taste, and sentiment. David Potter has argued that white southerners shared an orientation toward the land (even those who indifferently cultivated it); a sense of personal independence; a pride in their Revolutionary heritage; an orthodox Protestantism; and a commitment to self-improvement, material acquisitions, and economic success. Moreover, when they were not bent on improving their lot, southern males played the same hedonistic cards regardless of rank. Cash's famous catalog of shared traits included the "tendency to frisk and cavort, to posture, to play the slashing hell of a fellow."[44] Planters'

41. Oakes, *Ruling Race*, 67–68. The mobility lessened in the late 1850s, when prosperity in cotton markets made the price of slaves soar along with planter incomes. See Lawrence Shore, *Southern Capitalists: The Ideological Leadership of an Elite, 1832–1885* (Chapel Hill: University of North Carolina Press, 1986), 55.

42. John Hebron Moore, *The Emergence of the Cotton Kingdom in the Old Southwest: Mississippi, 1770–1860* (Baton Rouge: Louisiana State University Press, 1988), 145; Minnie Clare Boyd, *Alabama in the Fifties: A Social Study* (New York: Columbia University Press, 1931), 249–51; letter, 1846, Alexander Melvorne Jackson Papers (M16), McCain Library and Archives, University of Southern Mississippi, Hattiesburg.

43. Quoted in Degler, *Place over Time*, 91.

44. Potter, *Impending Crisis*, 472; Cash, *Mind of the South*, 52–58. Potter attributes these attributes to most northern whites as well. Grady McWhiney argues that planters and yeomen shared the same leisure-time activities, especially those condemned by

relationships with poorer whites were often marked by courtesy and tact, partly because the poorer whites were often the planters' kinsmen who eventually expected to become planters themselves.

Distinctions in fact were more in "the process of becoming than realized" because most settlers sprang from the same general sources—in some cases "from identical sources."[45] In the social network of overlapping connections, extended kinships were important among migrating families, and it was inevitable that the unstable economy would benefit members unequally. It was a commonplace even into the twentieth century that every wealthy landowner knew of, acknowledged, and included in some of his family gatherings a poorer brother making do without black labor, a luckless cousin reduced to landless status, even yeoman kinsmen struggling to maintain their expectations despite makeshift economies.

An unpredictable economy had always encouraged considerable crossing of patrician and yeoman class lines. James H. Hammond observed in one letter that the families he knew were marked by a mixture of traits: "Genius and imbecility, Chivalry and poltroonery and meanness," and the same geography contained old families "undecayed" and others "decaying," new families "founded by successful overseers and factors," and others who became successful despite their irrelevant extended kin—"loafing fishermen, hunters etc." Hammond was his own best example of rising in the ranks. A modest Yankee schoolteacher, lawyer, and editor who married an heiress, Hammond, in the words of one critic, "succumbed to the myth of the Old South even before the South was old and before there was a myth."[46]

The evidence suggests that in the rawer West families tolerated even their poltroon kin with more grace than Hammond and his acquired class in the coastal enclaves. The machinery of inclusion (at parties, dinners, and ceremonial events), whether out of duty or festive need, operated to solidify the successful planter's public image of beneficence; but probably just as important was an ingrained sense of the precariousness of wealth itself. In those who had achieved much, fluctuating fortunes instilled an awareness of friends and kin who had experienced overnight ruin as well as spectacular riches. Indeed, it was not a rarity in this vola-

---

outsiders: hunting, fishing, gambling, drinking, and dancing. *Cracker Culture: Celtic Ways in the Old South* (Tuscaloosa: University of Alabama Press, 1988), 144–45.

45. Cash, *Mind of the South*, 39; Moore, *Emergence of the Cotton Kingdom*, 145.

46. Bertram Wyatt-Brown, *Honor and Violence in the Old South* (New York: Oxford, 1986), 64–65; Carol Bleser, ed., *Secret and Sacred: The Diaries of James Henry Hammond, a Southern Slaveholder* (New York: Oxford, 1988), 304.

tile economy for the same planter to experience in his lifetime multiple bouts of both boom and bust.

The diary of Sarah Gayle, a native South Carolinian married to a prominent Alabama political figure, offers a rich picture of the dynamics of class relations in the antebellum South. In 1828, in small-town Greensborough, before her husband was elected governor of Alabama, Mrs. Gayle noted many of the activities of the ladies, including their competitions for social leadership. "These little squabbles . . . are extremely unpleasant in a small society," she wrote, "and always take from their dignity." In 1829 she commented about a party attended by many new faces: "gentle & simple, pleb[e]ian & patrician were mingled in one undistinguished, somewhat mothey mass." The guests included "descendants of Pocahontas" and other exiles from Virginia, and Alabamians whose recollections went back to "log cabins, Indian Camps and all the privations of a lately settled Country." The entry provided Mrs. Gayle a chance to vent her irritation at an unnamed Virginian, dissatisfied with a crude Alabama, who "most unmercifully and often most affectedly sneers at the very state to which his interests bend him." Rather than disparaging the state's amusements, talents, and advantages, the newcomer, she concluded, should "frankly accept the perhaps rough welcome we have to offer, and make charitable allowance for the much which is lacking."[47]

The clear-eyed Sarah Gayle was no doctrinaire apologist for Alabama, however. Because of her own experience she understood the growing pains of a society long past its backwoods origins but not yet fully civilized. In an 1832 letter to her uncle in South Carolina, who was considering a move west, she advised him that his wife "will find but little polish, little style; and where pretensions are made to it, it does appear to me to be awkward." In her journal a few years earlier she recorded her pangs of "regret" over a "Mrs. Crawford": "[W]ealth has brought with it much formality and the tall & some-what ceremonious lady has taken the place of the frank, timid, & beautiful girl. The change is not to suit me." As an antidote to such pretentious transformations, Mrs. Gayle cited "the Leather Stocking of Cooper—keep *before* civilization," which brings with it "so much of form, and appearance & coldness that I am chilled." But perhaps her most astute insight into social awkwardness in Alabama after statehood is her 1828 entry about a certain "Mrs. Owen," scheduled

47. Sarah Gayle, diary, Gorgas Family Papers (Sarah Gayle Materials), William Stanley Hoole Special Collections, University of Alabama Library, University of Alabama, Tuscaloosa.

to go with her husband to Washington: "It is an ill-advised trip—she has all the requisites for being loved at home and not a single one for shining abroad. Raised in the country, when its character was wildest, she had no advantages either for cultivating her mind or manners." Mrs. Gayle concluded her thoughts about the lady: "She has native goodness, but no acquired graces—and it seems to me that the transformation from the free-spoken Louisa, who used to scamper over the woods with me, to the fashionable, bowing attendant at the President's levees is very great. I hope she may sustain the last character as well as she did the first."[48]

Although this articulate woman probably mingled across class lines with more purposefulness that many of her contemporaries, her observations show no political restraint, no fugitive expressions of mere *dutiful* socializing. Her candor in assessing her friends, her freedom from the rigid application of the "visitability" norm of the older patrician families, and her genuine curiosity in matters of religion, culture, and manners allow us pertinent glimpses into the realistic class behavior of her time and place. Mrs. Gayle's perceptive comments are echoed in numerous letters and journals, in Mary Chesnut's extensive diaries, in the Longstreet sketches narrated by Abraham Baldwin, and in the domestic interludes of William Tappan Thompson's Major Jones letters.

Less harshly satiric than Longstreet with *his* aspiring Georgians, John B. Lamar follows the Peablossom family as it struggles to balance country gentility and common sense in "Polly Peablossom's Wedding." When in the absence of an indisposed parson Captain Peablossom declares that the ceremony will be conducted by Squire Tompkins, his wife protests that in *her* day in North Carolina, "the quality" disapproved of marriages celebrated by mere magistrates. The Captain's response sums up the widespread sentiment recurring throughout the antebellum period of settlement:

> "None of your nonsense, old lady, none of your Duplin county aristocracy about here, now. The *better sort of people*, I think you say! Now, you know North Ca'lina ain't the best State in the Union, nohow, and Duplin's the poorest county in the State. Better sort of people, is it? *Quality*, eh! Who the devil's better than we are? . . . Why, darn it, we are the *very best* sort of people. Stuff! nonsense! The wedding shall go on; Polly shall have a husband." (*PPW*, 20–21)

48. Sarah Gayle to William Haynesworth, December 31, 1832, Gorgas Family Papers (Sarah Gayle Materials); Gayle diary.

Merely to cite pretentiousness (as Mrs. Gayle with Alabama ladies and Lamar with his Georgians) is to reflect by negative example the common-sense ideal that the newer quality often found difficult to uphold. Nevertheless, the constant threat of snickers from envious neighbors and the economic reality of success that might not be permanent had little effect in restraining the newly rich from sometimes advertising their status. To be set apart from the common run was an urgency many achievers thought worth the risk of deflation.[49]

What such accounts confirm is that, except for its earliest years, the Old Southwest was never a classless site; indeed, the conventional protocols of class distinctions were self-consciously carried into the new country by Carolina and (especially) Virginia settlers. But they also confirm the persistence of a permeable society that discouraged those conventional biases. The very newness of society in the backcountry promoted cultural intercourse among diverse callings and classes less formalized than in older, more stable communities. It could hardly be otherwise for a region that on the eve of the Civil War was still emerging from its frontier stage. In Cash's tonic reminder, the same men who as children "heard the war-whoop of the Cherokee in the Carolina backwoods lived to hear the guns at Vicksburg."[50]

Diarists, correspondents, even some travelers, document the matter-of-fact intercourse among all whites during those in-between years. The porousness of the social geography benefited the humorous authors, not merely by providing substance for their sketches but by allowing them to take advantage of its loose structure in their personal lives. Both Joseph G. Baldwin and C. F. M. Noland were scions of respectable Virginia families whose new residences released them to prosper as they never could in the more closely monitored society they left. Even more relevantly, the flexibility of the Southwest provided Joseph and Matthew Field the kind of opportunities often closed to the Irish in the Northeast. Permeable social lines were a vital factor for A. B. Longstreet himself, the son of yeoman migrants from New Jersey who became educated, made friends

49. A contemporary preacher was not immune to his own tumefying when he commented that affected speech was always vulnerable: "Any excessive tumefactions of speech often collapsed ignominiously at the prick of some stinging joke" from alert yeomen. Quoted in William Henry Milburn, *The Pioneers, Preachers, and People of the Mississippi Valley* (New York, 1860), 401.

50. Cash, *Mind of the South*, 24. See also Degler, *Place over Time*, 56; Richard Aubrey McLemore, ed., *A History of Mississippi* (Hattiesburg: University & College Press of Mississippi, 1973), 1:410.

with sons of more highly placed families, and "married up." Though he could claim a distinguished ancestry (including a "Signer"), Johnson Jones Hooper by the time of his maturity was exposed only to declining fortunes in his North Carolina family; his parents were hopeful that his move to Alabama might revive their wealth. Like Noland in Arkansas, Hooper manifested his in-between status by freely associating, along with his educated peers, with what conventional southerners called "low company."

The educated elite never lost their dominative instincts in cultural interchanges, even in the newly opened lands, but the conditions permitted, even mandated, a freer, more relaxed involvement of planters, lawyers, doctors, and editors in the backwoods styles of their clients, patients, and customers than had been customary in the fixed social climate of seaboard centers. Taverns, boardinghouses, courtrooms—almost any public space—were necessarily sites of democratic elbow-rubbing. Men of the greatest local reputation sported with men of the lowest. In 1836 the governor of Georgia, who had received a petition for the release of a horse thief from prison, was told that it had been initiated by "the last quality of characters in the county" and that the few "men of note" who had signed the petition did so only to placate the man's wife.[51] The incident suggests that at the local level all males of whatever social standing could, for whatever reasons, cooperate in specific enterprises. It also suggests that in low-density-population areas (which is to say, most of them) a certain fraternization of "men of note" and the "last quality" was an expected feature of public life.

Even as late as 1860, when hundreds of fashionable Episcopalians gathered on a mountaintop at Sewanee, Tennessee, to dedicate the new University of the South, the ceremony attracted the unfashionable as well. One participant recalled that the festivities honoring education and religion were ringed by yeomanry "fighting, horse-trading, gambling, all conducted openly and vociferously and without the least regard for the ceremonies that were being conducted around the cornerstone."[52] Such counterfestivities were visual and aural reminders to the genteel that, though the social boundaries of southerners were no longer as porous as they had been in settlement times, the elite still shared their general space with lesser folk.

In the earlier decades of white settlement, planters, professionals, yeo-

51. Bruce Collins, *White Society in the Antebellum South* (London: Longman, 1985), 171.
52. Wyatt-Brown, *Honor and Violence*, 49, 79, 121.

men, and poorer whites may not have "mingled" in the sense often con-
noted by that word, but for amusement they all found themselves drawn
to the same occasions: musters, courthouse visits, hunting parties, even
camp meetings. From their written records, it is reasonable to conclude,
with Bertram Wyatt-Brown, that the quality sought out such entertainments from "the fear of being left alone, bored, and depressed," but there
is no reason to suppose that the nonquality of the new settlements were
immune to ennui.[53] Even though the written yeoman record is sparse,
what we have shows the same drive toward sociability as their betters.
There is nothing resembling scenery out of Watteau in the bulk of antebellum writing, either public or private, nor of an exclusionary class taking its stately promenades in it. The humorists' vision may have been
defective because of its concentrated focus on yeomanry manners and
values, but, as we shall see, their writing comes closer to social honesty in
depicting a time and place than the mythologists who invented a Ruined
Homeland.

iv.

The work of the mythmakers began earnestly only after the humorous
authors had done theirs. Longstreet was also tempted by the backward
glance (toward an earlier republic), but most of the authors who followed him had little appetite for some preferred past. Their creative
efforts were invested in mining the temporal amusements of a volatile
present that later readers, coping with the aftermath of war, would find
insufficiently relevant. Those readers were also Mark Twain's generation.
Though his career paralleled that of the poets, novelists, essayists, orators, and educators who embraced the Lost Cause mission, the heir of the
antebellum humorists rather famously showed little interest in a South
reimagined as sacred place. Though he has been aptly called the "untrans-
figured southerner,"[54] he wanted us all to know that Sam Clemens was
death on nostalgia.

Yet, as we also know, what has been called the Matter of Hannibal[55] exerted a powerful nostalgic pull on the professional author who had made

53. Ibid., 79, 121.
54. Simpson, *Fable of the Southern Writer*, 192.
55. Walter Blair, introduction to *Mark Twain's Hannibal, Huck, and Tom*, vol. 5 of
the Mark Twain Papers (Berkeley and Los Angeles: University of California Press,
1969), 11.

an undistinguished Mississippi River town his home from ages four to seventeen. *The Adventures of Tom Sawyer,* the village idyll of 1876, is the most coherent result of his backward glance—though for a boys' book, shadows abound: moralistic sentimentalism, casual racism, malfeasance of public officials. Someone once counted about a dozen corpses throughout its pages. For this national author, who flourished alongside both programmatic realists and sentimental romancers, idyll is always vulnerable to exposé.

In the waning years of the century, the squire of Hartford and world traveler ransacked his memory for a retrospective summary of Hannibal in his childhood. Written presumably for private reference, "Villagers of 1840–3" is both idyll and exposé. Despite its title, the summary is not of a frozen moment, but incorporates the Matter of Hannibal within a more extensive time frame, from about 1839 (when the author was four) to about 1853 (when he left home). The remembrance in 1897 of more than 160 residents is factual but rarely objective, and the text is that of a disappointed idealist more than that of a critical realist. Indeed, even as an *aide-mémoire,* "Villagers" has a thesis. Clemens calls antebellum sentimentality "puerile," but he quickly pronounces it "preferable" to "the ideals of to-day." Yet another of his stuttering parables of the fall, the document turns not on the Civil War as critical juncture—the defining event that predictably resonates in all southern memoirs of his generation—but the Gold Rush of 1849. Prior to that event, we are told, "money had no place" in the general life of Hannibal; the California fever "begot the lust for money," which became the "rule of life" that in turn generated the "hardness and cynicism" of the present.[56]

The vision of a village shattered by the news from California composes itself all too readily in a made-to-order schema, yet the individual entries belie the rigid contrast. Young Sam Clemens may not have been aware of it, but the importance of money for the villagers did not begin in 1850. One of the constants in these Rolodex résumés is economic health and financial standing of community residents irrespective of the gold fever. John Robards grows up as a "valued citizen, and well-to-do"; Neil Moss, the "envied rich boy of the Meth. S.S.," descends into a "graceless tramp" living by "mendicancy and borrowed money"; Sophia marries "the prosperous tinner"; from his father, Jim Quarles "gets $3,000—a fortune, then," to set up a business, but becomes a "drunken loafer" instead; Clint Levering's brother lives to be "rich and respected"; one commission mer-

---

56. Mark Twain, "Villagers of 1840–3," in *Mark Twain's Hannibal, Huck, and Tom,* 35.

chant dies "rich ($20,000)." Threading the biographies are such phrases as "lived to have a family and be rich and respected," "Eventually rich," and "daughter married well." It is as if the moralizing Clemens—"To get rich was no one's ambition"—ignores what common sense tells us about human nature as well as the specific turns in the thumbnail sketches he has just penned. "Villagers" is merely one more text in the grand drama of declension that a mature Mark Twain had been documenting with increasing stridency for many years. His own era of ethical shabbiness becomes a kind of sad norm that he embeds with romantic melancholy. This particular segment of the Matter of Hannibal focuses on disasters, scandals (from middling to major), and harrowing details of families that begin substantially and decline into obscurity. A grim notation concludes entry after entry: "dead without issue," "all dead now," "Died," "and so died," "Got drowned." Even more chilling than the punctuating *memento mori* are Clemens's reminders of less satisfying closures: "Disappeared from view," "not heard of again," "Played out and disappeared," "departed never to return," "moved away," "drifted to Texas," "went mad and finished his days in the asylum," "Went deaf and dumb from breaking through ice." The specifics of "Villagers of 1840–3" sound less appropriate to the popular image of the nineteenth-century village than to the searing depictions we later find in Sherwood Anderson, Willa Cather, and Sinclair Lewis.[57]

We would like to think that, unlike the mythmakers' purified southern versions of pastoral idyll, Clemens's gloomy recasting of the village idyll is more trustworthy, more honestly reimagined. The revisionists' texts are vehicles of grand imaginings, some with unabashed design, others no more than ephemeral confections. Because the mythmakers ransacked not only their memories and family narratives but also partisan history, popular lore, genealogies, and testimonials at dedications of statues and cemeteries, their texts gathered force and carried authority as impersonal, collective truth. Though composed under the aegis of unblinkered skepticism, Clemens's village idyll, precisely because it seems so personal, so lodged in one man's memory, has the virtue of an intensive, singular vision, one equally tainted by imagination and aesthetic enlargement. The Gold Rush as the hinge that connects *then* and *now* is even more a structural convenience for the Presbyterian apostate than the Civil War is for the mourners of a lost civilization. In either case, however, we should not underestimate covert rage as well as longing. Both

57. Ibid, 23–40.

the notational realism of Clemens and the venerable romanticism of the revisionists issue from affective cultural upheaval and decline. Yet the energy to resist declension goes not to the famous foe of nostalgia, but to those apostles of nostalgia whose rebuilt structures allow them, spiritually at least, to reject defeat.

The recital of lost souls in Hannibal is passive. The gritty particulars of their brief careers, condensed in a manuscript text of thirty-four pages, reinforce the steadily deepening pessimism of the author's late maturity. As we see from the score of unfinished fragments, the Matter of Hannibal coheres only in a handful of completed works (notably *Tom Sawyer*), where Clemens could construct his village idyll despite wracking philosophical nihilism. Yet nostalgia, which he once contemptuously called mental masturbation, is nostalgia even when its operation is laced with pain. We may remember that the term itself is medical in origin: homesickness so profound that place becomes temporal as well as spatial.

Chapter 2

Southwest Humor and the *Cordon Sanitaire*

Cordon sanitaire. A line of watchers posted round an infectious district to keep it isolated and prevent the spread of the disease; a sanitary cordon.

—*Brewer's Dictionary of Phrase and Fable*

The best-known sketch among all the pieces from the Old Southwest, "The Big Bear of Arkansas," is also the sketch that, predictably, has attracted the most vigorous critical attention. Never mind that "The Big Bear of Arkansas" is typical neither of Thomas Bangs Thorpe's other writing nor of antebellum humor generally. It has the happy distinction of being self-contained, its narrative integrity free of any felt need for clarifying context. It may not be particularly funny, but it is still the finest single sketch in a body of writing that has always had to compete for space in anthologies: "Big Bear," like the best hitter in the schoolyard, is the first one chosen by literary managers.

One conclusion we could draw from the prominence of this tale, which has more depth and complexity than its frivolous cousins, is that it deserves to be team leader *because* it isn't particularly funny. That is, its value to us lies in its surprising ability to hold its own alongside more serious canonical items of its literary moment—Irving's "The Legend of Sleepy Hollow," say, or Hawthorne's "The Birthmark." We enjoy the irony at the heart of the tale: a champion bear hunter, for all his skills, fails to bag his biggest quarry, a mythic beast who simply dies "when his time comes." We like the fact that, though Thorpe's hero tells his yarn in dialect, the backwoods vernacular channels the same "themes" that resonate in other American texts written in conventional English—self-making; success and failure; identity and reputation; wilderness and civilization as sources of rival values; the diminishment of wilderness. Yet our admiration of "The Big Bear of Arkansas" has sometimes taken skewed turns to justify its importance.

i.

A student once remarked, after a session on Thorpe, that Jim Doggett's tale, embedded as it is within gentlemanly discourse, was too good to be held in "discursive bondage." If driven to it, certain deconstructionists of a few years back, whose theories the student had recently sampled, would have murmured approval. But just how much bondage does Thorpe subject his bear story to? About half of the sketch is Doggett's direct narration about his adventure with the unhuntable bear, uninterrupted by either narrator or audience. In slightly less space, in a query-and-response exchange, Doggett engages the crowd with some preliminary tall talk about Arkansas fertility. Even the introduction, with the narrator speaking "as himself," is a mere five paragraphs preceding the hunter's dramatic entrance.

The prose of Thorpe's narrator is neither obtrusive nor unduly literary. He generalizes about the "heterogeneous character" of passengers "jostling together" on the Mississippi steamers and then describes the variety:

> the wealthy Southern planter, and the pedlar of tin-ware from New England—the Northern merchant, and the Southern jockey—a venerable bishop, and a desperate gambler—the land speculator, and the honest farmer—professional men of all creeds and characters—Wolvereens, Suckers, Hoosiers, Buckeyes, and Corn-crackers, beside a "plentiful sprinkling" of the half-horse and half-alligator species of men, who are peculiar to "old Mississippi," and who appear to gain a livelihood simply by going up and down the river. (*TBT*, 112)

When he notes that a "man of observation need not lack for amusement or instruction in such a crowd," the narrator clearly identifies himself as such, one who has taken "the trouble to read the great book of character" open on "the well-known 'high-pressure-and-beat-every-thing' steamboat 'Invincible.' " Being amused and instructed is the private reward for a man of observation, and passing along to the reader the story of the hunter—"given in his own way"—is the public gift of an amiable, educated gentleman.

There are indeed discursive bonds that tie this narrating voice to Doggett's bear story, but they are not the restraining kind. Marking the gentleman is a controlled and balanced prose in which consciously parallel substantives of the passenger list suggest the crowded diversity of the men in the social hall who listen to the yarn. The rhythm of the introductory paragraphs is more familiar than formal. Even as this respectable English is calculatingly distinct from the vernacular of Jim Doggett, the narrator comes across as neither starchy nor stately. Only the fussiest schoolmarm in 1841 would have faulted this scribe for allowing such colloquial items as *plentiful sprinkling* and *high-pressure-and-beat-every-thing* to invade his own natural register. The narrator's subsequent fascination with the hunter suggests that he is just a *leetle mite* susceptible to tall talk, too, and rather easily held in thrall to the enticements of a lying oral imagination. If modern readers are more comfortable with what they imagine is the "more natural" language of uneducated speakers, it does not follow that the linguistic level of the narrators in Southwest humor is unduly formal, too nicely correct for even mid-nineteenth-century standards of compositional style. Stylistic contrasts in the sketches are always clear, as they were meant to be; but the separation between levels of lingual fluency, between the stand-in narrator and the (often) barely literate yeoman, is never as radical as we have often been led to believe.

An older version of discursive bondage theory centered on "The Big Bear of Arkansas" (along with similar frame tales) as a parable of contention between the elite and the rabble. Kenneth Lynn's influential thesis—that such humor was warning, not celebration, that the box structure itself functioned as a *cordon sanitaire* to contrast the "morally irreproachable Gentleman and the tainted life he described"—presupposed that the humorists were really satirists of a culture they deplored. In this political reading, the humor functions as a covert signal to decent citizen-readers who might be tempted to allow illiterate blowhards to affect values and policies better set in place and supervised by an educated leadership.[1] It is a thesis premised on the fact that most of the humorist authors

---

1. Kenneth S. Lynn, *Mark Twain and Southwestern Humor* (Boston: Little, Brown, 1959), 50–65. An earlier reading of the contrast between narrators and their yeoman

were Whigs and most of their subjects were Jacksonian Democrats. Yet even as Whigs, most of the them were willing participants in the culture they chose: not the Virginia or Massachusetts they left, but the Southwest and its crude potentialities they sought out. For any number of reasons the authors thrived in the amorphousness, even the chaos, of a place that was more hectic than civil in its settling process. They may have resented the raw terms of settling—having to accept as cultural condition the fact that social divisions based on class and family name were both elastic and permeable—but their texts fail to show such resentment.

The case for a Whiggish agenda in the humor depends heavily on the imagined aloofness of a genteel narrator, whose educated style serves as a self-imposed barrier against the vulgar camaraderie of his yeoman subjects. But the authorial personas are hardly genteel (though most of them are more or less educated), and their language is much too supple to qualify as the archly formal style that the *cordon sanitaire* presumes. The humorists are artists enough to manipulate language for effect, both with vernacular speakers and their stand-in narrators, but there is no reliable evidence that their linguistic and stylistic gifts are being put to the service of covert political ends. For the authors to make too much of stylistic separation would be to signal discontent with those very figures who so promiscuously populate their world. Cultural theorists tell us that "metanarrative" and "monologic discourse" are monitored by political control, an authoritarian power that confines, delimits, represses, and subsumes all other stories—in effect assigning roles for narrators and auditors.[2] In the body of writing we call Southwest humor, that power would lie with the author-narrators, the source of control for both creating and assigning roles. Such is the benefit of literacy. Yet as agents of political control, they are scandalously lax. Had they dedicated themselves, in the Marxist sense, to the kind of master narrative that brooks no alternative narratives, we should barely notice the yeoman types who clamor to tell their stories; but the authors conveniently allow them so many opportunities that some will hardly shut up.

It is true enough that we can assume that the better-speaking narrators in the sketches are at least inclined toward the Whig party and that the vernacular speakers are mostly Jacksonites. Yet, as David Simpson argues,

subjects can be found in Walter Blair, *Native American Humor, 1800–1900* (New York: Knopf, 1937), 62–101, 163–96.

2. David Carroll, "Bakhtin and Lyotard," in *The Aims of Representation: Subject/ Text/History,* ed. Murray Krieger (New York: Columbia University Press, 1987), 75–76.

representatives of all political groups were in effect "speaking the same language." After the Jacksonian era, custodians of the American language could no longer afford "to present the speech of the lower orders (usually dialect) as improper, ridiculous, or sociologically charged."[3] Because the humorists are cagier in playing their party cards than some of their later critics, we should take some care in pronouncing them ideological Whigs. Not all were even nominal Whigs. George Washington Harris, John Gorman Barr, and H. E. Taliaferro, for example, were stout Democrats. One Mississippi memoirist affirmed that "Governor McNutt was a Democrat of the Jeffersonian school."[4] The selective conservatism we see in A. B. Longstreet and W. T. Thompson is more akin to the social values of the old-fashioned Federalists than to the doctrinaire Whigs. Suspicious of Jacksonian democracy, Joseph G. Baldwin shared the belief of his class that political leadership should be in the hands of the educated, yet his career as well as his writing reveals a complexity that political orientation cannot fully explain. If he was active in the Whig cause before the party dissolved, Baldwin then chose to be a Democrat, not a Republican. There is little to suggest that he was doctrinaire in either role.

Even the conservative Johnson Jones Hooper was a political floater: first a Whig, then a Know-Nothing, later an independent states' rights secessionist. As his private hopes for an honorable ruling class untouched by predatory instincts were dashed in the competitiveness of his time, so were his ideals of governance. Hooper may not be as joyous in the opportunistic Flush Times as Baldwin—his view of human nature is appreciably darker than Baldwin's (and that of his audience)—but as "Johns" he enters vigorously into his task as biographer of the scruffy malefactor Simon Suggs, in effect acknowledging his "contamination." Captain Suggs himself is allowed to demolish the separation the narrator would like to maintain between gentlemanly honesty and yeomanry amorality. In his "autographic" letter he reminds "Johns" that he "ustur be as nisey a dimmikrat as ever drinkt whiskey"; now, he demands, "quit ritin' lies for the d—d feddul whigs, and come back to your ole princupels!" (*SS*,

---

3. David Simpson, *The Politics of American English, 1776–1850* (New York: Oxford, 1986), 146. James E. Caron argues that the distancing device is "more one of behavior, attitude, or temperament than economic class or political affiliation." "Backwoods Civility, or How the Ring-Tailed Roarer Became a Gentle Man for David Crockett, Charles F. M. Noland, and William Tappan Thompson," in *The Humor of the Old South*, ed. M. Thomas Inge and Edward J. Piacentino (Lexington: University Press of Kentucky, 2001), 181.
4. James D. Lynch, *The Bench and Bar of Mississippi* (New York, 1881), 134.

142, 147). Hooper belonged, in one scholar's words, "to a southern elite that never emerged."[5]

Partisan political rhetoric in these years could be incendiary when Whigs voiced their urgent fears that the excessive liberties of the noisier Democrats would undermine American governance. The Whiggiest of the humorous authors, however, usually refrain from any temptation to hector or lament. Their mingling in a time and place that thrived on mingling is unparochial. They rarely take as their subject political ignorance and wrongheadedness among the yeomanry, but when they do, they are circumspect and realistic, not ideological, assuming merely, with their readers, that they are dealing with "Jackson men." Whether insouciant or bemused, the author-narrators are never wrathful at hearing political opinions inimical to "enlightened" Americans. Some are generous, even permissive, in their tolerance. Outsiders—intellectuals, travelers, and distinguished visitors to the Southwest—were rarely as circumspect.

Consider, for example, Charles Lanman, the Michigan sporting author extravagantly admired by Irving for his depiction of picturesque scenery. In *Adventures in the Wilds of North America* (1854), Lanman has occasion to meet an old veteran of the Creek Wars, Adam Vandever, in the Georgia wilderness, reporting without comment on the raw facts of the old deer hunter's career. But Lanman cannot refrain from editorializing on the man's weak grasp of politics. When asked how he feels about President Polk (the Democrat who had won the election of 1844 by aggressively supporting the annexation of Texas), Vandever parries the question, saying, "I never seed the governor of this state," but assures the stranger that he had voted for "the general" (the Whig Zachary Taylor, who won in 1848)—"and that's all I know about him." The old warrior, however, clearly knows enough both to evade a leading question and to mollify the Whiggish stranger who asks it. Vandever responds with characteristic mountain punctilio, a kind of oblique politeness that the visitor fails to understand. Lanman can only be exasperated. "Very well! and this, thought I, is one of the freemen of our land, who help to elect our rulers!"[6] Many of the humorous authors, even those like Hooper who were political animals, may have been cultural Whigs, but they never indulge in the kind of political snobbery that Lanman betrays. In the relishing of their histor-

5. Johanna Nicol Shields, "A Sadder Simon Suggs: Freedom and Slavery in the Humor of Johnson Jones Hooper," in Inge and Piacentino, *Humor of the Old South*, 140–41.
6. Charles Lanman, *Adventures in the Wilds of North America*, ed. Charles Richard Weld (London, 1854), 151–52.

ical moment they appreciate, even honor, a fluctuating gentry, one that always had to contend with insurgent upstarts from the ordinary classes. Quite a few were themselves such upstarts.[7]

Only in one humorist, and largely in one sketch, does the spirit of the *cordon sanitaire* unambiguously dominate the narrative proceedings—and there it goes far beyond the matter of difference in how English is used. The author who shows the most complex negotiation of authorial space is H. E. Taliaferro, a Baptist clergyman and religious editor from North Carolina who enjoyed a reputation throughout the Southwest as an effective preacher and administrator. His doctrinal explication, *The Grace of God Magnified*, carried his own name on the title page; his major entry in regional humor, *Fisher's River (North Carolina) Scenes and Characters* (1859), is signed "Skitt," Taliaferro's boyhood nickname.

In this mellow volume Taliaferro is no parsonical sobersides intervening in the rambunctious pranks and yarns of Surry Countians, mostly because of the chemistry between the returning Skitt ("Who Was Raised Thar") and the old friends who never left the isolated valley. However well-known outside Fisher's River, the author can simply not presume any moral superiority he may have earned in his twenty-year absence; he cheerfully accepts the refusal of old neighbors to look upon him with undue reverence. In recording his teasing by Dick Snow, Skitt comes across as a sympathetic outsider who, once a vital member of a rooted culture, remembers and appreciates the intimacy (and lack of dignity) accorded him by those who remain. Although Taliaferro's situation requires little of the cross-cultural negotiation that we sometimes see in the relations between narrators and vernacular characters, it requires even greater tact for an acknowledged authority in moral leadership to present himself as an unsnobbish old boy once again engrossed by the drinking, lying, fighting residents, their courtship rivalries, and their religious indifference.

Sleepy Hollow lurks as a distant model for the backwoods community in several of the humorous sketches, but Taliaferro is almost alone among his humorist peers in sharing Irving's avuncular sentimentality about the inherent virtues of secluded villages that seem unresponsive to "the great torrent of migration and improvement" sweeping by them.[8] The charity

7. See Philip D. Beidler, *First Books: The Printed Word and Cultural Formation in Early Alabama* (Tuscaloosa: University of Alabama Press, 1999), 5–11, 87–101; and Johanna Nicol Shields, "A Social History of Antebellum Alabama Writers," *Alabama Review* 42 (July 1989): 163–91.

8. Washington Irving, "The Legend of Sleepy Hollow," in *History, Tales, and Sketches* (New York: Library of America, 1983), 1060. Taliaferro's attitude, unlike that of most

and goodwill that Taliaferro extends to his Blue Ridge characters make *Fisher's River* an exceptionally gentle example of antebellum humor. His Crayonesque mode (inspired by Irving's *Sketch-Book of Geoffrey Crayon, Gent.*) affects the tone of all the Carolina sketches. The double perspective of the returning native combines an empathetic heart-knowledge with the clear-eyed evaluation of experienced analysis. Skitt is a narrator who despite his intellectual and moral status permits the traits of his provincial figures to emerge with their own integrity, showcased in accomplished speechmaking and tale-telling.[9]

While characters, family connections, occupations, and leisure activities seem to have been faithfully reproduced in *Fisher's River*, Taliaferro evokes a milieu and mood out of the genial haze of nostalgia. It could hardly be otherwise. The Carolina country that Taliaferro leaves to make a career is an idyllic mountain community; the Southwest where he makes that career is a site of unstable frontier settlements. Surry County had been a coherent society of long-established residents; Alabama he found to be a swirling geography of violent boatmen, drunken layabouts, scofflaws, and opportunists of all classes, mostly unaffected by the smattering of law-abiding Baptists. If Fisher's River is an organic community when Taliaferro leaves it in 1829, it glows with a memorial sheen when he returns for a visit in 1857. The in-between years have seen Taliaferro pursuing a career in education, writing, preaching, and theological controversy. Skitt's narrating generosity lends a pensive ease to all the Surry County pieces.

Yet that generosity oddly disappears near the conclusion of the book. Gathered at the end of *Fisher's River* is a series of pieces set outside the Sleepy Hollow ambiance of his Carolina community. The final two, "Tare and Tret: An Alabama Tale" and "Ham Rachel of Alabama," are explicitly set in a part of the South where Taliaferro spent most of his adult years. While "Ham Rachel" is one of the most accomplished sketches in all of Southwest humor, it also signals a disturbing dissonance in the character of the author we have come to appreciate. For a narrator who in most of the

---

of the humorists, is that the crudity of the time and place possesses an integrity *because* Fisher's River is exempt from civilization, "remote from commerce, with its corruptions" (*HET*, 202). Irving is also a clear model for sketches by W. T. Thompson, Joseph B. Cobb, and Francis J. Robinson; see Edward J. Piacentino, "Sleepy Hollow Comes South: Washington Irving's Influence on Old Southwestern Humor," in *Humor of the Old South*, ed. Inge and Piacentino, 22–35.

9. Raymond C. Craig points out that while Taliaferro is not totally free of the customary condescension of most educated narrators, the voice we hear in *Fisher's River* is tolerant, even indulgent (*HET*, 58).

collection has entered wholly into a companionate society, self-portraiture is tonally crucial. To turn from the amiable tolerance guiding us through the nourishing life of his old village to the acerbic impatience of "Ham Rachel" is both disquieting and perplexing. It is as if we have suddenly laid aside a humorous book of character sketches, presided over by a permissive, compliant friend, and picked up a travel book documenting just how assaultive the primitive manners of backwoodsmen can be to civilized sensibilities. The reader inclined toward the Whiggish *cordon sanitaire* could wish for no better example than this sketch by a committed Democrat.

The narrator, finding himself at sundown on a rural stretch of road, is granted a night's stay by a farmwife who expects her husband, Ole John, momentarily to return from town. The piece is formally built on the narrator's blasted hopes for a restful night in this "quiet, good house." A cattleman, Ham Rachel, and some accommodating yeomen arrive to deposit the drunken master of the house with his wife, who for their charity invites them to stay for supper. Although he is edgy because of such tablemates and kept awake most of the night by rowdy wagoners who have camped nearby, the narrator is mostly discomfited by the strenuous efforts of Rachel to become better acquainted. He repulses all overtures, determined to reveal nothing about himself to the curious cattleman. What makes the confrontation vivid is the radical extent to which the narrator goes to discourage Rachel: indefatigable interest is met with belligerence. What begins as another variant of backcountry curiosity develops into a test of wills that makes the narrator appear petty, even childish, in his strained and witty putdowns.

HAM.	Ef I mout be so bold, whar do you live, Stranger?
STRANGER.	I "mout" live in New York, New Orleans, Mobile, or Montgomery, or any where else. *That's my business.*
HAM.	By golly! That's durned smart. But, Stranger, that answer don't co-robber-rate to yer looks. That ain't you. Ham Rachel won't answer a stranger that a-way. But I'll try yer agin, sence ye'r so ding snappish on that pint. Ef I mout be so bold, what sort o' biz'ness do yer foller, Stranger?
STRANGER.	That's too bold; but since you must know, it is my "biz'ness" to follow my nose—a pretty long one at that, you see.
HAM.	Wusser and wusser. Durn it, I'll drap you. You're as snappish as a par o' sheep-shears. (*HET,* 175)

The narrator's wise-ass retorts are configured like schoolyard taunts; the exchange, at least formally, goes to the stranger, since Rachel gives up his queries and leaves. But the victory is short-lived. The curious yeoman returns to the fray later in the evening and again on the following morning. Although there is no evidence that the narrator is aware of his self-diminishment in his own story, the space and speech given over to Ham Rachel serve to enlarge our sense of the Alabamian's dignity and to deepen his humane sympathy. The Christian perception of inner worth beneath an unlikely exterior belongs not to the narrator (who, though he refuses to admit it, follows the "biz'ness" of religion), but to this "lean, gaunt-looking specimen of freakish humanity." It is Rachel who acutely observes that the stranger's snappish responses don't seem to fit his gentlemanly appearance.

Rachel is a rebuke to the Christian gentleman in other ways as well. As the "attendants" to the drunken master of the house sit down for supper, it is Rachel who, "acting parson," says a brief grace before the hungry men begin eating. Later, when a noisy wagoner entertains his fellows with an impromptu mock sermon, it is Rachel who, rushing up to the narrator, protests the impiety. "They're mockin' old Eldridge," he says. "[H]e's no better nur them, but that's no reason fur them to make fun o' religion." (The narrator had already identified the "preacher" from his intonations as a Hard-Shell Baptist, but had taken the sermon as genuine: "'Give it to them thick and heavy,' said I to myself.") After supper, the narrator goes to his room, "determined to maintain my dignity and secrecy."

What Taliaferro's narrator exhibits is the kind of overt snobbery that the humorous writing rarely reveals. The most characteristic posture of educated and socially superior figures who find themselves in the midst of rawer specimens is tolerance, even joshing camaraderie. The stranger in this sketch is neither subtle nor amiable. He bewails the "waggish remarks and blasphemy" of the boisterous wagoners, especially in the presence of the lady of the house, but makes no effort to intervene to protect her sensitivity. "I left," he writes, "and retreated to another part of the house," where he resumes his reading. When rowdiness threatens again, he says again, "I left and went into another room." The garrulous Rachel drives him into principled nonaction: "My course was soon determined upon; I would have nothing to do with the crowd, and would have nothing to say to them; I would keep my own room." When, to be sociable, Rachel invades his room, "I still maintained my gravity," the narrator notes. His response is not merely aloofness, but undisguised scorn.

For all his professed dignity and gravity, the narrator stands revealed as a prig, incapable of even disinterested sympathy. In the dynamics of this encounter between gentleman and backwoodsman, Ham Rachel's curiosity is less troubling—and considerably less annoying to the reader—than the narrator's finicky withdrawal to preserve his privacy. There is no evidence that the narrator intends to dramatize his own priggishness; he seems hardly aware of how insufferable he is. Paying his "fare" after a sleepless night, he is further punished when Rachel volunteers to be his traveling companion until they reach the fork of the Eufaula road. "It has ever been my destiny," he declares, "if there is a bore in reach, he will find *me,* and cling to me like one's shadow." It is not clear why the Taliaferro persona, who is so tolerant of long-winded and often pointless story-telling in North Carolina, should be so exasperated when confronted with this Alabamian who, in the same spirit, lets fly "a diarrhoea of words and sentences." The indulgent Skitt, who in Surry County encourages the tall tales of Uncle Davy Lane and Larkin Snow and who overlooks such common failings as drinking and resistance to Christian conversion, becomes in Alabama a testy, impatient moralist. By Taliaferro's own accounting, Ham Rachel respects religious sentiment and is certainly more moderate in his pleasures than the sottish squire he hauls home.

When the two men reach the fork, the cattleman delivers a parting speech, eloquently human, that transcends the gaunt freakishness of his "type." The sound of cowbells signifies that he is a man of property, eager still to entertain the companion who is still a stranger:

> "[G]o home with Ham Rachel, and stay a long week. He can treat yer like a king on the best these deadnins affords. Do yer see these jugs? . . . Thar's plenty ov fiddles, gals, and boys 'bout here. I don't know whether ye'r married ur not: no odds; yer wife won't know it, and the gals won't keer a durn. You may sing, pray, dance, drink, ur do any thing else at Ham Rachel's. He's none ov yer hide-bound, long-faced cattle, which strains at gnats and swallers camels. . . . Come, stranger, the world warn't made in a day. . . . Come go wi' me." (*HET,* 178–79)

If Ole John's has been neutral ground, now Rachel extends a hospitality that is his by right of proprietorship. He offers the stranger a yeomanry Liberty Hall.

In the margin of my library copy of *Fisher's River* a reader has penciled a reaction to this scene: "Temptation resisted!" Indeed, with great consistency, the narrator resists this final appeal, as he has all previous efforts to draw him into an affective human relationship. Rachel offers the full array of human pleasures: music, food, drink, sexual indulgence, and "any thing else." As a Baptist preacher, the narrator might be expected to be morally appalled by such temptation; yet, as we remember from the Carolina sketches, he is remarkably unruffled by the frailties of the flesh. To give him his due, his response is not that of an outraged moralist horrified at the prospect of a week's worth of rural sybaritism. He thanks his would-be host with gentlemanly correctness: "Your generosity is great; but my business is quite pressing, and I must be going. Good-morning to you, sir; I am much obliged." While it is a chilly farewell, it is more consonant with the dignity of his self-image than his earlier exasperation.

As an independent sketch, "Ham Rachel" is merely a predictable ratification of the class snobbery sometimes attributed to the Southwest humorists generally. But as the closing episode of *Fisher's River*, it tends to cast suspicion on the narrator's goodwill and easy sociability in the pages that have preceded it. Moreover, the goodwill here belongs to the Alabama yeoman alone. For all his strenuous efforts to break down the steely resolve of the narrator, Rachel fails. What lends depth to this piece is the author's ability to override the affective limitations of his own stand-in (whose point of view necessarily defines the action) and to touch the reader (who senses the affinity that the narrator ignores). Ham Rachel, a man of practical morality who relishes the physical world about him, takes easily to those who customarily regard themselves as his superior, not with cynical deference but with the openness of one who is at home in the world. For him that is a world of connections. Even if the contacts are not always pleasant, they proclaim the wonders of diverse humankind that become the stuff of experience to be meditated on and marveled at. There is every reason to suggest that this Alabama yeoman feels profoundly his failure with a man who resolutely remains a stranger.

Unfolding outside the auspices of Crayonesque geniality, "Ham Rachel" is a remarkable achievement in which both narrator and yeoman, yoked by "a night never to be forgotten," are left poignantly unfulfilled. Because of the stock methods of characterization in the humor, the vernacular protagonist is more often than not a static if colorful figure, and the authorial narrator is always potentially more than a mouthpiece of the humorist, capable of having his humane breadth extended and enriched by those usually beneath him. Unlike visitors from the East and Europe, most of the educated narrators in the humor are never left entirely untouched by their encounters with backwoods figures. If they are stiffly pretentious, they become less so; if they maintain their snobbery beyond a certain permissible level of condescension, they get a comeuppance. In a few instances, notably Thorpe's "Tom Owen, the Bee-Hunter" and "Big Bear," Joseph Field's "The Death of Mike Fink," and several of Henry Clay Lewis's sketches in *Swamp Doctor,* the narrator's humanity is actually enhanced by the act of inscribing the experience. Many of the sketches, often with some complexity in psychological nuance, go further than verbal exploitation of vernacular idioms and backwoods storytelling techniques. They become the record of individual interaction in which the genteel figure proves to be emendable.[10]

ii.

If the metaphorical use of *cordon sanitaire* is inapt for most of the humorous sketches, its literal reference in southwestern society is to a mostly ideal barrier that visitors would have liked to see more of. Keeping the unwashed "democracy" at arm's length is alien to the spirit of the humor; it is not alien to the spirit of travel accounts, though travelers usually discovered its irrelevance. Exposure to ordinary citizens on their itineraries was usually something of a trial. Aside from the necessity of protecting their high self-regard, travelers sometimes expressed anxiety about their health while documenting squalid frontier conditions. Visitors were understandably nervous about diseases that were endemic to the South (malaria, yellow fever) and the frequency with which residents suffered bouts of fever, ague, and dysentery. In a region noted for its ill-trained doctors and the rural custom of self-diagnosis and self-dosage, outsiders were predictably appalled at the unsanitary conditions they found in public houses and in some steamboat accommodations. Hygiene and lawlessness were linked dangers. Even Natchez, which prided itself as the most civilized spot in the Mississippi valley, could not fully quarantine the notorious disorder of Under-the-Hill.

Towns away from the major rivers were no better than village crossroads in segregating the quality from the rabble. Almost without exception, travelers give vivid accounts of backwoodsmen talking too loudly, eating too fast, and spitting too near their boots. Visitors liked to entwine bad habits, health threats, and provincial diets into their censure of

---

10. None of this affective potential touches such notable figures as Sut Lovingood, Simon Suggs, and Billy Fishback, who dominate sketches in which the Crayonesque mode is rigorously eliminated.

democratic pretensions to equality. Southern spas were scenes of eclectic crowds for whom restorative health was never a sufficient motive for mingling:

> patricians, plebeians, first-rates, second-rates, third-rates: gentlemen whose manners savoured of the good old school, and others whose manners indicated their being copied from some new school, or—no school at all: legislators, travellers, others of literary name; men with name but little money; others who had money and no name;—citizens and families from every State in the Union—beaux and belles—the belles of this year, of last year, and the belles of the year to come . . . with a very partial sprinkling of responsible matrons, and irresponsible old gentlemen, to keep them in order.[11]

Although the study of the common run of southerners at their own routines was accepted as part of an educative experience, visitors would have enjoyed the spectacle more comfortably if steamboats, stagecoaches, inns, and public spaces had offered a more effective *cordon sanitaire.*

A concern for their own literal well-being, however, is not part of the humorists' experience. Neither is their metaphoric well-being. Although nineteenth-century decorum dictated that the humorists filter out of their writing many of the squalid details of frontier conditions, enough remains to confirm the pervasive slovenliness noted with such excitement by English visitors. Even the less sanitized impulses of William C. Hall and Henry Clay Lewis suggest rather than exploit the mean and brutish side of life in the new country. As we see in the cosseted travelers and as we know from historical accounts and from personal letters and diaries, a *cordon sanitaire* was rarely feasible. For the humorists, whose successive sites of operation were never elegantly urban, their willingness to mingle may have had less to do with choice than circumstance; yet the hygienic metaphor, especially when forced to do political duty, fails to explain the gusto of that mingling. The willingness to suspend one's sense of superiority, to be curious, to risk engaging in competitive banter with the undeferential commoner is crucial to the authors' experience in the space they tried to make their own. The humorists' aim in their sketches is not to scorn (or, for that matter, to warn against) the very subjects that made their literary effort worthwhile; it is rather to portray them in ways that demonstrate not only quaint differences, but also the logic and (sometimes) virtue of those differences.

11. Charles Joseph Latrobe, *The Rambler in North America* (London, 1835), 2:127–28.

Solomon Smith records one educative instance during his theatrical troupe's foray into East Tennessee. The manager hires an old tobacco-chewing doorkeeper in Greeneville, but suspects him of admitting to the performance most of the two hundred villagers without tickets. A "little pettish" after finding only seven stubs in the ticket box, he demands an explanation for the discrepancy. But the laconic, literal-minded doorman warns his employer against casting any aspersions on his honesty: "You engaged me to *keep your door.* . . . I had nothin' at all to do with the WINDERS—*and thar's where your hundred and eighty people came in.*" Smith finds that backwoodsmen can get a little pettish, too, and that interaction with them requires some negotiation in civility. Lewis's swamp doctor, Madison Tensas, enjoys the hospitality of the Hibbs family ("plain, unlettered people"), especially the old lady's passion for "talking horse." He also finds a friend in the son ("very illiterate" and "extremely ignorant on all matters not relating to hunting or plantation duties"). "We had become very intimate," writes the doctor, "he instructing me in 'forest lore,' and I, in return, giving amusing stories or, what was as much to his liking, occasional introductions to my hunting-flask."[12] And Thorpe's Jim Doggett acknowledges the narrator's genuine interest in his bear tales: "I am pleased with you, because you ain't ashamed to gain information by asking, and listening" (*TBT,* 118).

The formula of asking and listening is at the heart of Southwest humor. Some narrators are not averse to practical joking at the yokel's expense, but most of them find that physical coexistence requires tolerant accommodation, and some discover a comfortable pleasure beyond condescension.

The laconic yeoman is one enduring image from the new country—tight-lipped, grudging in giving information to strangers, sometimes injecting that impassive reticence with salty, hokey wit. This kind of response to ordinary sociableness is a sort of defense, protecting individuality and privacy, misleading the outsider who pries too much. A second image, recurring with even more regularity, is the garrulous yeoman, who, chattering in a spate of anecdotes and broken-off narratives, punctuates the flow of his experiences with vigorous rhetorical flourishes of local idioms and hifalutin eloquence. This loquacious side of the backwoodsman's encounter with the visitor is the response of marginal isolation, when solitaries need news and gossip from the outside and companionable parley—even if it is only with strangers. The model of

12. Sol Smith, "A Tennessee Door-Keeper" (Cohen, 72); Henry Clay Lewis, "A Tight Race Considerin'" (*SD,* 41, 44).

both principal types is enfolded in "The Arkansas Traveller," a witty dialogue born in political campaigning in the Ozarks in 1840.

> Traveller—Hello, stranger.
> Squatter—Hello, yourself.
> . . . .
> T.—How far is it to the next house?
> S.—Stranger! I don't know, I've never been thar.
> T.—Well, do you know who lives here?
> S.—I do.
> T.—As I'm so bold, then, what might your name be?
> S.—It might be Dick, and it might be Tom; but it lacks a
> d—d sight of it.
> T.—Sir! will you tell me where this road goes to?
> S.—It's never been any whar since I've lived here; it's
> always thar when I git up in the mornin'.
> T.—Well, how far is it to where it forks?
> S.—It don't fork at all, but it splits up like the devil.[13]

This fruitless exchange continues as the squatter plays the beginning of a
tune on his fiddle; only when the stranger proves he knows "the balance" of the tune by completing it on the fiddle does the squatter become
a voluble, hospitable host.

The initial popularity of this tale—which also flourished as a fiddle
tune and song, a frame for improvisational humor, a play, and a painting—comes from the classic contrast of gentleman and yokel, civilized
outsider and illiterate cracker; but its continued appearance in its several
guises derives from the demographic and historical assumption of *accommodation.*[14] As the tale unfolds, distinctions are adjusted by mutual need.
The canvassing outsider, lost in the wilds, needs directions and something
to drink from a taciturn squatter; the squatter, during an exchange that
goes nowhere, cannot complete a tune until the traveler does it for him.
The needs of both participants are thus met. The squatter, giving freely

13. Fred W. Allsopp, *Folklore of Romantic Arkansas* (New York: Grolier Society, 1931),
2:46–53.

14. The text, attributed to Col. Sanford Faulkner, appeared first in 1859 to accom-
pany a print of Edward Washbourne's painting of the rustic scene; see appendix in
Sarah Brown, "The Arkansas Traveller: Southwest Humor on Canvas," *Arkansas
Historical Quarterly* 46 (1987): 372–75. See also Mary D. Hudgins, "Arkansas
Traveler—A Multi-Parented Wayfarer," *Arkansas Historical Quarterly* 30 (1971):
145–60; and George Lankford, "The Arkansas Traveller: The Making of an Icon," *Mid-
America Folklore* 10 (1982): 16–23.

the information sought, ends by inviting the traveler into his primitive cabin for food and drink. The laconic yeoman has become the garrulous yeoman.

It is worth noting that the posture of deference in this piece belongs to the gentleman, not the yeoman. As in much of the humor and in some of the frustrated travelers' reports, the vernacular figure is never above the verbal tweaking of the outsider. Affected naïveté and the playful satirizing of respectable, pretentious language, beginning with Crockett (and Paulding's redaction of his larger-than-life persona as Col. Nimrod Wildfire), continue throughout most of the antebellum years as a reminder of a stout egalitarian past.

For most outsiders, there is of course rarely an urgency to seek *any* social accommodation with the creatures of the interior. They are visitors, one-time observers who are customarily eager to move on to other sites of greater interest. The humorists and their educated peers among what passed as the gentry may have personally viewed the backwoodsmen in a similarly detached way, but their recorded encounters are far more tolerant. The language of social control is rare among the humorists. They may believe with the reformers that "restraints are the web of civilized society, warp and woof" (Theodore Weld), that primitive societies remain so because they "manage their affairs by passion—not by reason" (James G. Birney); but they also know that largely unregulated behavior in their uncivilized geography contributes piquancy and interest in their own lives.[15] Whether for a few months or for a few years, they lived among men of unrestraint and in certain important ways were professionally dependent upon them. Some (Noland and Lewis, for example) apparently found no great onerousness in repeated socializing.

What we see in numerous sketches, then, is what we substantially miss in the travel books, gazetteers, orations, sermons, and official documents: a continual negotiation in cross-cultural encounters between backwoodsmen and authorial narrators (and the educated groups for which they are stand-ins). If the narrator is superior, it is at a level that is worked out in actual moments of intercourse, however brief. His literacy and professional status are taken for granted not only by himself and his peers, but also by the backwoodsmen in whose company he finds himself. The narrator is a figure in Southwest humor who knows and appreciates skills and talents that are not his. In this respect his greatest and most obvious

15. Weld and Birney quoted in Ronald G. Walters, *The Anti-Slavery Appeal: American Abolitionists after 1830* (Baltimore: Johns Hopkins University Press, 1976), 77.

superiority is in contrast to his counterpart in the travel accounts, who is little disposed toward asking and listening.

It is not that toplofty elites are missing in the humorists' world. A few show up as dandies, moralists, or the occasional Magnus Apollo of the village, and we see some of the more unbending as unreconstructed Virginians in *Flush Times;* but they are never figures representing the authors. They call attention to themselves *because* they are unbending, men of some pretension who, like Europeans in the backwoods, are little disposed to ask or listen. Cornelius Baldwin reported that, at an early age, his brother displayed resentment at the aristocratic manners of some Virginians. At sixteen, Joseph authored a three-act comedy intended solely "to ridicule" specific individuals who made much of their heritage and status, individuals who belonged to a conspicuous class of men that, Cornelius wrote, his brother "always held in supreme loathing and contempt." He found especially annoying the newfound "pretentious airs" of those who, having recently "got up in the world," "turned up their aristocratic noses at their old companions and occupations."[16] In *Flush Times* Baldwin's tact forecloses any direct assault on the old-line Virginians who dampened aspiring younger professionals; but his use of the word *surveillance* (suggesting a sense of social control he felt before his departure for the Southwest) is resonant of a feeling deeper than his genial prose indicates.[17]

Although authorial stand-ins in the humor are rarely foolish enough to be snobbish, they radiate strains of certain values we think of as shaping an earlier generation: discipline, reason, dispassionate analysis, a belief in fixed standards and hierarchy. But in almost every case these markers of Enlightenment principles are subordinated to such alternate values as imagination, ambition, subjectivism, even whimsy. Whether from expedience or inclination, these educated go-ahead men of the world, who as moderns support a national agenda of progress, allow themselves a wide-ranging tolerance for opinions and tastes not their own. In any culture, as some specialists tell us, the political imperative to divide values and their representatives into *high* and *low* is often riddled with compromise. In

16. Cornelius Baldwin's "Memoir of Jo G. Baldwin" is quoted in Eugene Current-Garcia, "Joseph Glover Baldwin: Humorist or Moralist?" in *The Frontier Humorists: Critical Views,* ed. M. Thomas Inge (Hamden, CT: Archon, 1975), 173.

17. "An old society weaves a network of restraints and habits around a man; the chains of habitude and mode and fashion fetter him: he is cramped by influence, prejudice, custom, opinion; he lives under a feeling of *surveilance* [sic] and under a sense of *espionage*" (*FT,* 229).

the Old Southwest, the authors and their narrators show few signs of ambivalence in their customary interaction with the resolutely ungenteel.[18]

Educated author-narrators never forget their social standing, of course, and their frequent and fruitful mingling with backwoodsmen is not the same as intimacy with social equals and professional colleagues. It may seem simple enough to cite levels of English usage as the evidence of some kind of comic sociodrama, but narrators and freer-tongued yeomen are not antipodal foils. Lingual levels are obviously meant to differentiate them—as they do—but the segregation is not simple. The respective registers have such latitude that their users dip freely in and out of them. Narrators in Taliaferro, Robb, Hall, Lewis, and others are invariably drawn to "talk down"; yeoman speakers in sketches by Noland, Thorpe, Warren, Baldwin, and others occasionally show off by "talking up." Imitating each other is a common tack for both the educated and quasi-literate.

Behind Plato's wariness of mimetic style was the fear of imitating "low-born" characters or otherwise unworthy models (that is, women, slaves, and cowards). When, the reasoning went, an author no longer speaks in his own person and imitates the speech of another, the shift may well threaten to legitimize a lower rhetorical mode (and its speaker). The antebellum humorists of course never hesitated to "imitate" women, slaves, or cowards, along with an assortment of unworthy persons Plato never knew; and they rather gloried in their stock-in-trade imitation— the speech of yeomen. Simply put, to grant space in any discourse to vernacular presence is to acknowledge its right to recognition. In this writing, however, it is more. Quoting is imitation. When the authorial stand-in begins quoting yeoman speech, he in effect momentarily suspends his own rhetorical mode and thus his authority. "To imitate a person is not just to mime a few characteristic mannerisms," writes one theorist, "but to assume another character, from grammatical person through social persona to psychological personality."[19] It is impersonation at its most fundamental level.

The humorists were not in the business of fretting that their impersonations might threaten the republic's health. The zest with which they shifted rhetorical gears is most obvious in the epistolary form, especially in the sustained performances of Noland's Pete Whetstone and

18. Peter Stallybrass and Allon White quoted in Rob Shields, *Places on the Margins: Alternative Geographies of Modernity* (London: Routledge, 1991), 5.

19. Meir Sternberg, "Proteus in Quotation-Land: Mimesis and the Forms of Reported Discourse," *Poetics Today* 3 (1982): 108.

Thompson's Joseph Jones. We see it as well in such first-person yeoman narratives as Robb's "June Bugs" and "Nettle Bottom Ball," Wing's "Squire Funk's Awful Mistake," and George Curry's "Panther Evans." Except for perfunctory interjections, McNutt's Jim and Chunkey yarns and Harris's Lovingood pieces all consist of a "low-born" rhetoric, mimicked so skillfully by the so-called responsible authority that it skirts the edges of transformation.

Even when the educated narrator chooses to summarize an incident in his own voice, he rarely does so with the sounds of what Kittrell Warren's Billy Fishback calls a "mighty quality tongue, real ristercratic mouth." The level may be excessively coy, or oblique, or in-house witty, but stuffily formal it is not:

> At Parson Bellow's night meetings it was not uncommon for persons "under conviction" to fall, and lie apparently dead for hours, and when they rose it was with a shout of triumph, "a clar and hopeful convarsion."

> [O]ur friend, after a hearty supper of ham and eggs, . . . felt very weary, and only looked for an opportunity to "turn in," though the mosquitoes were trumping all sorts of wrath, and no net appeared to *bar* them.

> I was led to believe, that one who knew a thing or two, had lately been to St. Louis, where he had learned that Gen. Jackson was actually dead, and that it was not "a darned Whig lie"; and that Gen. Cass was a colt out of the same old war horse, and they were a going to run him any how, and he was jis' naternally bound to be the next President, any way it could be fix'd; and he wanted all that could, to stand up to the rack, fodder or no fodder.[20]

Freely amalgamating idioms, clichés, puns, homophones, and other yeomanisms into their own levels, the authors craft styles of narration that are visible measures of social accommodation.

There is scarcely a form used in the humor that neglects the heard sounds of the colloquial majority in the Old Southwest. The presiding discourse is always subject to what linguists call "contamination." Almost before he configures a colorful yeoman character for the printed page—Simon Suggs, say, or Lije Benadix—the author-narrator must configure speech, for whose creation (or imitation) he is as responsible as he is his own proper style. Contamination, we might say, works in all directions: summarized narratives in which the author imbeds his own rhe-

20. H. E. Taliaferro, "The Convert" (*HET,* 158); Joseph M. Field, "Honey Run" (Cohen, 105); Solon Robinson, "The Pumpkin Dance and Moonlight Race," (Oehl., 219).

torical mode with idiomatic snatches from yeoman-speak; a standard-ized received level punctuated by argot derived from steamboating, law, medicine, banking, agriculture, merchandising, or religion; a natural ver-nacular littered with macaronic compounds and hifalutin coinages. All levels consort with each other with unastonished good cheer.

For the educated narrator the backcountry is the site of the ludicrous, the excessive, the uncivilized; but, as so many of the sketches show, it is also the site of the spontaneous, the kinetic, the unregulated—traits that held an attraction for many nineteenth-century Americans. The best of the humorists, practiced in the arts of impersonation, indulged them-selves in that attraction. The same phenomenon is at work when the author-narrator "quotes" the yarns of, or anecdotes about, interesting fig-ures who are closer to him socially and professionally, as in both *Swamp Doctor* and *Flush Times*.

The proliferation of "authors"—not all of them vernacular illiterates—attests to the constructed nature of the written sketch, but such facility is not a reliable guide in ferreting out political ideology. As we see in *Georgia Scenes,* several of Sol Smith's adventures, Thorpe's "Far West" letters, some of Lewis's Madison Tensas pieces, the earthquake story told by Baldwin's Cave Burton, and segments of Joseph Field's *The Drama in Pokerville,* surrogate authors make their bid for attention in a wide range of styles and accents. Much of the humor exploits types, personalities, and ethical codes that the literal author would be less willing to bother with were he in a fully civilized milieu. Despite misgivings and uncer-tain craft, the author is the author of *all* registers and styles. That within an inchoate and constantly changing demography he counts himself, some-times with some stretching, among the "quality" further smudges any sure political authority.

The gentleman narrator figure in antebellum humor may be mostly an authorial convention, but he is more varied than a stock device usually warrants. With convenience comes potentiality. His least persuasive role, it was suggested at a conference some years ago, is that of the "light-bringer," an American version of imperialism's cultural emissary to the dark places. But while there were contemporary groups, overlapping the authors, dedicated to the civilizing mission of America (and betraying the same mix of innocence and greed, of high-mindedness and hypocrisy that Conrad saw in Europe's cultural cadres), the humorists show no hint that they thought of themselves as light-bringers, shoulder to shoulder with preachers, Bible salesmen, agents for tract societies, abolitionists, and other reformers. Indeed, for all their ingrained sense of superiority, in the elbow-rubbing democracy of the Flush Times the authors saw more possibilities in the prevailing local culture and found literary forms for rendering it more useful (and less in need of amending) than did establishment leaders in the East. Their missionary spirit could be low-key because they matter-of-factly assumed that the commonality they mingled with represented a developing stage, not a permanent condition. Some, like Baldwin, were more blasé than others, but they all were more patient and more tolerant than cultural missionaries could ever be. The frequency with which the outsider in their writing is humiliated or repudiated by villagers attests to their regional distrust of Whiggish do-gooders (and even Democratic know-it-alls) who were out to change their world.

Except for a single article of faith—the defense of slavery—most southerners, Whig or Democrat, required no shibboleth for party affiliation. As we shall see, the humorists, modernists in a premodern society, may have considered institutional slavery (like agriculture) an unlikely resource for amusing tales, but the fact that they lived in and wrote about a region in which the white population of all grades supported chattel slavery called for a delicately balanced posture that rarely tilted to the rigorous national agenda of either party. The rise of the plantation mystique was not a substitute for a modern society, but its reverse. It effectively blunted the Whig policy to dampen western expansion (and therefore slavery), along with other principles: public education, economic diversification, and dilution of both casual and ritualized violence. The planters' resistance to Henry Clay's gospel of progress—a program in which business and agriculture would collaborate in modernizing the South—was a strong element in preserving the region's preindustrial habits of thought and action. Instead of a doctrine of self-improvement, the South favored group and family loyalty reinforced by political patronage and an embattled racial pride—what Alexander Stephens characterized as "downward progress."[21]

Someone once suggested that the raucous antics of backwoodsmen in the southwestern interior were debased versions of the forensic challenges hurled by the region's impassioned fire-eaters. Certainly both illustrated

21. Daniel Walker Howe, *The Political Culture of the American Whigs* (Chicago: University of Chicago Press, 1979), 255, 262, 132, 182–83; David Brion Davis, "Expanding the Republic: 1820–1860," in *The Great Republic: A History of the American People*, ed. Bernard Bailyn and others (Boston: Little, Brown, 1977), 483–87. See also Major L. Wilson, *Space, Time, and Freedom: The Quest for Nationality and the Irrepressible Conflict, 1815–1861* (Westport, CT: Greenwood, 1974), for summary accounts of partisan politics.

the South's frontier heritage of belligerence and cranky independence. Stubbornly committed to its singular agrarian economy and protected by aggressive rural biases (against foreigners, capitalists, and urban policies to monitor religion), the South differed as a premodern state from the rival North, and even on the eve of war its difference extended from seacoast cities and river towns to its backcountry.

The degree to which the humorists endorsed the Whig vision and mission over the Jacksonians' cannot be precisely calibrated. In a public sense, the only success for the Whig outsider in the South was total assimilation into the regional ethos. The process was common. Hostility toward northerners, at least before the abolition crusade in the 1830s, was rare in the South. Between 1776 and 1860 more than half a million northeasterners moved south, where, in the words of one historian, they were so quickly assimilated that they "almost lost their identity."[22] The most spectacular example of such assimilation was S. S. Prentiss, the Maine schoolmaster who, in moving south to improve his fortune, grew so acclimated to Mississippi that he became a fierce promoter of protective tariffs and lent his colorful style of oratory to the general cause of plantation interests. There is no evidence, however, that the non-native humorists were intellectually or emotionally committed to their adopted region in the Prentiss fashion. Conscious of the Democrats' selective egalitarianism, they personally liked the deferential mode based on old social hierarchies, but they had no clear-cut agenda for examining the dangers of folk independence with the kind of didacticism that would urge voters to keep the rowdy Jacksonians under a Whiggish thumb. They no doubt preferred order to disorder, as did all literate and cultivated men of their time, but their writing cannot be used as evidence that they approved institutionalizing the principle of social order. Village models of control (Dorothea Dix's insane asylums, Horace Greeley's phalanxes) were manifestly alien to a sectional culture dominated by yeomen; and it is not surprising that one of the principal motifs in the humor is the simultaneous frustrating of well-laid plans and triumph of free-floating desire. The writing celebrates energy, whatever motives lurk behind its composition.

In the world of the humorists, everyone—not merely the louts from Rackinsack and Upper Hogthief—has a story, and the authors are generous in carving out space for stories to proliferate. Some are ephemeral, most are apolitical, and a handful stand as impressive testimony to the

22. Fletcher M. Green, *The Role of the Yankee in the Old South* (Athens: University of Georgia Press, 1972), 4–5.

authors' immersion in an antebellum oral culture. The accelerated inflation of narratives, their fluidity, and often their seeming dissidence come
not from the clash of opposing political platforms but from the nature of
narrative itself, the capacity of one story to respond to or counter another
story. We should not fault these authors for being such lax superinten-
dents of Whig orthodoxy (which in the South was never very orthodox
anyway), but admire them for cheerfully endorsing the principle most
germane to their project: the commonplace aesthetic fact that referents
for any narrative are usually other narratives.[23]

iii.

Many of the humorists may have been Whigs, but their humor was not
Whiggish. Indeed, except as Swiftian satire, *Whig humor* may be an oxy-
moron. Too pinched for a frontier sense of humor, the most politically
savvy of Whig leaders were by gravitas possessed. Solemnity of purpose,
uprightness, and an abiding faith in discipline, improvement, and respectability characterized the ideological temperament that linked the
diverse Whigs. From about 1834 to 1854, Whigs constituted that bloc of
Americans who were "active, enterprizing, intelligent, well-meaning &
wealthy" (the words are Emerson's), dedicated to an almost evangelical
belief in the collective redemption of society.[24]

We have little reason to doubt that the southern humorists—those that
were officially Whigs—subscribed in some general way to party principles: a belief in education, social hierarchy, civic duty, public sponsorship
of physical improvements to ensure material prosperity. Since many of
them were lawyers, judges, doctors, and preachers, they clearly believed
in the power of institutions to effect social change. Like most Whigs, the
authors expected inequality in social conditions, not as the price for eco-

23. There is no master narrative, of course, either Whig or Democratic. Narrative in
antebellum political discourse is plural, fragmented, and distributed locally and re-
gionally. Even influential politicians adjusted easily "to whatever party held the purse
and patronage strings," and party loyalties were so weak that alignments were usually ephemeral. Robert V. Haynes, "Historians and the Mississippi Territory," *Journal
of Mississippi History* 29 (1967): 421.

24. *The Journals and Miscellaneous Notebooks of Ralph Waldo Emerson, Vol. 9, 1843–
1847,* ed. Ralph H. Orth and Alfred R. Ferguson (Cambridge, MA: Harvard University Press, 1971), 160. See Howe, *Political Culture of the American Whigs,* 4–37, for
the religious strand of Whig doctrine. Among conservative Whigs, Howe writes, the
custodial interest was in paternalism and in "improving discipline" (20).

nomic prosperity, but as an inevitability. The old paternalistic politics of deference, which was anathema to rabid Jacksonians, they accepted as a given in any well-regulated society; yet the very conditions of southwestern life eroded their automatic endorsement of such prescribed social continuities. For all their practical alignment with the planter class, the humorists found their affective life—and their most productive moments—in the pervasive styles of yeomanry values. Though they may have believed them to be retrograde, the patterns of rural pursuits, work and play, religion, courtship and marriage customs, sporting protocols, and storytelling techniques all, in the words of one scholar, "exhibited a general retreat from formalism, complexity, and sophistication," qualities which the Old South elite yearned for and which eastern visitors promoted as national norms.[25] Whigs easily thought of themselves as the party of civilization. Despite certain signs of Whiggery, the humorists have a mixed record in upholding such values as character building and self-discipline, caution, uprightness, and even advocacy of strong government. A faith in respectability fluctuates along with fortunes. And the kind of fervor that lent an evangelical cast to the party's political programs is nowhere evident in the humor.

No one can miss the tone of rectitude in *Georgia Scenes*, even as the narrator betrays Longstreet's soft spot for the rogues with whom he traffics so easily. But that penchant for scrupulous moral judgment as a component of humor, which carried over sporadically into the work of Longstreet's friend W. T. Thompson, has scarcely any purchase in the humor that follows. Even Thompson's Major Jones is too old-style, too homespun, in his conservative pieties to qualify for the Whig vision of moral redemption. Thorpe, Lewis, Francis James Robinson, and others construct a narrating presence that imitates the moral and social posture of respectability; their voices *sound* Whiggish even if they are not. But this presence is less an elitist alarm warning against Jacksonian values than a subversive mark of the authors' at-least-momentary release from the high-mindedness and religiosity of Whiggery as a secular creed.

Joseph Story, a Supreme Court justice during the Jackson era who held a traditionalist's faith in institutions to govern and protect their individual members, was predictably uneasy at newer sentiments that government existed at the pleasure of those outside its institutions. He could see only decline: "How can a Republic long continue, when the People . . .

---

25. Robert J. Higgs, *God in the Stadium: Sports and Religion in America* (Lexington: University Press of Kentucky, 1995), 60.

refuse to listen to the counsels of Wisdom and Experience?"[26] Did the shrewd authors perceive the Whigs' language of morality as political subterfuge? One historian has charged that the vocabulary of Whiggery had nothing to do with actualities and that "it was useful mainly as a disguise."[27] By the same token, the vocabulary of Jacksonian democracy, in its strident upholding of egalitarianism, could be perceived as a disguise for the ordinary self-interest of its promoters. Both parties owned oxen they preferred to keep ungored, and the art of deception was not the exclusive maneuver of Barnumesque showmen. What does it mean for an educated professional to linger, with some relish, on the lingual and behavioral crudities of backwoodsmen? to iterate the weakness, failure, or irrelevance of courts, churches, schools, and even families? to depict communal life only in its competitive phases of scamming, practical joking, and fighting? to talk like "them"? The southern antebellum humorist made it his job to do all these—and more.

One reading, the one that has dominated what we think of this body of writing, attributes political motivation to what is essentially satiric work. By his unrelenting focus on the chaotic state of a ragtag democracy unable or unwilling to uphold social order, progress, self-improvement, restraint, and public responsibility, the humorist exposes the inadequacy and unfitness of Jacksonians clamoring for ascendancy. Another reading attributes an aesthetic motivation that is essentially prerealistic. The humorist performs his job as reporter, as social historian and anthropologist manqué, inscribing an accurate record of residual social types on the margins before they become absorbed by the center. Neither reading is entirely satisfactory. The first requires us to grant more subtlety and calculation to the humorist than his discourse warrants. The second allows the humorist insufficient political sensitivity at a time when politics was a consuming passion.

The southern humorists were conservative, but hardly ideological Whigs. They were opportunists who, out of social and professional interests, enjoyed their alignment with the planter class, itself shaken by deviations from the national party. Even those who had come to the new

26. Quoted in Robert A. Ferguson, *Law and Letters in American Culture* (Cambridge, MA: Harvard University Press, 1984), 278–79.

27. Arthur M. Schlesinger, Jr., *The Age of Jackson* (Boston: Little, Brown, 1945), 279. See also Thomas Brown, *Politics and Statesmanship: Essays on the American Whig Party* (New York: Columbia University Press, 1985), 12–14 ff. Still useful is George Brown Tindall's summarizing account of the southern Whigs in *The Ethnic Southerners* (Baton Rouge: Louisiana State University Press, 1976), 121–24.

country from outside the South—Thorpe, Thompson, Robb, Sol Smith, the Field brothers—are temperamentally far removed from such Whig stalwarts as Horace Greeley, the industrious apostle of work, and Joshua Giddings, the evangelical congressman. Not all Whigs, from whatever region, were such stern exemplars of rectitude. Henry Clay himself was a slippery compromiser who often put his own career ahead of party principles, and the humorists who were Whigs, even the active officeholders, were more politically flexible than even their great leader.

In *Party Leaders*, Joseph Baldwin, who himself had chafed under the hereditary patriciate of old Virginia, describes Henry Clay as the "specimen of the parvenu" from Kentucky when that state was still a backwoods. Worse than his undistinguished ancestry, Baldwin writes, he refused to bear himself humbly, "asking no leave" and "acknowledging no precedence." The humorist makes Clay, as one of the "new men," more than a party leader. If the old-style elite saw him as a political "half-horse, half-alligator, and a little touch of the snapping-turtle," Baldwin emphasizes flexibility and brashness as *expedient* principles, useful tools in making one's way.[28] The perceptive chronicler of *Flush Times,* one of the "new men" himself, fashions Clay as a kindred spirit.

Although, as Baldwin admits, the "free manners and not over-puritanic conversation" in his new setting may not have strengthened his higher nature ("we leave this moral problem to be solved by those better able to manage it"), the young lawyer from the Old Dominion clearly revels in his biographical moment of vulgarity, opportunity, and "unmitigated rowdyism." The population of Alabama and Mississippi was, when he migrated, "standing knee-deep in exploded humbugs," as he describes his Flush Times. For a people in whom "the organs of Reverence" were almost entirely wanting, the characteristic stance is skepticism, "when the humbugger sees the intended humbuggee looking him . . . in the eye, and seeming to say . . . 'Squire, do you see any thing green here?'" (*FT,* 235, 88–89, 244). That kind of irreverent energy inflects most of the humor, and not solely as a cautionary trait of its democratic subjects. What one critic has described as the humorists' "collective attitude" is accurate: neither positive nor negative, theirs was a complex response of men "confronting not the follies of outsiders but an outrageously exaggerated version of values they partially shared."[29] Although the sketches

28. Joseph G. Baldwin, *Party Leaders* (New York, 1856), 311–12.
29. Michael Oriard, *Sporting with the Gods: The Rhetoric of Play and Game in American Culture* (Cambridge: Cambridge University Press, 1991), 90.

of each author are tonally different, all the humorists share a latitudinal mind-set that approves the zone of maximum liberty that the back-woodsmen occupy. There is no pinched restraint or finger-wagging in the humor, even when the heroes are clearly enemies of order and ratio-nal governance.

Letter writers in the new country often cite institutional disorder as a trait they must live with in beginning communities, but they invariably put their faith in the moral and social order once they begin to think of themselves, their settling and setting up, as part of *society*. The humorists, however, generally don't endorse that cheerful attitude. Military inept-ness is a given in the society that they depict; so are judicial ignorance, political favoritism, and common chicanery. In the private forms, allu-sions to preachers of all stripes are usually favorable or neutral; in the humor, the preacher is an almost universal whipping boy. The same is true of sheriffs, constables, and assorted peace officers. And, up to a cer-tain point, even lawyers and doctors fare less well in the humor than they do in the more casual testimony we find in daybooks, letters, and autobiographies.

Except for Longstreet, probity and moral earnestness are not conspicu-ous virtues among the humorists; dexterity and expedience are. Dexter-ity and expedience are telling descriptors of Thorpe, Lewis, Hooper, and the other first-rate humorists, partly because these authors—of whatever political persuasion—shared a time and place with thousands of other go-aheaders who wrote nothing. The humor does not emphasize skepti-cism, violence, and cheerful anarchism because such subjects served the program of Whig moralists, but because the authors lived in and made their way in that kind of society. The evidence shows that they rather en-joyed it.

Part II

The World the Humorists Found

Chapter 3

Migrating for Fun and Profit

I leave this rule for others when I'm dead,
Be always sure you're right—then go ahead!

—David Crockett

W hen Joseph Glover Baldwin arrived in Mississippi in April of 1836, he could not be sure he was right to swap his ancestral connections in Virginia for the dubious company of strangers who were already going ahead in the Old Southwest. But the newly opened lands were almost as attractive to aspiring professionals like himself as they were to yeoman farmers, better-heeled planters, and land speculators. "Seldom in history," writes Thomas P. Abernethy, "has an area been settled so rapidly." And for those professionals on the make—doctors, lawyers, actors, journalists, preachers—who would also become authors, the accelerated shift from the older states to the new was fueled by the same self-interest that made this "Great Migration" such a dramatic exodus.[1]

Blocked careers, restlessness, and the promise of new opportunities drew John S. Robb from Pennsylvania as surely as it drew Baldwin from

1. Thomas P. Abernethy, *The South in the New Nation, 1789–1819* (Baton Rouge: Louisiana State University Press, 1961), 465. See also Thomas D. Clark and John D. W. Guice, *The Old Southwest, 1795–1830: Frontiers in Conflict* (Norman: University of Oklahoma Press, 1996), 164–69.

the Old Dominion, H. E. Taliaferro from North Carolina, William Tappan Thompson and Henry Clay Lewis from Ohio, and Solomon Smith and the Field brothers from New York. The desultory search for a career stimulated the moves of Charles F. M. Noland of Virginia and Johnson Jones Hooper of North Carolina. Though delicate health sent Thomas Bangs Thorpe from New York to Louisiana, he prospered, in turn, as a portrait painter, newspaperman, and political appointee in his adopted region. In the new era even those humorists who were natives of the lower South—A. B. Longstreet and Francis J. Robinson of Georgia, Kittrell J. Warren of Alabama, and William C. Hall of Mississippi—seized advantages where they saw them.

From the first, David Crockett's popular motto—*Be always sure you're right—then go ahead!*—implied unfettered mobility, a liberty of what foreign visitors liked to call personal *locomotion.* The bear hunter and congressman, from his birth on the Tennessee frontier to his death in Texas, exemplified that mobility; but, more importantly, his motto came to symbolize the general antebellum spirit for *moving on. Go-ahead!* was a metaphor for American impatience, determination, and indefatigable energy. To be sure, the first part of the motto about being right was rarely remembered, beginning with Crockett himself. It was not right-thinking and -doing that made propulsive confidence a relevant motto. The go-ahead spirit was an ethical temperament linked to individual initiative, stubborn principle, even bellicosity. Above all, the motto stood for expectation of success even in the shadow of failure.[2] *Going ahead* was a recipe for anyone who would trample all the mean conditions along his path, but, like Captain Suggs's *making every edge cut,* it became especially germane for those with finagling on their minds. Although Crockett the man benefited little from the rabid speculation in which many of his contemporaries indulged, his martyrdom at the Alamo coincided with numerous other schemes churned up by expansionism. His motto ratified the courage of risk-taking at all levels, becoming a vernacular equivalent of Emerson's "optative mood." As a locution, *go-ahead* enjoyed an extended life on the waterways, where it merged with the symbolic power of the steamboat.[3]

---

2. The saying flourished after Crockett's death in 1836. A popular Alamo melodrama, *Davy Crockett: Or, Be Sure You're Right, Then Go Ahead,* enjoyed continuous stagings from 1872 to 1896 in both the United States and England. See Gregory H. Nobles, *American Frontiers: Cultural Encounters and Continental Conquest* (New York: Hill & Wang, 1997), 138; Richard Boyd Hauck, *Crockett: A Bio-Bibliography* (Westport, CT: Greenwood, 1982), 150.

3. A farmer in Alabama, when his end-of-the-year entries of profit and loss pleased him, appended a self-congratulatory "go-ahead, steamboat!" in his daybook. John G.

i.

In 1836, inspired by the example of A. G. McNutt, the future governor and humorist then enjoying "a large fortune" after having migrated to Alabama only eight years earlier, a fellow Virginian, James D. Davidson, briefly had his own "golden dreams of the South" as he indulged his speculative fever: "Have I caught . . . the famous *Davy Crockett Spirit,* which changes these wild woods and dismal Swamps into Cotton fields? Whether I have or not, I must now 'Go ahead!'" Anticipating Mark Twain's verdant miner in *Roughing It,* Davidson got lost in the woods, "wandering about in pine thickets—cane thickets, and all sorts of thickets" while dreaming of his productive acres. He lamented, "God help the life of a Land Hunter!"[4] During her travels in the United States, the Swedish novelist Fredrika Bremer was, like Tocqueville, more comfortable in New England than elsewhere, equating the go-ahead American with the Yankee, but her synoptic description of the Crockett spirit was especially relevant for all those who sought out the heady atmosphere of the Southwest. "He is a young man," she wrote, "who makes his own way in the world in full reliance on his own power, stops at nothing, turns his back on nothing, finds nothing impossible, goes through every thing, and comes out of every thing—always the same." Bremer cites with approval another observer: "all the enjoyments of heaven would not be able to keep an American in one place, if he was sure of finding another still further west, for then he must be off there to cultivate and to build."[5]

Tocqueville was puzzled by the striving to get ahead in a "limitless"

Traylor Diary (SPR 302), Alabama Department of Archives and History, Montgomery. Timothy Flint, *Recollections of the Last Ten Years in the Valley of the Mississippi* (1826, reprint, ed. George R. Brooks, Carbondale: Southern Illinois University Press, 1968), 59. William T. Porter, though he had trouble getting his readers to pay for their subscriptions, used the term to justify a price hike for the *Spirit of the Times.* Norris W. Yates, *William T. Porter and the "Spirit of the Times": A Study of the Big Bear School of Humor* (Baton Rouge: Louisiana State University Press, 1977), 32. The *OED* suggests that the term derives from competitive games, but in the volatile Southwest of the 1830s the impetus was not sportsmanship but self-reliant initiative of the ruthless variety— *go-ahead* so focused the self that it barely acknowledged others in the race.

4. Herbert A. Kellar, ed., "A Journey through the South in 1836: Diary of James D. Davidson," *Journal of Southern History* 1 (1935): 355–56, 367, 370.

5. Fredrika Bremer, *The Homes of the New World; Impressions of America,* trans. Mary Howitt (New York, 1854), 2:464. Bremer's analysis was improbably inspired by Bayard Taylor, whom we remember (when we think of him at all) more as the dandy and dilettante than the Viking adventurer; a theatrically grubby Taylor had just returned from the California gold fields when Bremer met him.

continent, but for one Louisiana planter it was seen as necessary. He remembered that as a young man in Nashville he was chastised by Crockett's nemesis, Andrew Jackson, for indecisiveness. Jackson told him, "[A]ct quickly . . . somebody may get in before you."[6] Michel Chevalier, another French visitor, came to the glum conclusion that the westering hordes lived a life of "sudden vicissitudes, of successes and reverses; destitute to-day, rich to-morrow, and poor the day after." Chevalier wrote: "Woe to him who trips and falls! he is trampled down and crushed underfoot. Woe to him who finds himself on the edge of a precipice! The impatient crowd, eager to push forward, crowds him, forces him over, and he is at once forgotten, without even a half-suppressed sigh for his funeral oration. *Everyone for himself!*"[7] The Austrian-born Francis Grund, on the other hand, liked the spectacle of go-ahead Americans, though he linked the help-yourself spirit not with Crockett but with an obsessive focus on business. Grund warned prospective emigrants that they must resolve in their minds "to find pleasure in business, and business in pleasure." He praised the reigning commercial spirit since it fostered "the greatest latitude of speculation, and the largest field for enterprise." The German sportsman Frederick Gerstaecker remembered before coming to America in 1837 an important sentence he had translated for his Leipzig tutor: "Money is the principal thing, therefore get money."[8]

Benjamin Latrobe confirmed the reputation of Americans for money-making. "Their business is to make money," the Englishman wrote in his journal. "Their limbs, their hands, and their hearts move to that sole object. Cotton and tobacco, buying and selling, and all the rest of the occupation of a money-making community, fill their time and give the habit of their minds."[9] One political appointee in 1847 sadly noted that speculation "pervades all classes—even Doctors, lawyers, and Divines—and farmers." A decade later, in one of many orations, the self-regarding A. B.

6. Alexis de Tocqueville, *Democracy in America* (1835; trans. George Lawrence, New York: Harper & Row, 1966), 283, 537; Wendell Holmes Stephenson, *Alexander Porter: Whig Planter of Old Louisiana* (Baton Rouge: Louisiana State University Press, 1934), 10.

7. Michel Chevalier, *Society, Manners, and Politics in the United States: Letters on North America* (1839; reprint, ed. John William Ward, Ithaca, NY: Cornell University Press, 1961), 216.

8. Francis J. Grund, *The Americans in Their Moral, Social, and Political Relations* (1837; reprint, New York: A. M. Kelley, 1971), 2:3, 103; Frederick Gerstaecker, *Wild Sports in the Far West* (Boston, 1866), 44.

9. Quoted in Liliane Crété, *Daily Life in Louisiana, 1815–1830*, trans. Patrick Gregory (Baton Rouge: Louisiana State University Press, 1978), 70. See also C. C. Robin, *Voyage to Louisiana*, ed. Stuart O. Landry, Jr. (New Orleans: Pelican, 1966), 36.

Meek fussily lamented that "this proud Southwest" had been vitiated by "the paltry passion for pounds and pence." Throughout society, he charged, the "great study" of farmer, lawyer, physician, merchant, and mechanic alike was the same: "how to double his profits." The westering of southerners, like that of other Americans, was generated by the well-publicized notion of material progress. No less than their Yankee cousins, "southern migrants were men on the make."[10]

One Mississippi Baptist admitted that "to make a fortune" was the first resolution of any importance he made as a young man; only after long struggle with what he termed his "almost inconquerable resolution to become rich," did he yield to the call of his church. On his way to Arkansas in 1825 "to make a permanent settlement," one Franklin Wharton was consoled to meet a fellow traveler who, "like myself, had once been in prosperous circumstances and now was seeking his fortune in the new country." Appropriating scriptural language from the Abraham story (he liked to record such passages as *I go among a strange people* and *I go to a new land*), Wharton pompously admitted that his intentions in going to Arkansas did "indeed participate of a pecuniary cast." An Irish immigrant in Alabama, soon after being admitted to the bar in 1845, acknowledged a similar single-mindedness but blamed it on his future wife: "For *you alone* do I desire the acquisition of wealth."[11]

Although he set great store by "unadorned" prose, Horace Greeley could strain metaphor with the best of the high stylists when he became exercised by the thought of squatters, "cider-suckers," Andrew Jackson, and the Old Southwest generally, where a parlous economy troubled him: "Why should Speculation and Scheming ride so jauntily in their carriages, splashing honest Work as it trudges humbly and wearily by on foot?" Other commentators worried about the ethical meaning of rampant speculation, reviving the suspicion common in the early republic about profit-taking from nonproductive labor. Many critics—Timothy Dwight

10. Samuel H. Laughlin Diary (MSS 61), Special Collections and Archives, Robert W. Woodruff Library, Emory University, Atlanta; A. B. Meek, *Romantic Passages in Southwestern History* (Mobile, 1857), 150–51; Grady McWhiney, "Reconstruction: Index of Americanism," in *The Southerner as American*, ed. Charles Grier Sellers, Jr. (Chapel Hill: University of North Carolina Press, 1960), 92. See also Russel B. Nye, *The Cultural Life of the New Nation, 1776–1830* (New York: Harper, 1960), 148.

11. Gen. Mark Perrin Lowrey Autobiographical Essay (M49), McCain Library and Archives, University of Southern Mississippi, Hattiesburg; Franklin Wharton, diary, Edward Clifton Wharton Family Papers, MSS 1553, 1575, Louisiana and Lower Mississippi Valley Collections, Louisiana State University Libraries, Baton Rouge; Alexander Melvorne Jackson Papers (M16), McCain Library and Archives, University of Southern Mississippi, Hattiesburg.

and Lydia Maria Child, for example—disapproved of the practice simply because it was a species of gambling.[12] Despite a bad press, Speculation seemed to be jauntier when it splashed honest Work on southwestern roads.

Travelers in the region who occasionally discoursed on speculation, however, were vastly outnumbered by those who carped about financial roguery, which ranged from bad-faith business deals to reckless investments, petty swindling, and dishonest swapping techniques. To many outsiders, appalled by a chaotic economy, the distinction between scoundrelly confidence men and run-of-the-mill settlers keen on bartering was blurred. Thomas Nichols (among others) declared that all Americans were obsessed with "swapping": "They are ready to swap horses, swap watches, swap farms; and to buy and sell anything. . . . Money is the habitual measure of all things." Yet those in the Southwest seemed to be singled out as particularly fond of the custom. Gerstaecker found that Arkansans would "barter any thing—lands, houses, horses, cattle, guns, clothes, even to the shirt and boot they have on—or, if you prefer it, they are just as willing to sell." The German got into the spirit himself by swapping his double-barreled rifle for "a very good long rifle . . . and a good sum into the bargain."[13]

The real problem with economic disorder, another German visitor declared, was that it led to democratic leveling.[14] Indeed, skepticism that democracy and social stability could ever be compatible lay behind many complaints about the excesses of individual conduct in the new lands. Even those Europeans who agreed that initiative and business acumen were more crucial than class in the go-ahead game were offended by breaches of etiquette. Pique over bad service on the road could trigger irrational criticism. In numerous travel accounts, within otherwise temperate chapters, surly table service or boat captains who ignored their own timetables could stimulate diatribes against democracy, often illogical. Ambrose Bierce's uncle in Alabama was sufficiently annoyed by a ferryman to declare, "Avarice is the ruling passion."[15]

---

12. James Parton, *The Life of Horace Greeley, Editor of the* New York Tribune (New York, 1855), 336; Ann Fabian, *Card Sharps, Dream Books, and Bucket Shops: Gambling in Nineteenth-Century America* (Ithaca, NY: Cornell University Press, 1990), 163–64.

13. Thomas L. Nichols, *Forty Years of American Life* (London, 1864), 403, 194–95; Gerstaecker, *Wild Sports*, 184.

14. Frederick von Raumer quoted in *Port Folio*, 4th ser., 16 (1823): 435–36.

15. *Travels in the Southland, 1822–1823: The Journal of Lucius Verus Bierce*, ed. George W. Knepper (Columbus: Ohio State University Press, 1966), 103.

Opportunities for making a secure place for themselves required the same spirit of enterprise among the humorists. Whether pursuing careers or their own restless urgencies, they participated in the same culture of mobility as other southwesterners. Crockett, the inadvertent author, may be our most conspicuous example. Like many backwoodsmen who seized the moment, Crockett elevated his chance to an uncommon level, finessing his native skills to become a celebrity from Tennessee to Texas, as well as eastern cities and Washington, D.C. Thomas Bangs Thorpe, the most resolute artist of all the humorous authors, forged his career, balanced between writing and painting, by his own geographical alternation between North and South. From Massachusetts and Connecticut, Thorpe arrived in Louisiana to make his home—in Baton Rouge, New Orleans, Jackson, St. Francisville, and Vidalia, in irregular and nervous succession. His seventeen-year association with Louisiana was punctuated by frequent trips to Philadelphia and New York City.

To his family's consternation, Johnson Jones Hooper fell into journalism and law, without much energy or satisfaction in either. With Chambers and Tallapoosa Counties as his base, he traveled much in Alabama: LaFayette, Wetumpka, Montgomery, Mobile, and a judicial district comprising six counties. But in the years just prior to the Civil War he restlessly traveled to Washington; Polk County, Tennessee; New Orleans; Columbus, Mississippi; Savannah; New York City; and Kentucky, finally joining the Confederate government when it moved from Montgomery to Richmond. Fully committed to newspaper work, William Tappan Thompson, who was identified with Georgia for nearly a half-century, arrived in Augusta after stints in Philadelphia and Tallahassee and moved on to Savannah, his final site, by way of Macon and Baltimore. Even the most austere of the authors, Judge Longstreet, was born in Augusta (the ultima Thule for backwoods Georgians), practiced law for a decade in Greensboro, his wife's hometown, and devoted his final years to writing impassioned defenses of the South from his home in Oxford, Mississippi. When after 1839 he entered a new career as a religious educator, Longstreet adopted the perambulating habits of his more modest brethren, the circuit riders, by becoming president successively of four institutions of higher learning. Most of the humorists' lives follow similar arcs. If the good judge found his happy hit in marriage, most of his peers had to scrabble with all the others seeking the main chance.[16]

16. These authors' regional identification was considerably more ambiguous than that of southern writers after the war. Only a few were actually born in the Old Southwest. Like so many of their fellow migrants, a large number were born in

ii.

In Missouri in the spring of 1846, a young Francis Parkman surveyed the thousand emigrants then at Independence preparing for their trek over the Oregon Trail. He termed the group a mix of "sober-looking countrymen" and "some of the vilest outcasts in the country." Fresh from Harvard, the Bostonian knew why *he* wanted to go west ("curiosity and amusement"), but he was "perplexed" about the motives that drove these others on their "strange migration": "an insane hope of a better condition in life," he speculated, "or a desire of shaking off restraints of law and society, or mere restlessness."[17] As modern historians have confirmed, the motives were clearly all of the above. Except for those generated by specific goals (cotton, gold, silver, land), most earlier internal migrations in the United States shared the assorted drives of the travelers to Oregon and California; and even in those particular instances the motives were considerably more diverse than what is suggested by such simplified catchphrases as "gold rush" and "sooners."

Migration is a physical process. In the antebellum era, at least, it was the itinerary for even the most ambiguous go-aheaders. For planter and farmer, speculator and artisan, professional and menial, to migrate was to expect success, even when past expectations had proved disappointing. Migrating could jump-start a stalled career or be the first step in a new one. Moreover, as Erik Erikson noted, the process was psychologically useful: "The size and rigor of the country and the importance of migration and transportation" help to develop the autonomy and identity "of him who is 'going places and doing things.'"[18] Though some foreign observers appreciated the magnitude of American migration and discoursed readily on the process itself, few of them ever came to terms with the conditions that made that process possible. Just why people took to the road, even in inclement weather, was an "astonishing" puzzle to Fortescue Cuming on his tour of the Mississippi Territory. He was predictably amazed at the democracy of such mobility—wagoners, packers, countrymen, families, merchants, judges and lawyers, legislators, and

---

Virginia and the Carolinas; but of the twenty-five authors represented in the standard anthology of this humor, eleven were not even southern by birth. See *Humor of the Old Southwest*, ed. Hennig Cohen and William B. Dillingham, 3rd ed. (Athens: University of Georgia Press, 1994), and various biographical dictionaries.

17. Francis Parkman, Jr., *The Oregon Trail* (1849; reprint, ed. Bernard Rosenthal, New York: Oxford, 1996), 11.

18. Erik Erikson, *Childhood and Society*, 2nd ed. (New York: Norton, 1963), 304.

even "the better class of settlers," all crowding the horrendous roads. Unlike Parkman, most natives, though they would also find the process astonishing, rarely found it perplexing. They were as equable as one young Virginia lawyer who, stopping at Louisville's Galt House on his way to Alabama in 1836, observed dispassionately: "It seems that the North is passing on South, so great is the number gliding down the Ohio."[19]

Except for the sharpers, whose home was the road, migrating was an impermanent state, the instrument of change, of transition. For settlers in a new country, the paradox of the frontier imperative lay in the restlessness that defined it. Success, the expected end, required migration, the necessary means. Energy, volition, eventfulness were under the aegis of means; settlement could claim only routine and hard work. If, as it is routinely thought, most eighteenth-century folk ventured no more than thirty miles from home, their nineteenth-century progeny made up for it by becoming nomadic. The tireless mobility exhibited especially by migrants into both the Old Southwest and the Old Northwest strikes us now as exceptional, accustomed as we are to a lingering stereotype made permanent by twentieth-century writers—the geographical rootedness of rural and village southerners and midwesterners.

The restlessness of Americans that Tocqueville coolly analyzed was more vexing to the Englishwoman Harriet Martineau. Expecting southern society to be languid and phlegmatic, she instead found it in ferment—"restlessly gay, or restlessly sorrowful . . . angry, or exulting . . . hopeful, or apprehensive." This lack of contentment, she concluded, "poisons the satisfaction of the stranger" in its midst.[20] Joseph Glover Baldwin himself was one of the restless, though there is no sign that he or his new friends poisoned the society for the strangers among them. In the turmoil of the boom, the Alabama and Mississippi country was a hospitable if temporary home for most newcomers. As *Flush Times* illustrates, the spirit of the migration experience affected all of society, even its most tangential and marginal members.[21]

19. Fortescue Cuming, "Tour to the Western Country (1807–1809)," in *Early Western Travels, 1748–1846,* ed. Reuben Gold Thwaites (Cleveland: Arthur H. Clark, 1904–1907), 4:62; Kellar, "Journey through the South," 351.

20. Harriet Martineau, *Retrospect of Western Travel* (1838; reprint, New York: Greenwood, 1969), 2:90.

21. Prior to 1840, prosperous settlers rarely migrated to the Old Southwest; most of the migrants were members of "southeastern rural middle and lower middle classes" of English and Scots-Irish extraction. John Hebron Moore, *The Emergence of the Cotton Kingdom in the Old Southwest: Mississippi, 1770–1860* (Baton Rouge: Louisiana State University Press, 1988), 131.

A proper Bostonian might consider the search for a "better condition in life" to be "an insane hope," but the hordes who actually undertook to do so had faith that it was worth the effort. Parkman's suspicion that the wagons migrating west also housed the unscrupulous and asocial was of course accurate, as was his speculation that merely a vague restlessness prompted the urge of many to move on. Such a patrician could not imagine that ordinary Americans might share his own motives for travel: "curiosity and amusement." Timothy Flint, the itinerating professional, found virtue in migration: it cured sedentary complacency. Because "traversing long distances" expanded the mind, Mississippi Valley settlers could thank that "spirit-stirring" experience for making them more tolerant than the "shrinking, stationary and regular" residents of the civilized east.[22]

In 1838, the *Democratic Review* reported a stirring Fourth of July speech by Edwin Forrest, commenting that the famous actor properly understood the mission of this country: "to shed the light of her moral truth, by gradual progression, into the remotest corners of the earth, for man's emancipation."[23] The sentiment was lofty enough and the language vague enough to satisfy Whig patriots as well as Democrats. The continent had not quite been secured for moral truth by 1838, but the mission—at least the rhetoric to pursue it—clearly had a life of its own. The ongoing restlessness of the country would continue for several more years as emigrants moved from old states to new, settled, and moved again in intermittent sequence.

Examples abound, each one a chapter in determination. On a steamboat in Arkansas, B. L. C. Wailes encountered a former overseer in Mississippi who, having made $50,000 from the sale of his land and slaves, was preparing optimistically to move on to even greater success.[24] One William Ramsey came to the Mississippi Territory in 1808 and, following his opportunity, moved with his family eight times in the next twelve years. Though the peripatetic fortunes of the Lides of South Carolina have their share of gaps, their narrative of migration has more coherence than

22. Timothy Flint, *A Condensed Geography and History of the Western States or the Mississippi Valley* (1828; reprint, ed. Bernard Rosenthal, Gainesville, FL: Scholars' Facsimiles & Reprints, 1970), 1:211–12.

23. Rush Welter, *The Mind of America: 1820–1860* (New York: Columbia University Press, 1975), 47–48.

24. Letterbook, B. L. C. Wailes Papers, Mississippi Department of Archives and History, Jackson; see also "South Mississippi in 1852: Some Selections from the Journal of Benjamin L. C. Wailes," ed. John Hebron Moore, *Journal of Mississippi History* 18 (1956): 20–30.

most. In 1835 Eli Lide moved his family to Dallas County, Alabama ("the finest place for a merchant" he had seen, he wrote his brother back home). Three years later his daughters were attending temperance meetings and piano recitals "to cheer us up." In early 1840 Lide began to complain of hard times because of President Jackson's suspension of specie credit and recommended that his brother might do better to "go off . . . in the cane break or somewhere else." None of the family by this time was fully satisfied, Lide's sister wrote: "I have no idea that we will stop short of red river." With some exasperation, she urged Lide to go to California, where "he would be obliged to stop" since "he could go no further." After considering California, Florida, Mississippi, and Louisiana, Lide finally decided on Texas. He left Alabama in 1854, leading a party of about one hundred migrants.[25]

Both visitors to the Old Southwest and its recent residents chronicled the general spirit of restless mobility. Early accounts—soon after the second war with England, when migration began in earnest—document the migrating impulse before it became linked to national mission. Most of the émigrés from Virginia—what Joseph Baldwin called its "surplus talent"—had preceded the humorist's own move in 1835. These restless political expatriates, writes one scholar, "found the combination of economic need and dreams of grandeur irresistible."[26] While appreciating its obvious vigor, foreigners and some native-borns saw internal migration as a serious flaw in the American character.

J. M. Peck, a compiler of emigrants' guides, warned prospective settlers, wherever they chose to go, against catching the fever of restlessness that made society in the new countries so unstable. Those who "move about from place to place, to find a better location, never become satisfied." Once a district for residence has been fixed upon, he wrote, "resolve to abide there contentedly." Peck's blunt advice often went unheeded.[27] Joel R. Poinsett, one of Tocqueville's informants, suggested that rich soil seemed

25. Clark and Guice, *Old Southwest*, 172–74; *The Lides Go South . . . and West: The Record of a Planter Migration in 1835*, ed. Fletcher M. Green (Columbia: University of South Carolina Press, 1952), 35–36.

26. Richard Beale Davis, *Literature and Society in Early Virginia, 1608–1840* (Baton Rouge: Louisiana State University Press, 1973), 306.

27. J. M. Peck, *A Guide for Emigrants, Containing Sketches of Illinois, Missouri, and the Adjacent Parts* (Boston, 1831), 176. As late as the Civil War, Peck declared that he knew hundreds of men, "not fifty years of age, who have settled for the fourth, fifth, or sixth time on a new spot"; see *Forty Years of Pioneer Life: Memoir of John Mason Peck, D.D.* (1864; reprint, ed. Paul M. Harrison (Carbondale: Southern Illinois University Press, 1965), xxxvi.

paradoxically to encourage restlessness "in the hands of the man" who cultivated it, "as if the habit of moving, of upsetting, of cutting, of destroying, had become a necessity of his existence."[28] If, as Tocqueville wrote, such restlessness gave Americans generally a "provisional" quality, Charles Latrobe was not so measured. Internal migration, he wrote, had reached such a "quantum of restlessness" that it threw "the whole mass" into disorder. Latrobe disliked the "strange effects" caused by the fashion for the road, and what begins as a description of traveling inconvenience escalates pell-mell into a castigation of national character:

> ... these shoals of travellers;—the overcrowded watering-places;—those new lights in politics, religion and education; the innumerable speculations and consequent bankruptcies; the general impatience of government, and of moral as well as physical control. Hence this golden age of roguery and radicalism, cant, and *charlatanerie;* disunion, disloyalty, want of faith.[29]

Latrobe's catalog was echoed, less frantically, by others busily touring the country.

One indication of the significance of mobility among restless Americans is the frequency and ferocity of voices raised to oppose internal migration. The fear of a steadily expanding west had begun as early as the Constitutional Convention in 1787. Gouverneur Morris, the influential New Yorker, declared flatly that if "the Western people get the power into their hands they will ruin the Atlantic interests." Horace Greeley (who invoked the backwoods when he found it useful) attacked preemption as an outright recipe for "spoliation of the Old States." He personified the settler as a "thriftless, industry-hating adventurer" who, like the Indian before him, was uninterested in making maximum use of the land he occupied. The cheapness of land—$1.25 an acre for most of the relevant years—Greeley denounced as unjust robbery of the Old States that eventually helped to "debauch and demoralize" the new ones.[30] John

28. Quoted in George Wilson Pierson, *Tocqueville in America* (Baltimore: Johns Hopkins University Press, 1996), 538.

29. Charles Joseph Latrobe, *The Rambler in North America* (London, 1835), 1:86. See also Henry Bradshaw Fearon, *Sketches of America: A Narrative of a Journey of Five Thousand Miles through the Eastern and Western States of America* (1818; reprint, New York: Benjamin Blom, 1969), 375.

30. Morris quoted in Robert Lawson-Peebles, *Landscape and Written Expression in Revolutionary America: The World Turned Upside Down* (Cambridge: Cambridge University Press, 1988), 139; Greeley quoted in Robin, *Voyage to Louisiana*, 83. See also Welter, *Mind of America*, 307–8. Although the 1830 preemption law invited abuse as

Quincy Adams, the most vociferous of Tocqueville's informants, put the matter in the starkest terms. The former president predictably touted New England as the country's premier region because it was settled by "enlightened and profoundly religious men." He dismissed the West as being populated "by all the adventurers to be found in the Union, people for the most part without principles or morality, who have been driven out of the old States by misery or bad conduct or who know only the passion to get rich." Adams could have been thinking of Dwight's depiction of the Natchez Trace as "a grand reservoir for the scum of the Atlantic states."[31]

Although Tocqueville dutifully recorded such sentiments in his diaries, and, indeed, expressed his own concern that the draining of the old states might endanger stable republican government, in *Democracy in America* he was considerably more measured, and more optimistic, than the old Federalists who condemned migration. At times his language anticipates the doctrine of Manifest Destiny. What were for Adams mere "adventurers" become for the Frenchman "bold adventurers," who, escaping the poverty of their fathers' homes, had gone to "the solitudes of America seeking a new homeland there." However unkempt his settlements, this pioneer is the "product of eighteen centuries of labor and experience." Tocqueville even justifies the often heard scorn of the "passion to get rich" as motive. "To clear, cultivate, and transform" their continental domain, "the Americans need the everyday support of an energetic passion; that passion can only be the love of wealth."[32]

The promise of freedom is sometimes cited as the great westering motive behind the exodus from the older states to the new, but practical ambition generated mobility more than did high-mindedness. Robert C. Henry, a Kentucky lawyer, worked for months to nail down a likely judgeship in the new Arkansas Territory. In 1819 he wrote his brother detailing specifically what he expected in his "emigration to a new country." It meant of course "unspoiled forests & uninhabited prairies," but it also meant that since society was "in its infancy, a rude & indigested

Greeley described, preemption, according to one specialist, was the settlers' and squatters' right to improve and subsequently to purchase public land that "always belonged to them." Malcolm J. Rohrbough, *The Land Office Business: The Settlement and Administration of American Public Lands, 1789–1837* (New York: Oxford, 1968), 136; see also 201–11.

31. Adams quoted in Pierson, *Tocqueville in America*, 672. Dwight's sentiments in *Travels in New-England and New-York* (1821) were quoted as early as 1826 by, among others, Timothy Flint (*Recollections*, 128).

32. Tocqueville, *Democracy in America*, 621.

mass, which the hand of genius & merit could shape to its own purposes," it held great possibilities for his own kind of genius and merit.
To be a judge would be to have the "power to serve my friends"—to do
"almost as we pleased." Another migrant who was already an
Arkansan judge confided to his diary in the early 1820s that ambition,
need, and a hankering to revive a family name that had sunk into obscurity had led him from Kentucky to Tennessee and finally to "a new,
uncouth country," there (in a curious turn of phrase) "to wait with patience for what is out of reach of exertion."[33]

Some spokesmen for an older South, distressed by the upheaval, didn't
care that self-interest was a spur to migration. The fiery congressman
John Randolph of Roanoke, who boasted of never having voted to admit
a single new state to the old union, candidly saw territorial expansion
tantamount to increased democracy, and thus the decline of states' rights
and the small republic.[34] William Gilmore Simms, the South's most distinguished author, was of two minds about the new country. Although it
was a testing ground for character, he was personally wary of the tendency of his fellow South Carolinians to move west (this despite his father's choice to settle there rather than remain in Charleston).[35] He
shared the concern of many thoughtful southerners that young patrician
males were growing self-indulgent in the empty-minded leisure of plantation life, yet believed that the backwoods was no cure for the "opium
charm" of idleness, and that the easy availability of public lands only encouraged laziness and further mobility. Migration, even for the hardy pioneers who succeeded, tended to erode stability and dilute the traditions
of settled society. In an 1842 essay Simms wrote bluntly: "A wandering
people is more or less a barbarous one." He has one of his border characters echo that sentiment: "The wandering habits of our people are the
great obstacles to their perfect civilization." *Staying put* was particularly

33. Henry quoted in S. Charles Bolton, *Territorial Ambition: Land and Society in Arkansas, 1800–1840* (Fayetteville: University of Arkansas Press, 1993), 104; Elsie M.
Lewis, "Economic Conditions in Ante-Bellum Arkansas: 1850–1861," *Arkansas Historical Quarterly* 6 (1947): 256–57.

34. John M. Grammer, *Pastoral and Politics in the Old South* (Baton Rouge: Louisiana
State University Press, 1996), 59. Joseph Baldwin makes John Randolph, with "no faculty of assimilation or adaptation," a leader of all old-time Virginians opposed to democratic reforms; see Henry Adams, *John Randolph* (New York, 1882), 4, and Joseph G.
Baldwin, *Party Leaders* (New York, 1856), 270.

35. For Simms's several trips to the Southwest and a revealing analysis of his published impressions, see Mary Ann Wimsatt, *The Major Fiction of William Gilmore Simms:
Cultural Traditions and Literary Form* (Baton Rouge: Louisiana State University Press,
1989), 87–93.

important for the artist, who needed, Simms felt, a firm traditional base with its history, memories, and associations.[36]

Simms's friend Hugh Swinton Legaré made his own sad admission in Congress about the weakening of those associations: "We have no local attachments, generally speaking—nothing bears the *pretium affectionis* in our eyes." George Tucker, another southern novelist, weighed in as well against migration. A character in *The Valley of Shenandoah* (1824) dreads a possible move from Virginia to Kentucky ("that *el Dorado* of all bad managers"), where his unhappy family would be forced to "feast on bear-hams and buffalo hump." His didactic tale of 1829, "The Gold-Seeker," was written expressly from the premise that all points south and west of Virginia were regions of barbarism.[37] Even Timothy Flint, no stranger to roving, pointed out the deleterious effects of itinerants, whose gregariousness stimulated restlessness among younger villagers. This "contagion of example," he wrote, fostered "habits of extravagance, dissipation, and [in a witty turn of phrase] a rooted attachment to a wandering life."[38]

In his own wandering life Flint noted that one of the effects of mobility on the smaller river towns in the Mississippi Valley was their makeshift transience. Gerstaecker found that two "infant" towns in Arkansas had exactly the same number of buildings—"two houses and a stable." The courthouse in another town that had failed to attract population was about to "be turned into a corn-crib." Visitors' accounts are filled with descriptions of once-flourishing communities reduced to shabby make-do villages where only the listless remained after the go-aheaders had moved on to more promising sites. Indifference to permanent improvements meant the deferral of real development and stability of the lower South. On his second stop at Cairo, Illinois, in 1849, Ethan Allen Hitchcock complained that the river town was no better than it had been earlier in the decade: "three or four decayed wooden buildings including two stores—dry goods—whiskey plenty—and a few more contemptible shanties." Two grounded steamboats had been recycled as hotels, and half-wrecked flatboats served as saloons. "This is Cairo in 1849—the

36. John Caldwell Guilds, *Simms: A Literary Life* (Fayetteville: University of Arkansas Press, 1992), 85; John R. Welsh, "William Gilmore Simms, Critic of the South," *Journal of Southern History* 26 (1960): 210; James E. Kibler, "Stewardship and *Patria* in Simms's Frontier Poetry," in *William Gilmore Simms and the American Frontier*, ed. John Caldwell Guilds and Caroline Collins (Athens: University of Georgia Press, 1997), 215.

37. *Writings of Hugh Swinton Legaré* (Charleston, SC, 1846), 1:301; Robert C. McLean, *George Tucker: Moral Philosopher and Man of Letters* (Chapel Hill: University of North Carolina Press, 1961), 80, 101.

38. Flint, *Condensed Geography*, 1:215–16.

same as it was eight years ago, plus cholera."[39] Hitchcock's visit roughly coincided with that of Dickens, who mockingly turned torpid Cairo into "Eden" in *Martin Chuzzlewit* (1843–1844). As late as 1856, when a boat passenger went ashore in Cairo to buy a newspaper, he came upon "a *Man lying . . . in his blood, having* only a few minutes before been *Murdered*—supposed shot." The corpse was finally removed a half-hour later, but "no public fu[n]ctionary appeared." The diarist, a New York musician, noted the "perfect thrill of horror" in the ladies' cabins: "nothing would do—to express their profound grief," he wryly added, "but a half a dozen of Quadrilles, which they danced in the most bewitching manner."[40]

The most formal argument against mass mobility came from Horace Bushnell, a noted New England clergyman, whose "Barbarism the First Danger" established his reputation in 1847. Emigration, he wrote in his oration, promotes a "bowie-knife style of civilization." Continual resettlement leads to "disorganization" because a migrating people sacrifice their "old roots of local love and historic feeling," and the training of professionals declines into half-measures so that second and third generations are destined to "mix up extravagance and cant" while "their tastes grow wild" and their enjoyments "coarse." These "semibarbarians," he argued,

> roll on like a prairie fire before the advance of regular emigration; they have no fixed habits and do not care to appropriate the soil, consequently have no education or religion. They live mainly by hunting and pasture; and when a regular settlement is begun within an hour's ride they feel proximity too close, quit their hut of logs, which is in fact only their tent, and start on by another long remove into the wild regions beyond them.

Bushnell's gloomy scenario of social decline climaxed with a parsonical threat of wholesale infidelism: "Ere long," he warned, these "wild hunters and robber clans" will become the "American Moabites, Arabs and Edomites!"[41]

39. Gerstaecker, *Wild Sports*, 274; *Fifty Years in Camp and Field: Diary of Major-General Ethan Allen Hitchcock, U.S.A.*, ed. W. A. Croffut (New York: Knickerbocker Press, 1909), 355. Hitchcock's assessment of Cairo is repeated in numerous accounts: see, for example, Bremer, *Homes of the New World*, 2:98, 173, and Lester B. Shippee, ed., *Bishop Whipple's Southern Diary, 1843–1844* (Minneapolis: University of Minnesota Press, 1937), 130–31.

40. Anton Reiff Journal, MS 3274, Louisiana and Lower Mississippi Valley Collections, Louisiana State University Libraries, Baton Rouge.

41. Horace Bushnell, *Selected Writings on Language, Religion, and American Culture*, ed. David L. Smith (Chico, CA: Scholars Press, 1984), 155–56, 158–59.

Some of the more articulate American commentators, then, viewed migration with an eye as jaundiced as that of most English travelers. In the words of one historian, antebellum America heard from its "native Jeremiahs" as well as "supercilious foreigners."[42] To describe migration, as Timothy Flint did, as a "contagion" came casually to most pens, but a lawyer in the North Carolina piedmont gloomily literalized the disease trope in an 1817 letter, an account of how anxiety and confusion were pervading "all ranks of people": "The *Alabama Feaver* rages here with great violence and has *carried off* vast numbers of our citizens. I am apprehensive, if it continues to spread as it has done, it will almost depopulate the country." He concludes his vision of the plague: "There is no question that this feaver is contagious[;] as soon as one neighbor visits another who has just returned from the Alabama he immediately discovers the same symptoms." The attraction of fertile lands was finally a powerful *national* phenomenon: there was also "the Ohio feever" as well as that in Alabama.[43]

There is no evidence, however, that either the moral or political arguments against restlessness had any effect in balking road-happy Americans. During the restless century, 50 percent of the population moved at least once per decade.[44] Although the words *national mission* might never pass their lips, even the most stable citizens accepted migration into the new countries as an expression of their God-given rights and an opportunity to get rich in another place. If they read the warnings of detractors, whether supercilious foreigners or homegrown Jeremiahs, the restless migrants ignored them. Freedom to move was rarely a philosophical or moral matter for them. A few looked upon migration simply as a means of escape—from threats, disgrace, family problems, poor health—but most seized the moment out of economic necessity. "Having some disposition to grow rich," George Hooper in 1833 confessed to being tempted by the "glowing narrative" of new settlers in the Southwest. He arrived in Alabama the next year, and his own glowing narrative in turn tempted his younger, less reliable brother, Johnson Jones Hooper, to follow. George

42. Rowland Berthoff, *An Unsettled People: Social Order and Disorder in American History* (New York: Harper & Row, 1971), 204.

43. Charles D. Lowery, "The Great Migration to the Mississippi Territory, 1798–1819," *Journal of Mississippi History* 30 (1968): 182; "Ohio feever": Rohrbough, *Land Office Business,* 90–91.

44. James W. Oberly, "Westward Who? Estimates of Native White Interstate Migration after the War of 1812," *Journal of Economic History* 46 (1986): 431.

wrote their parents in North Carolina that the country was indeed promising for anyone with "a fluent tongue and abundant assurance."[45] When residents recorded the movement of neighbors to Arkansas, Mississippi, Texas, or Louisiana, the gloomy iteration didn't require specific reasons. They knew the migrants were hoping to better their lives *financially*.

So too the humorists. As professionals in their migration to the new country, they were governed by ambition, and they entered into the hustling life of the region with the same high hopes expressed by other middle- and working-class newcomers. It is not surprising that for all the diverse temperaments and talents among the newspaper authors, their humorous sketches are dominated by a common spirit: competition. The professional men who contributed their readings of antebellum culture were, like other migrants, engaged in their own "mad scramble for place and power" in the Southwest. In their writing, as one commentator has noted, virtually every activity "becomes a contest: not just horse races, cockfights, gander pullings, and poker games; but horse swaps and camp meetings, dances and weddings, pranks and steamboat trips. Everything is up for grabs: wealth and status to be won by enterprise not birth, an entire order to be determined by wit and opportunism."[46] Nearly all gestures toward an improved civil order are starkly challenged in the humor. Besides camp meetings, dances, and weddings, other group activities that historically lent coherence to communal life—court days, militia musters, local elections—are marked by aggressive self-interest.

Like many other kinds of imaginative literature, this humor is an italicized version of actuality—and inevitably a distortion. Yet historically, in the era of provisional settling, migration and money-getting were rarely to be separated. As surveyor general of the northern section of the Mississippi Territory (an old-boy post thanks to his friendship with Andrew Jackson and his service in the Battle of New Orleans), John Coffee was deluged by applicant letters in 1816–1817. One Virginian urged General Coffee to appoint his son as deputy surveyor, not because he was talented but because he could provide his father with information about the new country where he wanted to purchase land. He needed specifics, as he admitted, on "Soil, Climate, Situation[,] water, local advantages or any thing or Every thing Else I may wish to be Informed of." While some ap-

45. Johanna Nicol Shields, introduction to *Adventures of Captain Simon Suggs, Late of the Tallapoosa Volunteers; Together with "Taking the Census" and Other Alabama Sketches,* by Johnson Jones Hooper (Tuscaloosa: University of Alabama Press, 1993), xix–xx.

46. Michael Oriard, *Sporting with the Gods: The Rhetoric of Play and Game in American Culture* (Cambridge: Cambridge University Press, 1991), 51.

plicants boasted of their "correctness, punctuality, and expedition" and others of their extensive knowledge of both theory and field practice, a few honestly confessed that they simply wanted a reason to migrate—in the words of one Elisha Clark of Massachusetts, "having had a wish for some time to see that part of our Country." J. S. Doxey of Alabama wrote Coffee in 1822, asking for a renewal of his surveying job. After itemizing recent misfortunes, he announced: "I intend, should I live and be able, to settle myself in the course of two years, in your section of the State, where I can have good society and more conveniences."[47]

Michel Chevalier noted in 1834 that there was "not a family at the North, that has not a son or a brother in the South"; the next year, Boston editor Sarah Josepha Hale lamented that fine young men who should be the glory and strength of New England "go to find their graves in the marshes of the south." When a perceptive visitor concluded that the new generation in the Southwest was no less devoured with "the passion of making money" than the industrious New Englander, he doubtless knew that the migrating generation included New Englanders. Indeed, many Yankees (including James Henry Hammond) became southernized early and easily. Ethan Allen's grandson, Henry Hitchcock of Vermont, wandered down the rivers and settled in Mobile in 1816; two years later he was appointed first secretary of the Alabama Territory. When he arrived in Mississippi, S. S. Prentiss, a Maine schoolmaster, considered slavery a detested institution, but nine years later, in 1836, he was publicly defending it. Politically and socially New Englanders saw that it made sense to adapt to the new culture.[48]

Conservatives continued to see the southwestern settlers as the offscouring of the East: greedy speculators, disgraced businessmen, confidence men, adventurers, the poor and the needy. One writer admitted that, in earlier years, migration meant *fleecing,* which suggested a raw society composed wholly of victims and victimizers. When "we heard of a respectable man hieing to an unknown land," he wrote, the dominant image was that of the "speculator beckoning him to destruction." When migration grew to be a national phenomenon, however, the hieing hordes included men "who could not be easily deluded." Even the neediest

47. John Coffee Papers (LPR 27), Alabama Department of Archives and History.
48. Chevalier, *Society, Manners, and Politics,* 88; Sarah Josepha Hale, *Traits of American Life* (Philadelphia, 1835), 101; C. B. Walker, *The Mississippi Valley, and Prehistoric Events* (Burlington, IA, 1881), 245; William H. Brantley, Jr., "Henry Hitchcock of Mobile, 1816–1839," *Alabama Review* 5 (1952): 3–39; *A Memoir of S. S. Prentiss, ed. by His Brother* (New York, 1855), 1:225.

of the migrants, prompted by poverty rather than choice, found the move useful.[49] The Puritan notion that Americans were playing out some divinely ordered drama was secularized in the forward-moving nineteenth century to accommodate the westering experience. The kind of expansion that such a drama involved was ready-made for theatricalized rhetoric, as the testimony of Edwin Forrest and the editors of the *Democratic Review* shows. If making migration an epic drama came naturally to actors and stage entrepreneurs, the idea that mobility was involved in doing the Lord's business—was in fact the manifestation of divine purpose—came naturally to humbler accounts as well.

Because epic dramas require epic heroes, the character of the men charged with the revised American mission underwent revision as well. With migration flowing, in Chevalier's words, "with a wonderful power and an admirable regularity," the settlers' role, whether they discerned it or not, was to spread themselves over the vast territory "marked out for them by the finger of Providence" and to subdue it to their uses. In an address in 1837 before his fellow representatives, Hugh Swinton Legaré found "a grandeur" in the "irresistible onward march of a race, created . . . and elected to possess and people a continent." His paean to Manifest Destiny came in the middle of a speech lauding the credit system, which was then beginning to create economic hardships. "[P]eril and difficulty are the price which Providence exacts" for eminent success. Struggle brings forth "heroic virtues" for those disciplined enough to persevere in filling the continent "with the noblest of all populations"; and with a purified and elevated character, the march "rolls on, in its sure and steady progress, to the uttermost extremities of the west."[50]

By 1857, A. B. Meek of Alabama had transformed the gritty experience of migration to frontier romance, emphasizing pioneer industry and ambition.[51] For all the aplomb with which some affluent planters dismissed moneymaking, the southwesterner was no different from his northern cousin in relishing material success. As one recent historian has written,

49. James Hall, *Letters from the West* (1828; reprint, ed. John T. Flanagan, Gainesville, FL: Scholars' Facsimiles & Reprints, 1967), 171–72.

50. Chevalier, *Society, Manners, and Politics*, 99, 262; Legaré, *Writings*, 1:305, 308. The phrase "Manifest Destiny" was coined by journalist John L. O'Sullivan in 1845, but the sentiment was much older. Six years earlier O'Sullivan had published "The Great Notion of Futurity" in the *Democratic Review*—a "paean to destiny and mission." See Robert W. Johannsen, "The Meaning of Manifest Destiny," in *Manifest Destiny and Empire: American Antebellum Expansionism*, ed. Sam W. Haynes and Christopher Morris (College Station: Texas A&M University Press, 1997), 10.

51. Meek, *Romantic Passages*, 240–42.

only a keen interest of the southern elite in amassing money could have insured a "sufficient fortune to free themselves from labor—chiefly by buying it from others." Culture and breeding ratified money, not sloth. "Those who could make fortunes made them. Those who could not tried another line of work or moved."[52]

In little more than a generation, the "Back Inhabitants" of the Southwest were mythically transformed into prosperous opportunists feigning indifference to ambition. One politician in the 1840s suggested the ideological basis of expansionism when he observed that Americans were busily "filling up the grand outlines of a territory intended for the possession and destiny of the American race—an outline drawn by the Creator himself."[53] Southerners put their own accent on that aggrandizing policy.

Perhaps the most extravagant of the antebellum heroizing impulses, however, came from a foreigner, Tyrone Power, whose *Impressions of America* (1836) envisioned a great future for the South. For the Irish actor, the settling of the lower South was an ongoing high drama directed by the Almighty for the moral good of mankind. Engaged in clearing the wilderness, the new southerners were laying bare the wealth of "this rich country with herculean force and restless perseverance, spurred by a spirit of acquisition no extent of possession can satiate." Completely missing from this picture is the image, persistently popular in the American northeast, of the southerner as indolent and dissipated. Rather, these are settlers advancing "the great cause of civilization, whose pioneers they are." Power's dithyrambic prose surpasses that of Meek and most of the other southern defenders of expansionism. The actor's own phrase— "Unconscious agents in the hands of the Almighty"—would be echoed by the most impassioned nativists.[54]

Despite the aging Jeremiahs among them, most southerners embraced western expansion for practical purposes: new land meant more cotton

52. William C. Davis, *A Way through the Wilderness: The Natchez Trace and the Civilization of the Southern Frontier* (1995; reprint, Baton Rouge: Louisiana State University Press, 1996), 209–10. See also Daniel S. Dupre, *Transforming the Cotton Frontier: Madison County, Alabama, 1800–1840* (Baton Rouge: Louisiana State University Press, 1997), 86, and Carl N. Degler, *Place over Time: The Continuity of Southern Distinctiveness* (Baton Rouge: Louisiana State University Press, 1977), 57.

53. Major L. Wilson, *Space, Time, and Freedom: The Quest for Nationality and the Irrepressible Conflict, 1815–1861* (Westport, CT: Greenwood, 1974), 109. The speaker was Rep. Chesselden Ellis of New York.

54. Tyrone Power, *Impressions of America during the Years 1833, 1834, and 1835* (London, 1836), 2:215–16.

and more slaves in the short run, and in the long run a chance to rectify the South's waning political influence in Washington. To deny widespread migration was not merely to block the extension of slavery, but also, in one historian's words, to deny "that geographical mobility which was a saving technique, a habit and almost a virtue in itself."[55] If the national encouragement of southwestern expansion saw nothing amiss in annexing Mexico and Cuba, the southern version of Manifest Destiny might well have been fashioned by fantasts who dreamed of creating a vast slave empire out of Central America, Brazil, and the Caribbean. One Georgia editorialist at the outbreak of the Civil War declared that "destiny" demanded such a move and, though it might not require the sword, it had to be accomplished "because Providence designs the spreading out of African slavery into regions congenial and suitable to its prosperity."[56] After the war, remnants of such pastoral imperialism were seen in land-speculating entrepreneurs who had only this continent as their theater.

iii.

Since the primary attraction of the western country was its untapped potential for agriculture, the crucial test of all scouting expeditions for the migration-minded was fertility of the soil. Many of the on-the-road families from Virginia and the Carolinas were driven by widespread crop failure, some weather-related but most as a result of overcultivation. One diarist in 1845 quoted newspaper reports that "hundreds of families are daily and almost hourly passing by Ash[e]ville and the Warm Springs hastening West in pursuit of subsistence."[57]

When migrants to the new lands bought acreage and actually settled, their letters to kin and friends back home tended to be missives of self-congratulation, only barely concealed in breathless recitals of statistics and the missionary zeal to share good fortune with loved ones. From 1841 to 1844 Robert Fraser, a schoolteacher and modest businessman in the Sumter District, was bombarded by pleas from his enthusiastic kin to forsake South Carolina and follow them to Mississippi. The satisfaction

55. Bruce Collins, *White Society in the Antebellum South* (London: Longman, 1985), 97. See also Berthoff, *Unsettled People,* 129.
56. Lewis P. Simpson, *The Dispossessed Garden: Pastoral and History in Southern Literature* (Athens: University of Georgia Press, 1975), 80–81.
57. Laughlin diary.

of being in "this land of plenty" made his brother-in-law giddy ("I felt almost like strutting") when he first realized his good fortune: "You can repair your affairs in one year here as much as you can there in three."[58] Such comparative appraisals of fertility were a regular feature of letters home. One migrant to Arkansas who settled in Pope County in 1828 wrote to his sister in New Jersey that "nothing could induce me to live in jersey now for [I] can make more in one year here than I can there in five with the same labour." The Atkins brothers, who settled near Albany, Georgia, in 1839, urged their father in Virginia to move also: "you could make more here farming in one year than you would there in five."[59] "I regret that I did not moove five years sooner," wrote Sandford Wilbourn from Mississippi to a friend still stuck in Georgia. He was "mutch pleased" by his move and tactfully hinted that his friend might want to show similar good sense. "I am entirely clear of debt. & that is more than I ever could say when I lived in Georgia."[60] The sentiment—if not the colorful imagery—of another settler's letter in 1836 was repeated again and again: "When a man once gets to the limbs on the tree of fortune, 'tis not hard for him to climb in this country."[61]

Yet the most stirring of all the settlers' chamber-of-commerce letters must be that of J. M. Roberts, who in 1844 detailed just how the rich lands of north Alabama had transformed Talladega into a near paradise. With 900 acres of land (400 of them in cultivation) and a sawmill and gristmill, Roberts touted Talladega as "the loveliest valley in North Ala. . . . The scene is truly picturesque & beautiful." He claimed that "Society in this valley is as good as I would have it," and that "tho' no flag of Temperance reform floats in the breezes of this our pleasant vicinity, society is allmost void of drunkenness & the peaceful banner of sobriety & virtue" flies from "nearly every habitation." Roberts declared his neighbors to be "generally intelligent & [as if he spoke from experience] more so than they are in Georgia." As a peroration, he asked, "Then why seek ye another country, why not come & enjoy the host of blessings to be had in Talladega Valley." From among the possible destinations of the migration-minded, Roberts addressed the issue like a rhetorical Goldilocks, foreclosing

58. "Some Mississippi Letters to Robert Fraser, 1841–1844," ed. Margaret Burr Des-Champs, *Journal of Mississippi History* 15 (1953): 181–89.

59. Bolton, *Territorial Ambition*, 55; Atkins Family Papers, Georgia Historical Society, Savannah.

60. Sanford Wilbourn, 1846, Special Collections and Archives, Robert W. Woodruff Library, Emory University.

61. Davis, *A Way through the Wilderness*, 105.

all of the sites except his own: "For should you go to the more sunny South—pale faces, sickness & death assail. . . . Go to the far West and civilization . . . yet sleepeth.—Go to the North & chilling winds soon destroy the vitals of the Southron and about the east what can *you* say—will you not join me in saying that my Chariot wheels roll not backward."[62] The term "tide of migration" came often to the pens of travelers and local inhabitants alike. What was an imperfect metaphor (for those who saw the tide moving irresistibly in one direction only) became depressingly appropriate when the chariot wheels occasionally did roll backward.

After a few disappointing years and a succession of new steads, migration sometimes was followed by countermigration back to points of origin. The fertility of new acreage in the Southwest could not guarantee prosperity either for farmers or the vast support population dependent upon an agricultural economy—the tradesmen, skilled workers, and professionals who clustered quickly in towns quickly founded. The cheerful go-ahead spirit of migrants who tirelessly urged family, friends, and other stay-at-homes to share in their westering prosperity had its darker underside in instances of settlers merely subsisting, escaping earlier debts, incurring new ones, trying to stay afloat. The all-too-common counterpart of making money was losing it. Those who flocked to the new country were obviously more adventuresome and perhaps greedier than their cautious cousins in the settled states, but they generally showed no greater shrewdness in making and keeping money. Although dreams of making a fortune by moving elsewhere thread their way through the domestic prose of the period, they are punctuated by pervasive unease about economic security. Letters back home are often filled with allusions to old debts, business embarrassments, even the threat of lawsuits—details that support the assumption that financial failure was the strongest historical cause for original migration.

One hat dealer in Augusta wrote a despairing letter in 1844 filled with frustration at having to compete with "no less than 6 Hat Stores." Convinced that he would have to move elsewhere to "make any thing more" than a living ("and I ought to do more than that nowadays"), he added that his wife discouraged him: "perhaps you wont find any better place so I give it up. *but it will not do.*"[63] As we know from Baldwin's *Flush Times,* an economy based on credit and locally issued paper money could only

62. J. M. Roberts, May 28, 1844, McCain Library and Archives, University of Southern Mississippi.
63. A. B. Mallory, William S. Comstock Papers, Georgia Historical Society.

crash—as it did in 1837. In May of that year a northern governess in Mississippi recorded having tea with a low-spirited "Mrs. M." and her daughter, who lamented the family's financial loss and the imminent ejection from "their fine house." With some relish, she generalized in her diary on "the truth of reaction in all things." Never was "a change so sudden and so little foreseen—and yet it might have been expected from so much reckless extravagance." Because the "luxury of almost every class was astonishing," an "insult to their less fortunate acquaintance," it was now, she concluded, "their turn to envy the insignificant."[64]

One migrant's story is an instructive example of how *conditional* success and *mitigating* failure so often meshed. The resilience and patience required of small merchants in the Southwest of the 1840s and 1850s may be more pronounced in the career of Samuel H. Aby than in the general run of migrants, but his is surely not unique. Aby fled to Gallatin, Mississippi, in the 1830s to recover from crippling debts back in Virginia, but in 1840 he complained in letters to his parents, "times with me are hard enough" and he expected to "lose about $10,000" in his mercantile business. To an old friend he stoutly maintained, "I must . . . do the best I can, and only hope for better times." While he was candid about the poor record of his career, he wanted to stick to it: "if ever I sell goods again, I must have the cash down[;] this credit sistem has done me great injury." He proposed that his friend risk $4,000 to begin a new dry-goods store in another town, which Aby would manage for half the profits: "if I have my health I think I can yet make at least a small fortune." He petitioned for relief under the Bankrupt Act in early 1842, which, he wrote, would make him "a free man again" within a month. By now he was in Grand Gulf managing a new business and being hopeful: "I am still young enough to begin the world & have had experience to teach me how to act in future."[65]

Trade in the new town, however, proved to be "dull" and money "scarce" because of bank failures in New Orleans and a poor cotton crop in Mississippi. Wistfully, he wrote, "I hope I shall not always be pressed for money." By spring of 1845 business had become "tolerably fair." He was not only hoping for a good fall trade ("our very Salvation depends upon it"), but was also vowing to "make extra exertions to make sales." In 1847 Aby finally enjoyed an unusually brisk fall trade ("business never

64. Margaret Wilson Diary (Z/180), Mississippi Department of Archives and History.
65. Aby Family Papers (Z/1793), Mississippi Department of Archives and History.

was so good"); his hopes buoyed that he might at last "get out of my heavy liabilities." And a letter of May 1852 was upbeat: "perhaps things will be better here after." But the next year he was considering a move to Texas, since a proposed new railroad "will ruin our trade here."[66] Ever hopeful of an upward turn in his fortunes, this merchant modestly achieved his goal, but it is clear that, like the more prestigious planters, his debts always shadowed him, even in good years.

Aby's story is incomplete in his correspondence, but the fourteen years he spent in Mississippi endeavoring to make "at least a small fortune" betray his anxieties as well as his persistence. His well-to-do neighbors would have found passing interest in Aby's struggle (many of them duplicated his experience), but cultivated easterners and old-state political leaders would have found depressing both his anxieties and his persistence. Aby was incapable of seeing himself as part of the big picture that Horace Bushnell and other intellectuals were busily painting of the calamities awaiting those foolish enough to join the wholesale migration.

The new lands, touted for their game even as the soil was advertised for its fertility, are both the source of frontier character and its test. We know of the unresolved sentiments at the heart of *The Pioneers*, balanced between a proud sense of achievement with the inroads of civilization and an acute sense that the price of town-building has been the loss of the wilderness. Even J. J. Audubon wobbles ambivalently. Like Cooper's Elizabeth, he can scarcely believe the progress that his eyes record: "villages, farms, and towns," the "din of hammers and machinery," "hundreds of steam-boats" gliding the waterways in a short twenty years have replaced "the grandeur and beauty of these almost uninhabited shores." As Annette Kolodny has observed, Audubon is trapped between condemning and applauding.[67] Henry Fearon called "the western country" an "almost boundless theatre for human exertion," and, after studying migrants on their way to Alabama and Missouri, expressed the hope that it would not be "polluted" by the "iniquitous perversion" of those who claimed possession. Like Audubon, he seemed uncertain whether the spectacle of settlement was cause for alarm or awe. William Cobbett, who condemned Fearon for trumpeting the West as a "boundless theatre" beckoning British émigrés to indulge its dubious delights, doubted

66. Ibid.

67. John James Audubon, *Delineations of American Scenery and Manners,* in *Writings and Drawings* (New York: Library of America, 1999), 522–23; Annette Kolodny, *The Lay of the Land: Metaphor as Experience and History in American Life and Letters* (Chapel Hill: University of North Carolina Press, 1975), 76.

that the *"rapid* extension of settlements" would prove to be "favourable to the duration" of the American union. The irascible Cobbett, making a go of his "Ruta Baga" farm on Long Island, declared that if his fellow countrymen crossed the ocean to settle here, they should "take up their abode on this side of the mountains at least."[68]

Despite the extravagant diction summoned up to describe the "grandeur of the american empire," Gilbert Imlay saw the *wilderness enchanting* and the *wilderness delightful* of Kentucky primarily as future farmland, not tracts to be merely admired: "[Y]ou must view it as a creation bursting from a chaos of heterogeneous matter, and exhibiting the shining tissue with which it abounds." In the land he envisions, "fertile fields, blushing orchards, pleasant gardens, . . . commodious houses, rising villages, and trading towns" will be the most satisfying portion of that "shining tissue."[69] The westering impulse continued despite roadblocks—overlapping land grants, rival claims of national sovereignty, shaky Indian treaties, and inconsistent policy toward squatters.[70] The urge to "push beyond" official settlement lines intensified after the Treaty of Paris, becoming what is now called the Great Migration. The sheer volume of peripatetic settlers also intensified the famous spirit of unease prompted by neighbors who "got too close."

Fueled by folklore, the earliest instances became legendary. In North Carolina, Daniel Boone decided to move on when he heard that someone had begun farming twelve miles away. His restlessness functions more tellingly in the culture of migration than in the culture of settlement. One of his "neabors" in Kentucky said that Boone "did not stay [in] one plase long [enough] to get acquainted." By Crockett's time, the motive for frontier restlessness—being within sound of the rifle fire of too many neighbors—had been romanticized as gnarly independence and self-sufficiency. A Mr. Conwell, one of Frederick Gerstaecker's Arkansas hosts, told the young German that he had always preceded civilization, "first in Carolina, then in Kentucky, Tennessee, Missouri, and now in the Ozark mountains," and, noted the sportsman, "he complained that people were gathering

68. Fearon, *Sketches of America*, 213–14; William Cobbett, *A Year's Residence, in the United States of America* (1818–1819, reprint, New York: A. M. Kelley, 1969), 575.

69. Gilbert Imlay, *A Topographical Description of the Western Territory of North America*, 3rd ed. (1797; reprint, New York: A. M. Kelley, 1969), 44, 168.

70. If the Old Southwest experienced "some of the most avaricious episodes of land grabbing, political corruption, and moral effrontery in the history of the nation," it was because of assorted entrepreneurs (including the romantic Imlay) who saw financial advantages in conflicting national titles and transfers (Clark and Guice, *Old Southwest*, 67).

too thick about him, and said he felt a strong inclination to make another move."[71] Other pioneers voiced similar concerns. By 1832, when the entire region was open for white settlement, one Mississippian complained, "I cannot move without seeing the nose of my neighbor sticking out between the trees." One historian concludes that mobility was addictive to the nomadic, forever "beset by the urge to stay slightly ahead of the prongs of settlement."[72]

The evidence is inconclusive, but repetitive anecdotes indicate that mobility, if not quite an addiction, was not wholly a means to an end. It was a satisfying act in itself.[73] Because he is "restless and migratory," wrote John L. McConnel, the pioneer is "fond of change, for the sake of the change"; by the time his homestead is encroached upon by others he will have moved on. With "no affection for the soil" as such, he will make "multiple migrations before he dies." Farmers and artisans alike, even those who were not planning grand migrations, were often accused of neglecting their daily tasks, presumably out of boredom. A scientist noted the habit of all too many southern settlers of "rambling about instead of attending to their farms." Achille Murat described these wanderers as "cordial." Quitting a district "as soon as it becomes peopled," they "abandon their dwelling . . . and transport themselves—God knows where."[74] After only one year as the sole inhabitant of Michle's Ridge in Alabama, one Michael McElroy (known as Mickle Muckle), distressed at the prospects of overpopulation, sold his place and moved away. His property eventually became the site of Marion, the county seat of Perry.[75]

The record for mobility, however, surely belongs to the Lincecums of Georgia. The father, beginning in 1800, spent the better part of his and his family's life being dissatisfied with present acres. He dreaded, wrote his son, seeing anyone settling farther west than he. Though he liked one

71. John Mack Faragher, *Daniel Boone: The Life and Legend of an American Pioneer* (New York: Holt, 1992), 66, 326; Gerstaecker, *Wild Sports*, 288–89.

72. James E. Davis, *Frontier America, 1800–1840: A Comparative Demographic Analysis of the Settlement Process* (Glendale, CA: Arthur H. Clark, 1977), 85, 108. See also Alfred Bunn, *Old England and New England, in a Series of Views Taken on the Spot* (London, 1853), 142–43, and George W. Featherstonhaugh, *Excursion through the Slave States* (1844; reprint, New York: Negro Universities Press, 1968), 2:113.

73. Berthoff, *Unsettled People*, 129–30 ff.

74. John L. McConnel, *Western Characters, or Types of Border Life in the Western States* (New York, 1853), 112; Thomas Nuttall, *A Journal of Travels into the Arkansas Territory during the Year 1819* (1821; reprint, ed. Savoie Lottinville, Norman: University of Oklahoma Press, 1980), 58; Achille Murat, *A Moral and Political Sketch of the United States of North America* (London, 1833), 52–53.

75. Weymouth T. Jordan, *Ante-Bellum Alabama: Town and Country* (1957; reprint, University: University of Alabama Press, 1986), 25.

prospect west of the Tombigbee because it was "the wildest, least trodden and tomahawk marred country" he had yet passed through, he
never finally was at home anywhere. His migrations, with family in tow,
lasted most of his life, well into the period of stable community-building.
After about eighteen years of resettling, his son had entered into the spirit
of wanderlust: "We were in a perfect ecstasy over the prospect of a wagon
journey through a roadless wilderness."[76] Lincecum's story confirms the
fluctuating, sporadic process of settlement, but it also suggests the gratification of mobility itself: pulling up stakes was at least as attractive as
putting down roots. Tocqueville had guessed as much.

Pulling up stakes was in fact the single most vivid sign of social change.
If national figures worried about the effects of restlessness on the health
of republican government, a humble corollary was domestic anxiety over
preserving the civilizing virtues nourished by the home and local community. Timothy Flint concluded that repetitive mobility strained the
stability of "connexions."[77] While fleeing from neighbors became a celebrated quirk among the earliest migrants, most ordinary settlers sought
out the company of others. They knew from emigrants' guides (and their
own common sense) about the social politics involved in new communities. One of the most popular advisers warned newcomers against voicing "complaints about the country, and the manners and habits of the
people," or by telling them how superior such traits were "back home."[78]
Yet they also knew that trusting strangers, even when they extended
"unaffected hospitality," was chancy. When they articulate in their letters
the hope of finding like-minded, decent individuals in their new surroundings, as they often do, the unspoken fear is that they might not be
able to know them when they see them. Nostalgic memoirists in the postbellum era write glowingly of barn raisings, corn shuckings, quiltings,
and other events of a rural culture that connote a tightly knit communal
spirit.

Certainly over time customs of mutuality became stabilized as tools
for absorbing social antagonisms, but for most of the settlement period
those that demographers call "persisters"—the migrants who settled down
in at least a semipermanent way—were too scattershot to pay much attention to mutual enterprises. The primary task was basic subsistence at
the individual level. As census figures indicate, success, if and when it
came, was measured almost wholly in terms of "private gain and per-

76. The Lincecum story is succinctly told in Davis, *A Way through the Wilderness*,
83–85.
77. Flint, *Recollections*, 149–50.
78. Peck, *Guide for Emigrants*, 70.

sonal liberation," with scarcely a nod to social coherence. Geographical mobility encouraged a competitive spirit that generally prevailed over communal cohesiveness. Even camp-meeting spirituality encouraged individualism, "not the communitarianism necessary for urban life." Most communities in the newer areas were composed of individuals who, in the words of one critic, "shared many hopes, but few memories."[79]

Adventure lay with "movers," not "persisters," and adventure itself often trumped stability. As early as 1825 American restlessness had become such a repetitive refrain in English travel books that James Kirke Paulding could not resist mocking it in his satiric *John Bull in America.* The eponymous narrator declares that the liberated colonials spurn home, with "all its delightful associations," and "leave their kindred, friends, and household gods, to herd with Indians and buffaloes in the pathless wilderness. If they cannot live in one place, they try another—if they cannot thrive by one trade, they turn to another; and so ring the changes until they succeed at last." For Gerstaecker and his friend seeking out the Arkansas backwoods, succeeding was not even relevant: "Our mutual wish had only been freedom and the forest, rightly conjecturing that all the rest would come of itself."[80]

Pulling up stakes also had another dimension. If restlessness thwarted social stability, it also celebrated the free exercise of a prior virtue: radical liberty. Perhaps only in a rapidly changing society could freedom to change one's residence allow one also to change an occupation that had been determined by class affiliation and family tradition. The note sounded by antifederalist Thomas Cooper was repeated with variations both elegant and common for most of the antebellum years: "In America, a false step is not irretrievable; there is room to get up again: and the . . . stumbler looks round at leisure, and without dismay, for some more profitable path to be pursued."[81]

---

79. Steven Hahn, *The Roots of Southern Populism: Yeoman Farmers and the Transformation of the Georgia Upcountry, 1850–1890* (New York: Oxford University Press, 1983), 57–58. See also Davis, *Frontier America,* 17; Dickson D. Bruce, Jr., *Violence and Culture in the Antebellum South* (Austin: University of Texas Press, 1979), 68–69; David J. Russo, *Keepers of Our Past: Local Historical Writing in the United States, 1820s–1930s* (Westport, CT: Greenwood, 1988), 21–22; John R. Stilgoe, *Common Landscape of America, 1580 to 1845* (New Haven, CT: Yale University Press, 1982), 238; Timothy L. Smith, "Protestant Schooling and American Nationality, 1800–1850," *Journal of American History* 53 (1967): 680.

80. James Kirke Paulding, *John Bull in America* (New York, 1825), 188–89; Gerstaecker, *Wild Sports,* 133.

81. Thomas Cooper quoted in Imlay, *Topographical Description,* 186.

A British traveler in 1854 directly linked the two kinds of change common in America. "Happy in not being cribbed and confined," Americans can choose their locality from among thirty states; "and if one place does not come up to expectations, they can resort to another." Neither are they "indissolubly tied to any particular profession." Just as everyone assumes that every trade is open to all, so each individual is presumed "to be able to turn his hand to almost anything."[82] Another foreign visitor was especially struck by how clergymen felt free to give up their calling to embrace other professions. To see a "preacher turn lawyer" or "take to politics" was common. "Some turn traders, auctioneers, photographers, or showmen. Many become editors and authors." In fact, he concluded, there were few professions "in which you may not find ex-preachers." Sometimes the direction of versatility flowed the other way. One Dr. S. S. Houston of Alabama began his varied professional life as receiver in the public land office, then became a physician, which practice he gave up to become a lawyer, which he finally shucked to become a preacher. Achille Murat observed wryly that the young preacher "who marries a rich person throws off the gown and becomes a farmer or a merchant."[83]

Leaving the pulpit seems to have been less soul-wrenching than we might expect. The motivation of the Rev. John Owen, a Virginia Methodist, may be more circumstantial than most. The thirty-two-year-old parson moved from Norfolk County in 1818 with his wife, mother-in-law, two small children, and a few slaves, bound for "the Alabamma Terytory." In the nine weeks of travel he kept a journal, a gloomy record of poor health, wretched roads, runaway horses, broken equipment, and unflattering comments on the people he met and places he passed through in Virginia and East Tennessee. He halted briefly in Abington ("A sorry looking place & a poor set"), camped near the north fork of the Holston River ("No cleaver people all shifting and mean"), joined other travelers in Knoxville ("a poor Contemptible looking place"), before arriving at the Alabama line ("people poor rough &c"). The entries are brief. Owen notes his distressed psychological moods as often as his physical misfortunes: "All well tho in the dumps"; "in tolrable spirits"; "low spirited"; "my wife more fortitude than myself ashamd of it"; "in better spirits." Only once, however, does he choose to elaborate on his low spirits: "almost wish I was dead or that fate had bloted the day in which I was born out of the calendar & left a perfect Blank." Two weeks before he arrives in

82. William Chambers, *Things as They Are in America* (Philadelphia, 1854), 341–42.
83. Nichols, *Forty Years*, 372; Murat, *Moral and Political Sketch*, 131.

Alabama, however, he perks up: "Our trust is yet in God whose mercy is over us and we yet think he will send us deliverance in some way." Despite his wavering faith, John Owen was in some way delivered. He and his party arrived safely in Tuscaloosa. Although he remained a good Methodist, he gave up preaching as a profession to become a physician; before he died he also enjoyed successful careers as a bank agent, bank director, and mayor of the city.[84]

In his journal of 1843, a visitor to Georgia and Florida wrote to a friend of having met a popular congressman "just suited to the kind of folks you meet in the back woods." His entry: "Dresses very roughly & is ready for any thing that comes up—Can defend a Case, Make a prayer, Preach a sermon, and a good one. Smoke, drink and fight." It concludes with a token of the congressman's canniness as well as his versatility—a habit of calling a prayer meeting the night before a trial so that "the jury will believe all he says the next day." One man in whose cabin Charles Lanman spent a night in the Smoky Mountains was "an adept in the following professions and trades, viz., those of medicine, the law, the blacksmith, the carpenter, the hunter, the shoemaker, the watchmaker, the farmer, and he also seemed to possess an inkling of some half dozen sciences."[85]

Versatility extended to all occupations. Francis Grund took the Americans' variable skills—what he rather grandly called "universality of adaptation"—as a reason to admire the militia system. Members were able to make their own uniforms, mend their boots, manufacture their weapons, and share the labor in constructing fortifications and roads. And as early as 1807, Fortescue Cuming on the Ohio River met a wagoner who was also a bridge builder, and declared that it was common throughout the interior "for one man to have learned and wrought at two, and even sometimes three or four different mechanical professions, at different periods of his life."[86]

Except in Transcendental circles, American dramas of self-making are rarely moral or spiritual efforts to achieve. The national Chamber of Commerce bestows its Horatio Alger awards to those individuals who struggle from poverty to wealth, and the key to that success is trusting in one's

84. "John Owen's Journal of His Removal from Virginia to Alabama in 1818," *Publications of the Southern History Association* 1 (1897): 89–97.

85. A. T. Havens Journal, 1842–1843, Hargrett Rare Book and Manuscript Library, University of Georgia, Athens; Charles Lanman, *Adventures in the Wilds of North America,* ed. Charles Richard Weld (London, 1854), 162–63.

86. Grund, *The Americans,* 2:346–47; Cuming, "Tour to the Western Country," 4:173.

initiative to find opportunities and then using them for personal advancement. Behind the flexibility and versatility of self-making of the past two centuries, including the identity-rich confidence man, lies the indispensable figure of Benjamin Franklin. When Melville's Israel Potter meets this "pocket congress of all humanity" in Paris, the old doctor is already an icon of "multifariousness": "Printer, postmaster, almanac maker, essayist, chemist, orator, tinker, statesman, humorist, philosopher, parlorman, political economist, professor of housewifery, ambassador, projector, maxim-monger, herb-doctor, wit:—Jack of all trades, master of each and mastered by none—the type and genius of his land."[87]

Ironically, it was standardization that made possible the variegated self-release that Franklin's *Autobiography* so matter-of-factly celebrates. One unforeseen result of the mechanical uniformity of eighteenth-century printing equipment was the physical mobility of pressmen. Because he could do his printer's job in Philadelphia as well as in Boston, Franklin became the most notable runaway in our history. And forsaking the oppressiveness of his brother's city for the openness of Philadelphia was not merely a change in place; it was his chance to succeed in *other* pursuits. Franklin is our first great success story, the shrewd chaser of the main chance, the self-made man whose significance lies in his material accomplishments rather than his moral character. He also functions as a paradigm of generational rupture in American families long before the rise of industry. Not all uppity apprentices would be inventive enough to fashion a postal system or to organize a lending library or to devise bifocal eyeglasses, but his example gave honorable status to countless callings that the old elite scorned as beneath them. As James M. Cox puts it, Franklin saw "street drainage and street lighting as being equal to lawmaking and political theory."[88] The *Autobiography* traces its hero's contributions to public service, but it unapologetically emphasizes Franklin's orientation toward the goal of becoming wealthy.

87. Herman Melville, *Israel Potter: His Fifty Years of Exile*, in *Pierre, Israel Potter, The Confidence-Man, Tales* (New York: Library of America, 1984), 479. Gary Lindberg would add "publicist," otherwise demoting Franklin to mere printer, an "agent of exchange" who took credit for advances in knowledge of which he was only a promoter. *The Confidence Man in American Literature* (New York: Oxford, 1982), 81–82. One biographer, however, calls Franklin "virtue's agent." H. W. Brands, *The First American: The Life and Times of Benjamin Franklin* (New York: Random House, 2000), 271.

88. Jay Fliegelman, *Prodigals and Pilgrims: The American Revolution against Patriarchal Authority, 1750–1800* (Cambridge: Cambridge University Press, 1982), 10; James M. Cox, "Autobiography and America," in *Recovering Literature's Lost Ground: Essays in American Autobiography* (Baton Rouge: Louisiana State University Press, 1989), 17.

In its ironized way, American literature has refused to grant heroic status to the Franklinian character. It was left to another indispensable figure in our culture to do that. Emerson domesticates the indefatigable energy of the "type and genius" into a modestly generic "sturdy lad" of New Hampshire, who without grief or regret "tries all the professions, who *teams it, farms it, peddles,* keeps a school, preaches, edits a newspaper, goes to Congress, buys a township, and so forth, in successive years, and always, like a cat, falls on his feet."[89] Emerson converts a material economic fact in the 1830s—occupational uncertainty—into enabling potentiality. For Achille Murat, *every American* was a sturdy lad, who, like "cats, and parsons," always fell "upon his feet." The royal exile spent more time in the United States than Tocqueville, but both Frenchmen, even without Emerson's hortatory enthusiasm, articulated the make-do tenacity of the Emerson formula and found it admirable. For a country on the move, Tocqueville observed, there is no time for long apprenticeships in cultivating skills. Without a sophisticated division of labor, the same man must often "till his fields, build his house, make his tools, cobble his shoes, and with his own hands weave the coarse cloth that covers him." Because it is easy to change trades, one frequently meets those "who have been in turn lawyers, farmers, merchants, ministers of the Gospel, and doctors." Though the American may be less adept than a European, "there is hardly any skill to which he is a complete stranger."[90]

For Emerson, the sequential trying out of one's talents was verification of the spiritual buoyancy of the times; for many Americans it was, more simply—like migration itself—a natural and comfortable accommodation to whatever promise unlikely conditions could be made to yield. Edward Fontaine, Patrick Henry's great-grandson, migrated to Mississippi in 1836 to clerk in the Pontotoc land office. He became, in succession, an amateur portrait painter, a Methodist minister, an Episcopalian rector, secretary to President Mirabeau Lamar of Texas, teacher, naturalist, and hydraulic engineer advocating a jetty system for controlling currents on the Mississippi River.[91] Richard Smith Elliott, one of the minor humorists associated with the *St. Louis Reveille,* embodied both the extraordinary mobility and versatility of antebellum citizens. A Pennsylvanian, he is

89. Ralph Waldo Emerson, "Self-Reliance," in *Essays and Lectures* (New York: Library of America, 1983), 275.

90. Murat, *Moral and Political Sketch,* 340; Tocqueville, *Democracy in America,* 403–4; Robin, *Voyage to Louisiana,* 267.

91. Willie D. Halsell, "A Stranger Indeed in a Strange Land," *Alabama Historical Quarterly* 30 (1968): 61.

credited for thinking up the symbol of the log cabin for William Henry Harrison's famous campaign of 1840. He began his newspaper career as a journeyman under his father's supervision, after which he was a restless itinerant editor. He served as an Indian subagent among the Potawatomies in Iowa; became a lawyer in St. Louis; helped organize the Laclede Rangers for an expedition to Mexico in 1846–1847 and was one of the earliest war correspondents in America; became a geologist of sorts (a meteorologist convinced of the arable possibilities of the Great Plains); and hired himself out as an "industrial agent" to enlist support for a railroad company, as a publicist for a barge company, and, like Fontaine, a promoter of the jetty system to control the Mississippi. As "John Brown," he also found time to write amusing sketches.[92]

Indeed, for many of the humorous authors, writing was a third or fourth vocation: most of them were not only lawyers, planters, or preachers, but also professionals in other livelihoods. Beginning with Longstreet (lawyer, clergyman, and educator), most of the humorists followed multiple callings, not because they were naturally men of omnicompetent skills but because, like most of their contemporaries, they were temperamentally versatile, always on the alert to pursue new and better paths that would lead to greater success. Thomas Kirkman was a planter and merchant, Alexander McNutt a planter and lawyer (and governor). About half of the leading humorous authors were newspapermen (including the Field brothers, John Robb, T. B. Thorpe, J. J. Hooper, Francis Robinson, and C. F. M. Noland) in addition to their other professions. More catch-as-catch-can, George Washington Harris was at one time or another a jeweler and metalworker, a steamboat captain, a railroad conductor, and a manager of both a sawmill and a copper mine. Perhaps the most engaging of the jacks-of-all-trades was Sol Smith. This theater man began his successful career as actor, director, and manager with the kind of trying-out efforts of so many nineteenth-century men. He referred to himself as "a changeable sort of fellow," and one landlord decided that Smith belonged to "such don't-know-their-own-mind sort of fellows." He tried reading law, opened a singing school, published a newspaper. That temperamental mobility accompanied him even after he began his

92. See Elliott's memoir, *Notes Taken in Sixty Years* (St. Louis, 1883); Fritz Oehlschlaeger, introduction to *Old Southwest Humor from the* St. Louis Reveille, *1844–1850* (Columbia: University of Missouri Press, 1990), 26–27; and Nicholas Joost, "Reveille in the West: Western Travelers in the *St. Louis Weekly Reveille,*" in *Travelers on the Western Frontier,* ed. John Francis McDermott (Urbana: University of Illinois Press, 1970), 203–40.

theatrical career. At various times, the anecdotes show, Smith rose to challenges by momentarily acting in real life as preacher, doctor, and steamboat pilot.[93]

There is no reason to suppose that any of the humorous authors, including Longstreet, were immune to the buoyancy of the times. Though they may have held firmly to a sense of superiority in the midst of a society relentlessly dedicated to self-interest, the record shows that they were as versatile and shifting in their professional lives as the sharpers, impersonators, and confidence men were in theirs. Like most of their resilient fellows in the Old Southwest, they left themselves open to possibilities and promise. Moreover, an attraction to the restless and shady merely added to their interest in the openness of their society.

Finally, there is the testimony of the two professional authors, Washington Irving and James Fenimore Cooper, whose work in different ways made that of the unprofessionals possible. Neither writer was immune to the restlessness of migration nor to the new openness in callings, pursuits, and trades that it offered to ordinary Americans.

Wealth and material abundance, earned the old-fashioned way, is both a given and an ideological battleground in "The Legend of Sleepy Hollow." The conservative Irving conceives of his setting as a Dutch enclave determined to resist "the great torrent of migration and improvement . . . making such incessant changes in other parts of this restless country." The Dutch are "fixed"; hospitality and family warmth ensure the continuity of rural well-being. Ichabod Crane, the hungry go-getter whose materialism is more in tune with the national spirit, threatens the well-fed stability of Sleepy Hollow. In fashioning his comic hero as the apostle of progress, Irving makes his values clear: Ichabod must be expelled as the enemy of order.

In the economy of national types, Ichabod turns out to be the winner he fails to be in his own story. Irving borrowed from a barrel of comic types, mingling in his one brilliant character the ignorant schoolteacher, the gullible gourmand, the village handyman, the superstitious coward, and the fortune hunter; but he updated these familiar types by making Ichabod the modern aggressive materialist. Although this go-ahead Yankee is also prey to the lure of the new lands opening to the south, he is all dream and no action—a migrant and speculator wannabe. Fantasizing a quick marriage to the wealthy Katrina and an equally quick sale of her rich Hudson Valley farm, Ichabod plans to invest in "immense

93. Oehlschlaeger, introduction, 19–23.

tracts of wild land, and shingle palaces in the wilderness." Even before he proposes marriage, "his busy fancy already realized his hopes, and presented to him the blooming Katrina, with a whole family of children, mounted on the top of a waggon loaded with household trumpery, with pots and kettles dangling beneath; and he beheld himself bestriding a pacing mare, with a colt at her heels, setting out for Kentucky, Tennessee, or the Lord knows where!"[94]

If this gentle mockery links greed and migration, Irving's fellow New Yorker, James Fenimore Cooper, was more harshly negative. In *The Pioneers*, his narrative version of the settling of Cooperstown, the frontier village of Templeton is depicted as a heterogeneous settlement of willful, mutually antagonistic residents. Here Cooper equates versatility of occupation with shiftlessness—and both with migration. Judge Temple makes the case against one Jotham Riddel:

> "What, that dissatisfied, shiftless, lazy, speculating fellow! he who changes his county every three years, his farm every six months, and his occupation every season! an agriculturist yesterday, a shoemaker to-day, and a schoolmaster to-morrow! that epitome of all the unsteady and profitless propensities of the settlers, without one of their good qualities to counterbalance the evil!"[95]

Cooper concocts a more successful version of Riddel in *Home as Found*—Aristabulus Bragg, an unsentimental projector who speaks casually of "other callings" and "other expectations" (i.e., speculation in newer western cities). John Effingham, the author's surrogate, characterizes Bragg as one who is "filled with go-aheadism," considering "life as all means and no end." Those means are still in the realm of the possible when, at the conclusion of the novel, Bragg marries the Effinghams' maid: "they were to emigrate to the far West, where Mr. Bragg proposed to practise law, or keep school, or to go to Congress, or to turn trader, or to saw lumber, or, in short, to turn his hand to anything that offered."[96]

---

94. Washington Irving, "The Legend of Sleepy Hollow," in *History, Tales, and Sketches* (New York: Library of America, 1983), 1067. Daniel Hoffman asserts that such folk figures as Ichabod Crane "stave off death forever by simply changing their occupations"; in the Southwest, the resourceful Davy Crockett is the model. *Form and Fable in American Fiction* (New York: Norton, 1961), 93; "The Deaths and Three Resurrections of Davy Crockett," *Antioch Review* 21 (1961): 5–13.

95. James Fenimore Cooper, *The Pioneers* (1823; reprint, ed. Donald Ringe, New York: Penguin, 1988), 317.

96. James Fenimore Cooper, *Home as Found* (1838; reprint, ed. Lewis Leary, New York: Capricorn, 1961), 24, 430.

Bragg and Riddel possess ambitions Cooper regards as so paltry that he makes shiftlessness rather than initiative the engine driving the pioneer spirit. George Washington Harris gives a sinister turn to such professional versatility in an East Tennessee jack-of-all-trades. After festooning his portrait with comparisons to a black snake, a horse, a sick dog, and a raccoon, Sut Lovingood summarizes the career of one Stilyards: "He cum amung us a ole field school-marster," and, suitable to his devil-like transformations, he becomes a lawyer and racks up exorbitant fees for his services, until, finally, "he got sassy, got niggers, got rich, got forty maulins fur his nastiness, an' tu put a cap sheaf ontu his stack ove raskallity, got religion, an' got tu Congress" (*SL*, 37–38).

Yet Tocqueville would include Jotham Riddel and Aristabulus Bragg (if not Stilyards) as part of his generalized picture of restlessness, the spur of which among all classes was the "feverish ardor" for prosperity. "An American will build a house in which to pass his old age and sell it before the roof is on," he wrote. "[H]e will plant a garden and rent it just as the trees are coming into bearing; he will clear a field and leave others to reap the harvest; he will take up a profession and leave it, settle in one place and soon go off elsewhere with his changing desires."[97] The restless migrant, like a homespun Emerson, would be inclined to write *Whim* on the lintels of his doorpost—if he could write, and when he had a house.

97. Tocqueville, *Democracy in America*, 536.

Chapter 4

Creation States and How They Are Used Up

"My God, man, it is land, don't you understand, it is land, and land cries out for man's hand!"

—Robert Penn Warren, *All the King's Men*

When, in "The Big Bear of Arkansas," the cynical Hoosier asks the storyteller where the events in his fabulous anecdotes had happened, the "irresistibly droll" Jim Doggett replies, predictably, "Arkansaw." Where else, he demands, could they have happened but "in the creation State, the finishing-up country?" (*TBT*, 114). By 1841, however, when Thomas B. Thorpe wrote his famous sketch, all of the states in the Old Southwest had touted their fertility and edenic promise. For a time, at least, all the lower South was a sequence of creation states. In the Civil War inset story in *All the King's Men*, a hardheaded planter reminds his idealistic brother of that necessary fact. In freeing his slaves, Cass Mastern has allowed his own plantation to lie fallow, its cotton land crying out for man's hand. The exasperated outburst from a fictional Mississippian sums up the historic mind-set of the planter class in the 1850s.

The orientation of Thorpe's bear hunter anticipates neither of the Mastern brothers—he is untainted by abolitionist sentiments, and he cares nothing for cultivating the prodigal earth. His creation state has been made for hunters, not farmers. Gilbert Mastern's career reflects that of hundreds of real-life cotton planters, rising, in less than two decades, from log-cabin poverty to big-house prosperity. Both "The Big Bear of Arkansas" and the Cass Mastern story elide the narrative of agrarian migration and the troubled consequences for the diverse new occupiers of Indian lands. The Old Southwest was made safe for agriculture by the simple argument that the land that cried out for man's hand had been allowed for too long to remain untouched, despite God's commandment to make his creation productive. As roaming hunters, the native Americans were declared incapable of improving the earth: the "temporary occupants of the wilderness" must now succumb to permanent residents for its cultivation.[1]

i.

An early historian described the American population of Texas in 1825 as a varied crowd of the unpretentious. Circulating between one extreme (the "pioneer surrounded by his hardy family . . . brave, rough, honest, hospitable, not too reverent or respectful") and the other ("escaped criminals and vagabonds of the worst sort") were individuals of all grades of morality and opinion:

> Men who had known better days and had moved in cultured society jostled discordantly with the rough hunters . . . living almost exclusively on the products of the chase. There were men whom business reverses had driven from home; there were those who had fled . . . from the demands of creditors and . . . those who came . . . repudiating claims against them. The speculator, the merchant, the surveyor, the planter and stockman, with the sprinkling of black-legs and criminals . . . —these formed a community which can be found only on the western margin of Anglo-Saxon civilization.[2]

Almost every state in the Old Southwest hosted a grab-bag population, though the anomalous Texas situation probably ensured that its citizens

---

1. Frederick Merk, *History of the Westward Movement* (New York: Knopf, 1978), 186. Whites disregarded Native American systems of cultivation because they did not correspond to settlers' "repeated use of specific plots of ground under the supervision of a male owner." Conevery Bolton Valenčius, *The Health of the Country: How American Settlers Understood Themselves and Their Land* (New York: Basic Books, 2002), 195.

2. Lester G. Bugbee, "The Texas Frontier—1820–1825," *Journal of the Southern Historical Association* 4 (1900): 107–8. The same point is made about the Arkansas frontier in 1832 by Charles J. Latrobe, who compares it to the "back part of Kentucky" fifty years earlier. *The Rambler in North America* (London, 1835), 1:258.

were more motley than others. Anglo settlers had arrived in the Mexican state only four years earlier, but in five more they would outnumber native residents. Even with local variations in settlement patterns, this description of Texas applied to Alabama and Mississippi a few years earlier. In early settlement there always seemed to be a "western margin of Anglo-Saxon civilization."

As we have seen, the extraordinary movement of individuals and families from old homes to new is itself a record of the dominant view of settlers, who saw the opening of lands in the lower South and West as their chance to repair fortunes that had long been hostage to depleted soil. One observer noted that the Mississippi Valley, with its obvious fertility, was like "a huge loaded harvest-waggon" pulling the population to it: "Disappointed, ruined, and restless men of the States, and men of other nations press on to it as the great agricultural field of the world."[3] Despite the fact that migration involved a heterogeneous mix of trades and professions, that image signals the supremacy of farming as the absorbing interest of both the transient population and those who wrote about them.

The evangelist Timothy Flint, whose itinerant profession coincided with his indefatigable love of wandering, would have approved of the image of the "loaded harvest-waggon." Though temperamentally reluctant to put down roots, he was lavish in his praise of southwestern fertility. In corn-growing areas, he noted, "manuring is scarcely yet thought of," and he echoed the common belief that a thick, impenetrable canebrake was the sure sign of "the exuberant prodigality of nature." As with the soil, the waterways were also embarrassingly prodigal. In Cole County, Missouri, the fish of the Moreau River were reported so numerous that they "frequently choked" the waterwheels of mills, forcing the machinery "to stand still."[4] The same kind of prodigality that farmers found had its parallel for hunters in the woods. When at seventeen C. F. M. Noland moved to Batesville, the future Arkansas humorist wrote glowingly to his sister that hunting and fishing in his new home were better than any other place he had seen, and boasted of having gigged a fifty-pound catfish and a sizable buffalo fish. A decade later, Frederick Gerstaecker, who had

3. Frederick J. Jobson, *America, and American Methodism* (New York, 1857), 298–99. For a summary of migration to the Old Southwest, see Thomas D. Clark and John D. W. Guice, "Where smiling Fortune beckoned them," chap. 9 in *The Old Southwest, 1795–1830: Frontiers in Conflict* (Norman: University of Oklahoma Press, 1996).

4. Timothy Flint, *A Condensed Geography and History of the Western States or the Mississippi Valley* (1828; reprint, ed. Bernard Rosenthal, Gainesville, FL: Scholars' Facsimiles & Reprints, 1970), 1:26, 33, 81, 227; Alphonso Wetmore, *Gazetteer of the State of Missouri* (St. Louis, 1837), 63–64.

only hunting on his mind, took pains to praise the White River region in Arkansas as "the most fertile in America," producing more than sixty bushels of corn to the acre, pumpkins "larger than a man can lift," and trees measuring "from five to six feet in diameter."[5] This German would not have been one of the skeptics in Jim Doggett's audience.

Enthusiasts in every state and territory in the Old Southwest entered the "most fertile" competition. In northern Alabama, Anne Royall declared that the river bottoms of the Mississippi tributaries were "not exceeded in fertility by any in the world"; even bites of the troublesome giant "moschitoes" were "amply remunerated by the soil's overflowing productiveness." Like mosquitoes and varmints in the woods, southwestern men were made to match the prodigal earth. In the midst of the Mexican War, John B. Lamar observed in a letter to Howell Cobb that just as southerners liked to appropriate a share of military victories in which "they have had no hand," so do they identify with their soil-rich locality. Mississippians particularly, he noted, act as if they are the "personification of an acre of land which could produce a 500 weight bag of cotton without the aid of manure."[6] In New York City, the perambulating Major Jones runs into some fellow Georgians, including one Col. Bill Skinner, who, at home, "don't look more'n half so big as he does here, whar the average size of the men is much less than it is in our genial soil, whar men's bodys as well as ther harts git to be as large as ther Maker ever intended 'em to be" (*MJS*, 122).

His migrated kin persistently reminded Robert Fraser, the Carolina schoolteacher, that for any man "under the weather the valley of the Miss. is to him as a City of refuge, for here prosperity awaits industry & Economy." His brother-in-law wrote that accruing rich acres beyond his expectations had justified his decision to come west; along with all his neighbors, he was prospering "abundantly." A letter from a friend, however, hints inadvertently of the darker aspect of such success on the land. "You can now come and participate with us in the bounties of this country," he wrote. "Settle on my Lands, help me to reclaim them and wear

5. Leonard Williams, introduction to *Cavorting on the Devil's Fork: The Pete Whetstone Letters of C. F. M. Noland* (Memphis: Memphis State University Press, 1979), 23; Ted R. Worley, "An Early Arkansas Sportsman: C. F. M. Noland," *Arkansas Historical Quarterly* 11 (1952): 25–39; Frederick Gerstaecker, *Wild Sports in the Far West* (Boston, 1866), 157.

6. Anne Royall, *Letters from Alabama, 1817–1822* (1830; reprint, ed. Lucille Griffith, University: University of Alabama Press, 1969), 224; *The Correspondence of Robert Toombs, Alexander H. Stephens, and Howell Cobb*, ed. Ulrich B. Phillips (1913; reprint, New York: Da Capo Press, 1970), 83.

them out and then if you wish to go back . . . we will all pack up and go back with you."⁷

Reclaim them and wear them out: it was the Virginia pattern recurring in the "inexhaustible" lands of the Southwest. A few years earlier, Joseph Holt Ingraham, a Maine clergyman and historical romancer who had lived in Mississippi, had glumly predicted that the obsession with cotton and slaves would continue until "the lands become exhausted and wholly unfit for farther cultivation." The signs were already ominous: "acre after acre of what was a few years previous beautifully undulating ground" had deteriorated into "a wild scene of frightful precipices, and yawning chasms" and "an appearance of wild desolation."⁸ Even before 1800, suffering from poorer and poorer crops, the agricultural interests had begun casting their eyes southwestward. By the time of Jefferson's death in 1826, the fertility of Virginia had already been exhausted. Spurred by reports of a profusion of rich soil untapped and unclaimed, passage out of the Old Dominion over the mountains began even before the new territories were ready for white occupation. In 1817, James Kirke Paulding was already referring to the "race of stately planters" along Virginia's rivers in elegiac terms: "A few of these ancient establishments are still kept up, but many of the houses are shut; others have passed into the hands of the industrious, or the speculating . . . ; nothing now remains, but the traditional details of some aged matron, who lives only in the recollections of the past, of ancient modes, and ancient hospitality."⁹

Images of agricultural decay summon up a literally Ruined Homeland startlingly different from the spiritually ruined one that postbellum mythmakers imagined. Exhausted fields and moldering homes were the sad glimmerings of a prior fable: that of the American Eden. In 1666 George Alsop described Maryland as a paradise: no other spot on earth, he argued, can parallel this "Adamitical" fertility and multiplicity, "Natures extravagancy of a superabounding plenty."¹⁰ Edenic images were set

7. Margaret Burr DesChamps, ed., "Some Mississippi Letters to Robert Fraser, 1841–1844," *Journal of Mississippi History* 15 (1953): 181–89.

8. Joseph Holt Ingraham, *The South-West, by a Yankee* (1835; Ann Arbor, MI: University Microfilms, 1966), 2:86–87.

9. James Kirke Paulding, *Letters from the South by a Northern Man* (1817; rev. ed., New York, 1835), 1:41. See also Jan Bakker, "Some Other Versions of Pastoral: The Disturbed Landscape in Tales of the Antebellum South," in *No Fairer Land: Studies in Southern Literature before 1900*, ed. J. Lasley Dameron and James W. Mathews, 77–79 (Troy, NY: Whitson, 1986).

10. Quoted in Wayne Franklin, *Discoverers, Explorers, Settlers: The Diligent Writers of Early America* (Chicago: University of Chicago Press, 1979), 36.

early—Sir Walter Raleigh had imagined Virginia on the same latitude with Paradise, but most later residents redrew the map of paradise with a full appreciation of its postlapsarian realities. Nature's "superabounding plenty" was both promise and threat. Its human usefulness was contingent on the plow and hoe, and Chesapeake husbandry often carried with it a distaste for labor.

Images of the garden antedate the actual planting of Virginia, dominating the promotional pamphlets, so-called histories, and epistolary tracts, but both Robert Beverley and William Bartram acknowledged that the caretakers of Eden had to factor in human complacency and laziness, the same frailties that had followed the colonists from the old world. Although the very presence of alternate Edens farther west encouraged bad husbandry in Virginians of all stripes, inattention to practical matters did not prevent Beverley and others from composing purling descriptions of their own *locus amoenus,* idylls that invoked a classical tradition in which rural life was equated with wholeness, integrity, simplicity, and virtue. But even by the eighteenth century that pastoral model was frayed.[11]

Long before his death, Jefferson was witness to both the disastrous husbandry of his countrymen's planters and the crippling dependence of the plantation system itself on slave labor. In a warm climate, he wrote, "no man will labour for himself who can make another labour for him." To forestall what he feared might be an apocalyptic end, the state's most notable planter and slaveowner proposed, as a judicious if visionary alternative, the self-sufficient farm, its model caretaker the yeoman farmer, whom he raised up as God's "peculiar deposit" of real virtue.[12] The image of self-sustaining acres tilled by the yeoman farmer was most powerful as a forensic tool in Jefferson's writings—and in the imaginations of those who never much liked soil-tilling in the first place. From the earliest settlers onward, the major impetus was to convert the wilderness to productive fields as quickly as possible, to extract what they could from it and move on. John Crowe Ransom once wrote that although it was quite a southern thing to love nature, it was not southern "to fall into mysticism before it."[13] Whites of all ranks and callings subscribed to the

11. Bakker, "Some Other Versions of Pastoral," 67–76; see also his fuller study, *Pastoral in Antebellum Southern Romance* (Baton Rouge: Louisiana State University Press, 1989).

12. Thomas Jefferson, *Notes on the State of Virginia,* in *Writings* (New York: Library of America, 1984), 288–89. See also Lewis P. Simpson, *The Dispossessed Garden: Pastoral and History in Southern Literature* (Athens: University of Georgia Press, 1975), 28–31.

13. John Crowe Ransom, "Modern with the Southern Accent," *Virginia Quarterly Review* 11 (April 1935): 193.

doctrine that nature was to be *used*. That the methods of doing it were often foolish and self-defeating affected the doctrine not at all.

The yeoman ideal of the small farm had some resonance in the antebellum South, but it remained mostly an abstraction of pastoral republicans, who liked it as a trope for political economy and civic virtue.[14] History and technology intervened. Both the ambitions and realities of the agricultural settler had, finally, little to do with the Jeffersonian vision. The yeoman ideal would be countered not merely by what has been termed "agrarian cupidity" in the white dispossession of native tribes[15] but by the efficient use of new agricultural technology at the very moment when huge tracts of those former tribal lands were being opened for cultivation. While the rich Southwest would attract men uninterested in agriculture—speculators, merchants, professionals, mechanics—the front rank of migrants were farmers. The foreground of settlement throughout the lower South was cotton cultivation, for which fresh acreage was crucial to economic hope and shelter. Even as John Taylor was penning his *Arator* essays and John Randolph was orating in Congress, newer southerners, both Democrats and Whigs, were being seduced by the vision of expansion. They associated the prosperity of republican government with the plantation system, which, however flawed, required more and more land. The system became a powerful internal image of continuity with the great civilization that the new cotton masters believed had flourished in the older seaboard South. The ideal behind the general urge of the aggrandizing planter to fashion agriculture into a thriving way of life was not so much independence and self-sufficiency as it was leisure and economic prosperity.[16]

In much of the private writing, necessity conspires effortlessly with myth in the spectacle of migration, and both conspire with greed in semi-official sermons, tracts, and orations—all invoking the rhetoric of national policy. Part of what Sacvan Bercovitch calls America's "collective fantasy" is the convergent potency of *what is* and *what can be done to* an unspoiled wilderness and a thriving culture; the favorite premonitory image out of that uneasy junction is the frontiersman, "living in harmony with

14. John M. Grammer, *Pastoral and Politics in the Old South* (Baton Rouge: Louisiana State University Press, 1996), 11, 24–25, 42.

15. Clark and Guice, *Old Southwest*, 13. See also R. Lyn Rainard, "The Gentlemanly Ideal in the South, 1660–1860: An Overview," *Southern Studies* 25 (1986): 295–304, for the contradictory concepts of "natural man" and "cultivated gentleman."

16. Lewis P. Simpson describes the later developments in the Southwest as "agrarian capitalism in a world marketplace society." *The Brazen Face of History: Studies in the Literary Consciousness in America* (Baton Rouge: Louisiana State University Press, 1980), 117–21.

nature and yet the harbinger of civilization."[17] By the time the mission had a name, Manifest Destiny—making at least the continent safe for America—it was not a naked policy for evacuating Indian lands and European territorial claims, but a fully clothed policy in the apparel of spiritual preordination.[18] In the Southwest the collective fantasy was the plantation, an economic system that at once lay claim to agrarian virtue and cultural achievement, the radiating core of a new (revised) notion of virtue and simplicity.

Symptoms of a compromised paradise, however, both in the old seaboard South and its re-creation in the new deep South, are evident even in two of the seminal works that had stirred the European romantic imagination. John Filson's *The Discovery and Settlement of Kentucke* (1784) acknowledged Daniel Boone as the frontier's representative man, and Gilbert Imlay's *A Topographical Description of the Western Territory of North America* (1792) attributed the purity of government to the country itself, with its temperate climate and fertile soil. The new nation may have been, as Filson wrote, the land "where nature makes reparation for having created man," but it was also amenable to agrarian capitalism. Imlay was a sometime sales agent in Paris for American lands; and as land dealer as well as schoolteacher, Filson contributed to the rage for migration—and for settlers in the role of what Gregory H. Nobles calls "the shock troops of national expansion." Both men stand as representatives of the mixed motives of promoters during territorial expansion of the Southwest.[19] Nature commodified presumably could make simple and virtuous all men canny enough to possess it.

For every deeply affected observer who deplored the spectacle of patricians now struggling to "reconstruct" their fortunes "in the far West and South," ten waxed as eloquently as simple men could by focusing entirely on the fresh acres where, in the words of one, "abundance spreads the table of the poor man, and contentment smiles on every countenance."[20] Over time the mythic image of smiling Fortune beckoning newcomers to the Southwest favored not the poor man but the planter, who

17. Sacvan Bercovitch, *The Rites of Assent: Transformations in the Symbolic Construction of America* (New York: Routledge, 1993), 7–8.

18. Gregory H. Nobles calls O'Sullivan's 1845 coinage "an ideology of inevitability." *American Frontiers: Cultural Encounters and Continental Conquest* (New York: Hill & Wang, 1997), 139.

19. Robert Lawson-Peebles, *Landscape and Written Expression in Revolutionary America: The World Turned Upside Down* (Cambridge: Cambridge University Press, 1988), 50–51; Nobles, *American Frontiers*, 131, 149.

20. Charles D. Lowery, "The Great Migration to the Mississippi Territory, 1798–1819," *Journal of Mississippi History* 30 (1968): 178.

by the mid-1850s had made his economic well-being virtually synonymous with political power. Numerically, the rush to the new lands in the first third of the century was a phenomenon of small farmers, squatters, hunters, and herdsmen; yet the fablelike arc of fertility and decay, celebration and mourning, extended throughout the Southwest, where a new cycle would affect all classes of men who made agriculture the dominant urgency behind migration.[21]

The settling process produced a considerable body of writing from the participants themselves. The earliest stage came from the farmer's fact-finding excursion. Armed with a notebook for recording crucial information about potential sites, the farmer-scout documented his experiences as a kind of catalog of travel routes, expenses, and statistics bearing on topography, water sources, vegetation, and projected harvest yields. Now resting unobtrusively in widely scattered collections, these fact books—often leather-bound, their sheets smudged, compact enough to fit into a pocket—are models of rhetorical minimalism, practical discourse that comes as close to the truth of the geography it describes as human gifts allow. Self-interest compelled the farmer to make his scouting entries faithful reflections of *what nature was*. After the exodus, however, in the earlier stages of settlement, another kind of writing appears: letters back home. In these, as we have seen, the correspondent's interest was to stress the most sanguine features of the new home—its healthy climate and rich soil, and its "society" (either real or hoped for). These missives, often intricately composed, combine personal and family news and information that go beyond statistics, couched in conventional but jaunty idioms. Their rhetoric serves to confirm the writer's decision to move; but these authors, their prose bristling with excitement, also argue, with sweet reasonableness, that the recipient should exercise the same good sense: *you come, too*. Predicting that Alabama would soon be the "garden of America," George S. Gaines in 1814 wrote a relative urging him to "come out & select you a tract of land & bring all our friends with you if possible." Private entreaties reinforced the official policy of what one commentator has called "regional impresarios."[22] Such letters

---

21. Allen Tate once sketched out a project, never completed, based on his own family history, using as "fundamental contrast" ancestors representing both "the Va. tidewater idea—stability, land, the establishment" and the restless pioneer, who, while preserving that "idea," had "some energy left over, which has made modern America." *The Republic of Letters in America: The Correspondence of John Peale Bishop and Allen Tate*, ed. Thomas D. Young and John J. Hindle (Lexington: University Press of Kentucky, 1981), 52.

22. Malcolm J. Rohrbough, *The Land Office Business: The Settlement and Administration of American Public Lands, 1789–1837* (New York: Oxford, 1968), 115; Valenčius, *Health of the Country*, 13.

now sound overblown, overargued, and much dependent on cliché, but, even when the pastoral mode falls into patches of gilded entreaties, they too are finally utilitarian documents of the agrarian life decked out with a modest flourish of artifice.

New settlers were largely enthusiastic about their land choices in the western regions, regaling kin and friends back home with hearty news of their present situation, and later letters continue for a time to be punctuated with meaningful statistics: pounds of cotton per acre, new acreage purchased, soaring market prices—all in happy contrast to the writers' agricultural experiences back in Georgia, Virginia, or South Carolina. But after a few years, when their fields begin to betray signs of depletion, the search for fertile soil elsewhere begins again. The process of migration is repeated. In the swirling flow of arrivals and departures in the new country, domestic correspondence confirms historians' accounts of how the poor husbandry of the seaboard followed the settlers into the newer South.

A newspaper writer as early as 1828 complained that the abundance of cheap land had "begot a careless, slovenly, *skimming* habit of farming," especially in middle Georgia.[23] In "The Turn Out," A. B. Longstreet pays nostalgic tribute to the once fertile "evergreen belt" surrounding the log schoolhouse in Columbia County. His narrator, Lyman Hall, quotes the hospitable Captain Griffen in 1790: "These lands . . . will never wear out" and "will be as good fifty years hence as they are now." When Hall returns to the spot forty-two years later, the old schoolhouse is set in a "barren, dreary and cheerless" landscape of "deep washed gully," dwarf pines, a dying willow, and "a sickly bog" (*GS,* 49–50). By 1830 the Virginia pattern had been repeated in most of the older settled counties. More than a decade after *Georgia Scenes,* Longstreet decried (in his own voice) the sorry state of agriculture: "Pass through Georgia, and the eye is constantly offended by worn out lands, deserted fields, and decaying habitations."[24] Robert Finley, a Princeton educator lured to Georgia in 1817 to take the helm of Franklin College (later the University of Georgia), died the same year he was appointed, but he was there long enough to observe that Georgia farmers were poor caretakers of their acres, and

23. Quoted in James C. Bonner, *A History of Georgia Agriculture, 1732–1860* (Athens: University of Georgia Press, 1964), 60; see also 63. J. H. Moore makes the same point regarding Mississippi—about two decades of cultivation in row crops were enough to ruin hill lands in the state. *The Emergence of the Cotton Kingdom in the Old Southwest: Mississippi, 1770–1860* (Baton Rouge: Louisiana State University Press, 1988), 30–31, 86–87, 132.

24. A. B. Longstreet, *A Voice from the South: Comprising Letters from Georgia to Massachusetts, and to the Southern States* (Baltimore, 1847), 51–52.

he seemed to know why: "being principally emigrants from Old Virginia, they wear out a piece of land and leave it."[25]

While it took more than a century for farmland in the coastal South to be degraded, it required only twenty years in the rich Tennessee Valley in north Alabama. As early as 1822 one observer lamented the exodus of restless settlers who were leaving "this beautiful country, and going, some to Texas, some to Missouri, and some to Red River, and others, the plague knows where." Frederick Law Olmsted noted that the despoliation of Virginia and South Carolina was being repeated in Alabama, once a favored destination of migrants. Quoting a speech from *DeBow's Review,* he declared that the forests had descended into "senility and decay"; in Alabama the "freshness of its agricultural glory is gone; the vigour of its youth is extinct, and the spirit of desolation seems brooding over it." A Greensboro newspaper in 1851 reported uneasily that 343 families had moved to Louisiana, the majority of them from Alabama. A few years later the same paper noted, "scarcely a day [passes] that some dozen or twenty wagons . . . are not seen on our streets on their way to Texas, Louisiana, Arkansas or Mississippi." On a trip west, even the enthusiastic historian of Alabama, Albert J. Pickett, wrote back letters proclaiming Texas "God's Country."[26] But poor choices could also be made in Texas. A young Georgian who had followed his father west wrote to a friend that Sabine County "is mean as smelling the pole cat in the woods." Certain "fools & rascals & great liars" had flattered his father, who "had no judgement" in purchasing such poor land. "I will leave this mean country," he asserted, "an its mean smellings an I will run to Georgia by myself."[27]

It is not surprising that the arc tracing the shift of farmlands from fertile paradise to wasteland should elicit a parallel emotional response from those affected by it. The recurring bouts of promising optimism and mournful dejection, occasioned by the temporary expedient of changing

25. Quoted in E. Merton Coulter, *College Life in the Old South* (Athens: University of Georgia Press, 1983), 29.

26. Daniel S. Dupre, *Transforming the Cotton Frontier: Madison County, Alabama, 1800–1840* (Baton Rouge: Louisiana State University Press, 1997), 100; Frederick Law Olmsted, *The Cotton Kingdom: A Traveller's Observations on Cotton and Slavery in the American Slave States, 1853–1861* (1861; reprint, ed. Arthur M. Schlesinger, New York: Da Capo Press, 1996), 530–31; Minnie Clare Boyd, *Alabama in the Fifties: A Social Study* (New York: Columbia University Press, 1931), 21–22. In one decade (1850–1860), Alabama lost nearly 100,000 residents to Mississippi, Texas, and Arkansas.

27. Bonner, *History of Georgia Agriculture,* 70–71.

scenery, suggest something more than ignorance, or a refusal to learn, or a signal lack of interest in good husbandry, or impatience with even elementary techniques for prolonging the productive life of the soil. The repetitive pattern hints at something like a proto-aboriginal distaste for the agricultural life itself. Despite its traditional (and mythic) reputation as a land where cultivation of the soil has always been a rooted antecedent value, the South, in these years of expansion, seems to have been particularly susceptible to all the stratagems for impeding it. An agricultural journalist in 1856, complaining of the "incessant and never-ending" labor required to maintain productive acres in Mississippi, advised farmers to try their luck in Texas.[28] As long as they had their workforce tilling, dressing, and harvesting in easily taught rote methods, the planters could devote their energies to socializing and politicking. Humbler farmers had their own humbler evasions for staying out of the fields.

Less concerned with this recurring pattern were hunters, herdsmen, and some squatters—some of whom had neither strong desires for nor serious hopes of becoming landowners anyway. And, in a curious way, the cycle seems to have been less traumatic for the small farmer than for the planter, primarily because of his own ambiguous attitudes toward the places he settled. Characterized variously as *yeoman, cultivator, freeman,* and *husbandman,* and eventually *cracker,* this Jeffersonian ideal found himself divided between his attraction to the planter model and the temptation to dissipate his energies in the pleasures of the backcountry. He may have aspired to the status of land- and slave-rich planter, but he found considerable bonds of interest with the independence of trappers, herders, hunters, and other land-free spirits. If the natural priority for some of the new settlers was aggressive cotton cultivation in river valleys, the more casual tending of corn patches in the wooded uplands was the natural priority for greater numbers among slaveless farmers.[29] For both the free souls and the small farmer, however, the uncultivated woods were a persistent magnet drawing them away from their duties.

Evidence of an aversion to the grubbing realities of agriculture appears early, even among those families who knew no other life. The ethnic and

---

28. *Affleck's Southern Rural Almanac and Plantation and Garden Calendar, for 1856,* quoted in Bruce Collins, *White Society in the Antebellum South* (London: Longman, 1985), 90–91.

29. "As late as 1860, corn, not cotton, was the Old South's leading crop." John Solomon Otto, "Southern 'Plain Folk' Agriculture: A Reconsideration," *Plantation Society* 2 (1983): 33. One Georgian told a visiting Bostonian in 1822 that before cotton was introduced, his "sole reliance for profit was upon cattle and hogs raised for market." Jeremiah Evarts Diary, Georgia Historical Society, Savannah (original in Bureau of American Ethnology, Smithsonian Institution).

class biases of the patrician colonists account for much of William Byrd's disgust at the Scots-Irish in Virginia; not all of them were the infamous "Lubbers" he railed against, but it was a population the literate generally defined by laziness. Historically, we now know that it had required more than laziness to prompt such ordinary settlers to challenge the Proclamation Line, which London instituted in 1763, forbidding colonial settlement west of the Appalachians. In most of the newer areas of the Old Southwest the appeal of the uncultivated was more immediate than it had been in the more stratified seaboard South. The sometime farmer probably never worried his head over political economy or the new civilization he might be advancing, but most yeomen never lost their fondness for wilderness, for sporting in the very spaces that were being gradually turned into productive fields.

Most commentators believe that the idealized yeoman model failed because Jefferson could not foresee the injection (and rapid triumph) of market capitalism and technology in this most basic of human callings. The reason may lie in something more basic. Along with agrarian ambitiousness in both planter and yeoman lurked a kind of countering impulse, which, extrapolating from Jefferson, might be phrased as *no man will labor for himself if he can prosper contentedly by not laboring at all*. The go-ahead spirit, guiding both the national and individual drive for success, is the powerful impetus behind most projects; but Jefferson's "pastoral piety" came also to include the retrograde satisfaction, unimagined by the visionary architect of the good life, of loafing in a barely tilled geography—subsisting, that is, on the fat of the land while nominally improving its formal acreage. For preindustrial agriculturalists, we are told, leisure was "a highly valued commodity," since time away from tilling the soil was time free for hunting and livestock-keeping.[30]

The zealous energy behind migration did not necessarily translate into agricultural enterprise. For the English proprietors, working the land (or, rather, having it worked) was both premise and privilege; but their plebeian fellow Britons seemed content to have uncultivated nature sustain them: "the more they are befriended by the soil and the climate," Byrd wrote, "the less they will do for themselves." An Anglican clergyman was blunter: the "Scum" lived a "low, lazy, sluttish, heathenish, hellish Life."[31] The parson might have been describing George Washington Harris's feckless family a half-century later, but the Lovingoods are only the most

30. Otto, "Southern 'Plain Folk' Agriculture," 33.
31. Quoted in Nobles, *American Frontiers*, 103–4.

vividly drawn of the humorists' figures for whom working the land is an onerous necessity when great nature and chance fail.

Unambitious farmers they might have been, but the so-called Scots-Irish colonists resisted patrician coercion, going their own way, stubborn, intractable, and (in most views) arrogant in their ignorance. In some respects, however, they merely constituted a lowercase version of the grander English planters. New Englanders had always thought of their fellow colonists in the South as addicted to indolence and pleasure. One foreign visitor echoed that view when he observed that Virginians, "much given to convivial pleasures," were "jealous of their liberties," ostentatiously "impatient of restraints," and could scarcely "bear the thought of being Controuled by any superior power." As for their agrarian skills, the visitor charged that with barely "a tenth of the land" cultivated, even that part was "far from being so in the most advantageous manner." This comment in 1759 foreshadows the steady decline of agriculture in Virginia and that of the lower states settled by its "surplus talent."[32]

ii.

A few years ago, during a seminar session on Southwest humor, a student asked, "What do these people do when they're not hunting or hanging out?" "They're just farmers," another student volunteered, "trying not to work."

Despite the brash answer, which suggests that Byrd's dismissal of poorer whites still appeals to their privileged betters two centuries later, the question is pertinent. The figures of Southwest humor in fact do a lot of hanging out—more hanging and talking than actual hunting. For both characters and their creators, the great enterprise of building a cotton kingdom, the central historical narrative of antebellum southern life, would seem to be somebody else's story. It is not surprising that the author-narrators generally ignore all agricultural matters. Farmland and its uses, the salient factor preceding their arrival, may have been crucial to the region's overall prosperity (and their own), but it never stimulated their writing. Almost with one accord they seemed to agree that farming was not funny. These professionals' indifference to agriculture in south-

32. Andrew Burnaby, *Travels through the Middle Settlements in North America in the Years 1759 and 1760* (1798; reprint, New York: A. M. Kelley, 1970), 44, 53–55.

western life is in fact matched by that of their yeoman subjects, who usually betray no interest in the vital matter of cultivating the land.

Because tilling assumed an almost sacrosanct aura in antebellum oratory, as a calling that would be eventually enshrined in Lost Cause writing, the historical consecration of the planter meant a vastly diminished role for the yeoman, who for most historians was not farmer enough to earn his place in collective memory. The fiction earnestly promoted by Old South publicists—that southerners had scorned the moneymaking that so consumed the Yankee—generated the edenic reputation of a cotton South with garden images resuscitated from colonial Virginia and Maryland. Like many well-to-do planters before the war, the Mandevilles of Louisiana sought to project an image of wide-eyed propriety untouched by moneymaking concerns. On their way to White Sulphur Springs in 1854, the amiable family stopped in Cincinnati, impressions of which Henry Mandeville penned in a guileless letter to relatives back home: "Such an anxious striving to-get money community of bipeds" is a novelty, he notes, for one accustomed to "the lounging nothing-doing South."[33] As we have seen, however, moneymaking was a necessary concern with southerners, especially planters and their factors. As one historian reminds us, Jacksonian Americans in general did not see land as evoking images of a bucolic life. Land served primarily "the purposes of acquisition and ascent; it was a medium of production, consumption, and exchange distinguished mainly by its abundance and convenience."[34]

In countless daybooks and diaries, southwesterners seem to regard farming as oddly parenthetical. If the entries in their work records are stuffed with the mechanics of agriculture—preparing ground, sowing and planting, cultivating, and harvesting—they are always relieved by items about social events that they found more amusing. Landowners ride, hunt, and go fishing; they attend shooting matches; they entertain relatives and neighbors; they go to hear preaching (and record both the good and the bad); they go to county seats for gossip, political meetings, balls, and circuses. One female sugar planter and her husband record a visit to Donaldsville to meet Henry Clay and to Baton Rouge for a party convention; she reports hosting a dinner party for a California-bound neighbor with "the gold fever" and a fancy-dress ball at "Madame

33. Henry D. Mandeville Family Papers, Mss. 491, 535, Louisiana and Lower Mississippi Valley Collections, Louisiana State University Libraries, Baton Rouge.

34. Marvin Myers, *The Jacksonian Persuasion: Politics and Belief* (Stanford: Stanford University Press, 1957), 102.

Valerie's."[35] Plantation daybooks seem to have served as a kind of therapy for owners who, once freed of the obligatory listing of the hard facts of farm management (acreage yields, prices for seed, assignments of field workers, weather conditions, income and—mostly—outlay), could openly comment on issues and people, often with candor.

One lonely planter near Holly Springs, Mississippi, frets when his wife "and our babe" go for a visit to his father-in-law, and openly worries that a projected railroad to Memphis will ruin the profits of a toll turnpike he is building on his land. Another in Wilkinson County keeps track of his houseguests and neighbors who drop by for tea and where he is invited in return; he visits Woodville for, alternately, preaching and dancing, and he records hosting a frolic of "about one hundred persons" to celebrate the wedding of two friends. One planter's son in Louisiana doesn't even pretend to be interested in farming. His daybook is chiefly a record of reading, playing poker and billiards, visits to relatives who think he plays cards too much, and pungent remarks on events and people that bore him—a dancing school, a quilting party, a book peddler whose "fluent impertinence" only slightly amuses him, a priest who "never gets into the pulpit without a pocket full of Echoes."[36]

Daybooks of the barely literate farmers are not plentiful. Such record keepers are only fractionally luckier than illiterates in leaving written accounts. Unlike their cousins the squatters and loners, and unlike their cousins in the ambitious middle class, many of the plain folk of the settlement period were moderately well off—respectables who never aspired unduly to respectability. From the handful of documents preserved, however, we can extrapolate a general profile: law-abiding and pious, they paid taxes, labored at routine tasks, and participated in such communal ceremonials as church services, frolics, musters, quilting parties, marriages, infares, and funerals. They celebrated, but not for long, and they grieved, also not for long. Like most settlers in the new country, who gradually made the lower South into a region measurably more coherent than when they came to it, the unschooled and the undereducated worked to better

35. Ellen McCollam, diary, Andrew and Ellen McCollam Papers, MS 550, Louisiana and Lower Mississippi Valley Collections, Louisiana State University Libraries, Baton Rouge.

36. Esther Turner McElrarts, diary, McCain Library and Archives, University of Southern Mississippi, Hattiesburg; Dick Hardaway Eggleston, diary, Eggleston-Roach Papers, Louisiana and Lower Mississippi Valley Collections, Louisiana State University Libraries, Baton Rouge; John Robert Buhler Diaries, Autograph Book, and Notebook, MS 1311, Louisiana and Lower Mississippi Valley Collections, Louisiana State University Libraries.

themselves within the system that developed around them. A spirited Know-Nothing stalwart, James M. Torbert, of Macon County, Alabama, began an account of his activities, expenses, and thoughts in 1848 and continued for several years. The highlights of his life in the latter half of 1855 are quickly evident, despite the terseness of the entries:

Aug 6   We had an election today. Watts and the ballince of the American ticket, was ahead at our box, had Several fights, John Greathouse got badly Cut, Dick & Bill White done it Cottonham took a turn with John Cannady I was quite unwell all day.

Aug 8   Us poor Know Nothings are badly beat but I am Still, an american, I belong to that party, I wan't to die one and all My Children after Me.

Sept 2   Mrs Willborn Sister is down on a visit to See Mrs Wilborn, She is a right Sharp looking gal

Oct 27   Clara Still worse, She died at half past four at night. Oh such a death she Suffocated with Croup I am Satisfied She is in heaven, Gathering Corn

Dec 20   Drove of hogs in town asking 8c Pork is verry high[37]

Although daybooks vary in levels of literacy, most of them achieve their modest goal within a narrow range of compactness, from the laconic to the gnomic. When we read unsophisticated prose, we usually attribute its perceptible signs—random juxtapositions, chaotic orthography, inadvertent humor—to dense minds and tin ears. In our patronizing way we tend to call such writing "artless," taking heart in believing that it is at least candid and unguarded, as if the merit of imperfect schooling is sincerity. As we might expect, yeoman keepers of daybooks are grateful for good weather, which allows them to perform their duties, and anxious about market fluctuations in prices. What they fail to reveal is any enthusiasm for farm life as a calling. They are as eager for distractions as their planter neighbors, and some in their ragged entries display a cautious guile along with their sincerity.

John Traylor, an Alabama overseer who achieved his modest goal to be an independent farmer, from 1834 to 1847 kept a diary that was mostly a daybook: "thind coten," "halled a lode of corn to the hill," "commenced

37. James M. Torbert Papers, Alabama Department of Archives and History, Montgomery.

puling foder," "cut down a bee tree," "kilded hogs 1000 lbs," "worked in the gardin and halled manewer all day." All these entries, including those occasional diversions that punctuated his routine tasks, are succinct, declarative in purpose and effect. Juxtapositions that, in rhetoric, would be non sequiturs frequently occur, not for effect, but for economy of time and paper: "went to preaching to mount common an the sun was in clips," "went to tricum an bought me a gun for $17.00 an had the hedake." As in most private discourse, expressions of sexual need and activity are rigorously oblique (and sometimes coy), yet yeoman-style circumlocution in Traylor's diary seems to intensify rather than distance the emotional urgencies behind the entries. As an unmarried man in his twenties, Traylor is alert to both sexual opportunity and ritual conventions of courtship and marriage. Plain folk culture provided both, as we can see in one sequence of entries in 1834–1835:

Mar 6   went to a wedding at Mr. Monday Mr. Bullark was married to Miss Sarah Sprat for I see it don

June 13   went to . . . in far at Mr. Hardy an a fine in far it was

Sept 21   went to the singin to old town creek church an never got home until monday 12 oclock was on a corting spree

Dec 26   went to benton an went to Henry Lewes an staed all night Came home an brother Jackson Monday came with me an then we went to Mr. Meallings that night an had fun with the girls

Jan 8   it is oh mi tr love if yo wer to consent to have me—me the happest man on earth an if not the miserablest of the human race all hope is gone all joy is don

Jan 9   bilt a stable

Mar 19   comenced raining in the eavning Saturday. live an lern dy an forget all oh the trials in this wourld. I will see hur to morrow if nothing turns up mor than common.

Oct 23   went to Sister Springs church an never got home untell Monday an that is not all

Oct 31   Wha is to bee will bee Oh Hoo can tell what time ma do How all my sorrows yet ma end

Nov 17   packed cottin 10 bags an hade 75 bags packed. I was married this day.[38]

38. John G. Traylor Diary (SPR 302), Alabama Department of Archives and History, Montgomery.

Even in this nakedly informational writing in which farming is all chores, the author manages to strike flashes of affective eloquence that transcend his models, the literary conventions of romance and meditative piety.

As we might expect, most yeomanry farm records tend to be matter-of-fact listings, unlike the more meticulous entries of plantation books that calculated poundage and market prices. Both plain farmer and planter, however, show a keen consciousness of conditions they sense are beyond their control: election results, economic fluctuations, weather. They both expand the sheerly functional use of the daybook to include social activities that make their lives more interesting. Both groups are persistently noncommital in expressing any *liking* for what they do with their acres, and planters betray no more sense of responsible husbandry than do scrabbling farmers.

In agricultural terms, two visual scenes dominate the received impressions of the lower South. The first is the great house, surrounded by domesticated space featuring slave quarters, outbuildings, stables, livestock pens, and barns. This image, as we have seen, enjoyed its most effective life only after the Civil War, when its memorial reconstruction in literature, oratory, and creative memoirs became not simply a nostalgic reminder of loss but a continuation of the ideological battles of the 1850s.[39] The second is that inscribed by antebellum travelers and (occasionally) the vernacular humorists: a scruffy, unkempt space in a crudely managed clearing that features a log cabin much too temporary and frail to dominate its wilderness setting, which is itself punctuated with pigpens and worm fences that mostly fail to protect the vegetable patches inside them.

Historical accounts over the years tend to blur such dramatic contrasts. In less mythic records, the successful planter expands his modest manor house with extensions both vertical and horizontal, but the effect is unprepossessing: not enough windows, not enough glass in existing windows, unfinished rooms, drafty fireplaces, free-ranging farm animals sharing grassless yards with domestic debris. Even with its upgraded condition, the planter's big house achieves only minimal superiority over the "improvements" of his yeoman neighbor. For both grades of farmers, the home base is conspicuously expedient, momentary, functional—a landscape claimed, but whose shaping is provisional. That base is a visual illustration of the backwoods proverb: "Don't care keeps a big

39. Even in the first plantation novel, Isaac Holmes's *Recreations of George Taletell, F.Y.C.* (1822), the idyllic mansion house "is set firmly in a context of ruin." Bakker, *Pastoral*, 26–27, 38–39. See also Guy A. Cardwell, "The Plantation House: An Analogical Image," *Southern Literary Journal* 2 (1969): 5.

house." If preachers, editors, doctors, and lawyers who wrote sketches for the newspapers found their humor away from the plantation and farm, it is unsurprising that the Jim Doggetts, Mike Hooters, and Pete Whetstones found nothing funny in farming, either. Their roles as yeoman farmers in the sketches are so tentative that they make Byrd's lubbers seem almost industrious.[40] W. T. Thompson's Samuel Sikes "pretended to cultivate a small spot of ground," reports the narrator of "The Fire-Hunt," but those who pass his place notice that his corn and potato patches stand "greatly in need of the hoe." More prominent are "a huge pair of antlers" on the gable end of his cabin, a dozen fishing poles propped against the chimney, and coon- and deerskins on the unchinked walls "undergoing the process of drying" (*CP*, 161–78). The student's conclusion that the comic characters are farmers "trying not to work" is cannily accurate. At heart they are (to use their critics' pejorative) "reversionary"—men riding into the woods, hunting, fishing, trapping, partying, and engaging in all other activities that postpone more onerous agricultural duties. In 1818 Henry Schoolcraft described one of his Arkansas hosts as "a forehanded man for these parts, and a great hunter," but complained that nobody in his family could talk on any subject except "bears, hunting, and the like."[41]

Yet even as the yeoman, not the planter, becomes the symbolic center of the humor, the agricultural landscape of both figures becomes irrelevant. The "master" who occupied the apex of southwestern society occupies no space in the humorous sketches; but, then, neither the planter in his make-do mansion nor the squatter in his diggins has anything to do in the world the humorists created. Neither inspires yarns; neither occupies a favorable storytelling site. For their own and others' amusement, they leave the big house and the cabin, finding congenial companionship in public venues that ensure pleasure for their idle hours: law offices, courtrooms, boardinghouse common rooms, doctors' offices, village porches, churches, crossroad inns—all of which announce the priorities of bonhomie and good-natured competition. In short, farming is not a generative activity in the humor.

Disapproval of the shiftlessness of yeoman farmers is a common atti-

40. Many settlers supplemented their farming incomes by assorted tasks. Some engaged in "two or more occupations, and still others flitted from job to job or managed to avoid work altogether." James E. Davis, *Frontier America, 1800–1840: A Comparative Demographic Analysis of the Settlement Process* (Glendale, CA: Arthur H. Clark, 1977), 151.

41. Sarah Fountain, ed., *Authentic Voices: Arkansas Culture, 1541–1860* (Conway: University of Central Arkansas Press, 1986), 66.

tude, sometimes in hints from plantation diarists, who often use "lethargic" and "indolent" to describe their less well-to-do neighbors. They do so without acknowledging that even the most literate planter families among them, apart from their trusty workforce, also show no great dynamism in the cotton fields. The popular image of a white South divided between planters and crackers had its birth in social snobbery as well as the larger economic interest blessed by national policy—the mission of development, progress, economic stability, and civilization. It was the virtuous norm, and it could only misinterpret the presence of whites whose ways of life seemed to rebuff that larger mission. One traveler in the Arkansas Territory explicitly linked patrician and yeoman in a kind of classless irresponsibility. Joseph Meetch asserted that the fertility of the soil had bred so much wealth that it had "paved the way to habits of dissipation and gambling" to which the better classes were "much addicted"; as for the others, hunting bears was the "chief employ and Sole Amusement."[42] If we are to believe this visitor (and what his observing eye recorded was not unique), fertility was a given: cleared lands were for planters an exploitable resource, and for yeomen a standby source of subsistence when their Sole Amusement palled.

Unfamiliar as they were with the heterogeneous callings of the southwestern population, casual visitors could see poorer whites only as flawed replicas of respectable farmers. Unlike the "real pioneer" ("independent, brave, and upright"), his lubber cousins were "helpless *nobodies*, who, in a country where none starve and few beg, sleep until hunger pinches, then stroll into the woods for a meal, and return to their slumber." These contrasting views by James Hall are not atypical for both native and foreign visitors, yet his observation strikes a note of anxiety about the vocational leisure that the *nobodies* exhibit, one derived from folk wisdom that linked idleness and the devil's work. Though he admitted that the "jackal" backwoodsman was usually "as harmless as the wart upon a man's nose, and as unsightly," Hall suspected that this type was unduly susceptible to the criminal element that preyed on honest folk.[43]

In northern Alabama the question was more focused: Which kind of whites should benefit from the 1809 federal land sale that made settlement

42. Joseph Meetch, diary, 1826–1827, quoted in S. Charles Bolton, *Territorial Ambition: Land and Society in Arkansas, 1800–1840* (Fayetteville: University of Arkansas Press, 1993), 33–34. See also Grady McWhiney, *Cracker Culture: Celtic Ways in the Old South* (Tuscaloosa: University of Alabama Press, 1988), xiv–xviii.

43. James Hall, *Letters from the West* (1828; reprint, ed. John T. Flanagan, Gainesville, FL: Scholars' Facsimiles & Reprints, 1967), 271–72.

legal in the rich Tennessee Valley? A Fourth of July orator in 1811 regaled the celebrants of Huntsville (who would not have a courthouse for another seven years) with a flattering vision that he presented as having already come to pass: "look at the population," he told his scrappy audience, "how numerous, how orderly, how decent, how opulent, how responsible!" And he went on to explain this *fait accompli* with a significant contrast: "It is not merely a rude frontier, thinly peopled with hunters and herdsmen, the mere precursors of the tillers of the earth, but it is the tillers of the earth themselves, who bring with them the pleasures of social life, the arts of industry, the abundant means of easy and comfortable subsistence."[44]

A later generation of memoirists, invoking the homogenized pattern of pioneer life, stylistically endorsed the affective reality that the Huntsville orator alleged. Their lexicon rarely varied. Pioneers were *generous, stout, kindhearted, sturdy, respectable, law-abiding, temperate.* And at least one local Alabama historian in the mid-1880s also troubled herself to distinguish real pioneers from the touchy independents who had little stake in the settlement process. Mary Gordon Duffee, recalling this "daring class of men" in Jones Valley, had praise for their bravery, but likened them to "the savage in their blood-thirstiness." Uncomfortable with the increasing density of population, such men, she generalized, flee "as fast as the Indian on the plains." Duffee saw them as a representative species in every frontier settlement: "Semi-barbarous in their habits and inclinations; cultivating instead of subduing their ferocious tempers," they play "no important part in the opening drama of pioneer life and experience."[45] Duffee was the daughter of Matthew Duffee, contemporary of humorist John Gorman Barr and proprietor of Tuscaloosa's Washington Hall, where Simon Suggs bolts down "without mastication, the excellent supper served to him" in the dining room before he sallies forth for his evening of faro.

The Huntsville orator and his like-minded respectables had at least one thing right—a vast number of rural whites in the Old Southwest were not, in fact, planters or farmers. One large group was made up of woodsmen, who earned their way by logging, sawmilling, and cutting

44. Quoted in Dupre, *Transforming the Cotton Frontier,* 25, 11–12.
45. Mary Gordon Duffee, "Sketches of Alabama," 1885–1887, Special Collection, Samford University Library, Samford University, Birmingham, AL. A version of the articles appeared as *Sketches of Alabama: Being an Account of the Journey from Tuscaloosa to Blount Springs through Jefferson County on the Old Stage Road,* ed. Virginia Pounds Brown and Jane Porter Nabers (University: University of Alabama Press, 1970).

firewood for steamboats and railroads; and herdsmen who grazed their cattle on public lands were always prominent, though their numbers decreased as more acreage in the region became cotton lands. By the end of the eighteenth century, the Southwest was dominated by stock-raising. Another group comprised commercial fishermen and professional hunters who sold their catches to both towns and plantations. Quite apart from the historically silent white laborers, skilled and otherwise—carpenters, masons, gunsmiths, shoemakers, harness makers, and wheelwrights, among the craftsmen—we now know that there was an entire class of residents who, while associated with the land, chose to pursue their interests beyond the troublesome complications of options, titles, preemptions, and deed-registering of property owners. Besides hunters and fishermen, these included cattlemen, charcoal burners, and turpentiners. Scorned at the time as "roving, worthless creatures," these necessary but illiterate workmen now are cited as "forgotten ancestors" because they "deeded no property, kept no books and made no wills."[46] After several months in the Southwest, Frederick Gerstaecker arrived at his own conclusion about the settlers. They were, he wrote, "not very fond of hard work; in those wild regions they prefer rearing cattle and shooting, to agriculture, and are loth to undertake the hard work of felling trees and clearing land."[47] An anonymous writer declared in 1851 that settlers in the Tennessee mountains were good horsemen and hunters, "but the men, at least, are not remarkable for agricultural industry." Travelers who sneered at the debased status of such settlers failed to recognize, as one historian puts it, that their survival in a world still marked by "a paradigm of predator and prey" depended on stubborn will and self-possession.[48]

John S. Robb, a Philadelphia printer and journalist, is one humorist who explicitly addresses the slippery nomenclature. His professional restlessness took him to a wide variety of sites in the Old Southwest, but

46. Boyd, *Alabama in the Fifties,* 63–64; Frank L. Owsley, *Plain Folk of the Old South* (1949; reprint, Baton Rouge: Louisiana State University Press, 1982), 47–48, 105, 114. J. F. H. Claiborne gave one of the earliest accounts of the life and work of the southern herdsman in "A Trip through the Piney Woods," *Publications of the Mississippi Historical Society* 9 (1906): 514–15, 521. See also Forrest McDonald and Grady McWhiney, "The Antebellum Southern Herdsman: A Reinterpretation," *Journal of Southern History* 41 (1975): 147–66.

47. Gerstaecker, *Wild Sports,* 164.

48. Eugene L. Schwaab and Jacqueline Bull, eds., *Travels in the Old South: Selected from Periodicals of the Times* (Lexington: University Press of Kentucky, 1973), 2:394; Daniel Justin Herman, *Hunting and the American Imagination* (Washington: Smithsonian Institution Press, 2001), 103.

also beyond: to Detroit, New Orleans, Sacramento, and San Francisco. His base was St. Louis, where by 1845 he was writing for the *Reveille* as both serious correspondent and humorist. Like most of his fellow newspapermen in the Southwest, Robb appreciated the complexities of its diverse white population, but, except for W. T. Thompson, none of his contemporaries attempted, as he did, to define *cracker*. His effort, in the preface to *Streaks of Squatter Life* (1847), is lightly skewed to fit his own writing.

Although the humor in the *Reveille* generally made little of class distinctions, Robb was eager to clarify certain categories (even as he chose to smudge others). The contrast he draws between generic groups is not between the settler as respectable steward of his lands and the squatter as shiftless spoiler of land titles—the "actual settler," in fact, is practically synonymous with "squatter." His antithesis is the *border harpy*, which Robb describes as the "worthless and criminal" type lurking on the "outskirts of civilization" and preying on Indian and white settler alike.[49] Robb chooses to link the disorder and violence of the frontier to this class of predator, not to the squatter, so often maligned by movers and shakers. Robb lumps the harpy, as well as the unambitious farmer, into one category: *crackers*, the oldest and most comprehensive of the pejorative epithets.

Robb's settler-squatter, the frontier's "free and jovial character, inclined to mirth rather than evil," is the figure who most conspicuously supplies the "hilarity" at barbecues, campaign rallies, and frolics. Though that figure is clearly not the responsible custodian that politicians and entrepreneurs preferred as the occupant of new lands, Robb moves him from the margins of public policy into the very center of frontier life, consciously refashioned and invested with traits that most of the humorists found endearing as well as useful. Like his juxtaposed cast of characters, the narratives in *Streaks of Squatter Life* can be divided into those that are "humorous" and those that are "thrilling"; but the collection as a whole emphasizes the "humorous" doings of Robb's "free and jovial" characters (*SSL*, ix).[50] While he is willing to acknowledge the historical actuality and

49. By the sixteenth century, *harpy*, a term from classical mythology, had come to mean any rapacious person who preys on others. Robb passes over more vicious frontier predators, who in a few years would become a staple subject in the dime western, a genre popularized by Erastus Beadle (1821–1894).

50. Avery O. Craven, *The Growth of Southern Nationalism, 1848–1861* (Baton Rouge: Louisiana State University Press, 1953), 6–11; Clark and Guice, *Old Southwest*, 195. Considerable light on the material lives of ordinary southerners before the Civil War is shed in such memoirs as W. H. Sparks, *The Memories of Fifty Years* (Philadelphia, 1882), and F. D. Srygley, *Seventy Years in Dixie* (Nashville, 1893). Bibliographies of the

the cultural significance of the ambitious middling farmer, Robb sees in him (and in the even more ambitious planter) nothing worth literary effort.

Robb's preface to his important collection of sketches illuminates the priorities of the humorist authors generally. Although the prototypes for many of the cranky and "jovial" figures in Southwest humor would have been classified as "farmers" in the United States Census, for these authors the ordinary white settler had no story. The humorists stripped away most of the unpleasant and threatening connotations of *cracker* (indeed, rarely using it) and transformed his well-known indifference to farming into traits that made him witty, enterprising, even (up to a point) reputable. Seasoned observers, the humorists among them, who spent considerable time among these reversionary backwoodsmen came to understand that their leisure-oriented culture was *rural* but not *agrarian*. (Even cotton planters, the most prestigious in the lower South, never quite outgrew a homespun quality despite their conviction that superintending the land was the only really honorable occupation.) Recent historians have summarized these reversionaries in nonjudgmental terms: "They lived, so to speak, off the fat of the land while their herds went untended, devoting all their time to hunting, fishing, dancing, smoking, fighting, and visiting—not to mention the pleasurable activity of conceiving large flocks of little crackers."[51]

The plow and the hoe may recur as iconic tools in political speeches, congressional addresses, cultural essays, and (at one stage) even in the humble letters of pioneers themselves. They are functionless, however, in the humorous writing. The sketches project a stage in which the hard work of settling a new country is already an *achieved part* of its history. Even in those pieces that reflect a narrative time earlier than their composition—in Longstreet, say, or in Taliaferro—the settlement has already occurred, the homesteads are already established if not flourishing, the routines are already fixed. Village and rural life is cast in a light primarily historical. For respectable folk the wilderness has already been conquered. Nobody works. Indeed, the professionals show no interest at all in the quotidian lives of farmers—yeomen or planters. The sketches are interested in the special event, the anecdote worth repeating, the particular incident likely to supply amusement—in storytelling venues *away from* the fields.

---

plain folk can be found in Everett Dick, *The Dixie Frontier: A Social History* (New York: Knopf, 1948), and Thomas D. Clark, *The Rampaging Frontier: Manners and Humors of Pioneer Days in the South and Middle West* (Bloomington: Indiana University Press, 1964).

51. Clark and Guice, *Old Southwest*, 195.

A popular historian once declared that the waggery of the American tavern was the entertainment of "the loiterer." Certainly, those practical jokes, tall tales, and witty exchanges in groggeries and inns that we follow in writing from the Old Southwest are the products of leisure, and they proliferate among yeoman layabouts and professional men alike. The conduct of farming, even how the fields look, is a larger cultural context the authors choose not to address.[52] Taking for granted the relevant details of hardscrabble agriculture, they proceed directly to the actual lives of plain folk in their leisure.

Being a fractious pupil in school may have been the trigger that sent young Davy Crockett away from the family hearth, but escaping the dull rounds of subsistence farming was most likely also a factor. For all his sympathies with squatters, tilling the earth was not part of the frontier identity that Crockett crafted for himself. On the eve of his departure to the Texas Revolution, he pointedly tossed out his own parodic version of the boaster of fertile acres: "They say Texas is the place; and the land is so rich, if you plant a crowbar at night it will sprout tenpenny nails before morning."[53] He clearly knew farming, and he also knew it was not for him. Most of the humorists after Crockett focus on characters who, though they are slackers in the field, are enthusiasts in the woods. They may not all be Davy Crocketts, but even when their skills as hunters are spotty (as in Robb's old gold digger in "Smoking a Grizzly," Noland's Pete Whetstone, and Lewis's Mik-hoo-tah), they expand into their true identities only away from the hoe and plow—away from the stability of agricultural villages. Their identities are then ratified by group consensus, the companionship of rivals in which the bonding threads are competitive tales of bears, not boasts about yields of cotton or corn.

If the ideal for nearly all the spokesmen for progress and development was nature improved, that for hunters, herdsmen, even squatters was nature left alone. Progressives, of course, awarded more points to settlers who cultivated the land than to those who only hunted the woods. The chief argument for rousting Native Americans from their ancestral lands had been and continued to be one that was reduced to commonsense observation: having "done nothing" for generations with their lands, the native tribes deserved to be usurped by people who understood the biblical

52. Richardson Wright, *American Wags and Eccentrics from Colonial Times to the Civil War* (1939; reprint, New York: Frederick Ungar, 1965), 47.

53. By this time several sayings of Nimrod Wildfire (in Paulding's *The Lion of the West*) were being attributed to Crockett. See Franklin J. Meine, introduction to *The Crockett Almanacks: Nashville Series, 1835–1838*, ed. Harry J. Owens (Chicago: Caxton Club, 1955), xii.

injunction to make the earth prosper. The perverse "savagism" that Henry Schoolcraft described among early white residents of Arkansas amounted to reversion from responsible progress. Hunting, fishing, and herding were indulgences of irresponsible men with no stake in civilization. If the soil in Arkansas was "scarcely less fertile than Kentucky," as botanist Thomas Nuttall pronounced it to be, "favourable to productions more valuable and saleable," then not to exploit it was to hinder progress.[54]

In "The Big Bear of Arkansas," Jim Doggett perversely endorses Nuttall's judgment. Thorpe's hero affirms his state's prodigal richness, as well as its fertility as a source of frontier character—and as a test of that character. When Arkansas entered the Union in 1836, most of its residents were, like their counterparts in neighboring states, officially classified as farmers, some of them (in the Mississippi plain) involved in a market economy that depended upon slaves and cotton. The opinion that Arkansans were bad farmers, which appeared in almost all the early evaluations of the territory, continued into statehood: only human indolence could be blamed for such indifference to good fortune. Doggett's encomium echoes the reports of visitors and earlier residents alike; but when this "child of the woods" dismisses farming as the likely way to take advantage of the state's resources, he dramatizes the very reversionary traits that progressives so deplored.

Tonally, his story is even more complex.

Thorpe makes his hunter thoughtful as well as witty. Choosing his own terms, Doggett, in entertaining his fellow steamboat passengers, becomes both booster and critic of Arkansas, a bravura posture that is nevertheless complicated by self-doubts. Ring-tailed roarers are customarily too straight-ahead to be complex, and some are blowhards incapable of bemusement. Circuitous and curious, Doggett is ruminative enough to poke into the agrarian question, one of the real issues of southwestern settlement. But even as he celebrates hunting as the preferred alternative, he has enough self-knowledge to dramatize his own limitations as hunter. The Big Bear of Arkansas seriously erodes the image of a beneficent unspoiled wilderness, a favored icon in romantic mythmaking. His verbal extravagance about his state's fertility goes beyond mere brag: it adds up to a witty argument *against* cultivation.

Doggett's affirmation of "the *spontenacious* productions of the sile" stirs up not pleasurable garden repose but edgy discomfort. Its details suggest

54. Henry Rowe Schoolcraft, *Journal of a Tour into the Interior of Missouri and Arkansas* (1821; reprint, London: Argus, 1955), 80–81; Thomas Nuttall, *A Journal of Travels into the Arkansas Territory during the Year 1819* (1821; reprint, ed. Savoie Lottinville, Norman: University of Oklahoma Press, 1980), 85–89.

how unnatural this "State without a fault" really is. Prodigality breeds excess. As the hunter himself admits, "you can't preserve anything natural you plant in it unless you pick it young, things thar will grow out of shape so quick." The settlers' dream of the fat of the land is uneasily literalized: turkeys, too fat to fly, burst open their "gobs of tallow" when shot; bears, though "more greasy" in winter when they tend to waddle instead of run, nevertheless enjoy one continual fat season. As an image of the Garden, the conventional referent for most American myths of the wilderness, Arkansas evokes not innocence and abundance but a nightmarish celebration of a land east of Eden in which prodigality and depletion are grotesquely equated. The Big Bear claims the high ground. From his experience as a farmer he has found "the sile is too rich, *and planting in Arkansas is dangerous.*" It is not out of indolence that he no longer plants: "natur intended Arkansaw for a hunting ground, and I go according to natur" (*TBT,* 112–22).

Is it blessing or curse that Arkansas projects an unbearable material heaviness? If the critters are oversized, they are more vulnerable to predators; if the soil is fertile beyond even parodic distortion, it is "dangerous." Doggett's Arkansas seems finally more like a verbal construct than real geography. Nomenclature defining it as a state "without a fault" is innocent ballyhoo writ too large. But even in the hunter's own terms, Arkansas' most distinctive attribute—its natural excess—cannot help but inspire gross ambivalence.

In this respect, the Big Bear's precursor is not the half-horse half-alligator with his smug boastfulness—Doggett's aural aggressiveness ceases as soon as he gets the crowd's attention—but the real-life figure of Timothy Flint, the most clear-eyed of the early chroniclers of the Old Southwest who saw both its allure and its threat. This parson's measured observations of the Mississippi Valley and its population have the authority of one who is a realist as well as a moralist. In his *Recollections,* he often communicates his unease with the human accommodation to the region's plenty. "There is something," he notes, "almost appalling in this prodigious power of vegetation. For there is with me, in some manner, an association of this thing with the idea of sickness." Migrants from other climates, susceptible to ague, often lose "their native activity" and these "cadaverous" figures are seen "yawning and stretching, apparently almost incapable of motion."[55] Even with its carefully qualified diction

---

55. Timothy Flint, *Recollections of the Last Ten Years in the Valley of the Mississippi* (1826; reprint, ed. George R. Brooks, Carbondale: Southern Illinois University Press, 1968), 23–24. See also Valenčius, *Health of the Country,* 26.

(*something, almost, with me, some manner, this thing, apparently almost*), this passage bespeaks a troubling frame of mind.

While Nuttall's science aligns itself with ideas of conventional land use, Flint allows conscience to interpose itself against an agrarian agenda. If Doggett's perspective in "The Big Bear" can be said to carry an agenda for the state, it might be bluntly phrased as *leave it alone.* The texture and substantive implications of Thorpe's great sketch seem designed to discourage further immigration. It is as if Arkansas is summoned up to illustrate not perfection, but a homespun New World version of medieval luxuria—a proliferating, rank excess that is as unhealthy as it is awesome. In such a place, being prodigal and becoming functional are necessary coordinates.

Again, it is Flint who tonally anticipates the Big Bear. Although this good clergyman is reluctant to discourage migration, a kind of disquiet creeps into his observation that no country is "more fruitful in men, as well as corn" than this richly endowed area. Flint links lassitude and fecundity when he recounts how "a whole posse of big and little boys and girls" stumbles out of each cabin to greet the passing stranger. Tattered and unkempt, such "hosts" of "white-headed urchins" are visible evidence of the "process of doubling population, without Malthus, and without theory." Reiterating the favorable facts of climate and fertility, Flint assumes an apparent neutrality: "The climate is mild, the cattle need little care or housing, and multiply rapidly. Grain requires little labour in the cultivation, and the children only need a *pone* of corn bread, and a bowl of milk."[56] Yet even his neutrality is edged with foreboding. The garden of plenitude thrives almost too generously. While Flint's account is less provocative than Thorpe's, it still sets its author apart from the politicians and land agents, whose self-interest endorsed the official mission. Jim Doggett's whoppers may be intended to amuse strangers, but the enlargement of nature that gives them context carries a single baneful message: *fecundity kills.*

It is already too late for Doggett's economic realities, but his performance in the steamboat's social hall is yet a comment on the dominant agenda to convert every acre to cultivation. Official logic—that the tribal hunters might not have been dispossessed had they been savvy enough to cultivate their own domain—was a disingenuous justification that linked reversionary whites to their Indian precursors. Given that ominous analogy, Doggett's pointed but genial dissent is remarkably civilized. Behind the hunter's "explanation" lurks something more primal

56. Flint, *Recollections*, 23–24.

144 Fetching the Old Southwest

than amusing folk reason. The kind of unfettered liberty that constantly thwarts David Crockett's route to respectability is a vital impulse in a sizable class of southwestern yeomen who are largely indifferent to respectability. Although a majority in the backcountry of the Mississippi Valley grew corn patches and pastured livestock on the free range, one historian asserts that they "lived more by the gun than the plow, shooting deer, wild fowl, and fur-bearing animals by the thousands."[57] For most Arkansans the most tempting intervention of all, the simple need to escape into the woods, became a habit that latter-day William Byrds seized upon as evidence that lubberly whites had, alas, carried their Sole Amusement west of the Mississippi.

Many of the extant letters and daybooks of ordinary people are of course records of farmers who could be passionate in their drive to become successful, aspiring perhaps to the status of planter with a slave or two. Even as late as the 1850s, however, both marginal farmers and planters never repudiated a territorial fondness for escaping into the woods—sometimes even to hunt.[58] The attraction of good country for farming in Arkansas had always to compete with a game-rich wilderness. One traveler, passing through the state on his way to Texas, tried to hire a horse and carriage, only to find that the lone stable owner in town had decided to go turkey hunting on the other side of the river. A. M. Wynn of Alabama went to Arkansas in 1857 to visit his brother and tarried long enough to attend a land auction, where men bid "as if they had plenty of money and no poor kin." He then joined residents in hunting for deer in an area where cows, colts, and hogs mingled with wild game—"a fine place," he noted, "for bears, panthers, wolves, wild cats etc."[59]

"A fine place" was a judgment on the lips of both progressives and reversionaries. Even the term *new country* had one connotation for settlers and another for all those who were indifferent to the promise of fertile spreads. For settlers—subsistence farmers, planters, and ambitious professionals—it meant fertile land, available and affordable, settlements and

---

57. Roger W. Shugg, *Origins of Class Struggle in Louisiana: A Social History of White Farmers and Laborers during Slavery and After, 1840–1875* (Baton Rouge: Louisiana State University Press, 1939), 44.

58. McWhiney, *Cracker Culture*, 144–45. Even John A. Quitman was frustrated in his command of volunteers during the Mexican War because it deprived him of the leisure "to hunt grouse, pheasant, duck and turkey." Robert E. May, "John A. Quitman and the Southern Martial Spirit," *Journal of Mississippi History* 41 (1979): 173.

59. Gilbert Hathaway, "Travels in the South-West," in Schwaab and Bull, *Travels*, 2:447 [originally published in *Magazine of Travel* 1 (1857)]; Alexander M. Wynn, Wynn Family Papers, William Stanley Hoole Special Collections, University of Alabama Library, University of Alabama, Tuscaloosa.

towns that could supply urban amenities, and nascent political and social structures that could be shaped by canny leadership. For hunters, eccentric loners, and (occasionally) desperadoes, it meant the isolation of the backcountry, woods if not wilderness, which protected privacy and independence. For both kinds of migrants, *new country* was synonymous with *better,* a place where lives could be conducted in a hospitable environment. Because they came in all stripes, confidence men, adventurers, border harpies, and petty land speculators mingled freely and often profitably among both groups. Both the ambitious and the desultory responded to opportunity in a place where either a Joseph Glover Baldwin or a Simon Suggs might prosper.[60] As in Alabama and Mississippi a few years earlier, residents in Arkansas and Texas were a heterogeneous mix of mobile settlers, those who continued their westward migration out of economic ambition, and freer spirits who pursued woods and wilderness no longer available in the lower states.

In the antebellum years, the independent farmer was necessarily conceptualized as a benefit to the *wilderness.* His "central source of civic virtue" was not in using the backwoods as his playground, but in following the Creator's command to transform the land He made.[61] Prior to westward expansion, hunters represented savagism while farmers stood for civilization. "No Tartar ever loved horseflesh or Hottentot guts and garbage better than woodsmen do bear," wrote William Byrd. Charles Woodmason, an Anglican who preached morality and manners to those woodsmen's descendants in the 1760s, confessed that for all his efforts, they remained savages. In one outburst, this cleric charged that the backwoodsmen "range the Country, with their Horse and Gun, without Home or Habitation," and instinctively "follow Hunting—Shooting—Racing—Drinking—Gaming, and ev'ry Species of Wickedness. Their Lives are only one continual Scene of Depravity of Manners, and Reproach to the Country; being more abandoned to Sensuality, and more Rude in Manners, than the Poor Savages around us."[62] After Arkansas was opened to settlement, Henry Schoolcraft reiterated the theme: bear hunters and their ragtag families were indistinguishable from the Indians in "manners, morals, customs, dress, contempt of labor and hospitality."[63]

60. Bolton, *Territorial Ambition,* 5, 122. See also J. Crawford King, "The Closing of the Southern Range," *Journal of Southern History* 48 (1982): 53–70.

61. Richard Hofstadter, *The Age of Reform: From Bryan to FDR, 1916–1970* (New York: Knopf, 1972), 24–25. See also Valenčius, *Health of the Country,* 198.

62. Quoted in Herman, *Hunting and the American Imagination,* 37, 39.

63. Schoolcraft, *Journal,* 80–81. See also Richard C. Brewer, "Henry Rowe Schoolcraft: Explorer in the Mississippi Valley, 1818–1832," *Wisconsin Magazine of History* 66 (1982): 46.

Nineteenth-century logic said the backwoods must make way for the orderly succession of privately owned, well-regulated farms. Despite a powerful official priority, not a single figure out of our agricultural myth— planter or yeoman—casts the kind of impressive shadow of Boone, Crockett, Meriwether Lewis, Johnny Appleseed, or Audubon. At one time or another most of these were farmers manqué, but their fame rests largely on the lore of their unsettled energies—their restlessness, their mobility, their curiosity, their impatience with routine, their ambivalence to a life of stable domesticity. Defying the official agricultural mission, the age glorified not farming and farmers, but hunting and hunters. Had they been more articulate, yeoman farmers in Alabama or Mississippi might have repeated Emerson's sentiment: "Thank fortune, we are not rooted to the soil," and here "is not all the world."[64]

64. Emerson believed that man's "historic nobility" derived from his use of the land, yet he warned against painting "in rose-color" the occupational farmer: "He represents the necessities." In September 1858, "neglecting to say *No* early enough," Emerson reluctantly lectured at Concord's agricultural fair; variously called "The Man with the Hoe," "Cattle Show at Concord," and "Farmers and Farming," the speech (or pieces of it) was cobbled into print as "Country Life," "Concord Walks," and "Farming." *The Complete Works of Ralph Waldo Emerson,* Centenary Edition (Boston: Houghton Mifflin, 1903–1904), 5:118n; 7:130 ff; 12:133–67, 169–79. See also *The Letters of Ralph Waldo Emerson,* ed. Ralph L. Rusk (New York: Columbia University Press, 1939), 5:118–19, and *The Topical Notebooks of Ralph Waldo Emerson,* ed. Susan Sutton Smith (Columbia: University of Missouri Press, 1990), 1:257.

Chapter 5 ⊹━━━━ஃ

Fetching Arkansas

Fetch

n. A contrivance, dodge, stratagem, trick.

v. To go in quest of; to steal (Obs.); to succeed in bringing (Now rare); to move to interest . . . by some happy contrivance or telling feature; to "take," attract, be telling or effective; to close in upon, surround; to enclose, take in; to cheat (Obs.).

—Oxford English Dictionary

i.

In the flush of migration, many transient villages in the Old Southwest found themselves unsettled by their catch-as-catch-can population. The diversity might include a handful of residents who were potential builders of community, but they were usually outnumbered by shrewd adventurers and bustling risk-takers. Petty frauds especially favored the little river towns that sprang up to accommodate commercial activity on the Mississippi River. Over time the more imaginative and more devious alike decamped, leaving the field to enervated "persisters." Cairo became the favorite site of travelers' scorn, but it was not unique as a sanctuary for those whose rambunctious spirit had largely played out. In the general sordidness of these sites of boredom, instinct, and casual mayhem, those in Arkansas were often seen as especially makeshift and their residents the most feckless of all.

Through his young hero's realistic eye in *Adventures of Huckleberry Finn*, Mark Twain captured some of these accrued impressions, the most revealing of which coincide with the introduction of the King and the Duke. Before we meet them, these con artists have already experienced something of the cold charities of Arkansawyers. This section of the novel (chapters 19–23) features their performance of "The Royal Nonesuch," a kind of revenge on "those Arkansaw lunkheads" who can't appreciate a first-class show, played on opening night before a total of twelve people—"just enough," Huck notes, "to pay expenses." What they wanted, in the Duke's judgment, was "low comedy—and may be something ruther worse than low comedy, he reckoned. He said he could size their style."

New circumstances require a different kind of Shakespeare. The Duke scraps the balcony scene from *Romeo and Juliet*, the broadsword scene from *Richard III*, and "Hamlet's Immortal Soliloquy." In keeping with the scaled-down performance, the placards are physically reduced except for a final flourish, where the Duke paints "the biggest line of all":

> LADIES AND CHILDREN NOT ADMITTED.
> "There," says he, "if that line don't fetch them, I don't know Arkansaw!"
> (*MW*, 772)

And the Duke does know Arkansas. It is neither high culture nor altruism that prompts the old frauds to bring the Arkansas lunkheads around. That night, the house is "jam full of men in no time." They are treated to the spectacle of "Edmund Kean the Elder" prancing around on all fours, his naked body, reports Huck, "painted all over, ring-streaked-and-striped, all sorts of colors, as splendid as a rainbow." Though the men like it, and call the King back to cavort two more times, that's all there is.

As confidence games go, making an audience pay to watch a grizzled thespian gamboling on stage is not much, only a modest instance of go-ahead enterprise. But it is an impeccable example of the yeoman track of that dominant ethic of the Old Southwest. The play's the thing that catches the coins, but the play's the thing in itself, too—an amiable mix of prankishness and self-interest, all compacted in the Duke's operative word, *fetch*. If one of its meanings is *to bring around, to bring off successfully*, Samuel Clemens, the student of diction and dialect, compresses in that one verb an array of rich and extensive nuances. Like most things associated with the crafty old frauds, fetching Arkansaw, when reduced to bare bones, has no more disguise than the rainbow nakedness of the King. *To fetch* is *to hoodwink*.

What is interesting about this episode, quite apart from its splendid entertainment, is the series of premises behind it and its strategic placement in the narrative. What is sometimes forgotten about the Royal Nonesuch as con game is the mutual interplay between conner and conned. The audience's first impulse when they sing out "Sold!"—their cry of recognition that they have been cheated—is to rush toward the stage for revenge on the World Renowned Tragedians. But one shrewd man among them jumps on a bench and convinces them that though they have been sold ("mighty badly sold"), they ought not make themselves the laughingstock of the town; rather, they should talk up the show for its performance the following night "and sell the *rest* of the town!" Betraying an affinity for conning, the audience conspires with the primary conners to continue the game. Accordingly, on the next night the King and the Duke again play to a full house. On the final night the townspeople return, now concealing rotten vegetables and dead cats for a surprise curtain call. But the Duke knows Arkansas: "Greenhorns, flatheads!" he laughs, after he and the King make a quick getaway. "*I* knew the first house would keep mum and let the rest of the town get roped in; and I knew they'd lay for us the third night, and consider it was *their* turn now. Well, it *is* their turn, and I'd give something to know how much they'd take for it" (*MW*, 775). For the entertainers, it has been worth $465 for the three nights.

With the mix of playfulness and selfishness that he inherited from the earlier humorists, Clemens explicitly situates the game of yeomanry conning in a mingy social climate. The Longstreet school of authors, as we shall see, was largely indifferent to the specifics of place. But Huck is a superb observer of his surroundings. He notes that the Arkansas river town of Bricksville consisted of unpainted "old shackly dried-up frame concerns" set on stilts to keep dry when the river overflowed and unkempt gardens sprouting sunflowers, jimsonweed, broken bottles, and "curled-up boots and shoes"—a one-street town filled with tobacco-chewing loafers whose boredom is broken by siccing dogs onto pigs lazying in the muddy street or by "putting turpentine on a stray dog and setting fire to him." But boredom in the stagnant town is dissipated also by drunken old Boggs, by some accounts "the best-naturedest old fool in Arkansaw—never hurt nobody, drunk nor sober." In a pathetic parody of backwoods roarer rhetoric, his empty challenges are taken up by Colonel Sherburn, who coolly shoots him twice as the crowd presses in for a firsthand look at the drama.

That it is a drama is important. One consequence of the Boggs-Sherburn episode is that it immediately generates its own street-theater version, and the mock murderer, who also plays the mock victim, does it so well that "a dozen people got out their bottles and treated him." Another consequence is the attempted lynching of Sherburn, a halfhearted afterthought born not of rage but of the community's casually felt necessity to repay sullied southern honor. Just before the segments devoted to the conning by bogus royalty, whose theatrical imitations are uninteresting until their fraudulence actually works, Twain presents the antics of more serious performers whose authority and behavior are equally bogus, but which result in a literal death. Sherburn's tonic dressing-down of the lynch mob, an authorial sermonette on the cowardice of the common man, is itself morally ambiguous: the truth issues from the mouth of an armed, violent bully who assumes aristocratic airs. Although Huck records the colonel's withering speech, he does not comment on his courage, which is so clearly absent in the mob; he does note the sudden breaking up of the crowd, with the leader "looking tolerable cheap" as he runs after them: "I could a staid, if I'd a wanted to, but I didn't want to."

As a mere observer, Huck has been in no danger. He *could* have stayed had he wanted to. But for him this visual drama has a confusing moral import. Without a break, without commenting on how he feels, Huck says, "I went to the circus." Here the ambiguity of the visual drama is more comfortably theatrical—"the splendidist sight that ever was"—one that is candidly designed to make people howl "with pleasure and astonishment." Even when he is unable to read certain signs of artifice in the guise of real life—the "drunk" in the audience who turns out to be a skillful circus rider—and feels "sheepish enough to be took in so," and even when he continues to believe that the ringmaster himself has been fooled by one of his own employees, the masquerade is not cruel. The circus provides a kind of genial relief from the darker Sherburn episode that tropes the Royal Nonesuch section.

If the lynch mob is a mass of bogus men—the colonel identifies the leader as only "*half* a man"—the man who disperses them is only half a hero. Arkansas is seen as populated by half-men, as animalistic as the literal beasts whose torture supplies their chief entertainment. Thus, the con man in his role of prancing, parti-colored giraffe on the makeshift boards of an Arkansas courthouse exploits not just the taste but the very nature of bestial Arkansawyers, who in various ways conduct their own theatricals in the form of verbal challenges, murder, mob action, and rhetorical addresses pitched in tones of moral indignation.

Huck's sensibility is ahistorical, except for what it absorbs from Tom Sawyer. Twain, however, is fully aware of the historical moment in a river town (only lately a frontier) that sets loose scoundrels like the late Dauphin and the Duke of Bilgewater to prey on a desiccated population that, like the Bricksville crowds, usually deserves to be preyed on. He is also aware of the literary continuum that finds him, a quarter-century after their flourishing, the modern, sophisticated heir to the so-called gifted amateurs that triggered his career.

In light of the author's subsequent scenes of theatrical variety, the King and Duke's performance is penny-ante. So is the degree of fetching when the frauds first invade the raft. But the very presence of the uninvited royal guests soon ratifies for Huck and Jim the substantive implications of, and the richly promising occasions for, the exercise of fetching.

To fetch Arkansas was to know Arkansas, and to know Arkansas was to know the Old Southwest generally, since the filling up of the new lands after the War of 1812 was a sequential expansion by the same kinds of people: land-hungry sons of Virginia and Carolina planters who had worn out their soil; war veterans who made the trans-Appalachian migration to claim land grants promised by a grateful country (whose crafty congressmen had also promised the same tracts to their friends for speculation); enterprising yeoman farmers eager to establish themselves outside the social and financial restrictions of gentry-dominated politics; ambitious young lawyers and doctors who could pluck their victims from a disparate populace until they too could buy land and join the planter elite; merchants, boardinghouse operators, tavern owners, gamblers, blacksmiths, wagoners, hunters, and trappers.

To know Arkansas was to know the conditions of the time: raw, unsettled country relieved sporadically in the interior by stands, settlements, and villages and, along the waterways, by pretentious and shabby towns in a wobbly state of transience; a flexible social arrangement, shaped more by mobile customs of the road than by the fashions of the hierarchical East, with only spotty reference to such institutional norms as school, church, and court. Indeed, even the sustaining values of the family were submerged and subverted by the radical need of its individual members to do exactly as they pleased. What most newcomers to the lower South held in common was the instinctive principle, growing from the demographic stew of dispersion, that expedience and self-interest are stronger stimuli in human affairs than reason, benevolence, sympathy, or law.

These are the conditions that Samuel Clemens summoned up imaginatively and historically. By the time of his growing up in Hannibal, the vitality and chaos of the frontier had moved farther west, leaving it stunted like Bricksville, Pokerville, and their even shoddier cousins in Missouri and Arkansas—comatose towns shabbily governed by the conventions of a cramped respectability. But enough traces remained to remind the author of the flush times recorded by a prior generation of writers: the lingual legacy of the braggart and the storyteller, the agents of spasmodic violence, the juxtaposition of the ragtag and the pretentious. Most important among these traces of that earlier writing was a vision of human nature that is perhaps only one level above the Hobbesian. We have often been puzzled by how the ebullient accents of Mark Twain, the funny man, gradually became the hectoring tones of the scold, the comedian transposed into prophet, arraigning "the damned human race" for its ignorance and intolerance and for exuding its moral flatulence to the uttermost ends of the earth. But the author of the Mysterious Stranger narratives (1897–1908) can be recognized as early as *Huckleberry Finn* (1884), where the spectacular humorous effects cannot conceal the relish behind his exposure of a callous society in the Mississippi Valley.

The Arkansas sequences, both comic and serious, that reinforce the Royal Nonesuch episode have the cumulative effect of a vision, only imperfectly glimpsed by Huck, of moral anarchy as a human given. If Missouri is spared the cruelest, most loutish instances, that may be because Twain could not bring himself to spoil the nostalgic daydream of his own sad little river town that he memorialized in *The Adventures of Tom Sawyer* (1876). Arkansas was after all indisputably South, and a crude South at that, almost as if the rawest frontier circumstances of this one southwestern state could emblematically serve as the whole South. But the disagreeable picture of Arkansas in *Huckleberry Finn* is not finally petty state-bashing or even the hot air of regional competition that marked American society and literature in the three decades prior to the Civil War. Clemens was using antebellum Arkansas as the convenient image of a national character that in the 1880s was growing increasingly repulsive to him. He permits Colonel Sherburn to say it: "I was born and raised in the South, and I've lived in the North; so I know the average all around." In the North the coward "goes home and prays for a humble spirit to bear" his abuses; in the South juries refuse to hang murderers but wait until after dark and lynch them.

Once they enter the story, the King and the Duke preside over a panorama of scenes, the social import of which grows progressively darker. If the novel generally is a compendium of swindles in human trust, the Arkansas segments look both forward and backward. Just as this Arkansas anticipates Mark Twain as author from the 1890s to 1910, so it also recapitulates the social climate of the recent southwestern frontier as depicted with such gusto by Longstreet, Baldwin, Hooper, Thorpe, and their contemporaries.

It is Huck and Jim's bad luck (and our good) that the King and the Duke, exposed at the same place and time by an irate public, find refuge on the raft. The first thing that Huck finds odd is that "these chaps didn't know one another." Odd because, except for the forty years' difference in their ages, they look alike, dress alike, sound alike, and follow the same occupation: the petty confidence game. One has been peddling tartar remover that also takes off tooth enamel; the other has been caught with a "private jug" while conducting a temperance revival. Separate but equal in their enterprises (and their exposure), they now maximize their opportunities by deciding to "double-team it together." In getting to know one another, they first pool their inventory of specialties. "What's your line—mainly?" asks the older man.

> "Jour printer, by trade; do a little in patent medicines; theatre-actor—tragedy, you know; take a turn at mesmerism and phrenology when there's a chance; teach singing-geography school for a change; sling a lecture, sometimes—oh, I do lots of things—most anything that comes handy, so it ain't work. What's your lay?"
> "I've done considerble in the doctoring way in my time. Layin' on o' hands is my best holt—for cancer, and paralysis, and sich things; and I k'n tell a fortune pretty good, when I've got somebody along to find out the facts for me. Preachin's my line, too; and workin' camp-meetin's; and missionaryin' around." (*MW*, 744)

Any *line* or *lay* requires changing one's place and refining a rich variety of pursuits, and the process is often tantamount to switching identities. The transience of settlements, villages, and towns provides a situation ready-made for the confidence man, whose very identity lies in a denial of fixed character, an assertion of the values of amorphousness—as we see in Melville's *masquerado*, whose cynical use of the moral ambiguousness of the Mississippi world is one part of his creator's larger and darker vision.

The King and the Duke are blessed by versatility (which they claim with only modest preening), but in a climate marked by opportunism, even those who follow a single occupation must be prepared to vary their presentation and technique, even their identities, as often as they change their venue. Twain's formal doubling of the con man in his comic rogues is a nice touch, but, as a device, it was anticipated more than thirty years earlier in *Uncle Tom's Cabin* (1852). Only her religiosity keeps Mrs. Stowe from making Haley, her inept and constantly frustrated slave trader, from becoming a fully comic character. When Haley, however, turns to the bulldoglike Loker and the catlike Marks for help in tracking down Eliza and her son, Stowe introduces us to a pair of walk-on figures whose tandem operations give efficiency to what she scornfully calls the "catching business" along the Ohio and Mississippi. " 'You oughter see now,' said Marks, in a glow of professional pride, 'how I can tone it off.' "

> "One day, I'm Mr. Twickem, from New Orleans; 'nother day, I'm just come from my plantation on Pearl river, where I works seven hundred niggers; then, again, I come out a distant relation of Henry Clay, or some old cock in Kentuck. Talents is different, . . . but Lord, if thar's a feller in the country that can swear to anything and everything, and put in all the circumstances and flourishes with a long face, and carry 't through better 'n I can, why, I'd like to see him, that's all!"[1]

That the King and the Duke, when Jim's usefulness has run its course for them, add the "catching business" to their own repertory of talents may be Twain's sly homage to his Hartford neighbor.

ii.

If *The Confidence-Man* (1857) does little to clarify the mysteries of human identity, Herman Melville's most robustly cynical playing field suggests the protean ways in which *confidence* defined, informed, and subverted the rules and protocols by which Americans played the game. As both a corollary of American freedom and as a personal trait elevated almost to the ranks of the Virtues, *confidence* rivaled *go-ahead* as an antebellum catchphrase. "Confidence is the indispensable basis of all sorts of business transactions," says Melville's Philosophical Intelligence Officer. For all its misanthropic application in *The Confidence-Man*, this commonplace happened to be true, even aboard the *Fidèle*. And it enjoyed no greater press than in the 1837 speech in the U.S. House of Representatives delivered with straight-faced passion by the eloquent Hugh Swinton Legaré of South Carolina. The credit system, he declared,

1. Harriet Beecher Stowe, *Uncle Tom's Cabin or Life among the Lowly*, ed. Ann Douglas (New York: Viking Penguin, 1981), 128.

implies *confidence*—confidence in yourself, confidence in your neighbor, confidence in your government, confidence in the administration of the laws, confidence in the sagacity, the integrity, the discretion of those with whom you have to deal; confidence, in a word, in your destiny, and your fortune, in the destinies and the fortune of the country to which you belong.[2]

If Legaré's passion to define *confidence* sounds suspiciously like an entreaty, it is because the word had already entered cultural life as one deserving suspicion. The oratory here is in the service of returning the word to its rightful place at the very moment it is widely regarded as a synonym for manipulation and fraud, a laudable concept distorted into shady practice throughout all levels of society.

A modern geographer's principle—"There is no natural tendency to work together for the common good"—was prefigured in 1853 when Joseph G. Baldwin worked out his rationale for the circumstances he observed in both the Old Southwest and in California:

Society is kept together on a principle of universal distrust. Nobody has confidence in any body else. Hence no one being trusted, no one is deceived: and, therefore, no one has any right to complain of being taken in. It is a great mistake to suppose that confidence keeps society together: it is the very thing that keeps men apart. Nothing so harmonizes a community as a modest and well-grounded diffidence in each other's integrity.[3]

The erosion of confidence, especially the abuse of the gentleman's agreement in economic matters, had turned the deal-maker into the confidence man. If the immediate context of Legaré's speech is the national economic debate about paper money—President Jackson the year before had issued the Specie Circular, an act that required the federal government to collect hard currency for future land purchases and which would soon fuel a six-year depression—the larger context is anxiety about even the most trifling of moneymaking arrangements. Gone was the gentleman's "word" that had functioned as credit in an earlier era. The crisis of confidence, created by a dearth of hard currency and the inability of banks

2. Hugh Swinton Legaré, "Spirit of the Sub-Treasury," in *Writings of Hugh Swinton Legaré* (Charleston, SC, 1846), 1:306.
3. Maurice Halbwachs quoted in Yi-fu Tuan, *Space and Place: The Perspective of Experience* (Minneapolis: University of Minnesota Press, 1977), 167; Joseph G. Baldwin, "California Flush Times," *Southern Literary Messenger* 19 (November 1853): 667.

to extend credit, coincided with a widespread dependence on "paper promises"—cosignatures, personal notes, local bills of exchange, and other material evidence of reliability. A letter from a Mississippi overseer suggests the fragile interconnections of financial loans: "I have made a failier in Collecting what is Due me and by this menes will fall a little behind with you on the first payment."[4] Although it was a heady economic climate for the skilled confidence man, in the fragile social cohesion and unstable institutional life of the Old Southwest almost everybody harbored swindling potential. Though it doesn't always work, one defense against swindling is the literal sign of distrust—"Pay to-day and trust to-morrow" (the notice posted in Jeb Snelling's "shantee" in *Col. Crockett's Exploits and Adventures in Texas*). The sentiment is cynically recapitulated in Melville's blunter "NO TRUST" (the barber's placard in *The Confidence-Man*). In terms of a middle class anxious to discern genuine respectability from its pretend version, the Old Southwest was hardly different from the nation at large. Especially in the metropolitan East, according to one authority, the "cultural work of guarding against social impersonation was never done."[5] Although fear of the confidence man was probably disproportionate to the actual number of swindlers operating, there were enough publicized cases to make ordinary citizens wary. Duplicity and cunning turned even honest overreachers into predators.

In "Story of a Speculator," one of the moral tales in a privately printed memoir, an old man takes his nephew aside to advise him of appropriate conduct "in a community where one-third are bungling gamblers, and one-third are stupid dolts" (presumably the remaining third are sensible, practical men who are wise to the others). After a series of admonitions out of almanac wisdom and chapel morality, the old man betrays a sentiment that goes beyond the avuncular conventions of such genres:

> You will regard all mankind as exclusively selfish, and consequently, ever striving to get the advantage of you. Thus it will not only be excusable, but proper, that you use every advantage or good fortune you may have . . . over them, consistently, with the aforementioned code. Written laws are made for rascals, and should not bind men of honor.[6]

---

4. Robert H. Wiebe, *The Opening of American Society: From the Adoption of the Constitution to the Eve of Disunion* (New York: Knopf, 1984), 151; F. M. Glass Letter, June 20, 1858, Mississippi Department of Archives and History, Jackson.

5. James W. Cook, *The Arts of Deception: Playing with Fraud in the Age of Barnum* (Cambridge: Harvard University Press, 2001), 27.

6. [John B. Darden], *The Secret of Success, or Family Affairs; A Memoir . . . by a Mississippian* (Cincinnati, 1853), 42–43.

When the early republican virtues of candor and simplicity became useful guises for deception, trust in a man's word and a sincere face could no longer be taken for granted. Certainly it would take more than Legaré's oratorical zeal to convince Americans to renew their faith in confidence. Even authenticity now needed to be authenticated.

As a literary convention, the confidence man is prefigured in the works of Franklin, Royall Tyler, and H. H. Brackenridge, but its flourishing occurs in antebellum America.[7] Many outraged travel writers dutifully recorded their occasional hoodwinking with exclamation marks; more equably, the newspaper humorists made confidence men in their various permutations a part of the cultural landscape, implicitly summing up in one type the national anxieties about language, civilization, and even the coherence of American identity itself.

Mathew Carey met head-on, by reversing the charge, the complaint of some foreign visitors that conning and hoaxing were a New World phenomenon. The editor and publisher condemned European "Gentlemen of Fortune" for emigrating to the United States. These "mere men of pleasure, the *fruges consumere nati* of society," he wrote, should remain in the "great capitals of Europe [which] are the proper elements for this class."[8] The implication is curious: that homegrown Americans were somehow too innocent to learn the skills required of men who lived by their wits. Longstreet, Baldwin, Hooper, and especially Mark Twain knew better. They knew that those who consumed the fruits of the earth could be skanky as well as sleek, that in those amorphous times adaptability and jerry-rigged fakery could yield results quite as often as polished professionalism. By the mid 1850s, the once-clear distinction between confidence man and victim, hoaxer and hoaxed, had been smudged, and P. T. Barnum was a major player in this development. The next year Herman Melville would trace the complicity, even the mutual need, of the relationship. The "insinuating ventriloquism" of his "unrestrained actor" is a response to a world in which all figures

7. Studies of the confidence man are extensive. They include Susan Kuhlmann, *Knave, Fool, and Genius: The Confidence Man as He Appears in Nineteenth-Century American Fiction* (Chapel Hill: University of North Carolina Press, 1973); William E. Lenz, *Fast Talk and Flush Times: The Confidence Man as a Literary Convention* (Columbia: University of Missouri Press, 1985); Richard Boyd Hauck, *A Cheerful Nihilism: Confidence and "The Absurd" in American Humorous Fiction* (Bloomington: Indiana University Press, 1961); Warwick Wadlington, *The Confidence Game in American Literature* (Princeton, NJ: Princeton University Press, 1975); and Gary Lindberg, *The Confidence Man in American Literature* (New York: Oxford, 1982).

8. Mathew Carey, *Miscellaneous Essays* (Philadelphia, 1830), 145, 353.

with whom he traffics are also "actors whose roles seem unsubstantial at best."[9]

If the traditional con man comes down to us as a predatory isolato, freed of the nourishing bonds of family and community, in the moral and social amphibiousness of the Southwest he was often merely an italicized version of everybody else for whom opportunity was its own sanction. As Baldwin suggested, even professionals like himself got into the spirit of the times. As late as 1852 one "regular" doctor deplored the prevalence in Alabama of the "foul and frothy tribe of quacks." In Mobile alone the medical establishment was an unstable mix of regular practitioners, homeopathists, hydropathists, root doctors, and Thomsonians—the latter known as "steamers" who freely plied their patients with both external and internal stimulants. In 1843 a doctor in Pike County, Georgia, wrote to a fellow Thomsonian who was discouraged by a practice that had not been lucrative. "The fact is," he declared, "we must be *determined* to *get rich* before we go home we must *skin* these lazy Georgians, & by our enterprize & industrious habits acquire a competence before we think of going [back] to Maine." He went on to say that since the opponents to "our *System*" were more formidable at home than in Georgia— "you would be a *quack* there"—his advice was to "remain where you are, till you have not only overcome the prejudice of the community but, till, you have got your pockets full of money." In a postscript the doctor's wife added her own encouragement: "Do all you can and don't get them well to quick."[10] Not only confidence men but also perfectly ordinary citizens in the valleys of the Ohio and Mississippi loved to hoax visitors, who in the three decades before the Civil War endured drunken stage drivers, racing steamboat captains, and slovenly innkeepers in order to size up the character and manners of this new people. Especially vulnerable were British female intellectuals and genteel clergymen. On his American tour, Charles Mackay complained of the unavoidable class of men whose only pleasure seemed to be "to mystify, bamboozle, and hoax strangers."[11]

Charles Latrobe habituated himself to the custom of the country in

9. Mark R. Patterson, *Authority, Autonomy, and Representation in American Literature, 1776–1865* (Princeton, NJ: Princeton University Press, 1988), 191, 227. Daniel S. Dupre discusses the politician as confidence man in *Transforming the Cotton Frontier: Madison County, Alabama, 1800–1840* (Baton Rouge: Louisiana State University Press, 1997), 197–201.

10. Isaac M. Comings to Samuel H. B. Lewis, Special Collections and Archives, Robert W. Woodruff Library, Emory University, Atlanta.

11. Charles Mackay, *Life and Liberty in America* (London, 1859), 1:303.

trading matters, being forced, he wrote, to display his own talents for "jockeyship and cunning." The swapping contagion did not merely involve the exchange of horses, rifles, and saddles, but was indicative of a crisis of identity: "you could never be certain of an individual till you saw his face." Perhaps not even then. Latrobe tried to discriminate between the unthreatening squatter in Arkansas ("the rootless man, whose impulses led him to keep the outskirts of society") and the ominous throngs who mingled in the same "wilds"—murderers, public defaulters, speculators.[12] A French visitor, concerned with how easily these adventurers donned fraudulent identities in order to con others, gave his readers the cynical formula for sneaky business deals: "Be a cheat, get in your favor the popular prejudice, and you will make the wise flee to hide themselves until the moment when some new trickster comes and dethrones you." An émigré who made the Old Southwest his home for a few years was less concerned than his fellow countryman about such tricksters. New countries, he noted, always attract a "multitude of rogues and intriguers," sometimes becoming "the government"; but this "momentary evil" disappears with the coming of "villages, towns, universities," and permanent settlers and "honest people . . . regain the ascendancy."[13] If exploitation, acquisition, and chance are powerful urgencies of a whole people on the move, in a cultural moment in which the migrating professional participates along with lesser transients and itinerants, then the confidence man is not merely a marginal figure who sets about breaking communal taboos and disrupting social bonds for profit. He is, rather, a profoundly representative one. As we see in Mark Twain's Arkansas, the King and the Duke operate within boundaries that are already smudged, in the all-too-human space between civilized rules and tolerated conduct.

The dispersion of patrician sources of authority naturally followed geographical expansion. The distress about westward migration voiced by John Quincy Adams and others during Tocqueville's visit attests, as we have seen, to the shift from a politics of deference—based on family name and accomplishments—to a looser, ad hoc series of alliances, expediently made and unmade, that could accommodate the general jockeying for place. Conservatives charged that social mobility and expansionism

12. Charles Joseph Latrobe, *The Rambler in North America* (London, 1835), 1:175, 194–95, 258.

13. Philarète Chasles, *Anglo-American Literature and Manners* (New York, 1852), 170–71; Achille Murat, *A Moral and Political Sketch of the United States of North America* (London, 1833), 20–21.

contributed to demagoguery: that is, political newcomers seeking office with no credentials other than their name could hoodwink voters as easily as they could sell them medical nostrums or land that belonged to somebody else. The new competitiveness—in the trades and professions, on the hustings, in the marketplace, even in the forms of language appropriate to the times—was cause enough for anxiety and confusion, but it was also the occasion for liberation and challenge. A thin wall, observes one historian, separated "mastery from mania," and the edgy spirit, the repetitive pattern of success and failure, produced confident men and confidence men alike.[14]

Michel Chevalier, after Tocqueville the most dispassionate foreign observer of the social effects of decentralized power, attributed such keen-edged competitiveness to the protestant "spirit of individuality" inherent in republican governance. Individuals, he wrote, have no real common bonds: "The republic of the United States is subdivided indefinitely into independent republics of various classes. The States are republics in the general confederation; the towns are republics within the States; a farm is a republic in a county." Commercial interests, continued Chevalier, are distinct republics; militia groups are only "volunteer companies" independent of each other, just as sects are "fragments" of religious organizations. Even the family is an "inviolable republic," and each member "is a small republic by himself in the family." One authority has suggested that American social classes were ineffectually defined not because the country was united "but because it was too sub-divided to maintain them."[15]

One significant component in the historical development of the Old Southwest, however, scotched the exercise of American individuality and militated against the spirit of competition it fostered: this was land speculation, the biggest "fetching" of all. In the three decades after the second war with England, the removal of the Indian nations and their replacement by white settlers was a process that was billed as fair access to cheap lands; but speculators, working in often shady alliance with government land agents, legislators, and wealthy planters, were able to effectively corner this vast market for profitable resale because they had

14. Ronald J. Zboray, *A Fictive People: Antebellum Economic Development and the American Reading Public* (New York: Oxford University Press, 1993), 176–79.

15. Michel Chevalier, *Society, Manners, and Politics in the United States: Letters on North America* (1839; reprint, ed. John William Ward, Ithaca, NY: Cornell University Press, 1961), 356; Robert H. Wiebe, *The Segmented Society: An Introduction to the Meaning of America* (New York: Oxford, 1975), 92. See also Conevery Bolton Valenčius, *The Health of the Country: How American Settlers Understood Themselves and Their Land* (New York: Basic Books, 2002), 37–40, 263, and esp. Chapter 7, "Local Knowledge," for the effects of diversity on popular and scientific discourse on disease.

more capital than did ordinary settlers who needed land.[16] In 1817–1818, land companies in Alabama had no more enthusiastic speculator than Andrew Jackson. One of his agents commented blandly in a letter to the general that "speculation in land is superior to Law or Physic."[17] The comparison with medicine and law says something about the condition of the professions even as it serves to mitigate the wholesale swindling engaged in by land companies, some of them organized for the benefit of such respectables as James Madison, Leroy Pope, Thomas Bibb, and General John Coffee, surveyor general of the Alabama Territory. Doctors and lawyers may have been inept in their practices, but their professions at least were not *designed* for massive malfeasance.

Although the land speculator is the most prominent confidence man of the era, the humorist authors barely suggest the magnitude of his dissembling—in large part, of course, because, like the farmer, he isn't funny. Both Hooper and Baldwin knew the seriousness of the subject. In *Adventures of Captain Simon Suggs*, momentarily suspending the insouciant rhythms of Suggs's "biographer," Hooper intervenes in his own voice to arraign land speculators in Alabama, and Baldwin alludes to the enterprise in his bill of particulars of Flush Times practices. Unlike most subjects in the humor, however, making land speculation funny required reduction and understatement, not exaggeration. It is one thing to know what an investigator of Arkansas land claims reported—that the federal government had been "successfully plundered" in the "most unparalleled" record for "forgery, perjury, and subornation" by "great actors" in Little Rock.[18] It is quite another to make Simon Suggs, Jr., a fraud engaged in Arkansas land deals, as Baldwin does. Confidence men in the humorous sketches are funny because the stakes they play for are so pid-

16. Albert B. Moore, *History of Alabama* (University: University Supply Store, 1934), 81–82. In the 1820s Anne Royall wrote that well-dressed strangers in north Alabama were always assumed to be speculators, "as nothing else brings people to this country." *Letters from Alabama, 1817–1822* (1830; reprint, ed. Lucille Griffith, University: University of Alabama Press, 1969), 215. J. M. Peck was so aware of rampant traffic among speculators that he was pressed to disclaim any selfish interest in his *Guide for Emigrants;* he insists he had "no connection with the business of land speculation, or town sites." *A Guide for Emigrants, Containing Sketches of Illinois, Missouri, and the Adjacent Parts* (Boston, 1831), 7–8.

17. S. Charles Bolton, *Territorial Ambition: Land and Society in Arkansas, 1800–1840* (Fayetteville: University of Arkansas Press, 1993), 69. What Richard Slotkin calls "self-transcendence through capitalist endeavor" appealed to all ranks in the Jackson era; the investment entrepreneur was as much admired in the West as the profligate hunter. *Regeneration through Violence: The Mythology of the American Frontier, 1600–1860* (Middletown, CT: Wesleyan University Press, 1973), 413.

18. Bolton, *Territorial Ambition*, 72, 67–68, 74.

dling. Like his father, Simon Jr. is a small-bore operator who expends the kind of calculation and energy appropriate to more ambitious scams; the disproportion between scheme and result allows us to laugh at the conner.

Self-interest monumentally dominates the historical practice of land deals in Arkansas, and it extends comically to lesser players. One historian has succinctly summarized the attitudes of settlers throughout the Southwest, both the powerless and the politically astute. Manipulating federal land claims, even if it involved fraud, he avers, carried no great moral taint: "Citizens who ventured into a territory" reasoned that they "deserved to have what was there and . . . the role of the federal government should be to help them get it." Despite the price reduction to $1.25 an acre in 1820, the government sold public lands in such large units that only the wealthy could afford to buy. The western model remained "squatters versus speculators" for most of the antebellum era.[19]

That cultural climate contributed to the chicanery in the humor. The really avaricious and manipulative agents don't appear as actors in the sketches because the authors' scam artists are limited in ambition and skill; their success is always minor because they are never cunning enough to play for big stakes. One disgusted citizen described a prominent Arkansas politician in 1831 as "a srude cunning atterny at law and a man of considerable tallence and a grate speculator in land"—a verdict that could not be applied to Simon Suggs, Jr., and his fellow types who saunter through the humor. The comic speculators know that already. Though he is "srude" enough to get to Washington to oil his way among the powerful, Simon Jr. is not an overreacher. But to be a go-ahead person—and to stay ahead—requires seizing opportunities even if they glitter a little too brightly. Risk is part of the opportunity. As both the elder Simon Suggs and Sut Lovingood know, failure comes to everybody, even the clever perpetrators with ready wit and sharpened claws. As one distinguished critic puts it, the "out-tricked trickster demonstrates the vanity of expecting a final victory."[20] What is left is garden-variety fetching.

Some sketches build upon very familiar cultural assumptions. Urban temptations, for example, are a traditional threat in this fiction as in American writing generally, and yokels and greenhorns in the city, though they always go forewarned, generally succumb. As a conspicuous type in a society fast reorienting itself to horizontal structures of power, the urban confidence man stood as a danger to youth. Lines of authority in tra-

---

19. Wiebe, *Opening of American Society,* 147; Bolton, *Territorial Ambition,* 67–68, 72.
20. Bolton, *Territorial Ambition,* 67–68; Robert Darnton, *The Great Cat Massacre and Other Episodes in French Cultural History* (New York: Random House, 1985), 59.

ditional hierarchies of class and professional status were not self-evident. When such vertical structures are shaken, authority rests not in fixed status but in fluid identity, in mobility, in self-aggrandizement. Advice manuals (a mode appropriate to a crumbling hierarchical society) warned that tricksters were not to be trusted with one's faith or money.[21] In the Old Southwest the greatest anxiety about trust and deceptive appearances occurred in reference to New Orleans as the acme of urbanity; this theme shows up in visitors' journals and letters home, as well as in accounts by professionals and travelers of diverse moral orientation. For one "unlarnt Hard Shell Baptist preacher," this exotic, threatening city is "the mother of harlots and hard lots, whar . . . gamblers, thieves, and pickpockets goes skiting about the streets like weasels in a barn-yard; whar honest men are scarcer than hen's teeth; and whar a strange woman once took in your beluved teacher, and bamboozled him out of two hundred and twenty-seven dollars in the twinkling of a sheep's-tail; but she can't do it again!" (Cohen, 446).

Traps, however, are not always set and sprung in cities. Every settlement, village, and town is vulnerable to dissemblers, many of them relatively harmless poseurs. One Alabama memoirist remembered an enterprising trader who came to Tuscaloosa during the legislative session of 1837 to find House members wearing black armbands as a badge of mourning for the recent death of one of their own. "Seeing the magic influence of crape on the arm" in the "attention it received," especially in gifts of cigars, liquors, and oysters, "he at once assumed the character of a member, by wearing the badge, and soon found himself the recipient of many civilities, and being that way inclined, he made a good thing of it."[22] Making a good thing of it could be instinctive as well as premeditated; in the professional life of the humorists, it was likely to be both. When it came to the entertainment of practical joking, being *fetched* was sometimes merely a synonym for being *tuk in*. In 1868 Mark Twain himself was fetched by Edward Burlingame in a joke that turned on punning in a scriptural passage from Matthew ("If a man compel thee to go with him a mile, go with him Twain"), but like a good fetcher the author used the incident to his own advantage: "I have closed many & many a lecture, in many a city, with that," he wrote his friend. "It always 'fetches' them."[23]

21. Karen Halttunen, *Confidence Men and Painted Women: A Study of Middle-Class Culture, 1830–1870* (New Haven, CT: Yale University Press, 1982), 24.

22. William Garrett, *Reminiscences of Public Men in Alabama for Thirty Years* (Atlanta, 1872), 43.

23. *Mark Twain's Letters*, ed. Harriet Elinor Smith and Richard Bucci (Berkeley and Los Angeles: University of California Press, 1990), 2:261.

"The Horse-Swap" pits the energetic, fast-talking Yellow Blossom, who has heard enough half-horse half-alligator oratory to make it his own, against laconic Peter Ketch, an old hand at judging horseflesh. Longstreet's sketch is one of the high points in the humor: an artfully paced contest that captures both the physicality and the psychological sophistication of rustic rivalry. Since the wittily named Ketch knows that in such encounters an accurate description of his horse will be disbelieved, he uses truth as a tool, declaring that his old Kit is a "monstrous mean horse," the "scariest horse you ever saw," and "blind as a bat." Though the deal involves the exchange of equally poor nags, Ketch is the clear winner at the end of a complex pass-and-banter negotiation. When Yellow Blossom appears to have bested the old man by palming off a sore-backed horse, Ketch maintains "the most philosophic composure." His son, Neddy, keeps his peace as long as he can, but chagrined by the crowd's laughter and taunts directed at his father, and too young to have "disciplined his feelings quite so well," he blurts out the flaws in the family horse: "old Kit's both blind and *deef*, I'll be dod drot if he eint." The audience instantly redirects its derision toward Yellow Blossom (*GS*, 13–19).

In this droll account, in which two country fetchers con each other in mutual bad faith, Longstreet tilts the outcome to the one who is able to play a psychological game. He dramatizes an art that requires what neither Ketch's rival nor his son possess: experience and subtlety. Ketch wins the swap because the onlookers give him the victory; Yellow Blossom is finally *tuk in* because he is the object of public gibes from observers who have no stake in the contest except their own entertainment. They, like Longstreet, appreciate Ketch's *style*.[24] Further, this most moral of the southwestern writers is unperturbed by the fact that Ketch has used his own son as shill, playing upon his innocence and impatience until he contributes his bit at the right time. The final jab is the old man's, one that incorporates and honors young Neddy for his role in the game: "Come, Neddy, my son, let's be moving; the stranger seems to be getting snappish." The riposte is worthy of the expedient exit lines that W. C. Fields was later to perfect.

24. The "sale of worthless animals," especially horses, is listed as No. K130 in J. Michael Stitt and Robert K. Dodge, *A Tale Type and Motif Index of Early U.S. Almanacs* (Westport, CT: Greenwood, 1991), 177–78. The basic ingredients of "The Horse-Swap" recurred in later works; see Joseph Csicila, "An Old Southwesterner Abroad: Cultural Frontiers and the Landmark American Humor of J. Ross Browne's *Yusef*," in *The Humor of the Old South*, ed. M. Thomas Inge and Edward J. Piacentino (Lexington: University Press of Kentucky, 2001), 218.

It is a mistake to think of the Old Southwest, the restless domain of the happy hit, as the sole venue of shady horse traders. In Virginia, Peachy Gilmer, who wanted to buy a horse for his younger brother, wrote about how difficult it was to find a seller "upon whose Judt & integrity you can entirely rely," since it was not commonly thought immoral "to lie and cheat in horses & people."[25] That is, even in the Old Dominion one did not need to be a confidence man to live by his wits. The frontier fetcher is indeed rarely depicted as a villain out to circumvent legitimate authority, but as a "character" whose self-mockery is merely another expression of the initiative that a vital democracy valued. One could fetch without formal designations, reinventing oneself for the opportune moment. Though he inspired yarns, the expedient rural fetcher was too ordinary in his various guises to enter popular culture as a mythic type like the dreaded urban version, but he responded fully, in one critic's words, to the country's "unique opportunities for self-government, self-posturing, and self-creation." We should not forget that, despite his Old World urbanity, J. J. Audubon expediently donned deerskin fashions, encouraged his followers to refer to him as "the American Woodsman," and sat for portraits dressed as a Boone look-alike.[26]

The unsettling of a country on the move was a hospitable condition for fetchers of all stripes. For more than twenty years the nation was an expanding region almost literally in motion. An Argentine visitor in 1847 remarked that if God called the world to judgment, "He would surprise two-thirds" of the American population "on the road like ants." The great highway from Virginia to Alabama in 1818–1819, comments one historian, was more "like the route of an army of occupation than an ordinary public highway." Along the major routes of migration, the vast flow of people on the move resulted in a turnover every five or ten years of more than 50 percent of the population in many towns, making them staging grounds more than permanent communities.[27] Given the fluidity of circumstances in the historical Southwest, and its fluid social structure, it is not surprising that its writing so frequently revolves around identity.

25. Richard Beale Davis, *Francis Walker Gilmer: Life and Learning in Jefferson's Virginia* (Richmond, VA: Dietz, 1939), 67.

26. Lenz, *Fast Talk*, 1; Daniel Justin Herman, *Hunting and the American Imagination* (Washington: Smithsonian Institution Press, 2001), 164–65.

27. Lewis Perry, *Intellectual Life in America: A History* (New York: Franklin Watts, 1984), 208; Thomas Jones Taylor, "Early History of Madison County," *Alabama Historical Quarterly* 1 (1930): 494.

iii.

"There goes Smith, the *Attorney*," said a man to his friend; as a tall figure, slightly stooped, hurried by them.

"I beg your pardon," answered the friend, "that is the Rev. Mr. Smith, a *preacher*, I have heard him in Tennessee."

"Well, that's curious," replied the first, "for I'd swear *I* have heard him plead at the bar."

"Good morning Sol., how are you?" salutes another, as he hurries by a group of citizens.

"What did you call him?" inquired one of the party.

"Why, Sol. Smith," was the answer—"*old* Sol., the *manager* of the theatre, to-be-sure; who did you suppose it was?—I thought you knew him—every body knows old *Sol!*"

"Well that is funny," answered the second, "for *I'll* swear he officiated as a *physician* on board our boat."

"Well who the d—l *is* he?"

—John S. Robb, *Streaks of Squatter Life, and Far-West Scenes*

Playing parts was Sol Smith's game, but in the Old Southwest the game attracted amateurs as well as professionals. Going into new territory is always an occasion for defining a self anew and on the self's own terms, and sometimes those terms include lingual imitation, most commonly the aping of the language of respectables—bankers, planters, doctors, lawyers, preachers, editors, all purveyors of ready-made rhetorics. Used by professionals to allay the anxieties of mere commoners who need their services, specialty rhetorics are also ready-made for pretenders. If people rely merely on the confidence man's own word that he is what he says he is, the machinery of persuasion (such as it is) often becomes the specialized discourse of those respectables. John A. Murrell, the region's most notorious outlaw, sometimes posed as a Methodist circuit rider because, as he admitted, people were less inclined to haggle or to inquire "into antecedents . . . when dealing with a sanctimonious preacher eager to say 'an Amen over the sale'" of stolen slaves. (But it could go the other way, too. In order to dispatch the rowdies who were disrupting his services, the evangelist Peter Cartwright passed among the interlopers "in disguise" to learn their plans in advance.) Impersonating preachers was a favorite tack, and concern about fraudulence extended to the spiritual mechanics of camp meetings. For a time the southwestern frontier seemed to be an environment in which there were as many people on their knees as there were on their toes, simply because itinerant camp-meeting preachers knew how to relate familiar texts to emotional anxieties. George W. Henry, known as "the Holy Shouter," wrote that some confidence men were clever enough to "pass counterfeit money on ignorant men," but that "a genuine shout" during services was always known to the faithful, whose "sanctified ear" could not be deceived.[28] The frequency of religious bamboozling would indicate that sanctified ears were uncommon.

Hence, despite Henry's certitude, the proliferation of impersonation in Southwest writing and the easily dropped allusions to Blackstone's *Commentaries, crimen falsi,* perdition, and sanctification. Befitting any settlement's most distinctive professionals, legalese and sermonic patter were the idioms of choice for pretenders. Even ratty charlatans felt the urge to deck themselves out in costumes that signified "quality"; and their getting it not quite right, or mixing incongruous items of clothing denoting differing levels of respectability, was a conventional source of humor. Just as in real life in the new country, so in its fiction: surfaces were important for settler and stranger alike. Hooper's young Simon Suggs uses Baptist doctrinal language to gull his preacher father; Henry Clay Lewis's young intern uses medical lingo, which he is still learning, as a weapon against a Kentuckian with a toothache; Kittrell Warren's Billy Fishback, an illiterate army deserter, hires "an adept in the writing business" to forge an eloquent letter urging him to be a candidate for the legislature—a well-turned missive that repeats the clichés of political oratory, crafted to seduce a respectable family whose greed invites their gulling.

In their memoirs antebellum lawyers can be nostalgic about the jovial fraternal spirit of their profession, but even in the haze of remembrance rivals, opponents, and even partners are usually judged through a scrim of competition. One writer of the time described lawyers in the Flush Times as mostly "youthful adventurers, who had come into the field long before the ripening of the harvest." Since they were "not of much repute," they compensated by indulging in the low arts of trickery and shady negotiation.[29] Except for the disapproving tone, Joseph Baldwin saw his profession similarly. Though he had to trick and negotiate his way through a thicket of *quashing* maneuvers (by "the *out quashingest* set of fellows ever known"), this young "lawyerling" clearly enjoyed being among other

28. Frances Allen Cabaniss and James Allen Cabaniss, "Religion in Ante-Bellum Mississippi," *Journal of Mississippi History* 6 (1944): 201; William Henry Milburn, *The Pioneers, Preachers, and People of the Mississippi Valley* (New York, 1860), 383–84; Richardson Wright, *American Wags and Eccentrics from Colonial Times to the Civil War* (1939; reprint, New York: Frederick Ungar, 1965), 134.

29. John L. McConnel, *Western Characters, or Types of Border Life in the Western States* (New York, 1853), 349.

youthful discontents who had migrated south and west for opportunities. He alludes frequently to the fraternal geniality of his legal set, but his most telling anecdotes are those that celebrate fraternal competitiveness.

The humorists flourished in the same expansionist, volatile climate as their professional peers who didn't write: doctors, lawyers, educators, preachers, planters, all parlaying their skills in fields that were fluid and unmonitored. Of all the humorists, Baldwin most directly recreates the spirit of the age as he observed and lived it. The referent for his new era of "credit without capital, and enterprise without honesty" is the legal system, but his analytic, compelling essays in *Flush Times* are not restricted to the fortunes of the bench and bar; "the general infection of morals" taints an entire time and place. Above all, it taints him. This, at least, is what the self-dramatization of himself as a "lawyerling" would have us believe. Despite those confessional strains, however, his fetching incidents are mostly about the ordinary self-interest that "infects" an entire population in a region made to order for such youthful "craftsmen." At the very prospect of opportunities, Baldwin writes, "we brightened up mightily, and shook our quills joyously, like goslings in the midst of a shower" (*FT*, 240). Like Baldwin, Lewis as Madison Tensas confesses to a propensity for some mild fetching in his role as verdant physician, but that also is one of the effects marshaled to support his particular narrative persona. There is more canny logic than deception working in his heightened alertness to the main chance—he seeks out a practice in Louisiana's swamp country because "it had the promise of being a sickly one and highly suitable for a doctor" (*SD*, 112).

Whatever their calling, most of the humorists brighten up and shake their quills in the new country. Though most are less inclined than Baldwin and Lewis to generalize a spirit of the age, their vignettes of southwestern characters blithely exploit the ethical amorphousness of the time and place. What Baldwin depicts so coherently is corroborated piecemeal in sketches by Noland, Hooper, and other authors privy to the reality of flexible law. What Lewis documents in the makeshift practice of medicine in *Swamp Doctor* is reinforced in the work of Marcus Lafayette Byrn, another doctor-author, who was probably influenced by Lewis's sketches. To make up for his hit-and-miss professional skills, Byrn's "Dr. David Rattlehead" dispenses trickery and bravado, his tongue always ready with a tall tale.[30] The same opportunistic schemes

30. Despite heavy glossing from the perspective of folklore, a carefully prepared and useful text is David Rattlehead [Marcus Lafayette Byrn], *The Life and Adventures*

can be seen in Francis James Robinson's "Lije Benadix," John S. Robb's "Settlement Fun," and other sketches from shrewd old heads who knew as much (or as little) about purgatives and bottled cures as they did about stacking cards or horse betting. (Some pretend doctors, writes Baldwin, "did not know a liver from a gizzard.") Like George Washington Harris's preachers with their "papers," lawyers and doctors in antebellum humor embody a kind of fraudulent authority through title—assumed when not awarded—and through command of specialized language. They reflect the historical preprofessional stage of expertise in which practitioners were inept, raggedly trained, and in some cases as ignorant as their clients and patients. As the humorists perceived them (some of the humorists *were* them), doctors and lawyers were little more than a subset of con artists, those go-getting individuals capable of constructing a reality, of interpreting signs—superior to ordinary souls whose greater illiteracy invited exploitation. Their fictional accounts are humorous statements about sources of authority in the social flux of antebellum society. Doctoring and lawyering are, as Wai Chee Dimock puts it, fields of "knowledge" where the "recession of meaning goes hand in hand with the concentration of expertise."[31]

In a self-referential turn, some of the humorists often see themselves contributing to that same climate of spurious expertise. If they are never so grand as to refer to their flourishing as the redistribution of social authority, they are artful enough to realize that their claims are preprofessional and their spirited moment on the national stage something of a masquerade. Though good-natured, the pose of Baldwin and Lewis requires a bit of stooping. Their argot becomes a useful device for enhancing a career, but that discovery hardly makes them exceptional. The widespread hokum that ordinary men often used to get ahead also proved useful to professionals. For lettered and illiterate alike, pursuit of the main chance ran like a high-mettled strain throughout all social transactions. Although brute strength was an obvious way to claim position, as a method of self-presentation it lacked art. Partly because they are more intimate with them, the authors prefer to recount the dissembling techniques of a Billy Fishback or a Simon Suggs or a Sut Lovingood—impersonation, movable identities, well-plotted ruses, candor as a disarming

of an Arkansaw Doctor (1851; reprint, ed. W. K. McNeil, Fayetteville: University of Arkansas Press, 1989). See also Valenčius, *Health of the Country*, 175.

31. Wai Chee Dimock, "Feminism, New Historicism, and the Reader," in *Readers in History: Nineteenth-Century American Literature and the Contexts of Response*, ed. James L. Machor (Baltimore: Johns Hopkins University Press, 1993), 87–88.

weapon. Except for George Washington Harris (who ethically anticipates Mark Twain), the humorists are not always eager to discriminate between piety and hypocrisy, or between dignified demeanor and pretentiousness.

Peter Cartwright comes across as a particularly complex model, incorporating both brutal honesty and opportunistic dissembling among his backwoods targets. He became legendary for his stern opposition to idlers, New Lights, Arians, Calvinists, Immersionists, slave owners, Universalists, Deists, Mormons, Campbellites, and Methodist defectors who filed off to raise "little trash-traps called Churches." But he was never above impersonating "rowdies" or drunken "Philistines" as a tactic in doing the Lord's business. Staying unspotted by the world was never a priority for Cartwright as long as he could exercise his own brand of moral realism. Neither was the evangelist overly concerned that "thousands of thrilling incidents" attributed to him are false—such as his fight with Mike Fink. He protests its inaccuracy when a religious paper reprints the story, but is mollified when the editor replies: "It was good enough for me." If Cartwright wouldn't publish a true history, "it was no matter if others published a false one."[32]

Most of the protagonists in the humor are not travelers, but many—traveling confidence men, local confidence men, horse swappers, gamblers, courtship rivals, practical jokers—are adept at fetching. Beneath the conning devices in the discourse of insincerity—the rhetoric of persuasion, impersonations, the parceling out of selective credentials—is a rejection of reason or benevolence as a guide to conduct. Further, if fetching is a complex skill based on a simple premise (that in the social jungle self-interest is the highest good), it is not especially secret. Like Stowe's slave-catching duo, many practitioners are eager to admit to their schemes and tireless in specifying the process by which they execute them. Though they find their greatest pleasure in pulling off schemes, their second greatest pleasure lies in public reenactment—in the act of storytelling itself. Whatever the degree of plotting to trick or ensnare, fetching at its most artful is a public enterprise, a spectacle for others, an entertainment. Even the least delicious triumphs call for an audience.

Southwest humor is all about that second pleasure: reconstructing, retelling, reimagining. Storytelling by vernacular characters is by its very nature re-creation. It is no coincidence that fetching, though it functions as a test of one man's superiority over another, flourishes in the village

---

32. *Autobiography of Peter Cartwright, the Backwoods Preacher*, ed. W. P. Strickland (Cincinnati, 1856), 271–72, 312.

with more consequence than it ever does in the bush. Like most feats of derring-do, in which hunters take on beasts and backcountry roarers take on each other, even the practical joke is most effective when it unfolds within a group of men who become admiring witnesses. Reputation of all degrees must always be assigned by the public. George Curry's "Panther Evans" outstares a panther in the Mississippi wilds and bests another one, "fisticuff fashion," in his cabin; but it is his settlement appreciators who bestow the honorific name on him (Oehl., 128–30). Whatever the reality of Mik-hoo-tah's life-threatening episode with a bear, it is a private experience until it is recast for consumption by others, and the accuracy of the reconstruction is irrelevant. What counts is what the storyteller recounts. That fabulous moment in the career of a one-legged hunter determined to be crowned "Bear-hunter of Ameriky" is further recast in the terms of the swamp doctor, Mik's primary audience. Through Madison Tensas's art "The Indefatigable Bear Hunter," at least two removes from what it documents, becomes the codified version. As in all of this humor, the second pleasure is the pleasure of the text.

The humorists are insouciant when they report that some frauds, with the tolerance of their neighbors exhausted, flee to a yet newer country to pick up their lives in a different and more hospitable environment. They never wax indignant, as does one Edward Stiff, who after some apparently disagreeable experiences, lectures the new Republic of Texas for allowing such emigrants to practice their foul arts unmolested: "[I]f you wish for the happiness of your posterity, or any of the blessings of good government, frown into obscurity such men as have 'left their country for their country's good,' and have found an asylum in Texas." Had Joseph Baldwin chosen asylum there, Texas would have profited from his move. Though he eventually contributed his legal skills toward better government (in both the Old Southwest and in California), the author not merely refuses to frown into obscurity his Ovid Bolus, but sends his memorable scoundrel "on the lift for Texas." Stiff's mode is to hector both the scoundrel and the land that gave him asylum: "A naturally bad man in the United States or elsewhere," he declares, "will be a bad man in Texas; the depraved heart is not to be regenerated by breathing your atmosphere, nor is it the most favorable spot for reform."[33] In contrast, the genial Baldwin adopts a tone of mock mourning for the departed Ovid: "[W]ith a hermit's disgust at the degradation of the world, like Ignatius turned monk, he pitched his tabernacle amidst the smiling prairies that

---

33. Edward Stiff, *The Texan Emigrant* (1840; reprint, Waco: Texian Press, 1968), 96–97.

sleep in vernal beauty, in the shadow of the San Saba mountains. There let his mighty genius rest. It has earned repose" (*FT*, 19).

The humorists may be such reluctant moralists because dissembling is so common. They know that not all impersonators are confidence men out to swindle their foolish marks. Some are benign, even tedious, and appear in their sketches as local wags whose only claim to memorability is in their reputation for being chameleonlike for the hell of it. For the practical joker and those who appreciate his ingenuity, the trick may be the most innocuous form of fetching—as when a naïf is persuaded to stick his hand in a wag's pocket that contains a crawfish. Verdant innocents are easy targets; greater challenges invite greater satisfactions. To make dupes of rival wags, pompous men-about-town, or standoffish strangers is to draw upon resources of cunning, and the practical joker may sometimes share credit with conspiring accomplices. Humiliation is never an innocent act, and in village culture it usually requires aiding and abetting.

As an exercise in social control, depluming reputations and embarrassing men of dignity reveals the darker side of *making sport,* even among residents who enjoy the semblance of orderly society. The boardinghouse, for example, is a telling—and paradoxical—site for such group dynamics. In its impersonal hospitality it promotes its patrons' sense of comfort among strangers, but its very existence, catering to salesmen and transients, is a sign of social fluidity. Even in its hospitable environs, social intercourse requires the mannerly negotiation of relationships. Its members may occasionally adopt wit and joking as tools of coercion, but the disposition generally is to confront slaunchwise conduct with disapproval, even hostility. The norm may only be *pretend* gentility, but it favors respectability as a civilized alternative to instinctual rivalry among individuals and as a weapon for keeping violators in line. The artificial camaraderie of the boardinghouse theoretically absorbs the foibles and eccentricities of its individual members. Quirkiness among loners in the wild is to be expected (and even tolerated, say, when the idiosyncratic hunter finds himself in the village), but even ragtag urban clusters have a claim on *society,* in which codes of behavior privilege the group, not the individual. In the new country the village, not the bush, is the demographic norm, one that monitors oddities and other deviances.

In the anonymous "The Man Who Was Looked At" (1844), boardinghouse guests conspire to retaliate against a traveling businessman who is too overbearing in his selling techniques and too hoggish at the common table. They agree that at the evening meal all as one will silently adopt the same "countenance expressing the most intense amazement" each time the man puts food in his mouth; in their "ingenious wickedness," they reinforce their shocked stares by dropping their knives and forks. When the victim complains that the "gaze of successive petrifactions" makes him lose his appetite, the landlord protests that he can't control facial expressions. The landlord indeed has no control over the nonverbal gestures of his guests; as a passive act of hostility, impertinent staring has always been a reliable way to invade another's territorial space. The conspirators are successful because the passive punishment is jointly and unrelentingly administered. Though the butt of their plot is not especially sympathetic, neither is he depicted as one who deserves the psychological damage that results from his punishment. So effective is the game that the ostracized man becomes a Poe-esque, haunted figure "wandering about town," convinced that all eyes are watching him and muttering of passers-by, "what the d—l they were *looking at*?" (Oehl., 50–53). Social coercion in effect reduces a successful businessman to morbid debility.

In "The Man Who Was Looked At" the protocols of the group are no longer an abstract defense of society's codes but an aggressive response designed by conspiring rivals. An unregarding selfishness is answered by concerted self-interest. The very competitive instincts that social decorum was intended to neutralize are rereleased by orchestrated action. When the violator is expelled, a conforming status quo is comfortably reestablished.

It is precisely that orderly and predictable state that Longstreet's Ned Brace is determined to dismantle. If in "The Man Who Was Looked At" the many frustrate the one, in "The Character of a Native Georgian" the one frustrates the many. Lyman Hall, the narrator, remembering a visit to Savannah with his friend Ned Brace, describes one man's calculated derangement. Unsettling the other guests at their boardinghouse, Brace tries out a series of pranks, each one designed to subvert not only the routine rites of social conduct, but also the procedures for handling such violations. All Savannah is his theater, but he makes the boardinghouse his main stage as he injects unpredictability into all comfortable patterns of conduct. He surprises, bewilders, and annoys. In the bar he takes the most conspicuous seat, but remains resolutely silent in a circle of amiably chatting men. He asks for both tea and coffee at the table and for every variety of bread (battercakes, muffins, rolls, and cornbread), "mashing all together" in a childlike mess. He is discovered reading a child's primer with great concentration, and is delighted especially with "Little Jack Horner."

Responding to the consternation aroused by his bizarre behavior, Ned "confesses" to Mrs. Blank, the distraught but friendly landlady, that his "unnatural appetite" for practical jokes is debilitating. "Humor," he admits, "has been my besetting sin from my youth up." It is only a confession of sorts, another tactic that draws into his plot the genial landlady and her husband, both of whom are said to have "laughed heartily" at their jokester guest. With "two more to enjoy his humor," Ned is spurred on to "let himself loose" on the other boarders on his final evening in the city (*GS,* 23, 31, 32). Strangers all, the boarders are not special targets, and Ned has nothing to avenge: only the driving need to unsettle expectations. He becomes a lord of misrule for a middle class that acknowledges no need for carnival. There is, then, a splendid outrageousness in his free-form activities because they are untainted by personal gain. His antic mode is as close to play for its own sake as we find in a body of writing already keyed to practical joking. For all the merriment of those who are privy to Ned Brace's antics, however, the perpetrator stands revealed in an oddly disturbing light.

We may well conclude that his dull and complacent "victims" are so alien to eruptive irresponsibility that they *need* Bracian play for their own affective health. In the textual economy of the sketch, however, Longstreet leaves little room for such possibility. As modern readers, we are left with the whiff of desperation common to the psychological compulsive, and a suspicion that what had seemed to be a comic strategy—his confession to the landlady—is at bottom a truthful and lacerating self-analysis. The overheated diction of that confession is resonant: Brace admits that he has been unable to *conquer* his *self-destroying propensity,* which is *wrought into* his *very nature—completely and indissolubly interwoven* in *every fibre and filament* of his being; he has not been able to *subdue* his *ungovernable proclivity,* and all he does is in *subservience* to it (*GS,* 31). The passage sounds more like the final "statement" of Stevenson's Henry Jekyll than the testimony of a practical joker. We might also remember that to nineteenth-century ears, this confession, despite its rarefied locutions, would echo the homiletic language of the Methodist pulpit—the need to acknowledge the distorting power of sin. When he writes "The Character of a Native Georgian," Longstreet is not yet a parson, but, like most of his contemporaries, he knows about orthodox moral failure.

We are apt to pass easily over Ned Brace's condition as "sin," but we may see his pranks as signs of a deep-seated pathology.[34] Revenge (as in

34. Kimball King characterizes Ned Brace as a "brutal tease, an unruly aggressive clown pursued by subtle and ultimately unfathomable demons." *Augustus Baldwin*

Sut Lovingood's payback schemes) can be more efficiently fixed than motiveless behavior. It never occurs to Longstreet, however, to ask the questions that modern readers occasionally raise about this character: Just when does "strange conduct" cross the boundary from manners to morals? What is too much? What is hurtful? Dedicated as Brace is "to amus[ing] himself with his fellow-beings," his mode is to assume "any character which his humor required him to personate," a talent he sustains "to perfection." What he leaves behind after a memorable weekend is a series of improvisational scenes, each one featuring a different "character." But what *is* the character of this "native Georgian"? This fetcher baits a Frenchman, whom he insists is Obadiah Snoddleburg of Sandy Creek; when he goes to church, he becomes the master of the silly walk as he looks for a suitable pew and sings the hymns in his most discordant, hoarse voice; he creates uncontrollable laughter in the rear ranks of a funeral procession; and, joining a bucket brigade to put out a house fire, he pauses to drink from each bucket that comes to him.

The narrator insists that Ned Brace's pranks, though they may occasionally be mean-spirited, are never executed for material gain. Ned damages no one. Even the social destabilization he creates is temporary. His ubiquity in Savannah makes him the talk of the town, although "hardly any two" of those who witness his capers "agreed about his character." (Hall belabors the fact that his model is a real person whose "true self" is as uncertain as the written copy.) His only core is his compulsion to wear successive masks while performing. He has a manic need to unbalance the sureties that society must have—even at the risk of deadening conventionality. From Hall's perspective, Brace's hyperkinetic play is too calculated, too *performative,* to be anything other than a sometime rebel's cheerful attempt to force predictability into open-endedness. The narrator refrains from acting the hectoring moralist (as he does in "Georgia Theatrics"), accepting at face value his friend's fondness for playing practical jokes. The improvisations suggest the continuing possibility for changing a world that respectables consider already completed.

Ned Brace is the most enigmatic impersonator in Southwest humor. Less complex is John Gorman Barr's Old Charley Patterson, the "boniface" of Washington Hall in Tuscaloosa, who is just as addicted to making

---

Longstreet (New York: Twayne, 1984), 66. Some students at South Carolina College (later the University of South Carolina) apparently thought that the staid President Longstreet still possessed enough intuitive mischief-making traits to justify their calling him "Ned Brace." Hennig Cohen, "Mark Twain's Sut Lovingood," *Lovingood Papers* (1962): 21.

sport out of impersonation. His guests may be affronted by what they think are his lapses in respectability, but being *sold* by him bears no scars. Local acquaintances and traveling regulars cherish Uncle Charley's reputation as an unpredictable eccentric, as his fame spreads for putting "on any character called for": "Sanctimonious or jovial, sedate or excited, ingenuous or mysterious, joyous or sorrowful—the extreme of know-every-thing-ism, or absolute and unqualified know-nothing-ism, Saxon or Irishman, the man of business or the town loafer, the city gentleman or the country bumpkin—he was everything by starts, and as long as it pleased him" (*RT,* 24).

Unlike the simple assertions of identity that we see in the jokesters of Longstreet and Barr, Melville's allegorical bent in *The Confidence-Man* almost demands a heavy investment in the visible signs of masquerade: disguises, wardrobe accoutrements, symbolic props—all aids for the duping creatures of metamorphosis and old-fashioned cony-catchers. The impostors in *Huck Finn* are nonmetaphysical, and in the Mississippi Valley of Mark Twain's 1840s their schemes don't need material props. Except for the Royal Nonesuch performance (mounted with a bare minimum), the King and the Duke carry on their masquerades with a supply of theatrical outfits as threadbare as their carpetbags. They are the fictive heirs of Simon Suggs and his ilk, whose cons stem solely from *what they say they are.* A vigorous transparency in certain forms of role-playing (the matched boasts of screamers, say) often marks them of an earlier time and a prior state of social organization, and some of the writing from the Southwest, that of the humorists included, honors that earlier stage. But more complex forms of role-playing occupy the major attention of Longstreet and his humorist contemporaries.

Most of the public soirees described by Longstreet's narrator of domestic scenes are marred by snobbery, backbiting, and social climbing. In one sketch, genteel competition climaxes in cultural overreaching. As they tend to do in such pieces, fashionable guests in "The Song" gather about Miss Aurelia Emma Theodosia Augusta Crump, beseeching her to play the piano. The diffident young musician pleads lack of practice: "Mamma was always scolding her for giving so much of her time to French and Italian, and neglecting her music and painting; but she told mamma the other day, that it really was so irksome to her to quit Racine and Dante, and go to thrumming upon the piano, but for the obligations of filial obedience, she did not think she would ever touch it again." She nonetheless performs with showy energy and follows her instrumental offering with a song: "she screamed, she howled, she yelled, cackled," and when she begins the sustained "note of a screech-owl," the music-loving narrator flees the room. As he reaches the door he hears an admirer exclaim, "By heavens! she's the most enchanting performer I ever heard in my life!" (*GS*, 42–47).

One generalization about the humor, that it is "populated with those who do not know all they need to know," applies not merely to "naive country boys . . . [who] make fools of themselves," but also to village poseurs.[35] A theme emerging from the uncertain passage of the raw into the cultivated is the social moment that entraps natural innocent and parvenu sophisticate alike. Both Davy Crockett and Paul Beechim, Baldwin's High Knoxvillian, drink from their finger bowls; pianos are treacherous instruments not only for Longstreet's Miss Amelia Crump but also for Thorpe's Mo Mercer; dance steps challenge the heroes' *savoir-faire* in Noland's Little Rock and Robb's Nettle Bottom; courting rivalry requires that both Thompson's Joseph Jones and Harris's Sut Lovingood have a go at games of wit.

For most of the settlement period—if we are to believe Daniel Hundley—the planters were crass vulgarians, expanding their holdings without regard for coherent community building. Joseph Holt Ingraham puts the best face on Mississippi planters when he calls them "a plain, practical body of men."[36] By the late 1850s, however, these "cotton snobs" were laughable versions of Virginia gentry. Impersonating gracious country squires in an older coastal South may have begun as harmless imitation, the predictable response of ambitious men in any escalating economy, in which, after a period of hectic enterprise, the "new men" gradually assume the biases, tastes, habits, and language of more established ranks. If the process took longer in the Old Southwest, it was because even the establishment had to be invented from scratch. Impersonating the hospitality and the rhetoric of honor probably helped to sand away the rougher edges of the parvenu; but as we see in much of Mark Twain and in Joseph Field's "A Lyncher's Own Story" (1845), imitation soon lost its harmlessness. In *Flush Times*, Baldwin the Virginian is ambivalent about assigning comparatives, but he is always conscious of the distinctions. The type that Hundley excoriated—loud, arrogant, unmindful of others—is distastefully

35. Hennig Cohen and William B. Dillingham, introduction to *Humor of the Old Southwest*, 3rd ed. (Athens: University of Georgia Press), xxxiii–xxxiv.

36. Daniel R. Hundley, *Social Relations in Our Southern States* (1860; reprint, ed. William J. Cooper, Jr., Baton Rouge: Louisiana State University Press, 1979); Joseph Holt Ingraham, *The South-West, by a Yankee* (1835; Ann Arbor, MI: University Microfilms, 1966), 2:102.

noted in the accounts of many travelers, including Frederick Law Olmsted, the most percipient of the lot. For the New Yorker, Mississippi had come to represent "the worst of what was southern," and his vignette of young planter swells in Natchez, "lounging or sauntering, and often calling at the bar; all smoking, all twisting little walking-sticks, all 'talking horse,'" is meant to serve as a vivid general image of the type.[37]

A cultural historian has written that social decorum among the planters in the lower South became formally calibrated because it so flimsily masked social insecurity and relational fragility.[38] For whatever reasons, it was a posture that made much of public visibility in hosting entertainments and encouraging company. One of Olmsted's informants, a Mississippi planter himself, admitted that his neighbors were "all swellheads" who hired foreign gardeners and enjoyed talking about royalty they had socialized with in Europe.[39] The consolidating gestures of aspiring planters included appropriate speech, something several notches more elegant than the backwoods demotic they were accustomed to. According to one memoirist, a gentlemanly preoccupation with language led some to adopt speech that aped the dignity and (presumed) formality of royal courts. Such speakers, he remembered, never used "a simple and direct form of expression when they could possibly think of a stilted and high-sounding circumlocution that would even vaguely suggest their meaning." That pomposity contrasted markedly with speakers in almost every other class or calling: "They never attempted to state themselves, touching any matter, in that jocular, rough-and-ready, vulgar dialect of close, confidential companionship so effectively used on all occasions by newspaper paragraphers, stump-speakers, popular lecturers and even preachers."[40] Ovid Bolus, Baldwin's great liar, has never been a planter (though most other callings show up on his résumé), yet he tries out the ideal image that aspiring planters endeavored to cultivate: an air and bearing "almost princely," manners "winning," and address "frank, cordial and flowing." If Bolus is "a little sonorous in the structure of his sentences," the fluent diction has been preselected to "give effect to a voice

37. Gary A. Donaldson, "Antebellum Criticism: Frederick Law Olmsted in Mississippi, 1853–1854," *Journal of Mississippi History* 50 (1988): 319.
38. Dickson D. Bruce, Jr., *Violence and Culture in the Antebellum South* (Austin: University of Texas Press, 1979), 68–69.
39. Frederick Law Olmsted, *The Cotton Kingdom: A Traveller's Observations on Cotton and Slavery in the American Slave States, 1853–1861* (1861; reprint, ed. Arthur M. Schlesinger, New York: Da Capo Press, 1996), 420.
40. F. D. Srygley, *Seventy Years in Dixie* (Nashville, 1893), 315.

like an organ." Baldwin sees this "ready debater and elegant declaimer" as an Americanized Bolingbroke adjusting his skills to the backwoods (*FT*, 6–7).

The bearing, manners, and speech of Kittrell Warren's Slaughter constitute a confidence man's version of a Georgia gentleman set loose in the parlor of Old Dominion gentility. This on-again, off-again confederate of oafish Billy Fishback is a facile humbug and blackmailer, but his chief characterizing trait is his faux planterese. Warren loads Slaughter's conversation with such circumlocutions as "she's in the incipient stages of dementation" and "the cumbrous rubbish of filthy lucre." Fishback never understands what his confederate is saying, but then neither do the designated marks. Yet, knowing that pretentious language will soften the resistance of Major Graves, a planter whose daughter, slaves, and lands he has an eye on, the army deserter contracts with Slaughter to appear before the assembled Graves family and "put in . . . them jodarters about me bein a good egg." When the smooth talker arrives, the conversation begins with the two malingerers speaking of their recent battle experiences:

> "Well, Billy," said he, "it has been some time since we met before, and both of us have doubtless passed through a fearful ordeal during the eventful and sanguinary interim. . . . But the lowering future is yet ominous of events in which we, perchance, will be integrals of a most belligerent aggregation."
>
> "That's jest *my* notions."
>
> "And perhaps we may become the doomed victims of a cruel, relentless and crucifying bellicosity."
>
> "That's the very thing I was gwine to a sed." (*AS*, 56)

Major Graves is not guilty of such pretentious speech; his is fairly straightforward, befitting a respectable, if not patrician, Virginian. Warren's point is double: that pretend gentlemen are especially eager to inflate their natural speech to accord with perceived gentility, and that more speechifying "jodarters" are to be found in Georgia than in Virginia.

What Anne Royall reported as the game of *putinon* in the early antebellum years only intensified as the era progressed.[41] The most egregious players were outright frauds engaged in putting on new and improved identities, and, eager to rush the civilizing process along, the most inno-

41. Anne Royall, *Sketch of the History, Life, and Manners in the United States* (New Haven, CT, 1826), 1:53.

cent were aspiring middle-class matrons, whose put-on airs are frequently noted in letters and diaries. Though reluctant to submit herself to the *"whims, & why's & where's"* required of the "public house keeper," Eliza Clitherall was obliged to become a boardinghouse proprietor when her husband died. She appeared in the public rooms only when "Ladies" were present, and, even then, without much mingling: "a little tact, wou'd discover character, & I have been often amus'd at the airs put on by some who *wish'd* to be genteel, but cou'd not cast off their vulgarity."[42] Some of the richest segments of *Georgia Scenes* are Longstreet's satiric sallies at the expense of such distaff vulgarity.

As the lower South moved further away from its pioneering settlement stage, many of its successful residents indulged in momentary regret for the lost days they recalled. We see the wife of John Gayle, the Alabama governor, identifying with the Crockett books because of their picture of a barely populated backcountry, and Mrs. C. C. Clay, widow of another Alabama governor, engaging in theatricalized nostalgia even at presidential levees. In her memoirs she quotes with amusement Senator J. J. Crittenden of Kentucky: "'If I had my way,' and he sighed as he said it, 'nothing could give me greater pleasure than to hie me back to the wilds of dear old Kentucky! Ah! to don my buckskins once more, shoulder a rifle, and wander through life a free man, away from all this flummery!' . . . [H]e detected a speck upon his faultless sleeve and fastidiously brushed it off." Mrs. Clay reminds Crittenden that because of his fondness for "fat plums and plump capons, both real and metaphorical," he would not be happy in buckskin. Laughing guiltily, "like one whose pet pretense has been discovered," the senator has been caught in a fleeting *downward* impersonation of a type already absorbed by progress.[43] But Mrs. Clay herself is not immune to the same impulse. She scores her greatest social triumph when she goes to a fancy ball impersonating Ruth Partington, Benjamin Shillaber's comic female version of the Yankee cracker-barrel philosopher. Engaging in such theatrical moments of reverse social aspiration is a more confident form of putting on airs.

Arguing from a study of parlor etiquette, entertainments, and advice

42. Eliza Clitherall Papers, Alabama Department of Archives and History, Montgomery.
43. Sarah Gayle, diary, Gorgas Family Papers (Sarah Gayle Materials), William Stanley Hoole Special Collections, University of Alabama Library, University of Alabama, Tuscaloosa; Ada Sterling, ed., *A Belle of the Fifties: Memoirs of Mrs. Clay, of Alabama, Covering Social and Political Life in Washington and the South, 1853–66* (New York, 1904), 85.

manuals, one scholar has concluded that the middle class in Victorian America self-consciously understood that gentility was an assumed role, that "all parlor life was itself a charade."[44] One form of sentimentalism encouraged sincerity—genuine feelings candidly expressed—as an anti-dote to social hypocrisy, yet what was to prevent clever frauds from mimicking sincerity itself? This kind of charade could be played as well as others. In the swaggering southwestern society, where "the soaring, inflated, even boundless character of its affirmations" marked most of the antebellum era, many of the agents of control were themselves put-on artists. At a time of social flux in which men and women were "constantly assuming new identities and struggling to be convincing in new social roles," refined codes of acceptable behavior, in conduct, language, and dress, were always susceptible to widespread aping.[45]

If Warren's Major Graves is more guilty of greed than pretentiousness, so is the inept confidence man out to bilk him. In *Life and Public Services of an Army Straggler* (1865), except for Slaughter's brief performance, there is no relevant aping at all. Social hypocrisy so permeates the respectables in Warren's text that the blatant fraud who would fetch them is too illiterate to mimic (and even to comprehend fully) their modest parlor language. Army deserter Billy Fishback is by narrative chronology the last of the humorists' fetchers. Like the more successful Simon Suggs before him, he hopes to be taken for what he says he is. Although he may think he is convincing in his assumed social role, he has only the grossest clues to acceptable parlor performance. The country society that Billy enters and uses is not new Southwestern, but old Virginian. The Graveses are a respectable planter family with the command of language, manners, and ethics generally attributed to their class. With a daughter in need of a husband, Major Graves is sensible enough to have sized up the rustic schemer as a gawky, illiterate lad without prospects. However, after reading a forged letter that Billy has salted in his pocketbook (and which refers to him as the sole heir of a thriving plantation and a likely candidate for the next Georgia legislature), the entire family reevaluates the crude manners and speech of the "poor olphin." Suddenly the skulking straggler is "such a nice gentleman—so original and unaffected," who deports himself in "such an artless and independent manner" and draws his language

44. Halttunen, *Confidence Men*, 185.
45. John Higham, *From Boundlessness to Consolidation: The Transformation of American Culture, 1848–1860* (Ann Arbor, MI: William L. Clements Library, 1969), 10–11; Elizabeth Burns, *Theatricality: A Study of Convention in the Theatre and in Social Life* (London: Longman, 1972), 134.

"from Nature's pure, unwrought well-spring" (*AS*, 52). Nothing has changed except his—and their—prospects.

Warren's portrait of the Graveses is quietly devastating. In his self-presentation, with his filthy clothes and his oafish vernacular, Fishback is as obvious in his shamming as Simon Suggs. But if Major Graves and his gullible daughters are persuaded to close their eyes to such transparent fraudulence, friends and neighbors, without a stake in the outcome, have no such motive. Though in the Graveses' presence they flutter about in mock envy, among themselves the acquaintances of the deluded Caroline exchange their low opinions of her future husband. One friend declares she has a "great mind to tell" Caroline that the crucial letter (read until it is now nearly "worn out by finger-marks") is "an arrant forgery"; another, disgusted at hearing the "lordly lover" converse "so charmingly about his 'mammy' and his [cotton] 'crap,' his 'taters, water-millions' etc.," refers to Billy as "Count D'Orsay Chesterfield." The deserter's hygiene earns him no points, either. One matron would "bet he'd give all the Graveses the itch"; another declares "he smelt *so offensive,* with the tobacco juice running out at both corners of his mouth." For all his drawbacks, though, Fishback is not without wit. His favorite motto is worthy of Simon Suggs: "When I *fit* I fit fur the country so's to make the country fit fur me" (*AS*, 54, 48).

It is hard to imagine southern readers enjoying Kittrell Warren's little book in 1865. Written by a Confederate veteran from Alabama and published within months after Appomattox, *Life and Public Services of an Army Straggler* is informed by neither sectional piety nor patriotism. The humor is as scalding as Hooper's two decades earlier. The shabbiness of Billy Fishback has the virtue of moral realism; but Warren's unvarnished account of a coward in the Confederate Army who, during his tour of duty, is also a thief, liar, and inept confidence man must have struck some readers, still registering the war's stunning casualties, as harsh and unfeeling. In private, however, writing about the twenty thousand men who deserted during and after the Antietam campaign, an embarrassed Robert E. Lee confirmed Warren's unflattering picture of the southern *straggler* (a euphemistic term for the uglier *deserter*). Just before Sharpsburg in 1862, Lee wrote Jefferson Davis that "our ranks" had been reduced "by straggling," up to "one half of the original numbers." In yet another letter the general gave a kind of proleptic précis of Warren's fictional plot when he wrote that "a great deal of damage to citizens is done by stragglers" who abuse their charity, taking "all they can take from the defenseless, in many cases wantonly destroying stock and property." By

1863, after Gettysburg, Lee was more blunt, finally referring to these men as deserters, "a formidable and growing evil."[46]

Hooper's fetcher succeeds with his scams because his victims are, as the Duke calls Arkansawyers, such "lunkheads." The convention in *Simon Suggs* is that the captain's targets are so easily sold because, whatever their social status, they are not bright enough to see that Simon has accurately, and quickly, taken their measure as greedy opportunists whose misplaced pride is vulnerable to flattery. Billy Fishback's shrewdness quotient is lower than Hooper's captain, and his targets are (or should be) more formidable than legislators, preachers, students, and Creek widows. And yet this Virginia family is taken in by an inept fetcher. Though Major Graves never actually hands over his "money, daughter and negroes" to his prospective son-in-law, having hastily sold his land, he is eager to do so. And it is no credit to his competence that the final phase of the plan collapses. Only chance and Billy's cowardice intervene to save the family further embarrassment.

Natural social evolution decreed that the frontier should re-create civilized society, and the humorists explored the rawness and crudity of the new country made visible through its makeshift imitation of the properties defining older communities. Their texts are filled with the dynamics of mimicry. *Difference from* and *similarity to* constitute little dramas centered not only in the aggressive modes that polite society finds intolerable (the bragging, crowing, and snapping of erstwhile heroes; the practical joking of village eccentrics and layabouts), but also in the pathetic efforts at self-civilizing that respectables endorsed (balls and cotillions, musicales, charades, reading societies).

iv.

In the long tradition that discriminates simulation (telling lies) from dissimulation (concealing truth), the first is usually seen as more damaging to the social compact.[47] To make up stories out of whole cloth is some-

46. Alan T. Nolan, "The Anatomy of the Myth," in *The Myth of the Lost Cause and Civil War History,* ed. Gary W. Gallagher and Alan T. Nolan (Bloomington: Indiana University Press, 2000), 25. Nolan is quoting from U.S. War Department documents in *The War of the Rebellion,* ser. 2.

47. "To dissimulate is to feign not to have what one has. To simulate is to feign to have what one hasn't. One implies a presence, the other an absence." Jean Baudrillard, *Simulations,* trans. Paul Foss, Paul Patton, and Philip Beitchman (New York: Semiotext[e], 1983), 5. For a similar formulation, see David Ashby, "Playing with the

how thought to be more disrespectful of those who hear them than, say, the merely prudent, amiable instinct to conceal truth that might otherwise mar sociability. In fact, however, this "lesser" evil occupies a more treacherous terrain in social intercourse than outright lying. Dissimulating may not require more imagination, but it calls for more craft, much of it the sly and cunning variety.

In the discourse of insincerity, what both modes share is impersonation as a technique for presenting the self. To pretend to be what one isn't overturns the comfortable assurance that the individual possesses a unitary and stable identity. Nineteenth-century Americans still clung to the politics of sincerity, a dedication to the Quintilian principle in its trickle-down, commonsense version popularized by Hugh Blair and his American successors: that liars *cannot* be eloquent and that audiences *compel* the orator to speak truthfully.[48] The public linking of self and others was not merely a matter of ethics, but, according to Edward Channing, a pragmatic result of the orating situation: only an honest orator will be believed. In the hands of Emerson, the connection between self and the other flows, with intuited psychic energy, from speaker to auditor, from writer to reader, in the faith that regenerating potentialities are communicable from one person to another. Hawthorne, Emerson's Concord neighbor, severely undermines both the Quintilian premise and the belief in an undivided self—as we see, for example, in *The Scarlet Letter*, in which Dimmesdale's adoring congregation fails to penetrate the eloquent lie behind his Election Day sermon.[49] Indeed, what most of us accepted a generation ago as Dark Romanticism—the writing of Hawthorne, Poe, and Melville—is a vast literature of anxiety, skepticism, and horror, in which the self suffers fragmentation and in which communication from one psyche to another generates tropes of rupture and discontinuity. One critic has claimed that this body of darker writing, with its power struggles, secret sins, masks, obsessions, and aliases, anticipates Nietzsche's vision of the shrouded consciousness, forever engaged in a lying art: "deception, flattery, lying and cheating, talking behind the back, posing, liv-

---

Pieces: The Fragmentation of Social Theory," in *Critical Theory Now*, ed. Philip Wexler (London: Falmer, 1991), 70–97.

48. Jeffrey Steele, *The Representation of the Self in the American Renaissance* (Chapel Hill: University of North Carolina Press, 1987), 173–79; Janet Gabler-Hover, *Truth in American Fiction: The Legacy of Rhetorical Idealism* (Athens: University of Georgia Press, 1990), 37, 39–41.

49. Terence Martin, "Dimmesdale's Ultimate Sermon," *Arizona Quarterly* 27 (1971): 230–40.

ing in borrowed splendor, being masked, the disguises of convention, acting a role before others and before oneself."[50]

Happily, neither the fetchers of Southwest humor nor their creators waste time theorizing over their dissimulation, apparently performing Nietzschean tricks without knowing it. It is unlikely that even Judge Longstreet, the best educated of the humorists, gave a thought to the philosophical understructure of Ned Brace's antic madness among Savannah's respectables, or the village worthies of "The Wax Works" who pose as mannequins to avoid their tavern bills, or the performance in "The Fight" of Squire Loggins, the village fraud who plays oracle at best-man fights. Longstreet, more than any other humorist, took seriously the state of morality and society, but he steered away from *serioso* meditations; he could not, however, have written his scenes of native Georgians in village and town without acknowledging the power of insincerity that permeated that society. The cracker versions of polite society also accommodate persona manipulation and the tricky art of impersonation, all of which have little to do with unimpeded self-expression.

If the self in rupture, not some posited unitary self, is what makes the characters of our nineteenth-century canonical authors memorable— Arthur Gordon Pym, William Wilson, Dr. Rappaccini, Zenobia, Ahab, Pierre—their complexity comes from their obsessions, their secrets, their anxious trying out of alternate masks, their fitful ruses and negotiations. Most of the memorable figures in the humorous literature are comfortable with their uncomplex typecasting: the backwoods hunter, the braggart, the wily native, the knowing widow, the frontier confidence man. Their creators refuse to take seriously whatever obsessions may propel them onto the public stage. Except for a few instances (Longstreet's Ned Brace, most conspicuously), we must be satisfied with their surface deceptions and impersonations. What so many of these figures have in common is a constitutive reliance upon guile—they bluff, lie, mislead, deceive; they simulate and dissimulate—but the authors spurn any plumbing of their psyches, ruptured or not.

The threatening qualities of acting, we are told, are the same ones inherent in human nature: "deceit, irreverent mimicry and the power to arouse in others passions and emotions normally controlled." The very vigor of Southwest humor issues from the dynamics of insincerity, but the figures involved are not rendered complex because of it. This is an art of surfaces, and the interest of the authors remains on the surface, not in

50. Steele, *Representation of the Self,* 178–79.

exploratory digging to find out *why* their characters are insincere. This is perhaps another way of asserting the obvious: that types can't experience growth. To revert to E. M. Forster's inadequate classification, they are "flat characters," not "round" ones.[51] But it may also be another way of explaining why, despite the variety of their styles of insincerity, they remain types with a unitary and stable self. They can be so comfortable in their types because they live in and respond to a culture that is itself predictable, a predictability based firmly but paradoxically on the *fluctuating reality of instability.* In an unsettled (and unsettling) country, guile answers guile, a necessary weapon against others already armed.

Although they accept the conditions of their time and place for what they are, the humorists ignore the messy and often tragic circumstances that would make their Flush Times an American version of Hard Times. In a certain reading, Hooper's Simon Suggs would be regarded as one of the underclass victims of competition in a nation venturing into capitalism. Indeed, the shrewd captain occasionally sees himself as economic victim. When the larder is empty, he mutters, "D—n it! *somebody* must suffer!" Because the authors accept the cultural politics of fetching as a given in real-life survival and success, their writing is rich in the aesthetics of fetching. If they are not much interested in probing *why it is done,* they delight in depicting *how it is done.* Hooper, then, focuses entirely on his hero's craft, tracing his success in impersonating variously a born-again sinner, a wealthy hog drover, and a state legislator. Although duping his marks to get what he wants, Simon's wants are unambitious—a free champagne-and-oyster supper, a modest collection of money in a passed-around hat. His success, even in such threadbare endeavors, is remarkable, since Hooper goes to some pains, as we shall see, to suggest that the captain's impersonations should fool nobody. That they do is both a measure of the author's low regard for the intelligence and integrity of the victims and a tribute to the versatility of Simon's resources: his foxy insight into human nature, his wit, his on-his-feet improvisations. It is true, as Constance Rourke long ago observed, that masquerade was the "salient" tool for adaptive frontier types, but what is conspicuous in the written humor is how transparent that masquerade is.[52] If the swindler says that *somebody* must suffer, Hooper's grammar says that somebody *must* suffer, since all the somebodies in Simon's orbit are too venal or dumb to resist the most transparent scam. The reader is left to

51. Burns, *Theatricality,* 151; E. M. Forster, *Aspects of the Novel* (New York: Harcourt, 1927).

52. Constance M. Rourke, *American Humor: A Study of the National Character* (1931; reprint, New York: Harcourt Brace Jovanovich, 1959), 86–87.

admire (reluctantly, perhaps) just *how* this backwoods manipulator reels them in.

In the humor the confidence man is never quite the dreaded scourge of innocence, partly because (*pace* Sut Lovingood's theology) there are no innocents to scourge, but mostly because as a type he fits into a continuum that includes the village hearty, the public wag, the practical joker— all of whom are figures answerable to the makeshift conditions of an interim society trying to shed its primitive habits while adapting to the expedients of propriety and cultivation. Throughout the antebellum era, the conspicuously wealthy man was always vulnerable to snares set by the crafty. As John L. McConnel put it in 1853, "the rich man was rather a bird to be plucked, than a 'hero' to be worshipped."[53] In the humor, however, the stranger with larceny in his heart is a rare figure, even in a climate pulsing with rivalry and designs for trickery. Most perpetrators are as unambitious as their easy decoys, and whatever fraudulence their schemes put into motion is shared by those they defraud. When money is the object, as in Simon Suggs's artful dodges, the amount is so negligible as to be unworthy of most con men worth their salt. But the object of such schemes is often gratuitous play. The dupe exists for the sharper, who may be merely a bored practical joker or an impromptu impersonator beguiling the time as well as the victim. The point of Longstreet's story of the two horse swappers who gull each other is that the stakes are well-nigh worthless: what counts in the game is the "banter," the testing of trading skills. Simon's masquerade as a rich hog drover elicits only an evening's indulgence in faro and a handsome supper, but his real game is taking on and taking in what pass for Tuscaloosa swells.

Simon Suggs is a stranger in Tuscaloosa, though the reputation of his assumed identity, "General Witherspoon," precedes his arrival. The humorists generally refine and domesticate the image of the stranger that will become so formidable in the history and lore of a successor Southwest. That image comes down to us in a series of classic situations: names change; professions slide easily into one another; reputations are honored, resisted, challenged, tarnished, and honored again. A character will often call another "stranger," which simultaneously signals a tentative friendliness and a defensive suspiciousness. The term can refer to a traveler just passing through, waiting for the next steamboat or stagecoach, or to someone from an adjoining county or state whose business is unknown. The stranger may be neither rascal nor modest gambler looking to take on the locals, but a sizing-up ceremony proceeds apace in an

53. McConnel, *Western Characters*, 311.

often flamboyant exercise of psychological assessment and verbal facility—sometimes as overstatement, sometimes as under-.

The stranger figures prominently in the critical juncture between settler and migrant. The boundary between the sometimes respectable settler
and the often expedient stranger is historically a source of social tension.
Tests of good faith and authenticity were choreographed carefully, since
impugning the integrity of any reasonable-appearing individual might
violate the delicate code of honor.[54] For communities in which half of the
settlers were little more than strangers, the challenge was to shape a class
of responsible people out of that flux. Two of the visible signs of the elect
were property and conspicuous display, which, like sincerity, could be
feigned with a selective personal past and manufactured family tree.

In the humor, however, if there are threats of duplicity, they tend to
come homegrown. Because of the uneven pace of community building,
many settlements enjoy (or endure) a kind of rotational democracy that
lowers the usual barrier of distrust for newer members. Simon Suggs remains a stranger at the faro club for about two minutes. The Tuscaloosa
gamblers, Chevalier would say, form their own little republic whose protocols encourage easy access, even a rough-hewn camaraderie. So, too,
Ned Brace in Savannah. Though his calculated mischief causes consternation and unease in both the town's public spaces and in the communal
dining room, the very nature of the boardinghouse, as we have seen, is to
diminish distance among strangers. Wariness is always prudent where
strangers congregate, but inns and other public accommodations were
the recognized sites of conviviality, nourished by the good offices of the
proprietor.

Chicanery is such a common motif in the action of the humor because
the trickery is indigenous, homebred by neighbors and friends. A local
cousin and rival humiliates Major Jones before his intended bride for
being too slow-witted at parlor games; an avenging Sut Lovingood slips
lizards into the pants of Parson Bullen to ridicule him before his adoring
congregation; Madison Tensas and his fellow medical students, annoyed
at their overly curious landlady, wrap the mummified face of an albino
Negro harelip in a parcel that they know she will open. Even Baldwin's

54. Richard C. Wade, *The Urban Frontier: The Rise of Western Cities, 1790–1830* (Cambridge: Harvard University Press, 1959), 104. In substantial towns, gambling rooms,
serving "the double purpose of gentlemen's public assembly-room and *café*," were
open to all respectable-looking men for billiards, roulette, and faro, and the evening
invariably concluded, after midnight, with a supper to which both winners and
losers were invited (Ingraham, *The South-West*, 1:134–35).

great scam artist, Ovid Bolus, is not an outsider victimizing the home-folk. Despite his tales of perambulating adventures (the Seminole war in Florida, the Texas revolution, a romantic interlude in Cuba), he is as "native" in his Flush Times settlement as everybody else. By his own innate qualities this genial swindler can never be a stranger to those he so entertainingly regales. Bolus is a spendthrift of other people's money and a princely sponge ("It took as much to support him as a first class steamboat"), but he is the *community's* sponge—which is to say that these characters' creators had little inclination to belabor the scruffiness of settlements they at least temporarily called home.

As insiders, the humorists tolerate chicanery, especially the petty sort that flourishes under their noses, in part because they accept the working premise of their particular geography—that the population is expediently, democratically, receptive to whatever improvisational scheme for bilking each other may come up. It may not be Nietzschean in impulse, but there is a substantive reason why *human natur* is so repetitively invoked in this body of writing. The southwestern community had its flaws not because, as the bias of the travel writers would have it, it was born yesterday, but because it seemed to harbor in its small compass more than its share of ancient, diverse, recalcitrant human nature. In plumbing that nature more of the humorists than not, beginning with Longstreet, were moral realists before they were moralists. They would have understood the country singer who says that though he was born in the dark, it wasn't last night.

Judge Longstreet and Mrs. Trollope alike were confident that crude morals and bad habits would eventually be smoothed out and improved by civilized development, but only Mrs. Trollope regarded that future an unambiguous improvement. Almost to a man, the humorists acknowledge distinctive backwoods traits as potential embarrassments to the national program, but they also affirm the virtues of those traits as part of a primitive culture that has yet to be nationalized. Thanks to education, religion, and benevolent societies, notes Longstreet, the most disorderly of those traits were already in the mid-1830s being eradicated. Yet practical jokers and cagey horse traders emerge in *Georgia Scenes* as superior to the crude polish of village society in its determined march into modernity. The pictures of the disabling fecklessness of "charming creatures" and swooning men in an aspiring community all too willing to become civilized are the author's measure of the coming loss of energy and fortitude in the backcountry. The mixed sentiments of Longstreet are repeated in the authors who followed his lead.

Chapter 6 ↬≡🎜

Southwest Humor and the Other

> In small-town eyes all persons not belonging to the village are "strangers" and suspect; to the native of a country all who inhabit other countries are "foreigners"; Jews are "different" for the anti-Semite, Negroes are "inferior" for American racists, aborigines are "natives" for colonists, proletarians are the "lower class" for the privileged.
>
> —Simone de Beauvoir, *The Second Sex*

In a meadow near Ft. Laramie in 1846, Francis Parkman recorded a moment of relaxation away from the band of Ogillallahs with whom his party was attached. Watching a shoal of little fish in a mountain pool, he notes they were scarcely "sporting together" amicably but were "engaged in a cannibal warfare among themselves." Small ones fell victim to larger ones, which in turn scattered when the "tyrant of the pool," a three-inch monster, appeared with his "overwhelming force." He writes: "Soft-hearted philanthropists . . . may sigh long for their peaceful millennium; for from minnows up to men, life is an incessant battle."[1] The Darwinesque moment is allowed to stand without elaboration, though it points

---

1. Francis Parkman, *The Oregon Trail*, in *The Oregon Trail, The Conspiracy of Pontiac* (New York: Library of America, 1991), 246. Parkman may be recalling critic John Neal's complaint in 1825 that writers sympathetic to Indians cared not "two-pence about Indians," but were only following "the fashion to be philanthropical." Quoted in Sherry Sullivan, "Indians in American Fiction, 1820–1850: An Ethnohistorical Perspective," *Clio* 15 (1986): 244.

to Parkman's rationalization for a national policy that would make the entire continent safe for the white man. While its author is no philanthropist, *The Oregon Trail* is not notably hard-hearted. Like many of his contemporaries, Parkman viewed the ultimate extinction of the Native American as lamentable (perhaps) but inevitable (certainly). In the American scheme of things, the white man was destined to be the three-inch tyrant in a vast pool of minnows.

The trope of big fish eating little is more pungently articulated by Mike Fink four years later in a T. B. Thorpe sketch for Porter's *Spirit of the Times.* "It's natur' that the big fish should eat the little ones," muses the boatman. "I've seen trout swallow a perch, and a cat would come along and swallow the trout, and perhaps, on the Mississippi, the alligators use up the cat, and so on to the end of the row" (*TBT,* 177). In this fish-eat-fish world, "the row" is the food chain, ever the most common example of competition for survival in the natural world. Mike Fink is even less soft-hearted than Francis Parkman, and as a "big fish," the bare-knuckles riverman needs no trope to justify his enmity for the Indian. Exterminating the red tribes is for him one more round in a best-man game. Fink comes down to us as one of the roughs, his views unleavened by fancy language. Parkman, wasting no tears in his prescient recounting of the destiny of the Indian, in his half-dozen books never overcame a civilized contempt for the "rigid, inflexible" nature of the Indian that made his fate inevitable, but neither he nor James Fenimore Cooper were able to write of that fate without civilized sympathy.[2]

In her reading of Washington Irving's western journals, Eudora Welty noted that for all his meticulous eye for detail ("He seems never to have caught sight of a new Indian without noting it"), the famous author never immersed himself in the western scene, in the problem of Native Americans, or the daily doings of the ordinary men in his own expedition. Her succinct summary: "appraisal without rapport."[3] Although Parkman surmounts such romantic neutrality, a similar detachment informs

2. Jonathan Arac, *The Cambridge History of American Literature: Vol. 2, Prose Writing 1820–1865,* ed. Sacvan Bercovitch (New York: Cambridge University Press, 1995), 739. So too William Gilmore Simms (*The Yemassee,* 1835), Catherine Sedgwick (*Hope Leslie,* 1827), and Charles Fenno Hoffman (*Greyslaer,* 1840). Sherry Sullivan reads these sympathetic texts as subversive of the national agenda of progress, which to philanthropic minds had moved far afield from a past of heroic idealism ("Indians," 248–49). See also Lee Clark Mitchell, *Witnesses to a Vanishing America: The Nineteenth-Century Response* (Princeton, NJ: Princeton University Press, 1981), 5, 8–16, 31.
3. Eudora Welty, *The Eye of the Story: Selected Essays and Reviews* (New York: Random House, 1977), 179.

the young Harvardian, who relied for his information, support, and nourishment on men he would never mingle with back home. That detachment becomes the Parkman formula for effective white response to the presence of the Indian—trying to balance a humane sadness about the red man's plight with a realistic resignation that, whatever the national policy, his dispossession was unavoidable. Indeed, this formula became the dominant one in antebellum America. Removal of the Native American was accepted as a public-spirited way of forestalling the utter extinction of a race. Cooper's own justification for the Removal is gingerly summarized in *Notions of the Americans:* "A great, humane, and I think, rational project is now in operation to bring the Indians within the pale of civilization."[4] The paradox is self-evident. To bring the Indians within the pale of civilization it was necessary to take them outside the pale, beyond the benefits and customs of the rational, humane society then abuilding on the eastern side of the Mississippi River.

i.

The "Indian problem" in Jacksonian America had a long history. Native Americans as proto-occupants of the land were, as Roy Harvey Pearce put it, "all that civilized men could not be."[5] From colonial times, the perception that the Indians had "no real home" fueled settlers' fears of sporadic attacks from all directions. *Habitation*—a physical structure of great iconological significance—was a civilized Christian requirement for the colonists in both Massachusetts and Virginia. Beyond the fenced boundaries of property lay unstructured and (in William Bradford's words) "unpeopled" nature, a pagan model for "brutish men which ranged up and down." Without "setled habytation," the Indians ("little otherwise than the wild beasts") were ineligible for proprietorship, the material re-

4. James Fenimore Cooper, *Notions of the Americans Picked Up by a Travelling Bachelor* (1828; reprint, New York: Frederick Ungar, 1963), 2:378.
5. Roy Harvey Pearce, *Savagism and Civilization: A Study of the Indian and the American Mind* (Baltimore: Johns Hopkins University Press, 1965), 200. The vexed racial politics are explored in Richard Slotkin, *Regeneration through Violence: The Mythology of the American Frontier, 1600–1860* (Middletown, CT: Wesleyan University Press, 1973); Richard Drinnon, *Facing West: The Metaphysics of Indian-Hating and Empire-Building* (Minneapolis: Minnesota University Press, 1980); Louise K. Barnett, *Ignoble Savage: American Literary Racism, 1790–1890* (Westport, CT: Greenwood, 1973); and Brian W. Dippie, *The Vanishing American: White Attitudes and U.S. Indian Policy* (Middletown, CT: Wesleyan University Press, 1982).

minder of Christian history working itself out in the new world.[6] This sense of fatedness, a powerful colonial motif that would gradually evolve into the notion of Manifest Destiny, was a firm national conviction—providence had set aside the continent for white occupancy. One European traveler agreed with the "irresistible" argument that "actual cultivation of the soil and the establishment of fixed habitations" were legitimate requirements for America's "doomed people."[7]

When two novelists of the humorists' generation, Robert Montgomery Bird and James Kirke Paulding, contributed their voices to what Melville called "the metaphysics of Indian-hating," they were in effect countering a new wave of antebellum writing that *celebrated* rather than damned the aborigines. In rejecting the sympathetic views of such writers as Cooper and Simms, they revived the old colonial tenet that Indians, because of their resistance to white incursions on their lands, were the implacable enemy—mostly evil, certainly pagan, and probably less than human. In the mid-1830s, Bird groused that Cooper and Simms, who often depicted their fictional Indians as benefactors of the white race, even as part of the nation's unique identity, had transformed red men into "nature's nobles, the chivalry of the forest." In his preface to *Nick of the Woods* (1837), Bird declared that "the North American savage has never appeared to us the gallant and heroic personage he seems to others." Indeed, to counter that savagery, he created in that novel the character of Nathan Slaughter, a Quaker who exacts revenge in kind for the massacre of his family—an event that has changed "a man of amity and good will" into a "slayer of Indians, double-dyed in gore." Even to the hero, a Virginia gentleman named Roland Forrester, Indians are "the most heartless, merciless, and brutal of all the races of men." Within the narrative, Bird editorially scorns the fashionable image of the heroic red man that "poets and sentimentalists" have constructed. "Honor, justice, and generosity," he asserts, are characteristics only of men in "an advanced stage of civilization."[8]

Although he never created an Indian-hater with the ferocity of Nathan

6. William Bradford, *Of Plymouth Plantation, 1620–1647*, ed. Samuel Eliot Morison (New York: Knopf, 1952), 1:25; John Winthrop quoted in William Cronon, *Changes in the Land: Indians, Colonists, and the Ecology of New England* (New York: Hill & Wang, 1983), 56.

7. Francis J. Grund, *The Americans in Their Moral, Social, and Political Relations* (1837; reprint, New York: A. M. Kelley, 1971), 2:47–48.

8. Robert Montgomery Bird, *Nick of the Woods or the Jibbenainosay: A Tale of Kentucky* (1837; reprint, ed. Curtis Dahl, New Haven, CT: College & University Press, 1967), 28–29, 226, 189, 202.

Slaughter, Paulding in private was even more caustic. He lamented the national sentimentalism that had followed the forced evacuation of native tribes in the Southwest. To a correspondent in 1838, he observed bitterly that the "bloody Indian" could now safely "break his faith," plunder and burn "a district or two," massacre troops, scalp a few women and children, and expect not condemnation but "immortal honour." Conceding that his language was a verbal "explosion," Paulding nevertheless continued in the same vein, scornfully predicting that the Indian

> will be glorified in Congress; canonized by philanthropists; autographed, and lithographed, and biographied, by authors, artists, and periodicals; the petticoated petitioners to Congress will weep, not over the fate of the poor white victims, but that of the treacherous and bloody murderer, who will receive his apotheosis in the universal sympathy of all . . . the hypocritical followers of . . . old Johnny Bull.[9]

Though he wrote just as the Native American was becoming a more sympathetic figure in the American consciousness, Timothy Flint gave no ground in articulating the majority view from the Old Southwest. Calling "preposterous" the rhetoric of benevolent-minded statesmen who invested Americans with "guilt of having destroyed" the Indians and "having possessed ourselves of their lands," Flint believed that though it was proper to pity them and "practice forbearance to the end," we must always remind ourselves that "the causes of their decay and extinction are found in their own nature and character, and the unchangeable order of things." That order decrees that "savages should give place to civilized men" who know how to strengthen and improve "the social compact." Like drunkards, idlers, and disturbers of Flint's own society, the Indian who can neither "cultivate the land" nor "lead a municipal life" is merely "a charge and a burden" to civilization. That burden, in fact, had already been capably borne by the government, which deserved praise for doing "all practicable good" for this "devoted and unhappy race."[10] As historians have noted, the cultural fact of Indian removal became a wide-ranging moral problem in Jackson's America. Distinct from the can-

9. James Kirke Paulding to Gouverneur Kemble, June 15, 1838, in *Letters of James Kirke Paulding*, ed. Ralph M. Aderman (Madison: University of Wisconsin Press, 1962), 215–16.
10. Timothy Flint, *Recollections of the Last Ten Years in the Valley of the Mississippi* (1826; reprint, ed. George R. Brooks, Carbondale: Southern Illinois University Press, 1968), 132, 140, 151–54.

did posture of Indian-hating, predictable from long decades of outright racial war, the issue of the natives' place in a white civilized society was so vexed that the majority argument took on all the contradictory play we expect in a position generally understood as morally suspect. Policy papers of the 1820s and 1830s dance awkwardly around self-righteousness, guilt, expiation, and evasion. The nub of the problem was how to reconcile a nation's idealistic self-image as just and compassionate in Indian relations with the cruelty and deviousness that proved to be equally as effective as militia rifles.[11]

Thomas S. Grimke, campaigning for the Sunday School Union, was relying on a commonplace when he spelled out the undeviating direction of migration "from the east to the west" that had brought such progress throughout the Mississippi Valley. The approved direction of migration was an oddly reiterated concern. The authors of one xenophobic treatise reminded readers that "Power for ages has gradually been moving westward, exactly through this geographical belt." It was left to John L. McConnel, however, to find the greatest lesson in westering. Perhaps no popular commentator was so addicted to the long view as McConnel, who pitched prehistoric Fate against up-to-date Providence. Fate determined the disappearance of the Indians when their ancient forefathers "emigrated in the wrong direction" (that is, from west to east). Providence, favoring emigration from east to west, stood for "enlightenment, civilization, Christianity," whereas Fate represented "darkness, degradation, barbarism." The two finally confronted each other on "the banks of the Mississippi!" The extinction of the Indian was therefore decreed (the race was receding, McConnel noted, "at the rate of seventeen miles a year"), which meant that American policy, reflecting the popular will, was "not only inevitable, but *right* that it should be so." The blessings that had been continuously invoked for the creation of the American nation, McConnel asserted, still operated for its orderly advancement in the Southwest. To Daniel Drake, physician and cultural light-bringer, the dis-

11. See Forrest G. Robinson, "Uncertain Borders: Race, Sex, and Civilization in *The Last of the Mohicans*," *Arizona Quarterly* 47 (1991): 2; and Drinnon, *Facing West*, 95–98. Henry Hitchcock, a Vermonter who settled in Alabama, declared he could never support Jackson for president, yet he agreed with his policy for the southern Indians: "the govt ought to remove them west of the Miss," not for any arcane ethnographical reasons, but for what passed in 1826 as humane expedience. Since the Indians were "gradually dwindling off, . . . a pray to all the bad passions of our nation without getting any good," they should be somewhere "where the whites cannot interupt them." Henry Hitchcock Papers, William Stanley Hoole Special Collections, University of Alabama Library, University of Alabama, Tuscaloosa.

possession of the Indians seemed mostly a loss for scholarship: "[E]very hour reduces their number, and increases the difficulty of composing a history of this middle period, in the annals of the West."[12]

The inaccurate image of the Indian as an exclusively nomadic hunter was the stereotype that dominated most antebellum arguments. In substance and tone, Andrew Jackson's reasoning summed up generations of opinions: tribes should not be allowed to claim lands on which they roamed without "improving" them. A perambulating people that accepted neither boundaries nor man-made maps, so the logic went, was a part of nature, and the solution to the problem was to treat them *as* nature—to be conquered, like the land itself.[13] Retrospection helped in alleviating some of the tortured rationalizations for occupying Indian lands, but the passage of time did nothing to dislodge the notion both that it was inevitable and that it was the right policy for a modern state. In his memoirs a Georgia lawyer was candid enough about the forced evacuation in the settlement period. He admitted that it may not have been "the most moral" system, but it was "better calculated to people a country than any ever yet devised." And an old-timer in the Republic of Texas remembered that in 1828, when whites began encroaching on the hunting grounds of the "wild tribes," the conflict of the races was a replay of earlier ones east of the Mississippi, and one "destined to the same finale— the survival of the fittest." The whites, he admitted, were as "barbarous" in their "mode of indiscriminate warfare" as their enemy: "Extermination was the motto on both sides."[14]

Mike Fink's unremitting hostility toward the Indian is carefully historicized in "The Disgraced Scalp Lock." T. B. Thorpe maintains the sturdy

12. *Address of Thomas S. Grimke* (Philadelphia, 1831), 12; *A Voice to America; or, The Model Republic, Its Glory or Its Fall*, 3rd ed. (New York, 1855), 361 (authorship is attributed to Frederick Saunders and Thomas B. Thorpe, yet what the humorist contributed is not known); John L. McConnel, *Western Characters, or Types of Border Life in the Western States* (New York, 1853), 60–61; Daniel Drake, *Discourse on the History, Character, and Prospects of the West* (1834; reprint, ed. Perry Miller, Gainesville, FL: Scholars' Facsimiles & Reprints, 1955), 19–20.

13. William Boelhower, *Through a Glass Darkly: Ethnic Semiosis in American Literature* (New York: Oxford, 1987), 43–45, 62–63; *Papers and Messages of the Presidents*, ed. James D. Richardson (Washington, DC: U.S. Congress, 1897), 2:459; Wilcomb E. Washburn, ed., *The American Indian and the United States: A Documentary History* (New York: Random House, 1973), 4:2546.

14. George W. Paschal, *Ninety-Four Years: Agnes Paschal* (c. 1871; reprint, Spartanburg, SC: Reprint Co., 1974), 216; Noah Smithwick, *The Evolution of a State or Recollections of Old Texas Days*, ed. Nanna Smithwick Donaldson (Austin: University of Texas Press, 1983), 151.

perspective of the less passionate 1840s as he recounts an incident from the career of the notorious boatman a generation earlier. Long before it was entirely safe for whites to antagonize the diminishing Indian population, the reckless Mike mounts a provocative theatrical parody of Native American battle rhetoric in the presence of a band of sullen Indian outcasts. Giving a loud war whoop and "mixing the language of the aborigines and his own together, he went on in savage fashion and bragged of his triumphs and victories on the warpath, with all the seeming earnestness of a real 'brave.'" Mike's "pugnacity" is aroused by the taciturn and haughty demeanor of one Proud Joe, a renegade Cherokee "banished from his mountain home . . . for some great crime." With best-man grandstanding, the noted marksman shoots away the Indian's scalp lock, leaving its wearer stunned but otherwise unhurt. What for Mike is "a little sport" is for the humiliated Joe an act calling for revenge, which comes several months later and hundreds of miles downriver in an attack on the riverman and his crew. A boatman is killed, along with two Indians in the war party, one of whom is Proud Joe of the missing scalp lock. The outcasts had risked their lives, concludes Thorpe, threading their way south through alien tribal territory for the single purpose of avenging "the fearful insult, of destroying *without the life,* the sacred scalp-lock" (*TBT,* 170–80). Although in the eyes of both whites and Cherokees Proud Joe is a drunken, worthless outcast, Thorpe gives him dignity, if not heroism, while underscoring the boatman's foolhardiness in performing a rash act that culminates in the death of one of his own men.

The humorists were no more exempt from the general complacency about the Indian, or the tortured rationalizations of official racist policy, than most antebellum Americans, wherever they lived. But Jackson's policy of removal, which they matter-of-factly condoned, had for them an immediacy, a practicality, not felt by northeasterners, for whom it was mostly an ethical abstraction. There is little evidence that the humorous authors and their vernacular subjects differed fundamentally on this topic, which transcended partisan politics. As in most respects, yeomen may have spoken their minds more viscerally than the educated class, but all whites in the region, except perhaps for the most extreme loners in the bush, agreed that removal was necessary. Their very presence in former Indian lands demanded it.

Although Jackson's Indian policy affected all whites in the Old Southwest, the land rush that followed removal affected them unevenly. Prosperity through lavishly extended credit created what Joseph G. Baldwin called "the Rag Empire," which spurred "an emigration greater than any portion of the country ever attracted." While it lasted, "many of our countrymen came into the South-West in time to get 'a benefit.'" The people who benefited primarily, of course, were the speculators, land agents, and planters with credit. Most of "the gold-seekers were mere gold-diggers—not bringing property, but coming to take it away." As Baldwin makes clear, the hordes of lawyers like himself brought no property either, only an expectant enthusiasm. He notes further that "the public lands afforded a field for unlimited speculation," and with disputed Indian claims, treaty obligations, and preemption rights, the "flood-gates of litigation were opened and the pent-up tide let loose upon the country" (*FT,* 236–37).

The Removal and the land grab joined red man and white, vanquished and conqueror, in a nonmorality play. Dutiful claims kept Baldwin and his cohorts lively, but the outcome in their theatrical courts was as foreordained as the fate of the Georgia Cherokees a few years earlier. No new country could be bested in the sheer gaudiness of its crimes, he writes: felonies were "splendid," bank robberies were "gorgeous," forays on the treasury "superb," defalcations "august," land-office corruptions "magnificent." But gaudiest of all was the sham competition of Indian claims and white preemption rights. Manipulative speculators trumped both. Society in the Old Southwest may have been "wholly unorganized," without "restraining public opinion," and the law may have been "well-nigh powerless," but greed compensated for the frailty of all civilized principles: "And in INDIAN affairs!—the very mention is suggestive of the poetry of theft—the romance of a wild and weird larceny! What sublime conceptions of super-Spartan roguery! Swindling Indians by the nation!" (*FT,* 238). The ironic nouns and modifiers in this catalog (*poetry, romance, weird, sublime*) serve to separate the indictment itself from the author's rather chilling affective response to it. The jaunty energy of his prose disallows emotional sympathy, even the requisite mourning of a Francis Parkman, because victimizing the Creeks is only one instance of the era's "hyperboles of mendacity." One of the narrator's maxims acknowledges the harsh lesson that innocence is always hostage to greed in the competitive drama of the moderns: "He who does not go ahead is run over and trodden down" (*FT,* 229). If this sounds cynical, it also suggests behavior appropriately calibrated to the demands of a Darwinian world. It is the kind of working adage that describes rather than justifies.

Indians in most of the humor are in effect neutralized by the determined act of historicizing them as a subject. The humorists, with their preferred focus on the white successors—including the yeoman class, sharing

in the spoils of Native American lands with more ambitious farmers—
see Indians as mostly irrelevant. When they function at all, it is through
their presence as scattered remnants, residual reminders of the red man as
threat. The real thing had once existed in its historical moment. Present
dangers, even the brief Creek eruption of 1836, are emotionally referen-
tial in the hands of these authors—mock threats replayed as parody.
W. C. Hall, for example, simply uses Indians as another opportunity for
his Arch Coony to let off steam. This "durndest, rantankerous hoss-fly"
of the Yazoo hills, drawn to any fights in the vicinity, leaves his half-
emptied jug to "go an' pitch into er privit 'spute 'twene two Injuns (when
he didn't care er durn cent which wolloped t'other), an' lamin both on
um out'n ther mockasins!" (Cohen, 365).

Indians are reference points in much of the humorous writing. During
the Mexican War, C. F. M. Noland's Pete Whetstone comments in passing: "them ar Spaniards aint half as good as wild ingens." There are enough
casual allusions to indicate that, if anything, Noland may have been comfortably sympathetic with the Indians. In 1839, when the federal government had been fighting the Seminoles in Florida for four years (and
would continue for three more), Whetstone writes that he is glad to be
back in Devil's Fork, Arkansas, after a tour of eastern cities, adding: "But
home is a sweet place to even an *Injun,* as them Seminolys in Florida
have shown Uncle Sam." And in 1844 he uses the occasion of horse racing at Fort Gibson, on the western border near Oklahoma, to praise the
Cherokee nation: "Them ar Cherokees' are oncommonly friendly," he
writes, "and nobody that has the horses and truck, need be afraid of their
hair among them. I guess they have got two schools to our one, and you
can't sling a dog through the cracks of their houses" (*PW*, 150, 187). Noland's hero reflects the tension between the races along the contact zone.
Two years earlier, Cherokee agent Pierce Butler, pressured by the Arkansas governor to halt Indian "outrages" against whites along the Oklahoma
border, responded that the "industrious" Cherokees were "neighborly
disposed," and that difficulties stemmed from "a plundering predatory
class" of white settlers.[15]

As for most of his fellow humorists, the "Indian problem" was primarily recent history in the life of Johnson Jones Hooper. He had been born
in North Carolina during the Creek War, and his arrival in Alabama in
1835 coincided with the government's grand operation to evacuate Creeks,

15. R. Douglas Hurt, *Nathan Boone and the American Frontier* (Columbia: University
of Missouri Press, 1998), 208.

Cherokees, and Chickasaws from their homes in the Southwest to designated areas beyond the Mississippi. Hooper thus found himself an eyewitness to the chaotic speculation in Indian lands that paralleled the Removal. In the Old Southwest the Native Americans—those who stayed, hanging on, on their own—were visible reminders of the general dispossession that the Indian Removal Act of 1830 ensured. Despite isolated incidents, the end of the Creek Wars in 1820 had changed the tenor of settler life, and Hooper, like a less-focused Baldwin, embraced the Flush Times as a spectacle promising advancement. In his writing the Creeks in Alabama are more victims of white expedience and fraud than they are bloodthirsty savages. In tones that range from bemused observation to parody, the Simon Suggs sketches force the subject of Indian danger back into present history.

The Indian war whoop, the old aural cue of enemy attack, has already become part of adolescent make-believe games in *Adventures of Captain Simon Suggs*. Young Simon, joyously escaping the paternal hearth on his pony, Bunch, celebrates his freedom by rising in the stirrups to give "a tolerably fair imitation of the Creek war-whoop" (*SS*, 30). Even the potential violence of the Indians is more farcical than serious. An older Simon is on hand at the great council in which all the tribes of the Creek Nation, in self-parodic imitation of their own warpath mode, pass much of their time in singing, dancing, intramural rivalry, whooping, and fighting—"with clubs, rocks, knives, teeth, hands and toes" (*SS*, 73). Later, Captain Suggs and his Tallapoosy Vollantares attend a Creek ballgame to bet on which team will win the purse—a shot pouch temptingly filled with silver. When he learns that the leaders of the two opposing teams have conspired to attack "all the white men present," the nimble Simon preempts the plan, exchanges his old pony for a fine Creek bay, and grabs the purse for himself (*SS*, 114).

The most extensive example of how the Indian functions in Simon's adventures is Hooper's account of the so-called Creek uprising of 1836. Though the incident quickly became a footnote, it was a significant historical event. J. Marion Sims, a doctor only recently settled into his practice in Mount Meigs, Alabama, wrote to his wife on May 11 about the "disturbances" and expressed his indignation at the cowardly response by white males. "The whole country is in a perfect uproar," the doctor wrote. "Women and children are flying in every direction," leaving their houses and homes "to be plundered by the ruthless savage." He continued: "*Any* man who would openly refuse, under such circumstances as these, to march to the rescue of his fellow-citizens, would not justly be entitled to the protection of the community in which he lived, much less to the affection that any *fair friend* might bear him."[16] Hooper would have shared Dr. Sims's low opinion of the local militia, but his tone is bemused and ironic. Instead of Sims's sympathy for "the consternation of the inhabitants," we see mostly a diverting scorn for a populace capable only of misreading and exaggeration. Hooper underplays the "disturbance" by reporting it in the passive voice: "Early in May of the year of grace— and excessive bank issues—1836, the Creek war was discovered to have broken out." Despite a few fatalities in Tallapoosa, the event in his hands is largely a theatrical lark exposing human foolishness and cowardice among the white population. Hooper writes that a large number of citizens throughout the state were "excessively frightened": "Consternation seized all! 'Shrieks inhuman' rent the air! . . . The yeomanry of the country— those to whom, as we are annually told, the nation looks with confidence in all her perils—packed up their carts and wagons, and 'incontinently' departed for more peaceful regions!" (*SS*, 82–83).

Even in the private writing, Indian "scares" often elicit anecdotes about terrorized whites, many of them wry memorials to settler determination and courage. Anne Royall, writing from Huntsville in 1822, passed on to her correspondent "an amusing anecdote" from earlier incidents involving the Creeks in Alabama, in which a "mischievous ill disposed" jokester spread the word that a large body of Creeks was within a day's march. The news struck panic:

> Some left their calves fastened up in the pens, and some their horses in the stable, some their horses in the plow; most of them taking their flight on foot. . . . One man took another man's child, and left his own. . . . Some of the women mistook other men for their husbands, and some husbands mistook other men's wives for theirs. One stout fat woman, though she had horses and slaves in abundance, picked up her youngest child, and taking it in her arms, on foot outstripped every man and horse in company.

Royall concluded her letter by reporting that a thousand people on the road to Nashville were within a day's journey "before they were undeceived." There was not, she wryly noted, a single "hostile Indian within an hundred miles."[17] In farce, false alarms are always occasions for

16. J. Marion Sims, *The Story of My Life*, ed. H. Marion-Sims (New York, 1884), 380–81.
17. Anne Royall, *Letters from Alabama, 1817–1822* (1830; reprint, ed. Lucille Griffith, University: University of Alabama Press, 1969), 243–44.

dramatizing human cowardice, and Royall's letter reflects the visual choreographing of the theater.

By Hooper's time the Creek threat was sporadic, recalled in the luxury of memory in the circles of tale-swapping settlers and the mechanics of stage farce among the humorists, who cast the danger of Indian predations in the same key as the ferocity of raftsmen. Hooper's mode is unremitting buffoonery, contrasting sharply with that of Green Beauchamp, one of the original settlers of Barbour County, two counties south of Hooper's Tallapoosa. Writing thirty-seven years after "our Indian troubles," Beauchamp remembers "Sunday, 16th May, 1836," when Methodist services at New Hope Church were interrupted by a runner who "bawled out in a startling voice" that one community had been burned and "the whole country would be overrun by Indians in a very short time." The large congregation scattered, and by one o'clock a hundred men had assembled "to defend the place." Beauchamp ends his account with: "No Indians made their appearance." The title of his sketch, "A Stampede in a Church," has its own comic resonances, but the author, here as elsewhere in his reminiscences, is mostly intent on clarifying local pioneer history, details of which were already in dispute in 1873. At only one point does he attempt to exploit the comedy of the disrupted service: "the crowd did not stand on the order of going, but got out like hornets from [a] hornet's nest."[18] Unlike Hooper, Beauchamp finds nothing amusing about New Hope's popular preacher having to vacate his pulpit. The humorist, on the other hand, with no urgency to be a clarifying chronicler, makes the most of his preacher, "the Reverend Mr. Snufflenosey," who futilely begs the congregation for a horse before "dash[ing] off precipitately afoot"—ahead of "fifty frightened women" (*SS*, 84).

Perhaps more than any of his fellow humorists, however, Hooper was conscientiously alert to the plight of the dispossessed Creeks. For the most part, Indians are merely a topic in his writing, not figures to be either admired or condemned. In only one segment does he drop the satiric evenhandedness of his persona to excoriate in his own voice a southwestern type, the land speculator. In a little inset story, Hooper relates the hoodwinking of "Sky-chief," a stubborn old Creek who refuses either to sell his land or to be "contaminated" in any way by consorting with the whites. His resolve weakens when one Eggleston, a partner in the Columbus Land Company, declares his love for the chief's daughter

18. Green Beauchamp, "Early Chronicles of Barbour County," *Alabama Historical Quarterly* 33 (1971): 61–62.

and marries her with her father's blessing. Once Eggleston has persuaded the old man to "certify" the land to him, he deserts his wife and the tribe. This event (which may or may not be fictional) inspires Hooper to pen an unusual diatribe against all land speculators, "from whose fangs there was no final escape!" He exults in the subsequent bad fortune of the wily tricksters in a remarkably candid paragraph that merits quotation for its very rarity:

> And where are these speculators NOW?—those lords of the soil!—the men of dollars—the fortune-makers who bought with hundreds what was worth thousands!—they to whom every revolution of the sun brought a reduplication of their wealth! Where are they, and what are they, now! They have been smitten by the hand of retributive justice! The curse of their victims has fastened upon them, and nine out of ten are houseless, outcast, bankrupt! In the flitting of ten years, the larger portion have lost money, lands, character, every thing! And the few who still retain somewhat of their once lordly possessions, mark its steady, unaccountable diminution, and strive vainly to avert their irresistible fate—an old age of shame and beggary. They are cursed, all of them—blighted, root and trunk and limb! The Creek is avenged! (*SS*, 69–70)

Writing in 1845, Hooper chooses to ascribe the ruination of speculators not to the Panic of 1837 and the general economic collapse, but to "retributive justice" occasioned by a Creek curse.

No other passage in all of Southwest humor is equal to the intensity of this one paragraph of moral outrage tucked into the satiric account of the niggling Simon Suggs. Moreover, the authorial censure carries a touch of wish fulfillment. Although the 1837 crash reduced the profits of venturesome capitalists, there is little historical evidence that as a class they were damaged as thoroughly as Hooper depicts. "Speculation" throughout the region was for a time a political shibboleth that dissuaded some ambitious men from seeking elective careers in government, but clever operators managed to overcome the taint. As one historian has noted, speculation in itself was never sufficient "to make a man unpopular in the community where he practiced it."[19]

19. Mary Elizabeth Young, *Redskins, Ruffleshirts, and Rednecks: Indian Allotments in Alabama and Mississippi* (Norman: University of Oklahoma Press, 1961), 169–70. Simon's schemes are picayune even compared to those of his fictional son, as imagined by Hooper's admirer Joseph G. Baldwin in one of his *Flush Times* sketches. Though his father made "Captain," Simon Jr. gets to be called "Colonel" for his dealings with the Choctaws. More ambitious than his father, the son wins a spare law license in a

The great white paternalism of federal involvement was institutional- ized in 1824 when Congress established the Bureau of Indian Affairs as the arm of a government committed, at least for a time, to the integration of Native Americans into general society. Ironically, in light of its subse- quent history of mismanagement and corruption, the bureau's mission was educative: to teach English, Christianity, and (through the ambigu- ous system of reservations) citizenship. Earlier "intercourse acts" had sought to regulate treaty-making, trade, and commerce between the races to discourage white swindling, but federal wardship over the Indians vacillated generally between protectionism and exploitation— one mark of the nation's divided sentiments on the issue. What remained consistent was the lurking faith that removing the Indians from their own lands was a compassionate directive that finally had little to do with political policy or even presidential decree.

Indian-hating aside, the popular attitude toward official relations with Native Americans was a measured combination of humane regret at the dispossession of the Indian and, with more than a touch of determinism, resignation to its inevitability. Yes, the white race had abetted the de- grading of the red man, but in the rule of superior succession, civilization would have its way. Whether presented in positive or negative terms, the Indian comes across in the writing of the period as, in one critic's words, "a creature burdened with such a timeless identity that his very im- mutability spelled his doom."[20] As in most matters ideological, the hu- morists steered a moderate course. Neither the heroizing impulse nor the residual demonizing of the "savage" has much currency in their work. As genial wits they correctly saw that the larger national questions of as- similation or segregation lay beyond their purview. The settlement process in the Old Southwest had eradicated the practical problem of Indian hostility. Long historical memory ensured, however, that for the race generally the image of threat was emotionally prior to sympathy; and for the humorists, as with most Americans, the Removal itself, so conspicuous in its operation, proceeded abstractly, a "generalized

---

faro game, migrates to Arkansas, and becomes an expert in "criminal practice." Elected solicitor for the "Rackensack district," he is appointed agent for Choctaw land settle- ments and marries the daughter of a distinguished "prophet and warrior, and head- man" in the territory. "Simon Suggs, Jr., Esq.: A Legal Biography" (*FT*, 114–41) is funny because Baldwin shows how Suggsian family traits finally flower into success, but part of the humor lies in the parallelism of Baldwin's own candid attraction to the "legal Utopia" of Alabama in 1836 and young Suggs's admiration of litigation-rich Arkansas in 1852.

20. Wai Chee Dimock, "Melville's Empire," *Raritan* 7 (1987): 109.

process" divorced from "human control and human reality."[21] If not solved, the problem had at least shifted, and was now the concern of white settlers west of the Mississippi.

ii.

Several years ago a fellow southerner whose specialty is nineteenth-century folklore observed that the antebellum South (and most of the postbellum as well) was comfortable with only two ethnic groups: Native Americans and African Americans. Aside from the sanguine *comfortable,* the statement sounds about right. But to whites in the Old Southwest during the settlement period even red and black faces were discrepant. For a long time thereafter, these groups were the only people of color, indeed the only "alien" ethnic groups, to disturb southerners' image of themselves as members of a coherent culture, one whose traditions and values, modified by strains of mostly British stock, would continue without much dilution until at least World War I.[22] The two ethnic minorities that dominated the region's antebellum history were always placed outside the culture that its dominant population called home. The historical irony is stark: what was racially alien was, in one instance, as old as the majority culture and, in the other, older. As the rest of the nation became a complex of all kinds of civilizations, the antebellum South depicted itself in austere terms: civilization against savagery. In that perspective, Native Americans and African Americans were different orders of otherness. The two races had disparate histories of contact, and their subjugation followed dissimilar patterns. Yet both groups were preserved as functions of the necessary Other—the source of legend and entertainment, threat and fear. F. N. Boney has observed that white attitudes fell easily into a formula: "Good Indian=Long-Gone Indian, Good Negro=Sambo Slave." Joseph B. Cobb, the sometime humorist, lumped both "alien" races into the same category, but made a distinction: Indians were more degraded than black slaves, "noted for cowardice, and craft, and meanness

21. Michael Paul Rogin, *Fathers and Children: Andrew Jackson and the Subjugation of the American Indian* (New York: Knopf, 1975), 171, 247–48.

22. Thomas D. Clark and John D. W. Guice, *The Old Southwest, 1795–1830: Frontiers in Conflict* (Norman: University of Oklahoma Press, 1996), 169. A brief summary of immigration patterns can be found in *Encyclopedia of Southern Culture,* ed. Charles Reagan Wilson and William Ferris (Chapel Hill: University of North Carolina Press, 1989), 541–42.

of every description." What is to be remarked in the writing of the humorists, however, is the tangential presence of both minorities. We see not merely the absence of strategies for reconciling national ideals and social practice in the matter of race, but also a determined refusal to recognize the problem.[23]

One of the hopeful pieties in early national policy had been an extravagant expectation that, over time, the Indian would be assimilated into American civilization. From Davy Crockett to George Washington Harris, however, as for most writers, the Indian remained the Other. The Removal was a watershed in the relationship of white Americans and their red predecessors. Although it was a national issue widely debated, after 1832 the subject was rarely front-page news in the Old Southwest. The humorists largely ignored what most white settlers regarded as an uncomfortable problem that had finally been solved. The persistent remnants, those individual Indians who for various reasons lingered on in uneasy coexistence with the dominant whites, are a felt presence in some of the sketches; but except in the work of Thorpe and Hooper, as we have seen, they never function as figures of action. It might be noted that the characteristic "traits" of the Indian—violence, undependability, hostility, and a slavish devotion to his own atavistic lore and habits—resemble those of the backwoodsman as some contemporaries depicted him. If many of the authors confidently presumed the backwoodsman would eventually merge into the general population, they never show such confidence about the red man.

The humorists dealt with racial minorities largely by acceptance and evasion: accepting the destiny of the Indian as a *fait accompli*, as unalterable history; and evading the moral thorniness of slavery as a problem whose solution was yet to be determined in a future that was still unreckoned.

In contrast, the Yankee brahmin James Russell Lowell, a well-known enemy of slavery, had no recourse to elaborate strategies of negotiation for what he saw as the motive for the Mexican War. For all his success

23. F. N. Boney, "The Ante-Bellum Elite," in *Red, White, and Black: Symposium on Indians in the Old South*, ed. Charles M. Hudson (Athens: University of Georgia Press, 1984), 90; Joseph B. Cobb, *Mississippi Scenes; or, Sketches of Southern and Western Life and Adventure, Humorous, Satirical, and Descriptive* (Philadelphia, 1851), 177. Philip D. Beidler suggests that in their humorous texts Baldwin and Hooper tended "to sublimate racial guilt out of slavery and into contemplation of the injustice done native tribes." *First Books: The Printed Word and Cultural Formation in Early Alabama* (Tuscaloosa: University of Alabama Press, 1999), 100–101. See also Johanna Nicol Shields, "A Social History of Antebellum Alabama Writers," *Alabama Review* 42 (July 1989): 163–91.

with the dialects and idioms of New England in *The Biglow Papers*, Lowell was never seen as a humorist in the popular sense, nor did he see himself as such. He was in fact both a wit and a humorist, but he was a resolutely high-minded author before he was either.[24] Even the best of the humorists were never mainstream, just as their texts were never canonical. As amateurs, they were not noticeably burdened by the ethical responsibilities that many of their serious contemporaries took on as (in Mark Twain's phrase) "teachers of the great public."[25] The humorists' refusal to make much of nineteenth-century racism in their work is no doubt a comment on these authors' easy affinity with the region's white elite; but, as one scholar has shown, even canonical authors who address race as an ethical issue betray enough unease to make their narrative resolutions less than resolute. Forrest Robinson asserts that *The Last of the Mohicans* and *Adventures of Huckleberry Finn* are texts that enact all the contradictions implicit in the gap between national ideals and social practice. Cooper and Twain composed strategic resolutions that wobble between defense of the social construct and criticism of its inadequacies. Moreover, the enthusiasm of their first readers suggests that their contradictory positions caught the spirit of the age. If both creators and consumers of these texts affirmed their faith in freedom and justice (openly esteeming innocence and humility), they also upheld the priorities of civilized order and the necessary rights to execute them, thus tolerating the "abuses of civilization and its power."[26]

What is missing in the humorous sketches, with their only glancing acknowledgment of African Americans and Native Americans, is the pressure of "deeply divided affiliations and loyalties."[27] Just as it tolerates considerable disorder without authorial intervention, so this writing

24. See the excellent introduction to *James Russell Lowell's* The Biglow Papers *(First Series): A Critical Edition*, ed. Thomas Wortham (DeKalb: Northern Illinois University Press, 1977).

25. Being such a teacher did not, of course, prevent Twain from voicing his own hostility to Indians—as we see in the character of Injun Joe in *The Adventures of Tom Sawyer*. The tenderfoot persona of *Roughing It* drolly casts himself "an Indian worshiper" because of Cooper's fiction, but with some investigation into that "mellow moonshine of romance" he realizes the "truth": the Goshoots are "treacherous, filthy and repulsive," descendants (alternately) of the gorilla, kangaroo, or Norway rat. See chap. 19 of *Roughing It*, ed. Franklin R. Rogers and Paul Baender, vol. 2 of *The Works of Mark Twain* (Berkeley and Los Angeles: University of California Press, 1972).

26. Forrest G. Robinson, *Having It Both Ways: Self-Subversion in Western Popular Classics* (Albuquerque: University of New Mexico Press, 1993), 3, 15. See also his *Bad Faith: The Dynamics of Deception in Mark Twain's America* (Cambridge, MA: Harvard University Press, 1986).

27. Robinson, *Having It Both Ways*, 139.

bypasses narrative situations in which the authors would find themselves in a dilemma, faced with supporting the power arrangements of society while exploring their failure to uphold justice. These authors only rarely offered themselves as social and moral critics, even of the subversive kind. Harris and Noland, whose humorous texts are the most politically inflected, rarely wavered in the primary purpose of their sketches—to amuse. Like most Anglo settlers in the region, the authors may have been "comfortable" with blacks, but, like most of their countrymen, they gave no thought to the possible absorption of the race into the dominant culture. If the Indian is a recessive figure in the humor, it is in part because the Removal effectively historicized the issue. The African American, however, a more persistent presence in the authors' world, had yet to be historicized. Although their world was a de facto biracial society, the humorists rarely identified slavery as an institution either to be defended or criticized. In the same era that the minstrel show flourished, real African Americans in the Old Southwest are seldom sources of ethnic humor in the newspaper sketches. Slaves appear as part of a social matrix, another condition of the authors' world, like climate and geography.[28]

In Longstreet's retrospective Georgia, the conduct of race relations is dominated by what was, by 1835, old-fashioned protocol—not the inflammatory posture of defense, but the cultural habit of whites who see themselves as guardians of their charges. Though their discreet privacies occasionally frustrate the paternalistic curiosity of both narrators in *Georgia Scenes*, slaves are never the butts of jokesters. They are not even subjects in the narratives. As the author's stand-ins, Lyman Hall and Abraham Baldwin display all the easy grace and unapologetic condescension of a favored class whose style in stewardship of a system long in place is more insouciant than passionate. Having no substantial roles to play and few speaking lines, blacks are more ambiance than they are characters. None of Longstreet's male characters, for example, bother themselves with the disciplining of slaves. That regulatory task, when it occurs, falls to Georgia matrons, and such matrons are favorite targets of the author's satire; they are depicted as imperious and shallow mistresses whose threats to their uncomprehending house servants are abusive and perfunctory. Those domestics with names—Flora, Rose, Clary, Aaron—are otherwise undifferentiated beyond their fidelity and long-suffering patience.

28. The walk-on African American in John Gorman Barr's "Relief for Ireland!" (1857) is not a slave but a free black in Tuscaloosa, who nevertheless suffers the community's easy label of thief when town jokesters execute a prank on an Irish shoemaker (*RT*, 143–61).

Of the two narrators, Baldwin, the delineator of domestic sketches, finds several occasions to arraign matrons of the "better sort" for being inconsistent, fickle custodians. Some are merely inept and irrational, like Mrs. Slang of "The Mother and Her Child," who prefers to assume that her irritable baby is crying because his black nurse has spitefully hurt him.

> "You, Rose, what have you done to this child? You little hussy you, if you don't tell me how you hurt him I'll whip you as long as I can find you."
>
> "Missis I 'cla' I never done noth'n' 't all to him. I was jis sett'n' down da by Miss Nancy's bu—"
>
> "If you say 'Miss Nancy's bureau' to me again I'll stuff Miss Nancy's bureau down your throat, you little lying slut. I'm just as sure you've hurt him, as if I'd seen you. How did you hurt him?"
>
> Here Rose was reduced to a *non plus*; for, upon peril of having a bureau stuffed down her throat, she dare not repeat the oft told tale, and she knew no other. She therefore stood mute. (*GS*, 90)

Others, like Evelina of "The 'Charming Creature,' as a Wife," are so indulgent of their servants that the household becomes a chaos. This sketch is structured as an unamusing morality tale that traces the consequences of the obsession of the narrator's lawyer nephew, George Baldwin, with a vain young woman, the "only child of a wealthy, unlettered merchant" who has learned from her parents "what a perfect beauty she was." The marriage is a disaster; the young husband loses his energy and purpose and, though once a promising lawyer, dies a drunkard. The narrator, with considerable emphasis, mounts his case against the "charming creature" by measuring her lax superintendence of the house servants against that of the hero's mother, who is clearly the paradigm of female white authority:

> Every thing under her care went on with perfect system. To each servant was allotted his or her respective duties, and to each was assigned the time in which those duties were to be performed. . . . Her children were permitted to give no orders to servants but through her, until they reached the age at which they were capable of regulating their orders by her rules. She laid no plants to detect her servants in theft, but . . . saw that they were well provided with every thing they needed, and she indulged them in recreations when she could. (*GS*, 54–55)

Mother Baldwin has Longstreet's blessing as well as his narrator's.

A few nondomestic blacks, mostly musicians and racetrack employees, show up in *Georgia Scenes*. In "The Dance" Abraham Baldwin pays tribute to Bill Porter, "a negro fellow of much harmless wit and humor" known through the state for his skill with the violin, and in "The Ball" he is impressed by a hired sextet, "all blacks, but neatly dressed." In "The Turf," Hall's experience with a "pert little blackamoor" recalls the ancient comedic device of the wily servant who knows more than his master. Eager to learn the names of the owners and the pedigrees of the horses entered in competition, Hall is foiled by an uncooperative "aged black" whose countenance plainly says that he has "many deep things shut up in his brain, which the world had long been trying to pry into, in vain." But the narrator's luck improves with the appearance of a black youngster, who, armed with "all the secrets of the turf," tells Hall what he wants to know, and considerably more, for "twelve and a half cents" (*GS*, 7, 84, 104–5).

As in so many aspects of Southwest humor, *Georgia Scenes* is the model text for the treatments of race that follow. The letters of William Tappan Thompson's Major Jones assume without emphasis the planter as humane master. In Pineville, racial relations, though formally dictated by hierarchy, proceed casually. As a modest planter, Joseph Jones runs his operation with common sense, neighborliness, and an understated appreciation of his responsibilities. What the young planter takes for granted in Middle Georgia, however, is severely tested when his creator sends him north to expand his cultural horizons. In almost every urban site, Major Jones is insulted by impertinent white ethnic workers (mostly Irish), but he is primarily affronted by free blacks, who offend by not being subservient. As a southern journalist who was born and educated north of the Ohio River, Thompson understood how the psychological dynamics of northern racial relations would assault the comfortable complacency of southern planters, especially those as naive as Joseph Jones.[29] The benevolent hero is especially hurt, puzzled, and angered by the independent, undependent behavior of free blacks.

Two black servants, Sol and Abe, frequently accompany Alexander McNutt's Jim and Chunkey on their hunts, primarily to make camp and cook, though as characters they are presences only. There are house servants as well in sketches by Joseph Field (who also confirms the historical record that black and white steamboat hands worked side by side), and a servant in John S. Robb's "Fun with a Bar" leads a chorus of laughter from onlookers who witness Dan Elkhorn's drunken sousing when

29. See Carl R. Osthaus, "From the Old South to the New South: The Editorial Career of William Tappan Thompson of the *Savannah Morning News*," *Southern Quarterly* 14 (1976): 237–60. Major Jones's experiences with northern blacks are discussed in more detail in chap. 13.

his canoe overturns during some energetic courting (Cohen, 179–84). When on a boat trip Fenton Noland's Dan Looney is accused by a towns-man on the Illinois side of being "one of them nigger-drivers," he decides to fight the man because the town sports a "disunion" flag; Looney con-cludes that the "abolitioners" are among those who talk "too sassy . . . about dividin' these United States" (*PW*, 208–9).

Unlike the ethnic pieces of the northeastern stage and press, where, as dependable sources of humor, the Negro was as prominent as the Yankee, the Jew, and the Irishman, in the southwestern sketches African Amer-icans are never major players. As we shall see, in only one of the primary humorists of the Old Southwest—Henry Clay Lewis (and in only a hand-ful of his pieces)—does the region's most conspicuous ethnic group fig-ure prominently. In the others they recede into the background as an assumed but unstressed thread in the social fabric. In planter culture, blacks had the anomalous distinction of being both Other and family. Historically the economics of slavery required dominant whites to do-mesticate an alien race, simultaneously set apart because of their skin and incorporated into the family because of their value as property. Such a code, permeating all classes, may have been conceptually contradic-tory, but in its curious way it largely removed African Americans as sub-ject matter appropriate to Southwestern humor.

Why this should have been so is not entirely clear. Like most Amer-icans of the time, planter families considered slave talk and slave logic amusing—occasions for personal diversion. In a society structured liter-ally in black and white, the performances of individual slaves as sources of fun were appreciated largely within the family. The minor role played by blacks in the newspaper humor follows the social reality of plantation slaves: however crucial to the economy, slaves in their several capacities as field hands, maids, cooks, nurses, and general servants were also un-seen—a psychological phenomenon that a later writer would trope as *in-visible*. As both Other and family, the slave was a primary part of the planter's demonstrated mastery.[30]

Although William T. Porter's disapproval of politics in the humor of the *Spirit of the Times* is usually taken as a ban against mutual sniping of Democrats and Whigs, it silently attests to the jovial editor's fear of getting his paper involved in the era's most heated issue. We have no evidence that the contributors from the Southwest chafed under this restriction.

---

30. Bertram Wyatt-Brown, *Honor and Violence in the Old South* (New York: Oxford, 1986), ix.

They may well have felt that the southern position on race was sufficiently covered in the voluminous discourse in books, orations, and pamphlets explicitly ideological. And while Porter is the best-known editor who officially discouraged mixing humor and politics, most of the southern editors also preferred to print amusing reports of squatters, local braggarts, hunters, and other marginal whites over those featuring comic slaves. Even though the humorous authors generally thought of themselves in a loose alliance with the planter class, their chief subject continued to be the yeomanry. In that context, the scarcity of blacks faithfully mirrors their world.

Unique in his use of slaves in the lower South, Henry Clay Lewis not only recognized the inescapable presence of blacks in his bayou world, but also tapped generously into the deep reservoir of ordinary racism that most of his fellow humorists avoided. In one of his least grotesque sketches, "Cupping on the Sternum," Lewis allows a black slave to function like the white Kentuckian who, in another sketch, needs a tooth pulled, or like the rehearsing gouger in Longstreet's "Georgia Theatrics"—as a verbal opponent in a test of wills with the narrator. A young intern acts on instructions to treat the "Negro girl Chaney," suffering from inflammation of the lungs, by cupping her "very freely over the *sternum.*" Having not yet taken a course in anatomy, the ignorant intern assumes *sternum* to mean *buttocks.* Even Chaney knows that her lungs won't be helped by having her buttocks cupped (a nineteenth-century procedure to draw fluids by scarification with a partial vacuum glass). Despite her reasonable protests, the arrogant know-it-all performs the procedure. When he learns of his mistake, he is embarrassed, not by the unnecessary pain and humiliation visited on the patient, but by not knowing that his preceptor had used the Greek word for *breastbone.* Chaney remains the humiliated patient whose girth is a source of fun. "Just imagine," writes the intern, "a butcher's block five feet long and four feet through at the butt converted into a fat bouncing Negro wench"; in the cupping "no blood flowed, nothing but grease, which trickled out slowly like molasses out of a worm hole." Because this episode is framed by the doctor as inept professional, the early reader would have been less alert to the racism that turns patient into victim than to the narrator's verbal levity in the cruel punning at the end. The cups, he writes, "were too in*fatu*ated to draw blood" (Cohen, 417–18).

Southwest humor abounds in pranks of extreme cruelty—to horses, dogs, ganders, pigs, Kentuckians, Millerites, Mormons, salesmen—and the evidence suggests that the most graphic examples of physical mayhem were popular *because* they were extreme. By common agreement, the most visceral scenes are those staged by George Washington Harris—not those in which other humans suffer, but those in which animals endure casual torture and dismemberment, as we see in the exploding foxhound in "Sut Lovingood at Bull's Gap": the tail comes down on Sut's hat, the head rolls down the hill, the forelegs continue "runnin moshuns" fifty feet in the air, the innards hang "in links" on the cabin chimney, and the "paunch cum down permiscusly like rain" (*HT*, 149–50). But because they focus on humans, the most outrageous examples in the humor occur in Lewis's dark sketches. As a matter of course, this author echoes the planters' frequently aired complaints about their slaves' laziness and irresponsibility and the corpulence of their ailing females, most of whom are thought to be "malingering." Though some of the blacks in the swamp doctor's account are uncharacterized, they most often are described with almost gothic intensity: gross, malformed, crippled, and evil—like semi-human emanations from the miasmic bayous of their creator's swamp world.[31]

iii.

In one respect, because they were so clear-cut, "natural," or "traditional," white attitudes toward African Americans were rarely ambiguous in the writing from the Old Southwest. There is, however, yet another wrinkle in the antebellum "Indian problem." The agrarian bias at least provided a *place* for black slaves, inhumane as it was. Indians, however, had no place. For the colonists the nomadism of the Indians had been a quasi-theological problem; it was also, more practically, a source of ordinary anxiety for succeeding generations of settlers: *where would the marauding heathen turn up next?*

Somewhere—everywhere, in vast and "unpeopled" expanses—wandered numerous tribes for whom the European idea of *patria* was irrelevant. Without man-made structures, *patria* could not exist. In the iconography of the moderns, the stand and the crossroads store that succeeded it stood in opposition to pathless woods. Even as a crude beginning, a human structure on a road, as much as a settler's cabin in sight of the road,

31. The most astute analysis of the darker side of Southwest humor remains Alan Henry Rose's *Demonic Vision: Racist Fantasy and Southern Fiction* (Hamden, CT: Archon, 1976). See also Edward Watts, "In the Midst of a Noisome Swamp: The Landscape of Henry Clay Lewis," *Southern Literary Journal* 22 (1990): 119–28.

was a harbinger of civilization, a material token of white presence super-imposed on the natural scene of nomadic natives. The term *pathless woods* was topographical nonsense—Indians throughout the southwestern woods rather famously made paths, most of them so directionally useful that subsequent roads of their white successors followed them. But the image that carried over from colonial days still suggested the woods as a "space of circulation" that could not be controlled like the channeled certainty of roads.[32]

Contrary to evidence in parts of the Southwest, the argument for the Removal turned on the conviction that the red race had neither the desire nor the skill to "settle down," to turn the lands they nominally claimed into productive fields. The complaint is suggestive of the Lord's own in the parable of the coins. Passive preservation, useless as a tool for self-betterment, was seen as clearly inferior to ambitious investment. A Maine migrant to Arkansas in 1825, condemning the "wretched and squalid be-ings" who had failed to cultivate the fertile lands they lived on, bluntly concluded that "the advancement of civilization, and the steady and pro-gressive extermination of the Aborigines, are two chains closely linked."[33] To possess a country was to conquer the wilderness. The Indians had not done so.

More disturbingly, however, many recalcitrant whites were not doing it, either.

By the time of the humorists, the white (re)settlement of the Old South-west was not complete, but the monocultural pattern of the process was already fixed. Race, the sine qua non for the society in the making, could be handled in certain time-sanctioned and straightforward ways. Unlike Indians and Negroes, even the most lubberly whites were regarded as potentially assimilable in a future and progressive order. The majority of the residents were not planters but plain folk, some of whom, however, might become planters within a generation, thus serving almost inciden-tally as models for the new white egalitarianism. Modest success stories featured dirt-poor farmers who, after they had accrued sustainable acre-age by hard work and persistence, became responsible men of their com-munities, founders (for later generations) of pioneering respectability. But what of those hardy types who resisted settlement canons of respon-sibility and respectability?

In the Old Southwest an entire category of unambitious whites became

32. The phrase is Boelhower's in *Through a Glass Darkly*, 61.
33. Franklin Wharton, diary, Edward Clifton Wharton Family Papers, MS 1553, 1575, Louisiana and Lower Mississippi Valley Collections, Louisiana State University Libraries, Baton Rouge.

even more irksome than the Indians. White leadership followed familiar cultural attitudes, endorsing permissible ways to handle the intractable fact of race: removal of the Indian, domestication of the African American into family. When the problem concerned their own kind, however, policy makers faced a dilemma. To fit the idealistic self-image of the Republic, the Founders were credited with having eliminated social rank and economic status as relevant categories—they had unsanctioned, as it were, the reality of class distinctions. But if one's own race was as refractory as that of the Indian, and if marginal whites projected unsettling pictures of restlessness and complacency, were they not as disruptive of the agrarian mission as the Indians? It was, like the Indian question, a dilemma with a long history.

In running the dividing line between Virginia and North Carolina in 1728, William Byrd observed wryly that the more savage Carolinians watched the surveying apprehensively "lest their Lands Should be taken into Virginia," where they would be forced to submit to "some Sort of Order and Government; whereas, in N. Carolina, every One does what seems best in his own Eyes."[34] Byrd's model for human order was a hierarchical (and idealized) Virginia, with its respect for economy, government, and religion—precisely those virtues that light-bearers would continue to bring to the southern frontier, and the same ones that for many years backwoodsmen would continue to resist. Like the Puritans before him, Timothy Dwight was a light-bearer in his own New England, chastising restless white men who rushed from civilized centers to the remotest margins because they were "too idle; too talkative; too passionate; too prodigal; and too shiftless" to abide by the restraints of civil order. Even when the "forester" became a "proprietor"—the visible sign of respectability—he was all too eager to sell out and move on because he was unwilling to undertake the "sober industry, and prudent economy, by which his bush pasture might be changed into a farm."[35] Dwight's Connecticut rhetoric is somewhat more measured than Byrd's nearly a century earlier in Virginia, which excoriated the sloth and ignorance of the lubbers. The point is the same.

For Dwight the margins were still the habitat of fallen men, nature

34. William Byrd, *Histories of the Dividing Line betwixt Virginia and North Carolina*, ed. William K. Boyd and Percy G. Adams (New York: Dover, 1967), 74. See also A. James Wohlpart, "The Creation of the Ordered State: William Byrd's (Re)Vision in the *History of the Dividing Line*," *Southern Literary Journal* 25 (1992): 3–18.

35. Quoted in Albert J. von Frank, *The Sacred Game: Provincialism and Frontier Consciousness in American Literature, 1630–1860* (Cambridge: Cambridge University Press, 1985), 50.

unredeemed by steady habits. Cooper's Leatherstocking novels, following John Filson's Daniel Boone story *The Discovery and Settlement of Kentucke* in 1784, suggested the ease with which the wilderness could be conquered, yet the heroic Boone-Bumppo image never quite replaced the earlier anxiety over white degeneration in the wilds. Urbanites were dismayed at discovering pockets of shocking primitivism in the fastnesses south and west of civilized boundaries. The difference between their views of the Indian and the backwoodsman was that the first in some atemporal sense was bereft of civilization, and the second, participating in the customary process of mankind, had of his own accord reversed the movement, sinking *into* barbarism *out of* a civilized state. One English traveler wrote that such "outcasts" in their "disgrace" could be found "on the western frontiers, from Pennsylvania inclusive, to the farthest south." Into the humorists' own era, cultural spokesmen continued to express dismay over such pockets of "anti-culture" in all these "inclusive" hinterlands. The more sanguine among them placed their trust in farms, schools, courts, and churches, which might redeem those "'primitive,' nonconforming whites who seemed to live like Indians."[36]

The humorous authors were not light-bearers in the manner of Byrd, Dwight, and governmental promoters of agrarian culture. For all their general agreement with the agents of order, they betray in their sketches little pedagogical urgency about discord. The unconforming and restless "proprietors" usually manage to divert and amuse them. In time, it appeared, the problem would presumably take care of itself, but a certain tautology tended to fray the dominant long-term view the humorists shared: backwoodsmen would no longer be marginal when the region no longer had a backwoods. In their own way the humorists contributed to the cultural work of isolating for close inspection the radical individualism of the peripheries. If the Indians in the "pathless woods" had been demonized even after they established permanent settlements, the backwoods people in crossroads and hamlets were exoticized as a harmless Other that could be regarded with benevolent curiosity because, unlike the threatening Other, they were redeemable, even at their stage of hu-

---

36. Rodger Cunningham, *Apples on the Flood: The Southern Mountain Experience* (Knoxville: University of Tennessee Press, 1987), 86–87. See also Perry Miller, *Roger Williams: His Contribution to the American Tradition* (New York: Atheneum, 1962), 201; David Brion Davis, *Antebellum American Culture: An Interpretive Anthology* (Lexington, MA: D. C. Heath, 1979), 253–54; Thomas D. Clark, "The Piney Woods and the Cutting Edge of the Lingering Southern Frontier," in *Mississippi's Piney Woods: A Human Perspective,* ed. Noel Polk (Jackson: University Press of Mississippi, 1986), 61.

man progress. What the new states needed was the bracing order of institutions to turn all white members of society into earnest supporters of the national mission, to make backwoodsmen more amenable to civilizing norms. But policy makers, prodded by speculators and planters, could not afford the luxury of the long view. How to assimilate the marginal whites, how to inspirit them with the self-evident values of an efficient agrarian economy, were tiresome issues for a political leadership that suspected that, at bottom, sweet reasonableness was a gambit unlikely to appeal to men so balky, so contrarian, even when their own self-interest was at stake.

Many early backwoodsmen may have conventionally viewed the Indian as their enemy, but politicians tended to link both groups as a common deterrent to orderly society. Both were renegade populations that held too little respect for cartographical boundaries, pursuing their interests beyond and despite proclamations, decrees, treaties, and land grants. Both embraced a nomadic lifestyle that spurned the virtues considered necessary to the planting of outposts in the wilderness, without which nature was an inappropriate milieu not merely for the "white Indians," but for all whites who ventured into it.

Botanizing near the confluence of the Ohio and Mississippi Rivers in 1818, Thomas Nuttall linked Indian and backwoodsman in almost synonymous terms: the "primeval solitude" of the wilderness had been penetrated only "by the wandering hunter, and the roaming savage." In that same year, a U.S. congressman voiced a widespread impatience with the Indian problem when he declared that the "sons of the forest" had only two options—"be moralized or exterminated." We hear an ominous echo of that sentiment nearly a century later in a newspaper that recommended a solution to feuding in the Virginia backwoods: "The majority of mountain people are unprincipled ruffians" for whom there are only two remedies: "education or extermination." The editorial pointedly concluded: "Mountaineers, like the red Indian, must learn this lesson."[37] By settlement standards the anti-agrarianism of backwoods hunters and herdsmen—and squatters who wanted to remain squatters—merged effortlessly into a class generally perceived as primitive, irresponsible, and lazy. Even when squatters became "proper farmers," they tended to resist necessary diligence, reluctant to curb their independence and liberty

37. Thomas Nuttall, *A Journal of Travels into the Arkansas Territory during the Year 1819* (1821; reprint, ed. Savoie Lottinville, Norman: University of Oklahoma Press, 1980), 48; Cunningham, *Apples on the Flood*, 109–10.

of movement for the beneficial values thought necessary to advance a modern society.

The mobility of ordinary citizens had always struck foreign visitors as an assertion of the radical liberty of democracy. For national leaders looking toward stability and economic prosperity, that kind of restlessness undermined progress. Because it showed no interest in transforming the wilderness into something else, the hunting culture, red or white, was antithetical to either town-building or plantation-making. A nomadic way of life was not settlement but primitive gratification of immediate desires.

iv.

One of the commonplaces about the settlement period in the Old Southwest is the homogeneousness of its new residents.[38] Ethnic diversity was always greater in the parallel setting of the Old Northwest, although neither of the rapidly expanding regions could match the urban Northeast for the eclectic mix of races, religions, and nationalities. From the perspective of William Henry Milburn in 1860, that had been all for the good. This commentator attributed to Providence the making of settlements by "the proper and distinctive Anglo-American forms of worship" prior to the influx of "strangers" so that later "absorption" and "fusing" could occur without conflict.[39] When the narrator of "The Big Bear of Arkansas" refers to the *heterogeneous* steamboat passengers, it is clearly a relative term, even in Thorpe's experience. To equate diversity on the Mississippi with Wolvereens, Suckers, Hoosiers, and half-horse half-alligators is not quite the heterogeneousness that Thorpe himself, even in 1841, would find in New York City, to which as a northeasterner he periodically repaired. The spectacle of Major Jones in New York, Philadelphia, and Boston struggling to cope with dialects and manners alien to his sensibil-

38. The census of 1820 showed that only about 12,000 unnaturalized foreigners lived in the South, while more than triple that figure lived in the North. Charles S. Sydnor, *The Development of Southern Sectionalism, 1819–1848* (Baton Rouge: Louisiana State University Press, 1948), 3. By midcentury nearly half of the population in Alabama, Mississippi, and Louisiana was born outside those states; only about 80,000 foreign-born lived in these three states, three-fourths of them in Louisiana. Frederick Jackson Turner, *The United States 1830–1850: The Nation and Its Sections* (1935; reprint, Gloucester, MA: Peter Smith, 1958), 214.

39. William Henry Milburn, *The Pioneers, Preachers, and People of the Mississippi Valley* (New York, 1860), 458.

ity is not merely the conventional comic situation of the naïf in the city. It is also a condensed image that reinforces the makeup of the South as it was developing, a demography of difference that underlay the cultural assumptions of the Longstreet generation of authors.

Most of them were born between 1810 and 1825, and although only a few years separate them from Sam Clemens (born in 1835), that decade or so was significant in shaping the tone, expectations, and even the content of their respective prose. If the condition of authorship changed, so did the nation itself. The assorted humorists took their cue from Crockett and Longstreet, the bear hunter and the judge. Although one was barely literate and the other an educator, they were both shaped by the cultural patterns—language, attitudes, decorum—of the eighteenth-century republic in which they were born. The careers of the humorists, proud moderns all, coincided with an agrarian age already benefiting from, even as it was threatened by, transitional technologies (whose values they enthusiastically embraced). Our greatest humorist flourished in a time and place that saw the nation consolidate itself as a fully modern industrial power (about which he was ambivalent). Although the continuities are clear, Clemens developed an aesthetic that bore fewer and fewer traces of the newspaper sketches that had influenced his early work.

While the Longstreet generation was generally content to remain amateur authors, amusing a popular audience with their "drollery," their great successor was never satisfied with that limited legacy. Travel away from it was one antidote to the complacent homogeneousness of the South—and the provinciality it fostered in Clemens's growing-up years—but it was also a means of countering his popular reputation as a mere "buffoon." Mark Twain became cosmopolitan over a career-long exposure to the same spectrum of national and international types, customs, and culture absorbed less self-consciously by his contemporaries Henry James and William Dean Howells. From the anonymous contributor of "The Dandy Frightening the Squatter" (1852) to the recipient of an Oxford degree (1907), Twain succeeded in turning his imitative role as newspaper humorist into that of professional man of letters. If his southern roots meant that he once matter-of-factly thought of house servants as "niggers," polished experience taught him to expand his thinking: his princely establishment in Hartford was run by a diverse staff of six servants—two African Americans, three Irish, and a German.[40]

40. Justin Kaplan, *Mr. Clemens and Mark Twain: A Biography* (New York: Simon & Schuster, 1966), 182.

Mark Twain was the kind of mesne lord who no doubt extracted private amusement from his employees, and in his writing he occasionally exploited character traits and speech idioms from what his era popularly categorized as ethnic and national types. We can hardly call his humor *ethnic,* however, at least in the way we have come to use the term.

Ethnic humor, the product of a largely urban environment and a disparate population, found its natural venue in the long-settled Northeast, in those cities that Major Jones visits and finds so perplexing. Here newspaper humor, like the popular stage, specialized in eliciting fun from minorities. Jews, Germans, Irishmen, Frenchmen, and African Americans were favorite targets of these sketches, some of which involved casual cruelty and humiliation, and some of which turned on competitive styles of oral wit. Scenarios were regularized through repetition. They ply the stereotype of the wily Jewish merchant caught in the (often unsuccessful) cheating of Christians; they focus on the trading tricks of, say, one Irishman by another, from formulas borrowed from older Yankee tales; they feature African Americans as sparring partners with Anglo types in episodes that turn on malapropisms and mispronunciations.

More than a half-century ago, Simone de Beauvoir observed that the category of the Other is "as primordial as consciousness itself." No group, she wrote, ever sets itself up as the One "without at once setting up the Other over against itself."[41] The machinery of ethnic humor, deriving from the ancient human need to make distinctions between *us* and *them,* energizes much of antebellum popular culture, including the nationwide contributors to Porter's *Spirit of the Times.* That principle channels the impulse of urban humor into a tirelessly circulated round of well-defined stereotypes. Its force, however, is attenuated in the rural population that the Longstreet school celebrated. In the sketches from the Southwest the One/Other opposition functions mostly in shadow versions, when the outsider shows up as an alien incursion into an isolated society. Opposition is mostly intramural—southwesterners never lacked the tribal exercises that made, say, the Devil's Fork superior to Chapel Hill Township (as in the Pete Whetstone letters) or, throughout the writings, the spirited competition in fighting, hunting, horse racing, and courting. One of the curiosities of this humor, conditioned as it is to flourish in a climate of competition, is how its flourishing transpires within so restricted a range of *us-them* relationships.

41. Simone de Beauvoir, *The Second Sex,* trans. H. M. Parshley (New York: Knopf, 1957), xvi–xvii.

In that society, it is as if two clearly delineated groups—Indians and black slaves—had been deprived of their relevance as convenient Other when the majority culture effectively finessed the category. Which is to say that it resolved (at least to its own satisfaction) the issue of difference by extermination and removal in one instance and by familial incorporation in the other. Compared to the historical modes of pacification in resolving such troublesome matters, there is a certain abstract, halfhearted energy in the humor when *difference* is dispersed in a loose collection of types, most of whom serve as emissaries of "the North." The outsiders who occasionally wander into the rustic precincts that the humorists made their own are sometimes encyclopedia salesmen, urban dandies, quirky religionists, Irishmen, or Frenchmen; and though historically he is as much a remnant as the left-behind Indian, the Yankee (still predominantly cast as peddler) had the power to generate animosity as late as Sut Lovingood's experiences of the 1850s.

The level of antagonism toward outsiders, however, is generally subdued, especially in the sketches of the 1830s and 1840s, a slant that may derive from the kind of tolerance that had been necessary in the migration period. In a new country, without a stable base of old residents and their standards, the immediate and tangible anxieties required in the very act of resettling fostered indulgence for all stripes of political and religious creeds, folk habits, eccentricities, and dialects. As in so many other instances, George Washington Harris is a noteworthy exception here. He is one of the earliest writers to sheathe his sketches in the sort of smug xenophobia that came to stand for hamlet culture in the next century, the kind of social notation that would radiate in writing from the South and Midwest. Although he is toughly judgmental of all his fellows, including himself, Sut Lovingood is particularly malicious in his unrestrained scorn for outsiders—Irishmen, New York dandies, Nashville Jews, North Carolinians, Yankee peddlers, and New England women (as well as having a nearly feral rancor toward Abraham Lincoln).

Northeastern schoolteachers came to be common figures in planter homes, tolerated for their pedagogic gifts despite widespread suspicion (after *Uncle Tom's Cabin* in 1852) that they were social do-gooders who harbored racial views identical to Harriet Beecher Stowe's. But in the humor, even abolitionists, the bête noire of southern pamphleteers, are no more than shadow enemies. Miss Charity is a politically ambiguous character in the most interesting sketch about a (suspected) female abolitionist, an inset episode in Joseph G. Baldwin's profile "Samuel Hele, Esq." The lawyer, who holds "great contempt for all prejudices except his own, and was entirely uncramped by other people's opinions or notions, or whims, or fancies, or desires," devises a scheme for ridding the community of a recently arrived Yankee schoolmarm, who presumably has brought south with her advanced ideas about slavery shared by "Mrs. Harriet S——." Though he is mostly an irascible grump, Hele, like many of his fellow professionals, has a knack for extravagant waggery, and the presence of a sentimental abolitionist in his midst stimulates his best parodic performance. With mock earnestness in a teatime chat with Miss Charity, he depicts his town as a typical instance of the hellhole that Yankees had long considered the South. Its "total depravity" includes personal immorality, theft, ignorance, backbiting, whippings, assassinations, and mistreatment and murder of slaves. Hele's performance has the desired effect. Miss Charity books passage the following morning on the northern mail stage (*FT*, 284–303).

Unlike Yankee schoolmarms, who might entertain alien notions about social arrangements, southern females were expected to be docile and subordinate, ceding gracefully the right of place to males upon whom they depended for their own position.[42] Gender orthodoxy made the "separate spheres" doctrine a part of the harmonious order of nature, cutting across class lines. A majority of southern women remained unpedestaled, performing the hearthside and nursery duties expected of them. Rural women joined men in clearing, cultivating, and harvesting; village women, especially in the late antebellum era, worked in cotton mills and shoe factories. Widows frequently assumed the operation of inns, boardinghouses, grist mills, ferries, and other businesses.[43] Only

---

42. A well-balanced account of the image(s) of the southern woman can be found in Anne Goodwyn Jones, "Dixie's Diadem," chap. 1 of *Tomorrow Is Another Day: The Woman Writer in the South, 1859–1936* (Baton Rouge: Louisiana State University Press, 1981). Atypical though she might have been, Mary Boykin Chesnut was, at the outbreak of war, "a woman of discerning intellect and great charm, a woman of strong opinions, strong loves, strong hates, and very little to do that she considered useful." Elisabeth Muhlenfeld, *Mary Boykin Chesnut: A Biography* (Baton Rouge: Louisiana State University Press, 1981), 72. Less celebrated examples of southern women who found much to do that was useful are discussed in a multidisciplinary collection of essays, *Negotiating Boundaries of Southern Womanhood: Dealing with the Powers That Be,* ed. Janet L. Coryell and others (Columbia: University of Missouri Press, 2000).

43. For a midcentury statement of the separate spheres doctrine, see Henry W. Hilliard, *Speeches and Addresses* (New York, 1855), 276–77, 481–96. For a summary of the historic roles of women, see Kenneth R. Johnson, "White Married Women in Antebellum Alabama," *Alabama Review* 43 (1990): 3–17. See also Maxine P. Atkinson and Jacqueline Boles, "The Shaky Pedestal: Southern Ladies Yesterday and Today," *Southern Studies* 24 (1985): 398–400; Anne Firor Scott, *The Southern Lady, From Pedestal to Politics* (Chicago: University of Chicago Press, 1970); and the bibliographical essay by

the lady of the Big House unambiguously occupied the pedestal, a position that some modern feminists tend to fold into the "Other" file. For all the mythic pieties, even the lady was an unlikely Other. Cosseted and idolized, she was a regional treasure in Lost Cause writing, the angel of the Big House exempt from the vulgar cares besetting her menfolk. Purified of rank desire, she was submissive and dignified, but, in a pinch, resourceful and courageous. If southern womanhood was an amplified version of generic Victorian womanhood, the image persisted longer in the Ruined Homeland than elsewhere. The reality of the southern lady was of course always more complex than the image burnished so tirelessly by southern orators, but only in the final decades of the twentieth century did revisionists remind us of just how inhuman the myth had made her—how harsh the constrictiveness demanded by a planter patriarchy and its progeny, and how high the price she had to pay for cultural sanctification.

It is doubtless true, as more than one authority has argued, that gender protocols in the South affected white women of all classes, and that the code of behavior in both rural and village society varied only insignificantly. But, except for bursts of irony, idealization was not the business of the Southwest humorists. In Longstreet the mythic southern lady is glimpsed only in the interstices of narratives about Georgia matrons. The author's judgment of aspiring middle-class village women is considerably fiercer than that of his yeomanry generally. Through his narrator, Abraham Baldwin, Longstreet's contemporary Georgian society is pilloried for its genteel affectations modeled on "European abominations" in fashions, music, dance, parenting, and general taste, which have routed the candor and honesty of old republican values. Most especially he targets the "weakly, sickly, delicate, useless, affected" females who have become models for all American women, not merely Georgians (GS, 43, 6). If Longstreet suggests that the progress of social refinement is a falling away from the franker decencies of an older time, that sentiment is more explicit in the work of the judge's younger friend William Tappan Thompson. Mary Stallins, the inamorata of Thompson's Joseph Jones, is proper in her demeanor, but she shows little interest in subordination. Although in the presence of her suitor she dutifully blushes when her mother uses the word *stockings*, her subsequent behavior is close to that of the crusty

Jacqueline D. Hall and Anne Firor Scott in *Interpreting Southern History: Historiographical Essays in Honor of Sanford W. Higginbotham*, ed. John B. Boles and Evelyn T. Nolen (Baton Rouge: Louisiana State University Press, 1987), 454–509.

old widow. As wife and mother, Mary Stallins acknowledges the conventions of refined southern womanhood, but they never cramp her style.

In the humorists' world the plain-folk woman, without a pedestal to stand on, is freed from the stricter canons of respectability, just like her male consort. By and large the females—ordinary wives, doughty mothers, randy widows, vivacious girls—are forceful, spunky, independent souls pursuing their own ends with the same indifference to mainstream codes of restraint and propriety as the males. Rarely victims, they are equal-opportunity subjects.[44] When William C. Hall's Sally Hooter is possessed by the idea of wearing a bustle (and a roll of sausage must serve the purpose), her comeuppance is a painful dip in a pan of hot mush. Neither the pride of this female nor its resolution has the delicacy of a "charming creature." When other wives, daughters, and widows among the plain folk are caught in postures of pretension—as in sketches by John S. Robb and George Washington Harris, in Kittrell J. Warren's pieces about Billy Fishback, and, notably, in the dry-goods scene with the wives of the rivals in Longstreet's "The Fight"—they are trounced for aping the shallow airs of the quality.

Hall's Mike Hooter admires old Miss Lemay's fearlessness of snakes: "she didn't care er dog on bit for all the sarpints that ever cum er 'long." She may be chagrined when news gets out that a snake has bitten her while she was squatting in her yard, but when Mike gets too vocal in his amusement about *whar?* she feels no compunction in taking him "kerbim right 'tween the eyes!" When a snake bites her, the *snake* dies (Cohen, 369–75).[45] In the Missouri backcountry the dozen daughters of one Squire Squegle are both aggressive and talented. They can "fell trees, yoke cattle, plant, plough, shuck, grind, . . . ride in a mule race, build cabins, flay coons, scalp wolves"; and although their "nice accomplishments" include dancing and courting prospective suitors, any one of these belles is able to "knock down an offender, strip him of his janes; kick him out of doors; give him to the world with a pair of sable eyes" (Oehl., 45–47). When they go to frolics, younger women may have the same weakness as charming creatures for fashion finery, "starn-cushions," and dancing

44. A surprising exception is George W. Harris's sentimental portrait of a "good woman" in "Trapping a Sheriff" (see chap. 15).

45. Hall's anecdote of Miss Lemay's poisoning of the snake is yet another witty reversal of the patristic tradition glossing the enmity of woman and serpent; see Elaine Pagels, *Adam, Eve, and the Serpent* (New York: Random House, 1988). A secular age reduces the harsh misogynistic punishment to a kind of folklore in which the continuing enmity is a source of humor (as in the comic strip *B.C.*, in which the "fat broad," armed with a club, beats the snake senseless).

conventions, but, says one of Robb's storytellers, they are not "your pigeon creaturs, that a fellar dassent tech fur fear of spilin' 'em, but raal scrougers—any on 'em over fourteen could lick a *bar,* easy" (Cohen, 179–84).

Though yeoman husbands often use derogatory terms for their wives (*ol 'oman, Old Quilt, ole Petticoat*), widows and wives typically need little protection from their menfolk, either physically or psychologically; in time-honored comic convention, even vulnerable daughters reject such protection, which they know is mostly perfunctory. It never occurs to Hall's Sally Hooter or Robb's Molly Dennison to defer to a code of womanhood that includes docility. They act out their needs, not in spirited rebellion against such a code but as if that code were irrelevant. They are rewarded in kind. In these gender protocols, the strong male characters court, admire, challenge, tolerate, and willingly accept equally strong females in their day-to-day lives.

Although female yeomanry occupies a place in the hierarchy paralleling that of better-off counterparts on the plantation, a lower status allows women greater flexibility when they want to act on their desires. In Henry Clay Lewis's "A Tight Race Considerin'," Mrs. Hibbs is just as embarrassed as a quality lady would be about exposing too much flesh. That possibility, however, does not prevent her from participating in an enthusiastic horse race one Sunday with a visiting parson. She wins the race, but is pitched "like a lam for the sacryfise" through an open church window, leaving "her only garment flutterin' on a nail in the sash." Less farcical than his fellow humorists in characterizing females, Lewis depicts Mr. and Mrs. Hibbs as an ordinary planter family, well-to-do and generous, but also "plain, unlettered" Virginians in their Mississippi exile. Mrs. Hibbs is a teetotaling wife and a pious church member; she is also "the daughter of a man who had once owned a race-horse." That heritage lets her speak her mind whenever either "religion or horse-flesh was the theme." The values of this "long-tongued" woman are awkwardly balanced between piety and pleasure (*SD,* 42–53). The tension in that balancing is more pronounced because she is female, but it is similar to that of plain-folk men whose behavior bobs inconclusively between an ingrained permissiveness (part of what Longstreet called the honest virtues of an earlier republic) and a fickle allegiance to a protestantism that monitors such social evils as drinking, dancing, and gambling. Lewis's narrator, Madison Tensas, is of course not torn between piety and pleasure. He makes Mrs. Hibbs as impartially kind as her husband and honors her for it. Her exposure, down to her "last kiverin'," may be embarrassing, but the reader ends the sketch as an invisible confederate of Mr. Hibbs, who in the fever of the race improves his wife's chances of winning by leaping on her horse and whipping it with a sapling—unmindful of the cost to her churchgoing apparel. At the end we feel, along with the author, not that the old lady has been punished for her pride, but that she has been rewarded for her spirited participation and great pleasure.

The benign condescension that pervades most of these humorous sketches also allows the narrators to indulge themselves with the females' indifference to the codes of their more genteel counterparts. It would be tempting to read the latitude we see in the portraits of independent-minded females as subverting the constrictive conformities governing women's lives in the antebellum South, but there is little evidence for such a reading. The educated authors betray no overt dissatisfaction with the social and economic structures of their society. We do, however, find frequent expressions of momentary class envy, when the narrators immerse themselves imaginatively in the frontier energy of a population uninvolved (as they see it) in the forging of a progressive civilization. Because of fictional heightening—artful manipulations of an observed yeomanry culture—many of these sketches are a species of fantasy. Both males and females attracted the authors because of what they necessarily saw as less inhibited, rawer aspects of life in the margins. Females, however, with the additional virtue of their sex, lent such wish-fulfillment a keener edge. The female in the humor can be a credible Other so rarely because she is thoroughly integrated in the masculine world of yeomanry.

Both educated narrator and vernacular storyteller share their region's homogeneity. In the inside world of the sketch, with its easy settlement perspective, the Other is the outsider. He may be Mormon, Millerite, peddler, salesman, dandy, or the occasional foreigner—any figure of the great world who impinges upon the cultural uniformity of this society. And he is offered up as the predictable butt of settlement joking. Among outsiders, Mormons and Millerites are favorite targets. In one sketch, one of Father Miller's adherents (not "backward in proclaiming his opinions" about the Second Coming) harangues a steamboat audience as he stands before a huge chart. The "learned lecturer," we are told, "subtracted the bear from the dragon, added the goat to the beast, multiplied the horns by the legs; which, with the figure's 'ten toes,' Nebuchadnezzar, Napoleon Buonaparte, and the Clay Convention, gave the year 1844 as clear as mud!" (Oehl., 41–44). Poking fun at the sect's penchant for esoteric numerology is innocent satire. More disturbing is Lewis's "The Day of Judgment," which depicts the disruption of the berobed faithful assembled for a camp meeting at the edge of a swamp. On an extended carousal, and itching to punish false prophets for "singing, screamings, and glorifications," some drunken medical students choose a stray mule as their agent. They saturate his hide with turpentine and tar, wrap his neck and head in a wet sheet, point him in the direction of the camp meeting, and set him on fire. The Millerite assembly erupts in chaos. Madison Tensas adds a detail that shows the faithful to be crafty as well as foolish: some have purchased goods "at twelve months' credit, thinking they would be in 'Kingdom Come' before the notes fell due" (*SD*, 59–64). Moral exposure of the "knowing ones" strengthens the jokesters' justification for such a prank, but the painful death of a dumb animal arouses no second thoughts.

Because they pose an economic threat, Mormons in their pre-Utah settlements in Missouri and Illinois are more rigorously victimized. One piece in the *Reveille*, "Puss-Eyeism vs. Mormonism," describes a practical joke on an itinerant preacher from Nauvoo. The perpetrators disrupt the preacher's service with twenty tomcats dressed up as imps from hell. Suspicion of his being a likkering saint because of his "bottle nose" is an exculpatory detail like others often cited to justify the hostility of older residents (Oehl., 58–60). Settlers in Jackson County, according to the *Missouri Gazetteer*, were forced to "rise in arms and expel" Mormon invaders because they were suspected of making "overtures" to slaves and Indians. Violent measures, adds the compiler, were "fully justified" to counter the sect's "disgusting folly" and "outrageous villainies."[46] In their perspectives on such outsiders, the humorous authors were more circumspect than communal spokesmen, but the practical jokes they describe are often fueled by the same attitudes.

In the overall picture, however, such outsiders are almost incidental. To educated readers throughout the United States, those who passively enjoyed the humorous sketches from the region and those who actually joined in producing them, the vernacular characters themselves were a kind of collective Other. Solid in their own world and radiating their own energy, the entire array of colorful figures is understood as *them*.

While Southwest humor may be at least a cousin to ethnic humor, we need to remark its most striking departure. Its simplest feature, which is also its greatest anomaly in specialized humor, is its field of operation: the types generating the fun come not from a pool of minorities, but from

46. Alphonso Wetmore, *Gazetteer of the State of Missouri* (St. Louis, 1837), 93.

the majority. Because we see the action and the characters from the point of view of narrators drawn from the educated professional class, the vast yeomanry of the humor's time and place is itself the Other. The gentlemanly narrator is, as he must be, the confident representative of superiority. He already has modernity and progress on his side, and with the power of the pen he is the voice of civilization.

As members of the powerful few, the newspaper authors are tolerant of nonconforming, primitive behavior, which they comfortably see as surmountable hurdles. To describe Southwest humor as kinder and gentler than its urban counterpart would be misleading. The very authors who refuse to judge their subjects never hesitate to revel in the comedy of debasement, with inventive methods of personal embarrassment, but the initiators of such schemes are more apt to be rivals within the yeomanry than educated spokesmen like themselves. Practical jokers are of course disrupters, troublemakers, lords of misrule, yet they are *native* disrupters. Womenfolk may occasionally agitate and annoy, yet they are *native* agitators. In the long view, the authors preferred to see "settlement fun" as intramural fun.

Only in our own time have we become ruefully conscious that all varieties of cultural dominance, even the well-meaning ones, are equally unable to "interrogate" the culture of the Other. Jean Baudrillard attributed this failure to the centrality of the West and its assumption of itself as *universal*, the primary model against which all other cultures become "vestiges of its own image."[47] As we have seen in the comments of spokesmen both official and personal, the writing from and about the Old Southwest in one respect is akin to other nineteenth-century cultural forms; that is, it romanticized, aestheticized, or exoticized the backwoods and its people. But the humorists rarely assumed that such difference was something to be valued on its own terms. Moreover, life at the edges of settlement was seen literally as "vestiges"—quaint, amusing, or embarrassing—of an older stage of America's history and far removed from the new spirit of economic progress and social consolidation. That perspective was part of a general commitment that also justified exploitation, usurpation, rampant development, and spatial colonization.

On the eve of the Civil War, Keziah Brevard, suffering ill health even as she anguished over a slavery system in which she participated, confided to her diary: "Judge L Georgia scenes are near—sometimes I laugh over

47. Jean Baudrillard, *The Mirror of Production,* trans. Mark Poster (St. Louis: Telos Press, 1975), 88–89.

them until I cry—at this moment I feel no desire to open them." This shrewd South Carolina plantation mistress, who maternally fussed over the welfare of her slaves, gloomily speculated that the history she was living through—her state had just seceded from the Union—might be divine retribution for past sins.[48] By 1860 it is not surprising that Judge Longstreet's humor failed to cheer her. None of the antebellum humorists would have been capable of doing so. Though they participated fully in the dominant national program (and relied on the familiar stereotypes of marginals who didn't), the humorous authors significantly lack the solicitous spirit of cultural missionaries. By the critical standards of the late twentieth century and after, they too never "interrogate" the culture that inspired their work. Neither do they depict it as an urgent incongruous element to be pacified, converted, and absorbed. In one critic's words, as "gentleman humorists, they wrote political realism as they saw it; and they also wrote it as they didn't see it."[49]

48. *A Plantation Mistress on the Eve of the Civil War: The Diary of Keziah Goodwyn Hopkins Brevard, 1800–1861*, ed. John Hammond Moore (Columbia: University of South Carolina Press, 1993), 45, 10–15.
49. Beidler, *First Books*, 101.

Chapter 7 ✦

Scenes in Course and Field

Life at the West and South is a teeming theme for Magazine writers but the cleverest and most amusing have certainly been of a
sporting nature. The curious and often rich provincialisms of dialect are here most appropriate, and are most vividly brought out
by scenes in the Course or in the Field.

—William T. Porter

i.

In the first number of what would become the favorite venue for most
of the newspaper humorists, William T. Porter issued his "Prospectus"
for a new publication devoted to "the cause of fashion, of pleasurable entertainments, of taste and recreation." His plans for *Spirit of the Times &
Life in New York* in 1831 reveal a clever entrepreneur fully conscious of
marketing opportunities. Porter promised variety to readers of leisure and
reputation, those who formed a potentially coherent audience, even as he
specified the newspaper's coverage: the "divertisements of life," which
would include all pursuits that satisfied an "appetite for pleasure, and
indulgence," and a willingness "to enter into occasional follies." The new
paper would feature such sites as theaters, museums, "and other fashionable places of resort"; the turf, the ring, and the pit; scenes of fishing
and fowling; and the court, "civil and criminal." A century later, this
journalistic scheme would have been equivalent to a merger of *Field &
Stream* and *Esquire.* Although Porter promised to promote writing that

would "paint 'life as it is,' without the artificial embellishments of romance," there is no evidence that he entertained any proto-Howellsian notions of realism; his commitment to writing about scenes and people "faithfully portrayed" was largely an effort to acknowledge human activities neglected by "the politicians, the theologians and the literati of our country" in their higher-toned "oracles." Even if the new paper celebrated pleasure, it would do so, Porter promised, "without wounding the feelings" of any reader, in a language "always chaste."[1]

Porter was in effect making his bid to join the nationalistic campaign for an indigenous literature, which had been vigorously waged since 1821 when Sydney Smith snobbishly dismissed American art in the pages of the *Edinburgh Review*. The capacious spread of subjects to be covered in the *Spirit* is indirectly linked to the editor's astute observation about the still-formative nature of American society. If its serious character is still unfixed, Porter argues, there is even more variation "in its games and amusements, which are the last habits acquired by a new people." And in a prescience worthy of the frontier theorists a generation later, Porter proposes to explore the ragged line where nature and civilization meet. If the staff of the *Spirit* had nothing else to do, he asserts, "we should have our hands full in watching and giving an account of [civilization's] encroachments on rustic manners, and showing the exact point where the refinements of society meet and overthrow the austerities and rudenesses" of the mountains, lakes, and deserts, where the "wilderness is thickening with population." Despite its obvious self-interest, Porter's vision of his new publication is consonant with the efforts of Cooper, Irving, and their successors to establish a national body of writing. Rather than trivializing the national mission, the *Spirit of the Times* would assist "in the great work of building up a sound physical frame for the Republic." It is a dexterous leap. Porter suggests that his focus on "pleasurable entertainments" is designed to inculcate "the *mens sana in sano corpore*" in the "care-worn and sedentary citizen."[2]

1. Quoted in Richard Boyd Hauck, "Predicting a Native Literature: William T. Porter's First Issue of the *Spirit of the Times*," *Mississippi Quarterly* 22 (1968–1969): 77–84. Quotations throughout this chapter from Porter's rare first number are from Hauck's reprint. For a general overview, see John Rickards Betts, "Sporting Journalism in Nineteenth-Century America," *American Quarterly* 5 (1953): 39–56. Though "racy" and "lively," the language of the backwoods and frontier that festooned the humorous sketches was apparently chaste enough. In accordance with publishing conventions of the time, colorful expletives were allowed, but such words as *damn* and *hell* were reduced to "d—n" and "h—l."
2. See Richard Boyd Hauck, "The Literary Content of the New York *Spirit of the Times*, 1831–1856," Ph.D. diss., University of Illinois, 1965.

If, apart from the matter of healthy minds and bodies, his vision ingeniously imposed a conceptual unity in advance of its actual appearance, the *Spirit* in its real and long life never lost its ebullient grab-bag diversity. It is important to remember, however, that Porter's chief interest was American sporting literature, especially writing about horse racing. The editor's passion in championing this "pleasurable entertainment" lent a prestige to the racetrack at a time when many Americans associated racing with sleazy touts, gamblers, and lowbred adventurers. Since one of the motifs of the *Spirit* was the reiterated assurance that properly managed racetracks were respectable as well as popular, Porter campaigned to rid these sites of "'mule-races, and Foot-races, and Gander-pullings, and Cock-fights,' [staged only] to swell the receipts" of the gate. Although he filled his pages with items on fishing, marine sports (rowing and sailing), and wolf-, panther-, bear-, deer-, elk-, and foxhunting (and even cockfighting),[3] Porter's great love remained what his contemporaries called *talking horse*. To foster his fascination with horse racing, Porter encouraged all kinds of contributions: news of sales, pedigrees, transactions by turfmen and breeders, statistics of races, articles on the practical training of horses, veterinary information, and, on occasion, racing controversies. Through his efforts, he later boasted, the value of bloodstock over the years increased by 30 percent; the sustained attention had reinforced the honesty of jockeys and promoted the collegiality of the nationwide racing fraternity. This racing missionary, who emphasized a genteel track, himself penned two notable sporting pieces, both of them on famous horse races (those between Wagner and Grey Eagle and between Boston and Fashion), complete with allusions to Halleck, Byron, and the classical authors. Both C. F. M. Noland before he invented Pete Whetstone and George Washington Harris in his pre–Sut Lovingood days began their writing careers by contributing sporting epistles to the *Spirit*.[4]

The glamour of field sports, and especially the track, was not morally persuasive for all readers—or potential contributors. Judge Longstreet, for example, would have been an unlikely correspondent for Porter's paper. In "The Turf" he finds the presence of respectables at racetracks an

3. Norris W. Yates, "*The Spirit of the Times:* Its Early History and Some of Its Contributors," *Papers of the Bibliographical Society of America* 48 (1954): 117–48; Mark A. Keller, "Reputable Writers, Phony Names: Identifying Pseudonyms in the *Spirit of the Times*," *PBSA* 75 (1981): 198–209.

4. John T. Flanagan, "Western Sportsmen Travelers in the New York *Spirit of the Times*," in *Travelers on the Western Frontier*, ed. John Francis McDermott (Urbana: University of Illinois Press, 1970), 168–86.

occasion for sober satire. In a close race between Eclipse and Bertrand, Eclipse falls, killing his rider; "without a competitor," Bertrand gallops for the pole, his rider bearing the purse "on high, backwards and forwards," before the spectators. "'I declare,' said Mrs. Blue, as her carriage wheeled off, 'had it not been for that little accident, the sport would have been delightful.'" General Grubs laments that such "amusement is not more encouraged!" Longstreet allows his narrator, the otherwise decent Hall, mingling with the quality without comment, to succumb to the moral insensitivity of the fashionable crowd (*GS*, 109).

For all the editor's patriotic sentiment, the earlier volumes of the *Spirit* are heavily weighted toward excerpts from British papers, including *Bell's Life in London*, upon which Porter modeled his paper.[5] He appropriated speeches, poems, even stories of regional English life, and serialized fiction of Thackeray, Dickens, and other popular authors, along with accounts of British turf and field sports. He admitted that, literarily, the British sporting magazines "beat us a long way," although after more than a century, their themes had become "exhausted," and even London papers were turning to sketches about buffalo and bear hunts in the United States.[6] If over time he devoted more and more space to reports from the domestic field, Porter continued to reprint British items, however exhausted. That dual commitment is reflected in his 1846 edition of an English work, Peter Hawker's *Instructions to Young Sportsmen* (1814), which omitted much of the English material to make room for American sporting prose. And though he was alert to a more lively and direct mode of reporting outdoor amusements, he never rejected solid pieces written in the British tradition, the archly witty and allusive style favored by the amiable elite.[7]

Porter's sister reported that the significant change in emphasis came in 1847, when original sketches became "thoroughly American."[8] Foreign

5. Francis Brinley, *Life of William T. Porter* (New York, 1860), 144–45, 104–5.

6. Norris W. Yates, *William T. Porter and the "Spirit of the Times": A Study of the Big Bear School of Humor* (Baton Rouge: Louisiana State University Press, 1977), 13.

7. See Leland H. Cox, Jr., "Porter's Edition of *Instructions to Young Sportsmen*," in *Gyascutus: Studies in Antebellum Southern Humorous and Sporting Writing*, ed. James L. W. West III (Atlantic Highlands, NJ: Humanities Press, 1978), 81–102. Cox argues that the inspiration for updating Hawker came to Porter in 1844 and that his two humor anthologies (1845, 1846) "impeded" the return to "the roots of Porter's interests"— the world of "manly, outdoor sport" (86, 92). See also Brinley, *Life of William T. Porter*, 202, 270.

8. Brinley, *Life of William T. Porter*, 69. See also Shirley M. Mundt, "William Trotter Porter," in *American Newspaper Journalists, 1690–1872*, ed. Perry J. Ashley, vol. 43 of *Dictionary of Literary Biography* (Detroit: Gale Research, 1985), 362–66.

excerpts on racing, along with much horse-racing material in general, may have been funneled into the *American Turf Register,* which Porter bought in 1838, before it ceased publication six years later. By 1844 the *Spirit* had been enlarged to twelve pages, which accommodated more regional correspondents. From the beginning, Porter was receptive not only to pieces detailing regional sporting events but also to personal narratives featuring characters, lore, and scenery of the backcountry. He was convinced that an "exhaustless supply" of copy lay on the American frontier—adventurers of the settlers, incidents of travel, examples of singular manners. However marked the change in 1847, Porter's influential anthology, *The Big Bear of Arkansas, and Other Sketches,* had appeared two years earlier, with its significant subtitle: *Illustrative of Characters and Incidents in the South and South-West.* Like his contributors in the south and west, Porter privileged writing that linked character and action to the varieties of climate and "peculiarities of scenery unhackneyed by a thousand tourists."[9]

In the *Spirit,* then, the line between sporting items and comic tales from the hinterland is not very distinct. While statistical summaries of heats and races are primarily reportorial, such informational pieces gradually grew into discursive tales, often involving owners, rivals, sporting bloods (with names disguised or fabricated), and wagering on outcomes of races. That is, the purely factual base is extended dramatically to show human beings caught at pressure points that reveal interesting character traits. In some pieces, the discursive format is extended further, into digressions that elaborate the characters of the participants in give-and-take bantering and anecdotal sayings. Sometimes a correspondent from Alabama or Louisiana, writing to the *Spirit* to report particular events, begins as a reliable reporter (much in the manner of the modern newspaper stringer), only to try out his talents at sketching the social scene. Then the report becomes both factual and imaginative, in effect a literary sketch about the colorful crowd at, say, the Selma track, captured in type by an observer who is accurate, imaginative, and gifted in rendering, not merely reporting, the scene.

By 1840 Porter was making little distinction between purely sporting epistles and pieces that freely mingled the verifiable and the imaginative. They were all glimpses into "life at the West and South." Yet five years

9. Porter's *Spirit* featured articles by Henry William Herbert, J. J. Audubon, T. B. Thorpe, and others. See editor David C. Estes's introduction to the standard Thorpe text, *A New Collection of Thomas Bangs Thorpe's Sketches of the Old Southwest* (Baton Rouge: Louisiana State University Press, 1989).

later, when Porter gathered his handsome selection of humorous pieces for the *Big Bear of Arkansas* anthology, there was no smudging of generic lines. Most of the twenty-one sketches have nothing to do with the turf— indeed, little to do with any of those "amusements" earlier readers knew as field sports. A few lingering strands in Thorpe's title story or McNutt's "Chunkey's Fight with the Panthers" hang irrelevantly from these humorous sketches. Most, like "Cousin Sally Dilliard" or "Pulling Teeth in Mississippi," bear no resemblance to the sporting epistle. Leisure patterns of rural life that only a few years earlier had been matter-of-factly rendered as "sporting nature" had expanded demographically and sociologically.

Published by Carey & Hart of Philadelphia, Porter's anthology was the most influential volume on the development of local-color regional writing since Longstreet's *Georgia Scenes* a decade earlier. If Longstreet had been a reticent scribe of humorous incidents, Porter was a virtual godfather, prodding, pleading, encouraging, even taunting dozens of correspondents to drop their inhibitions about authorship. No humorist himself, this affable editor was the facilitator and publicist of those who were (or could be) humorists. As the good entrepreneur, not hesitating to take credit for the flowering of the humorous sketch, Porter made his preface a kind of literary history of its development, one in which "the novel design and scope" of his weekly publication played a pivotal role.[10] "In addition to correspondents who described with equal felicity and power the stirring incidents of the chase and the turf," he writes, the *Spirit*

> enlisted another and still more numerous class, who furnished most valuable and interesting reminiscences of the pioneers of the far West— sketches of thrilling scenes and adventures in that comparatively unknown region, and the extraordinary characters occasionally met with—their strange language and habitudes, and the peculiar and sometimes fearful characteristics of the "squatters" and early settlers.[11]

10. Brinley, *Life of William T. Porter*, 197; John Porter Bloom, "Sources for Western History in *The American Turf Register and Sporting Magazine, 1829–44*," in *Travelers on the Western Frontier*, ed. John Francis McDermott (Urbana: University of Illinois Press, 1970), 187–202. Norris W. Yates speculates that Porter's example in both *The Big Bear of Arkansas* (1845) and *A Quarter Race in Kentucky* (1846) encouraged some of the authors represented in them—Thorpe, Robb, J. M. Field, and Sol Smith, among others— to collect their sketches in their own books (*William T. Porter*, 53).

11. William T. Porter, ed., preface to *The Big Bear of Arkansas, and Other Sketches, Illustrative of Characters and Incidents in the South and South-West* (Philadelphia: Carey & Hart, 1845), vii–viii.

The contents page was meant to suggest the heterogeneity of amusements throughout the raw interior of the South and West. If the title of a
sketch was not self-explanatory, Porter supplied a subtitle that specified
its geographical origin (i.e., "A Story of Georgia"); of the twenty-one selections, only three bear no sign of origin. The substance of the sketches,
however, reveals that "gentlemen" behave and speak the same all over,
that backwoodsmen in Missouri display some of the same idiosyncrasies
as their counterparts in Georgia, and that all of them—narrators and storytellers alike—have the same linguistic fondness for a handful of certain
idioms and images.

As even incomplete files of the *Spirit of the Times* show, the growth of
the humorous sketch was rapid. Dominated by Porter's high-profile paper,
the vitality of the periodical exchange system is suggested by the sheer
number of contributions submitted in direct response to earlier published
pieces. A readerly one-upsmanship—or, as Porter put it, a "generous feeling of emulation"—also solidified many of the conventions of the humorous sketch: the clever prose affected by the amiable author; the unstressed
class distinctions that emerge between the narrator-correspondent and
the vernacular-speaking storyteller; and the (imperfect) typographic reg-
ularization of dialect. Despite Clarence Gohdes's impressive argument a
generation ago that newspapers more than oral yarns provided "the peculiar shaping force as well as the chief medium through which native
American humor developed," we still like to think of this writing as spilled
folklore. Like most other forms of writing, the primary inspiration of the
humorous sketch was prior writing, not nature.[12]

ii.

Porter's inclusive sense of appropriate materials in the preface to *Big
Bear* reflected a journalistic trend generally. "Outdoors writing" meant
specific accounts of particular sports, but it also meant individual experiences "in the wilds" that we see in such books as William P. Hawes's
Sporting Scenes and Sundry Sketches (1842) and Charles W. Webber's *The
Hunter-Naturalist* (1851).[13] The mainstay was first-person reports of the
chase and the turf, but *sports* accommodated even accounts by pioneers

12. Clarence Gohdes, *American Literature in Nineteenth-Century England* (Carbondale: Southern Illinois University Press, 1944), 91.
13. Daniel Justin Herman, *Hunting and the American Imagination* (Washington: Smithsonian Institution Press, 2001), 159.

from newer sections of the nation. Opening up his pages to frontier reminiscences, the editor delicately ignored the probable extent to which these amateur authors used their fancy to heighten historical accuracy. What he frankly preferred was liveliness in the "sketches of thriving scenes and adventures" and their cast of "extraordinary characters" speaking a "strange language." That kind of latitude in the potential scrambling of fact and fiction would have a heartening effect on most of the humorous contributors.

One such piece makes explicit Porter's enlarged definition of *sporting*. "My First and Last Turkey Hunt" is a farcical account of a bumbling Louisville sportsman who forswears all turkey hunting after his one attempt ends with the destruction of a settler's "*tame* turkeys and chickens" that are roosting in their customary apple tree, "all unconscious of the awful fate" awaiting them.[14] Some of the later contributions, however rural, did not even pretend to be sporting. For example, alongside rambunctious accounts, the *Spirit* continued to publish Irving-like scenery pieces such as Dick Dashwood's "Sports of the Prairies," which was mostly an exercise in Crayonesque aesthetics ("undulations of the prairie, wrapt in heavy folds of mist, tinting everything with silver, rose in confused heaps, like the waves of the ocean subsiding after a storm").[15] Similar pieces, rife with gentlemanly diction—with many *exhalations, mantles, nocturnal slumbers*—testify to Porter's liberal editorial policy. Indeed, the editor never turned his back on what can only be described as dilatory prose from genial, fun-loving gentlemen. Even Charles Fenno Hoffman, a professional writer, mingled unhurried travel rhetoric and scenic description with the reproduced lingos of bear and panther hunters: "Wild Scenes in the Forest and Prairie" is a sketch without a narrative nub, but it suggests the breezy tone that Porter favored in his columns.[16]

Natt. Phillips's "Wedding and Deer Hunt in Kentucky" turns on the unlikely doubling of topics announced in the title. Built upon the technique of deferral, the sketch proposes to recount a deer hunt, but Phillips must first write about a wedding, which itself spawns a series of digressions. What matters is the literary pacing, the self-conscious authorial interruptions to the digressions: "But I am straing from the dance" and "Well, I have bin pretty much like the fellow that worked three days on a piece of iron and steel for a broad-axe, and at last it came out a Frow, so I

14. *Spirit of the Times*, December 18, 1847, p. 507.
15. *Spirit of the Times*, December 4, 1847, p. 483.
16. *Spirit of the Times*, April 6, 1839, p. 62.

have bin so long at this confounded weding . . . so now for the *Deer Chase.*"[17] Despite his self-description as "the No. 1 Deer-slayor," one Jaikup Leggins contributes a piece that is only marginally a sporting epistle. This Alabama correspondent begins "A Night among Wolves" on a note of mild, perhaps even mock, disapproval: "Seeing as how you are free-kwently publishin some mortal long yarns and big tails consarnin the adventures of all manner of folk, agin the birds of the ar and the fishes of the depe, I thort I mought not be considered bold to ventur on a letter to you miself."[18] This correspondent later contributes a proper sporting epistle, "Camp Hunting in Mississippi" (signed, more conventionally, as Jacob Leggins, and excising other misspellings). Here he attempts to give the kinetic flavor of a deer hunt by using present tense and stacking quotations from members of the hunting party:

> Now we see the buck . . . ahead of the hounds . . . stretched like leather thongs! . . . Up we come, dogs, men and horses. . . . "Look out! he's for a fight! No shooting! you'll kill a hound! Take care, boys, he's getting wrathy! . . . There's a dead dog! poor Trueboy! he's used him up! Yes, and there goes Sounder, as dead as a herring! Look out, he'll kill your horse! D—n it, take care, man."[19]

Not all contributors were pleased with the broadening coverage of "sporting interests." "A Young Turfman" from Natchez complained that he was "beginning seriously to fear that the time honored" racecourse was to be "abandoned entirely to Buffalo hunts, trots, foot races, etc., etc.," and he urged contributors to return to the "sports of the Turf."[20] A writer from Cincinnati begins his piece: "*Oh, Elevated Spirit!*—Since it is the fashion now-a-days for every one who has shot *at* two or three woodpeckers or has fished for a couple of hours in some meandering brook . . . [to write up] the wonderful event in the columns of the racy 'Spirit,' suppose I tell you about *the boy that shot the Deer.*"[21]

Porter was never above self-promotion. From week to week, he larded his pages with approving squibs from other journals—one editor declares that Porter is "the father of the *funny* literature of the day"; another affirms that he has "yet to see the man that has formed its acquaintance,

17. *Spirit of the Times,* February 8, 1840, p. 583.
18. *Spirit of the Times,* October 16, 1847, p. 395.
19. *Spirit of the Times,* January 15, 1848, p. 555.
20. *Spirit of the Times,* July 31, 1847, p. 267.
21. *Spirit of the Times,* September 4, 1847, p. 321.

who is not an enthusiastic admirer" of the *Spirit*. One waggish admirer wrote to praise Porter in his efforts "to destroy evil and ameliorate the condition of mankind"; another asserted that the *Spirit* was "the most charming hebdomadah of which the country boasts."[22] Although Porter's serialization of British novels and reprints of hunting and adventure stories from across the Empire lent the *Spirit* a tone of urbanity, it was clearly the homegrown sporting and humorous sketches that sold the paper. By the time the *Yankee Blade* in 1847 praised Porter's policy of including "a greater amount of original facetiae and rib-tickling sketches than any other journal," the bantering tone had become as important as substance to the *Spirit*'s readership.[23]

In his preface to *The Big Bear of Arkansas*, the editor notes that most of his contributors, "country gentlemen, planters, lawyers, &c. 'who live at home at ease,'" are comfortable with their public scribblings; but with more than a hint of frustration, Porter confesses that he must deal with some authors who refuse to be named in public.

> We are utterly precluded, by repeated injunctions of secresy, from giving the "name" or "local habitation" of any one of those not designated in the introduction to the respective sketches. Their modesty should be esteemed. ... Most of them are gentlemen not only highly educated, but endowed with a keen sense of whatever is ludicrous or pathetic, with a quick perception of character, and a knowledge of men and the world.

Most of all, they are *writers*, possessing a power of originality in transferring to paper striking and effective pictures. As a choice made by talents with no superiors "on either side of the Atlantic," secret authorship is clearly vexing to these writers' chief enthusiast.[24] For a man with the combined zeal of agent, editor, publisher, and publicist, the insistence on "secresy" was daunting.

The editor's ambition and tolerance combined in such a way that tone and literary effect came to dominate the contents of the *Spirit of the Times*. Porter liked the clublike convention of pseudonyms for his contributors, although he would have liked it better had their use been *only* convention. Whimsical names added to the air of gentlemanly insiderism, but ideally, he felt, they should not mask—at least for long—the real identities behind

22. *Spirit of the Times*, March 20, 1847, p. 42. *Hebdomadah* is an obsolete term used here to mean a weekly publication with the force of authority.

23. *Spirit of the Times*, March 13, 1847, pp. 26, 31.

24. Porter, preface, xi–xii.

them. Just as obvious was Porter's delight in being able to name two of his contributors: Thomas Bangs Thorpe and C. F. M. Noland, who had already attracted national attention for their sketches of Mississippi and Arkansas, the latter "so recently reclaimed from the wilderness."[25] The most dependable correspondents the *Spirit* would have, these two enjoyed respectable social status. Their immersion in backwoods culture was as restrained as their prose. Thorpe was the most Irvingesque of the southwest writers; and, as "N. of Arkansas," Noland was both observant and gentlemanly in his turf reports—even his Pete Whetstone is a backwoods character more endearing than crude. Bold in claiming significance for the kind of writing he champions in the *Spirit,* Porter is safely conservative in placing Thorpe and Noland in continuity with the reputable Cooper and Paulding.

Even hunting sketches, which often began with the trappings of actual chases, hedged their veracity with wry monikers instead of real names, and the convention of claiming exaggerated success reinforced artful lying in general. One of the keys to the popularity of Porter's paper was the unexamined line separating actual and fictional events. Acceptable enough among those who trafficked in light literature, playing fast and loose with the truth could be an affront to solemn readers and writers—notably, Horace Greeley. "Multitudes" of popular scribes, suggested the famous editor, had falsified the character of Abraham Lincoln by making him a witty raconteur. In his sixteen years of familiarity with the man, he wrote, he could remember no "jocular narrations or reminiscences" from him, an observation that perhaps says more about the chilling effect of his company than it does about the president. The affable Porter remembered Greeley, newly arrived in the city as a printer's apprentice, as "a youth who could have gone on the stage, that minute, as Ezekiel Homespun." Even a stint in the *Spirit* office seemed perversely to confirm the Whig journalist as a sobersides. The function of writers, Greeley declared, was to "sing and shine as enlighteners and monitors of their fellow-beings." Porter's cultivation of truth-stretchers among his sportsmen and humorists could only be a temperamental affront to the social activist who once wrote: "A new book is only to be justified by a new truth."[26] Not a single original contributor to the *Spirit* would have qualified as an

---

25. Ibid. Thorpe, whose southern residence was chiefly in Louisiana, wrote many sketches based on activities and scenery in the lower Mississippi Valley.

26. Horace Greeley, *Recollections of a Busy Life* (New York, 1869), 226, 405, 434, 451. See also James Parton, *The Life of Horace Greeley, Editor of the* New York Tribune (New York, 1855), 124, 418–33.

enlightener and monitor, and by Greeley's standards, all their assorted collections would remain unjustified.

Within some sketches much is made of the truthfulness of anecdotes, but the editor, knowing that internal insistence on truthful reporting was itself a comic convention, wisely refrained from putting a fine point on the matter. He even published with great delight a series of contributions from "Mount Mendacity." In "Woodcock and Varmint in Louisiana," one author, "Easy," describes shooting a panther. "This is a glorious country for game of all kind; I only wish I had Pete Whetstone here, and some more chaps from the Devil's Fork, I'd show them sights."[27] "Easy" moves in and out of (presumably) actual events into the kind of competitive challenges to both real and fictional persons so common in the pages of the weekly.

The *Spirit* continued to attract readers (some of them, when dunned several times, even paying for their subscriptions) far beyond the audience for the editor's two collections of humorous pieces. Whatever the intrinsic merit of the anthologies (and it was considerable), their publication functioned largely as a shrewd entrepreneur's marketing device to drum up additional subscriptions. Their contents pages bear witness to the comprehensive distribution of settings throughout the nation's newest states. And Porter is correct when he claims in the preface to the first collection that his correspondents in the *Spirit*—already in 1845 a longer-living paper than its several rivals—include "a large majority of those who have subsequently distinguished themselves in this novel and original walk of literature."[28] Porter had no reason for modesty. Of all the major humorists associated with the (misleadingly termed) Big Bear school, only A. B. Longstreet and Joseph Glover Baldwin did not profit from his promotional fervor and largesse.

iii.

The appeal of the *Spirit* was nationwide. In 1856 Porter probably exaggerated his claim of forty thousand subscribers, but his weekly reached not merely the eastern seaboard and the Old Southwest but also the newer Southwest—the far-western reaches (mostly in military camps) and the Pacific coast.[29] Its popularity among southern readers derived in

27. *Spirit of the Times*, October 12, 1839, p. 379.
28. Porter, preface, viii.
29. Yates, *William T. Porter*, 29–30.

part from Porter's attraction to their projected image of leisurely conviviality as they pursued "manly sports" and other outdoor amusements.
The canny editor returned that image of himself in chatty editorials and
introductory notes to reprinted sketches. Although the *Spirit* was a masculine enterprise, at least one southern woman enjoyed reading it. The
liberal-minded Mrs. Gayle of Alabama, known during her husband's
campaign for governor as "the novel-reader," devoured Mrs. Opie, Mrs.
Sherwood, Scott, and Irving along with the usual fare by religious writers. But this very public lady also wanted amusing reading material,
complaining to her husband that she was not getting enough newspapers: "I like the Spirit of the Age—it is humorous—none of the *fee-fau-fum*
gravity of a ghost."[30] Presumably Mrs. Gayle meant Porter's *Spirit of the
Times*. It is unlikely that this southern lady would have found amusing
W. H. Channing's *Spirit of the Age*, a reformist weekly concentrating on
antislavery, temperance, and other gravities. Though she does not say so,
the New York *Spirit* presumably went to her husband, one of hundreds
of subscribers that the editor aggressively courted in the South.

Porter *was* "Mr. Spirit" for all regions, but the high regard for the weekly
among southern readers was, above all, a matter of discreet politics. When
in 1835 he declared that the *Spirit* was designed for the elite of American
readers ("gentlemen of standing, wealth and intelligence—the very corinthian columns of the community"), Porter did not specify region, but
southerners took it as a bias they could be comfortable with.[31] When he
wrote in 1839, "Into this page we intend to cram every good thing said,
sung, or done, 'in these parts,' placing Fun 'well up,' and Politics 'no
where,'" they were assured that the *Spirit* was one northern paper that
would remain free of abolitionist sniping at their peculiar institution.[32] If
Porter's public fondness for the South in the *Spirit* was usually indirect,
his actual fraternizing links to the southern planter class were unambiguous.

In 1838, with the avowed purpose of making his association with his
southern contributors a personal matter, Porter made the first of several
tours of the South and West. It was, notes one scholar, "something of a
triumphal procession" for the editor, who acknowledged the "unremitted
attentions" paid him by gentlemen in Georgia, South Carolina, Alabama,

30. Sarah Gayle, diary, Gorgas Family Papers (Sarah Gayle Materials), William Stanley Hoole Special Collections, University of Alabama Library, University of Alabama,
Tuscaloosa.
31. Yates, *William T. Porter*, 15; Flanagan, "Western Sportsmen Travelers," 185–86.
32. *Spirit of the Times*, March 9, 1839, p. 1.

Mississippi, Kentucky, and Louisiana. As a result of that goodwill trip, Porter declared that "we shall be better enabled than ever to cater [to] the tastes and wishes of our Southern readers." His early friendship with George Wilkins Kendall in New York was also an important personal link in Porter's contacts south and west after Kendall became the influential editor of the *New Orleans Picayune;* two of Porter's brothers would write for the *Picayune.* An editorial in the *Spirit* after Porter's death in 1858 made explicit what the tolerating formula had been all along. The editors (or perhaps the editorial was the sole work of T. B. Thorpe) angrily attacked "agitators" in the North who were sneering at southern mores and customs. The editors admitted that the "public men of the South . . . had a preponderating influence" on the literary character of the *Spirit,* partly because of the popularity of outdoor sports among "the refined and wealthy."[33]

Though it was Porter's favorite sporting venue, the turf in the South was not in fact a very exclusive affair. Especially in the fluid social arrangements of the late 1830s, horse-racing enthusiasts were not all corinthian columns. The tracks drew huge yeoman audiences, who often outnumbered the quality (conspicuously after the 1837 economic downturn) and whose fiery activities offtrack often rivaled the formal heats in excitement and interest. As Porter discovered, the planters of the newer South, who had enough money and leisure to pursue hunting and to frequent the racetrack, were also literate enough to read (and occasionally write) sporting epistles. His courtship of the South was not an ideologically perverse turn for a New Englander. The prestige of the slavocracy appealed to many enterprising young men north of the Ohio, some of whom, like S. S. Prentiss, emigrated south as an abolitionist-minded person, only to become totally identified with the new planter culture. In Porter's case, however, political allegiance seems almost irrelevant: as entrepreneur, the editor knew that the success of his publications—the *American Turf Register* as well as the *Spirit of the Times*—depended upon the readership and goodwill of southerners, for whom turf interest was likely to be free of the moralistic criticism occasionally directed at eastern racing activities. To shy away from political subjects was simply good business sense in an era that was always on the verge of regional conflict. When Porter abruptly left the *Spirit* in late summer of 1856 (for reasons still not entirely clear), he put the old journal he had been associated with for a quarter-century in the hands of George Wilkes, founder of the *Police*

33. Yates, *William T. Porter,* 34–35, 199.

Gazette. The *Spirit*'s earlier tolerance of slavery was replaced by a distinctly pro-northern position that acknowledged no community of interests with southern planters. The *Spirit* not only lost many of its former correspondents from the South and West; there was also a noticeable decline in editorial coverage of events in the South.

Porter's apolitical policy had made possible a rich outpouring of sketches from contributors who felt comfortable with him. Of course, Porter's sensitivity to political coloring in his paper was itself political; his neutrality was a statement of sympathy for a society that was rapidly moving apart from the rest of the country. The new *Spirit* expired in 1861. A year after its demise, the *Spirit of the Times* supplied unexpected comfort to one Mississippian, who wrote home from a Virginia battle site that a bullet had "thussed through" his canteen, his haversack, and a copy of the *Spirit* that he had stuffed in his coat pocket. Had he been a more serious reader, the bullet would doubtless have lodged at an appropriate text in his pocket Bible.[34]

In a sense, the "fun" of the *Spirit*—increasingly concentrated in bantering sporting sketches and humorous anecdotes from the lower South—safely displaced national political anxieties. Though he may have been sympathetic to the political ideology of his southern readers, Porter knew that for all the elitist assertions, frontier conditions still obtained in most communities left behind the actual frontier line. "Life at the West and South is a teeming theme for Magazine writers," he wrote in 1840, with its "curious and often rich provincialisms of dialect." After his discovery of the first sketches of Simon Suggs in an Alabama newspaper, he wrote that he wanted their author as a regular correspondent to join others who had made the *Spirit* "far more famous for original wit and humour than its being the 'chronicle of the Sporting World.'"[35] John S. Robb, Johnson Jones Hooper, and C. F. M. Noland, among those in Porter's stable, occasionally alluded to national politics in their pieces, but their dialectal, freewheeling heroes had nothing to do with the "manly sports" of southern "aristocrats." With their creations, these vernacular backwoodsmen shunted aside, at least momentarily, serious focus on both class and politics.

34. Jerrie Gage, June 7, 1862, Gage Family Letters, Department of Archives & Special Collections, University of Mississippi, Oxford.
35. Eugene Current-Garcia, "'Mr. Spirit' and *The Big Bear of Arkansas:* A Note on the Genesis of Southwestern Sporting and Humor Literature," *American Literature* 27 (1955): 333–34. See also Current-Garcia's "'York's Tall Son' and His Southern Correspondents," *American Quarterly* 7 (1955): 371–84.

iv.

The adventures of sportsmen in the wild were ready-made vehicles for a venue devoted to "fun and frolic." Hairbreadth confrontations of man and beast could be comic or heroic. The yarns that recounted them tapped into the often ambiguous relationships of hunter and hunted. If skillful, the vernacular storyteller, a type that developed in part from the figure of the hunting guide, could make dialect a sustained and supple narrative instrument. It is easy enough to see the relationship between the sporting sketches in Porter's *Spirit* and the humorous pieces that often use the bear and deer hunt as a frame. In both, the literate narrator offers space for a vernacular storyteller; in both, beast and man tangle, often in amusing and choreographed ways and sometimes in the whimsical exchanging of traits. In both, the sturdy questioning of the romantic motif of nature as a "world elsewhere" ensures a cohesive lighthearted tone.[36] Nowhere is the considerable overlap of forms more evident than in the bantering, mock-pedantic style that can veer wildly between factual reportage and satiric fantasy.

Gentleman sportsmen, even those described as "capital fellows" or "witty raconteurs," rarely betray what they regard as the seriousness of their subject. One sketch, for example, in which two gentlemen go fishing, is mostly devoted to lazy singing of "fine airs," the languid baiting of minnows, and snatches of learned repartee.[37] The Charlestonian William Elliott is properly praised for his astonishing range in *Carolina Sports by Land and Water* (1846). Despite William Gilmore Simms's strictures against the "excessive vivacity" of his prose, Elliott approaches his subject with the seriousness of a real devotee without lapsing into ponderousness. This loosely structured book on hunting and fishing in the low country also faithfully imitates the naturalists' scientific description of fauna; includes anecdotes, essays, and yarns that are practically short stories; and even offers a meditation on the civilizing value of sports. (Its full title was *Carolina Sports by Land and Water, Including Incidents of Devil-Fishing, Wild-Cat, Deer and Bear Hunting, Etc.*) "Field sports are both innocent and manly," Elliott writes in his conclusion. Moreover, such "country amusements" are "promotive of virtue" because they redirect men away from

36. As in many other respects, Thorpe's "Big Bear of Arkansas" is a significant exception. Both the educated narrator and the yarn-spinner affirm metaphysical mystery as an unplumbed aspect of great nature.

37. "An Angling Reminiscence," *Southern Literary Messenger* 19 (1853): 366–69.

immorality. None of his acquaintances who participate in them, he asserts, "has been touched by the vice of gaming!"[38] This patrician may have been sensitive to the linking of "country amusements" and carousing. The Virginian George Tucker, in his account of southern leisure, equates the turf, the cockpit, the chase, and the gaming table. A visiting cleric observed that southerners generally "hasten to the woods for a day of field sport and an evening of dissipation."[39]

As Elliott's admirers point out, his eclectic book is rarely moralistic, but richly textured with lively dialogue, colloquialisms, and tales both touching and funny. *Carolina Sports* is the product of a distinguished man whose authority in real life is carried over effortlessly into unambivalent authorship. Elliott's embrace of authorship is a refreshing attitude in a region that was unusually suspicious of professional writers. The Charlestonian's reputation as a sportsman was apparently enhanced by his authoring a number of pamphlets on agricultural and political topics, reviews of current books, and a poetic drama set in Renaissance Italy. Even as he relates semi-hoaxing tales inspired by slave folklore, Elliott maintains a certain gravity, an obviously personal demeanor that tonally unifies the assorted genres in his book. The bantering mood of a contemporary commentator ("I never read fewer lies in a real sporting book," he wrote, "and these are told very gracefully") is closer to the tone of *Carolina Sports* than that of a later admirer who, solemnly approving the book's patriarchal validation, extrapolates the bravery and generosity of Elliott's fisherman-hunter into a paternal concern for his "fellow human beings" back on the plantation.[40]

The patrician authoritativeness of this southerner is mostly missing in other books by gentleman sportsmen, including those of Henry William Herbert, the bellwether figure and the most influential of all antebellum sportsmen. An Englishman, educated at Eton and Cambridge, Herbert was

38. William Elliott, *Carolina Sports by Land and Water, Including Incidents of Devil-Fishing, Wild-Cat, Deer and Bear Hunting, Etc.* (1846; reprint, Columbia: University of South Carolina Press, 1994), 247, 250–51. Simms is quoted in Theodore Rosengarten's introduction, xxvii.

39. Mary Ann Wimsatt and Robert L. Phillips, "Antebellum Humor," in *The History of Southern Literature,* ed. Louis D. Rubin, Jr., and others (Baton Rouge: Louisiana State University Press, 1985), 146–47; Louis D. Rubin, Jr., *William Elliott Shoots a Bear: Essays on the Southern Literary Imagination* (Baton Rouge: Louisiana State University Press, 1975), 195–212.

40. Lewis Pinckney Jones, "William Elliott, South Carolina Nonconformist," *Journal of Southern History* 17 (1951): 380; Jacob F. Rivers III, *Cultural Values in the Southern Sporting Narrative* (Columbia: University of South Carolina Press, 2002), 4, 17.

forced into self-exile for failing to honor debts incurred as a result of his dandyish lifestyle. For a time after he came to the United States, he taught classics at a Manhattan academy and wrote extravagant adventure novels; but even with reduced funds, shod in his "Cavalier boots with King Charles spurs," he managed to cut an imposing figure among the young-bloods of New York City, once besting a professional jockey at a city track. His real impact, however, was as "Frank Forester," the name he used first in 1839 when he began writing sketches on horse racing, sculling, hunting, and fishing in *The American Turf Register and Sporting Magazine.* Because the first Forester book, *The Warwick Woodlands* (1845), emphasized the technical aspects proper for sportsmen, the author was credited with establishing the appropriate codes of dress and implements for the gentleman sportsman. A friend described his peculiarities in attire—"bright-hued cut-away coats, with glistening buttons, *outre* waistcoats and dashing pantaloons." The flashy image only reinforced Herbert's insistence upon establishing rules of behavior for proper outdoorsmen.[41] Before 1827 only one American hunting book, *The American Shooter's Manual,* acknowledged hunting as a worthy activity. The Frank Forester books spawned others that detailed personal experiences, gave technical advice, and entertained their readers with narratives of both fiction and nonfiction. One authority declares that Herbert made hunting and woodsmanship "not just respectable but redemptive," a lesson that would be institutionalized in the Boy Scouts.[42]

Unlike Herbert, Charles Lanman of Michigan, a dedicated apostle of Isaak Walton, is never quite the dandy in the big woods, but he never forgets his image as the gentleman sportsman, indulgently conscious of the figure he cuts: "My cap and buckskin shirt are on, the latter gathered round my waist by a scarlet worsted belt. My powder-horn and shot-pouch are filled with the nicest kind of ammunition, and in my hand is my valued little gun (bought expressly for myself), polished bright as a sunbeam." Lanman, who gave up a promising mercantile career in New York City to travel, explored and wrote about most of the mountainous areas of the country. He published his angling adventures and other sketches of the wild in various journals, especially the *National Intelligencer,* before collecting them in book form. Washington Irving, after reading *Essays for Summer Hours* (1842) and *A Summer in the Wilderness*

41. Robert H. Boyle, "The Sports Pages Began with Him," *Sports Illustrated,* June 5, 1989, pp. 14–17; Wimsatt and Phillips, "Antebellum Humor," 146.
42. Herman, *Hunting,* 70, 71, 178. As books in the Forester mode, Herman cites in particular those by Charles W. Webber, John Krider, and Elisha J. Lewis.

(1847), wrote Lanman admiringly regarding his sketches of "savage life," the fishing and hunting anecdotes, the "adventures of trappers and back wood men," and the "whole arcanum in short of indigenous poetry and romance."[43]

These accounts are characteristically structured as sporting expeditions, temporary life on the trail that facilitates Lanman's meeting trappers, mountaineers, hunters, and professional men; and though his favorite geography is eastern Canada, upper New York, and the Great Lakes area, Lanman has extensive segments covering rambles in the upper South. His style is commendably straightforward, less grave and pretentious than that of some of his contemporaries who took to the woods; but, in the approved mode of the day, American nature is invoked as a species of European architecture. In North Carolina, Lanman writes of a rocky ledge: "you might fancy that you looked upon a ruined castle, a decayed battlement, or the shattered tower of an old cathedral." Irving, who could hardly better this mode himself, declared to Lanman, "You are in fact the picturesque explorer of our country."[44]

If the spectacle of American forests was awesome principally in terms of European cathedrals, the symbolic meaning of Great Nature also revealed itself generally in comfortable patterns nearly a century old. Like that of Parkman, Cooper, Longfellow, Richard Henry Dana, Horace Greeley, and many others, Lanman's native scenery invited moral glossing that suggested cultural "laws." Like most cultivated tourists, this piscatorial sportsman exploited the spiritual effects of topography unavailable to English Waltonians. What he borrowed from those writers, however, was an appropriate lexicon for framing those effects in an Old World rhetoric of the sublime. Tallulah Falls in Georgia elicits an impersonal prose that dutifully draws the lesson of picturesque nature; amid the "gloom and horror," rainbows, and fierce air currents, Lanman observes that "the roar of the waterfalls, eternally ascending to the sky, falls upon the ear like the voice of God calling upon man to wonder and admire."[45]

When writing of Michigan, Lanman's prose grows memoiristic: the nostalgic note of boyhood recalled absorbs all the sentimental tags of the

43. Charles Lanman, *Adventures in the Wilds of North America*, ed. Charles Richard Weld (London, 1854), 146; Washington Irving, *Letters: Vol. 4, 1846–1859*, ed. Ralph M. Aderman, Herbert L. Kleinfield, and Jenifer S. Banks, *The Complete Works of Washington Irving* (Boston: Twayne, 1982), 293–94.

44. Lanman, *Adventures*, 161; Irving, *Letters*, 609.

45. Lanman, *Adventures*, 146.

English poets of a generation earlier, the standard diction of the romantic traveler. That bulwark requires little spontaneity, as if natural feeling demands an even more vigilant hedging by the language of convention. Michigan is evoked by garlands of dependable locutions: the songs of wilderness birds and *ever-murmuring* streams are a *perpetual anthem;* the inhabitants are represented by the *secluded husbandman* hunting the *noble buck;* the *picturesque* Indians are celebrated for their *unaffected assemblies* and *simple games* and their skill with the *net, the hook, and the spear.* Lanman even allows himself to conclude his sketch of his native state with a kind of dream vision, punctuated by poetic snippets, which ends like most versions of that venerable genre: "The spell is broken;—my dream, and my book about the wilderness, are both ended."[46]

Freely offered opinions come as easily to gentleman sportsmen as to the generalist travelers on tamer treks. Perhaps because they are ostensible masters of certain specialty skills—fishing, hunting, planning wilderness camps—they tend to evaluate everything in their ken, never hesitating to pass judgment equally on scenery, men, and social phenomena.[47] Unlike their contemporaries the scientists, who at least imagined themselves operating objectively, Lanman and his fellow sportsmen saw both scenery and people through a lens that had proved useful in the civilizing mission of all activists. Storms at sea, western vistas, cataracts, Indian mounds, the Hudson Valley: all manifested a God of Power. For all the freshness of the native scenery celebrated by Irving and Cooper, whom most of the sportsmen imitated, their way of looking at it was comfortably derivative, even as it reflected contemporary political doctrine. The sublime had always affirmed a generalized spirituality, but to interpret it in terms of Manifest Destiny was to link aesthetic principles of long standing to the national mission.

Lanman spends much of his time experiencing the wilds "on foot, on horseback, and in canoes," adventures that may be rare for a former merchant but that are not inconsistent with his century's zeal in using expeditions for personal testing. What this fishing enthusiast brings to his experiences is a firm commitment to mainstream values of social hierarchy,

46. Ibid., 60–64.
47. Lanman, the confident dispenser of advice to fishermen, strikes the same note of authority when he turns to art. Although he discusses technical lapses in Thomas Cole's *Course of Empire* series (some figures are "poorly drawn and arranged"), the sportsman praises Cole for the grand conceptions that make him an appropriate model for younger painters. *Haw-Ho-Noo; or Records of a Tourist* (Philadelphia, 1850), 152–64.

Anglo-American superiority over the world's peoples, and the felt impulse to voice these beliefs. Knowing that one measure of wealth—the condition of residences—is suspect in the South, Lanman devises his own rule of thumb for measuring relative prosperity in the Smoky Mountains. "A rich man seldom has more than one dog," he writes, "while a very poor man will keep from ten to a dozen"—a rule that he also applies, with the same insouciance, to children: "The poorest man, without any exception, whom I have seen in this region, lives in a log-cabin, with two rooms, and is the father of *nineteen children,* and the keeper of *six hounds.*"[48] Such bemused ethno-snobbery is less a trait of Lanman as an acute field observer than it is a cultural assumption common to the educated classes generally. More than many of his fellow sportsmen, however, Lanman frequently goes beyond mere assumptions with disarming directness. In North Carolina and Georgia he admits that it made him happy "to communicate what little I happened to know" to the mountaineers, but it pains him to ponder "their uncultivated manner of life." With refreshing candor he concludes: "Give me the wilderness for a day, or month, but for life I must be amid the haunts of refinement and civilisation."[49]

As with Lanman, the shadow of Washington Irving falls across the career of David Hunter Strother, an artist and writer from Virginia so enamored of the New Yorker that he chose to call his writing-and-sketching self "Porte Crayon." "A Visit to the Virginia Canaan" (1853), in which Strother introduced his pen name, is an account of six sportsmen on a fishing expedition into the Virginia interior. Strong on scenic description and characterization, the piece includes a garrulous talker and a corpulent gourmand whose game bag is fuller going out than on the return. Like the scribes of most of the late antebellum sporting literature, Strother crafted a style that is unapologetically genteel. Despite the obvious fact that the expedition in "Virginia Canaan" is a social occasion, his chief commentator suggests that Strother participated in a generic convention in sportswriting: sentimentalizing the superiority of a "romantic attachment to rural solitude."[50] Significantly, "Virginia Canaan" and Strother's later sketches appeared in *Harper's Magazine,* not in Porter's *Spirit.*

48. Lanman, *Adventures,* 160.
49. Ibid., 209.
50. Cecil D. Eby, Jr., *"Porte Crayon": The Life of David Hunter Strother* (Chapel Hill: University of North Carolina Press, 1960), 77. See also Mary Ann Wimsatt, "Antebellum Fiction," in *The History of Southern Literature,* ed. Louis D. Rubin, Jr., and others (Baton Rouge: Louisiana State University Press, 1985), 103.

When he gathered his several pieces into *Virginia Illustrated.* (1857), Strother harkened back to conventions of eighteenth-century novelists who created narratives out of travels and capitalized on the American Victorian fondness for manicured descriptions. His most effective and incisive portraits are of those figures outside his own class—African Americans and North Carolina backwoodsmen. Though Strother could not avoid becoming the patrician beneficiary of the Old Dominion's colonial snobbery, he, like his fellow sportsmen, could amuse his audience with irony and gentlemanly self-deprecation in casting himself and his well-to-do companions as tyros in the woods. (T. B. Thorpe's bear hunter, we remember, has his own take on the marksmanship of sophisticated gentlemen: "They'd miss a barn if the door was swinging.")

A more interesting and ambitious author of sporting in the wilds is Charles E. Whitehead, whose *Wild Sports in the South* (1860) first saw print as articles in the *Spirit of the Times*.[51] Intelligent, sensitive, and observant, Whitehead is a conspicuous example of the patrician who took the role of sportsman seriously as a class privilege. He avoids stuffiness by fashioning a persona that was always attractive to William T. Porter: the confident, accomplished gentleman who can belittle his woodsmanship because his class affiliation allows him the indulgence of modesty. Though his prose is often magisterial, the tone conveys his whimsical expectation of his own near-failure and open admiration for the fidelity and enterprise of those subordinates who ensure the success of the expedition. Like most of his sporting peers, Whitehead enters nature in fine nineteenth-century style, which is to say, with genial companions and a retinue of servants and dogs. The most important character in his book is "Mike the Spook," a lanky, taciturn, and dependable guide with skills learned by living in the wilderness and fighting the Seminoles. The author's chief companion is "Poke," the stocky Dr. Pollock, a gentle scientist who seems "to know everything" and who scorns the use of common names for the fauna they encounter. (Whatever their grounding in reality, the characterizations of both the guide and the doctor show clear compositional descent from Cooper. Despite his resemblance to Natty Bumppo, Mike becomes a credible and effective figure in his own right; Whitehead is less successful in differentiating Dr. Pollock from Obed Bat of *The Prairie*.) With his grave demeanor, native wisdom, and wry, understated sense of

51. Charles E. Whitehead, *Wild Sports in the South; or the Camp-Fires of the Everglades* (London, 1860). The general title of the individual sketches in the *Spirit* was "Camp-Fire Stories." A lavishly illustrated edition was titled *The Camp-Fires of the Everglades or Wild Sports in the South* (Edinburgh, 1891).

humor, Mike gives Whitehead's book the vigor it needs. He had agreed to become guide, we are told, not only because he liked the author but also because of "mere curiosity" in watching Whitehead and his doctor friend performing avocationally in the wilds the tasks he has spent a lifetime perfecting.[52]

Like other books of its kind, *Wild Sports in the South* is an adaptation of multiple genres: natural history pieces shaped by the personal essay; newspaper reports of hunting expeditions in the forests; and the adventure romance inspired by both Cooper and the antebellum plantation idyll. It is also a rustic page out of tale cycles like the *Decameron*, in which each of an assembled group takes his turn in spinning a yarn appropriate to his character. That the book moves with any narrative development is somewhat surprising given the wide variety of forms that it draws on. The expedition itself becomes a naturally evolving narrative alternating rhythms of momentum and rest. The hours are divided between actual forays (for bear, turkey, deer, and, in unplanned moments, wolves and panthers) and a succession of camps (where the group enjoys amiable bantering, storytelling, and basking in the enveloping sounds and sights of natural creatures not worth the hunt). A lawyer with a naturalist's inclination, Whitehead notes sporadically—when the party tires of yarns and hunts—the natural life of the Florida peninsula. In his topographical surroundings, the author is as alert to the mockingbirds, ducks, snipe, and herons as he is to the larger game that draws him to the Everglades.

The guide's story, "The Panther's Cub," is appropriately told in a passable yeoman vernacular that avoids the exaggerated diction common to similar tales in the humor. Mike's yarn is not merely affecting, but also effectively tied to present action. When later in the expedition Mike is forced to shoot an attacking panther, he knows from the cat's configuration that it is the same "cub" of his story, grown older by four years, a turn of fate that brings out the meditative side of the guide. He delivers what amounts to a funeral address over the dead animal: "Yer forgot me, but I didn't forgit you, no how at all, little yaller back, and now yer dead, poor thing. Wall, wall, we'll all come to that soon, only let's have our traps packed and ready." In contrast, the narrator chooses to sketch the natural history of the muskrat. He ends: "When I had finished my history, I looked around upon my auditors, and found they were all asleep."[53] Except for the author's pleasantly self-deprecating touches, the matching tales and

52. Whitehead, *Wild Sports*, 11.
53. Ibid., 85, 136.

tellers emphasize literary models over credibility. There are entirely too many exclamations of joyful anticipation and clapping of hands ("A story—a story!").

Hunting, as most of these books make clear, is a gentlemanly activity, a ritualistic demonstration of what has been called "self-assertion and social authority." A correspondent in 1829 urged young readers of the *American Turf Register* to "spend their leisure time in the *open field*" rather than in saloons and oyster cellars.[54] The outdoors became a testing ground for (mostly) urbanites intent on measuring their diligence, self-restraint, and Americanness. Herbert's promotion of field sports ("the manliest" amusement for preventing "over civilization" and "sloth") appealed particularly to southern planters, who sometimes fretted that a leisurely lifestyle might be encouraging irresponsibility and effeminacy in their sons. For A. B. Longstreet at Emory College, the antidote to dilettantism was "healthful, useful, instructive bodily labor." According to one memoirist, the southern father, in order to forestall "enfeebling self-indulgence and luxury," typically taught his son to shoot, ride, and hunt "as soon as he left off petticoats." There is no evidence that Alfred Bunn's devastating profile of "Young America" had much effect in the South, but the visitor's acerbic analysis was consistent with how Frederick Law Olmsted viewed sons of well-to-do southerners. Bunn depicts the poorly supervised young male as a species of the useless snob who

> has his clothes from England, his boots from France, and his hats at home, which he considers the best in the world. He wears that hat a little on one side, and has a tooth-pick in his mouth which he sucks as he goes along, "for want of thought." He calls every one of his own age "old fellow." He sings a bad song, tells a bad story, but makes up for either deficiency by thinking very highly of himself.[55]

54. Herman, *Hunting,* 136. See also Michael P. Johnson, "Planters and Patriarchy: Charleston, 1800–1860," *Journal of Southern History* 46 (1980): 45–72.

55. Frank Forester [Henry William Herbert], *Field Sports of the United States* (New York, 1856), 26; *Address Delivered before the Faculty and Students of Emory College, Oxford, Ga., by Augustus B. Longstreet* (Augusta, GA, 1840), 15–16; Reuben Davis, *Recollections of Mississippi and Mississippians* (1889; reprint, ed. William D. McCain, Oxford: University and College Press of Mississippi, 1972), 156–58; Alfred Bunn, *Old England and New England, in a Series of Views Taken on the Spot* (London, 1853), 282–83. A New Yorker summed up the southern medical student as a long-haired, foulmouthed verdant who outside his region becomes "a puzzle to professors, a terror to landladies, and a munificent patron of grogshops." Conevery Bolton Valenčius, *The Health of the Country: How American Settlers Understood Themselves and Their Land* (New York: Basic Books, 2002), 180.

Sporting activities became an effective weapon against self-indulgence and luxury, yet most of the authors (beginning with Herbert) stressed *appropriate dress.* Being manly did not mean dressing boorishly. Elisha J. Lewis in his *Hints to Sportsmen* (1851) advised hunters to keep their hands "white and smooth" by wearing gloves: "nothing," he declared, is more vulgar than to see "a coarse, scratched and scarred hand."[56]

The appearance of William H. H. Murray's *Adventures in the Wilderness* (1869) signaled an end to the genre before it metamorphosed into the ecological treatise. In gathering his periodical pieces, Murray took pains to differentiate his account of sporting experiences from all the reports that had gone before. In his introduction he asserts that readers are in great need of outdoors writing "unencumbered with the ordinary reflections and jottings of a tourist's book, free from the slang of guides, and questionable jokes, and 'bear stories.'" Though as a New Englander and Congregational minister his distaste for those aspects of sporting literature may have well been moral, it is more likely that Murray was simply tired of the books' easy aping of each other. His *Adventures,* he makes clear, is not meant for the idle hours of armchair sportsmen.[57]

The title of Murray's very first chapter affirms that departure: "Why I Go There,—How I Get There,—What I Do There,—and What It Costs." The prudential Yankee learnedness of Henry Thoreau is soon succeeded by a straight-talking, practical enthusiasm for wild sports that anticipates Theodore Roosevelt's agenda less than a generation later. This author names all the necessary items of clothing (flannel undersuit, camp shoes, buckskin gloves), sporting outfit (rifle, fly rod, landing net, "flies"), and dependable merchants for buying tackle (such as J. Conroy, Fulton Street, New York City), and gives a reasonable itinerary for reaching the Adirondack wilderness with the least grief. But the most aggressive change is Murray's attitude toward guides, countering most sportsmen, who—at least in their written accounts—set great store by their illiterate, yarn-spinning, woods-wise guides. The truculent Murray advises his readers not to tolerate the "ignorant, lazy, low-bred guide," who is "forever *talking.* He inundates the camp with gab. . . . He is possessed from head to foot with the idea that he is *smart.* . . . He is always vulgar, not seldom profane. Avoid him as you would the plague." To ratify his advice, the au-

56. Quoted in Herman, *Hunting,* 136.

57. William H. H. Murray, *Adventures in the Wilderness* (1869; reprint, Syracuse, NY: Adirondack Museum/Syracuse University Press, 1970), 7–8. See also Roderick Nash, *Wilderness and the American Mind,* rev. ed. (New Haven, CT: Yale University Press, 1973), 116.

thor appends a list of the names and post office addresses of *approved* guides, those "worthy of patronage."[58]

This muscular Christian is not always the curmudgeon about the genre he scorned, and he retained some familiar aesthetic features: word pictures of the wilderness, profiles of acquaintances in the expedition, and kinetic descriptions of perilous stages that a sportsman must be ready to undergo—running the rapids in a canoe, say, or trying to shoot a loon during a thunderstorm. Surprisingly, Murray even includes an interpolated yarn told around the campfire by a stranger who joins his party unexpectedly. Although T. B. Thorpe judged the book "twaddle," *Adventures in the Wilderness* is a practical guide.[59] Inheritors of Murray's approach are diverse: health-and-recreation therapists, YMCA camp programs, the grittier successors to Karl Baedeker's travel guides, and the merchandisers at L. L. Bean and Abercrombie & Fitch (in its earliest incarnation). Had Willis & Geiger—purveyors of safari gear—issued a catalog in 1869, Murray would have been an ideal writer of copy.

For all the good advice, this late entry in sportsmen's writing ends sourly. From some mysterious compulsion—perhaps his Christian honesty—Murray includes the texts of many letters generated by his newspaper articles two years earlier. Most are harshly critical, complaining that his version of camp life in the wilds is inaccurate, exaggerated, misleading, and unrealistic. Readers of the *Spirit* of a generation earlier would have recognized in these letters the chaffing pattern of claim and response, assertion and challenge, and the brio of epistolary competition. What they would have missed was a good-natured tone. The rivalry that Murray dutifully records does not consist of stilted mock challenges by genial sportsmen with arch pseudonyms, but charges of bad faith hurled by angry and disappointed readers in the plain language of outrage. In an appendix, Murray files his reply to what he calls his "Calumniators"; it is appropriately grave, with a trace of parsonical indignation over aspersions to his veracity. *Adventures in the Wilderness,* with its neutral and echoing title, brings to a solemn end the cheerful amateurism of American sporting prose.

Frederick Gerstaecker is a sportsman of a different stripe.[60] He is not only not a gentlemanly amateur writer; he is also a foreigner whose most

58. Murray, *Adventures,* 32–33, 39–40.
59. Quoted in Herman, *Hunting,* 197.
60. The spelling of the German sportsman's name is rendered variously as *Gerstäcker, Gerstaecker,* and *Gerstaeker.*

celebrated books on the American Southwest were written in German. In translation, such books as *The Pirates of the Mississippi* and *The Regulators of Arkansas* are rich both in folklore and in realistic detail in their explorations of backwoods life. And his first book, despite its title, *Wild Sports in the Far West,* barely resembles the collections of outdoor adventures reported by Lanman, Elliott, and others. It is not quite a travel book, the form most foreigners in America preferred, but neither is it the product of a well-to-do man firmly assured of his place in a structured society.

This German hunting enthusiast traveled widely in the United States, particularly in the Old Southwest. "Of all I had seen in America," he notes before returning to Europe, it was Arkansas "which pleased me most," and his book, accordingly, focuses on that game-rich area. A single sentence suggests just how far afield *Wild Sports in the Far West* is from most travel books of the time: "I was passionately fond of field sports, and [my brother] often severely blamed my useless loitering about in the woods, seriously representing to me that I could not go on so for ever, and that I should be forced, sooner or later, to settle somewhere, and become a useful and reasonable member of society." The governing diction grows out of a settlement culture, an attitude that equates field sports not with a gentlemanly tradition but with a more primitive stage of civic development. Later, his brother even offers to help Gerstaecker "settle somewhere"—"to hang up the rifle, and take to the axe." Moreover, the wandering sportsman understands (and agrees with) the bias behind his brother's offer. Though he refuses it, he too associates field sports with restless mobility, a "wild and unsteady life" that is not conducive to a society of "useful and reasonable" men.[61]

As we see from the accounts of Whitehead and Lanman, and as we see also from the contemporaneous squibs in Porter's *Spirit,* Gerstaecker's notion of field sports was anachronistic, akin to the frontier habits of an earlier generation of Boones and Natty Bumppos. Field sports may not have been a leisure activity restricted to the elite, but their assumptions and protocols emerged from a gentry culture that had little relevance for this German. That spirit is suggested by one commentator's definition of *sportsmanship:* a code for those in power who play not to win or lose but to strengthen cultural bonding among like-minded men. Being a *good*

61. Frederick Gerstaecker, *Wild Sports in the Far West* (1854; reprint, Boston, 1866), 374, 370. The original German account, written in 1844 soon after Gerstaecker returned from the United States, was based on his detailed journals of his American years, 1837–1843. The first English translation appeared in 1854.

sport confirms "the legitimacy of power."[62] Both in its setting and its narrator's self-definition, Gerstaecker's book is anomalous. In an Arkansas backwoods resistant to gentlemanly missions, its author reenacts, in the late 1830s, belated adventures out of Boone, Crockett, and Cooper (whom he had avidly read in German).

He has a guide known as Slowtrap and a dog he calls Bearsgrease. For days at a time along the Arkansas-Texas border he feeds on wild turkey and deer meat, which, lacking salt, he seasons with sprinkles of gunpowder. Gerstaecker cites one instance in which he and Erskine, a companion, flush a bear, which promptly kills four of their dogs. As he plunges his knife into the bear in an attempt to save the rest of the dogs, the howling, wounded prey knocks him senseless. When he awakens, he finds Erskine dead, along with the dogs and the bear. With a dislocated arm he passes the night keeping a fire going to prevent an attack by circling wolves, until he is rescued by some Indians. Bear hunting, as Crockett suggested, could be a dangerous sport to men and dogs alike. Hand-to-paw combat is rare in most sporting literature, though it punctuates some of the tall tales told around the campfire.

There is yet a further oddity about Gerstaecker. A young man without any well-defined goal, he plans his journey to America in 1837 as his *Wanderjahr,* except that this itinerant visitor bounces about the Southwest for nearly seven years. For most of that time he is a hunter in Arkansas, and while his adventures there sound (and probably are) authentic, they are also necessarily selective, subject to the same kind of self-dramatizing instinct we see in one of his letters of 1838. After listing an extensive series of jobs in America, Gerstaecker writes: "Here I stalk through life like a wild animal—like the panthers in the wilderness."[63] At that time *here* was Cincinnati, where he was then a silversmith.

In *Wild Sports* he is wont to write occasionally that he craves company, that he longs "to fall in with human beings, to eat bread, and taste salt." If at times he revels in his loneliness, he is also dissatisfied, dreaming of "a warm bed, a sound roof, and the society of fellow creatures." But even in the selective record of *Wild Sports,* he satisfies these cravings frequently. The very restlessness that propels him into the woods regularly brings him back out. He makes himself known to the considerable community of

62. Michael Oriard, *Sporting with the Gods: The Rhetoric of Play and Game in American Culture* (Cambridge: Cambridge University Press, 1991), 26.

63. James William Miller, ed., *In the Arkansas Backwoods: Tales and Sketches by Friedrich Gerstäcker* (Columbia: University of Missouri Press, 1991), 6.

Germans who preceded him to Arkansas, and his text throughout is enlivened by skillful word pictures of old settlers, including an ancient man "who had fought under Washington in the war of independence." His vignette of "lying Bahrens," an Arkansas frontiersman who amuses him with tales of marksmanship and the fertility of Arkansas soil, comes from prolonged exposure to his company. Gerstaecker is even tolerant of a young man whom settlers suspect of horse-stealing: for all his cloudy reputation, he is pronounced "a good fellow, and a capital sportsman."[64]

If in most ways this German's concept of sport has little in common with that of more conventional chroniclers, he is at one with them both in literary self-consciousness and the psychological need for the society of other capital sportsmen. Gerstaecker passes the time during a rainy season reading *The Pilgrim's Progress* and volumes of American biography. At one point he simultaneously inserts himself into a hackneyed literary campfire scene—"stretched under the starry skies beside a crackling fire in the forest, my trusty rifle and faithful dog by my side"—and meditates on what it has cost him to follow game as a sportsman. "The future offered no inviting picture; alone, in the endless wilderness, I stood, with hair turning gray—a solitary hunter, leaning on my rifle, separated from all I loved." This moment ends as literarily as it began: "Old Hawkeye," he muses, "must have had many a sorrowful hour." Even as he identifies with Cooper's mythic hero, Gerstaecker assumes the pose of Daniel Boone in the portrait by William C. Allen.[65]

If Frederick Gerstaecker comes down to us as an anomaly, Alabama's Thomas Dabney in his daughter's "memorials" is a veritable paradigm of the planter sportsman. Without irony, his daughter writes: "Managing a plantation was something like managing a kingdom." Among other roles, Dabney is the generic southern sportsman, devotee of fishing and hunting, organizer of a hunt club, and host at an annual autumn deer hunt, an event for showing off his accurate rifle eye and entertaining a party of intimates. The deer hunt is important more for its appurtenances and its bonhomie than for shooting game: "A wagon with four mules carried his servants and a marquee large enough for twelve men, bed, camp-chest," and provisions for men and beasts for two weeks. The huntsmen, "leaving all care behind, were as full of practical jokes as schoolboys," Susan Dabney Smedes remembered, and the host regaled his party

64. Gerstaecker, *Wild Sports*, 87, 154, 249.

65. Ibid., 288. Miller, *In the Arkansas Backwoods*, xiii–xviii, supplies a clarifying chronology of the sportsman's Arkansas years, which is muddled in *Wild Sports*.

with stories of previous hunts "full of adventure."[66] If this straight-faced account sounds like a near parody, it is because the image of the antebellum planter with his careless command of servants, friends, and dogs in big house and big woods alike has so long been fixed and predictable. The hunt is as ordered as a cotillion. In Simms's satiric novella, *The Golden Christmas* (1852), a boar hunt is a diversion so stylized that its organizers call it a "tournament" of competing "knights," each one armed "with boar spear and *couteau de chausse*." The most memorable fictional appearance of the hunt is in *Go Down, Moses*, where Faulkner at once honors and satirizes it. By enveloping the expedition in a rustic elegance that grows more and more ragtag, he suggests the sense of depletion in a recurring rite. The spatial depletion of the Mississippi wilderness in which the symbolic hunt is encased is both source and consequence of the rite.[67]

The old pleasures of the sporting outdoors that are keener because of their diminishment are not restricted to Susan Smedes or to the other genteel custodians of tradition. Most antebellum accounts take for granted the hunting of game. The long shadow of the shrinking frontier extended to the governor of Mississippi as late as 1861. Governor Pettus, observed an English visitor, "hunted deer and trapped in the forest of the far west, and lived in a Natty Bumpo or David Crockett state of life"; moreover, this "grim, tall, angular" man "very rightly made the most of his independence and his hard work."[68] The articulated pleasures of wilderness in the Old Southwest are mostly celebrations after the fact, when the literal shrinkage of wilderness has become obvious. In *Wild Sports in the Far West*, only the testimony of Slowtrap, with his historical perspective as both hunter and migrant (from North Carolina to Kentucky to Arkansas), awakens Gerstaecker to the mournful process of depletion. "It was about this time of the year," muses Slowtrap,

"and the game we saw made our hearts bound: numbers of bears, deer, and buffaloes; while the turkeys could hardly get out of our way. It would tire you to tell you of all the sport we had, for no country in the world

66. Susan Dabney Smedes, *Memorials of a Southern Planter* (1887; reprint, ed. Fletcher M. Green, New York: Knopf, 1965), 102, 92–93.

67. William Faulkner, *Go Down, Moses*, in *Novels, 1942–1954* (New York: Library of America, 1994). Mary Ann Wimsatt discusses Simms's comedy of manners about the "fashionable folly" of the low-country elite in *The Major Fiction of William Gilmore Simms: Cultural Traditions and Literary Form* (Baton Rouge: Louisiana State University Press, 1989), 176–79.

68. William Howard Russell, *My Diary North and South* (Boston, 1863), 299.

could boast of more game than Kentucky thirty years ago; but now it is no better there than it was then in North Carolina, and five years hence, a man who wants to shoot a bear in Arkansas, will have many a weary mile to tramp."[69]

With the exception of this German's anomalous book, there is a stately progression that structures the adventures of gentleman sportsmen, which tend to emphasize leisure moments—for both proper preparation and for meditation, as well as for the creative space necessary to make the adventures meaningful. These books require no formal objectivity, no dispassionate eye for assessing people and events, but, cued by Frank Forester, class affiliation demands a sense of fair play in judgments. The author's knowledge of horses, wild game, firearms, and geography is a given in these accounts. For quaint details or common lore, the sportsman usually defers to the guide, quoting him or summarizing his perspectives with good-hearted condescension. Porte Crayon especially was skillful in transferring heard dialect to written form, but though he enjoyed the sketches of Ham Jones and Johnson Jones Hooper, he never thought of himself as a humorist. His prose is the writing of a man aspiring to the regard of his public. And, in general, there is nothing tentative about such sportsmen's prose. It marches solidly behind the guidon of Victorian orthodoxy in all matters cultural. If at times the authors occasionally press the limits of good taste in dress, what they write follows the standards and expectations of a large but select public eager to behave and improve.

v.

William T. Porter nowhere suggests that such accounts of wilderness adventures are stuffy. A number of them are in fact noted and reviewed in the pages of the *Spirit.* But if their subject was naturally attractive to much of its readership, their manner seemed increasingly old-fashioned

69. Gerstaecker, *Wild Sports,* 242. Mourning over the rapid decline of a game-rich wilderness edges many accounts. When Crockett says he killed 105 bears in less than a year, we tend to chalk up that fact to the embellishments of a canebrake roarer; yet that detail says more about pioneer hunting generally than about the self-publicizing hero when we compare it to Daniel Boone's record of 155 bears in a three-week period—"eleven one day before breakfast." Elliott West, "The American Frontier: Romance and Reality," in *William Gilmore Simms and the American Frontier,* ed. John Caldwell Guilds and Caroline Collins (Athens: University of Georgia Press, 1997), 35.

compared to the breezier styles of the humorists' contributions. Gentleman sportsmen pretended to regard rivalry with distaste, and they regularly deemphasized numerical signs of success. In contrast, hunting sketches in the *Spirit,* even those that sound entirely factual, invariably cite amounts and weights of game bagged. Like much of the humor, the typical sporting pieces were de facto exercises in competition, often framed as regional challenges. An army correspondent on a big-game hunt in Iowa with his dragoons reported a total of 104 deer, 57 buffalo, and 20 elk; another officer in Texas described a three-day jaunt that resulted in 10 deer, 51 geese, 69 snipe, some cranes and turkeys, and, for good measure, a panther weighing 160 pounds.[70] Yet many of the humorists whose major outlet was Porter's *Spirit* were as passionate about field sports as the more sedate authors, and a few of them wrote their pieces with appropriate restraint. In these sporting essays, reports, and squibs, the humorists might momentarily suppress their own competitive urges, but they always brandished their talent for the witty and the droll. The Frank Forester manner radiated through much antebellum writing.

The celebrated editor of the *Spirit* was practically the president of his own guild: his stable of contributors to the *American Turf Register* and the *Spirit of the Times* overlapped with sports-minded journalists on such regional papers as the *St. Louis Reveille* and the *New Orleans Picayune.* As we have seen, the line separating the humorists and the sportsmen was not always distinct; indeed, two of Porter's favorite humorists—Thorpe and Noland—also wrote many pieces on field sports. The readership of both the humorous sketches and the sporting epistles overlapped as well, even though the tone and substance of each varied considerably. More decorously written, field-sports prose carried an aura of greater seriousness than the flippant humorous pieces: it could be "droll" but not "ludicrous." Much of it avoided even the mock urbanity that constituted a kind of house style for the intramural network of authors and editors. Some of the sporting writers—Herbert especially—may have been men-about-town in their personal lives, but the style of the self-assured, comfortable country gentleman was generally the image they preferred to project.

When in 1856 Johnson Jones Hooper turned away from the amusing scams of Simon Suggs to produce (hurriedly) *Dog and Gun,* he had in mind a practical manual for hunters. Even as he takes his subject seriously,

70. Flanagan, "Western Sportsmen Travelers," 182–83.

Hooper is never quite willing to sacrifice his customary wit and sportive style when writing as himself, laying out points of instruction and advice. His little book is also a mini-anthology. Unlike Porter in his reworking of Peter Hawker's *Instructions to Young Sportsmen,* Hooper strengthens his authority with substantial excerpts from earlier experts. He also benefits, as he admits, from the "abundance of facts, feats, and general information" he found in the weekly numbers of the *Spirit.*[71] The humorist's liberal cribbing of others' material burnished the reputations of established sporting authorities, and such mutual reinforcement suggests the strong ties of a dispersed sodality, a network of like-minded fellows whose enthusiasm for the chase is typically tempered by a pervasive gentrified taste.

Dog and Gun is dedicated to Herbert, the magisterial dean of sportsmen, and, like some other volumes of its kind, it implicitly defines the protocols of a leisure activity taken as the hallmark of an established class.[72] Hooper would have understood perfectly the anxiety and occasional exasperation expressed by William Elliott, the patrician sportsman ideologically at odds with "the people." As a wealthy planter, the Carolinian grumbled about court decisions upholding the hunting rights of his poorer neighbors, who stoutly repeated the maxim of hunters' law: "I should follow my dogs where they might!" Fearing a depletion in the game supply, Elliott saw that gentlemanly hunting was threatened (and with it the gentry's cultural prestige). The prejudices of the people, he lamented, "are strong against any exclusive property in game," because, as he accurately noted, exclusive rights to hunting were associated in the popular mind with "ideas of aristocracy—peculiar privileges to the rich, and oppression toward the poor!"[73]

In his little treatise Hooper is by turns a patient mentor, an insider with tips for buying quality equipment, a digressive raconteur, and a hectoring Mr. Manners regarding sporting etiquette. In this latter role he is less willing than the typical southern planter to rely on the *implicit* codes for sportsmen. Stung by the easy way in which some Alabamians equated him with the disreputable Simon Suggs, Hooper may have been personally oversensitive—certainly his rhetorical tack reflects a class system less stable in his Old Southwest than in William Elliott's South Carolina.

71. Johnson Jones Hooper, *Dog and Gun: A Few Loose Chapters on Shooting, Among Which Will Be Found Some Anecdotes and Incidents* (1856; reprint, ed. Philip D. Beidler, Tuscaloosa: University of Alabama Press, 1992), 8–9.

72. Herman, *Hunting,* 179.

73. Elliott, *Carolina Sports,* 254–60.

In the older coastal South, the reader of a book like *Dog and Gun* would not have to be reminded that hunting is properly for sport, not for food, or that language and style are important clues to behavior even in the field. Proper nomenclature for all things sporting is itself, Hooper insists, an index to class affiliation: "the ill-bred fellow is detected by the ordinary dialect he affects," which exposes him and his ilk as "pot-hunting vagabonds." If the reader will only learn to "*Call Quail*, QUAIL!" rather than by the "misnomer, *Partridge*," he will be "one step nearer sportsmanship than the *commune vulgus* who kill him foully and serve him *more* foully, to wit: in hog's lard." (The true sportsman, we learn, delights in eating quail "dressed with a half-teaspoon of pale brandy.")[74]

Hooper's reiterated reminders about distinctions reflect the steady incursions of "the democracy" into those outdoors that by tradition the English (and their admirers in America) reserved for gentlemen. Sporting hunters and pothunters had been bluntly discriminated as early as 1818, when William Cobbett complained that most Americans were inclined to "*kill* things in order to *eat*, which latter forms no part of the *real sportsman's* object." The Simon Suggses of *Dog and Gun* are always generalized as *pot-hunters*. Hooper's prose bristles with recurring cautionary observations. In dog training, he who would scorn the whip would not know the difference in the field between "a perfectly well-broken pointer and a 'pot-hunting cur'"; "*bawling* at your dog" is an "ungentlemanly habit"; nobody but a "pot-hunter, ignorant and irreclaimable," would use long, small-gauged guns. In the same year as *Dog and Gun*, a sportsman wrote in the *Spirit* that animals should be honored to be shot out of existence by gentleman hunters and not "subjected to the tender mercies of the mere pot-hunter." The year before, Elisha Lewis, in his book *The American Sportsman*, attacked the pothunter as "disgusting" and "unmanly" because he lacked "etiquette, humanity, law, or even the common decencies of life."[75]

Along with his occasional puns and self-conscious digressions, Hooper's lapses into defensive asides are also part of the stylistic brio that makes *Dog and Gun* distinctively his. In context, the Latin tags that might otherwise seem affected (even by antebellum standards) are whimsically show-offy, as in the humorists' mixed-level discourse. In both his own prose and in that of the authors Hooper chooses to quote, the elevated

74. Hooper, *Dog and Gun*, 10, 9, 439.
75. Cobbett quoted in Herman, *Hunting*, 59; Hooper, *Dog and Gun*, 44–45, 41, 16; Herman, *Hunting*, 157, 154.

decorum of a proper gentleman's style can rarely sustain itself through a paragraph, sometimes even a sentence, before it happily confronts and absorbs vernacular locutions. (Characteristic yeomanlike phrases are encased in quotation marks, but others—such as "there you have it" and "a little under the mark"—are simply adapted into the overall middling style.) Even in addressing subjects generic to sporting manuals ("On the Shooting of Quail," "How to Choose a Good Gun") the author's voice belongs to a writer more than it does to a hunter. His command of the arcana of nomenclature validates Hooper as an on-site expert, but if experience is the source of his advice, its persuasiveness depends on style.[76]

An obsessive determination to discriminate the sporting life of gentlemen from the economic need of "pot-hunters" obscures a common trait in both—the high priority accorded to *leisure.* The slave-owning planter whistles to his hounds and rides out to his far acres; but that same privilege applies also to the hardscrabble farmer. Moreover, it is not always hunger that motivates the planter's ungenteel kin to lay aside the hoe and shoulder his rifle: the *sport* of hunting attracts him no less than his better-off neighbor. Both can be measured by one rule of thumb: woodland rambles take precedence over ploughing or picking. That shared inclination to take to the woods joins planter and yeoman in a cultural frame of reference.

Southern apologists in the late antebellum era were never quite consistent in their depiction of the planter and his values. Pictures of the planter gamboling in freedom in the woods, enjoying the leisure of his days (guaranteed by enforced labor), contributed to the edenic image of an agrarian lifestyle, one that contrasted sharply with the soulless mercantilism of its Yankee counterpart. One transplanted northerner reminded a friend in Pennsylvania that he had found it necessary "to commence the world anew" when he arrived in Mississippi a decade earlier. Though he has done well with his "planting Interest," he admits that he has yet to adjust to the fact that "Shooting Drinking &c is the order of the day mor particularly in the South & West."[77] Both the humorists and the sporting writers suggested what disapproving travel writers had explicitly noted—the vulnerable line between graceful leisure and laziness, the trifling dis-

76. The modern editor of *Dog and Gun* calls Hooper's work "a serious volume on a practical, manly subject." For whatever reasons, it enjoyed widespread readership, with six editions between 1856 and 1871. Philip D. Beidler, introduction to *Dog and Gun*, viii.
77. E. D. Walcott Letter (M45), 1828, McCain Library and Archives, University of Southern Mississippi, Hattiesburg.

regard of responsibilities and the arrogant assertion of rights.[78] Certainly if we are to believe visitors' observations, packs of haughty youngbloods enjoyed congregating at public sites, making a nuisance of their leisure hours—a kind of coterie version of the sometimes obnoxious crews of yeoman layabouts.

Unlike Hooper with his Alabama backwoods captain, Fenton Noland saw no need to be embarrassed with his Arkansas creation. Before he invented Pete Whetstone of Devil's Fork, he was a regular contributor of sporting dispatches (primarily turf news) to the *Spirit of the Times* under the name of "N. of Arkansas." His earliest known letter to the *Spirit* was a survey of southern racing stables in 1836.[79] There was never a question about Noland's expertise in—or passion for—horse racing. As secretary of the Batesville Jockey Club, one of his duties was to advertise races in Texarkana and Fort Smith, where alone on horseback or on foot he often went as an interested party. His fondness for racing spilled over from "N. of Arkansas" into the character of Pete Whetstone, whom Noland sent in 1839 to visit the famous sites at Trenton, Baltimore, and Louisville, hobnobbing in his earthy way with the same figures that delighted his creator: breeders, owners, managers, trainers, and other fanciers of horseflesh. Although his turf dispatches to the *Spirit* began as reportorial news, Noland early on reinforced his experience and his fund of technical knowledge with colorful glimpses of "the scene."

When Noland developed his Devil's Fork characters, he did not merely give Pete Whetstone his passion for horse racing. Enhancing Pete's credibility, the author allowed his fictional colonel to use real names of tracks, stables, horses, hotels, and steamboats, all of which would have been familiar to those who avidly followed "N. of Arkansas" (*PW*, 40). When Pete visits a famous track in the east, the scene is authentic because he consorts with the same real people as Noland; and when Pete announces that he is on his way to White Sulphur Springs, it is not fashion that draws him there but the same thing that drew Noland—watching races by new horses. Even after Pete became a coherent and credible contributor to "Mr. Spirit," Noland continued his own high-spirited dispatches, and, he reported, finally engineered a meeting with the fictional Pete, with whom he enjoyed many amusing sessions. From 1836 until his death in

78. Oriard, *Sporting with the Gods,* 103–4.
79. Leonard Williams, introduction to *Cavorting on the Devil's Fork: The Pete Whetstone Letters of C. F. M. Noland* (Memphis: Memphis State University Press, 1979), 23–24. See also Ted R. Worley, "An Early Arkansas Sportsman: C. F. M. Noland," *Arkansas Historical Quarterly* 11 (1952): 25–39.

1858, Noland became the most frequent and popular correspondent in Porter's *Spirit,* accruing some three hundred items.[80] Although in volume he outpaced his peers in sporting letters, Noland never gathered even his turf pieces into a book. The Pete Whetstone letters would remain uncollected until the late twentieth century.

Whereas Hooper and Noland were humorists who also wrote sporting sketches, Thomas Bangs Thorpe was a writer primarily interested in the natural history of the Southwest. His first book, *Mysteries of the Backwoods* (1846), omits "The Big Bear of Arkansas," the atypical but single most famous piece in the body of Southwest humor, though it contains the author's fine "A Piano in Arkansas." Nine years later, Thorpe included "The Big Bear" in his second collection, *The Hive of "The Bee-Hunter,"* but it is the work's subtitle that reveals his major interest: *A Repository of Sketches including Peculiar American Character, Scenery, and Rural Sports.*[81] One commentator accurately noted some years ago that Thorpe's writing generally is a "blend of realistic reporting and romantic faith in the power of primitive nature."[82] In a single passage from *Hive* we find a cluster of his favorite words and phrases: *vast interior solitudes, mighty continent, vast extent, wildest imagery, primitive wilds, mighty associations.* Unlike his fellow contributors to the *Spirit of the Times,* Thorpe preferred setting a natural stage without cluttering it with too many backwoodsmen. And unlike most of the travel writers, he showed little interest in the settlement process or the economic and social impact of migration on the Mississippi Valley.

Confronted by what he considers "primitive nature," Thorpe adopts the awe and sentiment, as well as the locutions, of such earlier writers as William Cullen Bryant and Washington Irving. As a discursive essayist, he never quite escaped the conventional tastes of an earlier generation. Yet if his prose style is usually unexceptional, it is rarely ponderous. For

80. Williams, introduction, 24. If Noland was chronologically the first gentleman humorist to contribute to the *Spirit,* he was also, judging from the flood of parodies and imitations he inspired, the most influential. See Lorne Fienberg, "Colonel Noland of the *Spirit:* The Voices of a Gentleman in Southwest Humor," *American Literature* 53 (1981): 232.

81. Estes, introduction, *A New Collection,* 47–55, provides the publishing history of Thorpe's two published collections. See Robert J. Higgs, "The Sublime and the Beautiful: The Meaning of Sport in Collected Sketches of Thomas B. Thorpe," *Southern Studies* 25 (1986): 235–56, for a fine account of the aesthetic principles governing the author's pieces on hunting and fishing in the Mississippi Valley.

82. Milton Rickels, *Thomas Bangs Thorpe: Humorist of the Old Southwest* (Baton Rouge: Louisiana State University Press, 1962), 179.

better or worse, it is a gentleman's style. Though more formally structured and rhetorically calculated in wit than their companions in Porter's
weekly, Thorpe's pieces are truly mediocre only when Indian legendry is
their subject, when all aspects of the writing are washed in a tepid *ubi
sunt* pathos. But if ancient Indians arouse his sentimentality, modern
ones can bring out a dispassionate realism, as in his explicit account of
the "Cumanche" hamstringing technique for buffalo hunting, a brutal
method that "wanton" white hunters readily adopted (*TBT,* 298, 283).
Although some of his hunting sketches are almost incidental to his interest in natural history (as evidenced by his descriptions of the wild turkey,
the alligator, the opossum, and the wildcat), the better ones are personal—by turns thoughtful, technical, and whimsical.

Unlike Hooper, Thorpe links the rude hunter and the sportsman in a
kind of ambivalent brotherhood. If the primitive rites of the buffalo hunt
feed the appetite of the ordinary white hunter's "habit and power to destroy," they are not lost on the sportsman, whose heart is also stirred by
"the latent fires repressed by a whole life" of respectability. And in an interesting reversal, Thorpe makes the *settlement,* not the *wilderness,* the
natural arena for hyperbolic rhetoric. The more primitive hunter, "surrounded by the magnificence and sublimity of an American forest, earning his bread by the hardy adventure of the chase," meets with "too
much reality to find room for coloring, too much of the sublime and ter-
rible . . . to be boastful of himself." While he may be separated from the
advantages of civilization, he is also separated from its "contaminations."
Thorpe asserts that *"boasting and exaggeration, are settlement weaknesses,"*
not the "product of the wild woods" (*TBT,* 151). One of Thorpe's devices
for negotiating the "contaminations" of modern hunting culture is to
project himself as the visitor, the guest, the amateur, in the society of
well-to-do southerners. Though he lived in the lower South for seventeen years, these are not wholly imaginary roles for the New York por-
traitist and writer. In "The Chase," a profile of the generic southern
sportsman, there is no reason to question, for instance, the sincerity of the
outsider who gazes upon the region's outdoor activities in "a transport
of admiration." The narrator can admire all the better if he never becomes truly skilled in southern field sports.

It is an easy posture, of course, but one that is wholly persuasive. In
one sketch he disclaims any great interest in the "excitement of the chase."
He admits that to "head a deer, or get a scare from an old 'he bar'" is a
mere prelude to what he most relishes—the campground at night, with
the fire doing its job on an immense haunch of venison, a bottle of claret

"stowed away under our jacket," and a woolen blanket for lounging. "We love to lie upon the lap of earth, and with our eyes dreamily viewing the firmament, and with our ears wide open, listen to the hunters' tales, who generally keep Truth on a full gallop to be any where in sight of their *facts,* or having distanced her entirely at the outset, cause her to abandon them for the evening" (*TBT,* 314–15). As Thorpe knows, repose after exertion is not only the typal situation in the humorous hunting yarns; it is also a constant in the sportsman's sketch, a segment that in detail is virtually identical in all accounts of hunting expeditions, whatever the game. His delight may be couched in a prose at once poetic and formally witty, but the moment is a characteristic one in the sporting forays of urbanites in the wilds.

Thorpe's persona is most revealing in a self-conscious reverie, "The First Hunting Trip of the Steamer 'Nimrod,'" in which the narrator imagines himself invited on a voguish adventure by the idle sportsmen of Barrow Plantation. Prompted by a news item in the *Spirit of the Times,* he ruminates on the notion of a steamboat expressly designed for sporting expeditions on Louisiana waters—one that would accommodate not merely a hunting party, but "twelve horses, and hounds to match." Snubbing the crude makeshifts of ordinary steamers (dismissed as "floating saw-mills"), the *Nimrod* would carry "into the wilderness the comforts of refined life, thus mixing up the life of a perfectly wild hunter, and the associations of the drawing room" (*TBT,* 136). In most of the written accounts, that happy mix might serve as the secret goal of all sportsmen.

There is humor aplenty in both *Mysteries of the Backwoods* and *The Hive of "The Bee-Hunter,"* but it rarely emerges from raucous backwoodsmen, and its verbal touches depend little on frontier vernacular—the staples of Thorpe's fellow humorists. "The Little Steamboats of the Mississippi," for example, proceeds wholly from the anomalies of size and mass. Despite its boastful name, the tiny mailboat *Emperor,* notes Thorpe, was one of the steamers "that 'run up' little streams that empty into bayous, that empty into rivers, that empty into the Mississippi." Feeling like a Lilliputian, the narrator observes that the ship's bell was "big enough for a Cathedral"; one passenger who comes on board adds "about three hundred" pounds to the displacement, and the captain of "enlarged ideas" commands in "a voice of thunder." Dinnertime boasts "the biggest roast beef, the biggest potatoes, and the biggest carving knife and fork that ever floated" (*TBT,* 253–56). "An Extra Deer Hunt in Louisiana" is structured like a southwestern gingerbread-man story. A wounded buck breaks from the hunters, takes to the open fields, and finally reaches the streets of a village. He is chased by the dogs, and a bellowing bull pursues the dogs; cows follow the bull, the calves ("knowing their anxious mothers wouldn't like to have them out") follow the cows, and a curious crowd follows them all until the buck expires at the courthouse (*TBT*, 127–28). From conceptual wit, Thorpe turns to situational humor in "My First Dinner in New Orleans," a sketch, like so many others, about personal discomfiture. Here the embarrassment is deferred beyond the episode itself. Under the mistaken notion that a hotel's gourmet courses are merely the public fare offered by its excellent kitchen, a stranger joins a private dinner party in the hotel dining room. The account becomes a hymn to gentlemanly hospitality and politesse (*TBT*, 203–6).

Thorpe's major humorous character is a bumbling newspaperman, "P.O.F.," whose sporting reports under the title "Letters from the Far West" constitute this author's most sustained comic writing. In this series of twelve imaginary dispatches from an actual expedition, Thorpe satirizes two genres familiar to antebellum readers: foreign accounts of travel in America and sporting letters from the wilds. The hoax also pokes fun at Sir William Stewart, the sportsman whose hunting party the narrator supposedly joins; Matthew C. Field, a fellow humorist and journalist who actually went on the trip; and naturalist J. J. Audubon, who didn't. Most of all, however, the humor is at the expense of the narrator himself. Gullible and impulsive, this tyro is subjected to more humiliation than most innocent victims in Southwest humor. When the sound of his spurs scares his first horse, he tries several more "steeds," all of which throw him. Dressed in clothes made of raw deerskins, he nearly suffocates when, in direct sun, they shrink on his body. He is chased by a bear and several buffaloes ("while I was looking out for a big bull, a big bull was in my rear, looking out for me"). He gets motion sickness in a canoe; he is attacked by hornets; he swoons several times. His chronic ineptness becomes a major source of comedy among the party. Trying his hand at taxidermy à la Audubon, he makes a mess of his specimens ("my quadrupeds look like sausages, and my birds like a roll of dough"). He confesses that Sir William "would not trust me to stuff a pillow." When Audubon gives him the origin of *buffalo* ("boeuf a'leau," from the beast's fondness for water), even the narrator thinks this bit of folk etymology the "best joke" of the trip—"except the idea of coming *out here for sport*" (*TBT*, 223–52).

The absurd notion of western hunting as sport is the narrator's recurring refrain. If, P.O.F. notes, the prospect of sport "inspirited all of us" at the beginning, it was largely because "the whiskey jug had been freely passed around." Along the Oregon Trail he decides that the "great fault of the Far West" was "that there is too much of it." By the time of the final letter, he can only conclude that he was "the most miserable dog that ever went sport-seeking in the Far West." But if the trip was a mistake, P.O.F. is also indefatigable in enduring it with puns and a kind of philosophic resignation. This self-effacing reporter turns out to be one of the originals in Southwest humor; one of his heirs is the naïf in Mark Twain's *Roughing It.*

David C. Estes sees more anxiety than humor in "Letters from the Far West"—that is, P.O.F. is not only too inept to adapt to the experience of the world he should be describing, but is also "linguistically powerless" both within the expedition and with the aliens who live in the West. It is a provocative reading, but to call this text a "nightmare of ultimate impotence in the face of nature's malevolence" is to ignore the tone of these funny and extraordinary letters.[83] There is more evidence of a non-anthropomorphic neutrality about nature than there is of malevolence. But it is true that the helplessness and foolishness of P.O.F., enveloping the humor, point to a disquietude beneath the normally serene surface of Thorpe's prose. In most of his pieces in which the instinct of wild creatures succumbs to the experience of men, his reporting is straightforward. In one sketch, however, the narrator sentimentalizes the conquering of a wild horse, whose muscular, glossy, and graceful beauty is pitted against the experience of a "horse tamer" whose job is to break him for human use. For horse, "it's nature"; for man, it's skill. This episode makes such an impression on the narrator that when the horse loses its freedom, he imagines he sees a "big tear [roll] down his cheeks" (*TBT*, 165). In no other piece is Thorpe so maudlin. His intuitive preference for nature over skill shows up occasionally in a flash of ambivalence, and there are enough of these to constitute a kind of covert undermeaning to his sporting anecdotes.

One of the questions raised in the interstices of Thorpe's work, from "The Big Bear of Arkansas" to the sporting essays, is What do we do with our environment?—not in the anachronistic ecological sense, but in a more elementary historical one. How does the settler in the rapidly expanding America of the 1840s fit into the spaces he has carved out of wild nature? To fill up the spaces, as we know from many apologists, was to obey biblical injunction while taking advantage of official land policy. For the Big Bear, going "according to natur" takes precedence over the

83. Estes, introduction, 26.

blessings of both God and government. Prodigality of nature, as Jim Doggett discovers, may mean more than pumpkin crops, and the title of best man among hunters is never definitive. What Thorpe's daydreaming narrator envisions with the *Nimrod*—the excitements of the "wild hunter" joined to the comforts of "the drawing room"—carries a disturbing meaning that may apply to all sporting narratives: forays into the forest are, simultaneously, escapes into wildness for those who have already tamed enough of it to be comfortable, and greedy exercises in domesticating the wildness that yet remains.

Just as the Civil War ended the humorous southern sketch as a productive and coherent body of local-color writing, so did it spell the end of the quasi-professional accounts of sporting in the wilds that were concurrent with it. Not only did war intervene and bring with it a new kind of modernity, but there were also fewer and fewer wilds, which had generated both genres. By the 1870s local-color prose had passed into gentler hands, three-quarters of them female, many of whom were writing boldly under their own names (few, certainly, with hokey pseudonyms) for an audience unrestricted by gender or profession. And gentleman sportsmen would evolve as well, some of them refining and consolidating the rules of all games that Frank Forester had begun with hunting and horsemanship, while others harmonized relevant sports with physical and spiritual training or with inculcating good citizenship.

vi.

Sporting literature, a kind of patrician alternative to the comic sketches of the humorists, is about *hunting in the woods*. It involves a gentleman hunter (who in the southern versions is also a planter) playing host to his friends in a party led by a yeoman guide for an extended trek into game-rich areas. The event is conducted as an entertainment consisting of lively conversation, comradely tale-swapping, drinking, and eating—punctuated by a few hours of actual hunting. This symbolic activity of the well-to-do confirmed an image of the planter as the entitled elite.[84] The yeoman guide sees himself (and is seen by his employer) as a facilitator whose experience and knowledge are expected to discover for others the most promising spots for hunting bear or deer. His subsidiary duties include

84. Bruce Dixon, "Hunting: Dimensions of Antebellum Southern Culture," *Mississippi Quarterly* 30 (1977): 259–81.

making camp and preparing meals suitable for roughing expeditions, and—if the party is lucky—telling tales also suitable for the occasion. Sporting scribes often concentrate on these guides and their vernacular expressions as one focus of interest; the better ones are also skilled in reproducing the guides' campfire stories as a patterned phase in the action-and-rest rhythm that structures their accounts.

The guide may be a mediator between the extensive woods and the urban bailiwicks of the sporting gentlemen, but he is not a protector of the wilderness. Faulkner's Sam Fathers is expressly conceived as a mentor figure, a wise scout who mediates an untamed wilderness for his betters among the planters and who is ultimately betrayed by a society that thoughtlessly makes the wilderness its victim.[85] But the writing of antebellum sportsmen shows no Faulknerian mourning over a diminished wilderness. In the sporting literature, not even the wise yeoman guide gives much thought to any mystical symbiosis of man and nature. He does well just to exhibit the traits of his type: a head full of lore and hands to apply it to present situations. The texts are notably silent about the virtues of human reverence toward, much less a sense of spiritual union with, great nature. If there is any symbiosis involved in the sporting literature, it is that between the vernacular guide and the genteel hunter-planter. Both are one in regarding the wilderness as theirs to use as they see fit.[86]

Unlike the sporting literature, the humorous sketches of yeoman hunters emphasize not *hunting in the woods* so much as *yarns about hunting in the woods*. Very few of the pieces actually occur as actions. A practicing novelist reminds us that the action of the first-person story is not the events in it "but the act of telling the tale." George Garrett continues: "What is happening, and indeed *all* that is happening, is that someone is telling a story."[87] What the humorist authors chose to do with the highly publicized activity of hunting was to isolate the event within a storytelling context. The focus of, say, "The Big Bear of Arkansas" is not really the wilderness where Jim Doggett's triumphs and failures occurred, but the social hall of a steamboat, where that action is remembered, recreated, and glossed, and where its impact is hedged and colored by the semi-

85. Myra Jehlen calls Sam Fathers a "scout betrayed." *Class and Character in Faulkner's South* (New York: Columbia University Press, 1976), 8.

86. For a contrary view, see Rivers, *Cultural Values*, 1–29 passim.

87. George Garrett, "The Best Way Home: Fact and Fiction in *Shiloh* and *All the Brave Promises*," review of books by Shelby Foote and Mary Lee Settle, respectively, *Sewanee Review* 110 (2002): 444.

participatory nature of the storytelling audience. Henry Clay Lewis's Mik-hoo-tah, who longs to become the "Bar-hunter of Ameriky," tells his sad story long after the event. The success of a one-legged hunter who bested some taunting beasts is juxtaposed against present need—he begs the swamp doctor to fashion him another leg to replace the one ruined by his late encounter. Neither Thorpe nor Lewis is much interested in the phenomenon of hunting in the woods, and if their yeoman characters are concerned with the activity it is only because of what it means for their reputation, which in turn depends upon their making the best case for themselves through oral interpretation.

The audience for yeoman stories of hunting varies significantly from that in sporting literature. Sportsmen such as William Elliott and Charles White-head, who recount the colorful sayings and tales of guides, have as audience those just like themselves; and in the modal shift from oral to written narrative, that audience is extended to the reader. In the humor, the hunter as employer is essentially lost; gentlemen and yeomen coexist as inter-dependent players on the southwestern stage. The narrators of the sketches are rarely planter types—not all are really gentlemen—but professionals whose contact with backwoodsmen and other yeomen is usually inciden-tal to the lives of either. In the humor, yeomen, even the lone hunter kind, never function as hired guides for well-to-do men; they interact with pro-fessionals for mutually functional reasons. They need a tooth pulled, or a case argued, or an adventure heard. In some cases (as in Lewis's "A Tight Race Considerin'") narrator and yeoman storyteller are friends.

Even in sportsmen's writing, although the planter may regard his yeo-man guide as entertainer and part-time jester, he never allows himself to imagine that guide as a kind of new-world squire to his knight or as a fool to his king. Egalitarianism in the new country had by the 1830s ban-ished the claims of Virginia-style patriarchy, and except for a handful of imitators of English hunting traditions, condescension was a mode only gingerly adopted by quality folk. Furthermore, in the dynamics of class relationships the guide is always mindful that his skill makes him useful, that he knows the woods better than his employer. In effect, his innate worth acts as a check to the normative superiority ascribed to the planter. Indeed, the woods become a democratized territory in which class and rank are held in momentary suspension. The hunting skills of the ver-nacular guide may at times eclipse the authority of the planter host, but they are *prior* skills that are literarily rendered by storytelling. Technical knowledge and experience are ratified only by *narrative* gifts to which the gentleman narrator of the expedition defers.

If sporting literature inevitably gives some of its space to yeomanry lingo and tale-telling, that is not the major object of its attention. When the editor of *American Sportsman* in 1872 touted hunting for its "unalterable *love of fair play,*" an avid contributor wrote in his approval, declaring: "Instead of being antagonistic meanings, the sportsman and the gentleman are . . . synonymous terms."[88] For most of the genre's publishing history, these terms in sporting discourse had usually been synonymous. Elliott and Whitehead devote most of their accounts to what *they* do and see in the woods. Their journeys combine the naturalist's sensitivity to flora and fauna and the gentleman's traditional fondness for hunting in the wilds. Hunting literature after the 1820s was a national, not a sectional, phenomenon, and while southerners were enthusiasts, so were urban professionals and businessmen in the North and East.[89] Behind most of the southerners' accounts lie the technical basics of Frank Forester, who, as we have seen, established himself as the most acclaimed authority on appropriate dress, weapons, and rules of behavior for gentry hunting. But in southern hands the protocols laid down with such élan were considerably informalized, softened by an impatience with rules, an inveterate love of narrative, and a reluctance to overvalue the sport. One sportsman visiting his uncle near Savannah wrote that he "went after Deer 4 or 5 times" to no avail: "But the way I massacared the Squirrels was a caution."[90] The texts of Elliott and Whitehead are peppered with anecdotes shaped as mini-dramas that feature gentleman participants. Hunting narratives in the humor, however, are inevitably focused on yeomen. It is their stories to which gentleman narrators give space, and the yarns about hunting in the woods rarely involve planters or even professionals aspiring to the planter class. As we shall see, narrators function mostly to introduce their vernacular storytellers and to supply colorful sidelights about them.

Even as the human relationships differ, both the sporting literature and the comic sketches share an important cultural trait: an antebellum attitude toward nature as a realm that exists for human use. In both genres nature is a given. Spiritualizing real estate was not a southern impulse; to attribute "ecological reverence" to antebellum gentleman hunters would be both facile and anachronistic. Despite sportsmen's occasional references to the fields, streams, and woods as conducive to man's pleasure,

88. Quoted in Rivers, *Cultural Values,* 65.
89. Herman, *Hunting,* 132–33.
90. E. J. C. Wood, N. S. Tyler Papers, Georgia Historical Society, Savannah.

and despite yeomanry preference for the deep woods over crowded settlements, great nature was seen as a topographical realm like any other. The notion of nature as teacher or spiritual guide was not one of the high Romantic legacies embraced in the Old Southwest. Indeed, except for those writers inflected by Transcendentalism, nature by itself was rarely portrayed as beneficent. For most of the antebellum population, from the speculator to the squatter, nature was mostly *potential*, huge parcels of land that awaited human improvement. Even Mike Fink, whose sorrows at the "betterments" echo Natty Bumppo, is mostly distraught because they were making irrelevant his profession and way of life.

There was little in this view, in fact, to make southerners different from most Americans. From Puritan thinkers onward, the task of Americans was to seek for and articulate design in the apparent chaos and irregularity of great nature. From cartographical mapping to settlement, the passion to domesticate nature was paramount, and behind it was the confident expectation that, however complex and forbidding, nature, in the words of Robert A. Ferguson, "could be circumscribed through intellectual control."[91] We neither expect nor get philosophical argument from sportsmen and humorists, but their idea of "control" was both more basic and less amenable to argument. What both groups responded to was a geography for their use and pleasure. The ecological view of man as responsible steward rather than exploiter became a significant concept only after the Civil War, and even then registered only spotty attention in the South until the twentieth century.

91. Robert A. Ferguson, *Law and Letters in American Culture* (Cambridge, MA: Harvard University Press, 1984), 189–90.

Chapter 8 ⤙⚏⚏

River Culture

"I have heard of your merchandising, your preaching, your acting, and your *doctoring*—did you ever try your hand at PILOTING?"

—Sol Smith, "Who's at the Wheel?"

i.

In *World Enough and Time* (1950), Robert Penn Warren concludes his story of the Kentucky frontier in the 1820s with a coda set along the banks and bayous of the Mississippi River. A misshapen territorial boss controls river commerce as well as pedestrian traffic on the Natchez Trace with a cutthroat gang of robbers and murderers. La Grand' Bosse (or Ole Big Hump) is a master of the keelboat. One day in 1811, he looks out of his swampy den to see the first steamboat passing on to New Orleans. To him it is a "preposterous, nightmare thing . . . puffing the black smoke and creaking and clanking." Adds the author: "it was the end of the great day of Ole Big Hump."[1]

If the novel's romantic leads, Jeremiah Beaumont and Rachel Jordan, enact a tragicomedy of a world well lost for love, the decadent boatman is too corrupt, too bestial, to enact anything dramatic. His story functions as a set piece, a *tour de force* that provides an analogue of human declension to the principals' disastrous love story. In this subsidiary figure Warren

1. Robert Penn Warren, *World Enough and Time: A Romantic Novel* (New York: Random House, 1950), 230–31.

explores the primitive obverse of his "civilized" romance, and to do so he taps into the major view of riverboat men in the earliest years of exploration and settlement in the Old Southwest. As a class they may have been, in one scholar's judgment, simply "a more or less normal frontier group," but in most contemporary accounts, they were outcasts, scruffy and amoral desperadoes operating in a space they claimed as their own, where the boundaries of justice were as shifting as the river channels of their calling. According to James Hall, one of the first chroniclers of the western frontier, these men represented "every species of filth and villainy" that regularly terrorized the settlers and villagers along the Ohio and Mississippi.[2]

Warren's La Grand' Bosse is a condensed image from which radiates a cluster of quasi-historical associations (*regulators, Cave-In Rock, Mike Fink, river pirate, Natchez Under-the-Hill*) that link all boatmen with outlawry. This fictional creature is also caught at the very moment in which mechanical innovation becomes the agent of change. Robert Fulton's biographer calls the steamboat a "transformative technology" that shaped the society that gave rise to it and ratified a belief in the nearly infinite power of "exploitation, expansion, and 'progress.'"[3] The historic transition from flatboat to steamboat culture is a crucial moment in American life, an economic change that also transformed American politics, agriculture, and social life. In a foreshortened way, the steamboat was augur—an ominous one for men like La Grand' Bosse, a propitious one for men of vision and industry who would succeed the disorderly boatmen. The steamboat represented modernity—and with it civilization, and, with civilization, rules for making profit. Boat culture was primitive, comfortably amenable to basic land-pirate behavior. Steam economics became complicated. La Grand' Bosse, writes Warren, was "simply the victim of technological unemployment."

From the earliest period, as we know from Timothy Flint, a great variety of "boats of passage" plied the western waters, but by 1828, when he wrote his *Condensed Geography,* broadhorns, or "Kentucky flats," had come to dominate river traffic.[4] That dominance was temporary. The steamboat

2. Richard E. Oglesby, "The Western Boatman: Half Horse, Half Myth," in *Travelers on the Western Frontier,* ed. John Francis McDermott (Urbana: University of Illinois Press, 1970), 265; James Hall, *Letters from the West* (1828; reprint, ed. John T. Flanagan, Gainesville, FL: Scholars' Facsimiles & Reprints, 1967), 230–31.

3. Kirkpatrick Sale, *The Fire of His Genius: Robert Fulton and the American Dream* (New York: Free Press, 2001), 202–5.

4. Timothy Flint, *A Condensed Geography and History of the Western States or the Mississippi Valley* (1828; reprint, ed. Bernard Rosenthal, Gainesville, FL: Scholars' Facsimiles & Reprints, 1970), 1:231–32. See also Harry N. Scheiber, "The Ohio-Mississippi

he knew to be a more efficient commercial vessel; its very capacity to haul increased tonnage also required greater caution in protecting valuable freight, which meant a more responsible crew and what James Hall called "men of character" to exact discipline from them. Flint's *Condensed Geography* appeared the same year as Hall's *Letters from the West*, and though the peripatetic preacher shared Hall's disapproval of the drunken brawls and intimidating bluster that gave the flatboatmen a high profile in the river towns, he rejected any judgment that imputed evil to an entire class of men. The coming of the steamboat, he writes, cast into unemployment "ten thousand" boatmen. By seizing upon the cultural implications of the new era, Flint helped to make the boatmen safe for nostalgic legend.

Although as a good Presbyterian he could not ignore the boatmen's excessive drinking and rowdiness, Flint is an early source for the mythologizing of the stereotype. Most of the romanticized features of boatmen and their calling that persist in the writing for the next half-century are his contributions: a great nature prior to settlement, the ever-changing succession of Chateaubriandized scenery along the riverbanks; the men's exchanges of "rude defiances" and "trials of wit" as their crafts pass each other; the sounds of boat bugles resonating on the shores. Subsequent fascination with boatmen, including the enduring visual images in George Caleb Bingham's *Jolly Flatboatmen* series, can be traced to Flint's elevation of the spirit of freedom and mobility the river world embodied.[5] By their very presence, both on the river and in the towns, the boatmen came to represent for envious stay-at-homes the romance of an unfettered life. Indeed, their attraction was "pernicious" for many daydreaming farmers' sons, who neglected their fields to lounge on the riverbanks, imagining themselves as fiddling boatmen hurling challenges.[6] Though Flint might allow himself nostalgia for the soon-to-be-succeeded boatmen, it was not yet the time to elegize them. Their potent attraction still threatened the priority in the development of the Southwest—cultivation of the soil.

By the mid-1830s, however, when steamboats triumphed commercially

Flatboat Trade: Some Reconsiderations," in *The Frontier in American Development: Essays in Honor of Paul Wallace Gates*, ed. David M. Ellis (Ithaca, NY: Cornell University Press, 1969), 277–98. For distinctions among the human-propelled crafts, see Leland D. Baldwin, *The Keelboat Age on Western Waters* (Pittsburgh: University of Pittsburgh Press, 1941), 39–42, 160–72.

5. John Demos, "George Caleb Bingham: The Artist as Social Historian," *American Quarterly* 17 (1965): 218–28.

6. Flint, *Condensed Geography*, 1:233.

as the major mode of water travel, the rambunctious flatboatmen had become fully realized romantic legends. In a piece in the *Natchez Courier* in April 1837, these men have already become figures of folk culture. "There is always amusement when a steamer and a flatboat meet," one steamboat passenger writes; "then Kentucky and Hoosier wit is peculiarly brilliant." After disposing of their freight and boats in New Orleans, he reports, flatboatmen return home as deck passengers. "Jingling their dollars" and bragging of bargains, they entertain the other passengers "with extravagant tales . . . which they call 'bamboozling.' " Although the "old race of *professional* flatboatmen . . . is passed away" and the present batch consists of farmers and their sons, they are still muscular men, hardy spirits following a trade that is laborious. Their appearance—with "their loose, coarse, brown trowsers, red or blue shirts, the sleeves drawn up to the shoulders"—is "exceedingly picturesque." Only a few years earlier Flint had worried that the life of the "professional" boatmen seduced farm youths to forsake their fields; by 1837 the farmers themselves have become part-time boatmen—no longer a "pernicious" type, but "a hardy, sober, industrious class, little understood and often grossly misrepresented."[7]

Henry Thoreau mythicized the boatmen he observed on Massachusetts waters as "fabulous river-men," in part because of their unfabulous need to carry all their possessions with them: "their very homestead is moveable."[8] On western waters the boatmen were sometimes celebrated, not because they practiced necessary economies, but because they ambivalently embodied the most radical liberty available in American life. Relatively few of the some three thousand boatmen who worked the Ohio and Mississippi Rivers left accounts of their lives. Most were illiterate. But, as if in compensation, their high visibility attracted a number of articulate scribes eager to be their celebrants. The touting of the representative remnants of a simpler frontier past coincided with the new technology that turned the steamboat into both a literal and symbolic hallmark of Jacksonian America. Historian Michael Allen has discovered, perhaps unsurprisingly, that the popular accounts, both oral and written, rarely suggest the actual situation of the real-life boatmen: "Primitive living conditions, sickness, navigation hazards, summer storms and winter ice,

7. *A Memoir of S. S. Prentiss, ed. by His Brother* (New York, 1855), 1:179, 180–81; Baldwin, *Keelboat Age*, 194.

8. Henry D. Thoreau, *A Week on the Concord and Merrimack Rivers* (1849; reprint, ed. Carl F. Hovde and others, Princeton, NJ: Princeton University Press, 1980), 210–11.

attacks by Indians and robbers, and a thousand-mile walk home through a dangerous wilderness" after each journey downstream.[9] The tellers and singers of tall tales and songs were not inclined to celebrate alcoholism, casual criminality, a diet even more minimal than the landsman's, and lice-infested clothing worn until it rotted off the body; and the literate authors whose details in letters and sketches contributed to the mystique of the boatmen were even more selective and more aggressively heroizing. It was part of the era's romanticizing of the frontier.

Most of the bad press came from travelers. Dispassionate observers noted the obvious vices, but finicky outsiders were offended by the drinking, smoking and chewing, gambling, cursing, and fighting among this "unterrified democracy," forgetting that such vices were identical to those they frequently complained of among backwoodsmen on shore. As early as 1818 one visitor disputed the accuracy of the most sensational stories about the boatmen's appetite for intimidation and physical violence.[10] A trustworthy chronicler in 1834 was also compelled to soften the image of brawling rivermen. Robert Baird insisted that while boatmen had grown more temperate, the traits of their class still flourished: "boldness, readiness to encounter almost any danger, recklessness to consequences, and indifference to the wants of the future, amid the enjoyment, the noise, whiskey, and fun of the present."[11]

Warren's La Grand' Bosse was a victim of technological unemployment, but there was a real figure who contributed to this fictional image, one who in popular lore became a kind of template for all larger-than-life boatmen. Mike Fink is to the western waters what Davy Crockett is to the western wilderness, and much of the writing about both in the almanacs seems to make little distinction between human and superhuman accomplishments. With its folkloristic base, the smudging of the line between the credible and the incredible is a striking feature of this flamboyant, highly energized writing. Romantic revisionism went on apace, despite one difficulty. In popular usage, *Kaintucks, half-horse half-alligators,* and *boatmen* were practically synonymous terms, but Mike Fink was neither a Kentuckian nor the perpetrator of all the sensational and brutal acts at-

9. Michael Allen, *Western Rivermen, 1763–1861: Ohio and Mississippi Boatmen and the Myth of the Alligator Horse* (Baton Rouge: Louisiana State University Press, 1990), 58.
10. Ibid., 207, 197. Boatmen went wherever "whiskey was plentiful, women were complaisant, and opportunities to demonstrate their manhood were available in profusion"—the usual pleasures of a masculinized culture common to the working class throughout the Old Southwest. Oglesby, "Western Boatman," 255.
11. Robert Baird, *View of the Valley of the Mississippi, or Emigrant's and Traveller's Guide through the Valley of the Mississippi* (Philadelphia, 1834), 116.

tributed to him. He was, however, the most feared, brazen, and respected boatman, with enough savagery attached to his name to complicate the heroizing impulse of contemporary writers. Mike's claim to fame as a frontier sharpshooter, writes one folklorist, "lay in the fact that most of his shooting wagers were sadistic pranks."[12] But a gambling spirit had little to do with much of his reputed sadism—shooting off a black man's heel because he disliked its shape; forcing his girlfriend to roll in a bed of burning leaves to discourage her flirting.

In 1828, only five years after Fink's death, Morgan Neville both documented and celebrated the man he nostalgically called "The Last of the Boatmen" in the *Western Souvenir,* a literary annual. In this first written account of Mike Fink, the educated narrator subordinates crudity and violence in favor of his subject's "daring intrepidity." Invoking comparisons to Apollo, Hercules, Roland, and Revolutionary War fighters, Neville takes the bully of oral repute and fixes him in a splendid legend as the performer of "a hundred fights, and the leader in a thousand daring adventures." Although he hints that an agrarian protection racket kept farmers along the banks "on good terms with Mike," Neville counters this "Black Mail" by casting his hero as a latter-day Rob Roy, "his great prototype." Neville also introduces the motif of progress and its impact on the river culture in which this American Rob Roy thrived. With his eyes focused on the "future destiny" of the west, the writer endorses the process with which "barbarism retreats before the approach of art and civilization," and he reports the death of Mike Fink in a bare-bones passage: "He went to the Missouri, and about a year since was shooting the tin cup when he had corned too heavy. He elevated too low, and shot his companion through the head. A friend of the deceased who was present, suspecting foul play, shot Mike through the heart before he had time to re-load his rifle."[13]

Although Neville's credibility was powered by his claim of early friendship with Mike Fink during their overlapping years in Pittsburgh, the chronology of his sketch is shaky. Most of the legends about the boatman, Neville's included, are imaginative reconstructions. Like some of the humorists' sketches, "The Last of the Boatmen" is cast as a "true" yarn by a genteel narrator basking in the reflected glow of his subject. Though only forty-five, Neville adopts the persona of an intimate old-timer regaling

12. B. A. Botkin, *The American People* (London: Pilot Press, 1946), 22.
13. Walter Blair and Franklin J. Meine, eds., *Half Horse, Half Alligator: The Growth of the Mike Fink Legend* (Chicago: University of Chicago Press, 1956), 52, 260.

other passengers on the deck of an Ohio steamboat. If he sounds a trifle too magisterial for his age, the pose seems to have been consistent. Joseph M. Field reported having heard Neville just four years later as "a noble old gentleman" reciting Mike stories.[14]

In his 1842 account "The Disgraced Scalp Lock," Thomas Bangs Thorpe sets the action thirty years earlier when the "last of the flatboatmen" was in his prime. He invokes a kind of poignance—occasioned by a forest-and-river culture succumbing to progress—as he replaces the reputed cruelty and crudity of the legendary boatman with a mournful sensibility. Thorpe's Fink anticipates his own displacement even before his confrontation with Proud Joe, a renegade Cherokee already displaced by progress. Moreover, Thorpe reinforces the tone of poetic melancholy by revising the corporate character of the entire class of men that Mike Fink so memorably represented. Thorpe's romantic tack, in defiance of historical fact, is to draw a neat exit line for the boatmen, which allows for a more sweeping revisionism. Not only are they "extinct and anomalous" by 1842; in memory they also have come down to us as brave, hardy, and "open-handed," a masculine beau ideal: "[T]heir whole lives were a round of manly excitement, they were hyperbolical in thought and in deed, when most natural, compared with any other class of men. Their bravery and chivalrous deeds were performed without a herald to proclaim them to the world—they were the mere incidents of a border life, considered too common to outlive the time of a passing wonder." Some of the foreign visitors a generation earlier would have been puzzled by Thorpe's group portraiture: "the manner modest, yet full of self reliance, the language strong and forcible, from superiority of mind rather than from education"—men of such "sterling common sense" that strangers were drawn to "court their society" (*TBT*, 170–71). Even southwesterners, especially older ones who were closer to the orally transmitted tales of Mike Fink, would have noted the author's studied efforts at sanitizing the rambunctious boatmen. Thorpe at once devulgarizes the half-horse half-alligator brag (to better fit the "bravery and chivalrous deeds") and supplies Fink with an *ubi sunt* temperament appropriate to a generic romantic poet.

Accordingly, the peerless boatman, needing excitement, declares himself to be "perfectly miserable, and helpless, as a wildcat without teeth or claws." He is tempted to declare war on the Choctaws "just to have something to keep me from growing dull; without some such business

14. Ibid., 15, 37.

I'd be as musty as an old swamp moccasin." His way, Mike is made to say, is to "walk tall into varmint and Indian, . . . and it comes as natural as grinning to a hyena. I'm a regular tornado, tough as a hickory withe, long-winded as a nor'-wester. I can strike a blow like a falling tree, and every lick makes a gap in the crowd that lets in an acre of sunshine. Whew, boys! . . . I must fight something, or I'll catch the dry rot" (*TBT,* 177–78). As tall talk goes, this is only modestly threatening. Before Thorpe's ameliorations, Mike Fink, as we shall see, was virtually the co-creator, with Davy Crockett, of the distinctive half-horse half-alligator rhetoric, and the riverman's in particular was as lingually brutal as his physical exploits. Mike became a recurring figure in the *Crockett Almanacks* (1835–1856), where he blandly sports arrogance, coarseness, contentious sadism, and cruel self-absorption—all reflected in his belligerent vows to remain "best man." Though Thorpe merely labels it *hyperbole,* tall talk was a special argot ratcheted up several notches beyond ordinary colorful vernacular, a rhetoric that took on a life of its own in antebellum discourse until it became a museum piece, like the exploits it celebrated, living on "almost exclusively as traditions" (*TBT,* 171).

If some of Thorpe's contemporaries were blunt in depicting Mike Fink as a "worthless and vile" perpetrator of ugly practical jokes and "destitute of any of the manly qualities" that progressive southwesterners thought appropriate, Thorpe himself ignores that harsh judgment. His sketch captures the moment when technology catches up with the boatman whose skill depends upon "physical force alone." But what also intervenes is Cooper's Natty Bumppo. A declining and bored Mike Fink laments "the desecrating hand of improvement" along the rivers: "What's the use of improvements? When did cutting down trees make deer more plenty? . . . Who ever found wild buffalo, or a brave Indian in a city? Where's the fun, the frolicking, the fighting? Gone! gone!" (*TBT,* 172). The inevitable progress that has removed Native Americans from the Southwest has also displaced the free-spirited boatmen. Thorpe's Mike Fink is reshaped to reflect two kinds of residual sentiment among the moderns—widespread ambivalence about fierce Anglo-Saxon primitivism and pity for the Indian. Because the strengths of both Proud Joe and Mike Fink are somehow elevated as antique virtues no longer relevant to civilization, Thorpe is able to balance the divided sympathies of his reader without (overly) sentimentalizing either antagonist.

The nostalgia that laces many of these accounts came from a perspective that required demotion (or, in Thorpe's account, the practical elimination) of the boatmen as a literal presence on the riverine landscape.[15] If they could be dismissed as functional only in a prior stage of development that had already succumbed to progress, they could be safely distanced and thus eligible for legends that made western history more interesting. More than a half-century after Mike Fink's death, when the boatmen were truly gone, a navigation historian could take a more measured view of their acknowledged leader, whose practical jokes were "exaggerated" versions of the antics of all his fellows. Though Mike's jokes were clearly "predations," they were marked by "a boldness of design, and a sagacity of execution that showed no mean talent."[16]

James Hall, the editor of the first western literary periodical as well as the compiler of several books of western lore, was eager to praise the same "improvements" along the Ohio River towns that Mike Fink lamented. A Philadelphia lawyer who rejoiced in progress, Hall was too close to the era dominated by boatmen to see them as romantic figures. Romance lay in the steamboat. The successor to the flatboat also gave rise to an important side business for marginal farmers: wooding stations to feed the hungry boilers. The woodyard, wrote an early historian, was almost as significant as the cotton field. Sometimes it was "a question which paid more, cotton or fat pine knots."[17] Yet of all the personnel featured in the romance of the river that Mark Twain would so memorably inscribe, the captains and pilots were the figures of prestige that suited both the technological development of the steamers and the improvements made along the banks to accommodate them. The raucous louts who commanded the flatboats were being succeeded by the more disciplined crews of the steamboat, the modern and efficient craft commanded not by riffraffish Mike Finks but "men of character"—ambitious, responsible, polite, industrious. When the well-bred daughter of a Vicksburg publisher became entranced by the handsome young pilot of the *Twichell*, his father, the captain, confided to her that he had given him a college ed-

15. Michael Allen points to 1823 as the hinge year separating flatboat dominance from that of the steamboat, but it would be cultural simplification to say that the steamboat put flatboats out of business. From the early 1820s to the Civil War, flatboatmen experienced "unprecedented prosperity." Allen quotes one boatman in 1848 saying his craft had been joined by so many other boats that they were "thicker than three in a bed—the river is full of us." Indeed, in a one-year span in 1846–1847 more flatboats worked the Ohio and Mississippi "than ever before or since." *Western Rivermen*, 4, 141, 171.

16. E. W. Gould, *Fifty Years on the Mississippi; or, Gould's History of River Navigation* (St. Louis, 1889), 48.

17. Mell A. Frazer, *Early Steamboats in Alabama* (Auburn, 1907), 21.

ucation to discourage his following the river, but that "his tastes turned that way" despite it.[18] Nearly every writer of newspaper humor would have accepted Hall's generalization of the boatmen as filthy and villainous (though they might not have accepted his tone) because they considered *themselves* ambitious, responsible, polite, industrious—in a word, *modern.* But they were also imaginative writers, and the success of the steamboat, and with it the decline of flatboat culture, gave them an excuse for some nostalgia.[19]

Joseph M. Field's sketch "The Death of Mike Fink" (1844) is almost a preemptive strike against the mythic heroizing of the infamous boatman. Strongly flavored by Morgan Neville's accounts both oral and written, Field's version emphasizes the professional displacement of one aging boatman and his subsequent disintegration. The sketch, rich and detailed, follows the general historical sequence of Fink's movements and some of the biographical circumstances of prior stories, but its strength lies in the author's own conceptual insights. That Fink's death has been variously reported ("in half a dozen different ways and places"), writes Field, is one of the signs that his life is being made larger by "the first gathering of the *mythic* haze . . . [that] invests distinguished mortality" with sublime attributes. Field argues that the specifics of the boatman's death had transformed a man into legend. The folk resurrection of the post-Alamo Crockett may be fresh in his mind when he announces that his purpose is to blow away the "mythic haze" of "the hero and the demigod" so that the skeptic will never need to inquire, "Did such a being really die?" Though he also grandly invokes comparisons of Mike Fink to classical heroes (Jason and Odin), Field yet insists on a perspective of the boatman as "simply human" (Cohen, 109–13).

The St. Louis newspaperman is no apologist for Fink, but neither is he an ardent debunker. Field knows that factual scrutiny is the enemy of romantic "enlargement of outline." His technique is a practical application of a historiographical principle laid down a few years later by his fellow humorist Joseph G. Baldwin. In *Party Leaders* (1855), Baldwin declares it a

18. Emma Shannon, October 6, 1857, Crutcher-Shannon Family Papers (Z/91), Mississippi Department of Archives and History, Jackson.

19. According to Allen, flatboating enjoyed its best years as the steamboat became dominant. Some boatmen became pilots and captains in the new era; those who still manned the flats used the steamboats as a dependable way to return home after a trip downriver; and flatboating attracted younger, more literate men who regarded a stint on the waters as a masculine rite of passage. Allen, *Western Rivermen*, 182, 142.

human weakness to use romance to "surround the illustrious men of the past. A man seen through the haze is a larger man *for* the haze. A familiar approach removes the illusion. When we come near great men, we see other things than the great parts, which, like mountain-peaks, at a distance, we alone behold. Few men can bear the scrutiny."[20] Baldwin's point is that Thomas Jefferson, the party leader referred to here, does indeed bear the scrutiny. Mike Fink, of course, is not a great man even in the humorous literature. But the facts of his diminution—in the far West, after his exile from the great southwestern waterways that framed his exploits—offer Field an opportunity to deepen the character of the man, to fill in the outline of frontier bully with a texture of pathos and sympathy.

A casualty of commercial technology, Mike Fink is literally out of his element in the Rocky Mountains. At Fort Henry on the Yellowstone, he must deal with a different kind of crew, trappers whose deference to his legend is weak and whose memory of his adventures is short. As hunter and trapper, Mike is subject to unaccustomed supervision, and his unruly behavior is not considered appropriate for the trading post and its military discipline. Professionally stripped of his riverboat command, Mike is unable to muster much command of himself. Field depicts a man in decline: "always a reckless dare-devil," the displaced boatman is old, "decayed in influence," alcoholic, "morose and desperate in the extreme." (The operative *desperate,* used four times in a four-page span, is an authorial gloss that explains the daredevil behavior of a man long past the time when such behavior is excusable, as boldness becomes cranky intimidation.) Mike's swaggering is little more than obnoxious bullying—not only of Major Henry within the fort but also of "his particular 'boys,'" the crew members who follow him warily and only so long as the association doesn't jeopardize their jobs with the fur company.

In a narrative meant to reduce the heroism of legend to the "flesh and blood" of a real man, Field rather easily traces a further reduction—to the man as animal. Unable to curb his raucous individuality and violent temper, and with his "exactions growing more unbearable every day," the aging boatman withdraws to "a sort of cave in the river's bank," well supplied with the whiskey that governmental regulations forbid within the fort. Unbearable at the fort, Mike becomes a bear in his cave. The "fort's a skunk-hole," he declares, "and I rather live with the *bars* than stay in it." In the pivotal crisis, at the drunken spring frolic where Mike and young Carpenter, now his sole companion ("my own cub," he calls

20. Joseph G. Baldwin, *Party Leaders* (New York, 1856), 100.

him), shoot cans off each other's heads, the alienated "boys" from the fort feel bold enough to taunt Mike: "Kill the old varmint, young 'un!" and "What'll his skin bring in St. Louis?" With his shot, Carpenter grazes Mike's head; instinctively, Mike fires a return shot that crashes through the youth's forehead. That he kills his only friend not only isolates Mike further from the community, but also triggers his own disintegration.

Field makes the aftermath worthy of the reader's sympathy for the troubled boatman. Edging the image of overbearing sot is that of the vulnerable father figure who appears to engineer his own death at the hands of his nemesis, Talbott, the fort's gunsmith and the most vocal in denouncing Mike as a "murderer." Though carrying his rifle when he approaches Talbott, Mike is more distraught than hostile, wanting nothing more than to talk about "my boy! . . . that I raised from a child—that I loved like a son—that I can't live without!" Mike protests that Carpenter's death was an accident: "You must let me show you that I *couldn't* do it—that I'd rather died than done it." But the gunsmith ("not a coolly brave man") is too agitated to hear him and fires his two pistols into Mike's breast. The last words of the grieving boatman are "I didn't mean to kill my boy!"

Both the plot action and the rhetorical configuration unspool a fully credible narrative of one man's decline, but Field also raises an issue of character that further reinforces it. Supporting the slippage from heroic to human to beastly are Fort Henry's dark hints of perversion. That Carpenter is a foster son of the boatman is a factual note that the narrative doesn't dispute, and the narrator circumspectly uses "companion" and "protégé" to refer to Carpenter; but the narrative incorporates as well the ambiguous authority of a public interpretation: "foul insinuations were made as to the nature of their connection; the youth was twitted with being a mere slave." If Mike's reference to Carpenter as "my boy" is primarily literal, Field must also have known it as one term for a young homosexual mate for experienced sailors. Mike is a product of the male world of the river in which the phenomenon of expedient sex was presumably no rarer than in the grander tradition of the sea—nor in the quasi-military society of the trading post and the hunting-and-trapping society, which were homosocial by their very nature. Indeed, the motives of the men at the fort "to withdraw Carpenter from Fink" are cloudy unless they suggest jealousy generated by sexual competitiveness. It is a strategy that Mike at least understands: "Some on ye's bin trying to part me and my boy, that I love like my own cub." The strategy succeeds.

Carpenter is "*pi*soned" against the old bear, and, as the narrator puts it, "much of their cordiality ceased."[21]

Giving credence to the fort's corporate insinuations about their relationship, however, does little to resolve the questions raised by Mike's shooting of Carpenter. Does the youth's alienation—from whatever motive—provoke Mike into deliberately missing the can on his head? Or do the ravages of alcohol, age, and emotional loss simply take their toll on Mike's famous marksmanship? The narrator's emphasis on Mike's grief would seem to return the dynamic back to the love (and generational tensions) governing father-son relationships—that is, to privilege Mike as authority over the community's view. Yet the narrative gaps allow Field creative license. He makes the old bear's behavior equally plausible as that of a distraught father or distraught lover.

Field's account of Mike Fink's last days was by default the official version, incorporating as it does the interpretation of the affair by witnesses, represented by Major Henry, the commandant of the post, and the little community of hunters, trappers, and functionaries within the fort employed by the fur company. That community, operating as a conservative force for civic order, necessarily views Fink, the old terror of the rivers, as a primary agent of disruption. Even in his anticlimactic phase, when he can no longer boast of being "a little bit the almightiest man on the river," his residual rowdyism, his capacity to threaten discipline throughout the ranks, makes him a formidable opponent of Major Henry. His "decayed influence" still has the power of intimidation. The post on the Yellowstone represents a civilizing institution as well as an economic one benefiting (primarily) Gen. W. H. Ashley's Mountain Fur Company.

Fort Henry is an example of how private business enterprise and governmental policy joined to promote consolidation in the territorial West. The public interest allowed and abetted the promotion of economic speculation; in the growth of Rocky Mountain and Plains commerce, the U.S. Army was conspicuous as protector, offering its benign aegis for trade with the Indian tribes of the west (or an aggressive presence when trade failed). In the history of westward expansion, the official agents of the federal government—the land officer, the Indian agent, the military commander, the geological surveyor—facilitate rather than oversee the schemes of the entrepreneur. What is significant in this linking of private and pub-

21. For an extended treatment of homosocial patterns in male culture, see Eve Kosofsky Sedgwick, *Between Men: English Literature and Male Homosocial Desire* (New York: Columbia University Press, 1985).

lic enterprise is its matter-of-factness. Even those Democrats who opposed
Henry Clay's American Plan—a system of public works (roads, canals,
bridges) that would be paid for by the federal government rather than by
private corporations or state treasuries—endorsed the beneficent role of
the military in the winning of the great west.

That matter-of-factness is clear in Field's account of Fink's death. It
seems that only the old man himself, possessed by "freaks" of impulse,
resents the constraints of order at the trading fort; it is a time when unregulated behavior is seen as atavistic. Even Fink's acquaintances accept
this shift in social emphasis, so that the old riverman stands as the lone
holdout in a society otherwise progressive. In earlier sketches the boatman disrupts respectable (and other unrespectable) men without serious
public consequences because conventional society is not much in sight,
and its values not strong enough, nor compelling enough, for its members to care very much. On the Yellowstone, Fink invokes the same appetitive rights that this lord of misrule has always insisted on. But the
time and place are now wrong. Mike Fink is the old-fashioned man in the
new society.

It is easy enough to say that "The Death of Mike Fink" is about how
the myth of the man kills the man—the moral lesson parsed in the classic
films about aging gunfighters in a nearly lawless West. Certainly the old
boatman must confront his own reputation even as he confronts his
newest opponents. But Field's sketch about the death of a legend is also
about the disintegration of a *class* of men who, in their freewheeling independence, once enacted certain national ideals. It thus resonates with
larger anxieties of its time and place: the ethic of *west* (the tangible site
still acting out the values inherent in an older principle of liberty) is gradually merging with the ethic of *east* (the source and symbol of a national
mission of modernity, progress, expansion, amalgamation).

Mike Fink is a marginal figure in the national transition from the generation of the Founders to the post-heroic years of consolidation, but his
role in the popular underhistory of the times is central. Born in the Revolutionary era, he is a spectacular example of how the common American could prosper in a republic fashioned and dominated by an innovative
patrician class. If the Founders' principled rebellion was always a trifle
remote as a model for illiterate types, its focus on individual liberty and
its promise of physical and professional mobility dissolved ethical and
social bonds for those assertive enough to demand unrestricted expression of desire. The dark side of liberty has always been an egoistic license
for compromising the liberty of others; in this sense Mike Fink, the bullying

primitive, is a case study of the national promise gone awry, with the cautionary lesson that individual desire without restraint is ultimately self-destructive.

In trimming the legend to man-size proportions, Field does not indulge in a genteel assault on Mike Fink; he in fact manages to make his study of human decline remarkably affecting. True to his determination to honor eyewitness testimony over reputed and overheard agents of history, he resists interpreting the known facts. The final paragraph on Mike's killer—a one-sentence coda—rigorously ignores the human interest inherent in the factual aftermath of Mike Fink's death: "A few weeks after this event, Talbott himself perished in an attempt to cross the Missouri river in a skiff." It is a tantalizing way to end a sketch about Mike Fink, the old master of rivers. Does it suggest retributive justice with a symbolic twist? If so, Field shows the utmost faith in *not* engaging in the glossing or moralizing that the mere fact invites. Narratively, of course, the death of Mike Fink's killer is another story. Here, in the bare-bones closure, interpretation is so inertly present that its affective potential remains just that.[22]

Mike Fink may have "toiled and rollicked and gouged his way through the world," but the very phrasing in this description suggests that he didn't do it all as Mike Fink. As most authorities now agree, the boatman's skills, activities, and sayings are notably generalized and generic: he becomes an archetypal example of all the "lawless, ignorant, rough mannered" roisters of the western waters, themselves folkloristic descendants of the fearless and ferocious Kentucky backwoodsmen.[23] His particular calling may be less important than the popular attitude associated

22. The circumstances of Fink's death were not resolved by Field, who three years after his 1844 correction of Morgan Neville concocted a romance serial for the *St. Louis Reveille* without answering any of the crucial questions. Despite Field's regard for factual reporting, nineteenth-century standards of objective journalism were conspicuously lax, and the creative Field was, after all, a theater man—actor, playwright, manager—before he was a journalist. Joseph M. Field, "Mike Fink: The Last of the Boatmen," in Blair and Meine, *Half Horse,* 105–34. In his "Recollections," unfinished at his death, James Haley White (1805–1882) remembers Fink and Carpenter as crack marksmen in St. Louis, where he watched their tin-can act. He also remembers in their company a "Levi Talbot," a cooper who stole Fink's blankets when he left the city, causing Fink "to swear vengeance against him if they ever met." This unglossed fact contributes additional motivation for the bad blood between the boatman and his eventual killer. James Haley White, "Glimpses of the Past: Early Days in St. Louis," *Missouri Historical Society* 6 (1939): 8–10. In the romance *Mike Fink; a Legend of the Ohio* (Cincinnati, 1852), Emerson Bennett casts a sanitized Mike in the unlikely role of rescuer and ally of a party of genteel respectables beset by the outlaws of Cave-in-Rock.

23. Leland D. Baldwin, review of *Mike Fink: King of Mississippi Keelboatmen,* by Walter Blair and Franklin J. Meine, *Western Pennsylvania Historical Magazine* 16 (1933): 146.

with flatboating—the tough but high-spirited rivalry that rhetorically co-alesced in the backwoods boast. As early as 1852, Ben Casseday, a local historian in Kentucky who included his own tale of the boatman in his *History of Louisville,* admitted that because "all the more remarkable sto-ries of western river adventure" were attributed to him, Mike Fink has had "to atone to posterity for many acts which never came from under his hand and seal."[24] Even the boatman's famous challenge to "out-run, out-hop, out-jump, throw down, drag out, and lick any man in the county" is generically indistinctive. As Walter Blair and Franklin J. Meine have shown, the Mike Fink stories were not satisfactorily frozen once the oral versions reached print.[25] The literary need for narrative coherence is frequently ignored in accounts that happily mingle fantasy and fact. (Even with all the unanswered questions, Field's 1844 piece is more compelling and credible than his 1847 serial, "The Last of the Boatmen.") In the end, like the actual careers of nineteenth-century outlaws and other badmen in the popular press, that of Mike Fink was so riddled with legend and hearsay, folklore and wish fulfillment, that the man himself never emerged as a cohesive character.

Some popular historians after the Civil War adopted the view that the boatmen were really pioneers who, for all their ragged independence, were important to the prosperity of the Southwest. If they all were in-deed like "the savage and reckless Fink," they nevertheless had a useful function in "working out the destiny of the West." Their "sometimes crim-inally violent" roistering came from a surplus of "merriment," not "mal-ice." Though "unpolished," they were really free, "just and manly," and were perfectly suited to the "lusty vigor" of the region in its early stages.[26] If this burnished image of the profane boatmen comes across as extrava-gantly polished, the revisionist sentiment behind it is only a fraction more romantic than that of Joseph M. Field and T. B. Thorpe before the Civil

24. Ben Casseday, *History of Louisville, from Its Earliest Settlement to the Year 1852* (Louisville, 1852), 72; Blair and Meine, *Half Horse,* 227. As early as 1818, one traveler wrote that the "cruel modes of fighting, prevalent among the boatmen of the west, are generally speaking untrue." Estwick Evans, *A Pedestrious Tour of . . . the Western States and Territories,* in *Early Western Travels, 1748–1846,* ed. Reuben Gold Thwaites (Cleveland: Arthur H. Clark, 1904–1907), 8:344.
25. Walter Blair and Franklin J. Meine, *Mike Fink, King of Mississippi Keelboatmen* (New York: Henry Holt, 1933).
26. W. T. Strickland, *The Pioneers of the West: or, Life in the Woods* (New York, 1868), 201; C. B. Walker, *The Mississippi Valley, and Prehistoric Events* (Burlington, IA: 1881), 246.

War. The humorists were fully participating members of the steamboat generation. As men of their time they admired the steamboat primarily as an efficient, comfortable mode of transportation, but in their sketches it also functions as a handy narrative device. An authentic technological triumph of the age became also a natural theater, a single captive space where segments of a vast population were drawn together to act or to be acted upon in an unfolding human comedy. What the steamboat was not was an object of nostalgia. That had to wait for writers of the following generation, notably Mark Twain. His humorist precursors indulged *their* romanticized instincts with the flatboat, and for the earlier boatmen they reserved a specialized set of feelings that safely honored what in their day that swaggering species of men represented: a recent past, primitive and occasionally sordid.

In "The Big Bear of Arkansas," Thorpe makes his Jim Doggett not merely a quirky hunter, but a harbinger figure. He encapsulates a conceptual *backwoods*, raised from a geographical entity to symbolic space—a great nature that is being eroded by settlement, by agriculture, by urban standards of value and competing kinds of expertise. Doggett is not and presumably never has been a boatman, but he effortlessly appropriates for his own purposes the attention-getting access to an assembly that he rightly expects to welcome him with mixed feelings. The narrator's recital—sensible, urbane, confident—suggests a comfortable adjustment to a world on the move, the *now* of change and heterogeneity, with the steamboat aptly serving as both vehicle and symbol. The Big Bear's intrusion into the amity of the social hall—his Indian whoop sets off talk about the "screamer"—is an influx of the recent past, and his tall talk, interrupting the civilized hum of conversation, is a reminder of how ragtag and provisional modern southwestern society still is. As Thorpe's writing incidentally shows us, the shift from flatboat to steamboat culture was neither abrupt nor well-defined.

The humorists were close enough to the earlier culture to appreciate it, and some were old enough to remember the boatmen before their eclipse. The depiction by an anonymous writer in 1851 hits all the notes familiar to the humorists: "plying the oar by day and the whiskey bottle and fiddle bow by night, they formed a class strictly sui generis, and a devil-may-care, roystering ready handed and open hearted one at that."[27] The generalized nostalgia contains, as we might expect, more than a hint of

---

27. Eugene L. Schwaab and Jacqueline Bull, eds., *Travels in the Old South: Selected from Periodicals of the Times* (Lexington: University Press of Kentucky, 1973), 2:400.

condescension, generated however not solely by the spectacular boat-men but, more profoundly, by the era they had come to represent, one remembered for its audacious energy, its cavalier independence that gave scarcely a nod to a larger common purpose. The regional, even na-tional, mission to extend the American realm rarely invaded the boatmen's consciousness. Only when that autonomous energy flagged, making room for a more corporate kind of drive, could the larger purpose be pursued. The momentum was taken up by movers variously desig-nated as "men of character" and "men of substance." Because most of the humorists were themselves men of character (and a marginal few were even men of substance), they shared in the succession, the inheritance of the moderns.

The most resonant link between the boatman era and the humorists is a character type. The half-horse half-alligator, as we shall see, was not re-stricted to the "Kaintucks" nor to the rivers, yet his generalized attributes as boatman conveniently provided the humorists with a touchstone for an entire period.[28] As writers, they instinctively perceived that the obvi-ous marks of the flatboat era were lingual—or, more precisely, what in oral high-talk became verbal in their reproducing hands. If Thorpe and his humorist contemporaries could not bring themselves to condone the barbarism of the Mike Finks, retrospectively they could at least admire the physical, unbuttoned vigor of their lingo.

ii.

There was a yell at us, and a jingling of bells to stop the engines, a pow-wow of cussing, and whistling of steam—and as Jim went overboard on one side and I on the other, she come smashing straight through the raft.

—*Adventures of Huckleberry Finn*

No moment better spotlights the coexistence of the steamboat and its man-powered predecessors on the great western rivers than this climac-tic passage in Chapter 16 of *Huckleberry Finn*. The literal crash symbolically

28. The stylistic signature of the half-horse half-alligator type belongs to Davy Crockett, symbol of the wilderness, not the river; and the first self-conscious humor-ous sketch is James K. Paulding's anecdote of a wagoner and a batteauman from a lit-tle town on the Shenandoah. The half-horse half-alligator character type is discussed in chap. 12.

condenses the lingering professional tensions of an era in river culture that has already become "the heyday of the steamboating prosperity."[29] Like his creator, Huck knows the steamboat pilots and their tag games—aiming at flatboats "to see how close they can come without touching," but they do touch sometimes; "the wheel bites off a sweep, and then the pilot sticks his head out and laughs, and thinks he's mighty smart." Huck identifies with the boatmen, though the little raft he and Jim find for their trip down the Mississippi is not even a distraction for steamboat pilots. By the time he reaches the surface after the crash, the steamboat has already started her engines again, for, says Huck, "they never cared much for raftsmen."

This passage also signaled a compositional crisis in 1875. Seven years would pass before Mark Twain picked up the action at this point to complete the novel. In the interim he journeyed back to the great river to visit old haunts while completing *Life on the Mississippi*. The return invigorated the author's creativity both for the (more or less) nonfictional book and for *Huckleberry Finn*. To flavor his account of river life, Twain "throws in" a projected chapter from the unfinished novel—an episode in which Huck slips aboard a flatboat to try to find out just where on the river he and Jim are: they need to stop in Cairo, and they don't know where Cairo is. The chapter, which Twain decided finally not to use in the novel, is a *tour de force* of riverboat tall talk, a set piece (like the earlier diatribe of Pap Finn) that illustrates the author's ear for dialect and its resonating rhythms. In its gaudy excess, the flatboatmen's tall talk suggests an older style long departed from the Mississippi. Indeed, it was a style that became passé for the humorists a generation earlier—cause enough for their nostalgic indulgence about the men who gloried in its use. For Twain, the elaborate riffs are open not to nostalgia, but to satire.

In the 1870s and 1880s Twain preferred to identify himself with New England (and his home as Hartford). As a southwesterner, he had lived long enough to see the flatboat succeeded by the steamboat, which in turn had lost its own dominance. This chronology allowed him, as we shall see, to make the flamboyant brag—the style that Thorpe, Field, and their contemporaries enjoyed—available to full-scale satiric assault. But if the re-creation of screamer rhetoric is show-offy fun for a writer proud of his linguistic mimicry, Twain's evaluation of the boatmen is serious—and virtually indistinguishable from that of his humorist predecessors.

29. Mark Twain, *Life on the Mississippi* (MW, 717).

These uneducated "rough and hardy men," writes the former steamboat pilot, were "heavy drinkers" and "heavy fighters," "coarse frolickers in moral sties" along the riverbanks, "elephantinely jolly, foul-witted, profane" and "prodigious braggarts"; but, for all that, they deserve honor for being "honest, trustworthy, faithful to promises and duty and often picturesquely magnanimous."

Flatboat culture was so safely historic that Twain felt little of its nostalgic pull, but the same cannot be said for the Mississippi itself and the steamboat that came to symbolize it during his early maturity. The romance of steamboating of course has its own history. At one time or another, a large number of our nineteenth-century writers found their way up or down the Mississippi on a steamboat, but it is Mark Twain who is the Laureate of the River. The glamor of steamboating enticed the boy in Hannibal and recurred as memory to the old writer in Hartford; for five of those years in between it was less glamor than hard work as he struggled to learn the river as a professional pilot. Until it was closed by the Civil War, the Mississippi was literally home to Twain. This man who was, variously, prospector, newspaperman, travel writer, humorist, "teacher of the great public," "jackleg novelist," and (briefly) soldier, remembered that experience as a pilot as his single most satisfying job. For all his exaggerations, jibes, satiric thrusts, recitation of facts, even an occasional mean-spirited demolition of others' reputations, *Life on the Mississippi* is primarily a hymn to the river. And for all his awareness that the great river in 1882 is still the great river, that hymn is most stirring when Twain succumbs to the memory of what the river was—and, despite its meanness and shallowness, what river culture was when he was one of the moderns. Though he was death on sentimentality, Twain was not immune to his own brand of nostalgia. Hardly anyone in nineteenth-century writing who remembered steamboating was so immune.

It is no wonder that contemporary accounts, both published and private (those recorded in diaries and correspondence) are so filled with references to the steamboat. It was a means to an end, an economic "motive," but it also became an end in itself: a "floating palace" that offered accommodations superior to most land hotels and (with few exceptions) even the tentatively grand houses that were going up in the lower South; a theater of astonishing variety that rivaled the Parisian outdoor cafés for people-watching; and a dominant, high-profile, material emblem of the new age. "Kings' courts have rarely been the scene of more reckless extravagance" than the Mississippi steamers, according to one memoirist. "It was simply magnificence gone wild. It was the quintescence of extravagance, dignity, formality, courtesy and debauchery combined."[30]

Traveling from North to South and West followed a predictable pattern, one which William Mercer's 1816 trip from Baltimore to New Orleans illustrates. A young surgeon, Mercer went by stagecoach to Pittsburgh, where he boarded a flatboat to Cincinnati; from Cincinnati he went on horseback to Louisville, where he boarded a steamboat for the final leg. His diary describes the early phases of river travel before steamboats became floating hotels. From Louisville to Natchez, Mercer was on the *Washington*, "the first steamboat of the flat-bottomed type to appear on the inland waters of the Ohio-Mississippi system." It took a month. For all the delays—caused by sandbars and a boiler explosion—Mercer decided that steamboat navigation was "singularly adapted to the western country, where the rivers are deep and impetuous, and their banks covered with an inexhaustible supply of fuel."[31] Although the steamboat was most crucial to the economy of the region and nation as a carrier of freight, the glamor of the era was associated with passenger traffic. Unlike many eastern steamboats, those in the west carried both freight and people. For purely practical reasons—speed and comfort—it was the vehicle of the modern age.[32] It was cheaper than the stagecoach and, given the notoriously unregulated drivers the stage lines relied on, less dangerous. If the steamboat had attained the height of its glory by 1840, it had done so for practical, not romantic, reasons.

Its appeal was broadly based—for planters (on business and pleasure trips); families (on visits to relatives); professionals, mechanics, and artisans (on their way to better opportunities); merchants, farmers, and hunters (on short hops); eastern visitors (for health, adventure, or scouting purposes); foreign visitors (for firsthand evidence to use in books they were writing); light-bringers (abolitionists, preachers, bible salesmen); and a wide array of professional gamblers, slave traders, speculators, adventurers, and confidence men. As we see in Melville's definitive fiction

30. F. D. Srygley, *Seventy Years in Dixie* (Nashville, 1893), 307.
31. Edwin Adams Davis and John C. L. Andreassen, "From Louisville to New Orleans in 1816: Diary of William Newton Mercer," *Journal of Southern History* 2 (1936): 390–402.
32. James Neal Primm, *Lion of the Valley: St. Louis, Missouri* (Boulder, CO: Pruett, 1981), 168. One foreign visitor credited this "most perfect system of transportation" with reducing "the distance not only between different places, but between different classes." Michel Chevalier, *Society, Manners, and Politics in the United States: Letters on North America* (1839; reprint, ed. John William Ward, Ithaca, NY: Cornell University Press, 1961), 204.

about the crisis in trust, steamboat travel became the symbolic locus of a society in flux, where strangers mixed more freely and with fewer communal restraints than obtained in settlements, villages, and towns. Adventure lay in the very uncertainty regarding diverse passengers. One proper young lady on a steamboat in 1850 reported her titillation at a raucous party in an adjoining cabin, fearing that she might hear "something I shouldn't like to hear."[33] Despite the potential threat behind the pleasant face and seductive tongue, the steamboat was the favorite site for antebellum mingling. The congregating (some of it wary) included everybody who took passage except the very poor, who negotiated whatever terms they could manage for deck accommodations. For some patrons the steamboat was a convenience, for others a treat, and for still others an opportunity for self-betterment through skill, fraud, or assorted dark designs.

In the life of the nation, the steamboat was not simply a water vehicle, but a very material proof of American progress. *Moving under its own steam* became a favored celebration of initiative. As a striking testimony to native innovation, energy, and independence, the steamboat was a source of pride for Americans. Though a few foreign visitors commented on the romance of steamboating, most Europeans were strident in their complaints about overcrowding, bad food, and worse company. The steamboat was, for example, an especially unpleasant site for visitors unaccustomed to tobacco-loving Americans, who, remarked one, "expectorate . . . as if they were toxopholites."[34] For those who found disagreeable the egalitarian principles of socializing, the steamboat was a concentrated site of enforced sociability.

Descriptions of the social mix on steamboats were rarely neutral. For a few natives and many foreigners, their fellow passengers, to use a favorite word in its nineteenth-century meaning, were entirely too *promiscuous:* too much, too many, too different. Society "of all kinds" was only the mildest term of disapproval; most travelers' accounts specify details of dress, speech, and behavior that offend, a tangible diversity that is itself evidence that the steamboat was no mere symbol. If mobility was a chief

33. Josephine Mandeville, letter, July 5, 1850, Henry D. Mandeville Family Papers, MSS 491, 535, Louisiana and Lower Mississippi Valley Collections, Louisiana State University Libraries, Baton Rouge.

34. Alfred Bunn, *Old England and New England, in a Series of Views Taken on the Spot* (London, 1853), 266–67. More serious than spitters were gamblers. Thomas L. Nichols discussed the wide range of gamblers, from the professionals to the most desperate amateurs. *Forty Years of American Life* (London, 1864), 1:170–71, 296.

trait generally of Americans after the War of 1812, the steamboat was the vehicle of choice once it became a practical means of transportation. One traveler declares he will refrain from adding to the litanies of disgust at life aboard steamboats ("others more competent to the task, have contrived to make them sufficiently notorious"), but he cannot refrain, and goes on to list features that make water travel disagreeable: common towels for passengers' toilets, barbarous table manners, drunkenness, incompetent stewards, stubborn captains, and a mixed society "to be designated by the single term, bad." For another traveler society "of all kinds" includes many men "most uninviting in their aspect"—men with "dark-lantern looking faces, with hollow cheeks, deeply sunken eyes, long hair, and grisly unshaven faces." Others seem merely "bilious." Those from whose waistcoats protruded bowie knives and revolvers are labeled "'border-ruffians,' or slave dealers."[35]

Moritz Busch, though not exhilarated by his fellow passengers in 1851, shows more composure than most in registering his motley companions. Admiring the boats' magnificent carpets, he thinks it oddly democratic that the "roughest and most repulsive," as well as the "most refined aristocrats," walk upon them. At dinner he sits with "a half-savage Hoosier from Indiana," a "pale and pious" Jesuit from St. Louis, a gold miner just returning from California decked out in a "red silk Spanish sash," a "crowd of professional gamblers," a stiff army major, a "smiling, fat Dunkard" (whom he engages in a discussion of hog breeding and the sacrament of baptism), some Methodist preachers with "chalk-white neckcloths," two loafers with dirty collars, and a smattering of "tree-tall, rawboned, coarse fellows from the forests of western Kentucky."[36] A clergyman who has had a joyless experience on a steamboat shares none of Busch's beguilement. When he tries to individualize his fellow passengers, his vexation lets him only summon up more types: "a Baptist clergyman, a Mormon elder, Green the Reformed Gambler." He continues: "Tom Thumbs, Jack Falstaffs & living skeletons, tall Kentuckians and short pigmies, drunkards, dandies & loafers, oh! such a crew!" As for the real crew, he finds the "deck hands of a Mississippi steamer . . . as hard apologies for human beings as I ever saw. They glory in a 'row,' a 'fight'

35. James Stuart, *Three Years in North America*, 3rd ed. (Edinburgh, 1833), 2:297; Frederick J. Jobson, *America, and American Methodism* (New York, 1857), 300.

36. Moritz Busch, *Travels between the Hudson and the Mississippi, 1851–1852*, trans. and ed. Norman H. Binger (Lexington: University Press of Kentucky, 1971), 209–10. This German traveler explicitly made the riverman a marine version of the backwoodsman, and both types he called "rough forerunners of civilization" (221).

or 'spree'," and, except for "their fine singing," he can discover "no charm about this class of men." In his compulsive calling of the roll, this bishop seems driven to exasperation simply by writing down the types he encounters, but even he perceives them all linked to what the new country now means: "One & all have chosen one motto 'Go ahead' and they do it too."[37]

What visitors to the Southwest objected to on the waterways was mostly what they found annoying in the vast interior: crowded sleeping arrangements, indifferent hygiene, bad food, boring society ("loud brag" alternating with anecdotes about cotton and hunting), rude and self-regarding functionaries. Steamboat travelers had two additional complaints: unreliable schedules (and the captains' casual attitudes about them) and the interminable delays along the routes. Making light of such tribulations, Joseph M. Field concocted one journey, which, though imaginary, bundled together several actual trips. Related in the present and present-perfect tenses to convey immediacy, "Fast on a Bar" incorporates the delays of traveling on successive steamboats and the passengers' verbal contributions to the operation. The time between trips is boring, writes Field, but must be borne "before the smallest possible boat, charging the highest possible price, takes the 'tallest' possible number to the sweetest possible place—Cairo—for further *transport!*" (Oehl., 86–89).

More vociferous than natives on all matters concerning steamboat travel, foreigners were also more anxious about its physical dangers. Running aground on snags and sandbars, they felt, was not merely an inconvenience. It suggested the potentially lethal nature of other probable accidents like boiler explosions, fire, and falling overboard. Such fears were justified. Throughout the antebellum era, a five-year life for a new steamboat was considered good.[38] Occasionally, these accidents were not accidental. Some captains could hardly ever resist racing. Frederick Gerstaecker, with some experience as stoker, was particularly harsh in judging the readiness of steamboat officers to race at full throttle. Near Cincinnati he witnessed one such instance when the "obstinacy" of the captain in "stopping the safety-valve" on the *Moselle* resulted in an explosion and

37. Lester B. Shippee, ed., *Bishop Whipple's Southern Diary, 1843–1844* (Minneapolis: University of Minnesota Press, 1937), 131, 138–39, 123.

38. By 1831, when 198 steamboats plied the western waters, 150 had already been "worn out or lost by accidents." Francis J. Grund, *The Americans in Their Moral, Social, and Political Relations* (1837; reprint, New York: A. M. Kelley, 1971), 2:181. By the end of 1849, 550 steamboats had perished, at an average age of under three years. Primm, *Lion of the Valley,* 170.

the loss of "130 persons on the passengers' list" and "a number of steerage passengers" whose names were never recorded: "Thirty carts were employed in carrying their mutilated remains to the burial-places; for weeks afterward, bodies were frequently washed on shore. The force of the steam was so great, that one man was thrown over to the Kentucky shore, and another came down, head foremost, through a shingle roof."[39] After this experience, the German sportsman decided to try his hand at silversmithing on shore.

Such carnage is of course more lightly regarded in the humor. In one sketch, John S. Robb waggishly links the "general convulsion" of fire and water in steamboat explosions to Father Miller's predicted date for the "general blowing up" of the world: "[S]ome of the engineers upon our western waters, who had been used to blowing up its inhabitants, became a little frightened at the prospect of having to encounter in another world, the victims of steamboat disaster" (*SSL,* 148). If he could never muster that kind of caustic élan, Baron von Raumer at least steeled himself to display the same good cheer on steamboats as most Americans. He could overlook the danger, noise, and excessive spitting because his fellow passengers never lost *their* composure. Even when traveling "on the utmost western boundary of human civilization," they kept their sights on "the great object, viz. to *go ahead!*"[40] For British travelers especially, the Mississippi became a geographical marker between what most outsiders considered civilization and its paltry imitations among the unwashed; the steamboat was a diverse world in which the status of its temporary residents was as fluid as the Mississippi they rode on.

Among native critics, Peter Cartwright denounced the permissive spectacle of passengers drinking, dancing, blaspheming, swearing, and playing cards ("men and women too"). When the fiery evangelist, himself a product of the frontier, boarded a steamboat with a fellow Methodist preacher for the first time in 1828, he, like most travelers who penned their impressions, noted the "mixed multitude." But for him the diversity was heavily freighted toward categories of "infidels": ordinary unbelievers, "some Deists, some Atheists, some Universalists," along with the customary sprinkling of "profane swearers, drunkards, gamblers,

---

39. Frederick Gerstaecker, *Wild Sports in the Far West* (1854; reprint, Boston, 1866), 124. Lugubrious exploitation made good copy. A popular book in 1840 was Allen Howland's *Steamboat Disasters and Railroad Accidents in the United States,* which provided detailed accounts of high-profile catastrophes. Jack Larkin, *The Reshaping of Everyday Life, 1790–1840* (New York: Harper & Row, 1988), 230.

40. Frederick von Raumer, *America and the American People,* trans. W. W. Turner (New York, 1846), 426.

fiddlers, and dancers." In his autobiography, seeing "we were in a bad snap," Cartwright "reproves" two of the loudest profaners, who assure him they will swear no more in his presence. Never above theatrical tricks in preaching to rough-hewn audiences, he walks casually to the gaming table, which is presided over by an army captain known as "a professional infidel." Affecting ignorance, Cartwright asks him what "those little spotted things were." The apparent gull, disrupting the game with questions aroused by his feigned curiosity, shifts the discussion to more serious topics, and the officer finally proposes: "Sir, if you will debate with me on the Christian religion, we will quit all our cards, fiddles, and dances." Though the debate ends ambiguously, the good parson at least completes his journey in a more serene atmosphere.[41]

For travelers, from the truculent to the compliant, the days and nights aboard even the most opulent steamboats were often exercises in patience. Her own account suggests that Harriet Martineau was what we would now call a difficult customer. Even she, however, was not immune to certain delights of river travel. On a nine-day trip from New Orleans she discovers a handful of agreeable passengers, and her aesthetic sense is sparked by the interplay of evening lights (from the moon, brands on shore, lanterns on passing flatboats, and fireflies). But she is not tolerant of nosy women who inquire about her religion (referring to her Unitarianism, one is overheard to say, "she won't find it go down with us") or young preachers who are "ignorant," and she is irritated by rambunctious Kentuckians "and other western men." Mostly she is not charmed by Mississippi scenery: though she has "untiring eyes" for the more varied prospects along the Ohio, Martineau finds herself oppressed by the endless miles of "vastness and rankness" along the Mississippi. If for many visitors the steamboat was a floating Vanity Fair, for Fredrika Bremer the craft she boarded in 1853 was a Noah's ark, filled with "really mammoth oxen, . . . cows, calves, horses, mules, sheep, pigs, . . . turkeys, . . . geese, ducks, hens." Except for the disagreeable odors, she confesses that "the sons and daughters of Adam" were made comfortable. But she too is oppressed by the scenery. She notes that the "shores are low and swampy" at the conjunction of the Missouri and Mississippi. "It is horribly monotonous. The weather is gray and cold, and every thing looks gray around us."[42]

Monotony is the single note repeatedly struck in the travel accounts.

41. *Autobiography of Peter Cartwright, the Backwoods Preacher*, ed. W. P. Strickland (Cincinnati, 1856), 190–91.

42. Harriet Martineau, *Retrospect of Western Travel* (1838; reprint, New York: Greenwood, 1969), 2:167, 185–86, 217; Fredrika Bremer, *The Homes of the New World; Impressions of America*, trans. Mary Howitt (New York, 1854), 2:172–73.

William Howard Russell found that the Mississippi was "the most uninteresting river in the world" and that "not a particle of romance" could ever "vivify its turbid waters."[43] Charles Mackay, venting his own boredom with the "prevailing uniformity" of the flat wooded shores, inserts into his description a poem, widely reprinted in American newspapers, to illustrate the anxieties and perils of a Mississippi river trip. One stanza addresses the passengers' boredom:

> Weary were the forests, dark on either side;
> Weary were the marshes, stretching far and wide:
> Weary were the wood-piles, strewn upon the bank;
> Weary were the cane-groves, growing wild and dank;—
> Weary were the tree-stumps, charred and black with fire;
> Weary was the wilderness, without a house or spire;
> Weary were the log-huts, built upon the sand:
> Weary were the waters, weary was the land;
> Weary was the cabin with its gilded wall,
> Weary was the deck we trod—weary—weary all—
> Nothing seemed so pleasant to hope for or to keep,
> Nothing in the wide world so beautiful as sleep,
> As we journeyed southward in our lazy ship,
> *Dawdling, idling, loafing, down the Mississip.*[44]

Not all visitors to the Southwest were bored and annoyed by the monotonous scenery and the raucous society that steamboats attracted. One Virginia lawyer wrote in his diary that he enjoyed sleeping "on Board a Steam Boat, the rocking of the Boat and the lumbering of the machinery lulls me to rest." The passengers "have become very social. We all know each other, and have become familiar with the officers of the Boat. We while away the day the best way we can." In his quieter, more romantic moments, Timothy Flint also liked giving himself up to the gentle lulling of the river current, which could induce "a tranquillity highly propitious to meditation."[45] But for this itinerant preacher, reveries were almost a

43. William Howard Russell, *My Diary North and South* (Boston, 1863), 295. T. B. Thorpe agreed that the river is "always turbid," but chose the rhetoric of sublimity to plumb its "sameness": only in contemplating its magnitude can the Mississippi overwhelm the mind; the "great Aorta," "*altering,* but not *altered,*" proclaims "the wisdom and power of GOD" (*TBT,* 101–5).
44. Charles Mackay, *Life and Liberty in America* (London, 1859), 1:251.
45. Herbert A. Kellar, ed., "A Journey through the South in 1836: Diary of James D. Davidson," *Journal of Southern History* 1 (1935): 353–54; Timothy Flint, *Recollections of*

selfish indulgence. No one is more upbeat about steamboat sociability than Flint. His democratic benevolence so orients him to steamboat travel that he sometimes sounds like a nineteenth-century travel brochure. The green shores, he writes, "are always seen with the same *coup d'oeil,* that takes in the magnificent and broad wave of the Mississippi. Refreshments come in from the shore. The passengers every day have their promenade." The claims of wealth, family, and position are laid aside: "the worth and interest of a person are naturally tried on his simple merits, his powers of conversation, his innate civility, his capacities to amuse, and his good feelings."[46]

The most sanguine (and long-suffering) travelers view their steamboat trips as an educational experience. Harriet Martineau goes ashore to inspect a woodcutter's cabin "just for the sake of having been in Arkansas." Bishop Whipple admits that the "floating pens" have made him aware of "specimens of mankind entirely new and strange & of whose existence I was before entirely unacquainted."[47] Despite the homegrown moralists, Americans were open to the steamboat experience, and more tolerant of its democratic mix than were judgmental Europeans. T. B. Thorpe stresses the "heterogeneous character" of the passengers—a phrase that, from his pen, is more inclined toward approval than otherwise. "Starting from New Orleans in one of these boats," he writes, "you will find yourself associated with men from every State in the Union, and from every portion of the globe," and, like Bishop Whipple (but with more good cheer), he enumerates their types, which include both the shady and the respectable. Thorpe's generous neutrality elevates both the scene and his own capacity for experience: "a man of observation," he writes, "need not lack for amusement or instruction in such a crowd, if he will take the trouble to read the great book of Character so favorably opened before him" (*TBT,* 112).

The most productive man of observation was Frederick Law Olmsted, who in the 1850s made three southern trips totaling fourteen months. The result of his inspection tours in "the American Slave States" was the classic study *The Cotton Kingdom.* Among the travelers, Olmsted was virtually unique in his analysis of southern character. What the crowded steamboats on the waterways of Alabama suggested to him was not diversity,

the *Last Ten Years in the Valley of the Mississippi* (1826; reprint, ed. George R. Brooks, Carbondale: Southern Illinois University Press, 1968), 23.

46. Flint, *Condensed Geography,* 1:210–11.
47. Martineau, *Retrospect,* 2:188; Shippee, *Bishop Whipple's Southern Diary,* 133.

but a "very great homogeneousness of character" amid all the superficial differences of types. More than any people he had heretofore seen, he wrote, southerners were "unrateable by dress, taste, forms, and expenditures." The same individual could exhibit both the self-possession and graciousness of a gentleman and the coarse tastes of a boor. Olmsted of course was no ordinary traveler—he was exceptionally perceptive and patient—and the primary objects of his attention on interior steamers were newly rich cotton planters; but his alertness to poorer whites, a rarity among travelers, only confirmed his ideas about "the Anglo-Saxon development of the South-west."[48]

Sometimes it takes an experienced hand to read the book of Character. In one of C. F. M. Noland's Pete Whetstone letters, Dan Looney makes two new friends when he boards a steamboat to New Orleans: a "great big raw-boned fellow from old Kentuck" and a sickly, ague-plagued fellow "from old Virginny." With more river-travel experience than the Arkansan, the two instruct Dan about the promiscuous mix around them as they make their way down the Mississippi. "Mr. Looney," says one, "if you will jist skin your eye close, you will see all sorts of people, on a big boat like this." When Dan looks around, he is reminded of what he had once heard from "old Giles Scroggins": that "mankind was divided into five sorts—viz., quality, bob-quality, and commonality, rubbish, and trash." He announces that he sees "three sorts of people here, but two kinds are missing—I can see quality, bob-quality, and commonality, but no rubbish and trash."

> "Ah, Mr. Looney," said Old Kentuck, who was a mighty plain matter-of-fact man, "when you have traded mules to Orleans seventeen seasons in succession, you will be a better judge of rubbish and trash than you are now; for I would be willing to take $200 for the best pair of mules I have got on this boat, if them hairy-lip fellows over there, cutting up such shines, ain't trash, and the meanest sort." (*PW*, 207)

Old Kentuck is right. If Dan Looney had ventured out of Devil's Fork more often, he would know what his genial creator had learned from his varied pursuits among both the raw and the cultivated. Like many of his

---

48. Frederick Law Olmsted, *The Cotton Kingdom: A Traveller's Observations on Cotton and Slavery in the American Slave States, 1853–1861* (1861; reprint, ed. Arthur M. Schlesinger, New York: Da Capo Press, 1996), 215–16. As the editor points out, Olmsted perceived "Souths rather than *the* South," but unifying all the strands of southern society—races, regions, classes, professions—was the institution of slavery (xlviii).

fellow humorists—Thorpe, Field, Sol Smith, Henry Clay Lewis, and others—Fenton Noland was knowledgeable of (and comfortable with) the great spectrum of humanity that routinely patronized the steamboat.

The humorists particularly revered the captains, often singling them out for their openness, competence, and capacious tolerance. While James Hall saw fit to emphasize the early steamboat captain's role as disciplinarian, the humorists noted his role as equitable boss. However, if "trash of the meanest sort" violated the captain's rules of conduct, they might well find themselves deposited on a sandbar in the middle of the river. In *Col. Crockett's Exploits and Adventures in Texas*, Richard Penn Smith tells the story of one enterprising captain at Natchez:

> A steamboat stopped at the landing, and one of the hands went ashore under the hill to purchase provisions, and the adroit citizens of that delectable retreat contrived to rob him of all his money. The captain of the boat, a determined fellow, went ashore in the hope of persuading them to refund,—but that cock wouldn't fight. Without farther ceremony, assisted by his crew and passengers, some three or four hundred in number, he made fast an immense cable to the frame tenement where the theft had been perpetrated, and allowed fifteen minutes for the money to be forthcoming; vowing if it was not produced within that time, to put steam to his boat, and drag the house into the river. The money was instantly produced.[49]

Except for the most egregious violators—gambling cheats, horse thieves, counterfeiters—both the respectable and the shady could expect fair treatment from captains.

The tone of the humorous sketches reflects that same catholic spirit. In "Breaking a Bank," Sol Smith praises one Captain Summons as a "very clever fellow," which turns out to mean that he is a disinterested supervisor of games. Anxious that his passengers be "comfortably bestowed, well fed and well attended to, and *determined* that they shall amuse themselves 'just as they d—n please,'" Captain Summons is "clever in every way":

> If he happened to have preachers on board, he put on a serious countenance of a Sunday morning, consented that there should be preaching, ordered the chairs to be set out, and provided Bibles and hymn-books for the

49. [Richard Penn Smith], *Col. Crockett's Exploits and Adventures in Texas*, in *The Autobiography of David Crockett*, ed. Hamlin Garland (New York: Scribner, 1923), 264–65.

occasion, himself and his officers . . . taking front seats and listening atten-
tively to the discourse. . . . If there were passengers on board who desired
to pass away the time in playing poker, euchre, brag, or whist, tables and
chairs were ready for *them* too. . . . All sorts of passengers were accommodated on the Dr. Franklin; the rights of none were suffered to be infringed;
all were free to follow such employments as should please themselves.

When the preachers ask him to stop the gambling, Captain Summons responds predictably:

"Gentlemen, amuse yourselves as you like; preach and pray to your hearts'
content. . . . These men prefer to amuse themselves with cards; let them;
they pay their passages as well as you, . . . and have as much right to *their*
amusements as you have to yours. . . . Preach, play cards, dance cotillions,
do what you like. *I* am agreeable; only understand that *all games . . . must
cease at 10 o'clock.*"[50] (Cohen, 74–77)

In one sketch a captain rescues an "Arkansas defaulter" who is being
chased along the riverbank by a sheriff's posse, but he afterwards demands payment for his decision to intervene: "Now, Kernel," he explains,
"we expect you to stand treat for all hands! Hurrah! bring on the licker!"
(*PPW*, 195). These autocrats of the river were not to be trifled with, even
by newspapermen. Joseph Field once urged the public to boycott a certain captain who, he charged in the *Reveille*, had arbitrarily withheld
New Orleans papers from the St. Louis office. The captain sued for libel
and won, a Missouri court deciding that Field's diatribe was malicious.[51]

The steamboat was a favorite venue for card players—amateurs as
well as hard-core gamblers—and off-duty crew members, and often the
pilot himself, would sit down with the passengers in the social hall for a
game of euchre, or faro, or brag. Such participation rarely attracted complaints, even from those on board who morally disapproved of cardplay-
ing, since captains and pilots were autocratic enough to discourage
anyone from questioning their authority. In a letter to a boyhood friend,
Mark Twain affirmed that though all men are "*slaves* to other men & to
circumstances," the pilot alone "comes at no man's beck or call, obeys no
man's orders & scorns all men's suggestions." Independent even of the

50. The 10 p.m. curfew was in effect from the very first, when Robert Fulton posted
his regulations on the *North River* in 1808. Sale, *Fire of His Genius*, 134–35.
51. William H. Lyon, *The Pioneer Editor in Missouri, 1808–1860* (Columbia: University of Missouri Press, 1965), 81–82.

captain, the pilot was, in the words of one historian, "the sole and un-questioned commander" because of his knowledge of the river; treated gingerly by "the captain, officers and servants," the courtesy "was quickly conveyed to the passengers."[52] Some passengers, however—those who were already disconcerted by widespread reports of fires and explosions—were made all the more uneasy at the sight of the man in charge finding too much distraction at the tables.

In *Fifty Years on the Mississippi* (1889), E. W. Gould cites the "abundant testimony" of officers who indulged their passion for card games while on duty, and gives the following account (carefully censored even after the event had long passed into history):

> In the early spring of ——— the beautiful little side-wheel boat ——— belonging on the upper rivers, was returning to St. Louis from a trip to New Orleans, when she struck a snag at Ruckers Point, between Memphis and Cairo.
>
> The boat and cargo were a total loss, but no other casualty. Later developments proved conclusively that the pilot on watch, or who should have been on watch, was in the hall below playing *poker* with the passengers, and a steersman was piloting the boat, when she struck a snag, being too far out on the bar.
>
> Many such cases could doubtless be enumerated, but not many perhaps with such fatal results.

The humorists, of course, delete "fatal results" from their stories set on the waterways of the Southwest. Captains, when they appear in the sketches, are always authoritarians with little patience for finicky passengers, but they may be genial as well as skillful. If their fondness for card-playing has practical consequences, these never involve safety: they are only embarrassments. In "Slow Traveling by Steam," Sol Smith extracts considerable humor out of the behavior of the captain of the *Caravan*, who is so engrossed in an all-night game of brag belowdecks that he fails to notice that his boat, ineptly piloted through fog, is going nowhere, even as it consumes load after load of fuel—which are all bought at the same wooding station (Cohen, 65–70). Although most captains insisted on a 10 p.m. curfew for "games of amusement"—as we have seen in "Breaking a Bank"—some allowed players to continue throughout the

52. Leland Krauth, "Mark Twain: The Victorian of Southwestern Humor," in *The Humor of the Old South*, ed. M. Thomas Inge and Edward J. Piacentino (Lexington: University Press of Kentucky, 2001), 227; Frazer, *Early Steamboats*, 15.

night. Many "old stewards," asserts Gould, "can yet bear testimony to the fact that they have often found the same players still engaged in the fascinating old game of *draw* when they called their cabin crew at daylight."[53]

If some passengers thought of themselves as trapped on a Ship of Fools, others more cheerfully imagined themselves as royalty, indulging their whims in a floating palace and reveling in all the accoutrements designed for the comfort of a civilized elite. Among experienced writers, the metaphors of choice for steamboating stressed the marvel of technology that had conquered the most dangerous of rivers. "Gigantic specimens of art," Thorpe called the Mississippi steamboats, "bellowing over the swift and muddy current like restless monsters, breathing like the whisperings of the hurricane, clanking and groaning as if an earthquake was preparing to astonish the world" (*TBT*, 253). The recurring image of the steamboat as monster presents this icon of the modern as awe-inspiring, simultaneously fascinating and hazardous. In 1836, when one Alabamian saw and heard his first steamboat in Montgomery, he described it as "grunting at the wharf," a sound "resembling heavy breathing of a large elephant but ten times as loud."[54] Joseph Field elevates a race between two steamer pilots into a battle of behemoths, in which the most conspicuous symbol of the new is also an atavistic creature resurrected from extinction. Imperfectly controlled by their dueling masters, the rival boats race with lumbering fury:

> [T]he iron throats of the steamers are less hideous than the human ones beneath them. The . . . thwarted monster has now "taken a sheer in the wild current," and, beyond the possibility of prevention, is driving on to the bank! A cry of terror rises aloft—the throng rush aft—the steam, every valve set free—makes the whole forest shiver, and, amid the fright, the tall chimneys, caught by the giant trees, are wrenched and torn out like tusks from a recoiling mastadon. (Cohen, 108)

Even though the humorists show little explicit foresight of how this splendid emblem of the modern is destined to succumb, like the flatboat, to yet more modern successors, their dedicated recording of the social history of the steamboat and its cultural reverberations leads them to hedge their satisfaction. In their writing, the achievement of civilization

---

53. Gould, *Fifty Years*, 741.
54. Rhoda Coleman Ellison, *Bibb County, Alabama: The First Hundred Years, 1818–1918* (Tuscaloosa: University of Alabama Press, 1984), 105.

is always in the future. Like other travelers on the waters, they see the steamboat as an index of antebellum America, a gathered image of its traits and tendencies, but unlike most, they appreciate it as a shorthand emblem of mechanized progress, incomplete and ongoing. Canals and railroads may offer little visible competition in the Southwest, but as commercial rivals within the nation they lurk as the inevitable next stage in the continuities of the modern.

In 1841 a writer in *Hunt's Merchants' Magazine and Commercial Review* characterized steam navigation as the crucial element in the settlement of the trans-Appalachian west: "Steam navigation colonized the west! It furnished a motive for settlement and production by the hands of eastern men, because it brought the western territory nearer to the east by nine-tenths of the distance."[55] Like all farseeing observers with a stake in their subject, this no-nonsense journalist had his eye on the economic development of the region. Two pertinent points are worth making about this piece. First, the writer refuses to endorse the common wisdom that the cotton gin (along with the energized slave trade that resulted) was the great determinant in the rapid growth of the Old Southwest, arguing rather that the filling up of the Mississippi lands and their flourishing can be traced directly to the steamboat. It was that invention, he says, that ensured the prosperity of an area that only a few years earlier had been mostly Indian lands and European outposts. Second, in an article that appeared in 1841, the writer uses the past tense to make his claim. The implication is clear: the commercial contribution of the steamboat to the development of the lower South is regarded as a mission already accomplished. And it had been accomplished in less than a single generation.

For most of the antebellum years, the flatboat was seen as part of America's past, and to the sensibilities of most writers—essayists, travelers, journalists, and tourists—the steamboat was the triumphant, modern present. But *modern* is a comfortable, self-regarding category that obtains only so long as nothing more modern comes along, which of course it always does. And so it was with the steamboat.

Historically it has been convenient to use the Civil War as the breakpoint in the dominance of steamboat culture. This is partly accurate. The Mississippi was the lifeblood of the Confederacy. With the end of the

55. Quoted in Erik F. Haites, James Mak, and Gary M. Walton, *Western River Transportation: The Era of Early Development, 1810–1860* (Baltimore: Johns Hopkins University Press, 1975), 9.

sieges at Vicksburg on July 4, 1863, and Port Hudson two days later, the South was no longer able to supply itself. After the war civilian use of the great river resumed, with the steamboat the chief instrument in that economy. But it was, for obvious reasons, no longer a Flush Times economy. In fact the decade *before* the Civil War saw the economic importance of New Orleans, as a gateway linking the west with the rest of the nation, dwindling. It accounted for about 45 percent of inbound merchandise in the 1830s; by the 1850s that figure had fallen to about 28 percent—with more and more trade going to New York, Baltimore, and Philadelphia. The reason for the decline was *modernity.* By the 1850s the latest technologies were canals and railroads, alternatives that spurred a redirection of commercial activity away from the north-south axis to an east-west axis. At the same time that aesthetic improvements were enhancing the attraction of the steamboat, the era, in the words of one historian, "gave promise of its eventual demise even before it had attained its greatest glory."[56] Mississippi steamboat culture lost much of its national flavor and gradually became more regional in orientation. It never regained its earlier prominence in national life. It is that loss which made Mark Twain susceptible to the temptations of nostalgia.

iii.

As professionals the authors trafficked comfortably among fellow southwesterners who clung so noisily to their retrograde patterns that they constituted a prominent part of their ebullient era. The authors claimed as clients, patients, parishioners, and even as friends a wide range of individuals that most outsiders pronounced "primitive." Such mingling never altered the professionals' self-image as modern men. When these lawyers, doctors, clergymen, and journalists turned to authorship, however, they sought to capture in their newspaper sketches not the progressive development of the Southwest and their role in it, but the rawer stages less amenable to modern shaping. It is this selectivity that skews their pictures of their society.

Had antebellum humor been a true mirror of the culture that generated it, we should expect a prominent place for the stagecoach as a likely site for amusing anecdotes. In the Southwest, as elsewhere, it was the major

56. Robert E. Riegel, *Young America, 1830–1840* (Norman: University of Oklahoma Press, 1949), 165. See also Haites, Mak, and Walton, *Western River Transportation,* 10.

mode of travel. As far as the humor is concerned, however, the stage-coach might as well never have existed. It is true that Simon Suggs must board a stage to get to Tuscaloosa; the trip gives him an opening for one of his scams, and he must board the late stage out of Tuscaloosa to avoid being discovered in yet another (*SS*, 52–68). And Thorpe gives an amusing account of a precipitous winter descent in a stagecoach in the witty parable "The Way Americans Go Down Hill" (*TBT*, 215–20). But the humor generally ignores this traditional means of travel. Arguably, there is only one sustained narrative in which it is the central focus: John Gorman Barr's "New York Drummer's Ride to Greensboro'."

Barr's sketch concerns an elaborate practical joke involving a Tuscaloosa-to-Greensboro stage that goes nowhere. The victim is a weary New York salesman who, deprived of regular rest for several weeks on winter stage-coaches, is persuaded to board the Greensboro stage well before its 9 p.m. departure, securing his seat and getting some welcome sleep at the same time. The jokers—two young wags fond of "rough sport" and wild pranks (one of whom is named Tom Conning)—duly awaken their fellow passenger with a "stiffner" at each of the scheduled stops along the way, until the well-rested drummer finally emerges the next morning in front of the same Tuscaloosa public house from which he thought he had departed the night before. As do similar sketches featuring village pranksters, Barr's celebrates "dexterity in the management of game"; the local boys are "singularly precocious" in carrying through their plot in a "finished and artistic style" (*RT*, 93–108). This sketch, however, highlights the isolation of the (then) Alabama capital. The stageline is crucial in Barr's story because it was crucial in 1837, when the story is set. Except for a few months each year, interior rivers were too shallow for steamboats, and without railroads, the stagecoach was the only transport.[57]

Stagecoach inefficiencies are liberally noted in the travel accounts by both native and foreign visitors, and in the correspondence of local citizens who depended on this mode of transportation for (usually) brief trips. Americans seem to have understood and accepted as a condition to be endured the wretched state of public roads; that condition was inseparable from the problems with the vehicles' safety. Steeling his nerves against "the perils of Stage travelling—Cracked Skulls—broken bones—dislocated shoulders, &&," a young Virginian in the Alabama of 1836 made the best of the dangers: "I must risk them all." Writing of a childhood trip to Alabama, only recently detached from the Mississippi

57. Ellison, *Bibb County*, 107.

Territory, Virginia Clay recalls her impression of a "big pudding-shaped carriage" and remembers the journey by stage from North Carolina as "an interminable pilgrimage."[58] In the fall of 1859 a Mississippi student returning to his classes in Oxford reported to his father that he and a friend survived "being jolted about by the Stage for some fifty or more miles," and were really disturbed only once—"when we were called upon, by the driver, to assist in pulling the Stage off one of the horses that had fallen down."[59] Much ink was spilled in outraged reports of missed schedules. The same kind of ire arose in connection with steamboat captains' perfunctory attempts to honor times of departure; but, as we have seen, the man in charge of the boat nevertheless garnered respect and even awe. There was no such good press for stage drivers. They might only occasionally be as foolhardy as boat captains, but they were roundly condemned for their rudeness, short tempers, and (mostly) drunkenness.

Antebellum passengers, however, seemed generally more concerned about speed than safety. A young Natchez man wrote to his sister after arriving safely in New York, boasting of his luck in getting passage on speedy stagecoaches: "The finest Stages and the finest kind of horses and a pleasant party"; the mares, he added, trotted "11 ½ miles in 55 minutes." A New York clerk was grumpy because to get to Macon he was forced to take "a lumber waggon without cover" to Milledgeville: "8 hours in driving 24 miles." He finally arrived in "a large Jersey waggon drawn by 6 mules" that covered "10 miles in 9 hours, We all walked the greatest part of the way." One Alabama planter was not happy about either land or water travel. He complained that the stagecoaches were slow as well as crowded, and that a steamboat from St. Louis was splendid but "too slow—all the crack Boats pass us."[60] Next to walking, horseback, and paddling, the stagecoach is the oldest means in America for transporting oneself from one spot to another. For all its erratic schedules

58. Kellar, "Journey through the South," 370; Ada Sterling, ed., *A Belle of the Fifties: Memoirs of Mrs. Clay, of Alabama, Covering Social and Political Life in Washington and the South, 1853–66* (New York, 1904), 4–5.

59. Gage Family Letters, Department of Archives & Special Collections, University of Mississippi, Oxford. Another Mississippian declared that one night on a stagecoach was "always sifficient to kill or cure." John M. Anderson, letter, May 4, 1859, Aldrich Collection, Department of Archives & Special Collections, University of Mississippi, Oxford.

60. William F. Griffiths, 1835, Mandeville Family Papers; A. T. Havens Journal, 1842–1843, Hargrett Rare Book and Manuscript Library, University of Georgia, Athens; William Proctor Gould Papers, 1853, William Stanley Hoole Special Collections, University of Alabama Library, University of Alabama, Tuscaloosa.

and smashups, this vexing and unreliable mode was a substantial part of life, even in remote towns. Even country rubes knew all about stage-coaches. We can speculate that they make such rare appearances in the humor because they are *too* familiar, *too* fixed in the ordinary life of south-westerners to offer comic challenge.

But if the stagecoach barely grazes the consciousness of the humorists because it is so old-fashioned, why do they equally ignore the newest rival to the steamboat? Where is the railroad in the humor?

It is not as if railroads hadn't yet made it to the Old Southwest. By the time of the humorists, the railroad was no longer a new mode of trans-portation in the new country. It had already revolutionized the commercial life of the Southwest, emancipating settlements previously dependent upon navigable rivers.[61] And while the entire South would ultimately discover to its sorrow that it needed many more railroads than it had by 1861, several thousands of miles of track stretched from seacoast towns to various pockets in the interior. Where it was available, the railroad was accepted as a convenience for ordinary citizens in their internal move-ment about the lower South. Diaries and letters frequently allude to the practical advantages of taking "the cars," and often such travel is orga-nized as an expedition or special treat.

Prodded by James D. B. DeBow, the most conspicuous proponent of a diversified southern economy, dozens of prominent planters and mer-chants became enthusiastic spokesmen for campaigns to begin new rail-road companies and to urge those already in business to extend track. These formal sessions in the 1850s became known as the Southern Com-mercial Conventions; in 1852 in New Orleans over six hundred delegates agreed on the priority of the railroad as a key to general economic devel-opment.[62] As the entrepreneur behind the sessions, DeBow dutifully pub-lished their regular proceedings in his influential *Review.* In 1859, for the last economic convention before the outbreak of war, DeBow toured the South by railroad. He was convinced that this technology was both a practical means for diversifying the agricultural base and the newest symbol of progress and prosperity. For this trek, he traveled more than

61. Robert H. Wiebe, *The Opening of American Society: From the Adoption of the Con-stitution to the Eve of Disunion* (New York: Knopf, 1984), 141; Riegel, *Young America,* 173–81.

62. The impetus behind the conventions was the need to diversify the economic base of the South, weaning it from its chief reliance on cotton. The standard treatment is Vicki Vaughn Johnson, *The Men and the Vision of the Southern Commercial Conven-tions, 1845–1871* (Columbia: University of Missouri Press, 1992).

200 miles on the Mobile and Ohio and spent 42 hours on the Memphis and Charleston ("an admirable structure"). For the 138 miles from Atlanta to Chattanooga he took the Western and Atlantic, and made briefer runs on the Mississippi Central, the Southern Mississippi, and the "well-managed" but unfinished New Orleans and Jackson. At various points, DeBow was forced to use transition modes—steamboat and stage—but, though he was honest enough to note the lack of completion and convenient connections among the assorted companies, he was resolutely optimistic about the efficiency of rail travel and its prospects for the southern economy.[63]

Readers of the *Spirit of the Times* in the 1840s and 1850s would have taken for granted the significance of the railroad in the national interest—its primary impact on the economy was to speed up the flow of goods from production sites to widely dispersed markets. But the yokel letters to the editor, sketches, anecdotes, and other humorous contributions from the Old Southwest were well-nigh innocent of any interest in this most up-to-date mark of modernity.[64] Not only are DeBow's promotional instincts not evident in the work of the humorists, there also are few signs that the humorous authors see anything in the railroad itself—either its literal function or its symbolic appeal—that could lend itself to their kind of treatment. Even as cultural context, the railroad is rigorously excised from the sketches. DeBow's business was to make intelligent guesses about the southern future, to anticipate how present realities could be shaped to ensure a more stable, productive, and profitable society. Though their careers would almost surely benefit from the progressive agenda of the Commercial Conventions, the professionals who also performed as authors dealt with another kind of South. For them guessing the future involved nothing more than their conviction that backcountry inhabitants, whose deviancies from a modern age were their chief subject, would in time become indistinguishable in habits, speech, and values from everybody else. These writers' sketches are characteris-

---

63. James D. B. DeBow, "Editorial Miscellany," *DeBow's Review* 27 (1859): 112–18, reprinted in Schwaab and Bull, *Travels,* 2:479–87. The noxious odors and engine vibrations of even the most elegant steamboats were minor discomforts "compared to the miseries of . . . bone-rattling stagecoaches and early railroads." Primm, *Lion of the Valley,* 168–69.

64. With one curious anomaly: In one of Longstreet's post–*Georgia Scenes* pieces, "A Night in the Cars" (1842), an unnamed narrator, aboard a train from Augusta to Madison, voyeuristically details his evening watching a major, his portly wife, and pretty daughter sleep. Written for William T. Thompson's *Southern Miscellany* when Longstreet was already president of Emory College, this odd sketch is reprinted in *Mississippi Quarterly* 23 (1970): 169–74.

tically set in a recent past, because they sought to depict the backcountry before it disappeared. They had little *literary* stake in a future society of stability and progress. The tenor of their work lay in precisely the other direction: provincial upheavals, clashes of village egos, primitive satisfactions. The railroad may have represented the technology of the future, but it had no imaginative function in the humorists' writing.

The mode of transportation that is both context for and generator of the comic sketches remains the steamboat. Its function in this writing derives obviously from its function in the economic life of the region. For all the efforts of DeBow and the Commercial Conventions, the antebellum South was as massively dependent upon water transportation as it was upon one-crop agriculture. Following from these economic facts, the region clung to the images of the river and the steamboat as historical markers of cultural identity.

We might also remember that the humorists, like most residents of the interior, liked the steamboat for its sociable features. Unlike either the older stagecoach or the newer railroad train, the smooth-floating steamboat provided space for formal assembly or idle grouping. It allowed passengers to promenade as well as to congregate for conversation and games. In its forward movement toward a designated site, the steamboat encouraged the continuation of social activities associated with public spaces on land, from the drawing rooms of the quality to the doggeries of the commonality. Like other public spheres where *things happened*— boardinghouse dining rooms, courtrooms, militia fields, porches, stores, village streets, and professional offices—the social hall and boat decks were *stages*, both for the enactment of little dramas and their reenactment in tale-telling. The steamboat was what the humorists most cherished—a theater of possibilities.

Part III

The World the Humorists Made

Chapter 9 ✦═══❦

Authorship and Amateurism

All America has not one humorist.

—Philarète Chasles, *Anglo-American Literature and Manners*

i.

According to Francis J. Grund, Americans generally were deficient in humor. The one great exception, he noted, was their fondness for laughing "at the expense of their neighbours."[1] But the scene was hardly as dour as Grund found it. By the 1850s American humorists had proliferated like upstart crows. Most of them, in New England and the South, were gifted, if not fully professional, writers with good ears who made a fashion of appropriating the lingual habits and folk wisdom of semiliterates.

Inspiration lay in impersonation. The letter to the editor from an earnest contributor, for example, was a ready-made form, and inspired an unequivocal attempt to capitalize on the oral riches of the barely lettered. The initial appeal of Seba Smith of Maine depended entirely on the fiction that his letters were the work of a rustic peddler named Major Jack Downing, not the publisher of the *Portland Courier;* in the case of one of

---

1. Francis J. Grund, *The Americans in Their Moral, Social, and Political Relations* (1837; reprint, New York: A. M. Kelley, 1971), 1:123–24.

Downing's heirs, the misspelt letters were from Major Joseph Jones, not William Tappan Thompson, an Ohio migrant pursuing a newspaper career in Georgia. For *Georgia Scenes* (1835), A. B. Longstreet had relied on narrators close to his own educative level and literary style, but for *Major Jones's Courtship* (1843) his friend and associate found the Seba Smith formula a more useful strategy. The system of impersonation—a kind of false disclosure—became a common literary device for many of the humorous authors, who bore the burden of authorship even as they reveled in its pleasures. Anonymity and pseudonymity were (at least briefly) twin protective maneuvers that satisfied (at least partially) the urge for creative freedom unrelated to the authors' social identity. Even with rickety covers, however, the humorists were still authors of the left hand, professing a commitment neither to authorship itself nor to the kind of literary seriousness that only real writers had license to explore. What resulted from such ambivalence was a body of work that merely extended to the public papers their coterie reputation as capital fellows with a knack for storytelling and practical jokes. Of all the authors, only Longstreet seems to have been exempt from the fulsome testimony of peers about their common penchant for raillery, shaggy-dog stories, and mock versions of trials, sermonizing, playacting, and courtship rituals.[2]

Joseph Glover Baldwin was not an anonymous humorist, and he published his sketches not in newspapers but in a prestigious literary journal—the *Southern Literary Messenger,* whose roster of editors once included Edgar Allan Poe. Moreover, he disguised his collected pieces as memoir (a respected genre, below history and natural science, but above fiction and humor). Yet it is no accident that "Ovid Bolus, Esq., Attorney at Law and Solicitor in Chancery" enjoys pride of place, presiding over all the pieces in *Flush Times* (1853). He is the great liar who functions as the spirit of the age, densely symbolic of the fraud, chicanery, and other "reptile arts of humanity" with which the legal fraternity cheerfully identifies (*FT*, 87). Baldwin also wryly hints that authorship, as practiced, is one of the reptile arts.

This author admires his great liar's economy (though "never stingy of his lies, he was not wasteful of them," either) and his conscientious self-

---

2. Even Longstreet has lost much of his earlier image of solemnity. In his edition of *Georgia Scenes,* David Rachels refutes the widespread notion that the judge repudiated the humor of his famous book; rather, to the end of his life he appreciated his "literary bagatelle." David Rachels, introduction to *Augustus Baldwin Longstreet's* Georgia Scenes *Completed: A Scholarly Text* (Athens: University of Georgia Press, 1998), xxvii–xxix.

editing ("correcting" himself when he misspeaks or when he confuses dates and places); but he is most struck by the consummate style of his "*lyric* artist," who has long before ceased to discriminate between "the impressions made upon his mind by what came *from* it, and what came *to* it." Ovid Bolus suppresses the vanity that traps fledgling liars, who are wont to exhibit too much pleasure in an effective "hit." Exultation "betrays authorship; and to betray authorship, in the present barbaric, moral and intellectual condition of the world is fatal." Yet, Baldwin muses, Dickens and Bulwer-Lytton can do "as much lying, for money too, as they choose, and no one blames them, any more than they would blame a lawyer regularly *fee'd* to do it; but let any man, gifted with the same genius, try his hand at it, not deliberately and in writing, but merely orally, and ugly names are given him, and he is proscribed!" Behind the faintly syllogistic observations here is an ancient commonplace: writing is lying. Skillful liars are artists, and novelists and lawyers are liars who get paid for their skills; some verbal liars are praised, but oral ones are denounced. What just misses being articulated in Baldwin's account is the most telling equation: Bolus as authorial doppelgänger. As a lawyer, Baldwin is a liar "regularly *fee'd*" to practice; as an author, he is a liar whose reception by the great "Sovereign, the Public" he must await with some trepidation (*FT,* 17–18).

Sometimes, as we see in James K. Paulding, H. E. Taliaferro, John S. Robb, even Longstreet himself, writing is posed as a civic task, designed to serve the public rather than to satisfy personal ambition. So too with Baldwin, though he refuses to make much of it. The Flush Times, in 1853 already a past era, may not have been the project most historians were clamoring to undertake, but this lawyer-author demotes historians to "tame and timid cobblers," borrowers of others' goods "got without skill" (*FT,* 3). By midcentury there seems to have been a dearth of both cobblers and custodians of records that cobblers need to work from. An editorial writer in 1850 urged historians to pay more heed in preserving and guarding official documents: "Public men at least . . . must know something of what has been, or they must be noodles and nobodies."[3] *Flush Times* was never an official document, of course. Though it contains facts aplenty, it refuses to grant them status higher than non-facts, sentiments, prejudicial opinions, and the extravagant spin-offs that facts often inspire. For Ovid Bolus, "the partition wall between his imagination and his memory" had long been torn down, and his biographer doesn't seem

3. *Southern Literary Messenger* 16 (1850): 118.

to mind the freer space for circulation (*FT*, 4). If the extrapolated world that Ovid represents is too densely specialized, too stylized, to make for a true memoir, it is also too literary to pass as history. Baldwin discovers a congenial meeting ground under the very nose of the cobblers, where Clio and Thalia play well together.

To make scenes "thrilling" and regional types "extraordinary" and "peculiar," William T. Porter, as we have seen, encouraged stylistic heightening in contributions to the *Spirit of the Times*. In the pieces he collected in *Streaks of Squatter Life*, John S. Robb used the same method. Restrained (whether out of tact or modesty) from naming in his preface those who, gifted with "bright mind and able pen," had by 1847 already brought the backwoods to "speaking life," the St. Louis newspaperman clearly included himself, one of the most versatile of his fellows (*SSL*, viii). Even the most pedestrian minds with the least able pens conduct their mission with the spirit of the social historian.

But not quite. Any record of the times is also a record of the recorder. Even preserving the most trivial events and the crudest characters as a record of "what has been" does not ensure neutrality and dispassion. The humorists *liked* noodles and nobodies. "Anonymous," no less than the scribes of dusty chronicles, left his imprint through topic selection, word choice, and personal verbal tics. Even when humorous pieces appeared under such names as "The Turkey Runner" or "Solitaire" rather than Alexander McNutt or John S. Robb, the maker was asserting his authority over what he had made. Some of the favorite subjects—the backcountry hunter, the yeoman naïf, the nubile gal and her suspicious pa, the con man, the village know-it-all—were inescapable presences in the world of the professionals-turned-writers, and the formal line separating excavation and creation was often happily smudged in what they were eager to "preserve" in written form. The comic sketches, however, are neither found objects nor memorial reconstructions. If what is being preserved is oral, the maker cannot credibly think of himself as mere mediator: the fleeting matter he snatches from the ether is realized in the shape of another medium. What the humorists experienced in the daily conduct at the bench and bar or on the Methodist circuit led them to admire the vernacular tall tale and the storytelling gestures of the illiterates and semiliterates with whom they invariably mingled. Part of their impressive achievement lies in their ability to convey the oral art of the artless in their own artful verbal versions. None of them, however, is a court stenographer. None of the sketches is a transcription.

The humorists thought of their pieces less as printed versions of the oral tale and more as printed evidence of oral *tale-telling*. The defining feature of their strongest work is that it echoes the human voice. Its *spokenness* may account for the fact that plot—narrative in its most regulated, sequential form—seems never to be a priority in this writing. The one genre in Irving's work that these writers show little interest in cultivating is the fully developed tale, and especially ignored is the formal tale of the type that Poe, their early contemporary, defined and practiced. Poe's fiction (like Hawthorne's) is an art of *writtenness*, in which the rhythms of heard speech are notably inhibited. Despite Poe's admiration for *Georgia Scenes*, we would have to stretch his definition to call even the best-constructed of Longstreet's pieces "short stories." They all are instances of storytelling that seem to have bypassed the modern urge to codify and regulate, to isolate, exploit, and then exhibit principles of narrative-making. Our high regard for well-paced stories with clean resolution and meaning is a bias born of a conservative notion of narrative. If twentieth-century modernism was supposed to have shattered such bourgeois expectations, it never fully supplanted them: consider the number of readers who still prefer *Dubliners* to *Ulysses* or "That Evening Sun" to *The Sound and the Fury*.

For the writers who succeeded Longstreet, storytelling was less a modern art and more a return to the ancient conditions of communal life. The frequency with which they invoked the campfire as the primary venue for telling stories testifies to a kind of entertainment atavism, even though the humorists were moderns who favored settings more familiar in their lives—porches, boardinghouses, offices, social halls of steamboats. Venerable or modern, such sites encouraged the leisurely re-creation of both narrative nuggets and the oral dynamics that sweep up hearers as well as tellers.

Audiences are rarely passive in this writing (as we see in "The Big Bear of Arkansas"). Teller and listener share the same cultural presuppositions about storytelling protocols, and one important trait, at least in hindsight, is capacious tolerance. Even the printed pieces with a developed narrative core vary dramatically, from simple reported anecdotes to elaborate yarns reconstructed in the teller's "own words." The appeal of consoling familiarity explains why so many of the sketches begin the same way, but only a mediocre sense of composition can explain why more than a few promising pieces get entangled in their own syntax and stumbling pace, or why their resolutions often peter out in anticlimax. Even such popular single-author books as *Flush Times*, *Mysteries of the Backwoods*, and *Streaks of Squatter Life* contain some dispiriting, flabby sketches.

What we tend to interpret as self-indulgence or ineptness in the story-telling process, however, is not always a simple matter of skill. Just as oral performance is enclosed in a set of conventions, so its transfer to print carries, as we shall see, its own set of expectations and familiarities.

Yet storytelling was only one source of the humorists' pieces. One way to look at this body of writing is to see it as a florilegium, an uneven collection inspired by unstable and often overlapping forms. At the disposal of these authors was a vast generic pool into which they freely dipped. We have to assume that many readers, like the writers, were on easy terms with the Irvingesque sketch (and its predecessors in Addison, Steele, Johnson, and the early Romantic prose stylists), the travel account, the informal essay, the memoir, the confession, the action adventure set in exotic geography, the almanac, the emigrants' guide, the epistolary novel, the dream vision and its nightmarish underside. Patches of all these forms and others appear, often in altered states, in the body of humorous writing from the Old Southwest. They are all preexisting literary objects capable of being invoked, and sometimes shamefully used, often in jumbled succession.[4]

Certain items in this florilegium have long since lost their relevance. The most humble of the little pieces that once stood alone in ragged newsprint survive as narrative residue, unfathomable to modern eyes. Others, a fraction more ambitious, survive as concrescences—objects formed out of preexisting objects. As a glance at any given number of Porter's *Spirit* will show, some of the comic items were nothing more than perfunctory fillers, squibs that might be absorbed by another, more skilled, hand in an entirely different piece more coherently shaped. All of the newspaper contributions were in fact objects different from the objects that went into their making, but their very simplicity, their seeming innocence, rendered them familiar so that all degrees of literates could read them and instantly nod, chuckle, snort, and pass them on to a friend for his pleasure. The paradoxical virtue of the humorous sketch is that it passed muster not by the literary condition of what was new, original, unique—the standards that practitioners of high art at least aim for—but

4. Hugh Henry Brackenridge's *Modern Chivalry* (1792–1815; reprint, ed. Claude M. Newlin, New York: American Book, 1937), is an early example of happy generic muddling. See also Cathy N. Davidson, *Revolution and the Word: The Rise of the Novel in America* (New York: Oxford, 1986), 164, 174–75, 178; Edward Watts, *Writing and Postcolonialism in the Early Republic* (Charlottesville: University Press of Virginia, 1998), 27–50; Philip D. Beidler, "'The first production of the kind, in the South': A Backwoods Literary *Incognito* and His Attempt at the Great American Novel," *Southern Literary Journal* 24 (1992): 106–24.

by the psychological condition of *readers reading*. The comic letter or the loquacious hunter's report worked on the principle of familiarity so that readers in the process of reading could say to themselves, *we've been here before—maybe*. Solace lay in familiarity; the conventional, the expected, was unthreatening. But even the most undemanding reader could not give assent if he wearied from *too* much familiarity or if he lost his way in thickets of narrative confusion. The sole danger the author had to negotiate was that familiarity might breed contempt; he did not have to demonstrate uniqueness to lead the reader into easy complicity, but to supply a modest twist to reinforce the familiarity. The compliant reader thus became a back-up authority, second only to the author himself.

How to establish the terms for earning this kind of complicity might seem to pose a task worthy of only the sophisticates of literary art—a Henry James, say—and none of the humorous writers were such masters. Nevertheless, those who have survived, if only in the margins of American literary history, knew how to play to their readers' strengths as well as their own. They had the prescience to use the tried-and-true, the worn-out forms, the stereotypes and assorted conventions as building blocks of their modest structures. In a climate of cheerful plagiarism, the humorists took what attracted their magpie eye. From the voluminous trove of essays that was their common heritage to the ephemeral observations of travelers, gazetteers, guidebook compilers, and their journalistic peers, the authors selected the kinds of texts whose norms and patterns were already designed for readerly response, and upon these familiar structures they proceeded to fashion their own pieces.

Preferring the tale over the sketch, modern readers are troubled by authorial misjudgment when we hear that Hawthorne thought as highly of "Little Annie's Ramble" as he did of "The Minister's Black Veil." T. B. Thorpe was probably not much different from his more celebrated contemporary, yet he shows that he was fully conscious of doing different things when he wrote "The Big Bear of Arkansas" and, say, "Primitive Forests of Mississippi." The crux of all popular art is familiarity, but the gratifying pleasures of this humor stem from the robust way in which the sketch cribs from all prior forms—even the starchily informational ones—to activate its potential under the aegis of the unembarrassed muse. It is "only by being shameless about risking the obvious," observes Eve Sedgwick, "that we happen into the vicinity of the transformative."[5] Some

5. Eve Kosofsky Sedgwick, *Epistemology of the Closet* (Berkeley and Los Angeles: University of California Press, 1990), 22.

pieces unfold in that vicinity: Thorpe's "Big Bear," Taliaferro's "Ham Rachel," the Simon Suggs adventures, and the Sut Lovingood sketches. Many of the others are not transformative, but they repay our consideration by being amusing and conscientiously skillful.

ii.

That the humorists sometimes posed as stenographers is one measure of the self-consciousness of their enterprise. Determined to provide for Jim Doggett's "singular" manner and "excellent way of telling" a story, Thorpe precedes the Big Bear tale with "As near as I can recollect, I have italicized the words, and given the story in his own way," a disclaimer that attributes both originality and crudity to the central character rather than to the author himself. W. C. Hall prefaces one of his Mike Hooter tales with "we may be pardoned for following Mike in one of his most stirring adventures, related in his peculiar and expressive vernacular" (Cohen, 364). With this tactic Thorpe and Hall merely followed the practice that Longstreet had carefully (and ambiguously) spelled out in his preface to *Georgia Scenes*. The author of that important book is merely "A Native Georgian," and only the two stand-in narrators who are responsible for the contents have names. Whether anonymously or pseudonymously, the very inscribing of vernacular, however intense, is at once an act of rebellion against literary decorum and an apology for it.

Whimsical pseudonyms and the matter-of-fact assumption of a stylistic gap between author and subject may serve several functions in the work of these authors, but surely more telling than conscious purpose is the anxiety of authorship. In the uneasy waffling between *claiming credit* and *refusing responsibility* for the proffered text we see a strategy of compromise that had long been in place for southern professionals who liked to write unprofessionally.[6] The boundary lines between the amateur and the professional in the antebellum South were as unstable as the preemp-

---

6. Through narrative pacing, authorial dissembling, and the disposition of voices, Longstreet produced not merely *Georgia Scenes* but the terms of its making. As Poe foresaw, the anonymous volume was an "omen of better days for the literature of the South." It is only an imperfect instance of Foucauldian "transdiscursive" texts, but it fully established "the possibility and the rules of formation of other texts." Edgar Allan Poe, review of *Georgia Scenes*, in *Essays and Reviews* (New York: Library of America, 1984), 796; Michel Foucault, "What Is an Author?" trans. Donald F. Bouchard and Sherry Simon, in *Critical Theory since 1965*, ed. Hazard Adams and Leroy Searle (Tallahassee: Florida State University Press, 1989), 145.

tion claims in the land offices. If, throughout the nation, publication was often thought of "as a degrading sort of exhibitionism," southerners were even more prone than Americans generally in regarding authorship as an unsuitable calling for a man. Attempts to establish literary journals, for example, had always been hit-and-miss affairs. When William Tappan Thompson launched the *Augusta Mirror* in 1838, his first editorial stressed his hope that the venture might encourage "the production of southern talent and southern genius." The next year, in a Fourth of July address, Alexander H. Stephens toasted the enterprise as a "lonely but brilliant Star in the long and cheerless night of the literature of Georgia." The *Mirror* died two years later, an unhappy milestone in the record of other short-lived projects, from the *Southern Review* (1828–1832) to *Russell's Magazine* (1857–1860).[7]

Nearly the only fully practicing, professional author of reputation was William Gilmore Simms, who, even as he strove to make his name the equal of Cooper's, labored over an entire career to raise authorship in the South to the same level of prestige as politics and the law. As an editor, he made a vigorous effort to make the *Magnolia* a permanent periodical. Because of the nature of southern society, imaginative writing had always been subordinated to politics; as he loyally turned his talents in the 1850s to the defense of his region, Simms learned that there was no southern "intellectual community functioning apart from the political community."[8] Even as he did his intellectual best to oppose *Uncle Tom's Cabin*, George F. Holmes had to admit that southern authors were ill-prepared to counter

7. Robert E. Riegel, *Young America, 1830–1840* (Norman: University of Oklahoma Press, 1949), 407; Bertram Flanders, *Early Georgia Magazines* (Athens: University of Georgia Press, 1944), 31–32; Richard J. Calhoun, "Literary Magazines in the Old South," in *The History of Southern Literature*, ed. Louis D. Rubin, Jr., and others (Baton Rouge: Louisiana State University Press, 1985), 157–63. The "exceptions to sudden death," notes Calhoun, were the *Southern Quarterly Review* (1842–1857) and the *Southern Literary Messenger* (1834–1864). See also Sam G. Riley, *Magazines of the American South* (New York: Greenwood, 1986), 9–11, 233–39.

8. Louis D. Rubin, Jr., *The Edge of the Swamp: A Study in the Literature and Society of the Old South* (Baton Rouge: Louisiana State University Press, 1989), 82. Even Thomas Nelson Page, the elegant elegist of the Old South, understood that southern literary mediocrity resulted from the fact that the region's writers were too comfortably a part of their society. "Authorship in the South before the War," in *The Old South: Essays Social and Political* (1892; reprint, Chautauqua, NY: Chautauqua Press, 1919), 57–92. See also Charles S. Watson, *From Nationalism to Secessionism: The Changing Fiction of William Gilmore Simms* (Westport, CT: Greenwood, 1993), 55. Most writers lived near towns, earning livings as doctors, lawyers, or preachers. See Charles S. Sydnor, *The Development of Southern Sectionalism, 1819–1848* (Baton Rouge: Louisiana State University Press, 1948), 306.

Mrs. Stowe effectively because of their region's long tradition of "blighting indifference," which had "chilled all manifestations of literary aptitudes." A rapturous romantic writer when he was not being a lawyer and judge, Alexander Meek (echoing a young Longfellow) lamented that southerners regarded "poetry and nonsense" as "convertible terms." Unlike Simms, who resigned himself to tepid southern support, Paul Hamilton Hayne was progressively outraged at his lack of recognition. As a poet struggling to be professional, he began publishing before the Civil War; by 1874, when he approved of Sidney Lanier's judicious move to New York, he was venting his indignation at "these semi-barbarous latitudes": "with the *South*, I, as a literary man, have *done* forever."[9]

These were sentiments of writers, contemporary with the humorists, who actively *sought* professional status, but the committed part-timers, whatever their public stance, were also eager to be read (locally if not nationally) and to that end approached cautiously the widespread gentry bias against authorship. In one chapter in his *Southern Sidelights* (1896), suggestively titled "Literary Aspirations," Edward Ingle quotes a Virginian in 1834: "A man who has sense enough to write a book very often has too much sense to publish it." With his collection *The Old Bachelor* already in press, a nervous William Wirt confided to his friend St. George Tucker in 1813 that his fondness for belles-lettres might well damage his reputation, "either as a man of business or as a man pretending to any dignity of character." Tucker's predictable reply could not have been cheering: to indulge a taste for "the belles-lettres," he said, will not "advance the author in the public estimation, *but may have the contrary effect.*"[10] This response was the definitive statement on the matter for most of the antebellum period.

Yet Tucker himself, whose major professional work was a five-volume edition of Blackstone's *Commentaries* (1803), left the literary door ajar with

9. Harvey Wish, "George Frederick Holmes and Southern Periodical Literature of the Mid-Nineteenth Century," *Journal of Southern History* 7 (1941): 350; Meek quoted in Rayburn S. Moore, "Antebellum Poetry," in *The History of Southern Literature*, ed. Louis D. Rubin, Jr., and others (Baton Rouge: Louisiana State University Press, 1985), 123; *A Man of Letters in the Nineteenth-Century South: Selected Letters of Paul Hamilton Hayne*, ed. Rayburn S. Moore (Baton Rouge: Louisiana State University Press, 1982), 120, 144. See also comments on assorted authors in *History of Southern Literature*, 114, 122–23, 162, 173–74. As late as 1900, "gentlemen of letters" in the South outnumbered professional authors. Robert A. Ferguson, *Law and Letters in American Culture* (Cambridge, MA: Harvard University Press, 1984), 292.

10. Edward Ingle, *Southern Sidelights: A Picture of Social and Economic Life in the South during a Generation before the War* (New York, 1896), 199; John P. Kennedy, *Memoirs of the Life of William Wirt*, rev. ed. (Philadelphia, 1860), 1:307–9.

a strategy that would become useful for southern practitioners in the years before and just after the Civil War. If an author otherwise respected in his profession is tempted to publish something unrelated to it, he noted, it must be done in a special "manner": the writing must "appear merely as a *jeu d'esprit,* the effusion of a leisure moment, and without any view to profit or emolument."[11] That is, authorship is an "embellishment," just one more piece of evidence that a man has versatility, even genius, "beyond the professional walk." As Simms put it more bluntly in 1845, writing had to be "a labor of stealth or recreation, employed as a relief from other tasks and duties."[12] For every well-connected artist laboring stealthily—James M. Legaré, Alexander Meek, and Mirabeau Lamar, among others—there were probably twice as many writers unwilling to forgo either their literary talent or their calling. St. George Tucker's formula would prove to be the key. A public *attitude* would permit them to sidestep the vexing issue of professional authorship; so armed, they could be both professional men *and* authors. It was the solution that lawyers, doctors, editors, preachers, and a few planters found useful in the Old Southwest.

Social presence was always an advantage among southern respectables: not the silky graces that southern legend has invested in the cavalier-planter, but quickness of mind and tongue, a gift for repartee and the bon mot, and an impersonating knack for storytelling. Being known and admired for being a *bon vivant,* however, could be a mixed distinction. Although geniality and fluency were auspicious traits throughout the overlapping social networks, those same qualities carried the risk of making public men otherwise engaged in the serious issues of the day seem frivolous. One Alabama memoirist, the lawyer William Garrett, went to some trouble to cite all his acquaintances who enjoyed reputations for waggery and yarning skills—a state representative here, a circuit judge there—but he promptly put such gifts in perspective. One friend, he remembered, had qualities "of more than ordinary grade" that served him well in his various public offices, but, he added, "being a wit, punster,

11. Teacher and judge, Tucker was a closet dramatist; his efforts over many years— farce, sentimental comedy, satire—remained unpublished. See Meta Robinson Braymer, "Trying to Walk: An Introduction to the Plays of St. George Tucker," in *No Fairer Land: Studies in Southern Literature before 1900,* ed. J. Lasley Dameron and James W. Mathews (Troy, NY: Whitson, 1986), 87–100. See also Richard Beale Davis, "The Valley of Virginia," chap. 12 in *Literature and Society in Early Virginia, 1608–1840* (Baton Rouge: Louisiana State University Press, 1973).

12. Kennedy, *William Wirt,* 1:307–9; [William Gilmore Simms], *The Charleston Book: A Miscellany in Prose and Verse* (Charleston, SC, 1845), 3.

and a very social, companionable man, he lacked that application to study and to business so necessary to complete success."[13]

Garrett was not especially solemn, but his piety and respect for moderation were thoroughly conventional, reflecting both the traditional southern view of authorship and the middle-class Victorian posture of social responsibility. A little of Tucker's *jeu d'esprit* went a long way; too much simply betrayed the public man's shallow grasp of his social role. In his rather sour entry on Johnson Jones Hooper, Garrett demonstrates how the humorists' straddling solution to the writing dilemma didn't always work. Garrett disapproves of the character of Simon Suggs, "a cunning, unprincipled man" of "pretended piety and church membership!" Although "tens of thousands" of readers laughed over the captain's grotesque adventures, "not one of them . . . has had his reverence for virtue increased by the perusal." This distaste for the fictional scoundrel slides easily into disapproval of his creator, who had never "tended to a very moral course of life": "religion seemed never to have entered his thoughts" until his final days, when he "sent for a Catholic priest" for last rites—which for Garrett means that Hooper's dying hour was filled with gloom.[14]

The other part of the humorists' compromise—simply remaining anonymous—was a convention of long standing and short effectiveness. A Marylander in the late eighteenth century declared that it required "no small Degree of Resolution to be an *Author*" in a country where the calling is "a Mark of publick Censure, and sometimes a standing Object of Raillery and Ridicule." His solution was to write anonymously.[15] Even in a more receptive climate, both Irving and Cooper preferred anonymity, at least on their title pages; and in the South, Simms confessed to a friend in 1844 that anyone wanting fame "could never take a more certain way of getting himself disparaged than by placing his name to his articles." A few years earlier, when the Charleston author of *The Yemassee* decided to write a sterner, unromantic story of the violent southwestern frontier, *Richard Hurdis: A Tale of Alabama* appeared anonymously. Simms's rationale was that even friendly readers tended to equate an author's "personality" with what he produced, refusing to separate the man from his writings. The Alabama novel,

13. William Garrett, *Reminiscences of Public Men in Alabama for Thirty Years* (Atlanta, 1872), 152, 553.

14. Ibid., 527–28.

15. Bruce Granger, *American Essay Serials from Franklin to Irving* (Knoxville: University of Tennessee Press, 1978), 70.

he reasoned, departed significantly from its established author's social standing and cultural range.[16]

The ambitions of the humorous authors in the interior were not the equal of the southern professionals', but most of them fully understood the reasons behind the tactic of anonymity. Longstreet's *Georgia Scenes* was written by "A Native Georgian." Thompson's *Major Jones's Courtship* was "a Series of Letters by Himself." Even when the humorists used whimsical pseudonyms to join the guildlike circle of like-minded authors, their privacy (which most of them only halfheartedly sought to preserve) was always subject to being breached. Furthermore, the names the authors chose were never much of an accommodation to those readers who clung to the notion that writing was for ladies who had nothing better to do. Seeing "Phazma" or "Pete Whetstone" or "Solitaire" signed to amusing anecdotes did little to convince sobersided gentlemen of the dignity and probity of those who really penned them. Besides, the very whimsy of these pseudonyms invited exposure; the identity of the authors, like that of their precursors who invented the ruse, rarely remained anonymous for long.

As early as 1845, the identity of "Solitaire" was widespread in newspaper circles. When a rival editor sought to hire John Robb, the *St. Louis Reveille* noted: "The Mobile Tribune desires us, of all things, to send that way our 'Solitaire,' but it would be a downright *Robb*-ery."[17] As the text of *Georgia Scenes* shows, the splitting of himself into two surrogate personas, "Hall" and "Baldwin," was not just the simple convenience that Longstreet pretended, with the former in charge of anecdotes featuring men and masculine pursuits and the latter supervising those more domestic and feminine. The device also distanced the anonymous author both from the crudity and violence of backwoods life and the feckless affectation of village social life. The judge may have been convinced when his friend Thompson assured him that there was "nothing" that "savor[ed] of immorality" in his sketches, for he allowed him to publish additional sketches in the *Augusta Mirror* three years after his book

16. William Charvat, *The Profession of Authorship in America, 1800–1870*, ed. Matthew J. Bruccoli (Columbus: Ohio State University Press, 1968), 294–95; John Caldwell Guilds, *Simms: A Literary Life* (Fayetteville: University of Arkansas Press, 1992), 82–83. See also the relevant essays in *William Gilmore Simms and the American Frontier*, ed. John Caldwell Guilds and Caroline Collins (Athens: University of Georgia Press, 1997).

17. Nicholas Joost, "Reveille in the West: Western Travelers in the *St. Louis Weekly Reveille*," in *Travelers on the Western Frontier*, ed. John Francis McDermott (Urbana: University of Illinois Press, 1970), 212.

appeared.[18] Contrary to early biographers, while he refused to allow further editions of *Georgia Scenes,* Longstreet never regretted publishing his sketches.

For the humorists who followed—including Thompson, who invented a modest planter as his publishing persona—the distancing formula of employing surrogate authors was useful: an aesthetic device certainly, and one more nearly political than moral. The genial Major Jones delivered himself of Whiggish opinions that his creator himself voiced (without the misspellings) as a conspicuously public man at the *Savannah Morning News.* As we shall see, however, this often bumbling observer and rustic philosopher, comfortably situated in his community, was a character as well as a mouthpiece. If Major Jones's shrewd insights into fashions and foibles in his little society (in *Major Jones's Courtship*) and the larger society he encounters on tour (in *Major Jones's Sketches of Travel*) match those of his creator, his amiable naïveté also makes him subject to jibes and tricks and self-humiliation. The deflecting surrogate, despite his flaws, is allowed to preserve his dignity: he remains a source of humor as well as its target.

Unlike Longstreet and *Georgia Scenes,* Johnson Jones Hooper came to regret publishing his own bagatelle. While he showed little anxiety over authorship—for most of his career he wrote for and edited a succession of Alabama newspapers—Hooper was perhaps the most intense political partisan among the humorists. As his commitment shifted with developing alliances on the national scene, he preferred the ardent engagement of politics to writing. His biography suggests that the writing in some ways was meant to be a stepping-stone to higher public office, but his ambition was only sporadically realized: he won a race for solicitor, only to lose reelection; he was named secretary of the provisional Confederate Congress in Montgomery, only to be bypassed as secretary of the permanent congress in Richmond. Hooper came to suspect that his stunning success as the author of *Adventures of Captain Simon Suggs* had damaged him politically. He was probably right. His major character was a repellent frontier trickster, shiftless and cowardly, but one who must also have been perversely attractive to antebellum readers. Appearing in 1845, *Simon Suggs* by 1856 had gone through eleven editions. The canny captain of the Tallapoosa Volunteers mingles in a diverse company, operating in what his creator obviously regarded as representative slices of Alabama society. Simon keeps his competitive edge by devising schemes to ensnare

18. James B. Meriwether, "Augustus Baldwin Longstreet: Realist and Artist," *Mississippi Quarterly* 35 (1982): 356; Rachels, introduction, xxvi.

his victims, who are chosen without favor or discrimination—gentleman gamblers, patronage seekers, preachers, Creek widows, and gullible Jacksonian yeomen. But perhaps the most telling feature of this rustic con man is that, like Hooper himself, he is seeking public office.

The ease with which many readers conflated creator and character strikes us now as naive. Casting himself as the captain's patron, "Johns" Hooper volunteers his literary gifts to write a campaign biography, that hackwork mainstay of American political life. Simon Suggs (so his argument goes) now comes before the voters as candidate for sheriff; after a lifetime of involvement with the public, he deserves a reward. He's old, and he needs the money.[19] His success in the election is of course unknown; but Hooper had the example of Judge Longstreet's "Darby Anvil" (1838), a yarn about an ignorant blacksmith who, "without any qualifications," is elected to the Georgia legislature and who, by shrewdness and "low cunning," turns people's weaknesses "to his own advantage." The story is recounted by the narrator Baldwin, who is more inclined toward discomfiture than irony, and no reader would have confused author and character.[20] In *Simon Suggs,* too, the contrast between gentleman author and vernacular subject is clear. Only barely held in control by a consciously inflated style, Hooper's wit is brutal in its heavy irony. Hooper and his frontier scoundrel are quite distinct.

And yet, for all the irony, the author betrays a kind of affection for the wily captain. Exposure is laced with admiration, in part because Hooper's anatomy of shiftiness is more than a biography of one rogue in the social backwaters. Shiftiness is the property of all politicians, and Simon Suggs is only better at it, more skillful, than his victims, especially legislators and ragtag lobbyists. In the hands of amateurs (readers and writers) literary irony is a volatile technique. In Hooper's case, when the biographer of a political scoundrel decided to run for office himself, the association was inevitable.

The case of Hooper and Suggs demonstrates just how justified the humorists were in maintaining some distance between themselves and their subjects. Heavily ironic though he was in his mock biography, Hooper *was*

19. The ancient office of sheriff was the most desirable county position. Since one of its prerogatives was tax collecting, it was not merely a prestigious post but a financially rewarding one as well. See Ralph A. Wooster, *Politicians, Planters, and Plain Folk: Courthouse and Statehouse in the Upper South, 1850–1860* (Knoxville: University of Tennessee Press, 1975), 99.

20. "Darby Anvil" is an uncollected sketch from the *Augusta Mirror,* reprinted by Rachels (*GS,* 162–79).

the biographer. We can only speculate, but might the conflation of author and subject have been lessened had he, like Longstreet, invented a surrogate to author his satire? In the 1850s he signed some of his pieces "Number Eight"—pieces that poked fun at Irishmen, Yankees, and ugly women. In 1851 Thomas A. Burke dedicated his edited anthology, *Polly Peablossom's Wedding*, to Hooper "as a token of respect," but he was unable to convince him to send a sketch, new or old, for inclusion. The humorist's refusal is laced with something more than modesty. If he possessed "a single copy of any one of my sketches," he assured Burke, he would be welcome "to all I ever wrote, at their real value—nothing."[21] In a further effort to rid himself of his lingering association with Simon Suggs, Hooper undertook three serious projects: *Read and Circulate* (1855), a satire on Alabama Democrats; *Dog and Gun* (1856), an anthology of practical sporting pieces; and an edition of *Woodward's Reminiscences* (1859), historical essays by an old Indian fighter in early Alabama. But nothing he did as a politician or writer could shake the public's identification of Hooper with his most memorable and notorious character. In the words of the "Capting of the Tallapoosy Vollantares," Simon Suggs would "allers be found sticking thar" to Hooper "like a tick onder a cow's belly." Even with the coming of war, when he was named secretary of the Confederate Congress by acclamation, Hooper's pleasure was spoiled by one reporter's bland summary of events: "The Southern Congress has met, Howell Cobb of Georgia presiding and Simon Suggs of Montgomery clerk."[22]

Calculated anonymity, we might say, is stealth akin to voyeurism since its primary beneficiary is the unsigned author, relishing the reception of his work with a kind of gnostic indulgence. If an author's anonymity satisfies the sly urge to observe the reception of his text without exposing his ego or reputation, pseudonymity is impersonation, in which the author protects his ego by constructing an alternative identity, preserving the self while making a tantalizing gesture toward exposure. In adopting Madison Tensas as a pseudonym, Henry Clay Lewis went further than any of his contemporaries in giving dimension to a narrating voice. Despite the pervasive influence of Irving in *Swamp Doctor*, Lewis's crusty old persona is neither an addled eccentric like Knickerbocker nor an

21. Autograph book, Thomas Addison Burke Papers, Georgia Historical Society, Savannah.
22. W. Stanley Hoole, *Alias Simon Suggs: The Life and Times of Johnson Jones Hooper* (University: University of Alabama Press, 1952), 160.

avuncular romantic like Crayon. The fiction of these "odd leaves" is that their scribe is a quirky old man, lonely and unfulfilled. He refers to his "haggard old-bachelor looks," commenting poignantly on what he calls his wife: his "books and calling—rather a frigid bride" (*SD*, 28, 179). The author follows Tensas from orphaned youth to aging doctor, at each stage maintaining psychological consistency. The swamp doctor, gloomily anchored to a belief in the illusoriness of ambition and talent, is haunted by an obsession with human errancy. Though the character was an impersonation, the evidence shows that his dour authority belonged fully to Lewis, aged twenty-five.

The editors of the standard anthology of Southwest writing argue that the humorists' use of pseudonyms suggests the extent "to which basic materials were common property, a part of the folk heritage and popular currency of the region."[23] Like village culture anywhere, rural society in the Old Southwest, when frontier conditions had gradually succumbed to a more stable sense of community, was rich in nicknames, pseudonyms, and pet names describing attributes of character or behavior that proper names alone are incapable of carrying. The pages of this humor feature an unembarrassed parade of backwoods figures with such names as Onsightly Peter, Bela Bugg, Ovid Bolus, Sally Hooter, and Rance Bore-'em—all of which, however, owe less to the folk heritage of the Southwest than to the centuries-old tradition of the nom de plume, which would have been fully available to the witty contributors who signed *their* names "Wing" and "Sugartail" and "Thunder." The sophisticated authors participated in their naming culture as heartily as their illiterate yeoman brothers, yet they did so with a sense of literary history behind them. If colorful cognomens stud the prose of the sketches, it is because they have already been assimilated into the imaginative world of talented scribes who, however observant their eye or sensitive their ear, know too much to use court stenography as their literary model. The sketches may not always be fictional in a technical sense, but, however grounded in actuality and however modest their offering, their very printing betrayed creative ambition.

The convention of pseudonyms among the humorists is, on the one hand, a gesture of alliance with the place and people they know so well, but, on the other, it also sets them apart from the motley population whose presence and influence were impossible to ignore. The working

23. Hennig Cohen and William B. Dillingham, introduction to *Humor of the Old Southwest*, 3rd ed. (Athens: University of Georgia Press), xx.

premise of many of the sketches is the assumed gap between the author-ial persona and his subject: he may be privy to the habits and mores of the people whose world overlapped with his, but as author or surrogate he is different from and superior to them. In actuality, of course, the role of gentleman is more assumed than real. Few of the authors were gentle-men in the Virginia sense. In the promissory climate of the new country, these middle-class men—who were respectable (mostly), ambitious, re-sponsible, and educated (to some degree)—flourished, faltered, and began again in the all-too-familiar pattern of American self-making. In their case, identity and class membership were subject to the same negotiation that marked the general competitive spirit of the go-ahead times. Even the pedigrees of real gentlemen were often challenged or rendered irrelevant among men whose "organs of Reverence" were "almost entirely want-ing" (*FT,* 244). As Joseph G. Baldwin and Henry Clay Lewis admitted, young professionals dealt with felons, swindlers, deadbeats, and malin-gerers on a comfortable basis since "lawyerlings" and scrabbling new doctors were themselves as ethically suspect as the general population. Both authors were half in love with impersonation. If *gentlemanliness* was a debased currency in the Flush Times, all social ranks enjoyed a democ-racy of opportunity in larceny, quackery, and malfeasance. As we have seen, fetching was a condition of their time and place.

In a kind of Masonic logic, the pseudonym and the gentlemanly per-sona allowed the humorist to have it both ways. Such conventions both disclosed and protected actual identity. Richard Steele's insight—"It is much more difficult to converse with the World in a real than a person-ated Character"—was the result of political wisdom as much as it was an aesthetic tool. So too in the "personated" essays of his American succes-sors—Philip Freneau, William Wirt, and Joseph Dennie—whose author-ial examples resonate in the squibs, letters, and sketches of the humorous authors.[24] Pseudonymous authorship suggests a fraternal order of adepts whose primary audience is itself, but whose amiable nature compels self-exposure to readers beyond the insiders' circle. One effect of the scribes' teetering commitment to writing is that the use of the pseudonym ac-knowledges a radical democracy in which the putative author submerges his rightful claim as aesthetic maker into the greater authority of the made, a habit of art that celebrates product over producer. This generation of ambivalent authors, from A. B. Longstreet to George Washington Harris, may be the first in American literature to assemble a body of writing in

24. Granger, *American Essay Serials,* 6, 70.

which, for thirty years, the text takes priority over its creator: a Pete Whetstone letter over C. F. M. Noland, a Sut Lovingood sketch over G. W. Harris, a wang-doodle sermon over William Penn Brannan. Mary Chesnut's allusions to the humorists in her voluminous Civil War diaries are as often to episodes involving characters as they are to the authors: Major Jones in his meal sack on Christmas Eve, Simon Suggs's "integrity" as he makes off with the camp-meeting offering.[25]

iii.

If Hooper emerges as an aspiring politician struggling to separate himself from the loutish fictional character he created, the equally aspiring David Crockett finds himself saddled with the loutish public image that he had earlier encouraged. The example of the Tennessee backwoodsman and his multiple texts is not typical of the fluctuating boundary between professional lives and amateur authorship in the Old Southwest, but it dramatically yokes the issues that most of the humorists dealt with: authenticity, self-authorizing, purloined texts, nonchalant attributions, and, above all, the relationship between historical person and writing persona and the complicity of fact and fiction. Like many less versatile Americans, the historical David Crockett—bear hunter, Indian fighter, congressman, frontier humorist, war hero—was eager to inscribe himself in autobiography, to fashion himself even as others were fashioning him.

As we have seen, the name of Mike Fink bore much of the unsavory reputation of the boatman class to which he belonged. So, too, Crockett among the backwoodsmen. Moreover, the cultural symbolizing of Crockett began earlier. The "true David Crockett is an ideal, not an actual man," wrote one perceptive reviewer soon after the hero's death. "He stands in relation to the backwoodsmen, as the shadower forth of their faults and virtues." The assessment concluded: "His private qualities are forgotten and merged in those of his class and age—of whom he is the allegory and personification."[26] What makes Crockett different from Mike Fink is the calculation involved in his self-making.

In 1834 Crockett stoutly repudiated the popular *Sketches and Eccentricities of Colonel David Crockett of West Tennessee* of the year before, devised

25. *Mary Chesnut's Civil War*, ed. C. Vann Woodward (New Haven, CT: Yale University Press, 1981), 280, 17.
26. Unsigned review of *Col. Crockett's Exploits and Adventures in Texas*, [by Richard Penn Smith], *Western Monthly Review*, October 1836, p. 625.

probably as a campaign biography (one that actually handicapped
Crockett in his congressional race), replacing it with an improved account of himself, *A Narrative of the Life of David Crockett of the State of Tennessee*. In the unsanctioned *Sketches and Eccentricities* he is an author
several times removed: Mathew St. Clair Clarke pretends to be James S.
French, who in turn pretends to be Crockett. The authorial remove is
lessened in the *Narrative*. Although ghostwritten by Thomas Chilton, a
Kentucky congressman, the content has been judged to be Crockett's.[27]
The first book confirmed rather than invented the folkloristic image of
the tall-talking hunter; the second downplayed what Crockett believed
was damaging to both his political aspirations and his rightful dignity as
a man—the excessive brag that made him seem a shallow rustic. Crockett
affected an injured sensibility over the "false notions" perpetrated by the
Sketches and Eccentricities, precisely on the matter of tall tales and tall talk.
Its scribe put "into my mouth such language as would disgrace even an
outlandish African," he writes in the *Narrative*, and though he seems resigned that the "bundle of ridiculous stuff" in the earlier book cannot be
totally eliminated, he tries to counter its distortions by reinstating details
and language that will ratify "the *countenance, appearance,* and *common
feelings* of a human being" (*DC*, 4–5). According to this version of David
Crockett, to be human is to be political; to countermand the apolitical exploits ascribed to him in the *Sketches*, feats that in effect removed him
from the merely human, the author must stress his human virtues in the
political arena—honesty, compassion, dedication. In this re-siting of the
self, such virtues are dramatically enacted.

Crockett, however, is better at self-authorizing than he is at authorizing a book about himself. In the preface to the *Narrative* he cagily obfus-
cates his role as autobiographer. If the "vermin" critics are not pleased
with his spelling, grammar, or structure, he will accept their criticism; as
for authorship itself, he declares he will "hang on to it, like a wax plaster." But although the "whole book is my own, and every sentiment and

27. Richard Boyd Hauck, *Crockett: A Bio-Bibliography* (Westport, CT: Greenwood,
1982), 5; James A. Shackford and Stanley J. Folmsbee, eds., introduction to *A Narrative
of the Life of David Crockett of the State of Tennessee*, facsimile reprint of the 1834 volume
(Knoxville: University of Tennessee Press, 1973), xvi. Shackford's judgment that the
Narrative is the most dependable account of the hero is confirmed by Richard Boyd
Hauck, "The Man in the Buckskin Shirt: Fact and Fiction in the Crockett Story," in
Davy Crockett: The Man, the Legend, the Legacy, 1786–1986, ed. Michael A. Lofaro (Knox-
ville: University of Tennessee Press, 1985), 10. The definitive biography of the histori-
cal Crockett is James A. Shackford, *David Crockett: The Man and the Legend* (Chapel Hill:
University of North Carolina Press, 1956).

sentence in it," he confesses that "a friend or so" has been responsible for "some little alterations" in spelling and grammar. Since he hates "this way of spelling contrary to nature" (presumably according to rules of orthography rather than aural principles), and since grammar is "pretty much a thing of nothing at last," the alterations are merely trivialities of authorship (*DC*, 8–9).[28] But not entirely trivial: he reminds the reader that he has sometimes resisted such corrections, and that some sections of the *Narrative* remain just as he wrote them. Part of Crockett's strategy—and part of his problem in image-making—involves his need to combine honesty and naïveté; that is, to both confess to the truth of his reported adventures (the ones that have made him well known) and to pose as an inexperienced politician who has only his integrity to battle the duplicitous machinations of his enemies. He needs some of his notoriety as a backwoods brawler, but not so much that it would detract from his seriousness as a responsible leader. As all autobiographers should do, he intends to lay out his own "plain, honest homespun account of my state in life," including some parts that may not be very interesting. Everything will be true, but some segments may be more appealing than others (those adventures reflecting his "eccentricities"?). His aim is to reach more, and more discerning, readers than read and believed the earlier "deceptive" book. With his authorized *Narrative*, he will at least have performed the necessary act of putting "all the facts down, leaving the reader free to take his choice of them" (*DC*, 10).

As the modern editors of the *Narrative* make clear, the text incorporates a few mottoes and aphorisms already identified as Crockett's, a few frontier oddities of usage, and stylized grammatical lapses (some of them spurious) that lend it a Crockett flavor without permitting the whole to sink into the quaint illiteracies of syntax and diction popularly associated with the backwoods. Because the text is not oppressively burdened by them, sayings common to the western country, some of them subsequently attributed to Crockett ("salting the cow to catch the calf," say, or "root hog or die"), tend to energize the flow of narrative rather than draw attention to the locutions themselves. Except for the frontier flavoring, the *Narrative* is more akin to Franklin's *Autobiography* than it is to the *Sketches and Eccentricities* or to the later *Crockett Almanacks*. The style is a generalized

28. Crockett's attitude was common in the backcountry, where oral culture was always more important than writing. Many settlers were contemptuous of orthography—Andrew Jackson was said to have been suspicious of any man who knew only one way to spell a word. David Hackett Fischer, *Albion's Seed: Four British Folkways in America* (New York: Oxford, 1989), 716–18.

rural vernacular "consistent in its deviations from standard English," its idioms representative of "no single region and no specific class."[29] The authorizing prose of the *Narrative* may be contrasted to that of the *Almanacks,* in which the surrogate writer and editor Ben Harding claims to have the hero's blessing: "my friend, the Kernill, had dun so much to author-eyes me to stand as cheef cook and bottle-washer in this bizziness."[30] In the *Narrative's* understated use of images, those that make an impression ("like a duck in a puddle," "nigh to burst my boilers") are clustered in about ten pages, almost as if Chilton-Crockett were experimenting with vernacular effects. In general, the language of the *Narrative* is restrained without being genteel.

The authorized account, then, even though its subject is known for extravagance, runs the rhetorical risk of being "uninteresting." For Crockett to insist on his simple humanity is a more difficult task, at least when writing for a popular audience, than to parade his eccentric superhumanity. At one point, after recounting his electioneering activities in 1822, Crockett confesses, "I am fearful that I am too particular about many small matters"—all because he wants the world to know "my true history" (*DC,* 8–9). All in all, it is an awkward dilemma for both authors and politicians. Honesty of craft and profession here presupposes an interactive reader, who in choosing Chilton-Crockett over Clarke-Crockett must be aware that David Crockett of the State of Tennessee is in effect competing with himself.

Consider the curious linkage with which the revision-minded author concludes his preface. He claims that his *Narrative* should be included among the "messages, and proclamations, and cabinet writings" of the Jackson administration. "Big men," he writes, have more important duties than "Dotting *i*'s and crossing *t*'s"; and as the "'Government's' name is to the proclamation," so "my name's to the book" (*DC,* 6).[31] Crockett characteristically uses "the Government" as a scornful synonym for Jackson. What dominated his later career, as seen in the ambiguous preface to

29. Hauck, *Crockett,* 5–6. Hauck presents a persuasive comparison of Crockett's *Narrative* and Franklin's *Autobiography.*

30. For the complex relationship of Harding and Crockett, see John Seelye, "A Well-Wrought Crockett, or How the Fakelorists Passed through the Credibility Gap and Discovered Kentucky," in *Davy Crockett: The Man, the Legend, the Legacy, 1786–1986,* ed. Michael A. Lofaro (Knoxville: University of Tennessee Press, 1985), 21–45. James A. Shackford calls the *Almanacks* a "gargantuan hoax." *David Crockett,* 248–49.

31. As the editors of the *Narrative* point out, it was widely known that Attorney General Roger Taney and even unofficial members of the Kitchen Cabinet were the real authors of presidential decrees (*DC,* 172).

the *Narrative,* was an orchestrated political shift: the legendary back-woods hunter (Jacksonite) turned responsible politician (Whig), a pivot that required a corresponding turn in style. For almost the entire period covered by the *Narrative,* Crockett is a friend and booster of Jackson; a rather bitter break occurs in 1828, presumably over Crockett's support of West Tennessee squatters and perhaps his opposition to Old Hickory's official policy of Indian removal.[32] When Crockett wrote his account in early 1834, the break was still a nagging reminder of the political griev-ance he felt over his unsuccessful campaign in 1829 for reelection to Congress. In the *Narrative,* the shift in political alignment after 1828 col-ors the incidents of a much earlier time, not merely in those chapters that Crockett devotes to campaigning. To signify his total separation from Jackson, he twice uses the image of dog and master, the second time on the final page as an indelible reminder to the reader that Crockett re-mains "at liberty . . . without the yoke of any party on me":

> Look at my arms, you will find no party hand-cuff on them!
> Look at my neck, you will not find there any collar, with the engraving
> MY DOG.
>   Andrew Jackson.[33]

Less flamboyant than Clarke-Crockett, the Chilton-Crockett medium is a restrained vernacular inflected with the rhetorical urgencies of truth-telling that are more familiar in depositions of converts, turncoats, and defectors.

The balancing act alone makes the *Narrative* a remarkable achieve-ment, despite the considerable slippage in clarity as the text contends with multiple topics: the motives of political affiliation, the pride of hon-est self-portrayal, the enigmatic defense of surrogate authorship. Despite the fact that the commodification of Crockett began with Crockett him-self, his core identity remains elusive. We may conclude that by 1834 this backwoods hero was a cultural referent for too many diverse groups, an

32. In a letter of December 14, 1833, Crockett explained that he was no longer a friend of Jackson: "when I see him trying to destroy the best intrests of his Country to keep his party, I am off like a pot-leg." David Crockett Letter (Z/392), Mississippi Depart-ment of Archives and History, Jackson.

33. Horace Greeley charged that Martin Van Buren owed his election to the "impe-rious will of Andrew Jackson, with whom 'Love me, love my dog,' was an iron will." *Recollections of a Busy Life* (New York, 1869), 118.

icon for so many divergent needs that coherence was not possible, even with Crockett's own impressive efforts. What is clear is the sophisticated process that the *Narrative* enacts: the figure in the center is as self-consciously self-fashioning as the spurious Crockett of *Sketches and Eccentricities*. If throwing off pursuit is a useful trait for a bear hunter, hedging is even more useful for a politician.

iv.

As we have seen, authenticity, reliability, and confidence were blurred virtues in the go-ahead Southwest. Professionals, businessmen, and planters of the middle class were especially vulnerable to frauds because so many of them were greedy for social prestige as well as material success. Confidence men, cleverer than the hokey Simon Suggs, knew all about the "soft spots" of new gentlemen eager to embody such older values as generosity, hospitality, trustfulness, and a good name. The impersonator is a familiar figure in the humor of the time, and not solely because the type was a cultural shorthand for the contagion of dissembling in society at large. The psychology of impersonation began with the authors themselves. In 1853, writing of his years in the Arkansas House of Representatives, C. F. M. Noland recalled: "I once travelled from Little Rock in a four-horse postchaise, where I had been playing the part of legislator" (*PW*, 21). If Baldwin and Lewis acknowledge that as professionals they are not quite what they seem to be, both finesse the uncertainty this raises by giving their younger selves—the "lawyerling" and the medical intern, respectively—the arrogant ineptness of youth. Despite their fallback position of authorial ambivalence, they also suggest that even arrogant ineptness may be bogus.

Not all the humorists are as (murkily) self-revealing as Baldwin and Lewis. Some of the others who like to deny relevance in their role as author proceed as if they are relevant. Far from claiming a place for themselves in American letters, most of the southwestern authors present their lighter efforts (what Poe liked to call "risible" writing) as avocational. Yet the record shows that Longstreet, Taliaferro, Thorpe, and Kittrell Warren, among others, embraced authorship with more ambition than we might expect from mere literary comedians. Although Lewis's career was cut short by his early death, that list would also include Baldwin. After *Flush Times* recorded brisk sales, the author wrote his wife that he now had a chance of "being enrolled among the writers of the land"; he voiced his gratitude that critics were not treating the book "as a Suggs-like affair."[34] Baldwin as author was more forthright than most of the other humorists (the title page of *Flush Times* bore his real name), but, at one time or another, all of them were too assiduous in their writing to be dismissed only as amateurs. Theirs was a craft as well as an art. They relished pulling off the "game": the setting-up, the procedures, the revelation, the snapper. Just as they construct their vernacular confidence men (and those with seedy pretensions to the quality) as agents of dissimulation, so they shape their amateur careers as authors.

In no other body of antebellum writers is there such a reliance upon pseudonyms and personas. For the humorists, names and identities are often mere conveniences that mask their authority, appearing alongside mistaken or enforced identities, fraudulent kinships, and premeditated personalities, all of which may be projected into stories in which competition is no longer straightforward but is kicked into action by the exercise of skills drawn from a generous repository of dissembling. If the "personated" essays of Addison and Steele head the list of precursors of the antebellum humorists, their most immediate model was Washington Irving, who distanced himself by layering his tales with narrators. Even Geoffrey Crayon—the author of the *Sketch-Book,* according to the title page—is leery of telling stories in his own voice, relying most often on surrogate tellers to whom he can condescend. "Geoffrey Crayon, Gent.," fooled no one, of course, but as a transparent convention, he enlarged the aesthetic possibilities of the pseudonymous narrator. By the time of *Bracebridge Hall,* a reviewer was praising the skill with which Irving could play "four or five parts at once" with equal ease.[35]

Porter of the *Spirit* could not hide his mild exasperation with the caginess of his anonymous and pseudonymous contributors from the Southwest, and he must have been relieved to publish Solomon Franklin Smith, whose only disguise as author was as "Old Sol," named for the well-known character he played on stage. No humorist of the group embraced authorship with quite the exuberant aplomb of this impresario, a literal impersonator. His résumé included stints as farmer, printer, newspaperman, lawyer, and singing master, and his theatrical talents extended this list, enabling him to assume (with moderate success) the roles of doctor,

34. Eugene Current-Garcia, "Joseph Glover Baldwin: Humorist or Moralist?" in *The Frontier Humorists: Critical Views,* ed. M. Thomas Inge (Hamden, CT: Archon, 1975), 176–77.

35. Review of *Bracebridge Hall,* by Washington Irving, *North American Review* 15 (1822): 213.

preacher, civic moralist, and steamboat pilot. Both on stage and off, Sol Smith was a man of movable identities, roving from one base of operations to another (New Orleans, Mobile, Cincinnati, St. Louis), with forays into smaller river towns and towns in the interior. Even though most of his roles offstage were improvisational, this irrepressible man enacted them with the flair of Sam Patch, the stunt master who specialized in spectacular leaps over cataracts and who explained his prowess with the motto, *Some things can be done as well as others.* If that showman was only refining and practicing an American habit long in place, Sol Smith was his impressive avatar. Smith in effect literalized the milieu that travel writers metaphorically called a "theatre of opportunity," but he inscribed his diverse performances, as he well knew, in the only mode that could endure: writing. He gathered his comic anecdotes into two books—*Sol Smith's Theatrical Apprenticeship* (1845) and *Sol Smith's Theatrical Journey Work* (1854)—and a kind of curtain call that topped both: *Theatrical Management in the West and South for Thirty Years* (1868).

Comprising five "acts," this huge compendium carried the symbolic weight of southwestern life that Baldwin had discursively laid out in *Flush Times*, including the transience, violence, and social chaos of a society not yet fully civilized. The accounts of a trouper and his company not only sum up the notoriously fluctuating fortunes of the theater itself, but also serve conspicuously as a material correlative of the settlement period in the lower South. Although a love of tricks dictated many of the episodes in *Theatrical Management*, and although the author avoided the deliberate baiting of preachers and other light-bringers who sought to reshape the ragged incoherence of his society, Sol Smith never allowed coercive moralism to blunt his activities. He was roused to battle only when grave guardians sought to bring down the curtain on his company even before it went up. At one time, hearing that a constable had referred to the theater as "the devil's church," the actor picks up the motif of the interchangeability of moral instruction and entertainment, using as his chief text the principle laid down by an admirer, a New Orleans Irishman: "The Church in the morning—the Drayma at night, is my maxam, Mister Sol, and I'll stick to it!" (*TM*, 232 ff.). Despite the fact that it was a potpourri of anecdotes, Smith insisted upon calling his book an autobiography. With structural excess he included as front matter an elaborate dedication, a detailed table of contents, a photograph of the author (signed), and a preface; these are followed by a prologue, the five "acts," an epilogue, an appendix, and an epitaph. Decked out with fifteen illustrations, it is as much a mock autobiography as Hooper's *Simon Suggs* is a mock campaign biography. As author, Smith might be seen as improvising again, but he does so with the same readiness with which he pretended to be a Methodist parson or a pilot. For a man whose very life depended on impersonation, there is, not surprisingly, an inspiriting ease in his authoring.

If they suspected that, as midcentury authors, they were not quite the real thing, most of the humorists were happily unburdened by their dissembling. The good cheer with which they aped their professional peers in both history and fiction was occasionally diluted with apology, but their self-doubts were nothing like those lacing the consciousness of, say, Hawthorne, whose discomfort as a mere "writer of story-books!" was exacerbated by the ghostly rebuke of a solemn Puritan ancestor who had benefited his society as "soldier, legislator, judge."[36] Humor was only one mode for such authors as Longstreet, Thorpe, Taliaferro, the Field brothers, and Robb; and those authors who were exclusively "risible"— Smith, Thompson, Hall, and a few others—bothered themselves not at all with the conventional pose of reluctance. They showed the same unblushing ambition for their scribbling efforts as their contemporaries professionally committed to authorship.

v.

In dedicating *Streaks of Squatter Life* to Charles Keemle, John S. Robb honored the St. Louis newspaperman, in part because as a long-time resident of the west, Keemle could attest to the changes in the region that the author suggested—"its progress in every stage, from the semi-civilised state until the refinement of polished life has usurped the wilderness" (*SSL,* iii). Although the referents for *polished life* were as relative as those for *west,* Robb subscribed to the same article of faith affirmed by almost every one of the southwestern authors: the reality of "progress" as a principle in social development. From whatever chronological starting point, even Longstreet's in 1835, the characters and incidents described tend to illustrate former times as much as they do present conditions. As a crucial stage in the new country, usurping the wilderness, however imperfect the polish of the resident population, is a given in most of the sketches. The narrating perspective is urban, even if the narrative sites are not quite urbane.

Although they share certain presuppositions—notably an appreciation

36. Nathaniel Hawthorne, "The Custom House," in *The Scarlet Letter,* Norton Critical Edition, ed. Seymour Gross and others (New York: Norton, 1988), 9.

of historical changes within their space—the humorous authors are as diverse as any other group of writers, and a sense of their calling is usually tempered by the degree to which they seem comfortable in carrying their wares to market. When they assembled their individual sketches for book publication, their approach combined the same assertiveness and hesitation, the same rhetorical pose and polite demurrer, as that of full-fledged professional writers. Most of them followed the custom of penning some introductory remarks that might justify their efforts as modest but worthy. Some, like Thompson, Baldwin, and Thorpe, zealously involved themselves in the preparation and promotion of their books. The prefaces to their collected sketches are at best imperfect clues to why these humorists wrote, yet they ratify the ambiguous line they walked in clearing a space for themselves, even as tyros, in the world of letters.

For Joseph Jones the epistolarian, the hard work seemingly has been done by "Mr. Thompson," who "made a book out of my letters." Nonetheless, he feels impelled to write a preface that will be warm and welcoming to readers. A book "now-a-days . . . without a preface in frunt would be like a log cabin with no string hangin out at the dore." Having found himself at a loss "to put a good face" on the "heap of nonsense" that he has already written, Major Jones has done some research "to see how other writers" worked it; what he discovers is that all the prefaces "seem to be about the same." The authors "feel a monstrous desire to benefit the public one way or other," some "anxious to tell all they know about certain matters, jest for the good of the public—some wants to edify the public—some has been 'swaded by frends to give ther book to the public—and others has been induced to publish ther writins jest for the benefit of futer generations—but not one of 'em had a idee to make a cent for themselves!" (*MJC*, 9–10).

The letters may be "nonsense," but they are not lies, and the Major decides he won't lie in his preface either: the only purpose of "*my* book," he writes, is "*to sell and make money.*" Nevertheless, like any author, this one frets over what the critics might say, since "they always nabs a'most every thing that's got a kiver on" (*MJC*, 9–10). Fortunately, Major Jones is encouraged because his book has already been vetted by Pineville's own critic-about-town, old Mr. Mountgomery, whose measured criticism struck the author as fair-minded: "Your book is a very original perduction, and though it don't belong to the more useful and elvated branches of literary composition, . . . it's equally as good as one half . . . [of] what is published in this country, and not half so pernicious as some of it" (*MJC*, 117). The Major decides that the "nonsense" of his letters is his best protection against the "bominable critics." "I remembered," he writes, "ther was two ways of gittin into a field—under, as well as over the fence," and books "git into the world of letters jest as hogs does into a tater patch—some over and some under. . . . Seein as I is perfectly satisfied with the under route, I dont think the critics will tackle my book. If they does all I can say is, I give 'em joy with ther small potaters" (*MJC*, 10–11). Being satisfied with the under route is a relevant tactic for most of the humorists. Some of them, Thompson included, even managed to slip in what they would regard as nourishment with their small potatoes.

In contrast, Robb takes his authoring seriously. He neglects the pleasant fiction that he has been "importuned" by friends to allow his sketches to be published as a collection. Neither are his sketches the products of his "idle" hours—the customary disclaimer for gentlemanly authorship—but rather (in a hairsplitting distinction) of the "few short hours" beyond his regular duties. His dedication to Keemle refers to his book as "the first production of my pen in the field of western literature," suggesting an ongoing project that is no more casual than his writing as a professional newspaperman. He envisions other books to follow, capitalizing on the metier of descriptive and humorous sketches of "western character." If his first is met "with favor," he will respond with others. Moreover, Robb acknowledges the role of the critic in the professional life of the writer. He concludes his preface by lightly begging the reviewers to touch him lightly: in the language of "the Irish pupil, when about to receive a thrashing from his tutor;—'If you can't be *aisy,* be as aisy as you *can!*'" In 1847 this restless newspaperman (thinly disguised in one sketch as a "Wandering Typo") is still a fledgling author. The preface of *Streaks* shows a consciously determined if not yet a smoothly functioning writer. He does not apologize for his style, admitting that even with more leisure he could hardly claim "a capability to furnish any better," but he does remind readers that the "finished and graphic writers of our country" have missed an opportunity by ignoring the field his pen has invaded. Robb readily names the "abler pens" who haven't ignored it: Thomas Bangs Thorpe, Johnson Jones Hooper, Joseph Field, and Sol Smith (*SSL*, vii–x). It is among this fraternal order that Robb places himself.

Kittrell Warren's preface to *Life and Public Services of an Army Straggler* (1865), one of the late entries in Southwest humor, begins with an encomium to the soldiers of the late Confederacy—as if patriotism might buffer the depicted crudities of the ignoble Rebel who is his subject. The "language of praise can never over-reach" when writing about the merits of the southern troops, insists the author, yet his text candidly recounts the adventures of a ne'er-do-well Georgian, an army deserter, liar, and thief whose picaresque schemes are as depraved as they are funny. In justification, the author suggests that any vast army contains all kinds of men, some of them undeserving the "language of praise." Warren's oblique reminder is directed to "that class of people whose vocations have kept them uninformed about the grosser elements of human nature" (*AS*, 3).

As we might expect, the most striking front matter in these collections of sketches is that prepared by Sut Lovingood, whose preface and dedicatory page are the most extreme instance of rebellious *non serviam* in all of American writing. Sut's embrace of authorship is both a premonitory clue to and a summary statement of his radical sensibility. He is as incapable of ingratiating himself to distant readers as he is to his neighbors in his settlement. Sut is not subversive: he is direct, challenging, even militant, scornful alike of both "orthurs" and readers. Most authors he blasts as hypocritically modest in offering their work to the public like lambs, "whinin and waggin their tails, a-sayin they knows they is imparfeck." He grudgingly concedes that his collaborator is George Washington Harris, but depicts himself as the real author behind "our book." George merely "writes," a situation that the illiterate Sut must accept: "Usin uther men's brains is es lawful es usin thar plunder, an' jis' es common." As for his audience, Sut anticipates objections from readers who have a fear of the devil ("an' orter hev") and from those whose reputation can't stand "much ove a strain." Like most of the humorists, but with far more scorn, Sut is alert to the threat of literary critics. In a line that anticipates the resentment of struggling professionals of more recent times, the "book-butchers" are "orful on killin an' cuttin up," mostly because they are not up to being authors themselves: "they cud no mor perjuce a book, than a bull-butcher cud perjuce a bull." His true audience is the "misfortinit devil" who is poor, footsore, and burdened by responsibilities; if these truth-telling sketches can elicit just one laugh from him, Sut will consider himself paid in full (*SL*, ix–xi).

Though he is guilty of it, Sut considers preface-writing "durned humbug." It is tantamount to taking off his shoes before going into the "publick's parlor"—but, he adds, he reckons he can do it "wifout durtyin my feet, fur I hes socks on." The allusion to Moses, commanded to remove his shoes on holy ground, is mockingly modulated for an unworthy reading public whose standards and tastes are so debased that even Sut would dirty his feet if he entered its precincts unprotected. Harris allows his rebel author one final dip in the pool of prefatory conventions, an allusion to the traditional "go, little book," a gesture that always mixed au-

thorial arrogance and humility. The image of the book as boat Sut transforms into a nearly literal version—or as literal as is possible for a writer
in the landlocked Tennessee mountains: "Now, George, grease hit good,
an' let hit slide down the hill hits own way" (*SL*, ix, xi).

When Sut mentions his book as a "perducktion" (which he does three
times on his first page), he characteristically conceives of his literary enterprise in its materiality; but as author he is not alone in regarding the
book as a physical object drawing attention to itself. When Thompson's
rustic hero in 1843 receives in the mail "a big yaller package" of six pamphlets entitled *Major Jones's Courtship*, the book is just that, a blue-paper
collection ("with the title-page on the outside") of sixteen letters that the
editor of the *Southern Miscellany* is offering readers as a subscription pre-
mium. In this metafictional moment, while the new author is more interested in reading the admiring critical notices of his work, his wife is
distressed at the visual illustration of Joseph Jones: "It don't look no
more like you, Joseph, than you does like a cow." She covers the offend-
ing illustration by pasting over it a prettier face that she finds "in some
picter-book" (*MJC*, 115, 118). In his preface to *Georgia Scenes*, Longstreet
asks the reader's indulgence for the imperfect physical state of the text:
having foregone "examining the proof sheets" to speed up publication,
he warns (accurately) that the book contains "many typographical errors" (*GS*, 3). So, too, Baldwin in his preface to *Flush Times*. Under "the
tremor of a first publication," the author hesitates to offer "a sneaking
apology for the many errors and imperfections of his work," because
even though it was written in haste, "under the pressure of professional
engagements," no excuse can fully justify "errors and imperfections"—
though Baldwin in fact thanks the editor of the *Southern Literary Messenger*, in whose pages the articles first appeared, for undertaking the
messy job he should have done: "revising and correcting" as *Flush Times*
"passed through the press" (*FT*, vi–vii).

Thorpe was the most reluctant "humorist" of all the authors because
his literary sights were set higher. As we have seen, he thought of himself
first as a sporting writer and delineator of the characters and scenery of
the Mississippi Valley. His first collection, *Mysteries of the Backwoods* (1846),
contained sixteen sketches, only one of which ("A Piano in Arkansas")
qualifies as humorous; that same year he was generously represented in
William T. Porter's first American edition of Peter Hawker's *Instructions
to Young Sportsmen*. If most of his career was devoted to editing newspapers in the Southwest, he yet found time to be an author in the traditional sense, writing what he referred to in a letter to his publisher as

"standard literature." Along with dozens of articles, humorous pieces, and squibs, Thorpe wrote multiple books about the war with Mexico and a novel, *The Master's House; A Tale of Southern Life*. In all this compositional activity he behaved like any professional author, instructing his publishers about technical matters, writing letters to influential figures who might puff his work, and keeping tabs on how well he was doing against competitors. A mere amateur would not complain to his publisher about disappointing sales figures, as Thorpe did: "According to the present public taste, Irving's Scketch [sic] book would be a failure" (*TBT*, 50).

As an artist, Thorpe was eager to illustrate his first book. Even after he acquiesced when his publisher wanted to engage F. O. C. Darley, whose work had enlivened Porter's *Big Bear* volume of 1845, Thorpe yet insisted on having some input. "With myself at his elbow to give the exact character of our southwestern scenery," he wrote, "I cannot imagine better illustrations."[37] His interest in the production of *Mysteries* was detailed and specific: "I want the sketches set up in large type, heads of chapters low down on the pages, thick leads &c &c so that the work may be spread over as much surface as possible, and be in every respect a more readable book" (*TBT*, 50, 46). Since he had to leave New York to return to Louisiana before the page proofs were ready, he negotiated with Rufus W. Griswold, the indubitable professional of his time, to do that job properly.

These authors realized that the book was a stage in publishing far more important than the miscellaneous printing of their pieces in ephemeral venues. Prefaces by their very nature are not really prefatory but afterthoughts, and most of the humorists' prefaces reflect the bland poses that allowed them to be unauthorized authors; yet the customary presence of a preface was an opportunity for them to *suggest* their authority, however apologetic they might be, in a format with greater chance of permanence than newspaper publication. Inclusion in Carey and Hart's Library of Humorous American Works was one important measure of success even for Thorpe, who was continually dissatisfied with his publisher's singular focus on regional humor.[38] These eclectic authors were

37. Though he became famous for illustrating books by Irving and Cooper, F. O. C. Darley did his first work for Thompson's *Major Jones's Courtship* (1843) and Porter's *Big Bear of Arkansas* anthology (1845). John Tebbel, *A History of Book Publishing in the United States* (New York: Bowker, 1972), 1:252–53.

38. E. L. Carey and Abraham Hart published the Library of Humorous American Works, a series of paperback volumes that sold for fifty cents each. By 1849 eighteen volumes had appeared. A. Hart, the successor firm, continued the series, which in-

out to render "western life and manners" in sketches both scenic and dramatic, topographical as well as comic, and within those terms their mission was more aesthetic than utilitarian. Their gestures toward seriousness were justifications that say more about their awareness of the literary and cultural climate of their time than they do about their motivation to create.

The humorists could be prankishly indirect about why they wrote, improvising with false leads or aping the stylistic conventions and locutions of well-known authors. Yet most of them were serious once their careers reached a level of national attention that warranted the interest of New York and Philadelphia publishers. Their depiction of their moment in the Old Southwest may not have had the kind of historical accuracy some of them grandly claimed, but they were never unaware that their work was being read in many quarters as a truthful evocation of a region most readers would never visit. For such readers they promised a view of life "as it was," a rhetorical tack that justified their use of subjects and language missing from respectable writing. As practitioners of specialty topics, most of the authors (with the possible exception of Thorpe) did not present themselves—in the manner of Irving, say—as purveyors of literature.

Those who clung to the role of author with ambivalence enjoyed dealing with figures that they and their readers knew were unconducive to high art. The laconic Lije Benadix, Francis James Robinson's poor white gourmand in *Kups of Kauphy* (1853), is much too busy eating to be a storyteller, but the author clearly enjoys quoting his constipated hero as he dribbles responses to his doctors' questions. Cave Burton's earthquake tale in *Flush Times* may be "interminable," with its parts bearing "no imaginable relation to the ostensible subject," but the very fact that no "mortal man had ever heard the end of the story" has its own satisfactions for Baldwin. If there are seven historical David Crocketts, at least three of them promiscuously coexist in literary roles as author, subject, and editor. Harris allows his coauthor, Sut Lovingood, unlimited access to the demons lurking beneath his own respectable front, in effect blessing his outrages against all the faces of civility, including the publishing business. From Crockett's "author-eyes" gambit to Sut's "I now consider

---

cluded volumes by Simms, Hooper, and Lewis. Some of the plates were acquired by T. B. Peterson and Sons, which continued the series as Peterson's Library of Humorous American Works. See Grady W. Ballenger, "Carey and Hart," in *American Literary Publishing Houses, 1638–1899*, ed. Peter Dzwonkoski (Detroit: Gale Research, 1986), 1:80–83.

myself a orthur," these prefaces take their seamless place within the impersonating rhetoric that infuses so many of the sketches. To the degree that all authors are impersonators, those from the Old Southwest appear with facades as meaningful (or as meaningless) as those of lawyers, doctors, peddlers, preachers, ring-tailed roarers, and the other characters that became their subjects.

Taking humor seriously may be as misguided as dismissing it. The fact that the humorists—without exception—kept their day jobs even as they indulged their pleasure in sustained writing suggests that though their audience could never take their writing seriously, it was too personally important for them as authors to dismiss. If, in our begrudging literary history, they come down to us not as professional humorists, they are surely humorist professionals.

Chapter 10 ✦━━✦

The Languages of Southwest Humor

Then the wit—the rich flashes of humor and genius and poetry—
darting out often from a gang of laborers, railroad-men, miners,
drivers or boatmen! How often have I hover'd at the edge of a
crowd of them, to hear their repartees and impromptus! You get
more real fun from half an hour with them, than from the books of
all "the American humorists."

—Walt Whitman, "Slang in America"

i.

We like to extol the antebellum generation of humorists for their sustained efforts in the cause of American vernacular, those bundles
of speech-based idioms that would soon, in the hands of Mark Twain,
transform our literary language. Not only was this body of writing speech-
based, it also aggressively promoted dialectal forms from the least cultivated regions in a nation that for a half-century had been chafing from
English sneers about how Americans used their language. One critic has
suggested that "talk-filled forms of American writing" began to flourish
when, without much premeditation, writers began to follow the sounds
of ordinary speech.[1] Walt Whitman's observation suggests that writers had

---

1. Edward L. Galligan, "American Fiction and the American Idiom," *Sewanee Review* 105 (1997): 356–68.

perhaps been following such sounds too long. In "Slang in America" (1885), the aging poet grandly argued that underpinning all writing was a "lawless germinal element." It was never of course that part of language which gave force to his own distinctive style; and he was in fact using *slang* broadly to mean "indirection, an attempt of common humanity to escape from bald literalism." He wrote at a time in popular culture when Americans had made literary heroes out of Mark Twain and his fellow comedians: Artemus Ward, Josh Billings, Bill Arp, and others. He may also have been remembering the earlier generation of humorists who had celebrated "repartees and impromptus."[2]

In 1835, A. B. Longstreet emphasized two important points for readers opening the pages of *Georgia Scenes, Characters, Incidents, &c., in the First Half Century of the Republic:* that he was recording what he had been listening to, and that the speech he heard was not his. As an educated lawyer, he knew, wrote, and spoke "appropriate" English. Yet in this book that effectively initiated Southwest humor the respectable author, for all his mitigating notes, was clearly not uncomfortable with the mangling of the spoken language he heard and recorded. His contemporaries and successors would be even more indulgent of dialects and lingual styles not their own. Their sketches, which often began in what journalists regarded as proper English—the diction and cadences of gentlemen—usually made space for a demotic deplored by all educators and lexicographers. Some of the humorists were more than liberal in turning over their space to deviant speakers. By their very choice of form—the mock letter to the editor—William Tappan Thompson and C. F. M. Noland created pieces that consisted *only* of dialectal English.

The humorists usually offered their transcriptions of backwoods talk as genuine. As theorists tirelessly remind us, however, the actual thing— the oral performance being recalled—had already disappeared in the ether. Imitating subaltern language is both an act of interpretation and a project

2. Walt Whitman, "Slang in America," in *Poetry and Prose* (New York: Library of America, 1982), 1165–70. Perhaps because the *North American Review* paid him $50 for it, Whitman later called "Slang in America" "insignificant." Jerome Loving, *Walt Whitman: The Song of Himself* (Berkeley and Los Angeles: University of California Press, 1999), 436–37. See also David S. Reynolds, *Walt Whitman's America: A Cultural Biography* (New York: Random House, 1995), 319–21, 377, 563. The first authors of dialect writing to reach a national audience came from the Northeast: Thomas C. Haliburton (1796–1865), the Nova Scotian whom Artemus Ward credited with founding American humor in the 1830s, created the Yankee Sam Slick, the "clockmaker of Slickville"; and Seba Smith (1792–1868) of Maine, the creator of Major Jack Downing, whose common-man perspective on the politics of the Jacksonian era, as we have seen, influenced W. T. Thompson.

of reproduction. These authors foresaw (inaccurately) the inevitable absorption of such deviant talk into a stable, homogenized American English, an envisioned goal that honored an ideology invoked by a cluster of national honorifics: *progress, society, destiny.* In the meantime, however, extensive quotation of deviant speech *within* these authors' own normative style actually hastened an inadvertent process. By dint of repetition and sheer volume, the prominence of linguistic deviance nourished familiarization. Though it would never be assimilated completely, deviant speech was made amenable to a reading public. In the thirty-odd years following *Georgia Scenes,* dialectal "disorder" justified itself as somehow a more "natural order" of English.[3] There is little evidence, though, that the humorists thought of their use of dialect as a mission to promote a more supple American English. Despite the tag of "amateur" they preferred to wear (and which we have uncritically accepted), they were *writers,* and in the antebellum community of writers and readers, that meant individuals blessed with a rigorous command of "correct" English—a received formal level, structurally complex, allusive, and, at its heaviest, self-consciously literary. Although their speech no doubt resisted the urge to lie in state, much of their written work, though seldom ponderous, is as correct as literate discourse of their time was expected to be.

As do most other literary efforts, the humorous pieces formally discriminate written language from spoken. Whatever their dramatic effect, whatever we think about their unarticulated reminder that literacy is an authorizing mark of power, the very existence of two distinct levels of discourse in these sketches acknowledges the historically unresolved debate of what constitutes appropriate American English. As one commentator observes, even in the early Republic, citizens never had a clear sense of what constituted an approved "hegemonic, high-prestige" level of speech.[4] Teachers and editors as well as authors were sensitive to the fact that the long isolation of Americans was affecting the general speech of their British origins. Changes in pronunciation and in the meanings of

3. Although most antebellum travelers felt compelled to devote segments of their adventures in the Old Southwest to deviant spoken English, much of the outrage was spent by the 1840s. A bemused Philip Henry Gosse cited examples, and Thomas L. Nichols was more droll than exasperated with what he heard. To avoid typographical numbness, Nichols, like the humorists, incorporated overheard phrases into his own prose as indirect discourse. Philip Henry Gosse, *Letters from Alabama: Chiefly Relating to Natural History* (London, 1859); Thomas L. Nichols, *Forty Years of American Life* (London, 1864), 386.
4. Gavin Jones, *Strange Talk: The Politics of Dialect Literature in Gilded Age America* (Berkeley and Los Angeles: University of California Press, 1999), 9–10.

old words and phrases—shifts that time and the ocean made possible—were reinforced by continental space: in the former colonies the regional clustering of the population encouraged oral differences in speech as well as in everyday culture. In the eighteenth century (as in any other time) variations in spoken language, including slang, argot, and vernacular substitutions, were audible signs of a subculture; they were defining clues to values, occupations, and biases of groups embedded in what national leaders tried to define as the dominant culture. Demotic English was noted and tolerated, if not celebrated. Dialect could be considered a matter of neutral choice in the contest for an acceptable national language because of its cultural history: learned in the crib, dialect was an intimate part of one's identity.[5] Republican principles, at least in theory, demanded that one dialect be regarded the equal of any other; in practice, linguistic authority fell easily into the hands of literate experts, mostly New Englanders who would also soon be in the forefront of all reformist matters.

Although its political and social function is rarely broached, linguistic authority is a natural part of the reformist strain in early nineteenth-century liberalism, one that echoes a cultural truism—that purifying the language of the tribe usually involves purifying the tribe as well.[6] The middle-class hankering for cultural respectability, however, because it favored a stern monitoring of regional "barbarisms," often clashed with the ideological rage for cultural independence. The campaign to Americanize the mother tongue was never as radical as the conservative opposition pretended. One program for developing a national culture was to beat the British on their own terms (*our high art is equal to yours*); another was to deny the relevance of comparison (*as America is unique, so is its art*).

Even Noah Webster, who enjoyed a popular reputation as a revolutionary lexicographer, shared the programmatic tensions of most educated citizens. He frowned on "provincial accents" because they confused foreigners. To dramatize the country's unity rather than its diversity, he set about building rules for "the *general practice of the nation.*" In his campaign for "*proper* pronunciation of words," Webster may have seen American English as not uniquely different from its British parent, just better than

5. The most useful study of popular speech and democracy is Kenneth Cmiel's *Democratic Eloquence: The Fight over Popular Speech in Nineteenth-Century America* (New York: William Morrow, 1990). See also Christoph Looby, *Voicing America: Language, Literary Form, and the Origins of the United States* (Chicago: University of Chicago Press, 1996).

6. David R. Sewell, *Mark Twain's Languages: Discourse, Dialogue, and Linguistic Variety* (Berkeley and Los Angeles: University of California Press, 1987), 89, 110, 36.

it; but for all his suggested revisions of the inherited language, he was primarily concerned with the "uniformity and purity of *language*."[7] He commended scrapping the sacrosanct rules of grammarians (chiefly Thomas Dilworth's) as "erroneous and defective" in favor of his own (often minor) revisions in keeping with common sense and the needs of a new people. He found no virtue, however, in any linguistic corollary to political democracy. A declaration of linguistic independence and a program for shaping an already workable language with a uniform prescription of usage may be culturally incompatible, but Webster's success can be measured by the enormous popularity of his *Blue-Back Speller*, a democratic bible for language education. The *Speller*, which comprised the first part of Webster's *Grammatical Institute of the English Language* in 1782, was published separately the following year. By the end of the century it had sold more than sixty million copies, and it could still be found in southern schoolrooms as late as World War I.[8]

As for the democratic existence of rustic dialects, Webster, like the humorists after him, envisioned a future in which all dialects, including the high-status forms, would coalesce into a standard national language.

Twin fears—of the vulgarity of the rabble and of the preciosity of the elite—permeated most of the linguistic debates in the early Republic. In 1813 Jefferson was still advocating the priority of usage over grammar and tolerating "neology" (itself a new word) so that our language would reflect the diversity and novelty of American geography and culture.[9] Yet still thriving was the conservative position articulated a decade earlier by Joseph Dennie, who attacked one dictionary because it collected "every vicious word, and phrase . . . coined by the presumptuous ignorance of the

7. Thomas Gustafson, *Representative Words: Politics, Literature, and the American Language, 1776–1865* (Cambridge: Cambridge University Press, 1992), 314. Both Webster's *Grammatical Institute of the English Language* (1782) and *Dissertations on the English Language* (1789) were rhetorically part of his revolutionary enterprise, even as they reverted to British models for the proper use of language.

8. Michael P. Kramer, *Imagining Language in America: From the Revolution to the Civil War* (Princeton, NJ: Princeton University Press, 1992), 40–48. With tortured logic, one critic in the 1830s decided that the "truly frightful" adoption of "newfangled words" showed the consequences of "too exclusive an attachment to British literature." Peter Stephen Du Ponceau, *A Discourse on the Necessity and the Means of Making Our National Literature Independent of That of Great Britain* (Philadelphia, 1834), v, 37, 40–41.

9. In 1820 Jefferson declared to John Adams: "I am a friend to *neology*. It is the only way to give to a language copiousness and euphony." Seven years earlier he had rejected "what is called *Purism*" in favor of "the *Neology* which has introduced these two words without the authority of any dictionary." Thomas Jefferson, *Writings* (New York: Library of America, 1984), 1442, 1295.

boors of each local jurisdiction in the United States." From the beginning, the dialectal tradition stood in what David Simpson calls a "disjunctive relation" to literary forms perceived as high art. One nineteenth-century writer, who steered a diplomatic course to attract a British audience without aping the most slavishly correct forms, enumerated some of the devices he had tried to shun: "turgid diction, brilliant antithesis, unnatural conceits, affected figures, forced epithets, and, in general, all factitious ornament."[10]

The readiness of the early Republic to acknowledge the validity of regional variations was linked to egalitarianism and sometimes cited as its most conspicuous sign. That tolerance wore thinner, however, when the United States gained power as a nation looking to take its place in the world; its desire for dignity and effectiveness required it to speak with one voice in a language equal or superior to its parent's. Conservatives looked to homogenization—of grammar, usage, and pronunciation—as an adequate rebuke to the snobbery of the British. For much of the early antebellum period the work of dictionary makers, grammarians, and tastemakers was concentrated on codifying a coherent, expressive, and respectable American language. As late as 1820, a group of concerned intellectuals offered plans to establish an American academy whose watchdog mission would be "to guard against local or foreign corruptions" in the language and "to settle" orthography, in order to create a standard of writing and pronunciation that would be "correct, fixed, and uniform" throughout the nation. Edward Everett declared the scheme a "farce."[11] The weakness of this language of respectability was not its deference to the British model (a defensive but harmless tack), but its aggression. Its showy correctness and Latinate diction, its tortured wit and wordplay, its ponderous allusiveness all marked its users as mushroom men, me-too parvenus aspiring to a highborn culture that could only be reached by outclassing the original. Its flowering coincided with the gentrification of magazines; the affected elegance of the *Atlantic* and the *North American Review* was the seal of achievement for a language that honored the newly self-conscious chauvinism. Except in the hands of authors of the first rank, simplicity, economy, and restraint were prominently missing in much American prose. (Even Mark Twain, who hated such sumptuous airs, was occasionally besotted by stylistic bloat.) By the mid-1840s, stan-

10. David Simpson, *The Politics of American English, 1776–1850* (New York: Oxford, 1986), 32, 49, 94.
11. William B. Cairns, "On the Development of American Literature from 1815 to 1833, with Especial Reference to Periodicals," *Bulletin of the University of Wisconsin* 1 (1898): 33–34.

dard received English was already standardly received as pretentious English. And not everyone considered pretension a shameful trait.[12]

As an English scientist who settled for a time in frontier Alabama, Philip Gosse was tolerant of backwoods dialect, observing that dialectal peculiarities were a common phenomenon in all large countries and that they could be a "legitimate source of amusement, and possibly of instruction." John Sherman went further. In *Philosophy of Language* (1826) he argued that the true legislators of the language were not grammarians but the people themselves. Using the spade, pickaxe, and crowbar as homely metaphors for common speech, Sherman suggested that an aristocratic aesthetic could be routed by the democratic efforts of the humble laborer. William Henry Milburn, however, deprecated the possibility that language could be enriched by its common users. Notwithstanding the fact that his own rather dull prose profited whenever this former Chaplain of the Congress decided to use backwoods idioms—his book *The Pioneers, Preachers, and People of the Mississippi Valley* is liberally laced with pungent slang and extravagant metaphors suitable to his subject—Milburn declared that frontier locutions were "bombastic and unsound" and, even though they were occasionally humorous, merely displayed "deplorable and extreme barrenness of mind and poverty of thought."[13]

Although Benjamin Franklin anticipated Noah Webster in his proposals for revising English spelling (and with a system considerably more radical), a more lasting contribution was the example of his prose style. While he avoided the most vernacular diction as well as the most ponderously formal, Franklin championed a kind of Enlightenment version of the Puritan plain style, whose chief principle was clarity. Even this modestly reformist impulse was resisted. At the Philadelphia offices of the *Port Folio*, Joseph Dennie blamed what he saw as the degradation of literature on the almanac-happy Franklin, in whose hands "the vile alloy of provincial idioms, and colloquial barbarisms" debased "polished and correct language."[14]

---

12. Writing levels corresponded roughly to oratorical styles: "elevated" for poets and orators; "middling" for historians, "familiar" for comic writers. Although Jefferson approved this separation of styles, within a generation the first two were already regarded as pretentious. Jay Fliegelman, *Declaring Independence: Jefferson, Natural Language, and the Culture of Performance* (Stanford, CA: Stanford University Press, 1993), 27.

13. Gosse, *Letters from Alabama*, 109–10; John Sherman quoted in Simpson, *Politics of American English*, 135; William Henry Milburn, *The Pioneers, Preachers, and People of the Mississippi Valley* (New York, 1860), 412–13.

14. Quoted in Ronald Weber, *Hired Pens: Professional Writers in America's Golden Age of Print* (Athens: Ohio University Press, 1997), 19. Dennie's *Port Folio* was by 1820 the most successful of American magazines, and, like the *North American Review*, it scorned

Washington Irving's entry in the national language enterprise would seem to be an American text untainted by any vile alloy, but in fact the *Sketch-Book* (1820) was a kind of index to the tensions plaguing American writers in the early part of the century. The quip that it was the best English book yet produced by an American, a sentiment widely shared on both sides of the Atlantic, was seen as dismissive by the few tastemakers who wanted more energy in American writing. But conservatives admired the book because its correct, graceful style and its genial, antiquarian narrator bested the British at their own game. It is difficult for us now to imagine that Geoffrey Crayon's avuncular affectation stemmed from "uncouth new idioms," as one American critic charged.[15] Certainly Charles Joseph Latrobe did not imagine it. The son of the famous architect dedicated *The Rambler in North America* (1835) to Irving; his introductory letter, with its candid homage, echoes "The Author's Account of Himself" from the *Sketch-Book*. "I was content," writes Latrobe, to

> turn my back for a season on the society and scenery of the Old World; and looked forward with a sensation of undefined pleasure and curiosity to those western climes, whose characteristics were so different from any I had yet seen. I longed to wander among the details of that sublime scenery which the fancy associates with the New World, as so peculiarly her own: her wide-spread streams—interminable forests and foaming cataracts . . .[16]

By 1835 fewer and fewer people were using the term *New World* in that old-fashioned way, and the retrograde idioms that had served Irving so well in 1820 are resplendent enough here to be a bit fusty. Nevertheless, for all its dull predictability, Latrobe's prose is as "correct" as respectable critics wanted.

Diction was the aspect of language that endlessly fascinated the tastemakers. The Philadelphian Mathew Carey wrote a droll review of one London publication, James Leslie's *Dictionary of Synonymous Words and Technical Terms in the English Language,* a book which he thought exceeded "all the ravings of any former lexicographer." He listed some examples for *agitate* ("to bandy, to betoss, to conquassate") and a few other items, and for his finest example reproduced one full entry:

any appeal to a mass audience. *The Cambridge History of American Literature: Vol. 2, Prose Writing 1820–1865*, ed. Sacvan Bercovitch (New York: Cambridge University Press, 1995), 52.

15. Review of *Bracebridge Hall,* in *North American Review* 15 (1822): 212.

16. Charles Joseph Latrobe, *The Rambler in North America* (London, 1835), 1:6.

Beat: to pommel, to bang, to sugillate, to thwack, to trounce, to vanquish, to vapulate, to repercuss, to buffet, to curry, to firk, to fease or feaze, to lamm, to bray, to drule, to baste, to batter, to maul, to nubble, to belabour, to bump, to cane.[17]

Carey may have been amused, but such lexicographic ravings constituted a kind of ur-Roget for aspiring respectables in America.

A newspaper editor in Vicksburg, outraged at a fire that threatened to destroy most of the city, thundered his vituperation at the unknown arsonist as a "sneaking, savage, sanguine, scorbustic, scraggy, scrofulous, scurrilous, shameless, sinister, slouchy, slavish, slinking, slovenly, sordid, skulky, soulless, slubberede gullion." Even Johnson Jones Hooper found the incantatory catalog useful when, as editor of the *Montgomery Mail,* he exploded in exasperation over the stream of poetic effusions submitted for publication: "The toad harvest of Egypt, in old Pharaoh's time, were a blessing compared with our reams of diabolical, discordant, whining, snuffling, longlegged, shortlegged, hamelegged and lamlegged, nonsensical rhymings and grating, halting, bald, rhythmless, senseless and very blank verse!"[18]

Newly discovered synonyms and arcane professional terms encouraged a weakness for windy phrasing, almost guaranteeing circumlocution as normative for genteel style. Moreover, because of a history of tolerance for regional speech variations, especially colloquialisms and slang, some citizens appreciated oddities of diction whatever the source.

The phenomenon flourished from the other direction as well. The most celebrated users of backwoods English seized upon the logorrhea of their social betters to forge a distinctive humor that simultaneously poked fun at their pretentiousness and reveled in their excesses. The American sculptor Horatio Greenough, newly arrived in Italy for further study, wrote to Washington Allston in 1828: "I have many acquaintance among the first conversaziones of artists and dillettanti and long to shew them how nobly *we American apples swim.*"[19] The young artist's diction is a kind of capsule of permissible (and permissive) levels of language that flourished in antebellum America despite the campaigns to regularize usage,

17. *Port Folio,* 4th ser., 15 (1823): 372–73.
18. *Vicksburg Weekly Whig,* January 19, 1848, quoted in Carey Hearn, "Fire Control in Antebellum Mississippi," *Journal of Mississippi History* 40 (1978): 322; Hooper quoted in Rhoda Coleman Ellison, *Early Alabama Publications: A Study in Literary Interests* (University: University of Alabama Press, 1947), 39.
19. *Letters of Horatio Greenough, American Sculptor,* ed. Nathalia Wright (Madison: University of Wisconsin Press, 1972), 20.

spelling, and pronunciation. When patricians incorporated dialectal idioms in their discourse and backwoodsmen aped the bloated indulgences of genteel speakers in their harangues, the result was a tonal discordance that offended purists. By the time of the humorists, however, it was a stylistic commonplace.

By the mid-1830s the problem of transgressive diction and speech patterns was not an idiosyncratic novelty. For a century "deviant" English had been analyzed, lamented, scorned, and exploited by America's intellectual elite. Frontier vernacular was, if anything, too well known; it was an expected feature for tourists who ventured into the nooks and fastnesses of the nation's interior for amateur but edifying research. One American linguist, William Whitney, actually approved broadening the definitions of words: the "customary office" of a word, he declared, should not be constrictive but should cover "a territory . . . that is irregular, heterogeneous, and variable." The question was what deviant language and its inevitable identification with social class meant for the larger national purpose. On the one hand, it signaled the vitality and enterprise of the pioneering spirit; on the other, it delayed the agenda to make American language, however different from British, the vehicle for a culture equal to its origins.[20]

The Southwest humorists, however, had no dog in that fight.

If Longstreet, Thorpe, and Hooper were, as a matter of course, agents of mainstream culture, they yet had no comprehensive program to defend, redefine, or promote. They were readers and writers; they practiced their professions; they were party men who supported political candidates and sometimes held public office themselves. But there were no Coopers or Whitmans among them to articulate the future of American language and literature. By their own choice, their kind of writing was of marginal significance to any national agenda that would either repress or unleash deviant language. Their immersion in the issues of written and spoken English had an immediate and specific purpose: to convey the characteristics of a vast population by particularizing the regional in their habits, dress, and (especially) speech. What their humorous texts revealed was the vitality, not the threat, of dissonant voices. The pages of Porter's *Spirit of the Times* were no longer contested sites. An educated elite continued to write respectable prose, but the Jacksonian era expanded the boundaries of permissible English usage to incorporate, and

20. Whitney quoted in Gustafson, *Representative Words,* 27. By the humorists' time, mainstream style often featured "a slangy vocabulary . . . nestled inside a refined syntax." Cmiel, *Democratic Eloquence,* 60.

to alert the ear to, the rhythms of colloquial speech. Dr. Daniel Drake told a college literary society in 1834 that because of migration "new and strange forms" had been added to the "great reservoir of spoken language," which in turn had been "transferred to our literature, and widely disseminated."[21] Respectable style absorbed some of the virtues of the common styles—mostly an increased looseness and directness, which show up in the rhythms of such canonical figures as Emerson, Thoreau, and Melville.

The program to make American English respectable was always one of half measures and ambivalences, since the revolutionary fervor to create a language of national expressiveness was just as strong and lasted longer. While they rejected nonce words and neologisms, the traditionalists were powerless to halt the proliferation of barbarisms in the mother tongue. From the time of Cooper and Irving, it was clear that American writing had diverged from its British models, although the common language, with only a few adjustments, remained the sturdy instrument it had been a half-century earlier. Dr. Drake predicted that the American version of English, though "inferior in refinement," would gradually become "superior in force, variety, and freshness, to the language of the mother country." Although he was extraordinarily effective in rendering frontier dialects, William Gilmore Simms usually linked deviant tongues not to variety and freshness but to violence and anarchy.[22] In the end, what remained conservative was the system of grammar and syntax. What flourished with republican gusto was a diction of rich diversity that usually originated in the specifics of landscapes, occupations, and local history, not to mention the Anglo mangling of words and phrases picked up from Native Americans.

Even Irving, after ending his seventeen-year exile from the United States, turned increasingly to the distinctive vocabulary that his conservative allies so deplored. In his three frontier works—*A Tour on the Prairies* (1835), *Astoria* (1836), and *The Adventures of Captain Bonneville* (1837)—he attempted to acknowledge all the new words he heard in the West, even when they sat oddly in the context of his gentlemanly fluency. Drawing the reader's attention to this renegade diction was a set of fairly obvious

21. Daniel Drake, *Discourse on the History, Character, and Prospects of the West* (1834; reprint, ed. Perry Miller, Gainesville, FL: Scholars' Facsimiles & Reprints, 1955), 29.
22. Ibid.; David W. Newton, "Voices along the Border: Language and the Southern Frontier in *Guy Rivers: A Tale of Georgia*," in *William Gilmore Simms and the American Frontier*, ed. John Caldwell Guilds and Caroline Collins (Athens: University of Georgia Press, 1997), 118–44.

devices: enclosing the terms in quotation marks, setting them in italics, or glossing them with explanations or synonyms taken from standard English. Occasionally Irving inserted brief discourses on expressions he found particularly interesting (*hired trapper,* say, or *pork-eater*). As one scholar has pointed out, Irving was conceding, if not validating, the new status of American language that was still evolving naturally from the parent stock.[23] Furthermore, he was doing so in the face of a harshly disapproving Cooper, his fellow New Yorker, whose dialectal quotations from mercantile and lower-class characters in his fiction are (as we have seen in Chapter 3) laced with scorn.

Irving's frontier writing appeared simultaneously with the first wave of humorous sketches from the Southwest: Crockett's *Narrative* (1834) and Longstreet's *Georgia Scenes* (1835). The migrating hordes that filled up former Indian lands in the lower South were extending pell-mell into the plains, mountains, and deserts of the West. For Americans on the move, the same yeasty mix of races, classes, and occupations that marked their itinerant progress also defined a context of converging linguistic levels in which dissimilar speakers absorbed each other's diction and rhythms. In Southwest humor the prestige English most approved for literate citizens promised a refinement that was simultaneously sought and scorned. Like the material signs of antebellum success in the Mississippi Valley (grander houses, trips abroad, or annual treks to White Sulphur Springs), the cultivation of a fashionable style of both writing and speaking was one measure of the shift from *striving* to *achievement.*

The rural environment that affected even cities, however, ensured an uneasy, and often not very compliant, accommodation to a national style. As one historian puts it, "New residents from the rural South who settled in urban areas generally did not become citified; they countrified the towns."[24] Even wealthy planters resisted the kind of polish and seemliness adopted by their northern counterparts along the Hudson River and by eastern nabobs eager to shed the residual smell of animal skins or the grime of railroad yards. Kinship lines and sparsely settled geography conspired naturally to soften the more conspicuous marks of class difference. Although the speech of the successful, especially in the 1850s, inclined toward the gassy and orotund, shared blood and shared culture (a common fondness for hunting, loafing, riding, storytelling, and being so-

23. Wayne R. Kime, "Washington Irving and Frontier Speech," *American Speech* 42 (1967): 5–18.

24. Grady McWhiney, *Cracker Culture: Celtic Ways in the Old South* (Tuscaloosa: University of Alabama Press, 1988), 251–52.

ciable) made the language of the slave owner and the yeoman more alike than different. Except among the most self-confident, elevation in language, like elevation in class, was a goal only gingerly embraced.[25]

As we might expect, elevation is in short supply in Crockett's autobiography. As we shall see, that text is essentially Franklinesque, except that its plain style is self-consciously enhanced by kinetic mountain vernacular. Though freed of the restraints of correctness, it is the lingo of a temperament that never makes too much of the specialized words and turns of phrase that are the author's by reputation. Crockett (or his savvy collaborator, Thomas Chilton) demonstrates early on how a truly vernacular idiom can be used for sustained narrative. Longstreet, unlike Crockett, was no autodidact. As a lawyer, he was fully conscious of the stilted homogeneity of respectable style, which was rich in Latinate forms, literary allusion and quotation, foreign phrases, and complex syntax—an elaborate elitist norm in the post-Revolutionary era that nourished him. As a writer, however, he took some pains to make his two narrators, Hall and Baldwin, only minimally genteel. They write pretentiously only when their creator subjects them to mockery.

Although the prose in *Georgia Scenes* reflects its author's education and rank, it is familiar as well as correct. Its forthright style betrays its models: Addison's essays and Irving's sketches. One of Longstreet's narrators (Baldwin) pays homage to Crayonesque grace and whimsy in "The Dance" and "The 'Charming Creature' as a Wife"; the other (Hall) chooses subjects relevant to outdoor pursuits, such as horse-swapping, horse racing, and fights. But a gentlemanly tact, inflected with the moral imperatives of common sense, dominates all the sketches, even when Hall recounts the conversation of two "industrious, honest, sensible" farmers who find themselves drunk in town. Like the prairie-touring Irving, Longstreet's spokesmen use conventional orthographical marks to distance themselves from the speech of the uneducated. Longstreet even follows Irving in explaining his interest in non-genteel subjects. In his preface Longstreet announces that the sketches were written "rather in the hope that chance would bring them to light when time would give them an interest, than in the belief that they would afford any interest to the readers of the present

25. It can be argued that a fully achieved southern version of respectable style had to wait for the generation that came of age after Reconstruction, which produced the graceful, elegiac prose of, for instance, William Alexander Percy's *Lanterns on the Levee* (1941). Scott Romine, "The Aesthetics of Community: William Alexander Percy's *Lanterns on the Levee*," chap. 3 in *The Narrative Forms of Southern Community* (Baton Rouge: Louisiana State University Press, 1999).

day" (*GS*, 3–4). (The trouble with this explanation is not circumlocution but ordinary wordiness—one stylistic hint that Longstreet was not being entirely candid about his expectations for the book.) A clearer statement of his "aim" appears in his 1836 letter to T. H. White: to fill in a "chasm in history which has always been overlooked—the manners, customs, amusements, wit, dialect" as they strike "an ear and eye witness of them." If the real purpose of *Georgia Scenes* was to document and thus preserve for posterity contemporary manners, it is no more ingenuous than Irving's announced program to traffic in the crudities of ungenteel life in order to fix in words "a state of things fast passing into oblivion."[26]

One of the premises of the expected homogenization of regional dialects was that pockets of extreme difference would empty out into the mainstream in the course of cultural and economic progress. It was one thing to express such sanguine hopes for the future, however, and quite another to consider marginal groups in far-flung regions as appropriate matter for literature. To become nascent anthropologists was one way for middle-class scribes to justify their interest in backward cultures. Recording for posterity the ways of life of yeoman tribes before they vanished into the dominant culture was an acceptable project, even praiseworthy. For an imaginative writer to present himself as a social historian has never been an absurd tack, even in the nineteenth century, though modern readers are tempted to see that motive among the humorists as merely a maneuver that allowed respectable men to indulge themselves in what really attracted them: the nonrespectable in all its vernacular glory.

That may well have been the case. But what equally attracted Longstreet was the affectation of villagers who grotesquely imitated what they considered fashionable speech and manners. Skewering genteel airs, often with goodly injections of refined words and phrases, had its own history in the satiric tradition; but quoting (and thus crediting) the crudities of the unwashed democracy ran counter to the educative role of American linguistic missionaries. Longstreet probed the comic inevitabilities of a nation coming to terms with the modern. Negotiating the snares of approved speech became one important literary strategy for exploring the growing pains of country people adjusting to the values of sophistication that an age of expansion demanded.

---

26. Letter quoted in David Rachels, introduction to *Augustus Baldwin Longstreet's Georgia Scenes Completed: A Scholarly Text* (Athens: University of Georgia Press, 1998), xlviii; Kime, "Washington Irving," 9.

Although it is considerably more, *Georgia Scenes* is a document preserving some of those growing pains in one specific place. Neither the
rustics (who unselfconsciously express themselves in colloquial idioms)
nor the ambitious villagers (who try to rise above them) exhaust the
demographic range even of Georgia in "the first half century of the Republic." The remaining literate population presumably had so sufficiently mastered respectable English that it was outside Longstreet's
interest. As lawyer, preacher, and educator, the author learned to trim
his own language of the more ponderous effects of correct usage. Most
literate Americans of his time, however, held what now seems an exaggerated deference to stylistic authority, the norms promoted by the
schools and the eastern models of gentility. The enormous popularity
of the McGuffey readers is one measure of the pedagogical efforts toward standardization.[27] Moreover, warnings against vulgarity, profan-
ity, and obscenity came not merely from prudes. Even in their private
moments, as we see in diaries and correspondence, ordinary men and
women honored the strictures laid down in grammars, readers, and
spelling books. The most thorough study of antebellum private writing
reveals that restraint, piety, and decorum dominated American sensibilities, and these values extended notably to matters linking speech
and behavior.[28] Seen in the light of his general conservatism, Longstreet's supple traversal of nonstandard speech and his comfortable,
down-home version of respectable style make his first book an even
greater accomplishment than it is often taken to be.

In the humor the language of respectability prospers in a circle of genial mockery. The faux-bohemian William T. Porter liked to envelop his
dapper persona in a style of indirection, euphemism, and irony; the educated authors forged their own versions of macaronic formality. Accurate
and lightly ornate, the style was popular. Inflated and smart, versions of
it frequently showed up in chaffing correspondence among young well-
to-do gentlemen. A Savannah resident wrote to his sister in 1837 on recent
Independence Day events: "several Gentlemen have been consumed by
that glorious combustion which kindles from the thirsty heat of Summer

27. Stories in the readers were meant to be read aloud, and "remarks" for each selection focused on mispronunciations and dialectal forms that predominated in most
sections of the country: "Do not say . . . *fea-ters* nor *feat-tschurs* for *feat-yres*." This example is drawn from the *New Fifth Eclectic Reader* (1857), quoted in David Brion
Davis, *Antebellum American Culture: An Interpretive Anthology* (Lexington, MA: D. C.
Heath, 1979), 56.
28. Lewis O. Saum, *The Popular Mood of Pre–Civil War America* (Westport, CT: Greenwood, 1980).

and the frozen Julips of the City Hotel. One celebrated the Fourth by taking his Leap on that day. Hugh Rose is dead. a Martyr to the potent mixture of strong grog and conjugal felicity."[29] The yeoman figures, whose interaction with narrators frequently triggers the comic anecdotes, are out to compete any way they can, and one way they find amusing is through their own linguistic commentary on the style of respectable gentlemen. The narrators know that the mock inflation of some of the vernacular storytellers is merely another kind of comic deflation. Despite the deadpan razzing of such parodic expressions as *exflunctified* and *topliftical,* innocent readers usually perceived such extravagances as the natural diction of the unlearned. As travelers constantly told them, backwoodsmen enjoyed countrified exaggeration in everything they did.

ii.

To write from a people, is to write a people—to make them live—to endow them with a life and a name—to preserve them with a history forever.

—William Gilmore Simms

The ambition of Longstreet's generation of humorists pales when set alongside the professional agenda of William Gilmore Simms, who envisioned his career-long body of writing as nothing less than the inscribing of nearly a century of southern civilization in all its social and topographical diversity.[30] Without much planning, however, the humorists also went about their objective to "write a people." Like Noland's Giles Scroggins of Devil's Fork, who classifies social types, we have always made sense of the "frontier" authors by discriminating them from our canonical ones. It still pleases us to call these authors *amateurs* and their products *humor* of the Old Southwest, even if the terms fail to adequately describe our actual reading experience. The usefulness of such categories is provisional and always subject to second thoughts.

For the humorist authors, of course, the primary mission in writing a people was to give voice to a population that had *only* a voice: the voluble quasi-literates they had occasion to mingle with every day. Although

29. William Waring, Waring Family Correspondence, Georgia Historical Society, Savannah.

30. William Gilmore Simms, *Views and Reviews in American Literature, History, and Fiction,* ed. C. Hugh Holman (Cambridge, MA: Harvard University Press, 1962), 12.

the vast ranks of yeomanry were already, as it were, *speaking* a people, it required an educated ear, eye, and hand to translate their energetic oral culture into something more permanent. The authors presented themselves as authorities at that task, despite sometimes modest demurrers; but just as their impressions were only as good as the organs that recorded the scene, so the quality of transmission was only as good as their individual sensibilities and skills. Most of the humorists that we continue to read with pleasure performed their job from an orientation that was neither historical nor poetic in an overt sense, yet they managed to lend their sketches enough solidity and imaginative power to make their best efforts not merely permanent, but memorable. It is clear that all these writers—even those who, like Baldwin and Thorpe, resisted any deep immersion in the slang and colloquialisms of backwoods speakers—were not only fascinated with dialects not their own; they *liked* them.[31]

If we modern readers most admire the humorists in proportion to their flair for articulating backwoods talk, it is yet well to remember that their pieces usually offer more than that. They may occasionally fret over their effectiveness in approximating the talk they are trying to reproduce, but they never apologize for their own presence in sketches involving exchanges among figures both like and unlike themselves. They take for granted their right to direct, control, and shade each piece as it develops. Even in heavily monological texts that focus on particularized dialects, such as *Sut Lovingood's Yarns* and the letters of Major Jones and Pete Whetstone, the author never quite disappears from the page. Neither Harris, Thompson, nor Noland spurns authorial agency. With varying degrees of comfort, the humorists in general wrote as the nineteenth-century writers they were. What that means in formal terms is that they followed the convention of registering a consciousness in the scenes they dramatized, even in those (or especially those) dominated by actors and speakers more colorful than they.

Critics of antebellum southern humor have generally favored, over all the forms, the frame tale, in which an educated narrator, standing in for the author, prepares the context for an internal storyteller whose idioms then flourish in splendid contrast to his own. Yet ordinary readers with

31. Although Thorpe, the most ambitious of the writers and the most Irvingesque in style, did not hesitate to quote backwoods vernacular when sketching native characters, he relied more on indirect speech and descriptions of the unspoiled country that he associated with such figures. The essay was his most congenial form, as it was for Baldwin, who excelled in marshaling an engaged, ironic perspective in personal essays on his time and place. Few pieces in *Flush Times* depend on comic vernacular.

little interest in theories of class or gender also tend to gravitate to the frame tale, emphatically declaring the humorous authors humorous only by virtue of their standing aside and allowing vernacular speakers room to speak. The authors are sometimes viewed as too "stuffy" to be interesting when they write "as themselves." True, it was easy for the educated narrator to elevate his standard register with fancy diction, indirection, and inverted syntax. He knew, along with the tastemakers, that a quoted scrap of verse or an italicized (and untranslated) foreign phrase contributed to the effect of a well-mannered prose. Even if dialect no longer stands out quite as the deviancy that nineteenth-century readers experienced it as, some modern readers of the humor find the normative level of ordinary, educated discourse pretentious by contrast. The humorists would have been familiar with the embellishments that Irving, Cooper, Paulding, and Simms relied on as a matter of course. An even heavier diet of enriched elegance was readily available in the work of Edgar Allan Poe, E. D. E. N. Southworth, and such professional dilettantes as N. P. Willis, Bayard Taylor, and "Ik Marvel." But the fact is that few of the humorous authors wrote pretentious English, and when they did it was usually a calculated lapse intended to mock ornamental prose style itself. They may sometimes have been taken by the word "splendiferous," but they refrained from writing splendiferous prose.

When the authors wrote "as themselves," their prose was generally fluent and measured, innocent of the ornamental flourish that calls attention to itself. Even when they fell into allusive asides, in the fashion that all their contemporaries thought appropriate, they were rarely pedantic. Indeed, at least one strain of the vernacular storyteller's yarn surpasses any of the educated narrator's effects. Beginning with Ham Jones in "Cousin Sally Dilliard" and culminating in Simon Wheeler in Twain's "Jim Smiley and His Jumping Frog," this is the humor of verbal maundering, amplified by circumlocutions, repetitions, digressions, deferrals, and rural euphemisms. By comparison, the narrators write a utilitarian and unvarnished English.

If there is a parallel in the prose of the author-narrators, it occurs not in their ordinary personal styles but in moments of self-indulgence when they inject passages of stylistic wit into their sketches. When W. C. Hall introduces Mike Hooter, his Mississippi backwoodsman, he indulges in a verbal habit that celebrants once reserved for legendary heroes:

> In order that the world may not remain in darkness as to his doings . . . and fearing lest there may be no one who entertains for him that particularly

warm regard which animates us towards him, we have thought it incumbent on us in evidence of our attachment for the reverend hero, to jot down an incident that lingers in our memory respecting him—bequeathing it as a rich legacy to remotest time. (Cohen, 364)

In his mock campaign biography of Simon Suggs, Johnson Jones Hooper justifies the "pious task of commemorating" the life of a "living worthy" whose acts and character are not constrained "by the folds of their cerements" (*SS*, 7). When Kittrell Warren introduces his army straggler, he begins by wishing he could do so "in a fashionable manner," the hero "sumptuously appareled, reclining gracefully upon a magnificent ottoman":

I would have him a grand looking character. Intellect should beam from his lustrous eye, and nobleness peep forth from every lineament of his features. . . . Sweet breezes—excuse me,—delightful zephyrs, and pleasant aromas should woo him. I would have the sun retreating in good order into the fortress of night, followed by a Regiment of clouds and leaving "Sentinel Stars" under command of the Moon, as officeress of the guard to hold the position he was excavating. (*AS*, 5)

Studded with bemused borrowings from epics and mock epics, these are examples of refinements and images codified in prior texts and traditions, but woefully inappropriate for present contexts. The technique may not amuse us in the same way it amused contemporary readers, but it is the result of the authors' deliberation, not an overvaluation of what constituted proper style.

The humorists also made occasional use of gentlemanly banter, a register familiar to readers of the *Spirit of the Times.* In his editorial commentaries, William T. Porter set the tone for his contributors by projecting a patrician authority of insouciance—an urbane mode made popular by Irving and Paulding in *Salmagundi.* Americanizing the New Yorkers' eighteenth-century models, the Knickerbocker manner emphasized the artifice of the eccentric man-about-town, the ersatz rebel of fashionable society.[32] That display of wit, a sustained form of benign impersonation, became an important device for Henry Clay Lewis. As a last-year resident soon to seek his own medical practice, Madison Tensas describes

32. For several years "Salmagundi" was the title of a regular column in *Spirit of the Times,* but the wry, coy, mock-pompous style that Porter favored never became the stylistic norm for the more substantial humorists.

the resolve with which he and his fellow students are putting aside their sportive antics:

> No longer the sweet vision of midnight oyster-suppers illumined the mental horizon, obscured by the listening to of six long lectures daily. No longer at the "wee short hours ayant the twal" was our Gannymede summoned to evoke the spirit of the whiskey jug. No longer musingly reclining did we watch the airy genii of the best cigar, borne up heavenward on the curling chariots of their consuming earthly tabernacles. No longer—pshaw! to comprise the whole, we were studying for our degrees. (*SD*, 114)

Even an account of a simple hunt in the neighboring woods or a trip to the local racetrack conventionally included a mock nod to what generally passed as fine writing. It bespoke learning, liberal-hearted leisure, social position, and amiability—all assumed lightly, confirming the public image of the author as knowledgeable, educated, and firmly in control of both his life and pen. The gentlemanly amateur produced a prose readily identifiable as elitist, and by drawing attention to the most conspicuous rhetorical features that marked its approved status, he announced his detachment from and superiority to it. He put himself in the game by taking himself out of it. In "The Indefatigable Bear-Hunter," Lewis emphasizes a slightly different aspect of familiar style—its love of personification and related tropes, which he spins out into absurdity: "The sun, in despair at the stern necessity which compelled him to yield up his tender offspring, day, to the gloomy grave of darkness, had stretched forth his long arms, and, with the tenacity of a drowning man clinging to a straw, had clutched the tender whispering straw-like topmost branches of the trees—in other words it was near sunset" (*SD*, 168). Such instances remind the reader of how tedious and indulgent the show-off can be when he forgoes an economic plain style. The mockery itself was as conventionalized a mode as the lofty style it fed on; at some point in their writing, it was adopted by nearly every one of the Southwest humorists.[33]

To make too much of the contrast between proper English and its deviances is to affirm the notion of linguistic imperialism, in which gentleman authors overcompensate for the dialectal vulgarity of their subjects

33. Though they refrained from its excesses, the humorists had not forgotten the prevalent taste in fashionable writing two decades earlier—a florescence of what one Irving scholar, quoting William Wirt, has called "gaudy styles staggering under a 'gorgeous load of ornaments.'" William L. Hedges, *Washington Irving: An American Study, 1802–1832* (Baltimore: Johns Hopkins University Press, 1965), 29.

by heightening their natural level (by right of birth or training) into a bloated style that, in turn, heightens their privileged status. This is the sentiment behind the theory of the *cordon sanitaire*, as we have seen. Whenever the humor incorporates both a narrator and a storyteller, the narrative interest centers on the happenstance convergence of alternate levels of English in the same physical space, a kind of linguistic counterpoint to social mingling. Another kind of linguistic dynamic is at work in sketches of unmediated dialect (letters to the editor) and in pieces based on the games of professional animals at play (some of the chapters of Baldwin, Lewis, and Sol Smith.)

Among the humorists, it is T. B. Thorpe who follows most closely the protocols of conservative tastemakers, but even his tailored prose is rarely ponderous. In his topographical pieces ("Concordia Lake," "Primitive Forests of the Mississippi") and those on native fauna ("Opossums and 'Possum Hunting," "The American Wild Cat"), Thorpe manages to incorporate his affective responses to nature in mostly unadorned ways. When he chooses to adorn, however, the stylistic traits are perfunctorily drawn from conventions common to moral and sentimental aesthetics: describing the "great temple of nature" in terms of Salvator Rosa, chiaroscuro, the Pillars of Hercules, and St. Peter's Cathedral; relying heavily on locutions designed to suggest the picturesque (*grandeur, solitude, fearful admiration, picturesque display*); and carelessly using diction already exhausted by dignity (*anon, yea, o'er, wearied limbs, airy abode*). Such old-fashioned constructions are just intrusive enough to remind us that, overall, Thorpe is more felicitous than many of his models. The passive contemplation of natural history cannot totally avoid static scene-painting, and all of Thorpe's sketches in this mode emphasize informational accuracy over affective sensibility. Yet anchored to such human activities as hunting and fishing, they are, like the humorous pieces, often enlivened by Thorpe's obvious admiration for the expressive language of the backcountry.

We should remember, too, that with the exception of Baldwin, Thorpe was the least inclined of all the writers to think of himself as a humorist. Though his pursuit of a career was somewhat more desultory than we expect of our canonical authors, he presented himself not as a humorous author, but as an *author*. Even Porter, who chose "The Big Bear of Arkansas" as the opening piece for his first *Spirit of the Times* anthology in 1845, wrote to his publishers that the famous yarn "hardly gives one an idea of what [Thorpe] has done or is capable of. . . . Some of his sketches of *scenery*

. . . are equal to anything in the language." The editor's comment followed the author's own priorities. In the summer of 1845, as he was assembling materials for *Mysteries of the Backwoods,* Thorpe wrote Carey & Hart: "My descriptions extend over every department, prairies, swamps, scenes in the Mississippi, scenes inland, with the rural sports peculiar to the South West" (*TBT,* 45–46).

Whatever the topics chosen, Thorpe's compositional emphasis was not on the contrast between gentlemanly discourse and backcountry idioms; he consciously strove to integrate linguistic levels. In the author's first sketch (and his favorite), "Tom Owen, the Bee-Hunter" (1839), his efforts are often awkward. Before introducing his bee hunter in an odd mix of bumptious rural lingo and Leatherstocking seriousness, Thorpe establishes the circumstances with casual clichés of gentility: the narrator has been staying at a friend's mansion "to drown dull care and court the roseate hue of health" (*TBT,* 83). Such reliance upon the hand-me-down is more sleekly functional in the best of Thorpe's comic sketches: "A Piano in Arkansas," "The Last from 'Arkansaw,'" "The Way Americans Go Down Hill," and especially "Letters from the Far West."

What we see in such pieces is stylistic accommodation to the region and character they depict. In its very engagement with vernacular culture, Thorpe's controlling authorial style loses some of the legacy of ornate propriety to which most of his mainstream contemporaries felt some obligation. In the most successful integration of levels, the humorists are no longer orthographically circumspect in isolating words that offend linguistic canons. Sol Smith's "The Consolate Widow," for example, opens: "Between Caheba Swamp and Lime Creek, in the 'Nation,' we saw considerable of a crowd gathered near a drinking-house, most of them seated and smoking" (Cohen, 73). The backwoods locution has been silently absorbed into the author's own customary level.

The philologists' fear of "leveling," in which different registers mingled in the same text, was understandable: vernacular always degrades superior style. After the Civil War, when dialect writing became fashionable, the improprieties that threatened the standards of literary civilization were slang, barbarisms (variously defined), solecisms, and other low-status forms. But standard discourse was always susceptible to contamination by linguistic otherness. W. D. Howells, commenting on dialect "heard everywhere," observed that Americans continued to be "an intensely decentered people in our letters as well as in our politics." One critic has suggested that Twain's extravagant claim in his explanatory note to *Huckleberry Finn*—that he has faithfully discriminated among all the dialects heard in Missouri in the 1840s—is a burlesque of the literary rage for dialect writing in postbellum America. A British traveler, comparing uses of dialect in the United Kingdom and the United States before the Civil War, declared that dialects in America were not confined to particular locales, but were "equally distributed" among all classes and regions: "The senate or the boudoir is no more sacred from their intrusions than the farm-house or the tavern."[34] That readers in our time should consider the standard received English of Thorpe (or any other of the humorist authors) a tool of repression is, ironically, one mark of the triumph of familiar style in ordinary discourse today.

Although the rhythms and local diction of the backcountry softened the authors' formal constructions by giving their educated style a suppleness it would not otherwise have had, that style was also complicated by the specialty jargons that blossomed in the cultural instability of the Southwest. The doctors and lawyers who penned humorous sketches were especially addicted to professional terms and locutions, festooning their prose with arcane murkiness. Some of the genres of professional expertise—lawyers' briefs, doctors' diagnoses, preachers' homilies—were convenient and conspicuous rhetorics of composition that even strong stylists like Lewis and Baldwin could not resist flaunting. Argot-sprinkled texts served the authors' need for distinction even as they evaded comprehension.

Other clusters of specialty grammars contributed to variable and diffuse notions of usage. The casual citation of tropes, adages, analogies, and clichés—drawn helter-skelter from surveyors' reports, merchants' account books, tourists' scene-painting, speculators' brochures, old women's country counsels, and politicians' speeches—suggests a kind of floating hybridism of prose styles. Because each of the humorous authors, including the gloom-infected Lewis, tended to articulate a self that was amiable and versatile, their rhetorical habits were eminently adaptable. Far from writing a fussy, stilted prose that honored the precepts of purists, they accommodated their styles as readily as their lives to the variable democracy of their time and place.

Because of the large number of lawyers in the antebellum South, the language of the bench and bar exerted more influence on prose style than that of any other profession; and because the law had enjoyed a long dominance in Virginia, the Tidewater style, with its learned bombast and filigreed images, became the magisterial norm as it spread quickly with the

34. Jones, *Strange Talk*, 29 (quoting Howells), 3, 25–26.

surplus talent that moved south and west. Its effect on half-educated imitators was powerful—and funny to those willing to be amused. Charles Latrobe, exasperated at the rhetorical ineptness of rural practitioners, ridiculed the "big words meaning little, and out of place" in courtroom arguments that led meanderingly to "bathos—digressions without end." This fastidious writer never quite understood the forensic calculation behind such performances.[35] Both the ineptness and the calculation contributed to a rich comic vein that Baldwin mined with great success. Sensitive to the comic potentialities of lawyerly conduct and language, and operating in a frontier milieu of physicality and illiteracy, most of the lawyer-authors became expert in the patronizing imitation of backwoodsmen engaged in litigation. But they also plunged beyond the droll juxtaposition of specialized language in the mouths of illiterates to an implicit critique of the very discourse they habitually used themselves. This disposition for linguistic self-scrutiny softened what the missionary-minded regarded as the civilizing role of an educated elite. At the very least, it made the lawyer-authors more willing to traffic in linguistic deviance than were dictionary-makers and pedagogues. With that openness to backwoods argot came an openness to the deviance of the backwoodsman himself. Although the hierarchical impulse is never far from the surface of the narrator's enclosing discourse, it rarely interferes with his amiable good nature and curiosity.

One of the minor success stories that *Flush Times* celebrates is the victory in the courtroom of common sense and plain speech over the oratorical rotundities carried from the older states. Baldwin makes that stylistic outcome seem inevitable—a natural result of near-chaos in the judiciary. The legal profession in the Old Southwest, he writes, was awash in defective land titles, "universal indebtedness," disputed partnerships, claims and contracts that had to be reconstructed. And since the exigencies of the times required the law to be an "every-day, practical, common-place, business-like affair," the necessary mode of the profession had to be "[r]eadiness, precision, plainness, pertinency, knowledge of law, and a short-hand method" of getting at and through a case (*FT*, 237, 242). In Baldwin's scenario the practical mode routed "flights of ambitious rhetoric," "vain repetitions," "mock sentimentality," and "tumid platitudes"—all the traits of "the old fogies" who had once orated safely behind their

35. Latrobe, *Rambler*, 2:67. Solemn travelers made an inept mess when they attempted to imitate such performances. See, for example, Lester B. Shippee, ed., *Bishop Whipple's Southern Diary, 1843–1844* (Minneapolis: University of Minnesota Press, 1937), 37, 39.

established reputations. Baldwin emphasizes the new legal style in a gallery of profiles both historical and fictional—modern men all, who had the quickness to adjust to a cultural moment when "every man knew a little and many a great deal" about law (*FT*, 228, 241–46).

In fact, however, that gallery includes a number of old-style performers who manage to overlay the "every-day" and "business-like" conduct of cases with elegant vituperation, florid elocution, and gross windbaggery: the slangwhanging Cave Burton, who "went in for gab"; S. S. Prentiss, whose "brilliant declamation" in court and flights of metaphor, "anecdote, ornament, eloquence and elocution" on the stump made him one of the most popular speakers in the antebellum South; Tom B. Devill, with a reputation as "the most 'LIBELLIOUS' tongue" in his district; and, most memorably, Caesar Kasm, a cranky Virginian known widely for being an "inveterate opponent of new laws, new books, new men" (*FT*, 153, 202–3, 279, 24). Veering between self-congratulation and self-satire, Baldwin describes his neophyte performance as opposing counsel in "My First Appearance at the Bar." He summarizes in one page his defense of a butcher accused of stealing hogs. In a rancorous cross-examination, Old Sar Kasm briskly proceeds to quote the savory rhetorical excesses of the inept "lawyerling." Familiar with all the "gymnastics of deportment," Kasm is a polite man, but his politeness, notes Baldwin, has a "frost-bitten air as if it had lain out over night and got the *rheumatics* before it came in" (*FT*, 23). A skillful but malicious eccentric who later dies of apoplexy while abusing someone else's client, Kasm is remembered by the next generation mostly for his nastiness.

Baldwin was not alone in making much of the superiority of the new forensics over the old style, with its Blackstone-studded cadences; indirect, allusive, euphemistic, and metaphoric flourishes were the aural signs of a pompous gentleman in or out of the courtroom.[36] In 1833 Thomas Hamilton declared that oratory was "less an art than an impulse," but that in America it became an accomplishment for "political aspirants." John Adams wrote William Wirt that though oratory "will always command admiration," it "deserves no great veneration." Wirt was prescient enough

---

36. Although stump oratory was already designated a "Southern fashion" by 1840, the most egregiously florid speakers became a stereotype only after the Civil War, when C. Alphonso Smith, an English professor, did his part for the Lost Cause movement by stumping the South to lecture on its "sacred and priceless" heritage. Robert G. Gunderson, *The Log Cabin Campaign* (Lexington: University of Kentucky Press, 1957), 162; Waldo W. Braden, "C. Alphonso Smith on 'Southern Oratory Before the War,'" *Southern Speech Journal* 36 (1970): 127–38; Waldo W. Braden, *The Oral Tradition in the South* (Baton Rouge: Louisiana State University Press, 1983), 7–8.

to see how orators' recondite manner cried out for a more relaxed, natural style. Warning a young lawyer friend against pomp, ostentation, and pedantry, Wirt wrote: "Teach these young Virginians, by your example, the insignificance of their affected swelling and *rotundification* of frothy sentences," adding: "I lost the best part of my life indulging the frolics of fancy,—and the consequence is, that it will take me all the rest of it to convince the world that I have common sense."[37] Political oratory was as vulnerable to satiric diminishment as pulpit oratory, as we see in Major Jones's Fourth of July speech, Cave Burton (who anticipated the bloated style of "Senator Claghorn" of radio fame), and several of Davy Crockett's campaign rivals.

One of the minor joys of *Flush Times* is how its very modern author encapsulates the cultural transition from a florid legal style to what he characterizes as a simpler style better designed for a country "just setting up." The very vulgarity of the new society, "standing knee-deep in exploded humbugs," was not a suitable environment for courtroom histrionics in which "demagoguism and flimsy perversions" bored onlookers and juries alike (*FT*, 243–44). Yet Baldwin fudges the historical record. It would take more than a sensible attorney general from Virginia and a cadre of vigorous "new men" to rout a histrionic habit that appealed to so many southerners. In the 1830s Harriet Martineau was distressed that schools continued to teach the cultivation of "declamatory accomplishment" as essential for men ambitious for distinction. They should instead, she thought, teach sound reasoning to counter the bad taste of insincere oratory, the palest "glory of an age gone by." Even Alexander Stephens, displaying more wit than he would later show as Confederate vice president, felt free enough in 1844 to poke fun at the splayed gravity of southern speechifying. In a letter to his younger brother, still a law student, Stephens sketched out a mock stump speech for fledglings to deliver: ". . . and the burthens of government press equally upon every nerve (you are fond of medical figures) of this vast and extended people. Our fathers themselves (then you'll wax eloquent) foresaw the necessity of making changes even in the Constitution itself . . . [because of] the power which it lodges in posterity of suiting it to their condition."[38] Stilted expression flourished as readily as frontier tall talk and was just as subject to comic chaffing.

37. [Thomas Hamilton], *Men and Manners in America* (1833; reprint, New York: A. M. Kelley, 1968), 2:93; John P. Kennedy, *Memoirs of the Life of William Wirt*, rev. ed. (Philadelphia, 1860), 2:71.

38. Harriet Martineau, *Retrospect of Western Travel* (1838; reprint, New York: Greenwood, 1969), 2:247–48; James D. Waddell, ed., *Biographical Sketch of Judge Linton Stephens* (Atlanta, 1877), 74–75.

Contemporaries generally thought border lingo grew out of wilderness conditions as spontaneously as "the luxuriant cane." The line between serious expression and the game of *putinon,* however, was as permeable as the cartographic frontier line itself. Most forms of expression were cultivated as canebrakes never were.

iii.

The body of Southwest humor includes an astonishing number of entries in which the author-narrator, mingling with his own kind and using the same (more or less) cultivated language, recounts anecdotes of intramural hoodwinking, practical jokes, and social gaffes. Yet by general agreement, how we think about this humor depends upon the author-narrators' focus on vernacular speakers. Their most vital energies are expended when they run with those who indulge low-status traditions in expressive language. At its most theatrical—the boasting exchanges of backcountry roarers—that means the rendering of a special language to characterize the more spectacular backwoodsmen in the South and West.

Realism of spokenness is usually linked to lingual accuracy, but the humorists rendered *approximations* of speech patterns so that the reader could "match" the look on the page with his previous experience of dialect (often in other texts). The tallest talk of this humor, the kind memorialized in accounts of roarer performances, refutes the argument that the humorists' rendition of colorful backcountry language is the first true evidence of American realism. There may be lingual accuracy in much of their recording of speech patterns, but bruiser rhetoric is not by intent or effect realistic. The flamboyant boasts, the metaphors, the five-dollar words that communicate power rather than precision all have little to do with the commonplace profiling of a time and place. Whether the authors' general use of dialects in the antebellum South was realistic is still a matter of debate, but the hyperbolic idioms of roarer types are irrelevant to that discussion. Some of the attempts at spokenness are clearly more realistic than others. Museum curators like to quote the late James Short of Colonial Williamsburg, who maintained that *believability* was what most people have in mind when they refer to *authenticity.*[39] If the authors' general way with levels of language not their own is one of their achievements,

39. Barbara G. Carson and Cary Carson, "Things Unspoken: Learning Social History from Artifacts," in *Ordinary People and Everyday Life: Perspectives on the New Social History,* ed. James B. Gardner and George Rollie Adams (Nashville: American Association for State and Local History, 1983), 188.

it may be that dialect-writing in the antebellum years should be judged by its believability. The humorists may not always have liked the speakers behind the eccentric talk (though internal evidence shows they usually did), but they enjoyed the talk well enough to make their transcriptions seem like the real thing. Theirs is a realism of *effect* that is more than the accuracy of a grammar phonetically reproduced.

When in one of his *Reveille* pieces, Richard S. Elliott alludes to a story "that looked very much like things overdone"; when Joseph Field's Judge Magraw remarks that a story about a bird "was a *leetle* too feathery to swallow"; and when a "live Sucker" dares to say that Jim Doggett's yarns about Arkansas fertility "smelt rather tall," the point in each case is *believability*. All these extravagant stories, however, meet skeptical ears because the language that relates them is extravagant—as of course it is meant to be in the logic of the tall tale. In the chemistry between teller and listener, successful performance is expected to be built on the twinned talents of lying and being credible, but in the internal dynamics of the tall tale, neither screamer oratory nor gaudy stretching has anything to do with realism as a gauge. All the humorists' exercises in vernacular forms require artifice and an audience willing to admire it. Consider the sounds represented in the following excerpts:

> You see I didn't like them sorter doins much, me, myself, I didn't, an' I al-l'ays ef ever I got er chance at Arch I'd let him down er button-hole er two. (Cohen, 365)

> "Don't tell *me* 'bout Fashun or Bosting." (*SD*, 43)

> "Well, Potter, he kep er feelin' up, an' feelin' an' er feelin' up, sorter easy like, an' toreckly he felt somethin' in his han'." (Cohen, 374)

> "[S]o if he does git over it, he never kin eat nothin'." (Cohen, 383)

> "[H]e pertend to be er preacher!—his preachin' ain't nuthin' but loud hollerin' no how!" (Cohen, 365)

> "[T]his here is a critercle time; the wild savage of the forest are beginnin' of a bloody, hostile war, which they're not a-goin' to spar nither age nor sek." (*SS*, 85)

> "Stay, I'll tell you who he married presently—Oh, stay! why I'll tell you who he married! He married old daddy Johny Hooer's da'ter, Mournin'." (*GS*, 134)

As these examples show, the humorists were never sticklers for orthographic consistency. The spelling of dialect forms, especially in contractions, prepositions, elided consonants, and other recurring units of speech, was never regularized. (Innovations in orthographic nuances would have to wait for later writers specializing in dialects.) Some of the authors' inconsistencies may reflect slight variations in different parts of the Southwest, but most of them were purely instrumental: spelling that approximated sounds heard was sufficient, and it varied according to the humorists' compositional circumstances. Some conventions did develop into a handful of recognizable, reusable patterns: phonetic indications of the schwa and other indeterminate vowels, simple repetitions to indicate mental processes, intensive repetitions to clarify attribution, italics used for tonal emphasis.

When we think of the humorists' prose that features backwoods characters, we tend to remember the most extravagant excesses, especially in the insults and challenges of yeoman hearties. Yet the majority of the sketches dealing with vernacular consists of speech patterns that depict human interaction, not confrontation. Most of the transcriptions are noticeably lacking in diction that swaggers, as if the highly wrought flashiness of peacock backwoodsmen has been redirected into domestic channels. Even when competitiveness and conflict are the occasion, the emphasis is not on language that is special and prepared but on language assumed to be customary and at hand. Above all, the humorists instinctively sacrificed the notational accuracy that phonetics might demand in favor of what has been called "the delivery conditions of vernacular discourse," which is to say, its *rhythm*—tonality and stress and the sequence of parts.[40] Henry James once referred to regional American dialects as "instinctive and irreflective."[41] Yet written approximations, as James himself demonstrated, are the fruit of much conscientious reflection. The humorists sought to capture something of that unstudied sound in a wide variety of forms that would feature, in their own constructed versions, a "natural" vernacular. That art should render nature, an irony common enough in literature, is not inevitably programmatic, nor is it, in these authors, politically stealthy.

Of all the structures the humorists tried, the frame format, as I suggested earlier, has most often been seen as a device to draw attention to

40. Jones, *Strange Talk*, 4. Mike Hooter, for example, is meant to be colorful in his "peculiar and expressive vernacular," but W. C. Hall actually highlights the *flow* of his speech more than his quaint idioms. "How Mike Hooter Came Very Near 'Wolloping' Arch Coony" (Cohen, 365).

41. A 1905 commencement address given at Bryn Mawr, "The Question of Our Speech" was widely assumed to be an attack on American language generally, but Leon Edel argued that James's target was the careless speaking style of American girls. *Henry James: The Master, 1901–1916* (Philadelphia: Lippincott, 1972), 302.

the gap separating gentlemen and commoners in the Old Southwest. In that reading the most dramatic gap is lingual—between cultivated mainstream English and a cruder deviant vernacular. To be sure, the virtuoso tongue featured in the frame tale is an attention-getter, both for the audience within the sketches and for modern scholars, but its prominence in the humor has been as exaggerated as its political symbolism. What we see in the frame tale—the speaker of respectable English meeting the dialectal speaker in a public space—is set up to conform to the social actualities of the new country. And what we hear in the ensuing stretches of vernacular, despite the sometimes creaky machinery that allows us to do so, is usually a persuasive character whose speech gives us insight into the personality, condition, and affective life of men and women different from the author-narrator. This form is arresting not because of the obvious differences between the spoken English of the principals, but because *the narrator gives over his space to the storyteller.* The formal structure is not a self-protective screen for the author—there is no sign that any of the authors felt the need for protection from the rabble—but an earnest of his interest in the variegated population in the geography he shares with all newcomers. Human interest trumps political and social bias.

Unlike the screamer performance (a species of rural baroque that gratifies through sheer ostentation), the frame tale typically allows dialectal speech to enter the pool of available languages. That talk may not be on some approved list, but, for all the anticipated homogenization to come, neither is it endangered. It achieves its distinction in the quieter sketches, not by decking out homespun idioms with riffs of florid cadenzas, but by releasing the rhythms of backwoods speech into credible discourse. As we have seen, Jim Doggett is not above bolstering his reputation with bits from the half-horse half-alligator lexicon, but his talk is made believable by his reversion to the unfussy, heartfelt, and (presumably) more natural narration of his experience with the Big Bear.

The mock-yokel letter to the editor is arguably the most common form of antebellum newspaper humor, and probably the oldest. Newspaper editors gathered anecdotes, character profiles, and bright, pun-filled, talk-of-the-town gossip as readily as hard news. Straddling news and fiction without apparent strain, contributors responded with a diverse mix of sketches: personal accounts of adventures with bears, panthers, and untamed hunters in the bush; narrations of crossroads and village life structured conventionally with summary and quotation; eyewitness reports of special events—horse races, gander pullings, and shooting contests (and the crowds they attracted), and of court days, militia musters, and patriotic parades (and the politicians they attracted). But the mock-yokel letter exploited the newspaper itself—as stimulus, model, and venue, medium and message alike, it coalesced in a flurry of country arcana laid out with misspellings made at a more creative level than most real quasi-literate readers were up to.

It was a popular form in part because editors had long enjoyed the experience of receiving the real thing from citizens concerned enough to voice their opinions and literate enough to produce (sometimes barely) readable texts. Maimed in grammar, syntax, and spelling, the genuine letters were in fact "found" literary art, serendipitous missives that editors delighted in printing and which in turn inspired the literary variety. For much of the antebellum era and beyond, the line between the real and the fictional letter was sometimes thin enough to fool even educated readers.[42] The fascination with this form could be traced to its immediacy. It addressed an audience without benefit of mediation by its real author. More than any other type of humor, the letter relied on vernacular speech alone to convey characterization, and letter sequences (with their continuations and responses) became a favorite format of writers of vastly different talents.

The convention behind this mainstay of nineteenth-century newspapers was that the opinions expressed—in matter and manner—were not to be attributed to an educated professional. The language was self-contained, innocent of editorial polishing to make it more "readable" for ordinary subscribers; it was no place for the finicky editor with his emending *sic*. The creator conceived of a character whose deviant language ingenuously soared without interruption by censor, glosser, or other cultural custodians. The pose of guileless correspondent in charge of his own free-tongued style also carried with it the assumption that that style, unchallenged by the dominant alternative, would preserve its own integrity as a system. In the absence of a controlling narrator, the reader's degree of sympathy for the writer depended upon the character of the correspondent. It is the only form in the humor in which the author eliminates himself as sole authority, in the risky faith that the reader will be his stand-in, silently censoring or interpreting the deviant system in his stead. In this form the reader replaces the genteel narrator.

John S. Robb's "Settlement Fun" is a sequence of eight letters by one

42. Henry Prentice Miller, "The Background and Significance of *Major Jones's Courtship*," *Georgia Historical Quarterly* 30 (1946): 270.

Bill Sapper about the social scene in "Liberti, Miss Sury," a site, like many others in the humor, where boredom invites practical jokes (Oehl., 239–68). Sapper recounts to his cousin a series of tricks and their targets: a snooty Virginia widow, a pious deacon, a lubber feigning ague-sickness, and a country boy who arrives in the settlement for a career. Except for the struggle for dominance and control (which the practical joke generically assumes), comic exposure in these letters is relatively benign. Sapper provides enough details to justify the victimization of his targets. The country boy is arrogant in his ignorance ("I aint easy got ahead of in daylight"). Despite his complaining, the "lazy ager" patient continues "a eatin' his share of dodger, drinkin' his reglar ration of licker, and callin' hisself a new daddy about onst a year." Old Deacon White betrays his own weakness for sin even as he rails against dancing, drinking, partying, circus-going, and assorted other "evils of the present generation." Robb's narrating correspondent is a genial observer, never initiating the trickery, but always on hand as it unfolds. He maintains a sense of fair play and balance and keeps his eye peeled for mitigating "perticklers" that "display humin' natur'"—and Robb, in a pointed aside, has him add: "all fellars that rite ought to keep lookin' at that pint."

One of the "perticklers" is female sexual fascination. When the wife of Little Jo Allen, the village shoemaker, delivers triplets, the response among wives, widows, and spinsters alike devolves from congratulations to curiosity about the prowess of the lucky husband. Sapper reports that the leading "literary" woman "tuk to admirin' him so that she could scacely keep her hands off" him; even country wives come to town, besieging "his shop winder, *all* the time, and . . . peepin' in, and lookin' at him, and askin' his age, and whar he cum from?" Harried by admiration, the desperate shoemaker flees town but is quickly "rescued" by the efforts of the admiring wives, who force their husbands into a posse to find him. A measure of peace returns only when the town passes a resolution: "the wimen shall ony visit his shop once a week to look at him, 'cept the married wimen, who shall be permitted to see him twice a week and no offener, pervided and exceptin' tha want to git measured fur a par of shoes." The candid sexual interest finally benefits the shoemaker. Sapper reports that Little Jo is busier than ever—"he's had a parfect shower of work, for the gals all round the country keep goin' to him to git measured, tha say he *desarves* to be incouraged" (*SSL*, 156–61).

Robb's evenhanded treatment of "humin' natur'" is best exhibited in his story of old Widow Dent, a well-to-do descendant "frum the furst Virgini families" who inspires a campaign by a doctor and a lawyer "to try and cum it over the old widder in the matrimonial way." Neither makes any headway. The lawyer fails his test when he admits he was born in Indiana: "'Indianee!' said the old widder, tarnin' up her nose— 'I'm thinkin,' Mr. Mason, you'll hev to use a good deal of *sassapariller* to purify Indianee blood up to furst family Virgini standard.'" The new country is where even filioanxiety goes to seed. Even before the widow resists both of the "cute perfeshional fellers," conspiracy follows motive: "Thur warn't many people sick about, nur much lawin' goin' on," so Tom Massey, M.D., and Dick Mason, attorney, agree in advance "to share which or tother got her, and ary one 'ud rather had the *share* than the *widder*." After she loftily insults both of them, Massy and Mason persuade all the other doctors and lawyers in town to snub her, and the widow retaliates by throwing a party without inviting "a single perfeshional to it" (Oehl., 244–47). The farce of the ensuing spite fight is sufficiently amusing, but the real distinction of these letters is the way Robb confirms Sapper's penchant for deemphasizing maliciousness. When Lawyer Mason sings a scurrilous song about the widow in public,

> the wimin listened to him snortin' it out in the street, tickled at what a fool he was makin' on himself, and a kind of pleased to death at his makin' fun of the widder. . . .
> . . . It didn't sot the young gals back much to see the young fellars slightin' the widder, 'cause none on 'em liked her, she wur so pompous, but they thort the fellars wur etarnal mean for courtin' the widder's money, and they poked all sorts of fun at Dr. Massey and Dick Mason. (Oehl., 246–247)

In perceiving the dynamics of communal relationships, Bill Sapper is a superior observer. Generously acknowledging the complexities of divided sympathies, even in this trivial contest, he makes the entire episode psychologically credible. The chief virtue that Robb attributes to his letter writer is moderation. Although the mean-spirited professionals and the snobbish widow alike deserve their mutual humiliation, appropriate censure comes not from this monitor of judicious fun, but from the working out of the action as the level-headed Sapper sees and reports it. If in Freudian logic the practical joke is a hostile act, in "Liberti, Miss Sury," that act is in effect neutralized by the energy of an opposing act. Both jokes work, but neither party wins. "The widder is dreadfully hurt," Sapper concludes, "but it's ginerally thort that all hands hev quit about even, and insted of gitin' ahead hev only made '*fun* for the settlement'" (Oehl., 258).

A more cohesive group of mock-yokel letters is that of Noland's Pete

Whetstone in his extensive correspondence to Porter's *Spirit*. The character of this shrewd backwoodsman is established not only by the letters he writes to his enthusiastic editor, but also by a number of corroborating letters about him by the more gentlemanly "N. of Arkansas," a different perspective crafted by the same author. Before creating Pete (and afterward, continuing for many years), Fenton Noland contributed to the *Spirit* turf reports and colorful accounts of hunting, signed "N. of Arkansas." In February 1837 he submitted the first Whetstone letter and soon after (as "N.") wrote Porter that he had had the "exquisite pleasure of seeing your correspondent, 'Pete Whetstone.'" He then quoted from a speech that Pete supposedly delivered in Van Buren County, Tennessee. By September, Pete and N. were friends. On a visit to Batesville, N. says, he introduced "Mr. Pete Whetstone, of the Devil's Fork" to the ladies; then, as Pete reports in one of his letters, the two of them "played and danced till just afore day" before returning home (*PW*, 81–86).

By doubling himself as correspondent, Noland also in effect doubled the social and cultural range of his state—though both contributors seem equally addicted to horse racing as their major amusement. Items of interest to turf fanciers had ceased to dominate the columns of the *Spirit*, but news of the track continued to be one of Porter's passions. As one critic has observed, Pete's social interests and political attitudes and his enthusiasm for horse racing and outdoor life coincide with those of his creator: "to know Pete is to know Noland" (*PW*, 34).[43] If the invention of Pete freed the Virginia émigré to speak more bluntly, more colorfully, and more truthfully than he could tactfully do in his own voice, the resulting expressions never became those of the backwoods clown. Throughout the life of Pete Whetstone, as Noland continued to gloss his hero's contributions from his own point of view, his character was never belittled nor patronized by "N. of Arkansas."

In addition to horse racing, Pete's great interests are frolics, people watching, hunting, and politics. Like the generic backwoodsman of this humor, this one also enjoys the spectacle of fights. Unlike his friend and brother-in-law, however, Pete himself is no stomp-and-gouger. The phys-

43. Leonard Williams, introduction to *Cavorting on the Devil's Fork: The Pete Whetstone Letters of C. F. M. Noland* (Memphis: Memphis State University Press, 1979), 34. The credibility of Pete Whetstone was also enhanced by other perspectives. William T. Porter himself alluded to him as a real correspondent, seen in New Orleans with his friends Noland and William F. Denton; and Albert C. Ainsworth, a friend of Noland who wrote under the name of "Trebla," spoke of Pete in several contributions to *Spirit of the Times*.

ical bouts he relates (often more threatened than real) are usually triggered by political differences, which is just one instance of the kind of intense partisanship that makes him a distinctive and coherent figure among his kind in the humor.[44] On one occasion Pete describes the work of Locofoco agents in Devil's Fork, describing it in terms of a seduction by political missionaries who use such resonating phrases as "real friends of the people" and "equal rights." Only when the agents propose the equal division of property in Devil's Fork do the righteous Whigs rise up: "I tell you they used them awfully," Pete writes: "they beat, bruised, and amalgamated them until they looked like the last of an ill-spent life" (*PW*, 88). The Locofoco incident reveals considerable sophistication behind the country accents. Pete is not a participant in roughing up opponents, even radical Democrats, and in his account he is rustic enough to savor a five-dollar word, smart enough to use an adverb with preferred spelling, and attentive enough to cite a middle-class cautionary phrase made common by years of sermons and moral tracts.

An early biographer made much of how Noland, one of the "Virginians of the better class," was not merely at home with the "rude, rugged, fearless, yet honest and true" Arkansas backwoodsmen, but became their "idol" as well.[45] Recent authorities are more restrained, but generally confirm the ease with which Noland adjusted to frontier culture. His own prose is witty and graceful, if unremarkable, in keeping with his social status as the son of a man who was a friend of American presidents. The prose he gives to the hearty Pete Whetstone is a distinctive and entirely persuasive achievement.

In contrast to Thompson's Major Jones—as we shall see—Noland is uninterested in spelling-by-sound as an orthographic device of characterization. Pete Whetstone is no great speller, but missing in his correspondence are the elaborate constructions that in the Major Jones and Sut Lovingood letters serve as double entendres or as witticisms in their own right. "They agreed to leave it to Squire Woods," Pete writes in one letter; "now Squire Woods is up to snuff and makes no more of belting a quart,

44. When his Democratic affections soured and he switched his allegiance to the Whigs, Noland allowed Pete to voice strong opinions in 1837 about "Van Burenism" and thievery. Porter, who discouraged political debate in the *Spirit*, went to some lengths to warn Pete that he was "getting regularly *wolfish* in his politics," and to back off. Noland did so, and Pete continued to be Porter's favorite correspondent. Leonard Williams, introduction to *Cavorting on the Devil's Fork: The Pete Whetstone Letters of C. F. M. Noland* (Memphis: Memphis State University Press, 1979), 39.

45. Josiah H. Shinn, "The Life and Public Services of Charles Fenton Mercer Noland," *Publications of the Arkansas Historical Association* 1 (1906): 330–43.

than a methodist preacher would of eating a whole chicken" (*PW,* 61). This passage from a random letter shows its author as a literate rustic. He may well be a "rude, rugged, fearless" Arkansan, but the credibility of his character depends not on mock illiteracy, but on the colloquial rhythms of a speaker gifted with metaphors and turns of phrase appropriate to his condition.

About a fellow Arkansan, Pete writes: "You ought to see him *shovel victuals* into his mouth. Eating don't take away his appetite—three corn dodgers, four big biscuits with grease to make them go down, and a quart of coffee don't make a meal. He is one of your cranebuilt fellows, and walks with his head hung down as though his mammy weaned him too early" (*PW,* 80). Noland emphasizes here his hero's perceptive eye and, to go with it, a clarity of expression that is just colloquial enough to make the speaker believable. Some of the humorists, having a go at this passage, would unerringly have chosen *vittles, biskits,* and *fellers* to characterize backwoods speech; others would have added such alterations as *Eatin'* and *tu see 'im.* Pete's lingo is less a deviance from standard English usage than it is a regional variation. The color in his speech, keyed to metaphor and diction, derives not from ignorance of what polite society dictates but from a matter-of-fact pride in his own lingual level.

The narrative logic of the Whetstone letters is twofold: an elected representative from Devil's Fork will be a rustic in Little Rock; and most of the Arkansas legislature, whatever their pretensions, will also be rustic. It is a comic principle well established in *Georgia Scenes,* and its American ancestry dates from Royall Tyler's *The Contrast* (1787). Pete is aware of what he doesn't know, but, though vulnerable to social slights and embarrassments, is dignified enough not to be done in by them. At a legislative ball, after he has led one of the ladies to the dance floor, Pete belatedly realizes his mistake: "I wasn't in the right place. I got scared, and couldn't get the figure; says one of them, in a whisper, 'Mr. Whetstone aint up to *Kertillions*'; at that says I, 'ladies and gentlemen, excuse me if you please, I am in the wrong row now, for I never got higher than a reel in all my life'; at that they all commenced giggling: this made me mighty mad" (*PW,* 97). In this perennial comic situation, Noland exploits the parvenu's anxiety in social performance (though as a convention in Southwest humor, only dandies really excel in dancing, music appreciation, and teatime small talk). Yet he allows his hero to preserve both his individuality and his temper. In a linguistic grace note, *Kertillions* is conspicuously given to one of the Little Rock women, not Pete, who, at any rate, at another ball a few weeks later, has learned all the steps that the capital can offer: "Well, there is no mistake, but cotillions are a huckle-berry above reels" (*PW*, 102). By the very restraint of this episode, with its shrewd, understated insights, Noland manages to deepen his hero's character by giving him a knack for learning. He is a rustic who also knows how to spell *cotillions*.

Chapter 11 ⊹⟺⟀

Narrators and Storytellers

"Oh, ho! and so, my boy, you said nothin' about it, eh! Well that is rich, fond of *ritin'* stories, but never *tells* 'em, eh!"

—Obe Oilstone, "Pulling Teeth in Mississippi"

His manner was so singular, that half of his story consisted in his excellent way of telling it, the great peculiarity of which was, the happy manner he had of emphasizing the prominent parts of his conversation. As near as I can recollect, I have italicized them, and given the story in his own words.

—T. B. Thorpe, "The Big Bear of Arkansas"

i.

When hunting for specimens along the Ohio River, the ornithologist Alexander Wilson was compelled to find lodging wherever he could. He reported in 1810 that at one "wretched hovel" in Kentucky he was regaled by war stories told by his host, one of General Washington's former soldiers: "Such a farrago of lies, oaths, prayers, and politeness, put me in a good humour in spite of myself." As a species of oral storytelling, the farrago we call the frontier tall tale was always a sentimental favorite with visitors to the Old Southwest. Many of the early travelers remarked on the backwoods propensity for exaggerating the unique perils that natives faced in living there. Most of the stories were so consciously tall that foreigners concluded that the tales had less to do with actual life than with the sociable urge to entertain. On a trip to Georgia, one educated clerk was taken to visit nearby sights in Florida; from both captain and passengers, he wrote in his journal, "we had some large stories about alligators, moccasins, wolves, bears &c—they were also assisted by Maj Bell who said he had seen alligators so thick in a lake in the interior that it was perfectly safe to cross on their backs."[1]

Some travelers were annoyed by the repetitive efforts to entertain them with yarns about wilderness predators; savvier ones, as part of their educative mission, understood such storytelling to be a cultural habit, like dirking or gouging. If panthers and bears were sometimes suspected of being imaginary threats, both visitor and southwesterner could agree on the actual viciousness of mosquitoes. Harriet Martineau had to don gloves and prunella boots "all day long" to protect her from mosquitoes. The assaultive energy and size of these pests are deplored in nearly every travel book and in many personal letters. One clerk from Maine was pleased with his move to Louisiana, despite its being "notorious for musketoes, Aligators, and other amphibions, fowels, and animals &C." Some travelers repeated heard stories; others wrote their own. One wag in New Orleans wrote to a sister in Natchez: "Have you got any Musquitoes up in your part of the Country? if not I'd like to send you Some—of the real torturers—Species Galnipper—Bills as long as my Creditors & bite like the mischief—Cant read a line at night without Smokes & Cigars are money—So musquitoes are dunners of the worst kind, as they compell payment."[2]

The Species Galnipper of tall tales has also been a favorite topic in critical commentary, especially the kind that searches out motive and function behind a narrative's formal shape. Most critics agree that the tall tale was a mode of deception poised ambiguously between the credible and the absurd, a narrative that, though nourished by fact, justified itself in the filigree of fantasy. Although its monitory function seems clear—to mitigate fears by exaggerating them—its more immediate purpose was, like

1. Alexander Wilson, "Letter from Lexington," *Port Folio*, 2nd ser., 3 (1810): 509; A. T. Havens Journal, 1842–1843, Hargrett Rare Book and Manuscript Library, University of Georgia Libraries, University of Georgia, Athens.

2. Harriet Martineau, *Retrospect of Western Travel* (1838; reprint, New York: Greenwood, 1969), 2:128; D. H. Holmes, letter, March 15, 1837, Burge Family Papers (MSS 266), Special Collections and Archives, Robert W. Woodruff Library, Emory University, Atlanta; Gus Mandeville, letter, June 1851, Henry D. Mandeville Family Papers, MSS 491, 535, Louisiana and Lower Mississippi Valley Collections, Louisiana State University Libraries, Baton Rouge.

Alexander Wilson's host, to put people in good humor in spite of their disbelief. Discriminating lies from truth was a hearers' game that exercised "the mind for physical, economic, and psychological survival," according to Carolyn S. Brown. The storytelling site of the extravagant yarn, for both performance and reception, became the zone of the provisional, a theater of communication within a homogeneous culture in which was played out a cluster of "fears, desires, fancies, and values." Referring to "the business" of telling bear stories, the civil engineer Caleb Forshey explained why he enjoyed the company of hunters during his surveying treks in the wilds. "These woodmen," he wrote in his diary for 1839, had a great advantage "denied to most men," a generous freedom "from the restraints of public opinion *alias gossip* in telling the facts." Partly because "competition produce[s] emulation," their yarns were better around the campfire than in "a crowded community" with its skeptics. Forshey cheerfully posed a theory that bear stories "increase with our years! & hence, at the age of 80 a tale . . . will be four times the altitude, latitude & longitude of the same tale at 20 years!" By 1850, according to Brown, the tall tale was "a form of social ritual" as much as it was a style of storytelling.[3] By midcentury, when frontier fears and fancies had mutated into national anxieties, the conventional tall tale was no longer a therapeutic mode, but an expression of egoistic assertiveness.

What is most apparent in the written humor is the authors' attraction to and dependence upon the oral tale (tall or otherwise), a pervasive form of entertainment at all levels of society in the Old Southwest.[4] Even the least talented of the humorists conscientiously sought to reproduce the styles and sounds of the yarns they heard—sometimes by first imitating them in the company of professional cronies. Exaggeration and flam-

---

3. Carolyn S. Brown, *The Tall Tale in American Folklore and Literature* (Knoxville: University of Tennessee Press, 1987), 36–38; Diaries of Caleb G. Forshey, Mississippi Valley Collection, University of Memphis Library. I have examined the Forshey diaries in more detail in "The Underheard Reader in the Writing of the Old Southwest," in *Discovering Difference: Contemporary Essays in American Culture,* ed. Christoph K. Lohmann (Bloomington: Indiana University Press, 1993), 60–62.

4. John Bryant, *Melville and Repose: The Rhetoric of Humor in the American Renaissance* (New York: Oxford, 1993), 76; William B. Dillingham, "Days of the Tall Tale," *Southern Review* 4 (1968): 569; Henry B. Wonham, *Mark Twain and the Art of the Tall Tale* (New York: Oxford, 1993), 50. See also more comprehensive studies: Constance M. Rourke, *American Humor: A Study of the National Character* (1931; reprint, New York: Harcourt Brace Jovanovich, 1959), 33–76; James M. Cox, *Mark Twain: The Fate of Humor* (1966; reprint, Columbia: University of Missouri Press, 2002); James M. Cox, "Humor of the Old Southwest," in *The Comic Imagination in American Literature,* ed. Louis D. Rubin, Jr. (New Brunswick, NJ: Rutgers University Press, 1973), 101–12.

boyant delivery were the common marks of such tales, and though oral swaggering leached into all ranks and classes, its theatrical gaudiness was usually identified with backwoodsmen and yeomen without much claim to literacy. Even before these residents were sources for literate scribes, their performances were both admired and puzzled over. Some foreign visitors could not conceive of humor outside of civilizing restraints. In Alabama, after her host had entertained her with a story, the hard-to-amuse Harriet Martineau opined that humorists were abundant "in rare settlements and retired districts, where they can indulge their fancies without much suffering from public opinion."[5] However it was received, the oral yarn seems always to have been a hallmark (and a commodity) of the backcountry settlements.

Among the humorists the tall tale stands at one extreme, a species of bravado that aggressively *chaws up* more modest forms of storytelling. It is neither the most frequently used form nor the most characteristic, but it attained an early prominence largely through its focal heroes, Davy Crockett and Mike Fink, figures who performed extravagant deeds and to whom even more extravagant deeds are attributed. T. B. Thorpe's Jim Doggett and Henry Clay Lewis's Mik-hoo-tah take on some of the reflected sheen of those vivid figures, but the titles they give to themselves to proclaim their achievement (the "Big Bear of Arkansas" and the "Bear Hunter of Ameriky," respectively) are tested by the ordinary circumstances of real frontier life, and the men who claim them turn out to be merely human. Lewis's "The Indefatigable Bear Hunter" is not restricted to the basic contest between man and beast, nor is it solely about testing Mik-hoo-tah against Thorpe's Jim Doggett. It is a test of texts, and Lewis's hero claims his space and his victory over the Big Bear by virtue of his handicap. Doggett may be embarrassed in his final confrontation with his quarry, but Mik has to face his with *only one leg.* What keeps Mik-hoo-tah and Doggett from being mere parodies of the exceptional man is the skill of their creators in giving dimension—notably subtlety and poignance—to their announced roles. Lewis and Thorpe enveloped their intrepid hunters in a chastened present quite different from the heroic past that had already been pushed into a kind of irrelevant history.

At the risk of cultural solemnity, we might see Crockett and Fink themselves as parodies of the great nation-making leaders. After the deaths of Jefferson and Adams in 1826, the iconic national names were no longer those of Revolutionary heroes, but Clay, Webster, Jackson, Van Buren—

---

5. Martineau, *Retrospect,* 2:61.

about whom there was (and is) no consensus. Spectacular and mouthy, Crockett and Fink were as much a trivialization of fame as they were the embodied prowess of the present republic. In this scenario, the heroizing of the Founders' generation, with its disinterested devotion to the people, was succeeded by a celebration of frontier eminence in which asserted egos were either accepted or challenged. The stories from the interior become a kind of shadow myth, alternatives to a fantastic story that, though historical, seemed no longer quite germane. One declension is clear: the intellectualism, shrewdness, and communal resolve of the Fathers—a tale of tall men and tall events to be honored—devolved into the untaught and impetuous independence of Crockett and Fink—tellers of tall tales to be celebrated. As if in compensation, however, the process also endorsed the dispersed energies and potentiality of western space.

Yet the tall tales from this space are the most resolutely retrospective of all the forms of southwestern humor. Though William Gilmore Simms and other thoughtful southerners saw audacity and hyperbole as the marks of America's future, the tall tale that so conspicuously bears these qualities was the product of hunters and rivermen who were already near-relics of the past. Though his death in 1836 was gratifyingly appropriate to national heroizing, Crockett would in the future be more closely tied to the coonskin than to the Alamo, and Fink would disintegrate as a "river god" when he was superseded by technology. Only for a brief moment does the tall-tale hero embody the extravagance and plenitude of a continent destined to be brought under American hegemony. That he also harbors cruelty, arrogance, and vanity is neither accidental nor surprising. He embodies energy without the shaping pressure of institutions; he offers a model of achievement which, because it is stripped of communal purpose, is a fantasy of individualistic, anarchic desire.

In antebellum humor, what Huck Finn would call "stretchers" are considerably more common (if less dramatic) than extravagant tall tales. If in real life lying was a psychological weapon for survival on the frontier, in the ludic culture of the humorists it was mostly entertainment. In his profile of the quintessential liar Ovid Bolus, Joseph G. Baldwin demonstrates the general principle that while belief in self-aggrandizing stories is not necessary, a willingness to be amused is the only mind-set to have if one is not to be outraged or bored. Moreover, to pursue the lie, testing its veracity against hard facts, is as misguided as using it to discriminate good from evil. The ragtag residents of Baldwin's Flush Times are so willing to be amused by Bolus's repertoire that they pay for the privilege by picking up his tabs at the groggeries. Less willing—and less long-suffering—

are those who endure the "brassy pretension" of "Rance Bore-'em," who intrudes into others' conversations to top each anecdote he hears. Unlike the insouciant Baldwin, Francis J. Robinson's narrator concludes the sketch of his "Loafer Bore" with an exasperated prayer: "for the peace and quiet of any town, it should be the daily petition of its inhabitants, '*from such,*' Good Lord! deliver us! So mote it be, amen" (Cohen, 389).

Supervising all such talk, narrators reflect their creators' manipulations. The point about language as practiced by the humorists was not to create space for some new kind of writing—the achievement later admirers attributed to them—but to get a purchase on space already cleared, a substantial space that required leverage to negotiate its thicket of forms, texts, authorities, and establishments. That leverage was a vernacular that the authors could assert through the idioms of the backcountry. Nominally, the narrators subscribed to the regulatory standards of approved language and style, along with related conventions and scribal habits; but, in most cases, the humorists' focus on deviance in their unapproved speakers also altered their own stylistic practice as sponsors of vernacular characters.[6] No one, author or reader, was unaware of the fact that the humorists were choosing subjects that were unconducive to literary artistry. No one could pretend that he was writing or reading high art or even imagine that writing and reading these sketches was relevant to the direction of an indigenous American art—one of the perennial topics in intellectual debates since the earliest days of the republic. What complicated those debates was what also complicated the orderly development of republican morals and manners—namely, the all-absorbing drive to extend national boundaries and the urgent, continuing presence of a frontier.

The known and reported conditions of the frontier, wherever it happened to be in any particular decade, affected the publishing industry everywhere in the early nineteenth century.[7] Literary respect was tendered only to those writers adept in settled genres and conventional forms of language and syntax (that is, inherited English style). As Albert von Frank has argued, one of the persistent dilemmas of American artists was how to balance the use of provincial materials (for native vitality) with civilized

6. One theorist has speculated that language itself contains the capacity "to resist whatever hegemony it might have coincidentally served and supported." William Galperin, "The New Historicism: Comprehending the Incomprehensible," *Centennial Review* 35 (1991): 57.

7. William Charvat, *Literary Publishing in America, 1790–1850* (Philadelphia: University of Pennsylvania Press, 1959), 23–24.

and fluent style (for aesthetic universality). The frontier supplied an overwhelming mass of localizing materials—shapes, weights, densities, colors, names—that by their very newness resisted a universalizing style. Since they dealt with prescriptive expectations, lexicographers and grammarians were less vulnerable than writers and editors to the pressure of having to choose between what they knew was *style,* the mark of civilization, and what they suspected was *substance,* the new materiality of American life. One of the beneficiaries of this literary dilemma was what von Frank calls the "American provincial comic mode," in which a "sophisticated point of view is brought to bear on preposterously subliterary materials."[8] This formula did not guarantee quality, but it became the most reliable way for the amateur writer to explore, with some leisure, the intricate techniques involved in negotiating style and substance. The resources of American language were always diluted, as we have seen, and what indigenous treasures the authors uncovered were always reproduced through the scrim of aesthetic effect. The humorists were makers as well as discoverers.

ii.

When Parson John Bullen sticks up his handwritten wanted poster, offering an "AIT ($8) DULLARS REWARD" for the "karkus ove a sartin wun Sut Lovingood, dead ur alive, ur ailin," George takes one "for preservation." What interests the literate narrator of *Sut Lovingood's Yarns* is its "blood-thirsty spirit, its style, and above all, its chirography" (*SL,* 48–49). Most of the authorial stand-ins in the sketches are more interested in the sounds of quasi-literacy than in handwriting. The vitality of the frame tale in particular comes from the interchange between two principals, the narrator (who can write) and his backwoods subject (who usually can't). To turn again to the best-loved sketch in all the writings from the Old Southwest (and the one that lent its name to what was once perceived as the "school" of this humor), "The Big Bear of Arkansas" is the very model of a narrative pattern in which an educated, sophisticated, and cultivated man of the world confronts a backwoodsman, who then recounts an episode out of his experience in the woods. If not exactly a gentleman,

8. Albert J. von Frank, *The Sacred Game: Provincialism and Frontier Consciousness in American Literature, 1630–1860* (Cambridge: Cambridge University Press, 1985), 73–75, 85–86. Von Frank attributes this mode to Longstreet and Baldwin, but in fact it became the necessary tactic for all the humorists who used mediating narrators for their localized materials.

the narrator of these sketches is a respectable, tolerant sort of fellow willing to be entertained; as the author's surrogate, he also serves, from the reader's perspective, as "one of us." The backwoodsman—a yeoman farmer, a hunter, a boatman, anyone who is most at home in the relative isolation beyond towns and villages—may be ignorant of some of the most basic kinds of information that the narrator takes for granted, yet he is savvy, tenacious, and garrulous—and willing to entertain.

Thorpe's narrator, steaming his way upriver from New Orleans, finds his reading interrupted by the genial Jim Doggett, who is heard before he is seen ("we were most unexpectedly startled by a loud Indian whoop" coming from the bar). Amid a "confused hum" of broken phrases and with a "Hurra for the Big Bear of Arkansas," the backwoodsman propels himself into the company of a larger audience. His one-liners, all windy tributes to "the creation State," are received with appreciative skepticism by the "heterogeneous" passengers who seem to be from everywhere but Arkansas. Doggett's attention-getting style transcends the source that generates it—the roarer bombast from an earlier phase of commercial life on the great western rivers. And his tale itself is such that the teller must moderate the requisite hyperbole to make the style fit the substance of the yarn. With his focus on "an *unhuntable bar*" that "*died when his time come*," the champion hunter tells a story in which he turns out to be a failure in his biggest challenge (*TBT*, 112–22). Just as the slangwhanging excesses of frontier colloquialism are planed away in Doggett's yarn, so too are the more prolix properties of formal English in Thorpe's narrator, who has sometimes been charged with pretentious fussiness. His gentlemanly narration is in a recognizably respectable style, but its language, considerably chastened, not only coexists with but also nourishes its vernacular counterpart.

The narrator strikes an effective balance of reserve and curiosity as he elicits the story that Doggett is eager to relate to a deserving stranger.

> [C]onscious that my own association with so singular a personage would probably end before morning, I asked him if he would not give me a description of some particular bear hunt—adding that I took great interest in such things, though I was no sportsman. The desire seemed to please him, and he squared himself round towards me, saying, that he could give me an idea of a bar hunt that was never beat in this world, or in any other. (*TBT*, 117)

Unlike some of the other hearers assembled in the social hall of the *Invincible*, the narrator shows his interest to be neither cynical nor patronizing.

His unshowy prose, like his straightforward manner, complements rather than jars the verbal richness of the yarn-spinner. The decisive fact of "The Big Bear of Arkansas" is not a formal structure that pits gentleman against backwoodsman, but the momentary packaging together of narrator and subject when these explicitly unlike figures converge in the same space. Perhaps to the delight of discursive bondage theorists, the canny hunter by sheer forensic force seizes the moment from his social better. There is no verbal tug-of-war. The narrative switch from one kind of discourse to the other, almost formulaic, is as sociable as a president's levee.

Although Thorpe's is the best of its kind, the same sort of sociability can be seen in many of the frame sketches. Linguistic and stylistic rivalry between narrator and storyteller in the humor is a fiction, though it is one that the authors themselves sometimes encourage. We expect the educated narrator to draw his line—the price he exacts to give parity to the uncouth storyteller—but that line is never firm. Juxtaposition of stylistic levels is a convention we expect in all narrative situations in which patrician and commoner are joined, yet in Thorpe's case it feels less like a linguistic war than a comfortable détente; and though the social realism behind similar narrative situations may stem from an enforced democracy, the mood is often genial and collusive. In these juxtapositions, arguably, are the only sustained instances in which the rampant competitive spirit of the humor is dampened. In the psychology of democratic humor, homespun always trumps elegance, and the authors often trick us into hearing more aesthetic dissonance than they actually provide. There may be several reasons for this effect, but one, at least, is formal. If we admire the commanding authority with which Jim Doggett seizes his moment, it is worthwhile to remember that the backwoods anecdotes that are so aurally distinctive to the steamboat passengers exist for us only in their *graphic* distinctiveness in the text, in the propulsive *look* of an oral style that Thorpe inscribes in words. We should not forget that the author is the author of all levels of discourse—the straightforward English of the narrator and the deviating dialects of the bear hunter and of the assorted members of the audience in the social hall. Thorpe invents both himself and his subject.

Although it can hardly be said to promote a Whiggish *cordon sanitaire*, there are several reasons why "The Big Bear" is the best of the frame tales. First, Thorpe manages his characterization so that Doggett emerges as the most nuanced and complex of the several hunters of antebellum humor. Something more than a generic bear hunter who tells yarns in a colloquial mode, he is also given a tale whose complexity far exceeds his lingual manner. And something more than mutual tolerance marks the relationship of the hunter and the gentleman. Doggett "approves" of the narrator's curiosity, and the narrator has the grace to acknowledge yeomanry superiority in imagination and inventive language. Though the narrator's manner is genial enough, his attempts at verbal levity are pedestrian compared to Doggett's down-home vivacity. Gentlemanly wit consists of the overly familiar—a lively saloon becomes "that place of spirits." The hunter prefers anecdotes that generate more original word-play. In his garrulous entertainment of the crowd, he recalls one newcomer to his region and how the Arkansas mosquitoes "used that fellow up!" This Yankee, he continues, "took the ager," and "finally he took a steamboat and left the country. He was the only man that ever took mosquitoes at heart that I know of" (*TBT*, 114). Thorpe turns a perceived linguistic deficiency—the limited vocabulary of the backcountry—into wit by allowing his hunter in one breath to cram three different connotations into a simple verb. His puns casually top the understated gentility of the narrator's.

It is in his extended tale of the unhuntable bear, however, that this yeoman deftly demonstrates his complex character. In the silence that follows his story, the narrator attributes the "mystery" of the hunter-hunted connection to the "superstitious awe" common to "all 'children of the wood'" (*TBT*, 122). This fallback explanation, suggesting a too-easy reliance upon specimens and categories, makes the narrator seem lazy, but lest we judge him too harshly we should remember that the author's point is that the episode just related was a one-of-a-kind experience for Doggett himself. His telling reenacts that uniqueness. Not only has the narrator heard a unique story; he has also witnessed the recapitulation of a story alien to anyone's experience, certifying the juncture of nature and supernature enacted at what Celtic Christians once called "thin places" on the earth.

This hunter is indeed a child of the woods. It is a state of being that he takes seriously. Long before he declares of the mysterious bear, "I loved him like a brother," Doggett abides by the empathy that governs his outdoor life. Behind his narrative is a rhetoric of metaphysical organicism. In Thorpe's tale the anti-agricultural bias that permeates much Southwest humor is presented as a logic of cause-and-consequence: in producing misshapen crops (beets that resemble cedar stumps and potato hills that look like Indian mounds), the too-prodigal earth signals that nature intended Arkansas to be hunting ground, not farmland. And, says Doggett, "I go according to natur." This consonance with nature extends to his dog. Not sure whether Bowieknife was made "expressly to hunt bar or whether bar was made expressly for him to hunt," he decides "they were ordained to go together," like a newly married couple. Even his rifle is sentient—this "perfect *epidemic among bar*" must be watched closely, since "it will go off as quick on a warm scent" as his dog (*TBT*, 115).

It is no wonder that Thorpe's narrator never knows quite what to make of Jim Doggett. Antecedents such as Crockett and other hyperbolic loners suggest nothing of the meditative self-consciousness with which Thorpe invests his hero. Neither does Doggett betray the excesses of predatory human hunters such as those who became infamous a few decades later on the western plains, or those cited by Cooper eighteen years earlier in *The Pioneers*. Doggett shares nothing of the fashion of his own day, the wasteful, socially prestigious rage for game-hunting (gentleman sports-men would call him a *pot-hunter*). He was "drivin to hunting naturally," he says, because of the populous bears; and, being a quick study, he is now "the best bar hunter in my district." Because his skill has become, in the rural idiom, second-nature to him, telling strangers about bear hunts has become "somewhat monotonous now." In a kind of metanarrative reduction, Doggett quips that a bear story can be "told in two sentences—a bar is started, and he is killed" (*TBT*, 118).

But of course his big story about a hunt that was not monotonous requires more sentences to honor it. That this hunter does so is a measure of how consciously, artfully, and subtly fashioned the tale really is. The symbiosis of hunter and hunted occurs under the aegis of great nature, and although "The Big Bear" trails clouds of romantic sensibility, Thorpe never permits romantic sentiment to falsify the mystery. The relationship of Doggett and his bear is confirmed not by a grand union like that of, say, Ahab and Moby-Dick, but by the aggressive juxtaposition of banal nature with nature at its most mysterious. It was James M. Cox who first pointed out the remarkable scatalogical joke at the very heart of a theophanic moment, when the hunter is caught off-guard, literally with his pants down, just when he faces his greatest challenge and opportunity.[9] From "habit," Doggett, in the rural way, answers a call of nature, acknowledging a biological necessity that overrides all human will and skill. If, as he first speculates after the death of his prey, the bear "jist come in, like Capt. Scott's coon, to save his wind to grunt with in dying," his more considered judgment is that the bear answered his own call, which likewise took precedence over will and skill (*TBT*, 122). The seam-

9. Cox, "Humor of the Old Southwest," 109.

lessness of creation, an existential continuity of physical and spiritual nature, is thus affirmed in the most visceral of ways: the grunt of routine defecation is answered by the groan of a singular, preordained death.

From Crockett onward, when southwestern writers took bear hunting as their subject, they inevitably emphasized the techniques and processes of the backcountry way of hunting and killing. Thorpe's disregard of such details in his tale of the "best bar hunter" in Arkansas is an anomaly. In his interaction with the audience, Doggett's ingratiating mode is at best perfunctory; often he responds with weary patience, as if he is playing a preassigned role as entertainer to unworthy admirers. This hunter-hero is bathed in the kind of mellow, retrospective angst we see in western films about aging gunfighters who question their own reputation. All hunting stories by definition are about killing, but in "The Big Bear" the killing of woodland creatures is a *condition* of the narrative, a prior contextual fact, not a feature of the narrative itself. The death of the she-bear in the lake is almost as vaguely specified as the climactic death of *the* bear: Doggett fires at what he thinks is his big quarry, but the focus of the passage is Bowieknife's wrestling with the animal in and under the lake. We see a past (the source of this hunter's reputation), and we get a glimpse of a preparation (the weekend before the Monday that Doggett has set as a deadline for his final campaign), but we see *no hunter-initiated killing*. What we see instead is what we have had intimations of throughout the tale—*dying*.

Doggett is agile in his wit, but not gifted with the ebullience of many other vernacular storytellers. There is no stint in his brag about his state (one of the functions of the backwoods roarer); the very terms that make it noteworthy, however, are those that make it edgy: excess and threat. A persistent motif of danger, depletion, and death threads its way through the hunter's performance. His "good sized sow," a victim of prodigal soil, is killed by the percussive effect of a grain or two of corn that shoots up overnight where she wallows. Buzzards hover over the bones of what had been a "beautiful . . . hog the day before"; the thieving bear has grown accustomed to "help[ing] himself to a hog off [the] premises whenever he wanted one" (*TBT,* 117, 119).

Both beast and man are big, adjusted naturally to their geography. If mosquitoes in Arkansas are large, Doggett argues early on, "Arkansaw is large, her varmints ar large, her trees ar large, her rivers ar large." In the calculus of competition that fueled the settlement of the Old Southwest, *big* was, of course, the operative measure of *best*. Doggett's exaggerations are both like and unlike those that conventionally mark the storyteller.

Arkansas mosquitoes "used the Hoosier up," but the hunter admits that the big bear caused him to be "as nearly used up as a man can be." In popular terminology, *used up* is a shorthand description of emotional and physical damage to someone who has been bested. It began, however, as a more literal kind of humor. A common oral tale in the Old Southwest, one that predates the written humor, features a used-up widow who, just married, frightens her new husband on their wedding night when, in a corporeal striptease, she begins removing all her false parts: wig, teeth, bosom, leg . . .

By 1867, when George Washington Harris used the situation, it became a story that one Bob Dawson reports to Sut Lovingood.[10] On the night of his wedding to Miss Squills, "an old maid of the steel trap persuashun," Dawson watches with increasing anxiety as his new bride divests herself of false calves, false breasts (she calls them "palpitators"), false teeth, a false eye, and a wig covering a skull as "glossy as a billiard ball." As he thinks, "what next?" he gets the "most horrible idear that ever burnt an' blazed in the brain of man." Meaning to be reassuring, his bride says, "Don't be impatient, Robert love I is most through," but her words propel Dawson from the bridal chamber, "up—*out*—*gone* . . . down them stair steps six at a bounce in my shirt tail" (*HT,* 177–83). Hawthorne's variant thirty years earlier, "Mrs. Bullfrog," also features a belated bride; though she turns into a hoarse-voiced harpy when a stagecoach accident strips away her fashionable attire, her new husband is untroubled by her lack of hair and teeth because she still possesses a $5,000 dowry. The central trope is one with which Poe was also familiar. In his mordant tale "The Man That Was Used Up," a famous military hero, systematically stripped of a number of body parts, replaces them with artificial equivalents.

In Thorpe's tale, the term describes a spiritual malaise. The hunter, convinced that destiny intends the Big Bear for him, nourishes his used-upness to arrive at a deep-seated chagrin that he has been unequal to the challenge. The psychological devastation has its physical counterpart when he grows as cross "as a bar with two cubs and a sore tail." The failure, Doggett reports, "took hold of my vitals, and I wasted away" (*TBT,* 119–21). This experience of emotional and physical depletion is part of the aura of natural mystery, another sign of the curious mutuality between hunter and hunted, nature and supernature. Although the hunter

10. See Ray B. Browne, "Marrying a Substitute," *Lovingood Papers* (1964): 22–29. Dawson's shattering experience becomes Sut's explanation for never marrying: "I sleeps in a one hoss bed the ballunce ove my nights, aymen!" Browne traces the motif to an old music-hall song.

resists claiming himself the winner in his struggle with the Big Bear, he willingly accepts spiritual identification with it. The bear survives totemically by transference: by the time he tells the story, Jim Doggett has himself become the Big Bear of Arkansas.

Standing "midway between nature and civilization," he unites the two realms "not by what he has done," but "by what he *is*," according to one critic. The destiny of Doggett's quarry is the destiny of the wilderness. The bear succumbs through some internal necessity that must always remain mysterious; but under the aegis of great nature, beast and man spiritually accommodate each other. Unable to figure forth his own integrity except through cross-species mentorship, the bear seeks out his (potentially lethal) opponent as fraternal kin. That hunter-hunted dynamic provides a proleptic glimpse of a spirit moving across Arkansas, one that is more powerful than either one of them: the spirit of progress, modernity, and human culture as shaper of the wilderness.[11]

iii.

In writing about the importance of storytelling during his growing-up years in West Tennessee, Robert Drake remembers that "the best tales . . . seemed to get *told* (not *read*) when everybody was comfortable and at ease, not only with themselves but also with the universe." Drake is emphasizing the emotional ambience that encouraged the beneficent, unspooling ceremony of inclusiveness, a mood for deferring the petty discord of everyday routine. At some point almost every southern writer has testified to the influence of shared storytelling, especially the effect of unplanned, even improvisational, *talking*, as if their world contained stories merely waiting to be released by complying tongues—indifferent to audience, as if specific ears to hear were of little moment. Eudora Welty remembered her family's sewing woman, who "didn't bother about the ear she was telling it to; she just liked telling."[12]

11. Robert J. Higgs, "The Sublime and the Beautiful: The Meaning of Sport in Collected Sketches of Thomas B. Thorpe," *Southern Studies* 25 (1986): 253. The death of the bear presages the death of what J. A. Leo Lemay calls "that vital religion of nature" with the coming of modernity. "The Text, Tradition, and Themes of 'The Big Bear of Arkansas,'" *American Literature* 47 (1975): 341.

12. Robert Drake, "A Back Bedroom, an Open Fire, and the Art of Fiction," in *My Sweetheart's House: Memories, Fictions* (Macon, GA: Mercer University Press, 1993), 60; Eudora Welty, *One Writer's Beginnings* (Cambridge, MA: Harvard University Press, 1984), 14.

Yet, for all the illusion of spontaneity and the self-satisfying conditions of storytelling for its own sake, we know that there is no story without an audience. Spontaneity is a fiction sustained by both performer and scribe, but since performance depends upon the teller's relationship to his audience, the teller borrows from and capitalizes on the spontaneity of the audience (which presumably hears the story for the first time). Erving Goffman's rule for real-life situations applies as well to the humorous sketches that feature storytelling: "Effective performance requires first hearings, not first tellings."[13] If spontaneity is an illusion in storytelling, so is sincerity. Storytelling is a discourse that contains most of the assumptions and values of the society that generates it, including the competitive spirit. Like certain games that circumvent the trustworthiness of statements and gestures, storytelling circumvents the entire matter of sincerity. If poker invites bluffing, with gestures intended to mislead and oral clues to convey misdirection and false conclusions, sustained yarn-spinning is also a species of jousting in which the reliability of words cannot be an issue.[14]

One steamboating traveler in 1851 never quite appreciated the ambiance of tale-telling. Skeptical of a trapping yarn related by a "sharp" Kentuckian, Moritz Busch saw it only as another "atrocious lie" when he heard "the same anecdote claimed as a personal experience by another person a week later." Most of his fellow passengers understand the protocol, including the storyteller's solemn assertion: "I'll call myself a skinned polecat if it's not the naked, pure, shining truth!"[15] In storytelling, truth is *nowhar*. Spectacle, effects, performative skills are so prized that they become normative. Like the confidence ruse, oral performance is a competitive game, but credibility, crucial for working a con, is only marginal in oral narrative.

Gérard Genette claims that the oldest meaning of *narrative* is not an event recorded but the experience of "someone recounting something."[16] Most of the humorous authors, whose mastery of conventional narrative was notably thin, expanded imaginatively within the generous contours of that oldest meaning. The oral tale can never dispense with its commu-

13. Erving Goffman, *Frame Analysis: An Essay on the Organization of Experience* (New York: Harper, 1974), 508.

14. Erving Goffman, *Strategic Interaction* (Philadelphia: University of Pennsylvania Press, 1969), 108.

15. Moritz Busch, *Travels between the Hudson and the Mississippi, 1851–1852*, trans. and ed. Norman H. Binger (Lexington: University Press of Kentucky, 1971), 212–16.

16. Gérard Genette, *Narrative Discourse: An Essay in Method*, trans. J. E. Lewin (Ithaca, NY: Cornell University Press, 1980), 26.

nal context. Even in their written forms, the authors preserved the dynamic of an interactive audience—Thorpe's Jim Doggett entertains in the social hall of a steamboat; Robb's Dan Elkhorn favors his fellow hunters around a campfire; Baldwin's Burwell Shines, resplendent in his going-to-court clothes, tells a jury of his assault by hooligans. Such yarns require only minimal geographical detail, but the communal context that generates and shapes storytelling is strong.

Sol Smith's commonsensical observation on the southwestern social scene—"a fertile mind may make a great deal out of a limited amount of material"—also says much about the compositional tactics of the humorists (*TM*, 202). Thomas Kirkman's "Jones's Fight" is both a story of how matters of small substance can churn up substantial action and one that illustrates how an eager audience can spur action. A political enemy accuses Col. Dick Jones, a Kentucky judge, of having been a Federalist during the War of 1812. That such an unconscionable charge must be challenged is a conclusion by consensus. The decision of this prominent man to settle his differences when he next goes "over the mountain to court" becomes a community matter "narrated through the town." The case is taken up first by the "patriarchs of the place," then the "store boys," then the "young lawyers, and young M.D.'s," then the "good old ladies," and finally "the young ladies, and little misses." Robinson's "Lije Benadix" is a profile of a gluttonish cracker who, when he becomes constipated from eating too many plums, suffers in public. When his condition is "noised abroad," Lije is attended not only by a succession of doctors touting rival methodologies, but also by concerned neighbors "collected in the house and about the yard" to comment on the weeklong treatments: "Poor fellow! ef the plums don't kill him, the *doctor* and his *calomy* will!" (Cohen, 60–64, 377–84). Privacy is the enemy of humor. Not merely does the patient suffer publicly, his story emerges only through an interactive audience.

Even when there is only a single auditor to a tale, as in Lewis's "A Tight Race Considerin'," what makes the telling possible is camaraderie—in this case, the drinking and hunting of Madison Tensas and young Hibbs. Lewis's printed tale is a reconstruction of Hibbs's oral yarn, which is itself re-created, and which emphasizes, even in its narrative layers, the social collaboration (and consequences) of Mrs. Hibbs's spectacular horse race with a preacher. And in Baldwin's "Jonathan and the Constable," when a fellow lawyer tells the narrator, who has eavesdropped on private testimony, not to go "blabbing this thing all over town," the narrator confesses, "I thought I should have to norate it a little" (*FT*, 150).

The seal of privacy is always a fiction. In the storytelling world of this humor, to blab something all over town as opposed to "norating" it a little is a distinction without a difference. Just as fights, illnesses, legal testimony, sexual intrigues, and practical jokes can never be private affairs, so the stories about them never actually have any seals to be broken.

Although the oral tale can never dispense with an audience, its print version is sometimes meant only to illustrate the reputation of its singular teller. Less common is the written text that celebrates the cultural reputation of place. Taliaferro's Surry County folk (who, as North Carolinians, express their stout independence from "the fust famblys in Fudginny") are keepers of a tradition in which the tales themselves are more marvelous than the eccentrics who tell them. Of the tall tales that crop up in antebellum humor, Taliaferro's are the ones most clearly indebted to ancient convention and folklore. His laconic yarn-spinners—Uncle Davy Lane, Oliver Stanley, and Larkin Snow—betray their roots in inherited narratives, tales of heroic encounters with mythic snakes (whip and loop), whales, and river eels fond of crowder peas. These tall tales hang local lore on the well-polished pegs of Munchausenism.[17] And while Fisher's River is depicted as a long-settled community of kindly souls, the spirit of competition among its storytellers is undiminished. Taliaferro's favorite is Larkin Snow, whose ambition "consisted in being the best miller in the land, and in being *number one* in big story-telling." The narrator repeats two of his stories to show how "he held his own" with his several rivals, "even with Uncle Davy Lane" (*HET*, 124).

We sometimes like to think of the illiterate oral storyteller in America as a backwoods version of the Old English *scop* or the South American *hablador*: the preservationist and designated culture-bearer whose mind and memory hold all tribal history and wisdom. A documentary sampling of vernacular yarn-spinning—in memoirs and visitors' accounts—betrays nothing so purposeful or ceremonial. Southern garrulousness on the margins is scattershot and expedient, even when it seems to be compulsive. The storyteller is a competitive soul boasting of difference and superiority, even uniqueness. The preservationist in this era is not the ceremonial oralist, but the author of *written* texts, who, though innocent of any unifying motive that would link far-flung settlers in a feeling of community, inadvertently functions as the celebrator of an entire oral culture that he senses is already disappearing. He can be as garrulous as the vernacular yarn-spinner.

---

17. By 1835 Baron Munchausen's *Narrative of His Marvellous Travels and Campaigns in Russia* (1786) had been through twenty-four American editions. Brown, *Tall Tale*, 12.

The transferral of a tale *heard* to a tale *written* ranges from the most elementary to the most intricate kind of self-authorizing. "Thunder," the author-narrator of the frame story "Fighting the Tiger," begins his piece leisurely, as he relates his trip to Hot Springs—"this wonderful freak of nature's great laboratory." He then announces: "And now we will turn to the immediate object in writing this sketch, which is to embody a 'yarn' that came to my ears during this visit, as well as to give tangibility and shape to an incident in the hunter's life" (Oehl., 131). Although Thunder pitches his yarn to the expectations of literates reading, not to those of a community hearing, he self-consciously apes the often ragged nature of oral performance. The storyteller, beset by distractions, is willing to meander and to flirt with irrelevance. In Ham Jones's "The Sandy Creek Literary Society," the interplay between oral and textual authority begins when the records of a group organized for community uplift by one Squire Primm fall into the hands of the village innkeeper, known throughout the region for his expert mimicking of his pretentious neighbor. The oral telling has a punctilious priority over the written sketch, since the innkeeper has used it to amuse others in his "excellent house of entertainment" (*HJ*, 61). Yet in the transition from oral to verbal, Jones quietly subverts the origin, burying the putative narrator and assuming his own authority by producing the only version that counts: the tangible, material text. In Crockett's case, the programmatic remaking of the self to which the live backwoodsman devoted such conspicuous effort is cheerfully smudged in posthumous accounts. In the *Almanack* of 1841 he is both canebrake bully ("thar's a hot place in my gizzard, and my gall is reddy to bust, and besides all this my feelins is hurt") and national hero (a "Justass of the peace" welcomes him into his family as "a extinguished orthur"). The man whose brag and banter derive from the oral tradition of frontier storytelling is the same man pledged to scribal honesty, even when his authorship is faked and the author himself is dead.

As we have realized for some time, despite the lingering influence of Constance Rourke,[18] the sketches of A. B. Longstreet and the authors who followed him are not simply written versions of tales passed along from one folk group to another. Antebellum southern humor is a written art, whatever its sources in oral performance. The readers of these newspaper pieces in the 1840s were not necessarily privy to the performative contexts of oral folklore, and it now seems increasingly irrelevant to ponder the questions we once asked about their sources: are they attempts to

18. Constance M. Rourke, *American Humor: A Study of the National Character* (1931; reprint, New York: Harcourt Brace Jovanovich, 1959).

reproduce the exact conformation of stories heard? are they village jokes? are they whole-cloth inventions triggered by overheard phrases? are they salutes to locally famous real-life yarn-spinners? Despite the notorious typographical variations in nineteenth-century printing, the written story inscribed itself as text, which, if not immutable, claimed by its materiality an authority that supplanted all oral versions that *may* have preceded it. Signally absent in the texts, however, is an entire array of paralinguistic stylings inherent in the oral tale: shrugs, raised eyebrows, hand gestures, facial twitches—everything in the one medium that is not reproducible in the other.

Even the most honest effort to reproduce the event in writing smooths out, erases, or simplifies the kinds of ambiguities that oral performance always involves, and it introduces others more congenial to the print medium.[19] The quasi-literate (at best) storytellers who figure prominently in the written sketches celebrate a kind of self-awareness different from that of the educated authors, who modify the performative styles in the light of their own market. As Derrideans and others have argued, the act of listening as well as the act of speaking is the experience of dealing with "just-vanished sounds." The energy in those sounds comes from the fragmentation of narrative, its banal recapitulations and modest variations, its ad hoc spins, its irrelevancies and anticlimaxes, sometimes its pointlessness. What the writer achieves with his oral sources is not so much an intervention as an incarnation. Committing a tale to text, even in its crude, error-prone typography, is tantamount to freezing a mutable moment imagined in a new way.

One of the ironies of Southwest humor lies in its perpetual tension between what is heard and what is written. The authors, the only agents for preserving what they heard, embraced phonocentrism as the only viable excuse for their art. Not to affirm the priority of the spoken would be to offer themselves as nothing more than second-rate Irvings. The narrator figure may pretend to the objectivity of a detached observer, but he is never quite neutral. He knows that at some point the repeated oral tale must submit to strategies that in effect bar further extension in that antic mode. The author-narrator cannot do otherwise than shape what has been heard (or imagined as heard) to his own more comfortable medium, which means that his authority supersedes that of the storyteller. Even Jim Doggett's superb yarn is not allowed to rest in its captivating mys-

19. Walter J. Ong, *Interfaces of the Word: Studies in the Evolution of Consciousness and Culture* (Ithaca, NY: Cornell University Press, 1977), 133–34, 167.

tery without the narrator imposing what Derrida terms the "[m]ore rational, more exact, more precise, more clear" biases of the text.[20] (That it is an inadequate interjection is irrelevant.) The narrator, however conscientious in transcribing authentic sounds, must abide by the pressures of his own conventions.[21] None of the authors, including George Washington Harris, the most phonocentric of them all, could evade their own *scribal* destinies.

There is yet another fold in the ironies of the storyteller-narrator relationship. Despite some readers who would like to make them a function of folklore, the yarn-spinners of the humor do not emerge out of a true oral culture as anthropologists conceive of it: that is, backwoods orality is neither coherent nor ritualistic. The tribal consciousness that operates in, for example, certain Native Americans is only roughly applicable to the hunters, guides, and boatmen who gloried in their talk in the new country; of necessity, even the most illiterate among them maintained cultural links with the dominant textual culture. Some, like Lewis's Mik-hoo-tah, yearning for fame in a yellow-backed book, aggressively pursue those links with a medium that can stabilize their immaterial stories.

As a kind of competition, storytelling, like other forms, is essentially an intramural activity. Although the structure of their sketches confirmed the social porousness of the Old Southwest, the humorists, with command of mainstream English on their side, were usually content to make their linguistic markers a sufficient earnest of their superior status. At the same time, they sensed the logic behind the principles affirmed by a later commentator. Walter Benjamin reminded us that storytellers draw from experience "passed on from mouth to mouth," and that the best written versions are those that differ "least from the speech of the many nameless storytellers."[22] The humorists never allowed their egos to clash with vernacular performers in the kind of verbal dueling we see in Mark Twain's battle of wits with Mr. Brown, the pilot-boss in *Life on the Mississippi*.[23] Among themselves, these professionals apparently repeated

20. Barbara Johnson, "Writing," in *Critical Terms for Literary Study*, ed. Frank Lentricchia and Thomas McLaughlin (Chicago: University of Chicago Press, 1990), 46; Jacques Derrida, *Of Grammatology*, trans. Gayatry Chakravorty Spivak (Baltimore: Johns Hopkins University Press, 1976), 301, 50–55, 70–76.

21. See Alessandro Portelli, *The Text and the Voice: Writing, Speaking, and Democracy in American Literature* (New York: Columbia University Press, 1994), 12–15.

22. Walter Benjamin, "The Storyteller: Reflections on the Works of Nikolai Leskov," in *Illuminations*, trans. Harry Zohn (New York: Schocken Books, 1969), 84.

23. See Lawrence Howe, "Transcending the Limits of Experience: Mark Twain's *Life on the Mississippi*," *American Literature* 63 (1991): 420–39.

yeoman stories recast in their own oral mimicking of dialect, but in the company of dialect speakers, they never engaged the vernacular story-tellers at their own game. The authors knew their chief subject was some-body else's stories, and one of their functions, if they were to make them their own, was to provide space in which backcountry yarn-spinners could perform as effectively as their talent allowed. As the author's stand-in, the narrator was cast in a role that brings no applause. The text, his priority, had to be favored because it had a longer life, yet most of this humor owed its existence to talk, and most of its vitality lay in a written mode powerfully shaped by the rhythms of human speech. The authors seem to have sensed a theoretical bias that we think of as a recent vin-tage: that speech *should* be favored not because of some prior status, but because of its immediacy, its sensuous presence. To borrow Barbara Johnson's terms, literacy made them agents of cultural empowerment: the life of *logocentrism* was preserved through *graphocentrism*. "It may well be," writes Johnson, that it is "only in a text-centered culture that one can privilege speech in a logocentric way."[24] By virtue of his medium, the author-narrator, whatever his subject, was the agent of control and mastery.

In the affective moment, however, that power was strangely provi-sional. Even if he exercised his responsibility as a sensitive mediator be-tween the primitive and the cultivated with tact and empathy, the role of the narrator was often mitigated by the very sources upon which his telling depended: the rival power of the human voice and alternative modes of storytelling. Whether genial, bemused, or condescending in his encounters with more virile and colorful characters, the narrator in his social control is often compromised. Even the mastery that really mat-ters—the aesthetic—frequently succumbs to the storyteller whose ver-nacular dominates the terms of discourse, overwhelming and routing the civilized accents of the sponsor. The author's mouthpiece is rarely hu-miliated by the overpowering presence of his yeoman subject, but in the social context he is often rendered superfluous. Even though his medium is the permanent one, what logic and history tell us—that the narrator represents both the present and the future—is temporarily marginalized in the high profiling of vivid figures who represent cultural backwaters. It is not surprising that the narrator sometimes stands around awkward-ly, a second fiddle who knows in his heart that he has a better future than the star performer.

24. Johnson, "Writing," 47.

The usual activities worth "norating a little" were those whose very function depended on noise: horse racing, fighting, Indian alarms, camp meetings, hunts in the big woods, musters, storytelling itself. Even village activities conducted in ceremonial idioms—weddings, church services, funerals, courtroom trials—were mostly conditions waiting to be shattered by disruptive sounds. Sicily Burns's marriage to Clapshaw, Sut Lovingood reports, was "the worst one fur noise, disappintment, skeer, breakin things, hurtin, trubbil, vexashun ove spirrit" (*SL*, 96).

The privileged sense in most nineteenth-century writing is sight, and one critic has made the link between seeing and knowing part of a larger Victorian concern for mastery. Our technologies of representation, writes Peter Brooks, "always bear witness to that impossible enterprise of arresting and fixing the object of inspection." In antebellum humorous writing, however, the privileged sense is sound, beginning with its representation of the voices of the backcountry. If mainstream writing is an exhibit of storytelling in which mastery through seeing and knowing is the central struggle, that of the humorists is the struggle to know through hearing.[25] That struggle can result in conspicuous failure. Hearing is not always believing, as Longstreet demonstrates in "Georgia Theatrics." Overhearing what he takes to be a vicious fight just off the roadway, the narrator rushes into the bushes to intervene, preachily condemning such violence. But his ears have been deceived by a lone ploughboy who, in rehearsing a fight, has "played all the parts." His multiple impersonation is an audio performance whose success on the natural stage requires a curtain of green to mask the reality of his role-playing. That barrier to adequate sight lines both enhances the illusion that prompts the narrator's rush to judgment and validates the actor's graphic rejoinder: "You needn't kick before you're spur'd. There a'nt nobody there, nor ha'nt been nother. I was jist seein' how I could'a' *fout*" (*GS*, 4–6).

The most vivid voice in the humor is of course Sut Lovingood's, but it shares with others the fondness for duplicating the sequences of things heard, primarily the urgency of the storyteller caught in his stuttering compulsion to fill the air with his voice. If the narrative is rarely linear, it is not solely because the form is that of the shaggy-dog artist, but also because the teller must take the time to mimic the way in which the sounds of objects reach the ear: *crosh, spang, whang, kerbim, ca-chunk, cowollop, cawhalux!* Externally, too, the storytelling site of the frame tale, where oral

25. Peter Brooks, *Body Work: Objects of Desire in Modern Narrative* (Cambridge, MA: Harvard University Press, 1993), 106.

performer and audience interact, often refuses to be a passive scene. Listeners may be appreciative or skeptical, but they are rarely silent for long: they make themselves known by expressions of doubt, astonishment, or satisfaction in spurts of interjections, snorts, and challenges in kind.

The aural expectations aroused by the storytelling context make Jim Doggett's story of the unhuntable bear all the more impressive. When the hunter ends his yarn, Thorpe takes yet another inventive turn in a story whose complexity derives from a succession of such turns: "When the story was ended, our hero sat some minutes with his auditors in a grave silence; I saw that there was a mystery to him connected with the bear whose death he had just related, that had evidently made a strong impression on his mind" (*TBT*, 122). The uniqueness of this conclusion lies in the *signifying silence,* both internally and externally, of storyteller and audience. It is a rare moment in southwestern writing, in which much "vexashun ove spirrit" reaches us through sounds. Vladimir Nabokov, in an early story, allows his autobiographical narrator to generalize: "All silence is the recognition of a mystery."[26] Thorpe perceives something similar when the hunter finishes his tale. But if the educated narrator recognizes a mystery, Doggett does so first. Whereas the narrator must dispel the mystery according to his own rational lights, Thorpe allows his vernacular hero *no* interpretation. He may be a child of the wood, as the narrator easily categorizes him, but Doggett knows enough about the art of storytelling to quit when he is ahead of the game. Whatever "strong impression" the re-created experience has made on his mind, he will not squander success with an audience that greeted him initially as a loud-mouthed braggart. Doggett has learned how to modulate his voice, to pace his narration, and to surprise his auditors with the rhetorical effectiveness of climaxing silence. Finally, to "break the silence," he invites "all present to 'liquor,'" which is at once a self-ratification of his skills (of storytelling if not of bear hunting) and a sign of his victory over a tough audience. Both storyteller and narrator know that Doggett has earned his celebration, drinking "to his heart's content" with skeptical strangers now converted to "companions" (*TBT*, 122).

In its inscribing writtenness, Southwest humor thus benefits from imitating a culture of things heard. It makes art out of both the truckler and the blowhard, but its abiding weakness is for logorrhea wherever it shows up. The garrulous yarn-spinner may be interested in crafting intricate,

26. Vladimir Nabokov, "Sounds," trans. Dmitri Nabokov, in *The Stories of Vladimir Nabokov* (New York: Knopf, 1995), 20.

inconclusive tales, but he meanders and defers most probably because he likes the sustaining sounds of his own voice.

Certainly the literate author-narrator profits from his efforts to suggest the immediacy of those sounds. Of all the formal ingredients available to the nineteenth-century writer, the humorists' favorites are monologue and dialogue. Except for Thorpe and Baldwin, these authors are strangely uninterested in using realistic description to render vivid their imagined worlds: not merely representations of scenery and landscape, but also of physiognomy (the tics and gestures that discriminate a person from his general class), climate (seasonal differences), spatial specificity (architecture in nature, floor plans of dwellings), and all the other representations in print that an author uses when he determines to see and interpret *what is*. The rendering of speech is the major compositional feature that justifies our impulse to see these humorous sketches as the early stirrings of literary realism. (Even that feature is so intensely pursued, so intensively inscribed, that in certain hands—those of Henry Clay Lewis and George Washington Harris come to mind—the sketch attains a mutated weirdness that outstrips any conventional understanding of realism as a mode.) The humorists were unable to conceive of story outside the sound of the spoken voice, the rhythm of speech rendered, not merely conceptualized. After them, no major American author could ignore the vernacular claim on realism. If the storyteller is the central figure in oral culture, the author-narrator is the central figure in typographic culture; and the primary mission of the latter is to represent in print the configurations of the former—often its vitality, sometimes its poverty. Not all the antebellum sketches depend upon the serviceable mingling of educated narrator and vernacular storyteller, but they all exploit the authors' efforts to represent the spokenness on which they depend. Not all backwoods figures tell sustained stories, but they all *talk*.

If vernacular speakers emphasize sound—the way humans, animals, and objects make noises—literate narrators must manipulate their medium to suggest that emphasis. Yet the structure of writing, its permanence, contributes to a kind of order that talking rarely concerns itself with. As Walter J. Ong has argued, the sensory bases of the very concept of order are largely visual. Words are seen, not merely heard; they belong to the scribe who originates them, not finally to the talker whose sounds are evanescent and lost as soon as they are uttered. The author may try as he might to be faithful to the "rich but chaotic existential context" of oral utterance, but in the end, his representation of pauses and emphases, facial and body gestures, circumstantial details of setting, and the linguistic negotiation of informal conversation will be noticed: the words on the page must do double duty as carriers of substance and context.[27] In the humorist's struggle to know through hearing, translating sound into sight is the narrator's triumph, not the storyteller's. The material page continues through time, while the human voice it has captured in type fades into the ether. Sound *was;* writing *is.* To transform sound into sight is to triumph over the evanescent, but it is also to triumph, poignantly, over the author's inspiration and competitor whose glory is the transitory one of spokenness.

iv.

We can never recover the voices that by report were marvels of kinetic storytelling—or, alternately, astounding feats of discursive maundering. Whatever his reputation, the storyteller insisted on doing it his own way at his own pace. Though his performances are unrecoverable, we have clues in the written versions—notably in the assorted Crockett texts, McNutt's Jim and Chunkey stories, Hall's Mike Hooter yarns, and Brannan's mock sermons—of what the tales might have been in their oral life. If these traces of the oral medium suggest that even the most adept yarnspinners had their limits, we have even stronger evidence that the narrating medium had its limits. Certainly the authors' conceptual inventiveness in constructing a yeoman-inflected humor seems to have only rarely transcended the limits of its chirographic and technical machinery.

Because the storyteller is central to the humorists' enterprise, a few of the weaker scribes invest too much of their own imaginative capital in this creative totem, as if they are obliged to walk in the shadow of a greater precursor talent. Such phrases as "will lose much in the telling," "I cannot pretend to do justice to," and "I am afraid they cannot well be transferred to canvas" dot the prose of the more awkward newspaper pieces. Invoking the classic site for frontier storytelling, Richard S. Elliott rhapsodizes on a hunter's campfire in "A Buffalo Tale": "How welcome is the extravagant tale of wild adventure, or the humorous relation of some ludicrous scene!" But the gratifying pleasure exacts a price in self-deprecation: "At such times I regretted that I was not a story-teller!" (Oehl., 124). Many of the newspaper contributors could never quite decide how much con-

27. Walter J. Ong, *The Presence of the Word* (New Haven, CT: Yale University Press, 1967), 108, 136–37, 103–4.

text was necessary for transforming a heard (or imagined) oral yarn into a self-sufficient sketch. Baldwin's anecdotes featuring vernacular speakers in court testimony or legal consultation all too often err by providing insufficient context, as if the educated narrator is unwilling to expend his own creative energy in melding passing moments into a coherent piece. The sketches "Jo. Heyfron" and "Scan. Mag." exploit Irish lingo, not only as a kind of shorthand characterization but also as a substitute for narrative. "Old Uncle John Olive" is more fleshed out in its focus on a witty but illiterate yeoman, but even Baldwin's superb forensic gifts cannot disguise the fact that it is nothing more than a one-shot, squiblike sketch that could benefit from expansion.

More commonly, the attempt to capture the flavor of the storytelling art sends the author-narrator in the opposite direction: not toward condensed economy, but toward self-indulgent diffuseness. Mostly it is a matter of indirect discourse in which the narrator incorporates into his own register a few phrases of the yarn-spinner, just enough to suggest unhurried storytelling. The "setting up" is sometimes oblique, depending on intertextual allusions to prior pieces and authorial rivalry—as we see in many of the *St. Louis Reveille* sketches. Elliott's story about storytelling begins sluggishly with a salute to ancient antecedents (Caliph Haroun Al Raschid, the Chinese "Celestials," North American Indians) in an introduction that competes for space with its subject, the amusing tales of a "rare narrator" of the author's acquaintance. Joseph Field begins "Fast on a Bar" by establishing its river site entirely in pilots' verbal locutions ("collectors," "draught," "*last* bell," "the Mouth") that, though familiar to contemporary steamboat passengers, are largely lost on later readers (Oehl., 86–89).

The frame tale would seem to be the form with the greatest potential for highlighting startling stylistic contrasts. Yet it emerged as a form that effectively registered the decline of lingual ostentation, the ponderous syntax and diction of the more pedantic practitioners of textbook English. It is not odd that "The Big Bear of Arkansas" has become a defining text for the whole of Southwest humor. Despite its atypicality, this piece is an almost perfect example of how conversational style in the late antebellum years triumphed over the florid stiffness of earlier nineteenth-century prose. It was not the triumph that grammarians feared—the replacement of accepted and approved usage by the show-offy colloquialism of frontier orality. What Thorpe's piece achieved was less dramatic—a newer, more utilitarian style whose idioms of common speech had absorbed the formalities of heavy-handed correctness. To varying degrees, the same loosening of conventionally elegant English can be seen in other box-structure sketches.

To appreciate Thorpe's stylistic accomplishment, we have only to turn to those occasional sketches in which the two narrating levels do indeed jar. One egregious example of a tin ear occurs, oddly enough, in Robb's "Fun with a 'Bar.'" Its problem is not pretentiousness but its reliance on the clichés of storytelling convention. The setting, the much-used western campsite of bored hunters, is redeemed by a skillful tale told by Dan Elkhorn, a credible vernacular storyteller. But the otherwise talented Robb risks subverting this tale at the outset. In a prose so backward-sounding that the author seems unaware of his own words, the narrator fills his introductory paragraph with nineteenth-century poeticisms and verbal scene-setting derived from romantic painting: "The evening's repast was over, and as they stretched themselves in easy attitudes around their stack of rifles, each looked at the other with a kind of questioning expression, of whether it should be *sleep* or a *yarn*?" Because the encampment is bathed in the "silvery sheen" of a full moon, "investing . . . those vast solitudes with a strange charm," the hunters opt for a yarn: "Dan Elkhorn was the leader of the party, and all knew his store of adventure inexhaustible, so a unanimous cry was made upon Dan for a story. 'Come, Dan,' cried a crony, 'give us something to laugh at, and let us break this silence, which seems to breed a spirit of melancholy—stir us up, old fellow, do!'" (Cohen, 179). Fortunately, Dan obliges, and his fine yarn ends the sketch, which never returns to the deadening jollity of the narrator.

The difficulty in "Fun with a 'Bar'" is not Robb's inept handling of colloquial dialect but an uncertain control of his own lingual level. The lapse here is all the more curious since this professional newspaperman was also an old hand at writing humor. His undisputed mastery of vernacular in a wide range of frontier characters is evidenced by *Streaks of Squatter Life, and Far-West Scenes* (1847) as well as by sketches from the *Reveille* that he never collected: one in which an old matron is pleasantly done in by an innkeeper's "sweeten'd drinks" ("Not a Drop More, Major"); another featuring Jim Sikes, who courts the bustle-loving daughter of a suspicious neighbor ("Nettle Bottom Ball"); and yet another about Old Sugar, a whiskey-making extortionist ("The Standing Candidate"). Robb was also adept at reproducing the sounds of his own class in such pieces as "An Incident before Marriage" and "That Last Julep! A Short Temperance Story!" The sophisticated voice of "Swallowing an Oyster Alive" belongs to a city slicker who loves hoaxing the hicks; in this famous first sketch Robb allowed the narrator to assume without fancy turns the superior tone that readers expected in this stock situation.

Except for his rare lapse in the Dan Elkhorn piece, Robb betrayed no uncertainty in his ability to reproduce any level of speech he heard. Such authorial confidence, however, is altogether missing in a brief sketch by another professional newspaperman, George Wilkins Kendall. "Bill Dean, the Texan Ranger" is ineffective, despite its appearance in *Spirit of the Times.* Kendall pronounces Bill Dean the funniest wag among the Texas Volunteers in the Mexican War, and he clearly intends to honor that waggery; after his initial paragraph, however, he seems to withdraw from the effort. Dean's "speech or harangue, or whatever it may be termed," Kendall writes, "will lose much in the telling, yet I will endeavor to put it upon paper in as good shape as possible." That shape, as all humorists knew, was the orthographic imitation of colorful speech. Its success depended largely on the sensitivity and skill of the author in transcribing the words, sounds, and rhythms of a storyteller most unlike himself. One of the founders of the *New Orleans Picayune*, Kendall was a wag himself, by reputation a congenial and witty raconteur, but "Bill Dean" is a labored, pedestrian effort. Above all, it is self-conscious, petering out with an allusion to yet another of the Texan's tales that the author chooses *not* to repeat. Kendall ends with a tacit confession of yearning ineptitude: "if I could only make it as effective on paper as he did in the telling, it would draw a laugh from those fond of the ludicrous" (Cohen, 96–97).

That, of course, was the point of being a humorist on paper: to draw a laugh by approximating verbally the art of the oral yarn-spinner. Everyone involved in newspaper humor—authors, editors, readers—was fond of the ludicrous, but success depended on the authors' skill. Kendall's concession gives away too much. Compare Thorpe's quiet authority as the narrator who asserts that he has let Jim Doggett give the story "in his own way." We might question the imaginative scope of Thorpe's narrator, but he is not nervous about his ability to present his subject. He is as firmly authoritative in rendering yeoman dialect as he is his own respectable English. The same holds true for Skitt, Taliaferro's stand-in for most of the *Fisher's River* sketches, who emerges as one of the most confident narrators in the humor. Both Lewis in "A Tight Race Considerin'" and Hall in the Mike Hooter pieces are as relaxed as they are authoritative in their interaction with vernacular speakers. All of the humorists knew, and some of them (like Kendall) nervously acknowledged, the distinction between what they heard and experienced in real life and what ultimately appeared on paper. As the wide variation in quality demonstrates, much depended on each writer's talents—more precisely, on each writer's knack for filtering the believable colloquial sounds of his world through ordinary style and the rhetoric of his own profession.

Though the frame tale was a common structural arrangement for showcasing the mingling of linguistic levels, it was not the only form that did so. Structure was always less important to the humorists than texture; the sketches were at their best when the orthography and rhythm represented credible approximations of heard tales. The most common form was the simple anecdote in which an educated correspondent relates an amusing incident by liberally quoting a backwoodsman. Ranging in length from a squiblike paragraph to a complicated narration of many paragraphs, the anecdote was boilerplate, a kind of conceptual grid for much newspaper humor. Neither Baldwin's "Jo. Heyfron" (as we have seen) nor Joseph Field's "Honey Run" (based on the stock situation of strangers of different sexes having to undress in a cramped cabin) is narratively ambitious, but both authors sensed that the juxtaposition of language levels was the key to effectiveness. A simple extension of the anecdote form was the dramatized exchange structured as dialogue-and-summary, such as Longstreet's "Georgia Theatrics" and Robb's "Swallowing an Oyster Alive." Still another variation was the profile, a kind of backwoods version of the seventeenth-century "Character": Baldwin's "Ovid Bolus" (about the quintessential liar), Sol Smith's "Slow Traveling by Steam" (about a gambling captain too fond of "brag") and Thorpe's "Tom Owen, the Bee-Hunter."

Although Baldwin largely finessed the crucial interchange of vernacular and standard educated styles, his focus on the bench and bar in *Flush Times* allowed him to exploit dialectal variations, not merely in illiterate clients but in his own legal fraternity. Although his interest in backwoods talk was never primary, he found rich material in the simple discovery that being a marginal literate and practicing law were not mutually exclusive in the Old Southwest. In one of his finest pieces, "Cave Burton, Esq., of Kentucky" (his only frame tale), Baldwin fondly depicts "the Blowing Cave" who, in a market already "glutted with brass," was "the pure metal all through." A gourmandizing demagogue, Burton had "not much intellect, but what he had he kept going with a wonderful clatter." In reproducing his subject's "Earthquake-Story" Baldwin calculatingly diminishes much of that rustic clatter, "leaving out most of the episodes, the casual explanations and the slang"—which, he admits, makes it comparable to "the play of Hamlet with the Prince of Denmark omitted." The self-editing in the Cave Burton sketch, balancing the author's own style and the "wonderful clatter" of a quasi-literate politician, is memorable because it is not overloaded with dialectal variations for their own sake (*FT*, 153–76).

We may be grateful that narrators and storytellers were not conceived as existing in a polarized relationship. With few exceptions, the humorists enjoyed the kind of joyous noise churned up in the interaction of idioms. Indeed, as in "The Big Bear of Arkansas," the very notation of subliterate conversation often affected the inherited style of straight narration, softening its stiffer formalities. Longstreet's narrators may sometimes sound priggish, but their style is not especially fussy. In "The Character of a Native Georgian," Lyman Hall describes his friend Ned Brace, the practical joker, in typical style—correct, but without pretension, in the accepted discursive mode of his time. For sixteen years, he tells us, Brace "never involved himself in a personal rencounter" with anyone, "owing in part to his muscular frame which few would be willing to engage; but more particularly to his adroitness in the management of his projects of fun. He generally conducted them in such a way as to render it impossible for anyone to call him to account without violating all the rules of decency, politeness, honor and chivalry at once" (*GS*, 20).

By 1835 these savvy authors had tempered the orotund stateliness of elitist prose in a discourse available to most readers—the "middling" style of American public life. If we should doubt this accomplishment, we have only to dip into the volumes of belletrists and journalists contemporary with the humorists: Bayard Taylor, say, or Nathaniel Parker Willis, who were still enamored of high literary art as lexicographers and national leaders defined it. Although they accepted as their natural legacy the genteel prose of the early century, the humorists rarely followed its decorous solemnities except to indulge in good-natured mockery. Because they liked to think of themselves as moderns, they betrayed a brash self-consciousness even when their writing followed too closely the avuncular elegancies of Washington Irving (still a cultural icon in the antebellum South).[28] The prose of these authors is primarily that of mainstream American writing at midcentury, a style common to most of our canonical writers except for the more innovative (conspicuously, Thoreau and Melville).

The authorial surrogate may function as straight man to a slang-whanger. More often, however, like Baldwin's narrators, he likes his style to have a little color, too. Many of these narrators are vulnerable to the lure of Latin tags—a tribute to the pervasive influence of the bench and

---

28. The Knickerbocker shadow fell most heavily, as we have seen, on the topographical and sporting essays of T. B. Thorpe, the most reluctant of the humorists and the least southernized of the easterners.

bar in the South—and, because the authors were well-read in earlier texts, their stand-ins often enrich their sentences with quotations from Shakespeare (a runaway favorite), Milton, Pope, Dr. Johnson, Addison, Scott, Lamb, Byron, and Irving. Some allude to French novelists, contemporary historians and journalists, and playwrights and theatrical performers. In short, if the charm of rustic embellishment of matter and manner draws the narrator to his backwoods subject, the gentleman also has his own hoard of ornamentation to draw upon. Unlike the contributors of turf dispatches or statistical reports of exceptional deer hunts in the wild (the generic sources of so many sketches), the authors held no great store for mere facts and the simple narratives they generated. Like Tom Sawyer (who, Huck Finn noted, always "throwed more style into" his projects than his unread friends), these contributors liked to smarten up their comic accounts, for fear that flashy vernacular might throw in the shade any style that was *only* ordinary.

They dipped freely into expressions from the backwoods (to show their comfort with their time and place) while simultaneously cultivating their own guild-like argot, with its air of irreverence and a few dollops of old *Salmagundi* wit (to show their comfort with irreverent modernity). Such styles as the humorists developed ranged from the simple to the ornamental, but their puns, mock etymologies, mock sententiae, quotations in ironic contexts, and playful adaptations of foreign phrases punctured schoolmaster ponderousness. What they aimed for, and what the most successful authors achieved, was a confidential, cohesive tone that surmounted any particular rhetorical device.

Among Matthew Field's satiric pieces on theatrical experiences is this advice to stagestruck villagers: "Go out into the woods and practice your voice for roaring, much depends upon this. Get a slender, straight stick, . . . and learn to poke it at a tree, and as you poke study how far you can stride your feet apart without falling. Or, another way to practice for this accomplishment, is to poke the yard stick through a knot hole in the fence, from whence it is called *fencing*" (Oehl., 143). The other Field, brother Joseph, was both an actor and a newspaperman, addicted equally to both physical and verbal capering: "There is a spot, in the south-western part of this state, known as the *Fiery Fork of Honey Run*—a delicious locality, no doubt, as the *run* of 'honey' is, of course, accompanied by a corresponding flow of 'milk,' and a mixture of milk and honey, or, at any rate, honey and 'Peach' is the evidence of sublunary contentment, every place where they have preaching!" (Cohen, 105–6). Despite having neither a conscience nor a sense of humor, Billy Fishback is a humorous character largely by virtue of his creator's use of eighteenth-century devices in constructing the adventures of his Confederate deserter—moralizing tags, comic digressions, mock-heroic rhetoric, and an intrusive intimacy between narrator and reader. Kittrell Warren establishes his biographer-narrator as a confidential voice tracking the movements of his yeoman hero: "If Fishback suffered misfortunes, *we* were present with the balm of sympathy; if he reveled in a hortus deliciarum, the gates were not closed on us; if he 'played fantastic tricks,' *we* bore him company. In a word, wherever he went, *we* were *thar*. Not in the flesh, but in the *sperrit*. Whatever he did we *seed* it" (*AS*, 21).

Some rhetorical embellishments come when the humorists have fun with refined style by imagining it as an appropriate vehicle for their un-refined subjects. A language suitable for commemorating the life of a worthy, for example, is adopted by Johnson Jones Hooper when he presents to the world Captain Simon Suggs. There are, writes Suggs's biographer, "well-authenticated instances within our knowledge, wherein he has divided with a needy friend, the five or ten dollar bill which his consummate address had enabled him to obtain from some luckless individual, without the rendition of any sort of equivalent, excepting only solemnly reiterated promises to repay within two hours at farthest" (*SS*, 12). The syntactical dilation in this commemorative life of a backwoods confidence man is itself a commentary on the entire genre of campaign biography. Joseph Field is more restrained in his satiric mode, but his source is the same: the attenuating formality of genteel style. Here he writes about surly waiters in steamboat dining rooms who tend to disappear when needed: "I wish, in quiet wise, to give unto type, as the result of much observation, the grave reflections consequent thereon; and my manner shall be as unadorned as my matter is sweet and gracious" (Oehl., 89). Solemnity as satire occurs in segments of *Georgia Scenes* (particularly those with Baldwin as narrator), *Flush Times, Streaks of Squatter Life,* and most individual sketches in which an educated narrator views his vernacular subject from a bemused distance. Cropping up regularly are phrases such as "our present and elderly hero," "a sang froid that was inimitable," and "his heroic brow."

Buttressed by verbal wit borrowed from the oral yarn's higher-toned cousins, the written texts, capturing in print what one writer has termed "the perishable breath of oral tradition," called for talents different from as well as similar to those necessary for the performative acts that inspired them.[29] For all their bows to verbal equivalents of oral style, the

---

29. Frederick Turner, *Spirit of Place: The Making of an American Literary Landscape* (San Francisco: Sierra Club, 1989), 79.

humorists embraced their own medium with considerable gusto and, often, with a self-consciousness appropriate to their guild-like sense of belonging. As much as they relied on neighborhood gossip, tales swapped by wagging tongues, local raconteurs, and episodes that were "norrated about a bit," the authors also liked to show their independence of such oral troves by quoting literary texts and applying historical precedents to village doings. They would have been the first to admit that they gloried in their literacy.

v.

The oral tall tale in the hands of Mark Twain has been described as less a form than an imaginative arena of "formlessness, extravagance, and unbridled wildness."[30] This may be a critical stretcher. Both the social realism at the core of our greatest humorist and his sly calculation of aesthetic effect would have disallowed the kind of imaginative chaos that such a judgment implies. Certainly Twain's version has little pertinence to the work of his predecessors in vernacular humor, who were not especially attracted to the tall tale. Although their work is speech-dominated, most of the oral performances—except for the wildness of the half-horse half-alligators (as we shall see) and some of the extravagant flights in the later Crockett almanacs—are comfortably accommodated to the ordinariness of village and rural life as the authors depicted it. The impact of the oral tale is to be seen mostly in the transactive scene of performance and response. Even the Munchausens of Taliaferro's Fisher's River operate within the bounds of the familiar and the settled; and Harris's Sut Lovingood never imagines himself apart from the community he aligns himself against. Yarn-spinning, as we see in Hall's Mike Hooter stories and in those of McNutt's Jim and Chunky, need not be especially tall to be vivid and memorable for those who participate in the dynamic of performance and response.

Unlike the memoirists later in the nineteenth century, the humorous authors, with no retrospective revisionism, rarely evoked the ceremonial events or community-building occasions that helped to make settlements and hamlets cohesive. Their preference (in part because it was more narratively interesting) was to emphasize the spirit of tension and opposition, the contest for superiority that we see in such characteristic tales as "The Horse-Swap," "A Tight Race Considerin'," and "Parson Bullen's Liz-

30. Wonham, *Mark Twain*, 27.

ards." Yet despite the emphasis on what we often think of as masculinist discourse, we also find in this humor a noticeable strain of storytelling that runs counter to the dominant competitive one. Some stories do not even focus on the contest as narrative hook, and some storytelling sites are conspicuously free of auditors clamoring to choose sides or to bet on outcomes. These include some of Taliaferro's sketches, most of the letters of Thompson's Joseph Jones, Thorpe's "Tom Owen, the Bee-Hunter" and "Enemy in Front and Rear," and a handful of Sol Smith's pieces on the Southwest theater. These comic sketches may have done little to strengthen the collaborative needs of backwoods society, but they featured talk-based occasions that skirted the kind of discord that more aggressive storytellers invited. As we have seen, even with Jim Doggett, the most accomplished of the hunters-as-storytellers, the consummate masculine tenor of the telling site was processed through a filter of civil urbanity.

One of the gentler sketches in Lewis's *Swamp Doctor* is "My First Call in the Swamp," in which Madison Tensas must endure an evening of communal storytelling by six old ladies, all of them whiling away a long night waiting for the doctor's treatment to take effect on a patient in another room. After proffering his own yarns, the narrator notes, with some admiration, "what wonderful recitals they gave me in return!" The assembled matrons learnedly discourse on *yarbs, kumfrey tea,* and *sweet gum sav;* they agree on the "general correctness" of such observations that "we must all die when our time kums"; they smile at Miss Pechum's joke about her son, which turns on *bite, right,* and *fight;* and they listen enthralled to Miss Stiver's ghost story, which ends with a "beautiful maid" drowning "in a large churn of buttermilk" that her mother had set aside for market (*SD,* 150).

Although Tensas knows that one role of the rural doctor is to become a "repository of all the news, scandal, and secrets" of the neighborhood (which he can then distribute along with tonics and pills), his evening with the six old ladies is expressly not concerned with that. Their storytelling comes from their own repository; he is just the latest recipient of what falls from their "case-hardened tongues." And just as these participatory stories elicit the expected responses from the female contingent already familiar with them ("Blessed Master!" and "Lordy grashus!" and "Well, did you ever!" and "You don't say so!" and "Dear heart do tell!"), so the youthful male among them responds with his own "profuse . . . expressions of astonishment and admiration" (*SD,* 148–50). It is a satisfying venue for cooperative storytelling: the sickbed gives rise to the same impulse toward narrative entertainment as the social hall of a steamboat or a doggery porch. What is different is the lack of rivalry in the domestic narrations of the tellers—each is both teller and hearer, and all operate in a venue notably free of the tensions and incipient violence that attend most situations of masculine tale-telling. Instead of skepticism voiced by the auditors, what we get are ritualistic murmurs of encouragement to facilitate an atmosphere conducive to domestic storytelling.

Eve Sedgwick has labeled as "feminine" the kind of narration based on "the precious, devalued arts of gossip, immemorially associated in European thought with servants, with effeminate and gay men, with all women."[31] These are in fact the kinds of narratives that in the United States came into their own in the 1870s with the popularity of local-color fiction (whose most distinctive creators were women), but they also appeared in antebellum humor more frequently than we ordinarily imagine. We see it in Thorpe's "A Piano in Arkansas," Hall's "How Sally Hooter Got Snake-Bit," Robinson's "Lije Benadix," and Robb's "Nettle Bottom Ball." And we see its definitive treatment in Longstreet's "A Sage Conversation"—a sketch that, stripped of its mild ribaldry, could serve as a precursor text for Mary Wilkins Freeman.

"A Sage Conversation" is another Ned Brace piece from *Georgia Scenes.* The practical jokes of Longstreet's lord of misrule are different from all others in the humor, in part because they are psychological exercises in befuddling, but primarily because Brace's victims and occasions are almost randomly chosen to test his skills. As we have seen in "The Character of a Native Georgian," Ned's pranks are aggressively executed to disrupt the rhythms of human expectations and orderly routine. In "A Sage Conversation," however, his major joke is folded snugly within the protocols of feminine storytelling.

On one of their jaunts about the countryside, Brace and his friend Baldwin, the narrator, are forced to ask for a night's lodging at a house occupied by "three nice, tidy, aged matrons," who, after a "comfortable supper," engage the strangers in conversation. They touch on a wide range of topics and, just before Baldwin and Brace retire for the evening, finally turn to "marriages, happy & unhappy, strange, unequal, runaways, &c."

> "The strangest match," said Ned . . . with a parson's gravity, "that ever I heard of, was that of George Scott and David Snow; two most excellent men, who became so much attached to each other that they actually got married"—

31. Eve Kosofsky Sedgwick, *Epistemology of the Closet* (Berkeley and Los Angeles: University of California Press, 1990), 23.

"The lackaday!" exclaimed one of the ladies.

"And was it really a fact?" enquired another.

"Oh yes, ma'm," continued Ned, "I knew them very well, and often went to their house; and no people could have lived happier or managed better than they did. And they raised a lovely parcel of children—as fine a set as I ever saw, except their youngest son Billy; he was a little wild, but, upon the whole, a right clever boy himself—Come, friend Baldwin, we're setting up too late for travellers." (*GS*, 129–30)

After they retire to an adjoining shed with open chinks between the logs, Ned and the narrator listen as the old ladies puzzle over the fascinating story:

Mrs. Barney.	Didn't that man say them was two *men* that got married to one another?
Mrs. Shad.	It seemed to me so.
Mrs. Reed.	Why to be sure he did. I know he said so; for he said what their names was.
Mrs. B.	Well, in the name o' sense, what did the man mean by saying they raised a fine pa'sel o' children?
Mrs. R.	Why, bless your heart and soul, honey! that's what I've been thinkin' about. It seems mighty curious to me some how or other. I can't study it out, no how.
Mrs. S.	The man must be jokin' certainly.
Mrs. R.	No he wasn't jokin'; for I looked at him, and he was just as much in yearnest as any body I ever *seed:* and besides, no *Christian* man would tell such a story in that solemn way. (*GS*, 130–31)

There is nothing mean-spirited in all this; the butts of Ned Brace's joke are the three well-meaning rural women who have extended their hospitality to make their guests comfortable. Their only flaw is natural curiosity, and that is not enough to warrant any harsh comeuppance. And none is forthcoming.

The matrons' conversation continues with exchanges of neighborhood gossip: whose daughters married and to whom, speculated causes of remembered deaths, and the relative merits of remedies for coughs, ague, and pleurisy. On the following morning the men rise to find the three women already prepared for a new day, but the lady of the house needs clarification about the story that has left them all puzzled: "didn't you say last night, that them was two *men* that got married to one another?"

"Yes madam," said Ned.

"And did'nt you say that they raised a fine pa'cel of children?"

"Yes madam, except Billy.—I said, you know, that he was a little wild."

"Well, yes; I know you said Billy was'nt as clever as the rest of them. But we old women were talking about it last night after you went out, and none of us could make it out, how they could have children; and I said, I reckoned you would'nt mind an old woman's chat, and, therefore, that I would ask you how it could be? I suppose you wont mind telling an old woman how it was."

"Certainly not, madam. They were both widowers before they fell in love with each other and got married."

"The lack-a-day! I wonder none of us thought o' that. And they had children before they got married?"

"Yes madam; they had none afterwards that I heard of."

We were here informed that our horses were in waiting, and we bad the good ladies farewell. (*GS*, 135–36)

The explanation is smoothly executed. The riddle-like answer neatly finesses the biological puzzle but not the homosexuality, and Ned Brace's storytelling skill leaves both perpetrator and victims happy. Although the entire episode, harmless as it is, centers on a joke addict's self-indulgence— the need to get pleasure by playing on human vulnerability—it occurs totally within terms the perpetrator chooses to work within: the nurturing, noncompetitive context of feminine storytelling.

If the characteristic tales of raw challenge (roarer vs. roarer, hunter vs. bear) evoke the touchy masculine world of the Old Southwest, a less bumptious, more socialized world is evoked in a few sketches of displaced or shared authority. In these, the distinction is not always clear-cut between the storytelling act as *boast* (a competitive assertion of skill) and the storytelling act as *bonding* (a congenial exchange of guesses, innuendo, passed-along rumors, unsupported judgments, and fraternal lies). Unsurprisingly, Longstreet's narrator in "A Sage Conversation" is Abraham Baldwin, who usually relates stories focusing on women; the joker is the same Ned Brace who has earlier been seen as the friend of Lyman Hall, the narrator who focuses on masculine pursuits. Indeed, neither of the Ned Brace stories is masculinist yarn-spinning in the manner of "The Fight" or "The Horse-Swap." Ned's submitting of his weakness to the maternal offices of the landlady in "The Character of a Native Georgian" is a gesture that disrupts not merely the good people of Savannah but Longstreet's own neat parceling out of tales and tellers.

"Johns," the biographer of Simon Suggs, never occupies the same physical space as his hero, yet their intimacy is understood to be sufficient to allow him access both to the old man's scams and, on occasion, to his mental processes. Suggs's conventional operating space is masculine—the highway, the improvised military fort, the gambling salon—space dedicated to business and the games of authority and control, not sentiment. But Hooper sets Simon's most demanding performance at a camp meeting, a space triumphantly communal and androgynous, combining the domestic realm of feeling with the outdoors sphere of public discourse and aggressive competition. With his flexible sensibility, Simon presents himself both as rational cynic and sentimental believer, and we are given the precise moment when the first becomes the second. His conversion unfolds in tangible stages, allowing the assembled spectators to "enter as it were into his body and become in some measure the same person with him." The language is that of Adam Smith in his analysis of how imaginative sympathy is communicated.[32] Simon's impersonation of the Man of Feeling is his most adroit. Though it is all fake, the ruse emerges from a reservoir of emotion and technique that the old fraud draws upon regularly. That reservoir is as domestic in its resources as it is masculine.

One of the minor sources of poignance in "The Death of Mike Fink" is the *absence* of both willing ears and a storyteller with a coherent perspective. Joseph Field, unable to play narrator, is forced into the role of investigative reporter, gathering up strands of the story about the end of a quintessential masculine celebrity. In the all-male environment of the fort, Fink engages, in his customary way, with the competitive ethic he has always known; but the hero, now defined by his emotional attachment to another, acts out the role of aging parent-lover, suffering the domestic trauma of loss and grieving his way to his own death.

Most communities, however, were not so uniform in their hostility and rivalry as the fort in Field's tale. In clusters of settlements, hamlets, villages, and towns, there were always tellers and hearers, and they were always touched by the values of the hearth. The prickly Sut Lovingood, as we shall see, is the most antisocial figure in the humor, and yet, by its very specificity, his anti-domestic agenda is dependent upon the domestic. This village pariah is at his best in picking up clues in paternity and adultery cases; in exploring the love-and-lust nostrums needed to bed Sicily Burns or desperate widows (who never seem to be quite desperate

32. Mary Chapman and Glenn Hendler, eds., *Sentimental Men: Masculinity and the Politics of Affect in American Culture* (Berkeley and Los Angeles: University of California Press, 1999), 3.

enough); and in analyzing the coy itch of female flesh for preachers, sheriffs, and assorted males other than himself. Besides all that, no ordinary male could possibly know as many quilt patterns as Sut.

We should not be surprised at how pervasively the domestic impinges on the world the humorists made. Most of their sketches derive not from life in the bush and the ethic governing the males who sporadically inhabit it, but from life in the village and its pressures for carving out a progressive culture. Hunting yarns may first be told around the deep-woods campfire, but they are most likely to be repeated in the settlements, with their larger and fresher audiences. In a body of writing structured so signally on the affective sounds of storytellers, the dynamic that depends on willing ears flourishes best in villages and the cultivated rural spaces connected to them.

Chapter 12 ✦

Droll Specimens and Comfortable Types

[C]haracters of fiction should be descriptive of classes, and not of individuals.

—W. H. Gardiner

Trappers are like sailors—when you describe one the portrait answers for the whole genus.

—Albert Pike

When he reviewed Cooper's *The Spy* (1821) for the *North American Review,* W. H. Gardiner urged American writers to take advantage of the distinct types to be found in the growing nation: the Virginia planter, the "Connecticut pedlar," the "shaggy boatman *'clear from Kentuck','"* among others. When Albert Pike chose to describe mountain man Bill Williams, his model was Cooper's Hawkeye, already entered as a type in American culture. Nothing had changed fifteen years later in the sensationalist fiction of George G. Foster, who, gathering up the "refuse" and "fragments" of "every-day life," admitted that his brand of realism needed character types. The Bowery b'hoy, the Philadelphia rowdy, the Hoosier, the trapper, and the gold-hunter were already, he declared, "so much alike that an unpracticed hand could not distinguish one from the other."[1]

1. [W. H. Gardiner], review of *The Spy,* by James Fenimore Cooper, *North American Review* 15 (1822): 251–52; Albert Pike, "Narrative of a Journey in the Prairie" (1835), *Publications of the Arkansas Historical Society* 4 (1917): 66–139; George G. Foster, *New*

It never occurred to Foster's contemporaries in the Old Southwest that they were populating their comic sketches with anything *other* than types, and they were adding their own to those that Gardiner had recommended in the 1820s: the nubile backwoods girl, the fighting cockerel, the gullible rube, the pretentious know-it-all. They were always quick to fix any noteworthy "specimen" within an appropriate and enclosing category. These authors were of course not alone in their addiction to such a rhetorical habit. Everyone who ventured into the new country was so inclined.

Travelers were the most enthusiastic agents in disseminating the categories they thought useful for defining the new society abuilding south of the Ohio—although some types were only new sightings of old favorites. Unlike, for example, the Yankee peddler, who appeared in the Old Southwest in almost the same guise he had assumed in settled regions of the nation, the rustic naïf, newly tricked out with apt accents, was an updated type bearing the genealogy of assorted Jonathans from the earliest days of the republic. John Pendleton Kennedy recounted the story of a backwoods youth from Virginia who marched with his militia to Boston to aid Massachusetts at the beginning of the Revolution. This "overgrown, gawky lad, entirely illiterate," objected to the regiment's motto, which was worked into their hunting shirts. Since he thought "Liberty or Death" too bloodthirsty, the young man had his sister amend the motto to read "Liberty or be Crippled."[2] If the figure of Yankee Doodle in the Revolutionary song is one memorable account of the type, others are the peculiarly mannered heroes of Royall Tyler. In the humorous sketches the naïf is a popular recurring type not simply because his ignorance invites torment from experienced wags, but also because his confident self-assessment of "knowing a thing or two" insures his deflation.

Other localized instances modified from earlier types, cited in a wide range of both public and private writing, include the leisured planter (reproducing himself from colonial Tidewater models), the hunter and trapper (extending the role of loners from earlier backwoods), the Kentuckian (dating from the second war with England), and the yeoman layabout

---

York by Gas-Light (1850), quoted in David S. Reynolds, *Beneath the American Renaissance: The Subversive Imagination in the Age of Emerson and Melville* (New York: Knopf, 1988), 317, 464–65.

2. John Pendleton Kennedy quoted in Rowland Berthoff, *An Unsettled People: Social Order and Disorder in American History* (New York: Harper & Row, 1971), 256. See also David S. Reynolds, "The Reform Impulse and the Paradox of Immoral Didacticism," chap. 2 in *Beneath the American Renaissance*, esp. 56–68.

(migrating from William Byrd's Lubberland). Exiled from the Old Dominion to the raw new country, Major Willis Wormley in *Flush Times* has his origin in Sir Roger de Coverley in *The Spectator*, the incompetent, whole-souled, and overly generous representative of an earlier time and place. A harmless, lovable relic amid more up-to-date fellows, Wormley is still enclosed by his community's (and Joseph G. Baldwin's) approval. Some of the newer types emerged from the settlement stage in the Old Southwest, and others derived from the late antebellum years: the flatboatman, the steamboat captain, the land speculator, the slave trader, the overseer, the planter's idle son, the fire-eating orator.

Identifying specimens of established types was a convenient approach for travelers touring the lower South and writing books about what they saw, but, in letters and diaries, private citizens also found the shorthand method useful in their business and pleasure trips. Objectivity and the niceties of discrimination were not notable priorities in such accounts; bundling individuals into comprehensible groups was a quick way of processing the new. Anne Royall, a semipermanent sojourner in northern Alabama, attended a congenial party of Huntsville residents in 1818, where she found "the sweet girl, the grave matron, the sparkling belle, the conceited fop, the modest young gentleman, [the] veteran soldier, and a sociable old planter."[3] A flirtatious widow, Mrs. Royall relied on a system of recognizable types as an efficient means for orienting herself: of the seven guests, four attracted her interest for obviously personal reasons.

In the confines of a middle-class parlor Mrs. Royall made her identifying categories an instrument for assessing the dynamics of social life. More ambitiously, Tyrone Power, the Irish actor touring America, portrayed New Orleans as a magnet drawing all classes and types. After singling out the Yankee ("cautiously picking his way to fortune"), the Virginian ("reckless and humorous"), the "suddenly enriched planter of Louisiana, full of spare cash," and the "half-civilized borderers" in his *Impressions of America*, Power devoted considerable space to the "Kentuck farmer." With "a self-possession that is evident at a glance," Power wrote, this man of "rude independence" was destined to give "tone and manner" to the "grandest portion of the continent," bestowing to posterity "the thew and sinew of a giant."[4] By Power's time, thanks to the identification of flatboatmen with Kentucky, the "Kentuck" was a type more than

3. Anne Royall, *Letters from Alabama, 1817–1822* (1830; reprint, ed. Lucille Griffith, University: University of Alabama Press, 1969), 124.

4. Tyrone Power, *Impressions of America during the Years 1833, 1834, and 1835* (London, 1836), 2:147–48.

an individual. He could have been either a boatman or a farmer, and he might or might not have been from Kentucky. The perceptive actor, however, applied the predictive, self-evident traits of the summarizing category to launch his vision of an even grander category—the American.

To explain the social landscape of the lower South, John L. McConnel wove the specifics of narrative history into capsule portraits of the types responsible for making the region what it was by 1853. *Western Characters, or Types of Border Life in the Western States* has the curious effect of being both curtailed and protracted. McConnel supplies historical sweep with synoptic Characters in the seventeenth-century sense—as condensations of ideal categories: The Indian, the Voyageur, the Pioneer, the Ranger, the Regulator, the Justice of the Peace, the Peddler, the Schoolmaster, the Schoolmistress, the Politician. Putting the old static genre to work, McConnel elicits the potential for cultural development in each portrait. For example, the commander of the local fort, the "natural" lawgiver of the early community who enjoys "justice without form," succumbs to the "unhealthy pleasures" of the office-seeker when municipal regulations are enacted to protect "order and legal ceremony"—thus giving rise to the "loud-talking" politician. McConnel was not burdened by the duties of neutral judgment.[5]

Daniel Hundley was even more opinionated than McConnel. An Alabamian living in Chicago, Hundley composed his *Social Relations in Our Southern States* (1860) to argue for the region's social diversity. His protosociology was more than synoptic, since it openly described the vast range of middle-class southerners (whom most outsiders never quite understood) and poorer whites (whom most southern polemicists of the time pretended did not exist). By virtue of his own Cavalier heritage, Hundley made the Virginia-derived Southern Gentleman the baseline of character, value, and conduct throughout the South. This small group, however, was overshadowed by a more numerous (and more useful) middle class, a category that included merchants, professionals, skilled artisans, and farmers. Members of this group chose to rise in the world by becoming "half-fledged country lawyers and doctors," storekeepers, and parsons.[6] If these representatives of the middle class betray Hundley's condescension, his outright scorn was reserved for four types: the

5. John L. McConnel, *Western Characters, or Types of Border Life in the Western States* (New York, 1853).

6. Daniel R. Hundley, *Social Relations in Our Southern States* (1860; reprint, ed. William J. Cooper, Jr., Baton Rouge: Louisiana State University Press, 1979), 262.

Model Storekeeper, the Southern Yankee, the Southern Bully, and the Cotton Snob.

Unlike many of his contemporaries, Hundley used categories as weapons. If the principal mission of this secular preacher was to articulate "an ideal of the gentleman," as Fred Hobson has argued, his method was to attack all instances in which the southern population had fallen short of that ideal. His harshness in characterizing poor whites (a category just under the yeoman) was familiar enough by 1860, but it seems no more differentiated than Byrd's more than a century earlier: the "laziest two-legged animals that walk erect on the face of the Earth," a "pitiable sight to the truly benevolent, as well as a ludicrous one to those who are mirthfully disposed." His most withering contempt, however, partly because northerners so often confused this type with the Southern Gentleman, was lavished on the Cotton Snob: a well-dressed sot, gambler, and braggart, "haughty and overbearing," an example of sneering vulgarity and faulty breeding.[7]

Because the newspaper humorists preferred a playing field dominated by yeomen, most of their preferred types were variants of the provincial commoner. Their sketches have neither the programmatic motive nor the tonal grumpiness of Hundley. For these authors stereotyping was simply an efficient method for ordering their world—not a neutral one, certainly, but one that was fueled by neither a lazy expedience nor a rage to denigrate and censure. The humorists in fact participated fully in an aesthetic reality that most writers bow to even when they fail to acknowledge it— that character types are prominent referents in the cultural predisposition of all readers because they are epistemologically "prior to thought." Contrary to a conviction common to beginning writers, readers are not anxious about originality in the texts they open for the first time. Preceding any expectation of freshness, their prior need is for an anchoring dependability (*who is this person? what does he resemble?*). In a nearly unconscious act of mental association, readers dip into a pool of clustered images that culturally connect, refer, and relate: a pool of national and regional traits they already know about, types identified by race, gender, social class, speech levels, codes of dress, and physical attributes. In the popular genres—melodrama, the sentimental novel, tales of adventures and detection—the bald outlines of typal figures are less blurred by the

7. Ibid., 170, 181. Fred Hobson's perceptive sketch of Hundley can be found in *Tell about the South: The Southern Rage to Explain* (Baton Rouge: Louisiana State University Press, 1983), 63–81.

disguises of genius, the apprehension of character less deterred by psychological complexity.[8] Given the conventional length of the humorous sketch, the humorists were compelled to particularize their figures from the common pool of available types with more dispatch than their peers who worked in longer popular forms, but it was not an easy task to limn a striking character both effectively and quickly.

Even as they insisted on the singular nature of their selected heroes, the humorous authors understood that their ardent Irishmen, their randy widows, their country boys, their village savants, and all the others that populated their world were what has been called "precluded": characters who have no option to operate differently from the way they do.[9] Some of the types outrun expectations (such as Thorpe's great hunter), but most were expressly created to fulfill them. Baldwin's Irishmen may be hauled before the judge for drunkenness or shady trading, but they function mostly to reveal their canny knowledge of the law. The country boys of Matthew Field, Joseph Field, and John Robb may bravely declare their smartness, but they are always suckered into scenes where they can be humiliated. Society matrons in Longstreet's Georgia and Noland's Arkansas exist to have their faux refinements punctured. However skillfully drawn, and despite being expanded versions of their type, Jim Doggett and Mik-hoo-tah seem firmly to be what they fatedly are. Even their idiosyncrasies hark back to typal origins ("the hunter in the bush") more than they look forward to psychological coherence as a device in nineteenth-century novels.

It may be no accident that the figures who loosely represent contemporary culture (judges, doctors, preachers, sheriffs, schoolteachers) are the very ones whose roles are *most* precluded. Even characters who are merely functional, rightly and dutifully doing their jobs, are usually fated to perform ineffectually *because* they represent the newer institutional order. All characters in the humor are vulnerable to humiliation, but the humorists' preferential prey are those who perform roles necessary to a civilized society. As we might expect, Sut Lovingood is the great hater of leading functionaries, and he doubtless reflects something of his cre-

---

8. Walter Benjamin writes: "There is nothing that commends a story to memory more effectively than that chaste compactness which precludes psychological analysis." "The Storyteller: Reflections on the Works of Nikolai Leskov," in *Illuminations,* trans. Harry Zohn (New York: Schocken Books, 1969), 91.

9. Robert Darnton, *The Great Cat Massacre and Other Episodes in French Cultural History* (New York: Random House, 1985), 192; Michael Roemer, *Telling Stories: Postmodernism and the Invalidation of Traditional Narrative* (Lanham, MD: Rowman & Littlefield, 1995), 3–7.

ator's rage; but even the moderate authors were disinclined to waste much sympathy on institutional leaders. Baldwin and Longstreet were so equitable in their targets, so square-dealing with the society that generated the writing, that even their alliance with the agents of civilization was momentarily suspended. For Hooper and Robb that suspension was more than momentary. One recurring scene was a disrupted courtroom in which sanctioned conduct and protocol are resisted and demeaned. When a judge loses control of his domain, his very function is negated; since he represents institutionalized order, the social pieties that encourage civilization are mocked. The preacher in the pulpit, the doctor in his patient's house, the teacher at his desk, the judge on the bench: in much of the humorous writing these vulnerable sites are high-profile.

Although *versus* supplies the core energy in any kind of drama, from mystery to farce, so pervasive is the crunch of opposing cultural forces in the humor that even an isolated event usually emerges as spectacle. Because closet drama tends to be an alien form in these sketches, the anecdotal action unfolds in full view of the interested parties. All performances are well-attended because there are no uninterested parties and there is no public space that is not a potential stage. The backcountry could always provide what one critic has called "ephemeral theater": "The stage was a stump in the woods, the floor of a general store, a table in a tavern, or a political podium."[10] Even traditional occasions—camp meetings, militia reviews, balls and musicales, weddings, public hangings, funerals—could be easily subverted into impromptu farcical theater. Major Jones, in his resplendent commandant's regalia, falls off his horse in front of the ragged militiamen he is charged with whipping into shape; Captain Suggs's conversion scam must sway the entire assembly of the camp-meeting faithful. Although Col. Dick Jones's humiliating set-to with an opponent (in Thomas Kirkman's "Jones's Fight") is not a home game, its detailed reenactment occurs in the crowded streets of the town where he is known as the leading citizen. Pete Whetstone must learn the steps danced at Little Rock soirees, where (as we have seen) the fashionable guests whisper among themselves that "Mr. Whetstone aint up to *Kertillions.*"

No significant activities can be private: quiltings, parlor games, court hearings and trials, church meetings, even courtships must be conceived and enacted with as much public exposure as Billy and Bob's confrontation

10. Richard Boyd Hauck, *Crockett: A Bio-Bibliography* (Westport, CT: Greenwood, 1982), 115.

in the middle of town in Longstreet's "The Fight." The courthouse in the Old Southwest was an especially popular arena. A modern historian has described the trial as a "central ceremony" throughout nineteenth-century America, and the "courtroom speech its most visible ritual." Sol Smith's theatrical troupe reached only a fraction of the communities in the interior, but judicial circuits were everywhere. In Alabama, Achille Murat declared that, because legal fees were "trifling," attending court was the grand entertainment: "Talk of the theatre! it is but a very feeble and awkward imitation of a court of justice."[11] Baldwin makes the most of court proceedings as theater, but Hooper and Harris also find occasion for farcical courtroom antics. The battle for attention between a pretentious judge and irreverent workmen in Joseph Field's Jurytown competes with the staged disasters of the Great Small Affair Theatre in Field's Pokerville.

The authors used public occasions to intensify and vivify the competitive spirit that prevailed in everyday life. (It can be argued that stomp-and-gouge is only an extreme version of competition-as-norm.) From Longstreet to Harris, the world of the humorists is one of opposition, sometimes overtly hostile, sometimes cruelly playful, which the sketches feed on without significantly altering. In their hands the dynamic of society consists of the challenge and clash of individuals who share an extravagant sense of their own integrity, a touchy drive to say, do, and have what they want without the intervention of agencies that are set up to preserve, even in an attenuated way, the rights of all.

E. Anthony Rotundo's fine phrase "casual hostility and sociable sadism" describes nineteenth-century boarding schools for boys, but its pertinence extends to most venues where American males gathered together—prize fights, saloons, social clubs—and to most public sites in the Southwest as the humorists depicted them. Rotundo writes: "The men's world of play returned a man to a boys' world in its hedonism, its boisterousness, its frequent cruelty and competition, and its disdain for polite, 'feminine' standards of behavior."[12] Venting his frustration over the disappearing forests along the riverways, Thorpe's Mike Fink decides "to have a little sport at the Indians' expense" (*TBT*, 173). The riverman's malaise is neither triggered nor sated by matters of ecology, of course: primal battle is

11. Robert A. Ferguson, *Law and Letters in American Culture* (Cambridge, MA: Harvard University Press, 1984), 69; Achille Murat, *A Moral and Political Sketch of the United States of North America* (London, 1833), 249, 147.

12. E. Anthony Rotundo, *American Manhood: Transformations in Masculinity from the Revolution to the Modern Era* (New York: Basic Books, 1993), 35, 192.

his only real satisfaction. *Having a little sport,* which always proceeds at somebody's expense, is only one euphemism for the kind of recreational violence that blossomed on the frontier, especially at events that drew crowds from wide areas. The humorists acknowledged only a sampling of the rough sport in their midst, but there are enough examples in their depictions of early settlement to demonstrate the cultural fact behind them—the fragility of courts, churches, and schools, all institutions charged with curbing the most damaging expressions of a masculine world. The most telling kind of fragility is that of family relations. In this most basic unit of organized society, the family was no bulwark against an atomized culture of competition.

The image of the home as a nursery of values that prepares young Americans to take their moral and social responsibilities seriously is notably absent in Southwest humor. The father may be a model of rectitude, but if a marriageable female lives under his roof, he is invariably depicted as a conventional stage figure, the ornery and blustering barrier standing between delectable daughter and horny suitor. The father in Robb's "Nettle Bottom Ball" ("cross as a she *bar,* with cubs"), notes the narrator, could "lick anythin' that said *boo,* in them diggins" and could "out swar Satan" (Cohen, 177). The father in Harris's "A Sleep-Walking Incident" has a dignity befitting his role as head of household, but he betrays his formulaic essence when he accuses an overnight visitor of being *"jist like a cussed mink . . .* among my hens" (Cohen, 200). In Noland's Whetstone letters, the father is effectively eliminated, not merely as a role model, but as a character. In Whetstone's first contribution to *Spirit of the Times* (the only letter signed "Peter" Whetstone), "Daddy" is an offstage figure trying to "enter land" by scrounging loans from his friends (*PW,* 59–62). Noland finds no further use for Daddy Whetstone in the subsequent forty-four letters. In Hooper's *Simon Suggs* the drama of domination and submission begins in the home, when the son challenges and overcomes the father. In an effort to throw off the onerous yoke of his preacher father, young Simon accepts his "predestinated" role of frontier sharper. Vanquishing the old man, the renegade son sets out from home to realize his destiny (*SS,* 19–29).

Given the atmosphere of competition that charges so many of the sketches, it is not surprising that when we think of this humor we tend to remember its physicality—the payback schemes of the Lovingood sort, the encounters of yeoman hearties in no-holds-barred fights, confrontations that feature the human body urgent in its functions. We are fascinated by the visceral because, in Sut-speak, it is our *natur*. Less metaphysically, we assign priority to the physical because it best meets our expectations of what frontier life and manners were really like.

Hooper's wily captain, however, discovers that his destiny doesn't require violence. In point of fact, the most interesting dramas of mastery and submission in the humor are based on wit and calculation rather than the kind of violence the authors knew well. These situations may involve *consequential* violence, the sort that results from such tamer occasions as the practical joke. A blindfolded Joseph Jones plays a parlor game, "Brother, I'm Bobbed," as his envious cousin Pete whacks him repeatedly with a heavy book; the Widow Haycock suffers a buckshotted bottom and a $25 fine for violating curfew at Fort Suggs; a wag persuades a country bumpkin to gulp down a bottle of pepper sauce to kill an oyster that he imagines is ravaging his innards. Foolishness is usually the part of *human natur* that practical joking revels in, but, almost as often, so is the violence that often follows—pain, humiliation, and assorted assaults on body and spirit. In Taliaferro's "Josh Jones and Hash-Head Smith," dislike of a Quaker couple triggers Jones's fight with his friend Hash-Head, but the real mayhem comes when the Quakers' home is consequently devastated. Sol Smith insults a "mad bull" Irishman by calling him by his landlady's name; although Sol is at fault, he wins the resulting fight through "science"—and so skillfully that the defeated Irishman urges him to go on tour to "whip any man" who challenges him.

Travelers' reports, private diaries and letters, and histories alike are filled with references to spectacular examples of frontier violence, from bare-knuckled fights to crude, dangerous tricks by which rash young men let off steam. That Georgia as early as 1787 had made it a criminal offense to gouge eyes, bite ears, slit noses, and "cut out or disable the tongue" did not prevent raucous entertainments throughout the early decades of the next century.[13] The protocols for participating in "fistycuffs," the kind Longstreet made famous in "The Fight," were minimal enough: a cleared space sufficient for strenuous going-at-it and cheering from the sidelines. Cries of "Fair fight!" and "Form a ring!" announced the event as a communal activity, preferably on a street large enough to accommodate a large audience. In a *Swamp Doctor* sketch, however, those familiar cries are heard in the confined space of an office, where Madison Tensas, a senior medical intern, presides over a free-for-all by a gaggle of students he

13. E. Merton Coulter, *College Life in the Old South* (Athens: University of Georgia Press, 1983), 9.

has called to the preceptor's quarters to discuss emergency remedies for a poisoned patient. Although he reminds the students, as they pitch into each other on the office floor, that physical disagreement with their colleagues is "unprofessional" behavior, Tensas himself admits his temptation to lay "into the mirror to whip my reflection, I wanted a fight so bad." When the preceptor returns to his office, Tensas lamely explains that the student fray occurred "whilst consulting" (*SD*, 36–42).

As her diary entry for July 4, 1828, Sarah Gayle of Alabama wrote that the "holiday of free men hallowed and consecrated by all that is sacred to men and patriots" has become merely an occasion for "drinking quarrelling & electioneering"; Independence Day was now more for "carousal than any thing else." By 1833, when she was the governor's wife in Tuscaloosa, she deplored student pranks on that drunken holiday, which included shaving horses' tails and setting fire to professors' "harmless dogs and philosophic geese."[14] Antebellum students, most of them the ungovernable sons of planters, rarely needed national holidays to violate the rules of decorum that southern colleges tried to impose. Some of the recorded infractions at Franklin College in Athens, Georgia, were the result of ordinary high spirits among privileged young men; enough incidents appeared in official documents, however, to confirm Moses Waddel's conclusion in 1824 that he presided over a college of exceptionally unruly students.

"Rolling brick bats" in corridors, pulling down fences, drinking and gambling, "firing a cracker," and playing water games were the least serious violations at Franklin; but loud bouts of exchanged profanities, curses, and obscene singing often escalated into attacks on other students, servants, townspeople, even professors. Students would pelt their victims with stones and beat them with clubs. Though illegal, pistols were regularly carried and sometimes fired at human targets. Drunken students' food fights at grog shops and billiard parlors often led to fights with canes. As late as 1856 two students were fined for fighting "in the recitation room of one of the officers while the lecture was going on." One of the militant southern fire-eaters of the 1850s began his career as a notorious college bully in the 1820s. Robert Toombs so repeatedly carried

14. Sarah Gayle, diary, Gorgas Family Papers (Sarah Gayle Materials), William Stanley Hoole Special Collections, University of Alabama Library, University of Alabama, Tuscaloosa. For A. B. Longstreet's experiences with unruly students on several campuses, see David Rachels, introduction to *Augustus Baldwin Longstreet's* Georgia Scenes *Completed: A Scholarly Text* (Athens: University of Georgia Press, 1998), xxxiii–xxxix.

grudges, along with his pistol, knives, hatchets, and clubs, that he was dismissed from Franklin College in 1828. Yet for all the disorderly conduct recorded there—drunkenness, fighting, stabbing, shooting—dismissal without reinstatement was a rare punishment.[15]

Students at the University of Virginia did not stop at "swaggering and swearing and whistling." In 1833 one visitor noted that "these embryo-statesmen usually carry a dirk or a pistol" to reinforce their bad behavior. At the military academy in Pineville, Louisiana (which would become LSU), William T. Sherman, then an engineering professor, was regularly forced to quell bouts of insubordination among the cadets.[16] During the Civil War, Sherman characterized "the young bloods" as "good billiard-players and sportsmen, men who never did work and never will." War suited them, he continued, "and the rascals are brave, fine riders, bold to rashness, and dangerous subjects in every sense. . . . They hate Yankees *per se*, and don't bother their brains about the past, present, or future." A veteran confirmed Sherman's observation about the southern soldier's reluctance to submit to discipline. The volunteers were "hardy lovers of field sports," George Eggleston wrote, but they "were not used to control of any sort, and were not disposed to obey anybody."[17]

Among the theatrical stock figures in the humorists' depiction of their times, flamboyant fighters asserting their dominance stand out from all the rest. For these braggarts, rivalry is as verbal as it is physical. Their high-talking engagements are an American version of flyting, the ancient ritual in which matched opponents exchanged extravagant and extended insults. In the new country, superior prowess, and its formulaic linkage of boaster with well-known repositories of strength, animated dramas of mutual intimidation that began (and often ended) with language: "When *I* talk, fishes swim low and seek deep water; snakes and reptiles slink back to their dark corners; steamboats of one hundred horse power refuse to turn their wheel and float back into the channel. . . . When Old Sense speaks, the earth trembles, and Millerites think the day is coming" (*PW*, 180–81). Its most conspicuous form among the antebellum humorists is the rhetorical excess of combatants who came to be called *half-*

---

15. Coulter, "Justice in the High Court of the Faculty," chap. 4 in *College Life.*

16. E. S. Abdy, *Journal of a Residence and Tour in the United States of North America from April, 1833, to October, 1834* (London, 1835), 2:239–40; William Tecumseh Sherman, *Memoirs of General W. T. Sherman* (1886; reprint, New York: Library of America, 1990), 1095.

17. William T. Sherman to H. W. Halleck, September 17, 1863, in *Memoirs,* 363; George C. Eggleston, *A Rebel's Recollections* (New York, 1878), 31–32.

horse half-alligators. We now know that these dueling braggarts have their origins, not in frontier spontaneity, but in the literary imagination. Richard Boyd Hauck has traced the analogues of the half-horse half-alligator formula to *Beowulf, The Iliad,* and the commedia dell'arte, and its native provenance to Washington Irving's *Knickerbocker's History* (1809), where the savage mixture is attributed to backwoodsmen of Kentucky, who are said to be held "in great respect and abhorrence."[18]

i. Half-Horse Half-Alligators

"I'm a Salt River roarer! I'm a ring-tailed squealer! I'm a reg'lar screamer from the ol' Massassip'! WHOOP!"

—Walter Blair and Franklin J. Meine, *Mike Fink, King of Mississippi Keelboatmen*

By its very nature, boasting is mostly artful bombast. Mike Fink's version, though it does nothing to sweeten a character that by most accounts was brutal and sadistic, defines this bravura type in its lingual exuberance. Here, at its very beginning, are the synonyms that the half-horse half-alligators loved: *roarer, squealer, screamer.* Transferred from animals, these descriptors accord with the general backwoods habit of addressing others in approbative terms derived from animals (*coon, hoss, critter,* often preceded by *old*). In roarer transactions, however, they do more. They add to the fierceness of the human speaker at his most intense while simultaneously subtracting that fierceness from the donor beast.

One reason why so many eighteenth-century observers thought of backcountry residents as irreligious was their accommodation to unshaped nature. To succumb to rather than resist that nature was to be closer to the wild beasts whose space they shared than to civilized men. In *Modern Chivalry* (1792–1815), Hugh Henry Brackenridge made much of proper discrimination in separating humans from other animals. When he allowed his hero, Farrago, to insist that "a bear is a real bear, a sheep is a sheep; and there is no commixture of name, where there is a difference of nature," he rejected the verbal confusion of species. The half-horse half-alligator, proudly belligerent in the metaphorical confusion

18. Hauck, *Crockett*, 78. The earliest reference to the half-horse half-alligator may have been in Christian Schultz, Jr.'s *Travels on an Inland Voyage in the Years 1807 and 1808* (1809; reprint, ed. Thomas D. Clark, Ridgewood, NJ: Gregg, 1968), 2:145–46.

of such reversionary types, would be the nightmare realized.[19] Reversionary in settlements as well as in the wilds: Phillip January's "That Big Dog Fight at Myers's" (1845) features Iron Tooth, a roister who challenges a dog known as "the worst in any body's nolledge" by descending to dog-level. On all fours, he struts back and forth before the chained dog, "bellerin'" and "histin' up one leg agin the gate," hanging his tongue out, biting the dog's ear, "rollin' and tumblin' in the dirt"; finally, slipping his shirt "smartly up over his back," he attacks. The cowed animal breaks his chain, tucks tail, and scampers off (Cohen, 249–52).

In nineteenth-century travel writing the chief characteristics of the backcountry are often said to be lethargy and sloth; in the humor, however, those qualities are largely supplanted by waggery and spirited rivalry. What authors in both modes share is a kind of cultural shorthand: *place-as-destiny.* To the urbane visitors, topological nature was the asocial home of humans in the wild thriving on a par with the game they hunted (when the necessity of hunger drove them to it). For the humorists that space was a playground for pitting human skills against beastly equivalents—bears, panthers, wildcats, raccoons—whose traits they imagistically absorbed. William Penn Brannan, a Cincinnati portrait painter, made a benign equation of human and beast in his famous mock sermon, "The Harp of a Thousand Strings." Unlike the theologically suspicious Episcopalians (portrayed as turkey buzzards) and Methodists (squirrels), the tenacious Hard-Shell Baptists are possums. "Thunders may roll and the earth may quake," roars the preacher, " but that possum . . . clings furever" (Cohen, 443–45).

D. H. Lawrence thought there was "too much menace" in the American landscape, but the Southwest wilderness as the humorists reproduced it is almost as domesticated as Cooper's.[20] Stripped of the atmospherics of dread, escapades with bear and panther are recollected with little gothic frisson and much circumstantial realism. The expository mode, with loving magnification, re-creates the adrenalized moment common to all contests between man and beast. Some yarns, however, deliberately shred such moments of danger by deflating their threat. All that is chaotic, unknown, and menacing in the woods is shunted into a lower register, in keeping with, say, the manageable chores of the cabin and its

19. Brackenridge quoted in Robert Lawson-Peebles, *Landscape and Written Expression in Revolutionary America: The World Turned Upside Down* (Cambridge: Cambridge University Press, 1988), 132–33.

20. D. H. Lawrence, *Studies in Classic American Literature* (1923; reprint, New York: Viking, 1964), 51.

clearings or the base camp that crudely replicates hearthside amenities. Wilderness animals are useful to the metaphorical imagination. They are invoked, their characteristics beefed up and absorbed into their human counterparts, when the backwoodsman is out to prove his mettle. When he is in a tight spot with such creatures, however, one of his tactics is belittlement, a way of draining them of their more dangerous traits with domesticating idioms that reduce them to mischievous pets.[21]

In a real-life expedition, Meriwether Lewis tried this tack without significant effect. Seeing grizzlies for the first time near Fort Mandan, he wrote in his journal: "I expect these gentlemen will give us some amusement sho[r]tly as they soon begin now to coppolate." The domesticating mood passes after he is chased for eighty yards by one of the "gentlemen." In a sonnet to a lady grizzly, Matthew Field transforms danger into the conventions of love poetry:

> Ar-ow! O, gentle madame, I entreat
> You'll not disturb yourself, but keep your seat,
> And I'll excuse all ceremony. Pause!
> And on your grizzly haunches stand at ease;
> Pause, gentle bear, and paws off, if you please,
> And don't be too affectionate—because,
> However much I may admire your graces,
> I don't just now aspire to your embraces![22]

John Robb's Dan Elkhorn—drunk, lovelorn, and wet after a "he-bar" capsizes his canoe—is threatened by the beast that stalks him like a human hunter. He "seed I have no weapons," Dan recalls, and, "quietly calculatin' . . . how he'd best git me out of the water," the bear taunts the drenched man with a "snigger" and rolls him off a log before leaving: "off slid Mister *bar*, laffin' out *loud!*" (Cohen, 179–84).

The prey in W. C. Hall's "Mike Hooter's Bar Story" also plays human games. This bear not only blows "all the powder outen the pan" of the hunter's rifle and removes the flint, he also taunts Hooter with an obscene gesture ("with the thumb of his right paw on the eend of his smeller, and wiglin' his t'other") before sauntering off into the canebrake (*PPW*, 49–54). Alexander McNutt offers a variation on the oral defanging of

21. Lawson-Peebles, *Landscape and Written Expression*, 211.
22. Lewis quoted, ibid.; Matthew C. Field, *Prairie and Mountain Sketches*, ed. Kate L. Gregg and John Francis McDermott (Norman: University of Oklahoma Press, 1957), 201.

hostile prey. Chunkey, an early embodiment of the good old boy, finds himself being trailed by panthers, which are reduced in his yarn to less threatening animals: "They'd jump and squat, and bend their backs, lay down and roll, and grin like puppys." After wounding the female leader of the pack with a "slantindickler" shot in the shoulder, Chunkey is emboldened to continue the domesticating tenor of the episode: "Howdy, panter? how do you do? how *is* missis panter, and the little panters? how is your consarns in gineral?" Only after seeing his advantage does this amiable yeoman transform himself into a roarer: "Did you ever hearn tell of the man they calls 'Chunkey'? born in Kaintuck and raised in Mississippi? . . . If you diddent, look, for *I'm he!* I kills bar, whips panters in a fair fight; I walks the water, I out-bellars the thunder, and when I gets hot, the Mississippi hides itself!" (Cohen, 90–92). The hunter's patronizing of wild beasts is a reminder that metaphor can function as "weapons turned against reality."[23] Yet the tactic, for all its psychological consolation, derives from the manifest reality of backcountry life. T. B. Thorpe speculates that the "untameable and quarrelsome disposition" of the wildcat inspired the human boast "he can whip his own weight in wild cats," but he reverses the equation of the usual trope. The animal, he writes, has "the greediness of the pawnbroker, the ill nature of an old usurer, the meanness of a pettifogging lawyer" (*TBT*, 166–69).

The extravagance of language, however, could never quite disguise the physical consequences of *human* rivalry. Travel writers both foreign and domestic frequently noted how their steamboats were invaded by "the scum of the population," pugnacious men of the woods, rudely dressed and crudely mannered, mostly specified as "Kentucks." The most vehement critique came from the "American Navigator" himself, Zadok Cramer, who declared Kentuckians "brutal and irregular," "so bad and so detestable." James Stuart, who throughout his travels was assailed by sassy inferiors in every state, argued that the offensiveness of boatmen and other intemperate half-horse half-alligators arose primarily because they refused to ingratiate themselves with their betters, "stunning your ears with an amusing and fanciful lingo, which . . . is, after all, nothing but slang." Stuart also noted that this western specimen was getting scarce. Though he witnessed "many boisterous doings," he admitted, with some disappointment, "I never saw any one stabbed or gouged." Another British traveler who generally found "disgusting" the conversa-

---

23. Karsten Harries, "The Many Uses of Metaphor," in *On Metaphor*, ed. Sheldon Sacks (Chicago: University of Chicago Press, 1979), 172.

tion among "the lower classes near the Mississippi," struck a faintly wistful note when he wrote: "The half-horse, half-alligator race, that was brought up from infancy in the arks and flat-bottomed boats that navigated these western rivers before steamers were introduced, are off the stage now; but the language of the people is still sufficiently figurative, and sometimes unintelligible."[24]

The first writer to make a narrative out of this frontier contest by ignoring state origins completely was Irving's friend James K. Paulding in his 1817 account of "a waggoner and a batteauxman" whose "combustible" materials "strike fire" whenever they meet. This incidental passage in *Letters from the South*, a book of observations in epistolary form, sets the pattern for most of the succeeding writers: frontier fights are heavily verbal affairs. The first spirited gestures of the combatants (flapping hands, crowing like a cock, neighing like a horse) are perfunctory; it is the progressive insults that lead to physical blows. The wagoner boasts that he has the "handsomest sweetheart," the "finest horse," and a "better rifle than any man that ever wore a blue jacket." The blue-jacketed boatman "could have borne any reflection on his sweetheart, or his horse; but to touch [on] his rifle, was to touch his honour." Bested in the ensuing fight, the wagoner, with a bruised face and three fewer teeth, takes "the law" to his rival.[25]

Paulding acknowledges in a note the existence of other versions of the story. One involves a set-to between a boatman (who flaps his arms and crows like a chicken) and Davy Crockett (who shakes his mane and neighs like a horse). Textually mediated by no other interpreter, this is Crockett's story. He of course wins the fight, though he admits that his opponent was "a right smart coon." In motive, however, Crockett's yarn differs importantly from Paulding's. Whereas Paulding's boatman and wagoner are "men of rather phlegmatic habits" who require many insults to get them going, Crockett makes clear that he had been spoiling for a fight. Viscerally, it was *time* for a fight to satisfy his own "humour."[26] His rival takes defeat in good spirits, and promises to vote for Crockett in the

24. Zadok Cramer, *The Navigator; Containing Directions for Navigating the Monongahela, Allegheny, Ohio, and Mississippi Rivers*, 8th ed. (1814; Ann Arbor, MI: University Microfilms, 1966), 308–9; James Stuart, *Three Years in North America*, 3rd ed. (Edinburgh, 1833), 2:300; George W. Featherstonhaugh, *Excursion through the Slave States* (1844; reprint, New York: Negro Universities Press, 1968), 1:62.

25. James Kirke Paulding, *Letters from the South by a Northern Man* (1817; rev. ed., New York, 1835), 1:72–74.

26. Richard M. Dorson, *Davy Crockett: American Comic Legend* (New York: Rockland Editions, 1939), 38–39.

next election. Paulding, though, has little interest in the frontier extravagance, verbal or physical, that the roarer type came to represent. His fight is incidental to what it is made to represent: he frames the entire episode as a legal case. Letter 29 of *Letters from the South* is primarily an encomium to the two young lawyers who see it through the court, suggesting how the civilized forms of discourse handle the disorderly eruptions of more primitive forms.

Like Baldwin a generation later, Paulding argues that the shortest and most certain way for a young man of legal talents to attain eminence "before his head grows gray with age" is "to emigrate to some one of the new states, instead of running to seed in the cities." In Paulding's argument, to *grow up with the country,* the obvious advice behind the perennial injunction to *go west,* requires not simply mobility but a homing instinct for a destination where the ambitious and gifted can, at least temporarily, put down roots. To remain in the older states is to remain hostage to men who not merely "worship the divinity of gold, but adore a spurious counterfeit in rags." To emigrate to the new states, "tak[ing] root with the first planting of the community," is to exercise one's talents where the "invincible money-getting demon has not yet worked his way into the human heart" and where the young professional can derive his "dignity, respect, and consequence, from sources far more pure, noble, and elevated." Had Paulding been in Alabama at the same time as Baldwin or Hooper he could not have so confidently exempted the new states as sites where the power of money elevated "the lowest reptile to the rank of man."[27]

If Crockett's version is closer to the format as it later developed, the unlikely linking of Crockett, the "gentleman" of the canebrakes, and the elegant Paulding of the Hudson Valley would be collusive, not competitive, thirteen years later in Paulding's play *The Lion of the West.* By 1830 the half-horse half-alligator had been generalized as a backwoodsman whose speech and physical traits had less to do with birthplace than with the venues where they flourished: the deep woods and the river towns. The hero of Paulding's play is a Kentucky gamecock, Colonel Nimrod Wildfire, modeled after the most famous of the real specimens, Congressman David Crockett of Tennessee (and Wildfire himself describes his kind

---

27. Paulding, *Letters from the South,* 1:75–76. Paulding overvalued what he thought of as the American need to "put down roots." While the conservative need for stability may have been an ultimate value for the migrants, achieving rootedness was a protracted process. As we have seen, settlement and permanent home- and town-building were often preceded by several geographical moves that could total a decade or more of effort. Paulding also underestimated the greed that the frontier encouraged, as we see in *Flush Times.*

of fighting as "old Mississippi style").[28] For both Irving and Paulding, the backwoods was the backwoods, and, as in farce generally, Wildfire condenses and intensifies the telling traits of a character type. Even in Crockett's own books, which began to appear after Paulding's play, there is nothing quite like the verbal clotting of vernacular idioms that we get in the set pieces of *The Lion of the West*. Unlike the "men of . . . phlegmatic habits" of Letter 29, the comic colonel of the play is exuberant in both action and speech, and his boasts are so committed to the best-man principle that for him to think of taking "the law" in any situation would irreparably tarnish his gamecock image.

The complications of the relationship between Nimrod Wildfire and Davy Crockett demonstrate how the most famous tall talk in antebellum America was a literary phenomenon, not folklore. For all the tangled issues of authenticity involved in the several Crockett "autobiographies," one aspect is clear: Crockett was not above appropriating as his own the backwoods idioms popularized by other writers and politicians, becoming thereby both author and subject. If Paulding thought of his Kentucky hero as "a figure who knew he was a type," Crockett the author was even more self-conscious in shaping his actual self to the pattern of that type.[29] When the real man of the canebrakes, watching *The Lion of the West* from his theater seat in 1833, acknowledged the bows of actor James Hackett, his theatrical counterpart, he was also acknowledging the mock-heroic as a useful tool for advancing his political career.

The oral extravagance of the frontier braggart had by this time lost its aura of danger (the "abhorrence" that Irving noted), and Crockett adopted the ready-made type with some care. As we have seen, he was concerned that the blustery image not supplant his right to be taken seriously in Washington. Paulding's play, which celebrated decency over uncouthness, served Crockett well. Wildfire's speeches are boldly lifted and put in Crockett's mouth in *Sketches and Eccentricities of Colonel David Crockett of West Tennessee* (1833). On his first trip to the capital in 1827, when he was still a Jacksonian, this tall talker had entertained audiences with

> "I'm that same David Crockett, fresh from the backwoods, half-horse, half-alligator, a little touched with the snapping-turtle; can wade the Mississippi, leap the Ohio, ride upon a streak of lightning, and slip without a scratch down a honey locust; can whip my weight in wild cats,—and if any

28. Richard Boyd Hauck, "Making It All Up: Davy Crockett in the Theater," in *Davy Crockett: The Man, the Legend, the Legacy, 1786–1986*, ed. Michael A. Lofaro (Knoxville: University of Tennessee Press, 1985), 110.

29. Hauck, *Crockett*, 70.

gentleman pleases, for a ten dollar bill, he may throw in a panther,—hug a bear too close for comfort, and eat any man opposed to Jackson."[30]

In repudiating the *Sketches and Eccentricities* the following year with *A Narrative of the Life of David Crockett of the State of Tennessee,* Crockett tamed the inflated backwoods tall talk attributed to him, while making his (now) celebrated opposition to Jackson appear more consistent. The stylized language of the lout is replaced by an idiomatic vernacular that neither shames him nor reshapes him as a gentleman.

In *Col. Crockett's Exploits and Adventures in Texas,* a posthumous pastiche assembled by Richard Penn Smith for the publishers Carey and Hart in 1836, the beastlike properties of the type, because they were still commercially useful, were reattributed—not to the martyr of the Alamo, but to a young Crockett admirer eager to help his hero rout the Mexicans. When Crockett asks him whether he is a rhinoceros or a hyena, the young hunter replies:

> "Neither the one, nor t'other, Colonel, . . . but a whole menagerie in myself. I'm shaggy as a bear, wolfish about the head, active as a cougar, and can grin like a hyena, until the bark will curl off a gum log. There's a sprinkling of all sorts in me, from the lion down to the skunk; and before the war is over you'll pronounce me an entire zoological institute, or I miss a figure in my calculation. I promise to swallow Santa Anna without gagging, if you will only skewer back his ears, and grease his head a little."[31]

By this time the half-horse half-alligator, essentially defunct as a comic presence, has been expediently revived for jingoistic purposes. Swallowing the enemy alive was a popular image during the Mexican War. One lieutenant wrote from the front in 1846: "It appears that old Polk is really determined on swallowing Mexico without any grease. If he will give us the means, we are just the boys to do it."[32]

---

30. [Mathew St. Clair Clarke], *Sketches and Eccentricities of Colonel David Crockett of West Tennessee* (New York, 1833), 164.

31. [Richard Penn Smith], *Col. Crockett's Exploits and Adventures in Texas,* in *The Autobiography of David Crockett,* ed. Hamlin Garland (New York: Scribner, 1923), 318. The *Exploits* ("Written by Himself") has been described as a calculatedly fraudulent piece of bookmaking. Michael A. Lofaro, "A Crockett Chronology," in *Crockett at Two Hundred: New Perspectives on the Man and the Myth* (Knoxville: University of Tennessee Press, 1989), xxiii.

32. Robert H. Ferrell, ed., *Monterrey Is Ours! The Mexican War Letters of Lieutenant Dana, 1845–1847* (Lexington: University Press of Kentucky, 1990), 102.

Even in declension, the triumphs are largely verbal. Whether what he says is true or false, Crockett is primarily a speaking voice, not merely projecting a self but creating one by puns, wit, and metaphor. He refers patronizingly to a "Justass of the peace"; in a bear fight he gives his opponent "an awful fundamental poke" with a butcher knife; he tells his editor that the pieces in his trunk, left behind when he went to Texas, "ar awl true, and may be lyed on." He even uses wordplay to win an election to head a militia regiment. When his rival pledges to the men that he is ready "to lead them to the cannon's mouth," Crockett responds with a promise to lead them to the "mouth of a barrel of whiskey." It has been suggested that the colorful congressman was one of the first Americans to make a living as a celebrity,[33] but the reputation was a collaborative enterprise, both in his lifetime and in his posthumous lives. What survived Crockett's death in 1836 was the half-horse half-alligator reputation, but not its exclusive association with the Tennessee hero. He freely borrowed the tall talk of others as well as some of the frontier exploits generously attributed to him. (We like to remember that he didn't have to shoot the coon—that once Crockett announced his name, the coon came down the tree of its own accord. Yet in more reliable accounts, the anecdote is told of a Colonel Scott.) What Crockett tapped into was a widespread linguistic style of the backwoods and river culture, including that of his Ohio River counterpart, Mike Fink.

The bellicosity of the frontiersman—teamster, boatman, hunter—is condensed (if that word could ever be appropriate to roarer rhetoric) in the candid boast which dismisses restraint as a civilized virtue and elevates primitive physical rivalry as the primary measure of self-worth. As one historian has observed, the ordinary southerner believed that "if something was worth doing, it was worth overdoing," and the extraordinary southerner made belligerent excess an organic character trait.[34] Whatever his disaffection with Andrew Jackson, Crockett and the other avatars of the type perform and speak in the Jacksonian mode. When Mike Fink laments the tranquilizing effects of settlement ("Six months and no fight would spile me worse than a dead horse on a prairie"), the sentiment emerges out of a cultural moment cued by Jackson's own words: "I was born for a storm and calm does not suit me." If, when they saw fit, Jackson and Crockett used the formula as a career gimmick, it

33. M. J. Heale, "The Role of the Frontier in Jacksonian Politics: David Crockett and the Myth of the Self-Made Man," *Western Historical Quarterly* 4 (1973): 406.

34. Grady McWhiney, *Cracker Culture: Celtic Ways in the Old South* (Tuscaloosa: University of Alabama Press, 1988), 128.

was also useful to lesser politicians on the hustings.[35] In Missouri, Alphonso Wetmore was subjected to a perilous dunking when the raft of a state representative capsized in the Mad River. When asked if he was alarmed, the politician responded: "No, madam . . . I am a raal ring-tail painter, and I feed all my children on rattlesnake's hearts, fried in painter's grease."[36] Half-lament, half-boast, and with a sprinkling of confession, Old Hickory's self-estimate serves as a kind of headnote to the more heated expressions of ego that thread the writing of the Old Southwest: the extravagant identification of men with the wilderness and its animals, the boastful litany of comparatives, the escalation of laconic assertions of self-worth into rodomontade. The widespread habit of attributing such traits to unlikely individuals could become ludicrous. Sarah Gayle in 1830 could not decide whether she was offended or amused when a newspaper editor referred to her husband, the governor of Alabama, as a *"Scorer, a roarer a ring-tail'd roarer."* On a crowded New Orleans dock where Henry Clay was due to arrive, Bishop Whipple overheard many voices praising the perennial presidential candidate: "'he's a horse' 'he's a buster'——&c&c&c."[37]

While it was not the invention of the humorist authors, this most flamboyant mode in their repertoire derived from the early stereotype of half-horse half-alligator in its various permutations (hunter, trapper, riverman), which set the standard for both the composition and reception of Southwest humor. This "found" mode encapsulated the perceived character of the region so firmly that later sketches, even those diversifying the picture with more subtle depictions, often incorporated the earlier images as points of reference. The type was useful in 1837, for example, when Robert Montgomery Bird created Roaring Ralph Stackpole, a Kentucky horse thief in *Nick of the Woods.* A dramatist as well as a novelist, Bird brought a theatrical version of Stackpole to the New York stage in 1839. When Pete Whetstone, another fictional character, visits the city, he writes home to Devil's Fork, Arkansas, to report that he has seen *Nick of the Woods,* but "it warnt much—one feller was called *Captain Ralph Stackpole,* a ringtail roarer from Salt river—but if he had any fun or wit about him, he kept it to himself while I was there." Pete goes on to compare the stage roarer to "Old Ben from Spring

35. Edward Pessen, *Jacksonian America: Society, Personality, and Politics,* new ed. (Urbana: University of Illinois Press, 1985), 321.

36. Alphonso Wetmore, *Gazetteer of the State of Missouri* (St. Louis, 1837), 90.

37. Gayle diary; Lester B. Shippee, ed., *Bishop Whipple's Southern Diary, 1843–1844* (Minneapolis: University of Minnesota Press, 1937), 92.

river," who could "out *cavort* him to death" (*PW*, 136). Aside from the intertextual sniping, Whetstone's dismissal of Stackpole is a measure of the aging stereotype in popular lore.

The liberal opposition to the Mexican War did its part in making roarer rhetoric a relic of wilder times. The jingoism occasioned by the southern enthusiasm for that war prompted Emerson to observe that each of the American victories "converts the country into an immense chanticleer," although an Emerson scholar notes that cockerel brag-gadocio—"the sheerest commonplace of Southwestern humor"—remains "one of the most venerable of American postures."[38] Whether antiquated or conventionalized as a national trait, animal-related brag suffered in the late antebellum years. By 1840 migration, westward expansion, and economic optimism had made the Kentucky cockerel an endangered species. If the hunter of Crockett's *Exploits* is too promiscuously animal to be credible, the set pieces that imitated him and his kind of verbal excess, flashy exercises for artistic effect, were even more calculated to "be lyed on." For all the domestication of stereotyped oratory, however, the gamecock figure endured allusively (if not venerably) through the antebellum era, its ornery belligerence an oddity to be recorded. A traveler in Washington, D.C., in 1853 for the inauguration of Franklin Pierce added a footnote to his description of a capital flush with eager office-seekers:

We were told an anecdote of an individual who luckily got what he came here to hunt for—a place. A commissioner, deputed by law to examine the newly-appointed clerks, found seated at one of the official desks, a raw sample of Kentuckian manufacture, of about six feet four inches in stature, in his shoes, and the following dialogue narrated to us as nearly as we can remember, passed between them:

COMMISSIONER.—Do you know who was the ablest officer in the Phoenician Fleet?

KENTUCKIAN.—Can't say I do.

COMMISSIONER.—Can you tell the exact interest on three hundred dollars at eighteen and a half per cent. for three quarters of a day?

KENTUCKIAN.—No—I can't.

COMMISSIONER—Can you tell the precise distance between the sun and the moon, when one is rising and the other setting?

KENTUCKIAN.—No, I can't; but there's one thin' I *ken* tell yer, which is,

38. *The Complete Works of Ralph Waldo Emerson*, Centenary Edition (Boston: Houghton Mifflin, 1903–1904), 11:330; Joel Porte, *In Respect to Egotism* (Cambridge, MA: Harvard University Press, 1991), 192.

that I've licked five fellers since I've a been here, and I'm agoin' to lick you, if you ask any more of your * * * * * questions.[39]

By the time of the Civil War the type and his oratory had lost most of their defining traits. Although the isolation of Taliaferro's Surry County would seem to favor these preserved forms (along with folk tales), the roarer rhetoric seems generally too belligerent for his storytellers. The most pugnacious of them, the witty Johnson Snow, tanked with "Knock-'em-stiff" spirits, comes closest in his one-way oral battle with Parson Bellow: "I don't 'low man nur 'umun to pop thar fists in my face. No, by juckers! Hello, git out'n the track here! Rip shins and marrer bones! Wake snakes, the winter's broke! Ha, ha! here's at you! I can lick the whole possercommertatus of yer afore you can say Toney Lumpkins three times, by Zucks!" (*HET*, 94). Backwoods strength and resolve are here innate features, no longer traced to wild animals or mechanical steam power; and the inventive referents are set squarely in a settled, civil society and its cultural progress.

From the perspective of the civilized east, the half-horse half-alligator was in some respects a self-fulfilling figure. For most of the eighteenth century the American frontier remained what it had been for the Puritans: a site of barbarism (if not devil worship) where, in the absence of civil institutions, man was apt to descend fully into his animal nature. The wilderness beyond the habitable borders was neither inspiring nor romantic, but, in William Byrd's phrase, "a dirty State of Nature," home to "Wretches" and "Adamites." The frontiersmen, wrote Timothy Dwight, were solitaries unequipped for "regular society" because they were "too shiftless to acquire either property or character."[40] At a time when property and character were almost synonymous, the backwoodsman continued to shape his life like the solitaries and outcasts of earlier ages, appropriating the traits of horses, alligators, snapping turtles, wild cocks, bears, panthers, and assorted other beasts of the wild, as a triumphant announcement of self-worth.

It would be simplistic to credit Crockett alone with turning an anti-

39. Alfred Bunn, *Old England and New England, in a Series of Views Taken on the Spot* (London, 1853), 129.

40. William Byrd, *Histories of the Dividing Line betwixt Virginia and North Carolina*, ed. William K. Boyd and Percy G. Adams (New York: Dover, 1967), 46, 91–92; Dwight quoted in Albert J. von Frank, *The Sacred Game: Provincialism and Frontier Consciousness in American Literature, 1630–1860* (Cambridge: Cambridge University Press, 1985), 50.

frontier bias into the celebration of sturdy independence (Boone in real life and Natty Bumppo in fiction contributed their part), but his writings certainly did much to bury the fear and distrust of the postrevolutionary generation. It is his voice in his books and the *Almanacks* that negated some vicious character traits noted by Dwight (idleness, shiftlessness) and transformed others (talkativeness, passion, prodigality) into virtues. As the frontier contracted, and as the backwoods and river cultures were absorbed into a modern economy, many of the contentious amusements of the Kentucky cockerels became domesticated. One Alabama politician on the campaign trail, surprised that his breakfast egg contained two yolks, swallowed it in one gulp so he could later intimidate his rivals on the stump: "I *devoured* two incipient roosters at breakfast this morning at one mouthful."[41]

Best-man games had shifted to other versions of masculine testing—especially accounts of gunfights in popular westerns. Superseded by more subtle confrontations in the hands of Longstreet's generation, the kind of Jacksonian-era bravura that Crockett and Fink popularized was only a quaint memory by the 1880s. If half-horse half-alligator bombast never took itself seriously even in its heyday, it was yet an oratorical early-warning system for men of tough reputations. By the time Mark Twain let his young hero eavesdrop on some flatboatmen's talk in a chapter originally intended for *Adventures of Huckleberry Finn,* it was a wholly parodic performance.

Two of the boatmen, in the midst of their singing and drinking, decide to fight. As Huck records it, one jumps up in the air, cracks his heels together, and screams out:

> "Whoo-oop! I'm the old original iron-jawed, brass-mounted, copper-bellied corpse-maker from the wilds of Arkansaw!—Look at me! I'm the man they call Sudden Death and General Desolation! Sired by a hurricane, dam'd by an earthquake, half-brother to the . . . small-pox on the mother's side! Look at me! I take nineteen alligators and a bar'l of whiskey for breakfast when I'm in robust health, and a bushel of rattlesnakes and a dead body when I'm ailing! I split the everlasting rocks with my glance, and I squench the thunder when I speak! Whoo-oop! Stand back and give me room according to my strength! Blood's my natural drink, and the wails of the dying is music to my ear! Cast your eye on me, gentlemen!—and lay low and hold your breath, for I'm bout to turn myself loose!"

41. William R. Smith, *Reminiscences of a Long Life; Historical, Political, Personal, and Literary* (Washington, DC, 1889), 91.

His announcement, writes Huck, is punctuated with a little dance: the corpse-maker swells like a rooster and paws with his feet. His opponent, of course, must do the same thing, going around in a circle three times and swelling himself up before he too jumps up and cracks his heels together:

> "Whoo-oop! bow your neck and spread, for the kingdom of sorrow's a-coming! Hold me down to the earth, for I feel my powers a-working! whoo-oop! I'm a child of sin, *don't* let me get a start! Smoked glass, here, for all! Don't attempt to look at me with the naked eye, gentlemen! When I'm playful I use the meridians of longitude and parallels of latitude for a seine, and drag the Atlantic Ocean for whales! I scratch my head with the lightning and purr myself to sleep with the thunder. . . . [W]hen I range the earth hungry, famine follows in my tracks! Whoo-oop! . . . I'm the man with a petrified heart and biler-iron bowels! . . . bow your neck and spread, for the pet child of calamity's a-coming!" (*MW*, 241–42)

As Twain made clear by his decision to use the chapter in *Life on the Mississippi*, he treasured the raftsman passage not for its function in clarifying the plot of *Huckleberry Finn*, but for the way its language expressed a long-gone way of life. His laconic excuse in 1883 was that he wanted to illustrate "keelboat talk and manners," as if a particular mode, condensed in one place, might represent an entire cultural moment, one that had actually passed away by the time Sam Clemens became a pilot on the river in the late 1850s. What is to be remarked about the raftsmen set-to is its unapologetic derivativeness. At first, the reader is tempted to say, with Huck, *I been there before.* But of course with Twain the use of prior materials is never simply repetition. This passage is not really a suggestion of the "talk and manners" of an earlier time, much less a summary, but rather a full-blown, whole-hog re-creation of the celebrated lingo of the half-horse half-alligator rivermen.

Derived from oral tradition and such literary accounts as the Crockett *Almanacks*, the arcane diction passes through Huck's recording consciousness untouched by his limitations. Except for spelling that imitates pronunciation, the verbal pyrotechnics result in a set piece only minimally adjusted to Huck's capacities.[42] There is oratorical elegance; there is folk-

---

42. Because the emphasis is not on the credibility of Huck as vernacular storyteller but on the delectable play of virtuoso language, author and protagonist almost merge. Had the passage been retained in *Huckleberry Finn*, we would doubtless fret over the unlikely ability of a ragamuffin illiterate, however clever, to recall and discriminate among the amazing string of oral insults. The segment works in *Life on the Mississippi* because its focus can remain, persuasively, on the *talk*.

loristic genealogy; there is the catalog of deeds inscribed by superhuman legendry. The realistic vein of best-man rhetoric is here stylized into the troping hyperbole of cosmic intervention, and the linguistic result is a kind of poetry that transcends vernacular speech. And if Huck as storyteller-author is not a credible transmitter of some of the words that the child of calamity tosses out, neither is the child of calamity himself. Only Twain, who puts in the shade all precursors in the genre, could imagine a raftsman boasting that the "massacre of isolated communities is the pastime of my idle moments, the destruction of nationalities the serious business of my life!"

This is the longest of the written accounts of keelboat talk, even as it is the most inventive, the most blatantly showy. The oral shenanigans of Sudden Death and Child of Calamity are far afield of other gifted reporters' reproductions of similar performances, which is another way of saying that they lie very close indeed to the fantasy of genius. The point of all the versions is that the mutual challenge to fight is more important than the fight itself, which is sometimes anemic and always anticlimactic. For the literary recorders, the joke is that half-horse half-alligator clashes are *all talk.* (The historical record shows that the boatmen were, as Huck notes, "a mighty rough-looking lot" who were not, at least in river towns with many witnesses, "all talk.") Twain's joke turns on the ratio of *talk* and *fight:* the more the former is pumped up, the less violent the latter is apt to be. As Huck concludes the episode, the "swelling around and blowing" is followed by the rivals "edging away in different directions" until a much smaller man, tiring of it all, intervenes. After *snatching, jerking, booting,* and *knocking* the two about, the "little black-whiskered chap" humiliates them further by making them confess that both of them are "sneaks and cowards" (*MW,* 243). The third man is Twain's contribution, giving to Huck the kind of "snapper" that his creator's well-honed storytelling techniques perfected in prior texts. For the purposes of plot, Huck is the inadvertent audience of the parodic flyting aboard the boatmen's raft, but functionally it makes no difference that he merely overhears: he is in precisely the same position as the narrator in the older Southwest sketches, alternating direct quotation and indirect summary, along with editorializing touches. Structurally, what Twain does with his first-person narrative is to erase himself (or, more precisely, to pretend to do so) as genteel narrator. Huck is both narrator and storyteller.

The overheard boatman talk is both an artful distillation of what Sam Clemens heard and a species of flamboyance available to Mark Twain by way of the earlier humorists. What Huck overhears, however, is not what T. B. Thorpe's narrator heard on the *Invincible* in "The Big Bear of

Arkansas." Though both figures supposedly occupy the same time and place, the Mississippi Valley in the 1840s, for Twain too much history has intervened. In the extended mutation of river culture, the boatmen's vernacular, too dated to qualify as nostalgia, is mostly an exotic relic in need of embellishment. Like Tom Sawyer, Twain chooses to throw some *style* into it, and the result is not recapitulation but reinterpretation: an argot of excess augmented, exaggeration itself magnified. As we have seen, the humorists were close enough to the flatboat era to miss (if not regret) its passing and to infuse what remained of boatman culture with some measure of human dimension. Thorpe's Doggett has emotional range; Field's Mike Fink is a study in the pathos of dispossession. Twain's brilliantly managed *tour de force*, however, is another of his verbal constructions that exposes the shabbiness of antebellum southern society. It is a reminder that the South of the 1850s was alive with oral threat. The bloated, self-regarding rhetoric of fire-eating politicians fell on the ears of outsiders who happened to hear it as *all talk*. Scaled to a different register, the bluster of Sudden Death and Child of Calamity is of a piece with the bellicose scourging so favored by southern partisans.

ii. Best Men

> You English wou'd abhor that Plight,
> Who strain no Tackling, gouge, nor bite.
> Unknown to Britain are our Modes
> Of Fight, or, if she knows, explodes.
> Upright, her Bruisers ply their Fists
> And all is Peace, when one desists.

—Robert Bolling, "Neanthe"

Because Mark Twain's raftsman passage celebrates river tall talk as oratorical fun, most modern readers tend to see such self-aggrandizement as more whimsical than threatening. While English travelers knew about "our Modes / Of Fight," they rarely saw such masculine bravado as mere *talk*.[43] To many kinds of antebellum readers, the phenomenon had an acerbic edge. Many visitors to the Old Southwest regarded the animal-laced rhetoric as appropriate for expressive backcountry types mired in

43. See J. A. Leo Lemay, "Southern Colonial Grotesque: Robert Bolling's 'Neanthe,'" *Mississippi Quarterly* 35 (1982): 97–126.

the beastly circumstances of their world. For outsiders who remained puzzled by the nature of the natives, one recourse was to fall back on William Byrd's colonial lubbers as a model. One updated version of Byrd betrays its genealogy: "Low ease; a little avoidable want, but no dread of any want"; no industry; "little or no real capital, nor any effort to create any; no struggling, no luxury, and, perhaps, nothing like satisfaction or happiness; no real relish of life; living like store pigs in a wood, or fattening pigs in a stye."[44]

These are the words of William Faux, an English farmer scouting for places where his countrymen might settle, but similar sentiments are repeated in numerous accounts, both foreign and American. A traveling cleric on the stage from Augusta to Montgomery described the horses as "lean and scranky," and added: "Man and beast look alike, long, lean, and lank." James Puckett found a Flush Times Lubberland in northern Georgia, where the mountain settlers were "tall, sallow, gawky-looking"—"thin, cadaverous-looking animals, looking as melancholy and lazy as boiled cod-fish." The only energy he noted in these "long parsnip-looking country fellows" was the political squabbling in "their filthy taverns." The judgment of the English geologist with whom Puckett traveled was even harsher. George Featherstonhaugh declared that the ignorant Arkansas layabouts had only a single goal: "The immediate gratification of animal wants." Their scorn for order and cleanliness vindicated his antipathy to Jacksonian democracy; nothing, he wrote, "seems to appear more natural to democracy than dirt."[45]

Often perplexed by the sloth and apathy of the backcountry, outsiders brightened when they discovered a seemingly anomalous trait—a penchant for violence. Impressed by earlier accounts that depicted the interior as a virtual nursery of Crockett-inspired enterprise, they were delectably expectant when they stumbled upon dirkings, gougings, nose-bitings, and other such intramural exercises. A Vermonter in the early 1820s wrote in his diary that both the rich and "poorer sort" were fond of the same amusements—hunting, drinking, horse racing. "From these sports," he wrote, "quarrels often arise," and among the better class "a duel ends the strife," while among the common people the favorite mode is "gouging

44. W. Faux, *Memorable Days in America: Being a Journal of a Tour to the United States* (London, 1823), 417.
45. G. Lewis, *Impressions of America and the American Churches* (1848; reprint, New York: Negro Universities Press, 1968), 148; James Manuel Puckett, Jr., "Experiences of a Frontier Traveler, 1837," Hargrett Rare Book and Manuscript Library, University of Georgia, Athens; Featherstonhaugh, *Excursion*, 2:122.

and dirking."[46] The Old Southwest's reputation for masculine violence preceded Crockett, had in fact been solidified by the turn of the nineteenth century, and the waves of migration after the War of 1812 did little to alter the image of a primitive interior. Kentucky may have set the tone, but "wild regions" in all parts of the new country brandished a "great recklessness of human life."[47] One "superannuated deacon" recalled being forced to flee with his family from North Carolina after his father bit off a rival's nose. Arkansas turned out to be more congenial. The move allowed the family "to fight almost day and night to keep up the morals uv the country."[48]

Visitors vied in nominating settlements that were the most uncivilized, a competition that began early and lasted well past statehood periods. One antebellum historian wrote that before 1802, when the Baptists finally began to "soften and refine" the people, the Tensaw vicinity of Alabama was "the worst region that ministers ever entered." Two years later a visitor declared that settlers along the Chickasawhay and Tombigbee Rivers were worse: "illiterate, wild and savage," morally depraved, quarrelsome, and mutually distrustful. In 1826 a Presbyterian evangelist to frontier Alabama reported that Ditto's Landing on the Tennessee River was a town full of "the most desperately wicked, disapated people" he had yet met.[49]

It was not the backcountry alone that gave the Southwest its reputation for dissipation and violence. The Bostonian William Richardson in 1815 declared Natchez Under-the-Hill the "most licentious spot that I ever saw," adding that from this "filthy spot emanate all the contagious disorders that infest the town above." As late as 1808 doorways on the streets in upper Natchez, the most fashionable in the Southwest, still exhibited the skins of animals recently shot in the nearby woods. Even before it became fully American in 1798, Natchez was known for harboring

46. *A Narrative of the Life of James Pearse* (1825; reprint, Chicago: Quadrangle, 1962), 51–52. See the comprehensive study by Elliott J. Gorn, "'Gouge and Bite, Pull Hair and Scratch': The Social Significance of Fighting in the Southern Backcountry," *American Historical Review* 90 (1985): 18–43.

47. Stuart, *Three Years*, 2:266–68; Philip Henry Gosse, *Letters from Alabama: Chiefly Relating to Natural History* (London, 1859), 250–51.

48. F. D. Srygley, *Seventy Years in Dixie* (Nashville, 1893), 238–39.

49. Albert Pickett quoted in James E. Davis, *Frontier America, 1800–1840: A Comparative Demographic Analysis of the Settlement Process* (Glendale, CA: Arthur H. Clark, 1977), 135; James F. Doster, "Early Settlements on the Tombigbee and Tensaw Rivers," *Alabama Review* 12 (1959): 85–88; John R. Williams, ed., "Frontier Evangelist: The Journal of Henry Bryson," *Alabama Historical Quarterly* 42 (1980): 23.

criminals among its aspiring merchant class. "You will see camels as frequently in the eyes of needles as you will meet honest men in Natchez," warned Richardson. He described even the honest few, however, as "refractory" men whose "zeal without knowledge" made them offensively opinionated. Those who were appointed to keep order were often barely superior to those they regulated. By 1830 vigilante groups were as likely to thwart as to assist the established authorities who oversaw criminal cases, and not everyone welcomed the arrival of civil law that affected the "old way" of settling disputes.[50] In *Flush Times* a murderer complains to his lawyer (whose own "standard of morality was not exalted") that the "new-fool ways" had spoiled everyone's values: "*Law, law, law,* is the word,—the cowardly, nasty slinks; and then them lawyers must have their jaw in it, and bow, bow wow, it goes" (*FT*, 308).

Farther west, Arkansas also had a reputation for disorder and violence. Joseph Meetch, visiting there in its lawless territorial years, reported that travelers banded together for protection, arming themselves against marauders with "rifle, tomahawk, butcher knife and very often a dirk and brace of pistols." Frederick Gerstaecker, who arrived soon after statehood and remained for four years, described Little Rock as a "vile, detestable place" and wrote that the Mississippi boatmen "have good reason when they sing—'Little Rock in Arkansaw, the d—dest place I ever saw.'" The English traveler Fortescue Cuming recorded that bellicose natives were "similar in their habits and manners to the aborigines, only perhaps more prodigal and more careless of life." He offered a crisp vignette of one bruising fight (cribbed, in fact, from an earlier travel book): a stranger, seeing a combatant "with the tip of his nose bit off," commiserates with the man's bad luck. "'Don't pity me,' said the noseless hero, 'pity that fellow there,' pointing with one hand to another who had lost an eye, and shewing the eye which he held triumphantly in the other." Another foreign visitor in 1834 suggested that such violence was a relic of the "olden time" to which only Kentuckians were still addicted. But even as late as 1850 in Kentucky, Lady Emmeline Stuart Wortley was all ears to local tales of "murder, duels, executions, terrific fights with Indians, encounters with grizzly bears," deciding that "people here" were indifferent to "life in general."[51] (The Indian-and-grizzly details suggest

50. William Richardson, journal, Louisiana and Lower Mississippi Valley Collections, Louisiana State University Libraries, Baton Rouge; Robert V. Haynes, "Law Enforcement in Frontier Mississippi," *Journal of Mississippi History* 22 (1960): 30–31.
51. Joseph Meetch, diary, 1826–1827, quoted in S. Charles Bolton, *Territorial Ambition: Land and Society in Arkansas, 1800–1840* (Fayetteville: University of Arkansas

that Lady Emmeline might have been an easy mark for tall-tale artists still basking in their frontier reputation.)

If official categories show assault as the most common violation, one historian cites instances that suggest that the line was a thin one between dueling for honor and outright brawling.[52] Dueling at least was a ceremonial strategy for settling disputes among equals. The heterogeneous mingling of several classes, professions, and trades in recently organized communities exacerbated the tendency of an earlier culture to reward aggressiveness. A jury in northern Alabama might find a person charged with violent assault guilty and yet uphold the ancient code of public vindication by awarding the victim only a penny in damages. In capital cases, decisions of guilt were often followed by petitions to the governor for pardon (signed, sometimes, by officials of the court). In Huntsville in 1820 a shady tavern owner was convicted of murdering a prominent citizen, but Governor Pickens granted the murderer a pardon because, according to the petitioners, the victim had humiliated him with a horsewhip— a "disgraceful chastisement."[53]

Self-sovereignty was reflected in the country saying *every man is a sheriff on his own hearth.*[54] As an accepted discharge of passion and principle, backwoods violence involved no guilt on a personal level nor anxiety about social stability on a communal level. Violence was the immediate resolution to disputes; its expression was meant to end them. The planter elite may have devised elaborate protocols for its conduct, but measures taken in the name of self-sovereignty indicated the same precarious stability in social relations that marked lesser folk. A Philadelphia Quaker in the Natchez-Vidalia area ironically defined youngbloods as "chivalric gentry" who for hours dashed conspicuously about on "highbred horses" and who repeated tales of "bear hunts, 'great fights,' and occasional exploits with revolvers & Bowie Knives." A Louisiana planter reported a

Press, 1993), 33–34; Frederick Gerstaecker, *Wild Sports in the Far West* (1854; reprint, Boston, 1866), 95; Fortescue Cuming, "Tour to the Western Country (1807–1809)," in *Early Western Travels, 1748–1846*, ed. Reuben Gold Thwaites (Cleveland: Arthur H. Clark, 1904–1907), 4:137; Abdy, *Journal*, 2:296–97; Lady Emmeline Stuart Wortley, *Travels in the United States* (New York, 1851), 104–5.

52. Davis, *Frontier America*, 256; see also 262, 112, 270.

53. Daniel S. Dupre, *Transforming the Cotton Frontier: Madison County, Alabama, 1800–1840* (Baton Rouge: Louisiana State University Press, 1997), 149.

54. David Hackett Fischer, *Albion's Seed: Four British Folkways in America* (New York: Oxford, 1989), 765. See also Charles S. Sydnor, "The Southerner and the Laws," *Journal of Southern History* 6 (1940): 3–23; and William J. Cooper, Jr., *The South and the Politics of Slavery, 1828–1856* (Baton Rouge: Louisiana State University Press, 1978), 71.

dispute between two of his acquaintances, one who brandished a knife, the other a pistol, but a "few vulgar fisticuffs were the only substantial" results. A Savannah doctor recorded a "melancholy occurrence" in his 1832 diary: at a barroom, one Stark, "without any provocation," cursed one Minis (not present) for being a "damned Jew" who "ought to be pissed upon." The abused man later killed Stark and was accused of "willful murder," a charge the diarist declared "most unwarrantable."[55]

Confessing to his own participation in the "absurd and barbarous" custom of dueling, Henry S. Foote recounted the circumstances: "I found a vicious state of public sentiment existing in the Southwest when I went thither to reside in 1825, and I weakly and criminally yielded to it in opposition to my own inward convictions of right and propriety." Surveying the condition of women for the *Portland Transcript,* a Maine lady traveling in the South in 1838 was gratified when she heard one young man in Mississippi declare "that he, *a native of the South, had never thrown a card, been on a racetrack, or fought a duel.*" The denial of these specific activities, long touted as characteristic vices of southern bloods, shows that some males among them were self-conscious about their stereotyped reputation. And S. S. Prentiss wrote in 1828, soon after arriving in Natchez from New England, that southern males had too much time on their hands and that they lived "rather more *freely* than we of the North," but that they were "more moral" than their reputation suggested.[56] The careful wording suggests that Prentiss, soon to become one of Mississippi's great political orators, was already southernizing himself, living perhaps "more *freely*" than he had done as a Yankee schoolteacher.

J. Marion Sims, a physician searching for a promising place to settle in the Old Southwest, wrote his wife from Alabama in 1835 that Mount Meigs was "one of the most dissipated little places I ever saw." Below his window, at the very moment he was writing, some twenty drunken men "of the most profane cast" were fighting. This scene, he generalized, was typical of almost all "the little towns and villages in these new counties." Ten days later, however, he was still in Mount Meigs, having

55. Edwin B. Bronner, "A Philadelphia Quaker Visits Natchez, 1847," *Journal of Southern History* 27 (1961): 519; John Robert Buhler Diaries, Autograph Book, and Notebook, MS 1311, Louisiana and Lower Mississippi Valley Collections, Louisiana State University Libraries, Baton Rouge; Richard D. Arnold Diary, Georgia Historical Society, Savannah.

56. Henry S. Foote, *Casket of Reminiscences* (Washington, DC, 1874), 176, 184; Eugene L. Schwaab and Jacqueline Bull, eds., *Travels in the Old South: Selected from Periodicals of the Times* (Lexington: University Press of Kentucky, 1973), 2:340; *A Memoir of S.S. Prentiss, ed. By His Brother* (New York, 1855), 1:74.

been persuaded to locate his practice there. While a "great many vagabonds" frequent the town "for the special purpose of frolicking," giving it a "desperate" reputation, his new acquaintances assured him that in another year Mount Meigs would become a desirable place "because the society will in that time be excellent." Tyrone Power made a stopover in a place "bearing the unattractive name of Sodom"—a wild little Alabama village across the river from Columbus in Georgia—that would never promise excellent society. Both Sodom and Columbus, he wrote, were infested with "outlaws from the neighbouring States," their numbers too large to be controlled by the U.S. marshal. In the winter of 1831 Tocqueville recorded in his diary a conversation with an Alabama lawyer who confirmed the regional propensity for violence. There was no man in Montgomery, Tocqueville was told, "who is not carrying arms under his coat," prepared for the "smallest dispute." It was, he admitted, a "social state that is half barbarian." When the lawyer directed the visitor to examine his head, Tocqueville saw "the marks of four or five deep wounds."[57]

Even as violence etched itself on the visitor's consciousness, its eruption became commonplace in the rich literary depiction of "ordinary life" in the Old Southwest, finally exhausting itself through repetition. Parodying both the substance of the sketches in the *Spirit of the Times* and the editor who encouraged them, an anonymous writer in 1851 described a day in the life of his neighbors, who had drummed up

> two street fights, hung a man, rode three men out of town on a rail, got up a quarter race, a turkey shooting, a gander pulling, a match dog fight, had preaching by a circus rider, who afterwards ran a footrace for apple jack all round, and, as if this was not enough, the judge of the court, after losing his year's salary at single-handed poker, and licking a person who said he didn't understand the game, went out and helped lynch his grandfather for hog stealing.[58]

When a confidant told William Faux that people in the new country worshiped two selfish gods, "Pleasure and Gain," he may have simply con-

57. J. Marion Sims, *The Story of My Life*, ed. H. Marion-Sims (New York, 1884), 370–71, 374; Power, *Impressions of America*, 2:132–33; Tocqueville quoted in George Wilson Pierson, *Tocqueville in America* (Baltimore: Johns Hopkins University Press, 1996), 640.

58. Quoted in Frederick Turner, *Spirit of Place: The Making of an American Literary Landscape* (San Francisco: Sierra Club, 1989), 80.

firmed the touring Englishman in his belief that the term "Backwoodsmen" was synonymous with "Rowdies."[59] But the informant was suggesting a more subtle comprehension about the culture of the backcountry. Although Gain covered gambling, horse racing, swapping, and confidence games, as well as ordinary commercial deals, Pleasure came from these same activities. The kind of violence that appalled visitors the most—the rough-and-tumble fight as *sport*—may have spurred the betting tendency among those who enjoyed viewing it. For the participants, however, it was largely Pleasure.

Early travelers went to some trouble to describe the kind of fighting favored by backwoodsmen. Without much thought to provocation, one wrote, they used their fists as a major weapon, but they engaged also in tearing, kicking, scratching, biting, and gouging until the opponent was bested. Outsiders were often more distressed by the participants' stoic disregard of injury than by the violence itself. Even Timothy Flint, no stranger, was disturbed by the laconic acceptance of injuries and the combatants' "disgusting familiarity about mutilation." At a steamboat stop Flint overheard the disinterested conversation of a gathering whose subject was

> a tall, profane, barbarous, and ruffian-like looking man, and they emphatically pronounced him the "best" man in the settlement. I perceived that according to their definition, the question about the "best" man had been reduced to actual demonstration. I found, on farther inquiry, that the "best" man was understood to be the best fighter, he who had beaten, or, in the Kentucky phrase, had "whipped" all the rest.[60]

The most vivid of the early reports came in 1811 from Thomas Ashe, an Irish traveler who described one "actual demonstration," a clash between a Virginian and a Kentuckian. The Virginian "pitched himself into the bosom of his opponent, his sharpened fingernails on the skull of the Kentuckian"; with his "claws" in his rival's hair and his thumbs on his eyes, he gave them such a sudden "start from the sockets" that the Kentuckian "roared aloud, but uttered no complaint." The struggle continued, with the Virginian biting his opponent's nose in two pieces, then tearing off his ears. Finally, "deprived of eyes, ears and nose," the Kentuckian gave in. The victor, also maimed and bloody, was then "chaired

59. Faux, *Memorable Days,* 121–26.
60. Thomas Anburey quoted in Fischer, *Albion's Seed,* 736–38; Timothy Flint, *Recollections of the Last Ten Years in the Valley of the Mississippi* (1826; reprint, ed. George R. Brooks, Carbondale: Southern Illinois University Press, 1968), 73.

round the grounds" to the cheers of the gratified crowd.[61] The Ashe account recurs, with only minor variations, throughout subsequent writing from the Old Southwest. This particular form of backwoods testing of masculine worth was, as we have seen, sometimes preceded by the elaborate verbal challenges of the half-horse half-alligators, but as a yeoman sporting affair it developed independently as a serious contest without oratorical trappings.

When the region became a geography of real competition, the bouts between half-horse half-alligators, like other frontier phenomena, quietly receded as engagements irrelevant in the progressive climate of settlement. The irony of Pete Whetstone's dissatisfaction with Roaring Ralph Stackpole on the New York stage is that a theatrical type that had once supplied spectator pleasure had grown *too* theatricalized when compared to "real" roarers. That Roaring Ralph had ceased to deliver "any fun or wit" was, at least in Devil's Fork, a reminder that the point of such oratorical gaudiness was to entertain.

The reality behind the gorgeously embellished boasts of the backwoods roarers was, however, believable enough. James Hall summarized the general characteristics of the southwesterner with a single trait: "to give as good as he gets." Bishop Whipple judged most of the regional yeomen according to their "hardest specimens"—swarthy, aggressive, "genuine *busters*" savoring of "woodland life & hunting," and outdoing Crockett "at backwoods talk." Although truculent cockerels staged their contests to determine best-man status, the same intensity, pervasive in most settlements, went into a wide array of physical encounters by those less interested in oral ornamentation. The screamers were only the most theatrical of the best men. As performers, they drew full houses. In Alabama, Achille Murat observed that man-to-man "fisticuffs" always attracted lively audiences and that crowds, assembled for whatever purpose, rarely dispersed without a battle. "The next day," however, "beater and beaten are as good friends as if nothing had happened." One memoirist confirmed Murat's claim. Though fistfights were expected on Independence Day, election day, and militia muster day, such combatants remained good friends after the fracas: "The fights grew out of ambition to be the best man of the neighborhood, rather than animosity."[62]

This aspect of the best-man obsession, however, significantly alters the

61. Thomas Ashe quoted in Fischer, *Albion's Seed*, 737.

62. James Hall, *Letters from the West* (1828; reprint, ed. John T. Flanagan, Gainesville, FL: Scholars' Facsimiles & Reprints, 1967), 118; Shippee, *Bishop Whipple's Southern*

ancient principle of the western world that only equals can be friends. The rawest instance of domination and submission is the swaggering egoism of Davy Crockett on the campaign trail. He thrashes a recalcitrant supporter, who then votes for him and becomes a loyal friend. The same kind of friendship by intimidation appears in the *Almanacks,* in which a resurrected Davy in 1839 recalls his outrage at a squatter, one of a class of men whose rights the historical Crockett worked to ensure. Cognizant of the latitude commonly used to interpret "improvements" on claims, the squatter asks his congressman to testify that he has improved his holdings. In Crockett's narration, the squatter comes across as respectful, polite, even witty, but Congressman Crockett explodes with indignation at what he takes as low-level fraud. He calls the squatter the "offscowring of creation" and in high dudgeon makes him eat cow shit. What makes the episode so painful to read is Crockett's less-than-credible claim to stand "on the caracter of a gentleman and the univarsal dignity of human natur." The humiliation, effectively stripping both bully and victim of dignity, cancels out the abstract political principle. A smug Crockett adds, "I never had a better friend arterwards."[63]

When the humorists staged their best-man dramas, they instinctively drew upon a cultural context in which personal disputes were usually settled by physical combat, an elemental resolution of clashing masculine egos that, with only minor shifts in emphasis, was also the favorite form of public recreation. The bout itself, even without theatrical "vaunting," was entertainment enough. But whether it was to establish preeminence over a real foe or to win in a game with a designated opponent, the main event represented an older order, a prior stage of social organization increasingly threatened by the modern need for community building that progress dictated.

What the humorists importantly showed, however, is just how jagged the line continued to be separating the geography of that prior stage from the new country being claimed by civilization. Like the frontier line itself, settlement of the backcountry in every state in the Old Southwest occurred by fits and starts in unequal waves, often in leapfrog fashion. And like many of their professional peers, the authors lived, worked, and played in that ambiguous geography. In their own time the entire region was a patchwork of advance and stasis, of swatches of technological growth

---

Diary, 85; Murat, *Moral and Political Sketch,* 245; Richard Smith Elliott, *Notes Taken in Sixty Years* (St. Louis, 1883), 45.
63. Quoted in Dorson, *Davy Crockett,* 145–52.

alternating with patches of resistance, and always—even in the more so-phisticated centers along the Mississippi River—pockets of frontier life not yet honored by the apostles of the modern. Even the sedate Judge Longstreet recalled in 1870 that his boyhood ambition was "to out-run, out-jump, out-shoot, throw-down and whip, any man in the district."[64] As one of the original thirteen states, Georgia was not new country, and by 1835, when *Georgia Scenes* appeared, the frontier had long since moved west; yet the state had its backward areas, just remote enough to remind most Georgians of how persistent their old-fashioned habits con-tinued to be. Even the urbanity of Augusta and Savannah, whose market-ing economy depended upon the enterprise of less civilized Georgians, was tainted by countrified pretentiousness. Beginning with Longstreet, the authors capitalized on the ambiguities of primitive and modern, cat-egories that were both spatial and temporal. As moderns themselves, the humorists endorsed the cultural implications signified by *progress*, the byword most current in the settlement process. Civilized literates, they often found themselves in sites overrun by what they surely regarded as only semicivilized illiterates; but with the faith of expansionists they foresaw the gradual absorption of the primitive backcountry into the de-veloping mainstream.

They understood also the role of simple chronology. Like many nineteenth-century leaders who thought of their age as the culmination of progress, they were not hesitant to set their pieces slightly back in time, not as a narrative convention, but as a cultural cue that the recent past was the scene of customs superseded by those of the present. It is not un-common for a humorous piece to begin with a temporal marker ("In 18—" or "Those of you who will remember . . .") to situate the anecdote about to be told, especially if its substance is old enough to suggest differences in the then-and-now and recent enough to require no explanation of its relevance. Without being exactly precise, Longstreet was the most insis-tent of the authors in the use of such temporal cues. Some of his pieces are placed as far back as the end of the eighteenth century, a device that supported his point that particularly crude and violent amusements were now "rarely" seen, even in dark Lincoln County. In "The Fight" Long-street reduced the essence of frontier crudity to its base in physical vio-lence, celebrating even as he deplored a competitive spirit at its purest.

64. Longstreet quoted in David Rachels, introduction to *Augustus Baldwin Long-street's* Georgia Scenes *Completed: A Scholarly Text* (Athens: University of Georgia Press, 1998), xv.

This famous sketch, however, despite the bloody details the narrator willingly itemizes, is carefully framed by an almost courtly punctilio on the part of both combatants—the author's reminder that protocol governed bare-knuckle fights no less than duels among the gentry. Longstreet rejects the comedy of the half-horse half-alligator, and the speech of his two stalwarts, Billy Stallings and Bob Durham, is totally functional, a modulated backwoods courtesy with which they extend respect for each other as a worthy opponent. By rejecting the flyting formula, the author acknowledges that stomp-and-gouge is not "just talk." The combat is the real thing. Rendered (by narrator Lyman Hall) with all the detailed intensity of a realist, the fight itself has fewer of the comic effects that we see in several of its companion sketches. Longstreet carefully resists any attempt to nudge brutal physicality into humorous spectacle; the comedy of the piece lies rather in the context of the event. Though dark enough to illustrate unenlightened Lincoln County, the humor transcends locale because it arises, as in an older tradition, out of the exposure of ordinary human weakness.

If Billy and Bob are too respectful of each other to indulge in oratorical bombast, their wives' confrontation while shopping suggests a distaff version that serves to delight onlookers even more. The name-calling between the wives, a kind of best-woman bout before the main event, exposes pride of place:

> Mrs. Stallings and Mrs. Durham stept simultaneously into the store. . . . "Have you any Turkey red?" said Mrs. S. "Have you any curtain calico?" said Mrs. D., at the same moment. "Yes, ladies," said Mr. Atwater, "I have both." "Then help me first," said Mrs. D., "for I'm in a hurry." "I'm in as great a hurry as she is," said Mrs. S., "and I'll thank you to help me first." "And pray, who are you, madam!" continued the other—"Your betters, madam," was the reply.

The dispute escalates when Billy Stallings comes in to hurry his wife home. She is late, she says, because of "that impudent huzzy." "Who do you call an impudent hussy? you nasty, good-for-nothing, snaggled toothed gaub of fat, you," Mrs. D. replies (*GS*, 36). If the gentlemanly restraint of the matched champions threatens to defer their much anticipated fight, this adroitly trashy exchange is the spark that reignites their rivalry. Ransy Sniffle, a clay-eating busybody, is on hand to speed things along. Desperate in their boredom, Sniffle, the disciples in both "battalions," and most of the villagers hanker for the violence that showdowns always promise. Moreover, the weaknesses of character that Longstreet so economically exposes extend outside the sketch to the reader, whose guilty pleasure, just as spectatorial, is subtly satisfied by the ramifying strains of tension.

If, in their shrewd depictions of yeomen at play, most of the humorous authors seem content to be observers and reporters of best-man games— or, at best, off-site participants—Henry Clay Lewis boldly sends his Madison Tensas directly into the fray. What one critic has called the generic "raw affront and challenge" of Southwest humor is never rawer than in the swamp doctor's case.[65] No other humorous author is quite as candid as Lewis in self-exposure, in confessing to and illustrating his personal demons. On a private level, Tensas must cope with anxieties of abandonment and the indignities of orphanhood. More philosophically, he is forced to operate continually with the conviction that a "hidden divinity . . . shapes our ends" (*SD*, 26).

His adversarial stance begins in childhood and continues into his professional training. Convinced that general intelligence and facile wit are as valid as specific knowledge and hard work, the "young grave rat" pits himself as a combatant against the superiors examining him for his degree. He later finds himself competing against an older doctor in the swamps, but, more humiliating, he is wryly bested by an old woman who matches her own "'sperience agin book larnin'" (*SD*, 94). Tensas's swamp world, when it is not filled with threats, consists largely of tests, opportunities, challenges. Stimulating his competitive mode are "poverty, youthfulness, the stranger's want of loving sympathy," and a host of "forebodings" about his future (*SD*, 140), all of which propels the swamp doctor into proving himself best man against (in sequence) a landlady, his fiancé's father, a Negro dwarf, assorted matronly dispensers of "kumfrey tea" and sweet-gum salve, and even the patients who need his help. Lewis gives his tyro doctor some of the traits of that familiar target of jokesters, the country verdant sent to hunt snipe or to fetch a bucket of cold steam; and when Tensas compensates for his naïveté, his ignorance is compounded by an arrogance that afflicts all the region's credentialed professionals. In some instances the patient becomes victim when the doctor's fretful drive for authority and reputation outstrips his abilities.

"The Mississippi Patent Plan for Pulling Teeth" is the fiercest example of the swamp doctor at his competitive best. A flatboatman, a generic Kentuckian, needs a tooth pulled but refuses to pay more than twenty-five

---

65. Edwin T. Arnold, introduction to *Odd Leaves from the Life of a Louisiana Swamp Doctor*, by Henry Clay Lewis (Baton Rouge: Louisiana State University Press, 1997), xi.

cents—the going rate back home. The sparring over fees puts Tensas (not yet a real doctor) in ill humor, and the contentiousness is heightened when the ailing patient calls him a "young one," a presumptuous term coming from a social inferior. Although the patient-doctor relationship is set up as a rivalry, the site is not a neutral space. The doctor's office boasts an intimidating array of (mostly restraining) furniture and equipment and is filled with a partisan audience of other doctor-interns. Only when Tensas sees the opportunity for a practical joke does he agree on the Kentuckian's price for pulling a tooth. He asks his patient which tooth needs pulling ("an incisor, or a dens sapientiae? one of the decidua, or a permanent grinder?"), and, in an aside to his friends, he bets that his experimental "patent plan" will break either the patient's jawbone or neck. The victim is strapped into a chair and hooked up to pulleys, ropes, and a hand vise. "I should have spared him," Tensas admits, "but his meanness disgusted me." The punitive aura of the scene—the "patent plan" is a humiliating torture machine that requires massive stretching of the neck— is enhanced by the "consultants" who function as sadistic cheerleaders. Neither jaw nor neck is broken, but the inexperienced doctor belatedly discovers that the vise was attached to the wrong tooth. The boatman "had too much blood in his mouth to discover it" himself (*SD*, 81–86).

In Lewis's sketch, the kind of wrangling associated with frontier swapping and the rivalry common to physical bouts are both transmuted into a modern instance. The Kentuckian's tooth is painfully extracted, but it is the wrong tooth; the doctor gives his patient change for a counterfeit five-dollar Kentucky bill. Tensas feels that he has had the edge in the encounter. Although he has demonstrated his ineptness and in fact pays *his patient* for the operation, his good humor returns. In this case, fulfilling his determination to have "some fun" at the boatman's expense makes him best man. The question of medical malpractice is quite irrelevant.[66]

The frequency of physical tests in Southwest humor would seem to reinforce the democratic ideal—in a raw society, every man is equal to every other man. The rivalries involving ring-tailed roarers are merely the most visceral testing of that theoretical principle. Yet most of the memorable characters in the humor are adaptive types, less interesting as individuals than as representative aggressors serving as their creators' image of

66. In a typical sketch, Tensas would be said to have been *picked up*, the term applied to someone who gives good money as change for counterfeit bills. Further, since he is out for "some fun" himself, the exchange would make him a *duper duped*, a term that many of the humorists favored. Since he is both narrator and hero of this sketch, however, Tensas deflects both roles. For a concise sketch about the trials of dealing with spurious paper money, see John S. Robb's "Picked Up!" (Oehl., 95–97).

members of a competitive society. Longstreet's two great characters in "The Fight" are not in fact the combatants, but Ransy Sniffle, the clay-eating troublemaker, and Squire Thomas Loggins, the cagey oracle. Billy Stallings and Bob Durham, who share the village title of best man, are reluctant warriors without a trace of cockerel belligerence. But in stripping the combatants of their inflammatory language, their creator makes them heroes in the colorless way that heroes in conventional fiction often are. Without the intrusive intervention of Sniffle (the "sprout of Richmond") and the enthusiasm of their respective lieutenants, Billy and Bob would be content to be as ordinary as their neighbors. But not quite ordinary: one of Longstreet's great touches is in making both champions more gentlemanly than their wives are ladylike.

William C. Hall's tactic with Mike Hooter, his Mississippi version of the type, is to return the reader to the old motif of providing entertainment. If earlier roarers were marked by ebullient self-dramatization, a performative style never far removed from self-mockery, Hooter, who is both narrator and subject, retains that verve while allowing himself parodic license. Hall revives the type and makes it relevant to Flush Times Mississippi by locating his hero in Yazoo, one of the state's retrograde sections ("the durndest hole," "that ar devil's camp ground"), and by modernizing it—Hooter is honored locally as a farmer and preacher as well as a bear hunter and fighter.[67]

Despite his reputation in "the Yazoo" as a champion of the "knock-down-and-drag-out row," Hooter is mostly a skilled manipulator of delaying tactics and fruitful evasion, as we see in "How Mike Hooter Came Very Near 'Wollopin' Arch Coony." Because he so artfully constructs this "fight," Hooter trusts his bluster and best-man rhetoric will be barely noticeable for what they are: a safe substitute for the real thing. Though both would-be combatants excel in verbal abuse, no blows are ever exchanged between the champion and Arch Coony, "the durndest, rantankerous hoss-fly that ever clum er tree." The anticlimactic verbal sparring match is preceded by months of long-distance insults carried back and forth by "sheep-stealin' chaps" who, like Longstreet's Ransy Sniffle, crave action. When the action comes, after much deferral, the face-to-face meeting consists of mutual taunts and still more deferral, until the rivals, stripping to their galluses for better handholds, insist that the riverbank be cleared of debris. Mike himself cleverly recounts the delaying tactics,

67. See John Q. Anderson, "Mike Hooter—The Making of a Myth," in *The Frontier Humorists: Critical Views*, ed. M. Thomas Inge (Hamden, CT: Archon, 1975), 197–207.

including a joint agreement to fight on the other side of the river so that the ferryman can keep to his schedule. The only action that occurs is when the ferry operator, tired of waiting, finally pushes off to the other side of the river, pitching Hooter from his horse "kerswash into the drink!" The rivals are left shaking their fists at each other and continuing the abuse that each prefers (Cohen, 364–69).

Hooter dramatizes the shift from heroic mold to the modern one, constructing himself as a witty, wry, and resilient personality unafraid of self-mockery. Though Coony calls Mike's preaching "nuthin' but loud hollerin'," the expounder of scripture is a close reader of his own oral texts, insisting on the accuracy of the challenge that was corrupted in transmission by the troublemakers eager to be entertained. Hall allows his hero his requisite posturing, his pride, and his account of his rival's flaws without depicting him as an out-and-out coward. It is Mike himself who confesses to being outdone when Coony boards the ferry, leaving him with only his words as weapons, and it is Mike who explains why he couldn't wait for the ferry to return with Coony—"my wife she would be 'spectin' me at the house, an' might raise pertickler h-ll if I didn't git thar in time; so I jumped on my ole hoss an' put for home" (Cohen, 369).

Although Hall pays homage to the lexicon of rhetorical bits associated with the ring-tailed roarers, his Mike Hooter is consciously downsized to recognizably human dimensions. It is as if the celebrated bluster that lifted the rough frontiersman into legendary status had, after the passing of the frontier, been forced into domestic service. Hooter is locally famous, but in his settlement phase he is condemned to act out multiple roles simultaneously—cotton planter, bear hunter, Methodist preacher, and husband. His extraordinary energy must now be distributed among several functions. What this sketch shows is that the time for the violence of stomp-and-gouge had largely passed, and its vitality had migrated (even regressed) to its lingual counterpart. In this case, the bark *is* the bite; the rehearsal *is* the performance. "How Mike Hooter Came Very Near 'Wollopin' Arch Coony" is both a satiric replay of the staple frontier fight and a humorous recasting in the domestic mode in which even heroes are comfortably accommodated to home life.

What had not passed was the theatricality of masculine rivalry. Even in its domesticated forms, the jactation of best men was still the engine that ran flashy competition. Even the verbal set-to could never occur on a purely private stage. Taking the measure of mouthy challenges, giving it public voice, was one of the duties of the narrator. In Baldwin's "An Affair of Honor," Jonas Sykes, a bullying pretender at gentlemanly honor, is

"prodigal in the jaw-work and wind-work of a fight." He selects his enemies with care, and the more he is restrained by his partisans, the more
his wrath intensifies, "like a bull-dog chained" (*FT*, 192–96). Yeoman stalwarts were rarely so pretentious as to claim "honor" as motive for spectacles either lingual or physical, yet they, no less than the planters with
their arcane code, knew their status was never a private satisfaction of
being, but a condition of character ratified by others.[68] The confidence
man might pull off his swindles by persuading others that he was *what he
said he was*. Best men, however, had to be *what the community said they were*,
and their reputation was always provisional. Attributes had to be continually earned.

Longstreet's Billy and Bob have their respective "battalions," support
groups that follow each turn of their champions' struggle in the village
square; Hall's Mike Hooter and Arch Coony have friends "testifying" for
their man. Consistently, these occasions are communal gatherings, public
forums to witness the testing of those males in the hot seat. All such contests require audiences, whether they occur on village streets, at boat
landings, in boardinghouses, or in courtrooms. Like the physical set-tos
in the street, the dramas enacted before judges and jurors in the courtroom attracted partisans who cheered on their favorites, and those on the
winning side often continued the rivalry with convivial replays on the
street and in the groggery. As the object of adulation, the best man was
expected to pay for his victory at the higher bar by "treating" his supporters at the lower. The witnessing could be impersonal or partisan (it
was sometimes both), but it was rarely silent. If the sketches of Sol Smith
dramatize how interactively audiences participated in performances at
literal theaters, onlookers were even more engaged and vociferous in
metaphorical theaters. Longstreet reports that the "commingled shouts,
screams and yells" that had urged Billy and Bob on to victory turn into
"shouts, oaths, frantic jestures, taunts, replies, and little fights" in the replay of the event after the real thing (*GS*, 40). Hooter's claim of victory
over Coony is an amusing reduction of what it means to be best man, but
if outcussing one's opponent is the standard, he has witnesses to endorse
it: "the fellers what was along with me sed I beat him all holler!"[69]

68. Dickson D. Bruce, Jr., *Violence and Culture in the Antebellum South* (Austin: University of Texas Press, 1979), 189; Bertram Wyatt-Brown, *Honor and Violence in the Old
South* (New York: Oxford, 1986), ix, 14. See also Kenneth S. Greenberg, *Honor and
Slavery* (Princeton, NJ: Princeton University Press, 1996).
69. What one sociologist terms "replaying" occurs almost instantaneously in this
humor. Erving Goffman, *Frame Analysis: An Essay on the Organization of Experience* (New

Throughout all ranks and in all categories, self-confident notions of the self in the antebellum South had to be endorsed by public opinion. Even forensic gifts, whether natural or acquired, whether as orator, storyteller, or raconteur, were another set of externally sanctioned values that established individual reputation. As Bertram Wyatt-Brown argues, the importance of public image led gradually to uniformity of values and conformity of behavior—one of the natural consequences of civilizing progress. "Tyranny of the community," he writes, "governed Southern society," and its particular brand of democracy "placed primary stress on white, manly virtue."[70] Without much interest in such serious sociological consequences, and despite their stake in civilization, the humorists were mostly satisfied in going no further than to demonstrate human foibles that were exposed to all eyes.

iii. Leading Men

[T]here are always more leading men in small villages than there are followers.

—*Col. Crockett's Exploits and Adventures in Texas*

The physicality of best-man contests may not have been funny, even to contemporary readers, but one-on-one fights were familiar and predictable. Less obvious, and requiring more nuanced characterization, was the phenomenon of the leading man. As the humorists depicted him, the leading man was a village variant of the confidence man, a modest bamboozler using his shrewd reading of human nature as a weapon in the battle for superiority. He could be a liar, a thief, or an adulterer, but mostly he was just a self-regarding villager who manipulated his lesser fellows for egoistic satisfaction and public adulation. Historically, some leading men were out-and-out scoundrels whose mobility let them easily elude the stuffy ethics of settled communities. A New England lieutenant with General Taylor's forces in Texas in 1845 complained in a letter to his wife of a "Colonel Cook here, a leading man at this place, but an outlaw from the States," who was stoutly denying that he had killed an Indian chief. "All the people around here are rascals," the officer continued.

York: Harper, 1974), 504–6. See also Twain's description of the interpretive repetition of Sherburn's killing of Boggs in *Huckleberry Finn* (MW, 766).
70. Wyatt-Brown, *Honor and Violence*, 149; see also 14, 31–33.

"There is not a man of them who is not a renegade from justice from our country, some for crime, some for debt."[71] Most leading men were merely innocuous opportunists who talked their way into the tolerance of the village. Because his humbuggery is too transparent to hurt others, the heedless liar Ovid Bolus earned his own profile in Joseph Baldwin's gallery.

The leading men the humorists favored are amusing, not threatening—village figures who earn (and sometimes lose) their reputation within parochial confines. Vain and self-promoting, they are often deficient in tact. W. T. Thompson's Boss Ankles aspires to be the leading man in Pineville, as he already is in his small settlement, but the local wags quickly target him as an overripe naïf worthy of their fun. When they torment him with firecrackers and rockets, he declares that Pineville deserves its "monstrous bad name for meanery and shecoonery of all sorts" (*CP*, 47). Most leading men are always on the verge of overreaching, boring others with their display of acuity and worldly knowledge. Boss Ankles, however, who cannot even pretend to learning, can claim nothing but an assertive manner. Even though "The Fight" is the most unvarnished recital of the best-man contest in the humor, one of Longstreet's subsidiary characters, Squire Thomas Loggins, anticipates the recurring figure of leading man in later sketches. Trying to determine where the advantage lies between the evenly matched heroes, the managers of the opposing battalions seek advice from Loggins, the village sage known as "Uncle Tommy." The slow-talking old-timer "had never failed to predict" the victor in such fights. Though he says little, "that little was always delivered with the most imposing solemnity of look and cadence," sly glances, and meaningful facial gestures. His performance before a fight—the "aspect of profound thought" that can seemingly tease "truth from its most intricate combinations"—gives encouragement to whichever side asks his help (*GS*, 37).

Like all predictions, Uncle Tommy's are so hedged, so minimally specific, that they are worthless. His reputation must be sustained by the sage himself, after the fact, when he reminds the crowd of his prescience. After Bob's victory, the old man joins the celebrating battalion to jog the memory of the audience about "what—your—uncle—Tommy—said—before—the—fight—began" (*GS*, 41). He is the village's leading man because, like so many notable characters in the humor, he is a performance artist whose verbal talents are firmly based on his reading of human na-

71. Quoted in Ferrell, *Monterrey Is Ours!* 13.

ture. Like many others, he is also a humbug. But unlike such small-bore confidence men as Baldwin's Ovid Bolus and Hooper's Simon Suggs, Squire Loggins benefits not at all from his little fraud except to earn pride of place in his village. If most leading men in the humor possess vanity too obtrusive to be overlooked, the deception practiced by Squire Loggins is too innocent to merit the customary comeuppance by village watchdogs. Confident of both his technique and his audience, he never overreaches.

Democracy on the frontier has usually been interpreted as the general spirit of equality, popularized by an energetic "I'm-as-good-as-the-next-man" sentiment. Though in local elections the commoners often acknowledged superior men among them, a kind of grudging surliness made the exercise of traditional political leadership vulnerable. Not merely were aristocracy and family distinction rejected as appropriate credentials, but any sign of pretension, of ambition that would unduly raise one man over another, was fair game for deflation. As Catherine Zuckert argues, the competitive drive among "equal" men inevitably invited them to indulge a natural appetite for distinction, seizing upon any visible means for elevating themselves over their fellows. In that zone of tension, within a relatively narrow range of acceptable conduct, would-be leaders made their delicate way toward their goals. The "hope of mounting and the fear of falling" were both central to the nature of interlinked social relationships.[72] Men whose reputation transcended state and region had some protection because of their party affiliation, which buffered them from the most common ridicule. (Naming hunting dogs after Andrew Jackson or Henry Clay was an honoring of a great man, not a mocking gesture.) Politics on a purely local level, however, offered few barriers against democratic deflation.

Although the humorous authors, whose interest was largely social, rarely entered the political arena in exploring that zone of tension, the same ambivalent egalitarianism holds sway in their sketches. Since in a democracy *equal to* is a passive sort of distinction, merely to claim it lacks drama. And in the conflict of equals, where *equal to* is always insufficient, only the demonstration of *better than* will do. Lewis's Kentucky boatman is already out of his natural element. He must contend not with a fellow boatman but with an altogether different rival, one who comes armed

72. Catherine H. Zuckert, *Natural Right and the American Imagination: Political Philosophy in Novel Form* (Savage, MD: Rowman & Littlefield, 1990), 62; Robert H. Wiebe, *The Segmented Society: An Introduction to the Meaning of America* (New York: Oxford, 1975), 103.

with the wiles, stratagems, and attitudes of a *modern* species. If Madison Tensas betrays the inevitable condescension of the literate professional narrator, he also demonstrates that the struggle for dominance continues even more fiercely among the moderns, professionals who are doing their part to raise the tone of the margins even as they establish themselves in the competitive center.

The authors were fortunate in the mix of Flush Times society to count themselves as part of the elite. Being both literate and literary helped. The goofy verdancy of country boys, the sly logic of tippling Irishmen, and the flamboyant self-promotion of half-horse half-alligators were easy marks for their gifts. Yet, like other forms of popular culture, the humor rejoices in ridiculing upward as well as down. Some of the authors' best writing went into depicting the egoistic foibles of their own kind—which is to say those aspiring individuals in a world of fluctuating class lines. The very fact that the definition of classes was murky encouraged what one writer called "illiberal jealousy." The individual who considered himself "of the better file" walked circumspectly to avoid "mingling with the *canaille*"; the more uncertain he was of his status, "the more haughty and suspiciously" he stood aloof, measuring each stranger who advanced "within the limits of the prescribed circle."[73] Especially alert to the psychology of rivalry, the authors extracted comedy out of envy, distrust, resentment, and retaliation. Without figures of real power, the humor favors the faux elite, pretenders who take on the airs of truly superior men: gentlemen blowhards, ersatz wisdom figures, elegant professional trimmers, and Miss Nancy sorts.

In Ham Jones's sketch "The Sandy Creek Literary Society," a village squire yearns to raise the cultural level of his community. Acknowledged as "a man of pretty good sense," Benjamin Primm spoils the effect by "the largeness of his pretensions, and by a most ridiculous mannerism." For him, being a cultural arbiter means eschewing his natural speaking voice in favor of an oratorical register that the narrator calls "a *set talk* or harangue" uttered in a single "particular key." Sprinkled with more than an occasional *aforesaid*, his talk is "monstrous *precise* and *knowing*." Assuming the office of president of a literary society, Primm assembles the best of the village, a barely literate group charged with constructing a canon of appropriate books that will "promote *vartue* and *marality*." Under his hectoring leadership, the group finally agrees on such books as Pope's

---

73. Joseph Holt Ingraham, *The South-West, by a Yankee* (1835; Ann Arbor, MI: University Microfilms, 1966), 1:234.

Essays, Shakespeare's *Julius Caesar,* and Watts's *Songs and Hymns,* which the secretary duly inscribes in the "catterlog" as "Pope's Asses," "Joolus Seeser," and "Wats Sams and Hims." The squire will not admit novels because "they are very detrimental to the marals of the rising generation" (*HJ,* 61–68).

"The Sandy Creek Literary Society" is interesting not merely for its generic verbal humor. Structurally, the sketch incorporates a familiar situation when the village mischief-maker, the towheaded Bill Jenkins, torments Squire Primm with two practical jokes. First, he interrupts the literary conclave by letting loose Selim, the squire's horse, which its owner touts as a "powerful crittur" that will create havoc among ordinary horses if not restrained. The members rush out to watch Primm's horse bite, kick, and paw the other horses until he meets the innkeeper's smaller, tougher pony, which humiliates Selim. Later, at the Sandy Creek Church, while a kneeling Primm, a "practiced exhorter," leads the assembly in praying for the success of the "praiseworthy and commendable" literary society, the joker releases a hornet's nest into a rip in the president's pantaloons (the prayer meeting ends "promiscuously"). Although he suspects the "uneducated varmunt" as the source of disruption in both instances, Primm, "encased in his sevenfold shield of vanity," remains "proof against ridicule" (*HJ,* 64–65, 68). He advertises another meeting of the new society, but nobody shows up except a bored Bill Jenkins.

Paralleling the lingual violence of the book club, both practical jokes expose the squire's unearned dignity, and the "uneducated varmunt" becomes the village representative who sabotages the efforts of its leading man to transform a rawboned community into a cultured society. Though this "Jackanapes" is a brother to Longstreet's Ransy Sniffle and Hooper's Yellow Legs—fomenters of mischief and tormentors of frauds—Jones's Bill Jenkins also shares the subversive resistance to progress most familiarly enshrined in Irving's "Legend of Sleepy Hollow"—Jenkins plays a sneaky version of Brom Bones to Squire Primm's Ichabod Crane.

As "the great man of the village of Summerville," Thomas Kirkman's Dick Jones, a Kentucky colonel, has more to justify his pretensions than does Squire Primm. Despite a "universal smattering of information," he is a "specious" lawyer whose professional advancement has come from an obliging manner rather than "superior merit." A public man who once served as congressman, Colonel Jones now reigns as natural leader in his county. Though the seniors defer to his legal opinions, his real influence is upon younger lawyers (admiring his "dress and taste"), matrons (charmed by his "easy, affable, and attentive manner"), and impressionable young ladies (delighted by his "suavity and condescension"). He is, in short, "a very agreeable companion." Though his fondness for striking outfits is not enough to make Colonel Jones a dandy, certain "vagaries in clothing" suggest that this "Virginian bred and Kentucky raised" gentleman exudes "an air of harmless . . . self-conceit and swagger" (Cohen, 60–64).

The crux of "Jones's Fight" is *honor.* How should the colonel respond to the slanderous accusation of one Bill Paterson that he had been a Federalist during the War of 1812? Since the village elders believe that this widely circulated charge is "more than an honorable man could stand," Jones declares that the next time he goes over the mountain to court in the adjoining county, he will challenge the slanderer.[74] Though the issue is antiquated, the means of settling it is not. Since the Virginia custom of dueling is not an option, Colonel Jones must abide by Kentucky's more plebeian solution: the stomp-and-gouge fight. Yet the physical action, unlike that in Longstreet's "The Fight," occurs offstage. Kirkman focuses on the lawyer's long-awaited return from the circuit to report on the encounter. He returns a physical mess—his eyes surrounded by "dark green specks," his right hand in a sling, a finger on his left hand wrapped in linen bandages, his ears covered with a "muslin scrap," and his face swollen and "clawed all over." His affability, however, is "undiminished." Even when he is peppered with the questions Summerville wants answered ("Which whipped?" and "Who hollered?"), he remains unflappable. In lawyerly fashion, delaying tactics and rhetorical detail postpone the climax until Colonel Jones finally is forced to conclude the account for his hungry audience: "We had fought round and round, and about and about, all over the court-yard, and, at last, just to end the fight, every body was getting tired of it; so, at l-a-a-st, I hollered" (Cohen, 64).

More aggressive, though with slenderer reason for his pretensions, is Moses Mercer of Thomas Bangs Thorpe's "A Piano in Arkansas." This affable "oracle of the village" of Hardscrabble is always eager to dispel ignorance; but, unlike Primm's neighbors, those of Moses Mercer actively seek his judgment on all arcane matters—because he is known to have visited Little Rock. Cosmopolitanism commands deference in Hardscrabble. Mercer is away on a hunt when the Dolittles—a northern mer-

---

74. In his record of his American visit in 1807–1809, Fortescue Cuming noted at length the mutual animosity of Federalists and Democratic Republicans. The labels alone were sufficient for partisans of either side to be pronounced "capable of every crime." Cuming, *Tour,* 4:71–72. Although the time of the action of "Jones's Fight" is unspecified, the sketch appeared first in the *Spirit of the Times* in 1840.

chant and his family—take up residence in the village, reportedly bringing with them "a real piano." Excited but perplexed by this news, the villagers agree that it is probably an animal ("though a harmless one") and eagerly await the return of Mo Mercer to settle the matter. Once back in Hardscrabble, the oracle is pleased to talk of the piano "as a matter he was used to." The narrator continues: "[He] went on to say he had seen more Pianos in the 'Capitol' than he had ever seen woodchucks,— that it was not an animal, but a musical instrument, played upon by the ladies, and he wound up his description by saying, 'that the way the dear creeters could pull the music out of it, was a caution to screech owls.'" With Jim Cash, a faithful sidekick who hangs on his every word, Mercer decides to pay a visit to the Dolittles. They are not at home, but their absence allows the oracle to poke around the premises, finally spotting the piano on an open porch: "a singular machine . . . crossed by bars, rollers, and surmounted with an enormous crank." When Cash gives the handle a turn, a complacent Mercer pronounces the grating sound "Beautiful!" (*TBT*, 140–44). His talkative toady spreads the news among the curious, and Mercer's stock soars.

Yet to make the village know-it-all such a marvel of casual mastery, even with obliging neighbors, is also to plaster a kick-me sign on his superior back. When the new family invites the leading villagers to a soiree to hear Miss Patience Dolittle "perform on the Piano," Mercer, having been twice to the capitol, is of course invited, along with his adoring acolyte. All the "grace of a city dandy" is tested, however, when the young lady sits down to play upon an entirely different instrument. When a confused Cash asks her to identify the object on the porch, she blushes a bit as she says, "a—a—YANKEE WASHING MACHINE!" Mercer's stock sinks. The "great and invulnerable" oracle now hears only whispers and titters as the fashionable vices of "envy, and maliciousness" are sown in Hardscrabble. "Time wore on, and Pianos became common, and Mo Mercer less popular, and he finally disappeared entirely on the evening of the day, when a Yankee pedlar of notions, sold to the highest bidders, six 'Patent and highly concentrated' 'Mo Mercer's Pianos'" (*TBT*, 144).[75]

That we follow an "accomplished" pianist in her excruciating recital in Longstreet's "The Song" is testimony to the importance of the piano as an indicator of the *material* superiority of the community that can claim

75. The village know-it-all and his faithful follower are recurring figures. See, for example, Joseph Field's "Tom Harris' Wink" (Oehl., 97–101) and the anonymous "An Arkansas Original" (*PPW*, 119–21).

it. Dr. Sims, pursuing his career in the backcountry, wrote his wife that the "Alabama lassies" gamely "make a noise on the *piano*," and as late as 1856, on his way to Arkansas, a young eastern musician found a piano in a Memphis hotel and thought it worth noting in his journal: "The first I've seen since leaving Louisville."[76] Thorpe's point is not the rarity of pianos in the backcountry but that his leading man is a country poseur, which in the comic world necessarily invites retribution. Mo Mercer counts on his experience in Little Rock to give him the cachet he needs among his provincial neighbors. The "Capitol," as we also know from Noland's Pete Whetstone, offered a level of sophistication not otherwise available in Arkansas.

In Georgia, Augusta serves the same function for the Reverend Jedidiah Suggs, whose standing in his community has been considerably enhanced by his one-time visit to that *"ultima Thule* of back-woods Georgians." As Hooper notes, "no man could visit the city of Augusta without acquiring a vast superiority over all his untravelled neighbours, in every department of human knowledge." It is entirely in keeping with his character that, even as an adolescent, Simon Suggs is not impressed: "Bob Smith says them Augusty fellers can't make rent off o' me" (*SS*, 22–23).[77] In Thompson's "Great Attraction!" Dr. Peter Jones, though he has no "sheepskin license to practice the healing art," returns home to Pineville, after attending one course of lectures at Augusta, "rich in all the polish and refinement which a winter's residence in that Philadelphia of the south affords such ample opportunities for acquiring." Dr. Jones considers himself the model for manners and style. With his fashionable outfit, walking cane, and general reputation for "smartness," he enjoys "undisputed precedence" in the eyes of the young. Not only can he read the placards announcing the arrival of a "Great Attraction," his mastery of Augusta also authorizes him to prepare the villagers for the kind of spectacle they can look forward to. "He told them that it was a thing called a

76. Sims, *Story of My Life*, 378–79; Anton Reiff Journal, MS 3274, Louisiana and Lower Mississippi Valley Collections, Louisiana State University Libraries, Baton Rouge. Historically the sight of a piano in isolated hamlets was a rarity. It caused "great wonderment" in one settlement, according to an observer. One man thought the instrument was an ironing table; another assumed the pedals were pistols; another mistook the piano for a funny-looking chest for storing fine clothes. McWhiney, *Cracker Culture*, 122–23.

77. For different reasons, George Featherstonhaugh was also not impressed by Augusta, which he noted was a "long, straggling town" full of "small stores and low taverns"—everything to make the traveler "anxious to take to the roads again, be they ever so bad." *Excursion*, 2:115.

circus, derived from circle for horses to run round in—that it was a very wonderful thing—. . . that he had 'seed' a great many of them in Augusta, when he was at college, and knew all about them" (*CP*, 11–38).

On opening night, standing aside from the eager and "uninitiated crowd," the doctor maintains his air of "exclusive complacency," having cleverly reserved seats earlier in the day (which, he says, is "the universal custom in Augusta"). To the bevy of six young ladies whom he accompanies, he points out "the various fixtures of the ring, explaining their purposes," begging them "not to *be* skared" at the breathtaking acrobatics of the riders—"that was nothing to what he had seen in Augusta." When two village rowdies create their own ringside performance, the doctor helps the manager restore order by calling "upon the gentlemen present" to part them; later, when a drunk interrupts an act featuring a clown and a circus horse, the doctor himself intrudes into the ring, fuming that if the interloper "was in Augusta, they'd have him in the guard-house in less than no time" (Cohen, 21–30).

Though the first break in the performance was a genuine disruption, this one is not, but the doctor is unable to tell the difference—he attributes both of them to Pineville's lack of sophistication. Thompson reinforces the doctor's gullibility by having some ordinary villagers detect the ruse; the young men who answer his call to oust the "drunk" quickly return to their seats ("that chap belongs to the show, I can smell it on his breath!"). Single-handedly suffering his indignity, the doctor finds himself hoisted on the shoulders of the "drunk," unable to dismount or to forestall the raucous participation of the audience ("Is that the way they does in Augusta?"). The "drunk" turns out to be a circus acrobat as adept at disguise as he is at horsemanship. He sheds layer after layer of clothing, revealing first the guise of a woman "trigged out in a flounced muslin, and a fashionable opera hat," and finally, with the dropping of the dress, a costume of gilt and spangles. As the butt of the joke, Dr. Jones is "mortified" to be slower than his fellow villagers to detect the trick. Taunted by shouts and jeers, he must rise and acknowledge, "I was most oudaciously tuck in that time—that's a fact" (Cohen, 31, 36–38).[78]

Paul Beechim, the "village Beau Brummell" in Baldwin's "Justification

78. Dr. Peter Jones is the same character as Joseph Jones's cousin Pete in *Major Jones's Courtship*, where he is mostly envious and mean-spirited. The episode of the circus is a probable source for Huck Finn's adventures at a circus, where a "drunk" on a horse, after shedding "seventeen suits," turns out to be the "prettiest [rider] you ever saw" (*MW*, 770–71). See also Pascal Covici, Jr., "Mark Twain and the Humor of the Old Southwest," in Inge, *Frontier Humorists*, 243–44.

after Verdict," considers the cultural norm to be Knoxville, his home-town, "at once the Athens and Paris of America." That model of refine-ment is his constant referent in his exile in the new country, during which time he takes seriously his role as cultural missionary, reporting back to Tennessee his progress in teaching fashionable manners to his new neighbors. "Rusticity and vulgarity were abominations to him," notes the narrator, and though he is "an excellent fellow," his "high-church Knoxvillism" invites irreverence. Vain in his dress, like Squire Primm and Dr. Peter Jones, Beechim is "pretentious as to fashion, style and man-ners," pluming himself "not a little" (*FT*, 184–85). But this dandy is also a naïf. Self-deluded, he is an extreme example of the provincial who thinks himself cosmopolitan, and therefore both pride and innocence go before his fall. In both structure and characterization, "Justification after Verdict" is a richly textured piece. It features such familiar plot turns as the biter bitten and the yokel in the city, but, like "Jones's Fight," it is also a sketch in which the central event that generates the action occurs off-stage and must be reconstructed.

Beechim, the narrator's client, is charged with the public beating of one Phillip Cousins after the two friends' return from a trip to New Orleans. While accepting a guilty verdict, Beechim refuses to divulge any circumstances that might mitigate his punishment. What the guilty man wants is what nobody in the humor should expect—secrecy. The nour-ishment of privacy is always doomed, as it must be in the humorous world of full disclosure. The mystery of "what happened?" is finally breached in court by a third party, a fellow villager who happened to be in New Orleans at the time of the incident. The assault, he reveals, was Beechim's retaliation for being humiliated by Cousins at a fashionable restaurant. In this variation of a perennial favorite, the provincial dandy drinks the water from his finger bowl after being told by his waggish friend that it is "sop" for his fresh pineapple.

The scene in the hotel dining room is both funny and painful. Though Beechim himself is generally unobservant, the eyes of the other diners ("ladies, dandies, foreigners, moustached fellows") are predictably drawn to the mess he makes on his plate. Their laughter escalates when the gulled Beechim finishes his course and announces primly and loudly, "I think the pine-apple very good, but don't you think the sauce is rather insipid?" In his rush to escape the scene of his humiliation, Beechim cre-ates enough havoc to make the next morning's *Picayune* ("no names given"). The mystery solved, the judge declares, "Justification complete!" followed by "The Court adjourns for refreshment," which in this situation borders on the redundant. Beechim is exonerated for thrashing his friend, but the price is public exposure. "[Y]ou have saved my body but you have ruined my character," he tells his lawyer. "But . . . if—you—can—help—it—don't—let—this—thing—get—back—to—Knoxville" (*FT*, 177–91). Less an expression of comic justice than an occasion for public entertainment, the incident enters local lore, perpetuated by public repetition and, in a wider context, by Baldwin's written version, which will inevitably "get-back-to-Knoxville."

If the plot and characterization of Baldwin's piece are unusually complex for a humorous sketch, so is the reader's response. Like all dupes in such stories, the central figure gets his comeuppance for inadequate self-knowledge, yet his anguished cry—"you have ruined my character"—is an accurate assessment, since Beechim knows that all private aspects of character must be submitted to the public for verification. The verdict smacks of bad (if common) law: the judge recognizes that even if it has been sullied in fun, a gentleman's honor demands public retaliation. Like all the other leading men in Southwest humor, Beechim is snobbish and presumptuous, but not fatally so. Baldwin's narrator, no less than the judge, considers justice in this case as a kind of fair exchange. Cousins pays for his waggery with a bloodied head; Beechim pays for his vanity and self-delusion with public exposure. Yet, relishing that exposure, the narrator goes further, as if retribution must be meted out for anybody's extravagant faith in "that out-of-the-way, not-to-be-gotten-to, Sleepy-Hollow town, fifty miles from the Virginia line, and a thousand miles from any where else" (*FT*, 185). Beechim is not a villain, but in a democratic environment his desire for special status invites squelching. Being set apart is not a gift *conferred on* leading men but a state *affirmed by* leading men.

Baldwin's "gallery of daubs" in *Flush Times* also includes a would-be leading man—Cave Burton, an ignorant slangwhanging lawyer too dense to be embarrassed by his failures. In "Cave Burton, Esq., of Kentucky," the "Blowing Cave," who loves oysters even more than he does juries of "*the people*," indulges in the telling of personal anecdotes "as if he were at a love-feast" and shares a copious repertoire of gossip and "neighborhood reports." He believes his early sacrifices and renunciations in "getting to the backwoods" should endear him to *the people*; but the people fail to set much store "by so rare an article brought out at such cost." He has, notes Baldwin, "brought his wares to the wrong market." If he is denied gratitude, he is, more materially, also deprived of his share of oysters that arrive for a Christmas celebration. As he drones through a familiar story that no "mortal man had ever heard the end of," his fellow lawyers consume the entire shipment (*FT*, 153–76). If leading men have little success in their mission to raise the cultural standards of the community, it is usually because they are too pretentious. Cave Burton's case demonstrates that a fulsome identification with *the people* can be equally fraudulent—and just as vulnerable to exposure.

Best men are hostage to the cultural climate of competition in which their status is always subject to challenge. Leading men, however, except for Kirkman's Colonel Jones, are not expected to struggle to gain or retain their special position. Leading men pride themselves on their communal duty to share wit and learning, though that gift may be only a "smattering of information" (as in the case of Colonel Jones) or even misinformation (as in the case of Mo Mercer, who can't tell the difference between a piano and a washing machine). The "great man of the village" cannot resist the pedagogic mode and the easy condescension that goes with it. The Squire Primms and Colonel Joneses of Southwest humor never hesitate to accept public ratification of a self-image distinct from the commonality, and to sustain it they resort to individualizing tics of speech or mannerisms of dress. Longstreet's Uncle Tommy is sparing in his speech, but what he says is delivered with imposing cadences, pauses, and solemn body language. Ham Jones's Squire Primm is overly fond of *aforesaid* and (to avoid what he considers common dialect) regularly pronounces the "O as if it were an A" (*HJ*, 62).

Kirkman's Kentucky colonel ensures his image of superiority by wearing showy outfits that contribute to his swaggering air: they might not be admirable, notes his creator, but they lend "piquancy" to his presence. Thompson's Dr. Jones comes back from Augusta sporting "a cloth coat of the latest cut, pants to match, and a pair of stilt-heeled boots," wears "a black velvet cap" ("jauntily"), and carries a walking cane of "the most delicate polish" (*CP*, 18). If the ladies of the village regard Baldwin's Paul Beechim as "the glass of fashion and the mould of form," that is because the Knoxville exile is pleased to model himself irrelevantly on a sadly dated hero of fashion (*FT*, 185). Outfits are visual confirmation of function—the felt duty to dispense knowledge where there is ignorance. Special touches—in vests, shoes, hats, trousers—and unusual combinations of formal and informal wear serve as narrative telegraphs alerting the reader to the likely tripping-up of the figure who so indulges himself. Putting on a false front had a literal application for one Georgia "major" in the Old Natchez district. After being bested in a wager at a racetrack, he was humiliated when a Dutchman and a Yankee discovered that his "ferocious" appearance hid a "dickey" rather than a real shirt.[79] Like speech patterns, "vagaries in clothing" proclaim a man's special status among his peers; and, as in comedy generally, self-proclaimed distinction invites communal demotion.

Among other men, leading men are of course more tolerated than liked, but among matrons and young ladies, their dignified attentiveness and lively wit make them favorite companions. Best men are forced to make their mark among men; leading men find it easier to achieve stature among women. Though their actual opposition always looms as potential, leading men and best men usually occupy separate spaces in the humor. They represent different stages in the march of progress. Best men operate according to antique values of manhood based on personal courage, physical stamina, and skill. Leading men operate, however tentatively, according to *expectations*, often seeing themselves as the advance guard of a newer, better social order shaped by knowledge, civil manners, and virtues, assumed whether they are owned or not. The great temptation of leading men is to put on airs, and they tend to be exposed by the common sort who suspect that there is no Great Oz behind the curtain.[80]

In one piece in the *St. Louis Reveille,* however, the uneasy transition from one cultural stage to the other is dramatized explosively in the same space with the confrontation of a leading man and a best man. "Squire Funk's Awful Mistake," by an author who signed himself "Wing," is narrated by an ordinary spectator, who relates the event with great vernacular gusto. He introduces Funk as the village know-it-all: "He knew more about things, and told about 'em oftener, and took longer to do it in, and made it amount to littler when he'd got through, than the hull bilin' of lawyers, widers, pedlers, and pisoners of the county." Onto these traits the narrator grafts those of the pious hypocrite: "he was jest a livin' saint, and how the deuce they got on without him up in heaven, was a wonder!" The squire

79. Laura D. S. Harrell, "Horse Racing in the Old Natchez District," *Journal of Mississippi History* 13 (1951): 123–37.

80. Best man Davy Crockett borrows a leaf from the leading man's script in one posthumous appearance in the *Almanacks* ("Col. Crockett's Account of a Duel"), when at a public dinner he intervenes by interpreting for an Englishman a potentially insulting toast by a Frenchman. Though he also drinks from his finger bowl, Crockett is no ordinary bumpkin, and if the jumbled traits of conciliation, bullying, self-confidence, and intolerance make him an unstable character, the telltale mixture stands as a kind of symbolic embodiment of the American male as so many contemporary foreigners fastidiously depicted him. *The Crockett Almanacks: Nashville Series, 1835–1838,* ed. Harry J. Owens (Chicago: Caxton Club, 1955).

has "scraped up a mighty friendly acquaintance" with the wife of Jake Miller, comforting her and getting her "to jine church" while the husband is out of town "flatboatin', or a horse-stealin', or somethin' or other." Jake, the conventional ring-tailed roarer ("born on a raft, suckled by a squaw, raised on *bar* meat"), is the best man of the village who makes "a livin' by threat'nin' everything human with death that cum in his way" (Oehl., 117).

In "Squire Funk's Awful Mistake," it is old Funk who comes in his way. As we know, the threat of death in Southwest humor is always hyperbolic, but Jake need not even threaten death as long as the "everything human" about the squire can be reduced through the enforced good fellowship of merrymaking. In Cap'n Tod's grocery, while he and his cronies celebrate their return with "baldface" whiskey, Jake forces the squire to drink draw after draw of soda water and threatens to run a footrace with him when the "succumventin' old sinner" is fully bloated with gas. When the conciliating Funk proposes to "shake hands and forget old grudges," Jake ups the ante by giving the gassy squire a bear hug: "he got sech a *bustin'* hug that *everything went!*—all *aft* was a wreck. . . . There he lay, explosion behind, a bowie knife before." But what backwoodsmen called *natur* intervenes further in the humiliation of the squire. A coon dives under his beshitted coat ("it climbed twixt his legs fust thing . . . kase it's the natur of the critter to *hang on!*") and the storekeeper's bull terrier jumps in after the coon:

> Oh, hair and nails! you never see any thing shoot as Squire Funk did! There it was, terrier and trousers! Coon and Squire! till the varmint had worked itself clean up into his bosom, he, the durned gassy old locomotive! *explodin'* all the while, and, at last, pitching heels and head over a log into a pig puddle!
> . . . No one could tell which eend he was nastiest! (Oehl., 118–20)

As the random appearance of these backwoods types illustrates, the social complexity of the antebellum Southwest is economically condensed in the writing into a few behavioral models. Like roarers, yeoman fighters, and self-regarding village leaders, lustful preachers and lawless sheriffs are generic characters who are useful in various situations. Such other figures as the innocent rube, the experienced widow, the gifted blowhard, and the watchful pa's sassy gal are summoned as dependable types whenever needed, not because the authors are lazy (a perspective from the legacy of realism that many of us are ready to assume), but because their familiarity helps to fix a clangorous and propulsive world that the authors must negotiate. Conceptually frozen into verbal snapshots that effectively fuse diversity and growth in the new country, character types are more a utilitarian function of the humorists' art than they are marks of ineptness.

Despite their vague assertions that backwardness had (mostly) succumbed to progress, the authors aggressively freed themselves of agendas that would overvalue their feel for their own times. Even in the case of Baldwin, the most historically oriented of the humorists, his portrayal of the rambunctious era he lived through is mercifully untouched by a sense of developmental sociology. *Flush Times* inscribes not merely the halcyon years leading up to Andrew Jackson's Specie Circular in 1836, but also the economic chaos that followed. Ruin and confusion have the same weight for Baldwin as speculation and confidence, and his affective mind-set is the same in 1853 as it had been in 1837. Bust may be different from boom, but this chronicler defines collapse with the same alacrity as he does reckless prosperity. His contemporaries among the authors show even less concern about an evolving world. They counter their full-speed times, the instability of the go-ahead spirit, with an Irvingesque temper. When they construct their sketches, capturing the turbulent mood of the settlement process is not a high priority, however expediently they heed it for themselves. The texture of their prose connotes the settled, the slow-paced, the regularized patterns by which villagers conduct their lives. Yet in retrospect we can read the very presence of leading men in the sketches as an implicit clue to the evolving Southwest. Unlike Kentucky cockerels and stomp-and-gouge hearties, creatures who are manifestly shaped by a vigorous frontier, moral and social leaders of the community signify the passing of the frontier.

Preachers and deacons were the conspicuous (if flawed) moral leaders of communities in their earlier stages of settlement. Though they continue to be prominent throughout the smudged chronology of the humor, these exemplary figures are forced to share their position with showier and smoother-talking men who take upon themselves the more secular mission of cultural instruction. Musicales, dances, soirees, and stage performances are the favored venues for these silkier rustics.

Like the moral monitors of the community, the custodians of culture betray a fondness for hectoring those who stand in need of their example. The Dr. Joneses and Paul Beechims of the humor may lack self-knowledge as well as a knack for reading the world around them, and the Squire Funks, like so many representatives of order, may be crass hypocrites, but leading men think of themselves as community leaders at a critical time in the process of settlement, when mere preachers no longer suffice as appropriate figureheads. Their advanced status means of course that ordinary types are ever more alert to signs in them of rampant ambition and exaggerated self-regard. In a competitive culture, at whatever stage of development, leadership skills are always subject to challenge from others, just as they are hostage to human frailties that so often mar their determined efforts.

As we see, the humorists cast a particularly wide net for entrapping the conspicuous pretender. Their examples range from lowly claimants of superior status to the near-subtle, and it is this very range that makes the leading man the most culturally "natural" of the competitive games in the authors' repertory. If they can find little humor in stomp-and-gouge encounters, the humorists find almost too much in domestic scrimmaging for position. Indeed, the writing is rich in this vein partly because the authors are speaking to a condition that is national rather than regional. Magnifying and deflating were coordinates in nineteenth-century democracy. However contrary to the national creed, the drive for rank and special place assumed its own social momentum in all varieties of communal organization. And however respected and feared the most successful strivers and achievers may have been, aggrandizement invited reduction.

But the authors did more than adapt a bemused democratic perspective on the cultural pretenders. The awkward negotiations of cotillion and courting rituals that we follow in *Major Jones's Courtship,* the Pete Whetstone letters, *Georgia Scenes,* and the Billy Fishback stories in *Life and Public Services of an Army Straggler* highlight not only these rustic imitations, but also the very codes of social engagement that the imitations imitate. When Longstreet pokes fun at the artificiality of village behavior, he reveals what one theorist has termed the "restriction of vision" needed by any culture, a circumscribing that shields us all from the "essential relativism of all symbolic construction."[81] As leading men, the humorists, even the inadvertent ones, knew that their society and their place in it were neither permanent, inevitable, nor universal.

81. Roy Wagner, *The Invention of Culture,* rev. ed. (Chicago: University of Chicago Press, 1981), 59–60.

Chapter 13

The Yokel as Social Critic

> What would the honest men of the old time . . . think if they could
> read the newspapers now and see all the murders, and robberies,
> and all manner of rascalities that they's filled with every week?
>
> —William Tappan Thompson, *Major Jones's Courtship*

Major Jones's Courtship (1843) is at once the most cohesive volume of
Southwest humor and historically its most popular.[1] More than any
of the other figures who speak their minds without stint, the voice of William Tappan Thompson's vernacular hero fully accommodates the sensibilities of a genteel nineteenth-century audience. Unlike Fenton Noland's
Pete Whetstone, Joseph Jones is an orderly sort of hero whose adventures, such as they are, rarely edge into what respectable readers of the
time would consider vulgar. He is so much the stout defender of consensus social values that, except for his being a southern apologist, he embodies broadly national attitudes even more relevantly than Seba Smith's
Major Jack Downing, the good-hearted Yankee who inspired Thompson's

---

1. One measure of the sustained popularity of *Major Jones's Courtship* is the space
accorded to Thompson in the anthology *Oddities in Southern Life and Character* (Boston, 1883), edited by Henry Watterson, the urbane editor of the *Louisville Courier-
Journal*. Although he acknowledges the work of Longstreet, Harris, Baldwin, and
Hooper as characteristic of antebellum humor, Watterson devotes 110 of his 485 pages
to Major Jones.

creation. Although Major Jones is decently aspiring (which means making a studied effort to transcend the grosser side of *human natur*), his real appeal lies in his sanative common sense (which means exercising a healthy skepticism about games and pretense). As in the epistolary form generally, the integrated sequence of Jones's letters comes supplied with its own contexts, requiring no intervention by the real-life author and minimal inference by the reader.

i.

Although it was as susceptible to self-distortion and special pleading as most literary genres, the public letter, penned at whatever lingual level, was a stable form. The letters of Joseph Jones show a remarkable transparency of character. Relentlessly middle-class, he is a decent man who wants to be seen as decent. Responsible and patient, he is not unaware of liberties taken at his expense by his domestic establishment, and he is capable of anger at both strangers and acquaintances (notably, his cousin Pete, known as "Dr. Pomposity") when they are mean-spirited. Jones sees himself as a rational and respectable "filossofer"; his creator sees him as the salt of the earth.

The rural social matrix of *Major Jones's Courtship* complements the one that can be inferred from the village and country of *Georgia Scenes*, in which setting becomes indispensable for depicting a world barely emerging into a "polite culture." Longstreet unearths as much cruelty in that maladroit society, with standards that only self-satisfied "quality" folks can meet, as he does in the rawer population that resists such premature refinement.[2] While he clearly approves of the influence of civil institutions that are moderating the primitive tastes of the backcountry, he is just as clear in his contempt for the unearned social airs of the village. Never hesitant to unleash his didactic impulse, the author has his stand-in narrator in "The Turn-Out" long for the heartfelt honesty of his own salt of the earth, mourning the loss of "the generous hospitalities" of an earlier Georgia (*GS*, 48). Thompson's own praise of unpretentious behavior echoes Longstreet's nostalgia for simple republican manners. The two authors were friends who also admired each other's work. When Thompson's hero hears that a Charleston bookseller is advertising "Major Jones's

---

2. Louis J. Budd, "Gentlemanly Humorists of the Old South," *Southern Folklore Quarterly* 17 (1953): 233; Keith Newlin, "*Georgia Scenes:* The Satiric Artistry of Augustus Baldwin Longstreet," *Mississippi Quarterly* 41 (1987–1988): 33.

Courtship, by Judge Longstreet," he is quick to say that "the Judge never writ a line of my book," but adds: "I don't know whether he feels flattered by havin my writins attributed to him, but if he does, I am even with him, for I take it as a very grate compliment to myself" (*MJC*, 143).

Major Jones represents a middle class just emerging out of the earlier settler period. Like his yeoman brothers, he distrusts suave manners and oily-tongued rhetoric; he does not hesitate, for example, to indict both his mother and his mother-in-law for indulging in the "fool quality notion" of newly prospering farmers of moving to a town house in the winter. He is yokel enough to be frightened of riding trains and fearful of eating his fill at hotels where there might not be sufficient food to satisfy everybody. A kind of sturdy common sense rules most of his cultural observations. As a reasonably well-to-do planter, however, he shares some of the traits of the new class. He firmly supports slavery and southern independence; he is traditional in his attitude toward marriage; as a militia officer he is patriotic, overdressing in splendid, even ostentatious military attire on muster days. Moralistic rather than religious, he disapproves of drunkenness, horse racing, gambling, stomp-and-gouge fights, and all the parlor excesses of what he takes to be urban or aristocratic behavior. Although he is sometimes clearly a fool, Joseph Jones is always disinclined to suffer other fools. His pride is at least as prominent as his gullibility.

Judging from its popular reception in Thompson's own locale, we might guess that Major Jones's assorted values were quirky enough to be character-defining yet familiar enough to be credible in the settled Middle Georgia of the 1840s. Some later southern readers, swayed no doubt by the simplified class structure of southern romance and the heroic myth of the post-Reconstruction South, have not been entirely comfortable with what they hear as the tonal cacophony of the major's letters. They find it difficult to reconcile Joseph Jones's knowledge of foreign phrases and historical and literary lore with his atrocious spelling—or, indeed, to accept this rustic, with his land and slaves, as a member of planter culture when he is consistently depicted as naive, bumbling, and gentle. In addition, he conducts himself in ways contrary to the traits of planters that observers of the Old Southwest most often noted with disdain: arrogance, pretentiousness, self-indulgence, and a penchant for violence. The major is not even sports-loving.

In *Major Jones's Chronicles of Pineville* (1845)—a book that, despite its title, dispenses with both Major Jones and the epistolary form—Thompson sheds some light on these apparent anomalies. In his preface he writes that his new volume, expanding on "some of the peculiar features of the

Georgia backwoodsman" seen in *Major Jones's Courtship,* depicts a "few more interesting specimens of the genus '*Cracker.*'" By Thompson's time *cracker* had been a pejorative designation for poorer whites in the piney woods of Georgia and Florida for more than a half-century.[3] The author's ambiguous phrasing would seem to mean that the generalized *back-woodsman* and the more specific *cracker* are in his experience interchangeable. *Chronicles of Pineville* documents several characters who clearly fit both terms. Devoting a paragraph to the pejorative, the author goes to some trouble to discriminate between crackers who are "good people" (that is, individuals who are "brave, generous, honest, and industrious, and withal, possessed of a sturdy patriotism") and those who are "dissolute" and "vagabond." Like Longstreet, Thompson foresees a time when education will bring these piney-woods people (both the industrious and the vagabond?) into the mainstream. That integration, which will doubtless increase the cracker's "happiness and usefulness," will also mean his disappearance as a distinctive type. By "polishing away those peculiarities which now mark his manners and language," education will reduce the cracker to "the common level of commonplace people," thus removing him from consideration as a subject by such authors as himself. Only distinctive "specimens" are of interest to the "naturalist" (*CP,* 6). Thompson's characterization of a hero whose cracker traits exist comfortably with his reputable status may well be a more accurate image of the Georgia planter in the 1840s than that drawn by complacent romancers. In *Major Jones's Courtship* that comic mix is certainly far from the volatile one that will develop in *Absalom, Absalom!* in which Faulkner constructs tragedy out of yeoman grotesques with cotton-economy aspirations.

If Thompson's epistolary volume is the most cohesive book among all those by the humorists, it is also the most intensely domestic. Spectacular characters and elaborate yarns are absent, replaced by a speaking voice that never strains for metaphorical effect with unusual diction or extravagant imagery. Only in Jones's role as suitor does this man of unemphatic style hone the superlative mode, determined as he is to claim Mary

---

3. *Cracker* is one of the oldest epithets for white southerners of a certain class, dating back to Scotland where it meant, according to Samuel Johnson, a "noisy, boasting fellow." Oral lore attributes the term to Scots-Irish hersdmen who cracked their whips to control grazing livestock. See the entries for "Crackers" in the *Encyclopedia of Southern Culture,* ed. Charles Reagan Wilson and William Ferris (Chapel Hill: University of North Carolina Press, 1989), 1132, and the *Random House Historical Dictionary of American Slang,* ed. J. E. Lighter (New York: Random House, 1994), 1:503–4.

Stallins, who is "jest a leetle the smartest, and best, and the butifulest gall in Georgia." Jones conscientiously embraces the conventional behavior of country lover by blushing and getting "sort of trembly all over" when Mary of the "rougish eyes" comes into his presence, especially when she wears one of her "wichinest smiles" and when her "bright curls [fall] all over her snowy neck" and "her rosy cheeks." Her spunky good sense barely overcomes her stereotyped romantic image—the teasing, coy role a village culture has taught her to play. Jones hates it when she is the "coquet" (*MJC*, 85, 79, 92, 70).

In Southwest humor swains are always awkward in courtship, but Jones's clumsiness engages readers' goodwill as well as their appetite for fun. The major, for example, has none of the deficits that John S. Robb attributes to one Seth Tinder: denseness, insensitivity, and ugliness. Though he is "cute at driving a bargain," Robb's notions salesman has had little luck with nature—"she made him ugly without his consent, and wouldn't agree to any alterations." In "Seth Tinder's First Courtship: How His Flame Was Quenched!" the Yankee gallant is convinced that true courtship requires clandestine nocturnal visits to his ladylove's window. For all his compulsive voyeurism, however, he is unable to discriminate his beloved's voice from the growl of her father's watchdog, which seizes "the advantage and Seth's seat of honor at the same time" (*SSL*, 177–80).

The major's pursuit of Mary is more conventional. The courtship itself, though Jones would like it to proceed with propriety and unaffected decorum, is a country ritual held hostage by circumstance, chance, and the suitor's own limitations. Unlike his smooth-talking, out-of-town rival for Mary's hand, he is neither quick-witted nor graceful, and conducts his campaign simply by being sincere and pedestrian. Jones must pretend that he isn't jealous of his rival, but in letters to Thompson he feels free to declare him a fool "rigged up like a show monkey" and "a leetle too smart for this climate, I think." Overeager in playing lovesick, he is merely clumsy. Shinnying up a tree to retrieve wild grapes for Mary, he tries to "skin the cat" and ends up skinning his nose instead when he falls on a branch below; at a candy-pulling, he burns his fingers by distractedly plunging them into hot molasses. His courtship techniques are both predictable and innovative. Most Middle Georgians tried to outlast sleepy family members during evening social calls on their sweethearts, but they did not "give themselves" as Christmas presents by spending a cold night on a porch trussed up in a dusty meal sack. With masculine solemnity, the major does this and more as means to his great end. His strategy for winning Mary Stallins is successful. She marries him and, in time, gives birth to a baby, Henry Clay Jones.[4]

Among the several virtues of *Major Jones's Courtship*, Thompson's mastery of his characters' language is conspicuous. This volume is in fact one of the most reliable guides to southern ruralisms in antebellum speech, most of which seem to fall effortlessly from the hero's pen. The credibility of Joseph Jones's character—his decency, candor, and old-fashioned republican values—is due largely to Thompson's written version of a modest planter's oral delivery. Just as Jones dislikes extravagance in fashion (such as whiskers on men and bustles on women) and "bominable nonsense" (the practical jokes relished by most of his friends), so he distrusts language that is too fancy to be heartfelt. He revels in Mary's praise when she refers to him as her "only real distinguished" suitor in Pineville: "if my thography was only as good as my reterick I'd do fust rate" (*MJC*, 54).

His attitude toward both orthography and rhetoric, however, is merely common sense in Middle Georgia. "Drat the larnin, say I—genus comes by natur, but everybody kin larn how to spell, you know." In a metatextual turn, even after his letters to the *Southern Miscellany* are published as a pamphlet and the major shamelessly milks what he calls "my grate literary popilarity," his style remains the commonsensical expression of what "genus" he has always had. Despite an uncertain grasp of spelling, he betrays the autodidact's love of allusion. But when he indulges in quotation, he does so self-consciously, making a priority of what he thinks is a natural, unaffected writing style. When he quotes from *Macbeth*, he asks Thompson to excuse him: "I don't blieve in stickin in book larnin in every thing a body writes—but then ther is *some* times when jest common words won't express the full meanin, you know" (*MJC*, 96).

Retrospectively, what is most meaningful about *Major Jones's Courtship* is its rendering of middle-class life, which mirrors the era more accurately than does the work of other humorists. As we have seen, most of the authors skillfully refracted their milieu more than they reflected it; but in Thompson's book, the quiet assembling of incidents, attitudes, human

---

4. The major's morality was questioned in the *Spirit of the Times* by one John Smith, who observed how short a time had elapsed between the Christmas stunt and the baby's birth: "Now, Major Jones of Pineville, was that night you swung in the bag the first night you passed on the premises?" Jones responded indignantly, quoting his wife, who called Smith "a nasty mean wretch . . . casting slurs on decent people." David C. Estes, "Major Jones Defends Himself: An Uncollected Letter," *Mississippi Quarterly* 33 (1979–1980): 79–84.

interaction, and ideology is barely distorted by dramatic heightening. Even the major's particular "thography" and "reterick" are undramatic by design. This modest citizen knows that most of the time "jest common words" are enough to express his full meaning. In following this witness of his generation, some readers may welcome help from slang and dialect dictionaries, but his words—not the marvelous and rare, but those commonly used in the 1840s—become linguistic tokens of the times even as they lend credibility to the country protagonist who uses them. In their ordinary ruralisms, intensive repetitions and inflections, the letters to editor Thompson are impressive redactions of casual spoken English that would have been familiar to all of his readers:

> [T]hey like to tare all his clothes off his back. (*MJC*, 52)
>
> I tell you what, I was in a stew. (74)
>
> . . . my yaller britches busted all to flinders. (28)
>
> I scrooch'd down in the bag. (90)
>
> . . . cousin Pete—he's never said peas about the duckin I gin him. (49)
>
> I got my dander up a little the worst I've had it for some time. (100)
>
> I would jest as leav be spicioned of stealin a sheep, as to be put upon a criminal jury by the lawyers now-a-days. (133–34)

Even country comparisons that occasionally clot the expressive vernacular in many humorous sketches are in the major's letters used economically. Though they come from Jones's mouth, they are drawn from the fund of community lore that is too unexceptional to call attention to itself. A sulking cousin Pete stays in his room "in the daytime like a possum in a gum"; Pineville coon hunters blast their horns "like they was gwine to tear down the walls of Jerico" (*MJC*, 119, 48).

Jones is not without his little vanities. He rightfully considers himself superior to his flashier cousin Pete who, though cleverer in social situations, lacks character. Oily in his seductive mode, Pete is sour when his schemes are foiled. A bad sport, he resents Jones's dunking him in the branch, a retaliation for an insult that the major never regrets. As chief officer, Jones takes his duties seriously at the Pineville militia muster, which gives him a chance to sport a sumptuous uniform—new boots "with long legs," a "cocked hat" surmounted by red feathers, yellow trousers, and a blue regimental coat "titivated off with gold and buttons" (*MJC*, 25–26).

Yet Jones is not alone in his pride of command. The writing from the Old Southwest is filled with accounts of the militia, all of which emphasize the buffoonery of ill-prepared volunteers struggling to execute maneuvers, and most of which draw a conspicuous contrast between the resplendently dressed leaders and their jeaned-and-gallused men.

In what he calls "militia muddling and Potemkin pretensions," one historian of Montgomery musters describes the incongruity of a ragtag company, drilling with canes, cornstalks, and brooms as well as muskets, attempting to understand the commands of their leader "dressed in full blue and silver field officer's uniform on a finely caparisoned steed." A Mississippi memoirist recalled his role as an elegant brigadier at a muster, which, though it promised some "splendid evolutions," collapsed in rustic confusion.[5] Others contributed their own versions of militia buffoonery. Longstreet included in *Georgia Scenes* a piece called "The Militia Company Drill," attributed to one Timothy Crabshaw, in which Captain Clodpole "with great vehemence" barks orders that result only in snarled lines of men: "how did you get all into such a higglety pigglety?" (*GS*, 101). To ease offended sensibilities the captain sends for grog, which merely aggravates the snarls.[6] The Surry County volunteers in H. E. Taliaferro's "Famus or No Famus" must decide if their thirst for grog is stronger than their suspicion that the supplier, straddling his whiskey barrel on the edge of the muster field, has distilled it with his dead dog. "It was 'narrated' all through the country" that Hamp Hudson's dog Famus had fallen into a mash tub "and was drownded." As the day and the heat wear on and the performance of the troops degenerates, Old Stony Pint, the lisping hero of the Revolutionary War, decides for himself: "I thay, boyith, you can do ath you pleath, but ath for me, old Stony Pint Jimmy Smith, *Famus or No Famus, I must take a little*" (*HET*, 190–93).

Major Jones's account of his experience with his company is the most satisfying of the various accounts of militia muddling, primarily because

5. John H. Napier III, "Martial Montgomery: Ante Bellum Military Activity," *Alabama Historical Quarterly* 29 (1967): 114–15; Reuben Davis, *Recollections of Mississippi and Mississippians* (1889; reprint, ed. William D. McCain, Oxford: University and College Press of Mississippi, 1972), 137–43.

6. This 1807 piece, variously titled "The Ghost of Baron Steuben," "The Oglethorpe Muster," and "The Militia Company Drill," was reprinted in John Lambert's *Travels though Lower Canada and the United States of America in the Years 1806, 1807, and 1808* (London, 1810) and C. H. Gifford's *History of the Wars Occasioned by the French Revolution* (London, 1817) before Longstreet picked it up for *Georgia Scenes*. It has been called "the first American short story classic." Howard S. Mott, *Collecting Southern Amateur Fiction of the Nineteenth Century* (Charlottesville: Bibliographical Society of the University of Virginia, 1952), 4.

Thompson uses it to deepen his hero's character. Jones manfully endures humiliation at the outset when his peaceable steed, unaccustomed to drums and fifes or "cussin and shinin and disputin," reels and wheels, throwing its rider in the dust. Though his grand uniform is ruined and he is "bleeged to wear my tother clothes," the leader marches his men to an outlying field—away from the liquor supply—to "put 'em through the manuel." Like the other versions, Thompson's is pure farce. The Pineville volunteers, even those with guns instead of sticks, "didn't know nothing about military ticktacks"; the men "forgit which was ther right hand and which was ther left," and their helter-skelter marching becomes "a snarl, goin both ways at both eends." Like musters in many of the historical accounts, this one is interrupted by rival political candidates eager to give speeches. A stomp-and-gouge fight climaxes the disastrous exercises. Since the "betallion was completely demoralized," the commander decides that "the quicker I got out of that crowd the better for my wholesome." Turning the bruised and bleeding men over to their captains ("accordin to law"), he declares that he is "'sponsible for nothin that tuck place after I left" (*MJC*, 30–32).

Beginning with the militia muster, *Major Jones's Courtship* is, despite its primary narrative of courtship and marriage, very much a series of scenes of assorted village activities: parlor games, socials, practical jokes, court proceedings, dosing the sick with home remedies, Fourth of July festivities, coon hunts, side trips to nearby towns. Aside from the recorded flow of all that is ordinary, Thompson's social notation also touches on the exceptional (an earthquake and a comet, both omens supporting Father Miller's prophecy of the end-time) and on the impingement on Pineville of larger national concerns (exasperation with President Tyler and lamentation over "degenerated times" in Congress). That social notation is persuasive largely because of the sensibility of one upright and stolid recorder, but Joseph Jones is acute enough to make credible the specific kinds of villagers who contribute to the communal feel: the decent Squire Rogers, the competent Dr. Gaither, the village elder Mr. Mountgomery, and, usually in the foreground, the major's male friends, who, because of his ambivalent attitude, are also his rivals for masculine dominance. A square among swells, Jones is razzed and tricked, exploited by his peers for his naïveté—in episodes that, however, do nothing to diminish anyone.

The texture of Pineville life is perhaps most vividly encapsulated in the character of the major's mother-in-law. Mrs. Stallins's faith in Father Miller's prediction that the world will end in March of 1843 tries Jones's patience, primarily because the old widow wants his wedding to Mary postponed until after next April, when it would be safe. Even when it is "all sifered out on a piece of paper," Jones is determined not to let such "proffesyin" interfere with his plans.[7] The widow finally gives her approval in a letter, quoting her daughter:

> She ses, ef the world does come to a eend she couldn't bare the site, no how ef you wasn't thar, right by her. She ses moren that, she ses—and I declare I'm shamed to rite it to you, and I no you'll blush to read it, jest to no how the child does love you—she ses she couldn't di no how, 'thout it was in your arms, and you no if you was to gratifi her when the catasterfy cum, and wasn't married, peple wood talk. (*MJC*, 98)

Superstitious, flighty, and "notiony," the widow Stallins is a source of energy in the letters. A plainspoken remnant from the earlier republican period, she is clearly one of Thompson's favorites. Her reticence in her letter to Jones is a nod to the era's prudery in matters sexual, but she is embarrassed primarily because she has to write it all down. She shows no such reticence in conversation. When her daughters blush, trying to shush her up when she uses the word *stockins*, the old woman will have none of it: "Highty-tity! . . . what monstrous 'finement to be shore! I'd like to know what harm ther is in stockins. People now-a-days is gittin so mealy-mouthed they can't call nothin by its right name, and I don't see as they's any better than the old time people was" (*MJC*, 89).

Despite his occasional impatience with his mother-in-law, Major Jones firmly endorses her sturdy, old-fashioned sense of both propriety and values, as we see when the now-celebrated author is invited to deliver the Fourth of July oration in Pineville. He betrays only minor stage fright before sharing his patriotic sentiments, the text of which he sends on to editor Thompson. The speech vibrates with what historians have described as a widespread sense of declension in the antebellum years among ordinary Americans, many of whom spoke and spelled better than Joseph Jones. The present generation, Jones begins, has failed to live up to the achievements of "our ansisters"; our "free institutions and glorious republican principles" have been weakened by "the pride, the mean-

---

7. William Miller, after long study of biblical prophecies, fixed the date of the Second Coming sometime between March 21, 1843, and March 21, 1844. When both dates passed uneventfully, Miller admitted a miscalculation and fixed a new date, October 22, 1844, which also passed quietly. The Millerite remnant eventually became Seventh-Day Adventists. See R. Carlyle Buley, *The Old Northwest: Pioneer Period 1815–1840* (Bloomington: Indiana University Press, 1950), 2:483–84; and Robert V. Rimini, *The Jacksonian Era* (Arlington Heights, IL: Harlan Davidson, 1989), 96.

The Yokel as Social Critic *499*

ery, the rascality, the corruption, the foppery, the monkeyism, the treachery, the dissipation, and the tetotal disregard for morality, religion, and virtuous principles" (*MJC*, 138). In its cheerful mingling of abuses of unequal weight, this catalog manages to be Thompsonian at the same time that it adds substance to the rustic hero's character. A homily disguised as a patriotic speech, the oration condenses most of the major's beliefs; on lesser matters (and on less formal occasions) he can be equally as opinionated about manners and personal conduct. Thompson makes him a mixture of principle and expedience.

Jones is, for example, a dedicated temperance man in a community that has as many drinkers as Washingtonians, but he gives up tobacco only because the habit blunts his courting technique. When dancing is disallowed at an engagement party, the young folks play "games and tricks, and sich foolishness," which the major pronounces "a bominable sight worse than dancin" (*MJC*, 100). After visiting the college at Athens, where he sees entirely too much hair, he takes a public stand in his letters against "grate long frizzled locks," whiskers, "soap-locks," "pin-feathers," and all excessive natural plumage. His diatribe has what he considers the desired effect—an Athens correspondent writes him that because of his disapproval, the barbers have made "a perfect harvest of the hair crop" and the community is beginning "to look like civilized beings" again. (One disgruntled Savannah man, however, writes in to abuse Jones as "a beardless puppy" and "a pineywoods fool.") Jones is equally hard on women's fashions, especially bustles, which he thinks make the female figure look out of proportion, "like a bundle of fodder tied to the handle of a pitchfork" (*MJC*, 156–57, 148).

His obsessions with such newfangledness as men's beards and women's fashions lend an air of the crank to this rural social critic. Conservative in both manners and morals, Major Jones has little social "give." Compared to his friends and neighbors, he is indeed a crank. As the catalog of governmental abuses in his Fourth of July speech indicates, Jones is incapable of discriminating between the large and the small. By giving prominence to the widow Stallins's distrust of the "highty-tity" without any intervention by the man who records it, Thompson, like his friend Longstreet, makes language one of the benchmarks of a modern culture that opens itself to criticism. Avoidance of plain speaking and plain writing is as much to be condemned as "the meanery, the rascality, the corruption," and all the other vices of the new order. Yet his Georgia rustic, a great admirer of education, is eager also to educate himself, even if he suspects that colleges fall short of his expectations. After visiting both

Macon and Athens, he writes Thompson, "I'm more'n ever in favor of travelin," a sentiment that prepares the major for further adventures away from home eight years later in *Major Jones's Sketches of Travel* (1848). Thompson allows this genial crank, whose temperament must be vented on matters both important and trivial, to invade a national geography where he is neither known nor tolerated.

ii.

Pineville accepts the major's sometimes quaint but conscientious strictures, but his particular set of principles, tastes, and foibles is tested in a national society in which he represents everything that makes non-southerners wary. If Joseph Jones as a quasi-cracker planter is an anomaly in southern writing, Thompson's decision to make him a cultural critic in an era of sectional controversy was an even riskier move.[8] In *Major Jones's Sketches of Travel* the tireless epistolarian experiences a wide assortment of urban incidents to which he reacts with down-home common sense.

His creator clearly intends Jones to be so grounded in his principles that they overcome his quirky tastes and endemic naïveté. The major's visit to Washington becomes an occasion to voice democratic sentiments that transcend Whig, Democratic, and Locofoco party doctrines. It also provides the Georgian a chance to declare his middle-class views on art and culture, an anti-elitist position that presumably reaffirms the values of the early republic. Seeing the artwork in the rotunda of the Capitol is worth a trip to Washington, he decides, though he would like fewer symbolic re-creations of the nation's past and more "single figers representin our grate generals and statesmen." Among the paintings and sculptures that the major cites are "picters" of William Penn "swindlin the Ingins out of ther land, and Columbus cumin ashore in his boat, and old Danel Boon killin off the aboriginees with a butcher knife, and other subjects more or less flatterin to the national character" (*MJS*, 45). At the Smithsonian Institution, where he views the coat worn by Andrew Jackson, Jones praises the hero of New Orleans, not because of his policies ("I thought his politics was wrong"), but because of his vigorous patriotism.

8. See Carl R. Osthaus, "From the Old South to the New South: The Editorial Career of William Tappan Thompson of the *Savannah Morning News*," *Southern Quarterly* 14 (1976): 237–60.

Looking at an Egyptian sarcophagus that an admirer had brought to America "to bury Gen. Jackson in," he applauds the old general's refusal: "In the fust place, I don't think it in very good taste for to be in too big a hurry to provide a coffin for a man before he's ded; and in the next place, I've got no better opinion of old second-hand coffins than I have of second-hand boots." Jackson, he adds, is "too much a proud-spirited republican . . . to lay his bones in a place whar sum bominable old heathen King has rotted away before, and I glory in him for it" (*MJS*, 56).

Major Jones distrusts Yankees not because of their commercial savvy and petty fraudulence in trading, but because their public moralism is strident, meddling, and hypocritical. A provincial who puts his trust in the known, he is fearful of foreign immigration because he sees the old stock that fashioned a stable republic threatened with dilution. He is scornful of elitism in art and government because of his country bias for plain speaking and doing and his village propensity for the practical.

In most of the eastern cities Jones comments on the beauty of the women (the Lowell factory girls stimulate an erotic dream), but in Baltimore he notes that the "common opinion" that their women are "the prettyest in the world" needs to be revised. The change for the worse he attributes to the adulteration of native stock by "people from all parts of the world": "what does remain pure and unadulterated, aint more'n half so conspicuous now as it used to be" (*MJS*, 72). (The bias against foreign immigration is clearly Thompson's, since Jones is visiting Baltimore for the first time.) The Georgia visitor experiences "Yankeedoodledum" mostly as a site of prohibitions and intrusiveness. When Bostonians stare at his cigar "like it was a rattle-snake," he sees their disapproval as a telling clue to the larger cultural habit of domestic meddling into the lives of all people. And the Pineville native turns himself into a semiotic critic when he describes Boston's streets as having "a sort of starchy Sunday-go-to-meetin kind of a look" that suggests the "pinched up, narrow contrived appearance" of New England in general. He theorizes that the merchants' signs, in which the letters "is all littler in the middle than they is at the ends," reflect the Yankee pronunciation of words: both signs and sounds point to character, "as for instance, a letter *I* looks like a lady that was dyin of tite lacin" (*MJS*, 125–26).

Most of the southerner's extended criticism of mainstream American life comes out of a village orientation that clings to "unalterable" values and attitudes that have already been altered elsewhere. When Jones calls the Bunker Hill monument a "majestic pile" sacred to northerners and southerners alike, Thompson allows him to meditate on the spirit of liberty it symbolizes even as he comments on the contemporary abuse of that spirit represented by the "No smokin 'lowed here" signs. This theme is reinforced when from atop this "Sinai of American Freedom" the major sees the ruins of the Ursuline convent, a view that reminds him of the intolerance of "a people who have violated the laws and disregarded the principles which ther fathers died to establish in this country" (*MJS*, 128). His brief visit to Canada is also meant to reinforce, by negative example, the memory of what America resisted in the previous century. Although he is no more anti-Catholic than most nineteenth-century Americans, the Georgian sees Catholic worshippers in Quebec as reminders of institutional restraints against personal liberty in both religion and politics. In Kingston, the "sad countenances and mechanical movement" of drilling soldiers prompt him to speculate on Canadians' misplaced dedication to a "power that only tramples 'em," training them to be contented "in ther servile conditions" and to "glory in the shallow glitter of a crown that is upheld by ther own sweat and blood" (*MJS*, 182, 184).

What Jones most vividly experiences on his travels, of course, is the modern world. In Pineville he sees himself as the radiating center of his community. Though conflicts, practical jokes, misunderstandings, and personality flaws are to be suffered and endured there, the upright and slightly vain major is understood to be somehow synonymous with Georgia culture at large. When Thompson sends him packing, the direction is inevitably north because by the 1840s the rivalries between sectional ideologies are visible and audible in the ongoing national dialogue. In Pineville the major has his place—a rather comfortable berth in a static plantation economy—and his Fourth of July oration and other occasional strictures against hostile political and social progress are sermons to the converted. In Baltimore, Philadelphia, Boston, New York, even Canada (where monarchical sentiments are preserved rather than resisted), Major Jones must confront the *different*. What is different threatens.

His responses to difference constitute a critique of the mercantile spirit, political and moral hypocrisy, and the urban—a confusing environment of human density, raw competitiveness, and the accelerated pace of ordinary living for which the North of Thompson's time had already become the symbol. The rhythm of life in Pineville, one of the most thoroughly bucolic of all the villages in Southwest humor, is so infused with value that for the major the traffic at depots, wharves, and stations, where modes of transportation imperfectly connect, is a cacophonous barrage of grabbing, yelling, and hurrying, as hackmen and baggage handlers assume control. The raucous scene at every stop pummels this southerner's sensibilities like a blast from hell (*pushin and crowdin one another, and hollerin in my ear; bags and boxes . . . tumblin and rollin in every direction, rakin your shins and mashin your toes*); and every stop is yet "another hellaballo." In "sich a everlastin rumpus" the Georgian must endure aggressive entreaties to buy goods and services. He is gouged by drivers and baggage-men, who then taunt him for being green. Thompson allows his hero to confront each time the same dread, the same exasperation, and to feel the same slow-thinking determination to ward off such aggression by his own will. Mostly he fails. When he is driven to extreme frustration over the assaults on his luggage, he resorts to threats of violence: "I tuck my cane tight in my hand and kep a sharp eye on 'em, determined to defend myself to the last" (*MJS*, 108). Thompson portrays Major Jones as being dramatically pushed to such a stance, one that is clearly meant to prefigure that of an entire region. Such scenes become an emblematic condensation of the North: disputatious, noisy, irreverent, greedy, and dedicated to trickery and victimization for selfish profit.

The disparate adventures that constantly test his greenness also expose in Jones the exacerbated sensibility that visitors since the early years of the century had professed to see in southern males. To create humor out of a hotheaded response to perceived slights and a personal code based on exaggerated notions of honor requires a light hand, and on occasion Thompson playfully satirizes his hero as a stereotype of the thin-skinned southerner. Genial Joseph Jones of Pineville, on his first night in New York City, is not above showing high dudgeon at one of the more sinister tricks played on him—he is threatened by "a everlastin crowd of peeple" who refuse to believe his story that the baby he is holding belongs to a sick woman who has disappeared with his dollar to buy medicine. "I'm a stranger in your city," he tells them indignantly, "and I'm not gwine to support none of your babys" (*MJS*, 115).

Yet, as Thompson well knows, the crucial subject in arousing southern ire is race. The major is no firebrand on the topic—indeed, he presumes to deal rationally with it as a "filossofer." Inasmuch as he takes seriously both his constitutional right to own slaves and his moral responsibility to be a caring, humane slave-owner, he is clearly meant to be a middle-of-the-road planter of his time. But when he harps on his Christian duty to be *more* than kind to his blacks—that is, when he indulges them—the verbal formulas are not so much Thompson's as they are appropriations of the region's sentimental fiction. While Major Jones admits to being tolerant of his servants' indiscretions and occasional airs, he cannot extend the same liberality to strange African Americans. Even before he has left the South, he is subjected to a reprimand by a black steward on a steam-boat, who reminds him that smoking is not allowed "aft the machinery." Ignorant of nautical terms, the major at once assumes the role of domi-nant white planter ("my buck, I don't understand your gibrish") and in-stinctively threatens punishment (using his cane for "takin the measure of his hed for a nock down"). The scene taps into the ugly reality that the rigid southern hierarchy imposed on race relationships, but Thompson disperses it quickly by showing the black steward to be unintimidated: "the bominable fool begun to snicker," the major writes (*MJS*, 44). The in-cident suggests that Joseph Jones cannot control situations beyond his own turf, even when they challenge his most serious positions.

On a steamboat on the Hudson he is deprived of a coveted dessert of strawberries and cream when he calls out "boy" to his waiter, who, roll-ing his eyes "like he was gwine to have a fit of hidryfoby," carries the major's plate to another patron. The news spreads fast among the other waiters, who also ignore Jones's attempts to get their attention. Denied a proper end to his "monstrous good supper," the major ruefully warns his correspondent about prohibited forms of address in the North: "If you should ever cum this way a travellin," he warns, never say "boy, nor uncle, nor buck, nor any frendly, home name. . . . They're all misters here" (*MJS*, 46). Both steamboat episodes preserve the image of Jones as a comic character who, in the classic pattern of all Southwest humor, is vulnera-ble because he knows too little. Uncertainty of the way the great world operates takes an emotional toll on this supremely confident Georgian. The loss of his dignity as well as of his luggage lurks behind every ad-venture.

What Thompson does with his hero is bolder than it seems. He makes genial fun of what in the late 1840s is the iconic figure in southern ideo-logical battles with the North, and he does so by exposing the fragility of *gentleman* as a touted category in those battles. Major Jones is a slave-owning planter—albeit a modest one—but he is also a cracker. In real life, sophisticated planters who in these years journeyed with their families to watering places in the North did not expose themselves to embarrass-ment as Joseph Jones does, in part because they already knew, however intensely they disapproved of it, that free blacks were treated differently from the slaves back home. But it is precisely the yokel aspect of Thomp-son's southern traveler that makes him endearing. His discomfort in the presence of free blacks is predictable because of his thoroughgoing pater-nalism, his tendency to domesticate the racial issue in light of his own planter ethic.

Unlike Longstreet, who became a zealous tractarian as the Civil War neared, Thompson never defended slavery based on complicated Christian doctrine and scriptural exegesis. He allowed his hero to echo the more familiar defense—that the situation of southern slaves was superior to that of their free northern counterparts. This tack, contrasting the happy slave with the dour factory worker in New England, blended opportunism and moralism; but in these letters the argument is resolutely downhome. "[I]f my niggers wasn't better off and happyer on my plantation than these Northern free niggers is," writes Joseph Jones, "I wouldn't own 'em a single day longer." Writing from Philadelphia, he muses that his slaves back home have

> plenty of hog and hommony to eat, and plenty of good comfortable clothes to wear, and no debts to pay, with no more work than what is good for ther helth; and if that ain't better than freedom, with rags, dirt, starvation, doctor's bills, lawsuits, and the five thousand other glorious privileges and responsibilities of free nigger citizenship, without the hope of ever turnin white and becomin equal with ther superiors, then I ain't no filossofer. (*MJS*, 105)

As a statement of policy, Jones's plain speaking doubtless shadows his creator's position more closely than usual, but the passage is followed by a candid admission that is not policy at all, but personal confession. Since blacks are part of the southern scene, the major reasons, "I prefer bein master myself and treatin 'em well, to lettin them be masters and takin the chances of ther treatin me well" (*MJS*, 105). While many preachers and planters turned themselves into filossofers to mount strenuously reasoned defenses of their peculiar institution, the kind of self-interest that Joseph Jones reveals was of course a dominant motive for ensuring its preservation. Such disarming honesty reflects a southern opinion that was only occasionally expressed—usually in private. A slave-owner confided to his wife in 1848, "If we do commit a *sin* owning slaves, it is certainly one which is attended with *great conveniences*."[9] That such private admissions were rarely used to buttress formal defenses makes Jones's candor all the more remarkable.

Although the letters of Thompson's rustic hero are usually classified as "the humor of crackerbox philosophizing," the kind of cool dispassion that marks the horse-sense wisdom swapped around the cracker barrel

9. Quoted in Bruce Collins, *White Society in the Antebellum South* (London: Longman, 1985), 54.

of country stores is hardly Joseph Jones's mode. Although the major rarely blusters, on all social or political matters he voices his views with ardor. He is vulnerable to his own decent instincts, chagrined when he must admit to being "tuck in" by swifter individuals. In bourgeois Pineville he is occasionally insouciant about conflicting viewpoints in the home, but that only means that he has capitulated to Mary and his mother-in-law in the interests of domestic harmony. In his letters, Pineville is the moral standard of conduct for decent and right-thinking people. Traveling away from his stable geography is a processive movement that only confirms the rightness of returning to it. Individually and culturally he enacts the comic formula popularized by *The Wonderful Wizard of Oz:* to leave home is to ratify the necessity and superiority of home. Despite his thorough-going racism, the inherent decency of Joseph Jones is not diminished by his experiences in an alien geography. In his travels the core meaning of identity is reasserted in incident after incident.

One of the more revealing segments of *Major Jones's Sketches of Travel* is one in which the Georgian plays tourist by visiting Niagara Falls. This is Thompson's major effort to show that his hero, though a provincial auto-didact, is neither illiterate nor insensitive. In capturing the full flavor of America's love affair with iconic geography, these letters also insert the southern tradition of republican values directly into a national context.

By the 1840s Niagara Falls was the country's most famous attraction for both native and foreign visitors. The major already knows how he should respond to this natural phenomenon. Some of the humor, of course, comes from the major's vernacular version of that conventional response. But his response is not wholly vernacular. Except for its better spelling, Horace Greeley's account of his visit to the "mighty torrent" is no more perceptive than Joseph Jones's. In viewing the "avalanche of waters," "awe struggled with amazement for the mastery of my soul," writes Greeley. "God and his handiwork here stands forth in lone sublimity."[10] The intensity of the language and some of the same words and phrases appear in the account of nearly every visitor, including Thompson's hero. Like most of the reports from the 1820s on, in which Niagara Falls is described in conspicuously Burkean rhetoric, Joseph Jones's letters take note of the human experience of the sublime. The psychological impact of the spectacle—the sheer onrushing volume of water, the ear-shattering roar, the contrasts in visual perspective—was most often tinged with religious

10. James Parton, *The Life of Horace Greeley, Editor of the* New York Tribune (New York, 1855), 221.

awe, since the site at once reminded the spectator of his own insignificance and of the majesty of God as creator. "The power and presence of the Almighty seem fearfully manifest," one guidebook author wrote in 1842; in 1838 Caroline Gilman noted the spiritual influence of the Falls and was compelled to offer up a "simple and humble prayer"; and in the mid-1830s the skeptical Nathaniel Hawthorne, having purchased a "pilgrim staff" at a Falls souvenir shop, cast his visit in terms of *pilgrimage*, with the Falls a kind of shrine at which he could confirm both his unworthiness and his renewal in passive contemplation of "the mighty scene."[11]

That humor and awe are incompatible is a general aesthetic principle that Thompson follows, partly because his hero already lacks a sense of humor. Joseph Jones, like his fellow Americans, is determined to experience the awe of the Falls. His letters are filled with the requisite diction of a spiritualized Burke: *eternal flood, dark abyss, awful sublimity, mighty presence, stupendious scene of terrific horrors.* Yet, as one commentator puts it, awe is an emotion "we must not overdo": the sublime is "but a step away from the ridiculous."[12] The "silent awe" that Jones acknowledges gradually leads to exclamations "that seemed to cum from our mouths 'thout our knowin it, as if the very soul within us was amazed, and was givin utterance to its emotions, while our fisical naters was overwhelmed and paralyzed by the terrific display of the majesty and power of the Being that made the Heavens and the yeath" (*MJS*, 158–59). The disparity between elevated feeling and unrefined expression is an obvious source of humor that is usually not far from the ridiculous. By this time on his eastern trip, however, the rural visitor has already recorded his impressions of the cities, so his mild orthographical eccentricities have become more or less naturalized in the reader's consciousness. Only slightly do they undercut the rhetorical substance or its dutiful solemnity. What Thompson does with the major's experience at Niagara Falls is simultaneously to affirm the site as one of the republic's most cherished sacred spaces and to use his hero's simple, heartfelt candor not to deflate him, but to record an ordinary citizen's response to the nation's best-known attraction.

11. John F. Sears, *Sacred Places: American Tourist Attractions in the Nineteenth Century* (New York: Oxford, 1989), 14; Caroline Gilman, *The Poetry of Travelling in the United States* (New York, 1838), 110–14; Nathaniel Hawthorne, *The American Notebooks*, ed. Claude M. Simpson (Columbus: Ohio State University Press, 1972), 592. See also Nathaniel Hawthorne, "My Visit to Niagara," *New England Magazine* 8 (1835): 91–96; and Nathaniel Parker Willis, *American Scenery; or Land, Lake, and River* (London, 1840), 1:17.

12. Marcel Gutwirth, *Laughing Matter: An Essay on the Comic* (Ithaca, NY: Cornell University Press, 1993), 17–18.

One critic has observed that like most tourist spots Niagara Falls sometimes disappointed visitors, who articulated their response in irreverent comments. To maximize the physical effects of the Falls, its caretakers devised mechanical aids to intensify the site's sublimity on first impression: staircases, catwalks, and towers, all designed to emphasize the "mightiness" of nature.[13] Joseph Jones concerns himself with the problem of perspective. One evening, on the Table Rock jutting out "over the bilin flood below," he writes that he has trouble getting a "fixed idee of heights or distances," but that the Table Rock "helps the imagination to extend the scene upon a scale suited to its awful sublimity." The setting is so successful that Jones's experience of it continues that night in a frightening dream, and he spends the next day experimenting with perspective and scale. The more he looked at certain spots, he later writes, the more he "couldn't tell how big a thing was." A rock might look like a "mounting" one instant and a little later "no bigger than a goose's egg." The "magnitude of things at Niagary depends altogether on how a body contrasts 'em," he decides, and when he sees men clamber "about the loose rocks" below, "lookin no bigger than so many ants," he feels himself to be "no bigger . . . than a seed-tick in Scriven county." If he stayed there very long, he admits, "I'd git sich an insignificant opinion of myself, that I wouldn't dare to say my soul was my own." But, in a deft deflection, he adds: "I know some peeple that it would do a monstrous sight of good to go to Niagary, if for nothin else but to git a correct measurement of ther own importance in the scale of bein—if they didn't git ther notions tuck down a peg or two, then I'm terribly mistaken" (*MJS*, 158–59). The major's difficulties with perspective, his notion of the Falls' grandeur as a measurement of human insignificance, and his unsettling dreams while at Niagara are also related to the religious connotations of the site as a grand memento mori. As one commentator has argued, "the brink, the plunge, the abyss, the rising mist and rainbow" were understood "in terms of prevailing notions of the after-life."[14]

In addition to his negotiating of scale at the Falls, the major is allowed full exposure to the varied enterprises of the economic opportunists clustered about the site. He visits the Barnett Museum ("all sorts of varmints, and Ingin curiosities, and minerals and sich likes"), bargains with guides and hackmen, and expresses disapproval of an entrepreneurial Yankee who has constructed a mechanical miniature of Niagara Falls with enough

13. Sears, *Sacred Places*, 18.
14. Patrick McGreevy, "Reading the Texts of Niagara Falls: The Metaphor of Death," in *Writing Worlds: Discourse, Text, and Metaphor in the Representation of Landscape*, ed. Trevor J. Barnes and James S. Duncan (London: Routledge, 1992), 58.

space in his shop left over to stock "Yankee made Ingin fixins, sich as moccasins, bead-bags, *card-cases,* and a heap of fancy articles, sich as the Ingins themselves never dreamed of makin" (*MJS*, 162). Sic transit Gatlinburg.

What Thompson understands in the 1840s is what Niagara Falls most fully is: a sacred site capable of spiritual enrichment, but one whose attraction is not restricted to elitist responses. Like most other American monuments, the Falls is Barnumesque as well as Burkean. Its mixed nature—though lamented by Dickens, Mrs. Trollope, and other foreigners—makes it a distinctively democratic space. For all his hostility to Yankees, the text shows that Joseph Jones *likes* the Barnett Museum and is impressed by the economic ingenuity of all those go-aheaders who are helping to make the site an education for visitors. If the Falls is not innately symbolic of the bounty, the prodigality, and the power of the new world, its American handlers have made it so.

And the site is particularly suitable for Thompson's purpose. Just as Niagara Falls is sublime nature vernacularized and made tourist-friendly, so Joseph Jones is a decent, honest American whose middle-class values, despite his racism, allow him entry into the intricacies of philosophy, religion, culture, and ethics. Born in Ohio, educated in Philadelphia, and enjoying a professional life as a Georgia editor, Thompson in effect sets up his vernacular hero as an affectionate version of himself. That Jones is a representative American who happens to be Georgian only underscores the worth of homely values *prior* to sectional dissension along political and racial lines. It is no accident that his characterization stems directly from a Yankee predecessor. Of all the fictional figures in the humor, Joseph Jones is the most affectively retrospective, a nostalgic character fashioned explicitly to embody the southern interpretation of the enduring values of an earlier republic.

Major Jones is a linchpin voice in American humor. If he looks back only a few years to Major Jack Downing, the Down East rustic created by the editor of the *Portland Courier,* he also anticipates the transregional rustic type whose sayings filled countless columns in national newspapers after the Civil War. Although Seba Smith first envisioned his village seer as a Yankee peddler, the omnipresent symbol of untrustworthiness throughout the South, Thompson seems to have had no trouble in modeling Major Jones after this homespun commentator on public issues, especially politics. And the key to Major Downing—shrewdness in simplicity—became crucial to Major Jones's character. Thompson's creation also prepared the way for the national jesters whose chief purpose was to serve as caustic watchdogs exposing the foolishness of the country in its pursuit of unworthy goals, especially its embrace of venal politicians. Joseph Jones mounts his critique not as a general naysayer; he is an observer of the public scene who is also a particular man of a recognizable class and region. In the South of the 1840s that meant the perspective of a citizen who was also a defender of slavery and states' rights.

Although some of Major Jones's pronouncements are generic, stemming from the stereotype of the country bumpkin out of his element, most of them, those that help to define him as a character, are culturally and politically shaped. As the national popularity of Thompson's books shows, it was still barely possible in the 1840s to fashion a sympathetic figure who spoke as a slave-owner (albeit a kindhearted one), a viewpoint that was pervasively hostile to opposing beliefs.[15] However green he may be in his adventures beyond the confines of his backwoodsy planter culture, Joseph Jones is outspoken, candid, and sometimes heated in expressing his sentiments about northerners on their own turf.

He was not a consensus comic character—as Bill Arp, Josh Billings, and Abe Martin were to become—and his creator was not a consensus humorist as G. H. Smith, Henry Shaw, and Kin Hubbard were to become in the post-Reconstruction years. Neither fire-eater nor apologist, Joseph Jones was in some ways the accommodating face of the southern ideologue of his time. Unlike the fiercer partisans, he is quick to isolate what is repugnant in modern Yankee culture from an older set of values common to North and South, condensed in such material objects as the Bunker Hill monument and George Washington's coat; but like those partisans, he is a stout defender of a planter economy and slavery as its institutional base, and like some of them, he retains the provincial and homogeneous mind-set of the frontier. Although his experiences never alter his ingrained values, including those that are obviously racist, the major, unlike most naive figures in antebellum newspaper humor, benefits from having his ignorance dispelled. The sequence of letters allows development not merely of narrative action but of the hero's sensibility. His adventures in the world of urban America will never make him one of the moderns; he returns to Pineville not notably happier than when he left, but he *knows* more than he once did, and that knowledge enriches the domestic scene that he happily reclaims.

15. The first audience for Thompson's letters was local—Middle Georgians in and around Madison, the western terminus of the Georgia Railroad. It was not the backwoods, but the thriving "hub of a civilized rural and village world." George R. Ellison, "William Tappan Thompson and the *Southern Miscellany*, 1842–1844," *Mississippi Quarterly* 23 (1970): 159.

Chapter 14

Making Game with Simon Suggs

Men of Tallapoosa, we have done! Suggs is before you! . . . He
waxes old. He needs an office, the emoluments of which shall be
sufficient to enable him to relax his intellectual exertions. His military services; his numerous family; his long residence among you;
his gray hairs—all plead for him! Remember him at the polls!

—Johnson Jones Hooper, "Autographic Letter from Suggs"

Major Jones is virtually unique in his rectitude. Of all the characters
in Southwest humor, Joseph Jones of Pineville, whose doughty hu-
morlessness generates humor, is the only one who is never guilty of what
Anne Royall called the *putinon* game. Innocent himself of role-playing, he
is clueless about the impersonating habits of others. For him, the playing
of practical jokes and the pulling of scams are well-nigh indistinguishable: they are all "foolishness," because such activities seriously undermine the rule of honesty in public dealings. To turn from Major Jones to
Captain Suggs is to turn from a crusty upholder of family connections
and communal stability to a crusty exemplar of modern self-interest and
shuffling ethics.

Johnson Jones Hooper makes his backwoods sharper as mentally agile
as yeomanry enterprise will allow—and it allows for a lot, including a
vagrant morality that gives priority to improvisation and impersonation.
The major from Pineville is an honest man and the captain from Tallapoosa

is a fetcher, yet both characters share a jealous individualism that resists all efforts to balk them. To call Simon Suggs a "filossofer" would be to demean the earnest solidity of Joseph Jones, but the Alabama rogue, no less than the Georgia planter, trusts his forensic gifts to articulate and defend the rules that justify his actions. The major has his principles; the captain has his mottoes.

i.

The zest with which the humorists depict fetchers, as we have seen, suggests certain assumptions about society in the new country. First, even in the most resolute fetching, exploiting confidence required no sophisticated chicanery; in a climate charged with the will to believe, earnest simplicity was the best approach, sincerity the preferred form. Second, most fetching did not require dogged resolution because role-playing was pervasive and could be found in all ranks of society. Men who sported false identities played much the same game as many upright citizens, though their names might well be real and their zone of opportunity mostly free of hobbling circumstances (a financial bust here, perhaps, a sexual embarrassment there). When a con man was exposed, there was scarcely any outrage beyond the personal ire of the injured party, since to misrepresent was an endemic trait.

Most of the lower South planters looked to their models in the coastal Old South, but refinement—absorbing appropriate tastes—took more time than they usually had patience for. As both the studious Frederick Law Olmsted and the quirky Daniel Hundley noted, the respectable ranks were filled with men who presented themselves in a scramble of the genteel and the crude. Overnight cotton colonels, who took to refinement more readily than the general run, could be described as sailing under false colors. The so-called urbanites, who may have been fractionally smoother in self-presentation, had a mode of sincerity that was even frailer. We do not have to agree with one commentator's conclusion that in Victorian America "all parlor social life was a form of charade" to understand that acquiring gentility demanded the playing of roles.[1]

1. Karen Halttunen, *Confidence Men and Painted Women: A Study of Middle-Class Culture, 1830–1870* (New Haven, CT: Yale University Press, 1982), 185. See also Frederick Law Olmsted, *The Cotton Kingdom: A Traveller's Observations on Cotton and Slavery in the American Slave States, 1853–1861* (1861; reprint, ed. Arthur M. Schlesinger, New York: Da Capo Press, 1996), 216, 555; and Daniel R. Hundley, *Social Relations in Our*

What much of the humor documents is a bemused stripping of facades. One of its premises is that all conduct in a society of permeable class lines is necessarily an ongoing performance in which presentation of the self is an abiding, competitive priority. Through his mouthpiece Abraham Baldwin, Longstreet skewers the tawdry select of village society—the strutting males and attitudinizing females who, having emerged from frontier darkness into light, follow what they know of "fashion" in clothes, dance steps, and courtship protocols. Because he is a doctor, Major Jones's cousin Pete sees himself as one of Pineville's superior bachelors; as he modestly explains to one woman, "We's sceptible to female charms jest like common men, I can asshore you." Pete Whetstone is accustomed to negotiating masculine challenges on the Devil's Fork, whether at the racetrack or in free-for-alls, but in the newly refined capital he must also compete at dances and dinners with pompous dandies who, viewing him as beneath the lofty standards of Little Rock, are heard to mutter such exasperations as "I never seed such rude behavior in all my life."

Perhaps the most scathing picture of what passed as (barely) middle-class culture is found in *Adventures of Captain Simon Suggs.*[2] Not only does Hooper's flexible protagonist refashion his known persona to fit his immediate need—as a militia captain for his neighbors or as the chief of sinners for the pious—but he is also adept at *putinon* from scratch, with the complacent dash of a public man. To a stranger he can be a land speculator; to a state legislator he can be a wealthy hog drover. His venality comes decked out in genteel country airs. Simon makes impersonation a major device simply because it works.[3] One of Hooper's points is that the "respectables" in Alabama are unable to tell the difference between the real and the sham, because most of those who claim status are themselves sham. Simon's threadbare impersonations are equally effective

Southern States (1860; reprint, ed. William J. Cooper, Jr., Baton Rouge: Louisiana State University Press, 1979), 170–75.

2. An excellent study of the rare first edition of 1845 is Howard Winston Smith's "An Annotated Edition of Hooper's *Some Adventures of Captain Simon Suggs*," Ph.D. diss., Vanderbilt University, 1965. See also W. Stanley Hoole, *Alias Simon Suggs: The Life and Times of Johnson Jones Hooper* (University: University of Alabama Press, 1952).

3. Hooper's fictional fraud was probably inspired by his brother's friend, one Bird Young, locally famous for his rascality. An Alabama judge has speculated that at his hangout in the Dennis Hotel in Dadeville, Young embellished yarns about himself and Tallapoosa County for Jonce Hooper's benefit. Young was variously reported to have been flattered or annoyed by the fictional Suggs. Jack P. Solomon, "Simon Suggs," in *Tallapoosa County: A History* (Alexander City, AL: Service Printing, 1976), 72–73. See also Bobby L. Lindsey, *"The Reason for the Tears": A History of Chambers County, Alabama, 1832–1900* (West Point, GA: Hester Printing, 1971), 101–3.

among the venal and the pious. The captain's struggle with his antago-
nists succeeds because his creator allows him to use the very instrument
that is meant to counter the hypocrisy of social life: sentimentalism. In the
nineteenth century sincere social forms were seen as antidotes to the widespread aping of elitist manners and language; honest emotion, candor, and
credibility were recommended as visible marks of confidence throughout
the entire order of American society.[4] But as most of the humorists knew,
and as some of them dramatized, sincerity was merely another arrow in
the con man's quiver.

Adventures of Captain Simon Suggs is not only a mock campaign biography, it is also a truncated bildungsroman—which is also mocked. If the
ordinary "education novel" celebrates temporary rebellion against the
dominant values of social integration—its arc the progress from experi-
mentation to predictability, from instability to conformity—Hooper's
antic book is a ratcheted-up turn on the American version, a riddled form
that is always riven with ambiguity.[5] Shunning a sustained life-narrative
of Simon Suggs in favor of highlighted episodes in that life, this biographer revels in the fragmentariness of his rogue hero's career. If American
versions of the education novel are impure, ranging from the moral
earnestness of the socially aspiring hero to the outlaw spiritedness of the
picaro, Hooper's account of his protagonist is a travesty of the narrative
arc that returns the restless individual to his ordained place in a productive society. There is no closure in Simon Suggs's career, merely the
promise of a lively campaign for sheriff in an upcoming election, the outcome of which is unknown. Hooper's comic premise in the *Adventures* is
that his hero, a pettifogging coward, is a viable candidate for public office.[6] The clear implication is that worse men have attained even higher

4. Halttunen, *Confidence Men*, 186.
5. Consider Henry James's flirtation with radical politics in *The Princess Casa-
massima* (1886), a motif that complicates without clarifying his idealist hero, whose
commitment is truncated by suicide; or Melville's "cabbagehead" hero in *Redburn*
(1849), who, though he matures beyond foppishness and priggishness, never finds
his restlessness quenched. Without chronological growth or consistency, Mark Twain's
tenderfoot in *Roughing It* (1872) says and does things throughout his western adventures that are appropriate to both the adolescent and the careerist—and most stages
in between.
6. It is not surprising that Simon Suggs should be a candidate for sheriff. Ordinary
citizens running for office usually announced their candidacies "by emphasizing circumstances of hardship." See William J. Cooper, Jr., *The South and the Politics of Slavery,
1828–1856* (Baton Rouge: Louisiana State University Press, 1978), 58–69. Legal training
was not a requirement even for justices of the peace and some judges, and minimal

political prominence. As his various scrapes illustrate, the illiterate Simon has so much savvy that it would be foolish to dismiss him as a contender. "Mother-wit," he says, "kin beat book-larnin, at *any* game!" He needs no parental admonitions, heard by countless southern louts ("Apply yourself!"); he seems to have been born knowing the key for staying afloat: "Ef a feller don't make every aidge cut, he's in the back-ground directly" (*SS*, 53, 81).

It is in the home that Simon first learns how to make every edge cut. Over his impressive career he comes to see society as a loose conglomer-ation of individuals, each one trying to use either mother wit or book learning to leave the others in the dust. Simon takes powerfully to his deacon father's belief in Providence, but with a dour twist. What has been "predestinated," in his view, is a cutthroat world of appetite. When somebody scorns a belief in Providence, intones Simon, "you may be sure thar's something wrong *here*"—striking himself in the region of his vest pocket—"and *that* man will swindle you, ef he can—*certin!*" In his role as the wealthy General Witherspoon, he declares that "this little world of ourn is tollable d—d full of rascally impostors." He is convinced that all men are dupes, most of them having already been taken in by im-postors—roving preachers, politicians, gambling sharks—and that his chief weapon against being duped himself is his instinct for detecting "soft-spots" in his fellows. To that end he cultivates a knack for assimi-lating himself "to whatever company he [might] fall in with" (*SS*, 81, 59, 12). Such assimilation comes easily to Simon because Hooper provides a world for him that is ethically monochromatic. Though the "company" this hero falls in with varies in its social spectrum, accommodation re-quires less enterprise for Simon than we might expect because the situa-tions all arise from the same principles of conduct.

It is interesting that Hooper refuses to exempt the family—the conven-tional bulwark of nineteenth-century society—from those principles. The importance of the family to security, stability, and continuity was felt es-pecially in the Old Southwest, where such institutions of order as the church, the school, and the court were at times sluggish in their civilizing mission. But if, as our lore insists, ruthless struggle in frontier America,

---

literacy was sufficient for the office of sheriff—the most prized position because it not only was one of real power (as opposed, say, to "captain" of militia) but also was fi-nancially rewarding. Ralph A. Wooster, *The People in Power: Courthouse and Statehouse in the Lower South, 1850–1860* (Knoxville: University of Tennessee Press, 1969), 66, 99. See also Steven Hahn, *The Roots of Southern Populism: Yeomen Farmers and the Trans-formation of the Georgia Upcountry, 1850–1890* (New York: Oxford, 1983), 95.

no less than in the industrialized urban world, forced the family to become the center of nourishing values, the family of Jedidiah Suggs offers neither solace nor retreat. The Suggsian ethic militates against even the intimate cohesiveness of the family unit. Simon's wife and children are mostly a burden to him, a reminder (when he bothers to remember) of yet another claim on him for money. If they are in want, "*somebody* must suffer," and he trots off on his nag in search of easy sources. Conventional family sentiments are merely another tool to be used in Simon's schemes—a fact italicized by Hooper's ironic description of the captain as a man of "intense domestic affections" (*SS*, 118).

Indeed, it is in the home that Simon first learns that human nature is fueled by self-interest, vanity, and greed, and his mentor is his father. Jedidiah Suggs, a hardshell Baptist preacher who admonishes his recalcitrant son with the "strictest requisitions of the moral law," is easily led into exposing himself as an avaricious humbug (*SS*, 13). The crafty adolescent reasons from scripture right along with the old man; by equating a stacked deck of cards with predestination, he bests his father with his own beliefs. And by letting the inept Jedidiah try to shuffle the cards, Simon exposes him as a clumsy ignoramus participating in a game he considers sinful. In the bargain, he punctures the old man's boastful claim to worldly wisdom (based on the fact that the elder Suggs has once been to Augusta).[7] What begins as the son's attempt to escape a harsh switching for his gambling ends with his escape into the great world on a family pony. The humiliation of the father is so thoroughgoing that he drops from sight in the narrative, forgotten by the adult Simon, the man of "intense domestic affections."

Simon Suggs leaves home at seventeen by exercising his talents and wit *against* the home. For added measure, he repays his doting mother by lacing her pipe tobacco with a thimbleful of gunpowder. He rides away imagining the tumultuous scene he will not witness. He envisions his mother's broken spectacles and "blind-staggers" in a scene marked by

7. Although Hooper was having his fun with Augusta, one memoirist was quite serious when he described Savannah and Augusta as "Ultima Thules"; to have been to Augusta with a load of cotton, to have sold that cotton and purchased supplies, and then to have returned home without having been cheated of the balance "were evidences of integrity, and established a character which entitled the young man to future confidence." George W. Paschal, *Ninety-Four Years: Agnes Paschal* (c. 1871; reprint, Spartanburg, SC: Reprint Co., 1974), 112. "The honest yeomanry," writes the narrator of T. W. Lane's "The Thimble Game: An Omitted Georgia Scene," looked upon Augusta as a Paris or London: "The man who had *never* been there, was a cipher in the community" (*PPW*, 28).

key words (*jump, sputter, break, a-kickin', a-turnin', snortin', hollerin', cavortin'*) that foreshadow the kinetic career of a shrewd con man nourished in the home (*SS*, 31). If Simon's family values are unsentimental, it is because Hooper makes them qualitatively the same as those in the rest of his world. "Human natur' and the human family is *my* books," the captain remarks, "and I've never seed many but what I could hold my own with" (*SS*, 53–54). A Hobbesian world begins at home.

Once he leaves home, Simon disappears from public view for some twenty years. His biographer speculates that he may have lived part of that time in Carroll County, Georgia, where the "chief occupation of the inhabitants has been to steal horses," but in 1833 he shows up as a settler on the Tallapoosa River. Though he is now a land speculator without funds, Simon enjoys the challenge—"to buy, to sell, to make profits, without a cent in one's pocket" will be the test of his ingenuity (*SS*, 34–35). That testing recurs at subsequent stages of his career as Simon demonstrates his virtuosity in short takes. We find him swindling other land speculators and Creek widows and impersonating, in turn, a public official, a rich hog drover, and a born-again sinner. We may be surprised that a group of camp-meeting faithful can be so effortlessly taken in by Simon's phony conversion, but the episode, in "The Captain Attends a Camp Meeting," serves as one of Hooper's proof texts: gullibility is well-nigh universal, and it deserves its consequences.

From the worshippers' perspective the transformation of chief of sinners into fledgling preacher in a single session—the weeping Simon announces plans to start a church of his own—is an impressive sign that the Holy Spirit is working. From Simon's perspective, to admit that he originally came among the group "jist to make game of all the purceedins" is a necessary ploy to raise the ante in a game that is already rigged. If the whole proceedings are "a grand deception—a sort of 'opposition line' running against his own"—then his own deception must be better. His weapon is the rhetoric of sincerity (*SS*, 125, 122).[8]

Simon passes no moral judgment on such issues as true piety or sincerity of the faithful; he is even tolerant of his "opposition line." A real-life critic at an Alabama camp meeting, the sharp-tongued Anne Royall, set down in a letter her exasperation over the way visiting preachers "draw women after them."[9] But Simon does not condemn the preachers who

---

8. Sincerity is of course the tactic used by the King in Twain's version of making game of camp-meeting "purceedins." See chap. 20 of *Adventures of Huckleberry Finn*.

9. Anne Royall, *Letters from Alabama, 1817–1822* (1830; reprint, ed. Lucille Griffith, University: University of Alabama Press, 1969), 104. Even Peter Cartwright was threat-

spend more time among the pretty girls than they do "hug[ging] up the old, ugly women," because "Nater will be nater, all the world over; and I judge ef I was a preacher, I should save the purtiest souls fust, myself!" He is annoyed, however, when he is singled out from the pulpit in unflattering terms: "thar he stands, . . . a missubble old crittur, with his head a-blossomin for the grave!" Simon calls the finger-wagging preacher a "sassy, 'saitful old rascal!"—words that also describe himself. When in his testimony, Simon cites how he was "brought to a knowledge," the phrase echoes the language of nineteenth-century evangelical Christianity; but for Hooper the phrase emphasizes the quality his hero most conspicuously embodies: knowledge of himself and of the world he operates in (*SS*, 123–25).

If, however, an unsentimental appreciation of the reality of human nature is scarce among the camp-meeting crowd, the contrast is not made explicitly by either the tolerant hero or his creator. By inserting a minor character (unnoticed by Simon) who is visibly impressed by the confession and testimony of the old sinner, Hooper highlights the irony of the self-deceived. Mrs. Dobbs, a well-to-do "old lady in black silk," orders her house slave to fetch the master so that he can be nourished, along with her, by Simon's "precious 'scource." The old lady's threats to Sukey of "a hundred and fifty lashes" alternate with her effusive admiration for Simon's testifying: "Glory to my soul . . . it's the sweetest talk I *ever* hearn!" (*SS*, 126–27).

Simon's chief challenge comes during the seeming resumption of the Creek War. Disorder attracts his genius. Though the Creeks are nowhere in sight, he loves the hysteria of impending "attack," writes his biographer, "because he delighted in the noise and confusion, the fun and free drinking" (*SS*, 85). He also enjoys the power that comes his way when he wheedles himself into the leadership of the Tallapoosa Vollantares—again by playing the sincerity card. Threatened with slaughter by the Indians, his audience is persuaded by his no-nonsense appraisal of the reality of the moment. In his new capacity as captain he expropriates Taylor's store, renames it Fort Suggs, declares martial law, mans the perimeters with guards, and establishes himself as sole authority: "If any man or woman don't mind my orders, I'll have 'em shot right away; and children to be whipped accordin' t size." As for the women—"it's plain enough what *you've* got to do . . . look to the Lord and hold your jaws" (*SS*, 86–89).

---

ened by enraged husbands and fathers, who charged the evangelist of making "all the women in the country fall in love with him." *Autobiography of Peter Cartwright, the Backwoods Preacher*, ed. W. P. Strickland (Cincinnati, 1856), 144–45.

Simon takes his cue from the general fear, beginning with that of his neighbors, who had been listening to the Reverend Mr. Shufflenosey when they received the "woful tidings." The preacher yelled from the pulpit, "Will any of the breethring lend me a horse? . . . Wont *none* of you lend me one?" and, "obtaining no answer, dashed off precipitately afoot!" Hooper continues: "Then went up to Heaven the screams of fifty frightened women, in one vast discord, more dreadful than the war-squalls of an hundred cats in fiercest battle. Men, too, looked pale and trembled" (*SS*, 84). Simon turns a fabricated peril into a staged event that he both writes and directs. This is scam as theater. The greatest threat to the captain's assertion of military authority is not the "enemy," but high-spirited urchins underfoot and three dozen women "sobbing hysterically." While the menfolk have acclaimed Simon as leader, their women "said nothing—only frowned." The Widow Haycock, slipping out after curfew to retrieve a plug of tobacco left in her cart, is shot by a frightened sentinel, who then mistakes her yelps for a war whoop. Her wounds are superficial, but her violation of curfew is more serious: at her court-martial Captain Suggs sentences her to be shot for crossing "lines agin orders." Out of neighborliness and sympathy ("I never *could* bar to see a woman suffer!"), he finally reduces the sentence to a $25 fine (which he shares with his lieutenant). He is tormented by Yellow Legs, a sassy clay-eater who sprints about miming the captain's bribe-taking and taunting him for his cowardice: "Keep close to *him*, and you'll never git hurt" (*SS*, 109, 87). Simon's rhetoric of sincerity works better on some than on others.

In the Fort Suggs segment of this campaign biography, Yellow Legs and the glaring women are editorial reminders that not everyone is foolish enough to believe Simon's posturing. A similar built-in skepticism appears at the very beginning of the biography when Simon and Bill, a young Negro, are caught playing cards rather than working the fields. Simon deftly pockets all the coins of the stake, including Bill's, just as Jedidiah descends on them. Simon uses scriptural arguments to deflect his punishment, and Bill is left to suffer the old man's switching. Although he accepts the unequal punishment, Bill protests Simon's pocketing of the stakes, but there is nothing he can do about it. Bill accepts but is not fooled by Simon's games of self-interest. The women at Fort Suggs are skeptical but offer no practical deterrent to the new leader because, like Bill, they have no vote on the issue. The men in the Tuscaloosa gambling salon are also skeptical of the captain's posturing. The company is not initially inclined "to acknowledge . . . their pleasure at seeing Captain Suggs" despite his genial salutation and "rustic bow," until whispers spread that he is General Witherspoon, a wealthy Kentuckian. "The bare suspicion" that he is rich is "sufficient to induce deference and attention" (*SS*, 56–57). Their first instincts—to ignore the hokey stranger—are a commentary on Simon's general bearing. Their deference, however, explains why so unprepossessing a rogue can prosper and why most of Simon's victims deserve their fleecing.

Perhaps *because* he is a petty malefactor, Simon Suggs is remarkably clear-sighted in understanding his fellows, some of whom (unlike him) are striving to become respectable, even as they (like him) mask their own venality. Both his self-knowledge and his exuberant opportunism earn a kind of grudging respect from his biographer. Even if Hooper never quite gives his blessing to this old trickster who uses his superior knowledge of *human natur* to get what he wants, he manifestly prefers Simon to those foolish enough to become his victims. But however subversive his sympathy, "Johns," as he is called in the sketches, does not permit a governing point of view to mesh with Simon's own. The authorial perspective is best illustrated by what the biographer calls the "tom philosophy" of the cat that supervises the human chaos in response to the imminent "attack" at Fort Suggs. As rumors of the Indian uprising spread panic in the settlement, the narrator describes one householder's flight with a wagonload of featherbeds, chairs, pots, ovens, a wife, three daughters, and—at the apex of "animate and inanimate 'luggage'"—an old tomcat. Unperturbed by the cries of alarm ("they'll kill us! they'll skelp us! they'll tar us all *to* pieces! Oh, Lord! daddy! oh, Lord!"), the cat sits "gravely and quietly, the very incarnation of tom philosophy!" (*SS*, 83). From his own superior vantage point, the narrator accepts the eruptions of human folly without undue involvement or judgment.

Despite a streak of feline craftiness, Simon is too social to share his creator's tom philosophy. For a man whose gift of ready assimilation among "whatever company" he falls in with allows him maximum opportunity for detecting potential marks, social disruptions are congenial. Sociability and judgment are built into Simon's "riotous good fellowship," his natural operating mode, which is firmly held in place by the author's supervising tom philosophy of going along and taking things in stride. This perspective allows Hooper to hold in suspension both admiration and disapproval of both fraudulence and cowardice. American farce has always depended heavily upon *nudge-wink* as a controlling device; but in the Suggs chronicle, any overt moral stance is so enfolded in the narrator's broad waggery as to be nonexistent. Moral commentary, such as it is, is oblique and structural.

This rogue's Alabama is a morally fragile world populated by innocents, greedy sinners, and deserving victims. Hooper's shameless old man is the beneficiary of readerly tolerance because the major difference between Simon and the world he exploits is his superior shrewdness. As biographer, "Johns" not only creates a memorable fictional scoundrel, he also re-creates Simon's milieu, his satiric eye roaming dispassionately over windy politicians, purse-proud quality, morally tainted matrons, lecherous preachers, fawning office seekers, and unpredictable Indians. It is clear by the end of the *Adventures* that Captain Simon Suggs and his context are seamless. To use Hooper's recurring word, Simon fits *snugly* in his world. Except for his compulsiveness in battling the faro tiger and his short-fused, short-lived irritation with those who would thwart him, Simon usually projects an image of country cool. He shares with his generic cousins the yeomanry pleasures of drinking, idleness, roistering, and good fellowship. His confession to the camp-meeting faithful is a reminder of how Suggsian sincerity can usefully advance the schemes of a witty punster. He approaches them as he does each of his potential targets, to *make game*, to pick up some easy money with the least effort.

As the camp-meeting episode shows, making game is itself a technique. Too lazy to don disguises to facilitate his modest scams, Simon relies solely on self-presentation to persuade his dupes that he is someone other than a dirt-poor ne'er-do-well, or that a dirt-poor ne'er-do-well deserves to be a captain of volunteers or the preacher of his own church. He declines to lie about his impersonations. He warns the camp-meeting gullible that he has come to "redecule" them. On a stagecoach he allows an ambitious appointment seeker to *think* he is Mr. Smith, the legislator ("I hain't said yet I was him"); the ruse is modest but is enough to get him free liquor and a "loan" to cover his travel expenses, which will serve him well in the faro club when he gets to Tuscaloosa. Simon, writes his biographer, is "determined to place his own identity as General Witherspoon above suspicion, by seeming to suspect something wrong about Mr. James Peyton." While he never explicitly claims to be Witherspoon, the rich hog drover, he manipulates his "nephew" into proving his identity by having him answer some "test questions" (*SS*, 60). In all the "purceedins" he is in fact a transparent schemer—a dissimulator, not a liar—whose most useful gift is improvisation. To be sure, the assorted impersonations are mostly absurd caprices, extemporized theatricals whose makeshift tactics work almost too effortlessly. But they work for Simon because he detects the soft spots of his fellows and uses their assumptions and misapprehensions—in effect, assuming the roles that his victims assign him: a legislator who can be bribed, a wealthy Kentuckian who can be flattered.

"What's a man without his inteegerty?" Simon asks rhetorically. As

Hooper makes clear throughout the *Adventures,* his hero can indeed lay claim to a certain integrity. Rather than ignore the customary marks of character, the captain makes them principles for living as he judiciously recasts them. Not for nothing does he learn from his father the usefulness of being able to interpret and apply abstractions. When Jedidiah determines to punish his son for playing cards, he finds to his dismay that Simon is already a formidable exegete. The "rale smart" Simon assures his father, "I'm gwine to play cards as long as I live" because he is skilled at it; why should he be punished if he is so "predestinated"? To his father's conventional moral arguments Simon responds in the same terms, frustrating the dim old man, who finally must resort to paternal chastisement: "Your daddy's a-tryin' to give you some good advice, and you a-pickin' up his words that way." When the elder Suggs persuades himself that he can teach his son a lesson by playing a hand with him, Simon of course stacks the cards, thereby winning the moral argument, his freedom, and the family's pony. "[D]addy couldn't help it," he explains to his brother, "it was *predestinated*—'whom he hath, he will,' you know." Mr. Suggs agrees: "to be sure—all fixed aforehand" (*SS,* 29). Simon's tactic of *picking up words that way* is testimony not only to his keen wit but also, in a perverse way, to his honesty.

At one time or another, Simon proclaims his respect for civil institutions, magnanimity, benevolence, veracity, fidelity in friendship, and gentlemanly honor. Whatever the virtues—and circumstances determine their priority—supple abstractions come as easily to Simon's tongue as they do to the discourse of the country's movers and shakers. Plundering both Poor Richard and Ralph Waldo Emerson in a muzzy salute to his era's national spirit of enterprise and daring, the "indomitable Captain" is a vernacular reminder that the "cannoo" of American success and self-improvement is firmly tied to a materialistic "stob."

When a shrewd and experienced Simon declares, "Fair play's a jewel, but honesty beats it all to pieces," the homey adage registers a fact of Suggsian character: despite impersonations and wordplay, the hero's scams are never based on outright lies. Beginning at home, he allows the greed, hypocrisy, and pride of others to guide his scheming. He realizes his own self-interest by intervening in and monopolizing the self-interest of others. Even by the standards of a community that knows him well, Simon is a conning scoundrel, not a criminal (and barely a scofflaw). We learn near the end of the *Adventures* that the captain, hauled before a judge for gambling, has never been indicted. He "has the reputation of being dissipated and tricky," reports the solicitor, "but I think has never been in court" (*SS,* 41, 138).

Simon's superiority as con man derives largely from self-knowledge. He is not only aware of his reputation of being "dissipated and tricky" in his neighborhood, he also is smart enough to use that reputation for further trickery. If Jedidiah Suggs believes that his wayward son is an ignorant sinner already hooked by gambling, Simon argues for his release from paternal control *because* of his fallen state. At the camp meeting, aware of his reputation as the "chief of sinners" in that entire region, he admits he was drawn there for "devilment"—to deceive, to play tricks, to poke fun at the believers. Among the Tuscaloosa gamblers, he makes the act of authenticating itself a weapon by scamming the nephew of the real General Witherspoon. Outside his bailiwick Simon has a freer range for impersonation and adaptation, but even where he is a known quantity he never hesitates to make his reputation work for him. That most of the humor comes from the astonishing facility with which the scams pay off is a tribute to Simon's extemporizing gifts and native wit. He shows that deception (minimally mounted, even obvious) is deceptively easy. But the smooth road on which he gratifies his modest appetites also suggests something important about his creator.

If Simon's basic roguery feels more credible to us than any of his improvisations, that feeling is Hooper's as well. Gullibility may be an attribute independent of time and place—Simon says "Nater will be nater, all the world over"—but Hooper's own experience in public service, both his success and his failure, made that attribute seem all too relevant in the era of Jackson and Van Buren. Impersonation and gullibility, he implies, are snugly woven into actual southwestern society no less than in the writing that comes out of it. The biographer's suggestion in his opening chapter that mothers use a lithograph of Andrew Jackson as "a faithful representation of the Evil One" to discipline naughty children serves as a whimsical symbol of the structure of pretense built into the culture that countenances a Captain Suggs. The identification of Jackson with Satan, comments Hooper, is "an atrocious slander . . . on the potent, and comparatively well-favoured, prince of the infernal world" (*SS*, 9).

The crafty veteran's campaign biography does not have room for the "self-immolating patriotism" that inspired biographies of Jackson, Van Buren, Clay, and Polk in their lifetimes; it is, after all, a genial record of chicanery, land-office trickery, bribery, theft, cynical manipulation of the public trust, and false representation. The point is clear. Simon Suggs's time—and his creator's—is also inscribed by the opportunism of hundreds of lesser-known men, Democrats and Whigs alike, who made game of all proceedings but who led lives of quieter exploitation.

Some readers rightly point out that while the humor is genuinely funny, it is never amiable. The Alabama that Hooper adapts for his hero is considerably more cynical than the Arkansas that Noland creates for Pete Whetstone—the other world in the humor most inflected by contemporary politics. The laughter arising from Simon's world is more desperate than genial because, unlike Whetstone's, it is a world stripped of all amiable graces. From the hinterland that Simon calls home to the state capital where he goes for wider opportunities, the milieus he frequents are already compromised arenas in which mendacity, petty intrigue, bribery, and fraud are enacted on levels far higher than his own.

A comparison of Hooper's Old Southwest with Joseph G. Baldwin's is instructive. If anything, Baldwin depicts the time and place as substantially worse. The transplanted Virginian illustrates the chaotic "atmosphere of a new people" with a stunning bill of particulars: blackmail, murder, robbery, land theft, felony, swindling, defalcations, and larceny—a world in which profligacy "held riotous carnival." But Baldwin's persona, a willing co-conspirator in that carnival, is vivified by this wicked world: it was "a merry time," he remembers, in which he and his friends "shook our quills joyously, like goslings in the midst of a shower." The dark side of the new country ("wild and weird") led him to embrace the opportunism that encouraged a "range and energy to action" (*FT*, 85, 240, 229). Instability bred delight: the celebration of *Flush Times* was repeated, in varying degrees, in the sketches of Noland, Hall, Smith, Thorpe, Field, and many other newspaper humorists. Hooper is unwilling to allow his somber vision to obscure the comic performance of Simon Suggs, but he is also unable to see his society stimulated into useful energy by pervasive skullduggery. He is too dour to say, with Baldwin: "Those were jolly times." Among his fellow humorists, his brooding spirit is rivaled only by George Washington Harris and Henry Clay Lewis, who were compelled to emphasize the moral darkness of their era even as they tapped the resources of the ludicrous. Harris's acerbic rage orients the Lovingood brand of humor, and the swamp doctor's plangent melancholy vies head-on with his waggishness. If Simon Suggs's vulgarity and low cunning are of a piece with his real-life counterparts in Alabama, Hooper at least makes those qualities both bearable and witty by investing his hero with self-knowledge—and indefatigable optimism despite it.

For all the sanguine buoyancy of its hero, Hooper's *Adventures* depicts a society even less responsible than the hustling, go-ahead, real world of the Jacksonian era that we know from the writings of historians and the testimony of private citizens. Furthermore, the devious rivalry, the assiduous scrambling for dominance that we see in Crockett's reading of that world, creates in Hooper's text a circumscribed society of depletion and appetite. The competitive spirit remains, only to be expended on scaled-down goals, trifling profits. Compared to Sut Lovingood's wound-up-and-spinning performances, Simon Suggs's schemes are *ad hoc* and only occasionally challenge what amounts to an environing inertia in both the captain and his marks. Hooper's mean geography may never be quite Hobbesian, but only Harris surpasses his vision of benighted human relations. To extract humor out of a cultural moment more debased than that of most of his fellow scribes, Hooper uses a verbal machinery that hums along on the oral justifications of his hero. Stitching together all the schemes is a potpourri of cynical mottoes that illustrate the old fraud's use of sincerity as technique.

In *The Gay Divorcee* (1934), the first film to star Fred Astaire and Ginger Rogers, the mistaken-identity plot requires that a password be used by a Signor Tonetti, the "professional corespondent" in a divorce case. He will identify himself by saying, "Chance is the fool's name for fate." But the success of the ruse rests on the frail memory of Tonetti, a notorious scatterbrain. What begins as a password disguised as a proverb collapses in a series of mangled variations that are equally abstract, each one decked out with syntax in search of meaning:

"Give me a name for chance and I am a fool."

"Fate is a foolish thing to take a chance on."

"I am fated to take foolish chances."

"Chances are that fate is foolish."

"Fate is a foolish thing—take a chance."[10]

Because all these sayings are meaningless as far as offering practical wisdom to be followed, none is memorable enough to be carried in the mind for more than an hour. It doesn't matter, of course, since in this film the real turtle soup is no more important than the mock.

The proverb is a cultural condensation. With its built-in efficacy of the ancient and the honorable, it carries in its brevity the sanction of a preserved tradition of right action. Homiletic by its very nature, it does not need to be proved or demonstrated: it needs only to be quoted. The tried-and-true—history, morality, and even (occasionally) achieved civilization—is on its side, which is to say that proverbial lore resists innovation,

10. *The Gay Divorcee*, directed by Mark Sandrich, screenplay by George Marion, Jr., Dorothy Yost, and Edward Kaufman (1934; Turner Home Video, 1999).

experiment, newfangledness. In the humorists' world, however, all proverbs are mock. Folk wisdom in the sketches—in adages, mottoes, and
cautionary tags—is inevitably subjected to parody by vernacular figures
deliberately chosen to mangle them, the better to use them as self-serving
weapons.

When he made his famous assertion *Be always sure you're right—then go
ahead!* Davy Crockett took the practical woods wisdom that had preserved him in a milieu inimical to cultivation and transferred it into the
structure and idiom of the proverb, a form that requires cultivation. That
the first part of Crockett's proverb was largely ignored is a measure of
the inadequacy of that form as reliable guide in the culture of the Old
Southwest. Except in sentimental moments, the proverb's very presence
as serious statement was suspect. Crockett's did better than most, however; in its truncated form, it generated a phrase that people actually
found useful.

ii.

> What a plastic little creature [man] is! so shifty, so adaptive!
>
> —Ralph Waldo Emerson

> IT IS GOOD TO BE SHIFTY IN A NEW COUNTRY.
>
> —Johnson Jones Hooper

It is not likely that the leading man of Concord, Massachusetts, only recently emerged from his Transcendental phase, ever read the tales about
the eminently adaptive Simon Suggs, whose scams were invented by a
catch-as-catch-can author from La Fayette, Alabama. Johnson Jones
Hooper was never the leading man of his raw interior town—or, for that
matter, of the more ambitious centers, Montgomery and Richmond, that
drew him in his later political career. To find common cause in a New
England idealist and a southern cynic may be a stretch, but in fact the
condition of nineteenth-century man merited an obsessive concern that
resonated similarly in Emerson and Hooper. Emerson spent much of his
life fathoming the ways in which the "plastic little creature" might realize his divine potential while negotiating worldly snares, the "lords of
life" lurking in his every circuit. Hooper wickedly created a shifty hero
whose potential was as relentlessly secular as his practicality. Hooper's
formulation of human character reverberated from La Fayette to Nash-

ville, where Andrew Jackson, one of his satiric targets, fortuitously died the same year that the Simon Suggs sketches appeared in book form.

Van Wyck Brooks spoke for many intellectuals—in our first "cool" generation—when he described the serene sage of Concord as "fatalistically optimistic."[11] It was Emerson's optative mood that gave comfort and aid to chautauqua lecturers and their thirsty audiences, encouraged scores of wholesome newspaper poets, and established secular routes for pilgrims on spiritual journeys. If the shadow of his presence falls heavily on both Unitarianism and Christian Science, it also lurks on the alternative maps to self-realization drawn by syncretistic New Agers in every age. But perhaps the most telling mark of Emerson's cultural persistence is the assimilation of his memorable proverbs into the American mainstream. Though he saw through the paltry expedience of the "greasy adages" of Poor Richard, Emerson ensured his fame by peppering his complex discourse with canny condensations of higher (or common-sense) truths, and his own adages have since become almost as familiar (if not as greasy) as Franklin's.

We still like the idea that a man is better than a town and that every institution is the lengthened shadow of one man. We still justify our incoherence by damning a foolish consistency as fit only for little minds. We take heart in thinking the only sin is limitation and that evil is merely privative. We fully understand that, in most eras, to be great is to be misunderstood and that the world whips the nonconformist with its displeasure. Above all, our cynical hearts still vibrate to that iron string "Trust thyself." Some Emersonian affirmations were widely endorsed early ("it is not meters, but a meter-making argument that makes a poem"); others have been reluctantly embraced in our lifetime ("all history becomes subjective"); some that concern themselves with healthy relationships are still matters of dispute ("better be a nettle in the side of your friend than his echo"), the outcome depending on which teleguru is getting the highest ratings.

It may come as some relief to know that Emerson has yet to be found indispensable to the value system of Simon Suggs. Hooper's fictional southwesterner did not need a Yankee source to activate his self-reliance. Had he taken to learning, however, to supplement his mother wit, Simon would have known how to act upon one—or even two or three—of the Concord sage's prudential sayings: "Life is not intellectual or critical, but sturdy," or "Everything good is on the highway." The high-minded among

11. Van Wyck Brooks, *New England: Indian Summer, 1865–1915* (1940; reprint, Cleveland: World Publishing, 1946), 59.

the Emersonians—those who have always believed life to be intellectual and critical—deplored the vulgar uses to which their man was put, yet that loftiness did not prevent some of them (Harvard President Charles W. Eliot and Methodist Bishop William Lawrence, for instance) from vulgarizing Emerson as the patron saint of captains of industry and assorted self-made entrepreneurs.[12]

It was not a happy development for the robber barons to use Emerson as their fallback seer. "We permit all things to ourselves, and that which we call sin in others, is experiment for us" is a clearheaded observation of human frailty, not an economic prescription for healthy predators. Emerson would surely have been shocked at the spectacle of his own kind, the now-attenuated Brahmins, blessing with his words the materialist schemes of Jim Fisk and J. P. Morgan. But perhaps not. The man who lamented "the downward tendency and proneness of things" in the democratic century was the same man who accepted rather serenely in his everyday experience "the clangor and jangle of contrary tendencies." For most of his career Emerson did not view the world about him through an idealist lens. He accurately saw in his times the unfolding of all kinds of contrary tendencies, and he was loath to exclude any of them. Each morning, he noted, brought to Concord "the dear old spiritual world and even the dear old devil not far off." If he often found his account with sots and bores, it was because, like the devil, they were *useful:* "I open my eye on my own possibilities." Emerson may not have been shifty in the Suggsian manner, but he assuredly was adaptive.

Captain Suggs, a sleazier con man than the successful self-made men of the East, found life sturdy, if terribly random, and found most of his opportunities on the highway. He would have liked others of Emerson's "mottoes" had he known them: "In skating over thin ice our safety is in our speed," say, or "Man was born to be rich," or "All stealing is comparative." But, fully equipped with his own aphoristic power, he found no occasion to crib other men's mottoes to justify his own values or methods.

Much of Southwest humor involves itself, without excessive apology from its makers, in tracking the eccentric speech and habits of what even modern southerners refer to as "trifling" or "shiftless" people, those who are of "no account" in the moral and social schemes normalized by those who do count. From *Georgia Scenes* to *Sut Lovingood's Yarns*, the writing

12. See Len Gougeon, *Virtue's Hero: Emerson, Antislavery, and Reform* (Athens: University of Georgia Press, 1990), 340–43.

consistently features a marginal population in a broad swath of geography that by the 1870s had already been remade as a nearly monolithic region called the Old South. Except for its chary narrator, *Adventures of Captain Simon Suggs* is totally immersed in these marginal people. Backwoods farmers, innkeepers, gamblers, clay-eaters, aspiring bank directors, land sharks, militiamen, judges—whatever their place in Alabama society, they are utterly *trifling* specimens. But Hooper's dramatic locale is such a rich playing field for his rogue hero because unlike, say, Joseph G. Baldwin's Alabama, it has been virtually emptied of the *shiftless*.

Despite its frequent use by respectable southerners in real life, *shiftless* hardly applies in Hooper's constructed Alabama of the 1830s: his subjects are trifling, perhaps, but, in keeping with the fortunes of the word, not shiftless. In its coarsening connotative descent from sympathy and pity—when the term signified a lack of artifice in protecting oneself—*shiftless* settled down to scorn and disgust for the deprived and ineffectual poor on the part of respectables who thought they got that way because they were lazy. But in his scalding depiction, Hooper's vulgar society-in-the-raw seems bereft of people who are shiftless either in the obsolete compassionate sense or in the modern pejorative sense. Though more modest in ambition, his Alabamians are as consumed by self-interest as those in Baldwin's *Flush Times.* From the pokiest resident of Tallapoosa County to the slickest person in Tuscaloosa, this new country is dedicated to the ethics of personal advancement, which means overcoming rivals and other assorted barriers by engaging in as many shades of enterprise as can be imagined by resourceful men. All Hooper's characters are *shifters.* Unlike the Bricksville that Huck Finn described, Suggsian Alabama lacks shiftless citizens (in the older sense). What remains and what counts are the industrious achievers: apostles of law, politics and government, religion, commerce, and agriculture. There is scarcely a victim of Simon's wiles who is not wily himself; victims are merely rivals who have been momentarily outstripped.

IT IS GOOD TO BE SHIFTY IN A NEW COUNTRY: Alabama is the new country, and Hooper's point is that it is especially rife with cheats and frauds, usually masquerading as respectables, who ply confidence as a game to outwit the less effective players among them. The syntax of Suggs's favorite motto suggests that resourceful men, when they find themselves dealing with tricksters, are forced to rely on their own devices, the most useful of which is trickery itself. There is so little public outcry against his methods because there is so little to corrupt. Simon does not operate in a moral society. *Human natur* being what it is, the ethical conditions in "this little world of ourn" are not even neutral. Simon must respond in kind if he is to survive.

In a world being reshaped and redefined by science, survival is not an abstract subject for either genteel essayists or hand-to-mouth journalists. We are told that if, "in respect to his moral conformation," nature made Simon Suggs a beast of prey, "she did not refine the cruelty by denying him the fangs and the claws" (*SS*, 132). The new country is not merely scrubby Alabama. It is the new order, an impersonal capitalistic economy to which religious, political, even family principles are beholden. Hooper's backcountry, no less than Emerson's New England, is the world of the *now* where all men, though unequally armed with fangs and claws, are free to respond to their impulses, good or bad. Emerson's characterization of generic man—a plastic little creature, shifty and adaptive—would seem to be at once more benign and more ambiguous than what Hooper has in mind for his frontier sharper. But Emerson's resonant *shifty* is reinforced by two additional words that make it an unstable trait, somewhere between the admirable and the distasteful. Early science is the source of both terms, but Emerson is already using them in their expanded modern senses. *Plastic,* once a neutral word to describe the molding power of nature, now suggests the pliancy of human character, a susceptibility to influence that allows new shapes; and the biological *adaptive* now carries the force of calculated expedience. For much of his long career Emerson struggled to accommodate nineteenth-century science to his early belief in idealist thinking, and his writing for most of his productive years attests to his embrace of the modern in all its mixed circumstances. The ambiguous terms are apt: even in his posture of serenity Emerson studied modern man with a full appreciation of his perversity.

The *shifty* motto is Suggs's favorite because it has the force of a blanket application, a general rule that covers snugly the many separate citations he churns up for specific occasions. But all of his mottoes are variants of the "greasy adage," the debased vernacular form that Emerson resurrected as a major rhetorical mode. Laced with the idioms and rhythms of moral guidelines (the better to ensnare the unwary), Simon's mottoes function as pre-invested verbal capital to be drawn upon for whatever good thing offers itself on the highway:

> Honesty's the bright spot in *any* man's character!—Fair play's a jewel, but honesty beats it all to pieces!
>
> Prudence is the stob I fasten the grapevine of *my* cannoo to.
>
> Human natur' and the human family is *my* books.

Ef a feller don't make every aidge cut, he's in the background directly.

Honesty and Providence will never fail to fetch a man out!

Simon Suggs never forgits his friends—NEVER! His motter is allers, *Fust* his *country,* and *then* his *friends!*

At first blush, it looks as if the mottoes, stripped of their localisms, might serve as linguistic condensations of the civil and cooperative society toward which the Old Southwest nominally aspired. If we knew nothing of Simon except his mottoes, we would award him high marks for succinctly tapping into the ethical structures of neighborliness and communal virtue. Arguably, only one of the mottoes seems to suggest personal expedience over social values: "Ef a feller don't make every aidge cut, he's in the background directly."

In the go-aheader's philosophy, every opportunity must be seized because a competitor is always lurking. The "edge" metaphor derives from the single-mindedness of forest-clearing pioneers—as in one old settler's memory of a neighbor who tackled the forest around his cabin as if he "intended to make a hole in it": "Being an energetic man, every edge cut that could; and that which could not cut, bruised, and that which could not bruise, mashed; and that which could neither cut, bruise, or mash, set by and grunted for the balance."[13] Though he belongs to the settlement period, Simon reflects this earlier ethic. Though his energy is quite differently applied, he makes every edge cut; but he is not beyond bruising and mashing to get what he wants. We *do* know more about Simon than the adages he uses as weapons, and we know they are all expressions of self-interest. By its own constitution, the aphorism is generically one kind of "fragment"—*insight* as opposed to *system.* We need not overstress the obvious: Suggsian mottoes are self-referential. Although Emerson, ever alert to his own possibilities, also began with the self, the aphorism was for him a rhetorical tool, a compositional principle of reduction for getting to the bone (one biographer has argued it was the "supreme literary form for the self-evident").[14]

13. Quoted in F. L. Cherry, "The History of Opelika and Her Agricultural Tributary Territory (1883–1885)," *Alabama Historical Quarterly* 15 (1953): 207. This earthy pioneer might have been a "right hero" of Emerson's, one who would "deliver his message"—"if broken, he can at least scream; gag him, he can still write it; bruise, mutilate him, cut off his hands and feet, he can still crawl toward his object on his stumps." Ralph Waldo Emerson, "The Scholar" (1876), in *Complete Works,* Centenary Edition (Boston: Houghton Mifflin, 1903–1904), 10:261.

14. Robert D. Richardson, Jr., *Emerson: The Mind on Fire* (Berkeley and Los Angeles: University of California Press, 1995), 564. See the concise account of Emerson's apho-

Emerson's splendid adages, accreting in tumbling profusion, suggest how various he believed the techniques were for getting to the bone. And they were also monitory. If he could get there, others could too. Simon Suggs's aphoristic power begins and ends with the self. In the mottoes that are expediently functional, Simon names his "virtues" to support his impromptu impersonations of figures his culture regards as more respectable than himself. These, however, are no different at bottom from those mottoes he mutters to himself when in a meditative mood.[15] A practical blend of the premeditated and the *ad hoc*, Simon Suggs is a superior example of his type, and his mottoes are not idle catchwords but the chief intimations of how and why he operates. They do not signify some idiosyncrasy but a new and improved set of cultural imperatives that will ensure victory over his like-minded contemporaries.

Whigs may have cackled with glee at the linkage of Captain Simon Suggs and General Andrew Jackson, especially their manipulation of military heroics for political advancement. But Hooper, the former Democrat, was a satirist as well as a partisan. Popular stump politicians of all stripes and the political journalists who supported them were his targets, together with banking, speculation, Indian policy, piety, and social mobility. Tallapoosa is only a rawboned version of the great world observed by most of our respectable authors at midcentury. As the humorist's chief modern editor succinctly puts it, "Hooper and his readers embraced modernity."[16]

---

risms in Lawrence Buell, *Emerson* (Cambridge, MA: Harvard University Press, 2003), 154–57. Lawrence Rosenwald argues that the Emersonian aphorism is a kind of interactive test, teasing the reader into the role of "combatant aspiring toward initiation." *Emerson and the Art of the Diary* (New York: Oxford, 1988), 109. In a recent novel, Emerson, as a character, speaks even to his initiated friends—Longfellow, Holmes, and Lowell—in strung-together orphic adages. Matthew Pearl, *The Dante Club* (New York: Random House, 2003).

15. The most sustained passage of meditation occurs as Simon tarries in front of the Tuscaloosa shopwindows on his way to the faro parlor. Holding "occasional 'confabs' with himself" in Hooper's version of stream-of-consciousness, the observant captain muses on the colorful displays of "deffrunt sperrets," books, and placards advertising a "sirkis" in town (*SS*, 52–54).

16. Johanna Nicol Shields, introduction to *Adventures of Captain Simon Suggs, Late of the Tallapoosa Volunteers; Together with "Taking the Census" and Other Alabama Sketches*, by Johnson Jones Hooper (Tuscaloosa: University of Alabama Press, 1993), xxxviii.

Chapter 15

The World according to Sut

Daddy kill'd the blind bull,
    Human nater, human nater!
Mammy fried a pan full,
    Sop an' tater, sop an' tater.

           —Sut Lovingood

A n admirer of both figures once remarked that Sut Lovingood is yeo-man to Ned Brace. Longstreet's Georgian can neutralize his bizarre experiments in baiting the respectables by turning on his abundant charm; George Washington Harris's Tennessean, however, would rather lose in his bouts with respectables than cultivate winning ways. A century later, the erratic Ned Brace, with his compulsive shifts from antic bad boy to model gentleman, would have been a candidate for behavioral therapy. Sut Lovingood might well have benefited from therapy, too, but not be-cause of incoherence in either his mental disposition or his public image. Although both characters perform outrageously in the company of more conventional people, Ned succumbs to his demons, whereas Sut disci-plines his in the service of bravura creativity. The character of the native Georgian puzzles, even as it delights, his tolerant friends; that of the lanky mountaineer may annoy many of his neighbors, but they are never per-plexed by his behavior: they unhappily know all about his penchant for fomenting trouble. Ned's confessions never explain his dark psyche but only arouse even further mystery; Sut's are always grounded in a gloomy surety of what *human nater* is.

The one character in Southwest humor that more closely resembles Sut is Simon Suggs. For convenience, we call Simon a con man, primarily because he is adaptable, quick-witted, and self-serving. We usually call Harris's yarn-spinner a trickster, primarily because of his larky pleasure in concocting schemes to deflate pompous authority figures and others who cross him. Like most categories, however, these do not exhaust the richness of either character.

The Alabama militia captain is as professionally marginal as his social status. If he is really a confidence artist, we see him operating at an appalling subsistence level, one so tenuous that his bilkings are almost too modest to be called cons. Hampered by a fondness for amiable fellowship, he sacrifices profit for pleasure. Furthermore, his character flaw—"fighting the tiger"—is, like any gambler's, an addiction that threatens to wreck even his paltry scams. Like Sut, Simon skewers a backward society too protective of communal values. What the two significantly share is their down-to-the-bone reading of human nature. They know that the status quo is set by community leaders, mostly moralists and law enforcers, who are themselves more prone to human failings than the general population. Unlike Harris's ruthless dissection of his time and place, Hooper's exposure proceeds with insouciance. Quite apart from each writer's unique creative vision, Harris's *Yarns* and Hooper's *Adventures* reflect the demographic difference between Sut Lovingood's long-settled, largely static mountain enclave and Simon Suggs's go-ahead society in the making and on the make.

The differences between these two vernacular figures, then, are substantial. Though he is as self-serving and quick-witted as Simon, Sut is rarely adaptable. He is too focused, too intense, to show any country cool. He does not play pranks, even for small gains. He hatches plots that are the maneuvers of a principled and passionate hater. His fun-loving, such as it is, is grounded in resentment and revenge, and his victims tend to be specifically targeted rather than randomly chosen.

Coming upon him as an unendearing character, students frequently seek to explain Sut by remaking him into a backwoods Till Eulenspiegel. Although we may be astonished at his Rube Goldberg schemes of revenge and admiring of his wit and facile tongue, we rarely find warmth in reading his *Yarns*. Within a narrative that explicitly celebrates storytelling (beginning with the title), Sut refuses to ingratiate himself with his audience, dismissing any query with scorn and insult. (He even threat-

ens the life of one skeptic.) Long before Edmund Wilson declared him repellent,[1] readers more often than not found Sut distasteful—in part because of the cranky surliness that he flaunted even when pursuing Sicily
Burns, and in part because his misogynistic creator seemed to revel in recasting insubordination as a kind of ethic. Sut Lovingood is clearly more
than an antic trickster, and he is also more than a social irritant who gets
his kicks by kicking against the restraints imposed by preachers and sheriffs.

In the course of one tale, Harris waggishly identifies one of Sut's ques-
tioners as an "anxious inquirer after truth." The designation is sportive,
but it suggests something of the seriousness behind Sut's role as troublemaker.[2] It is easy enough to see his tricks merely as crude payback, which
they often are. Sut admits that his priority is physical pleasure (good
food and drink, especially when supplied by others, and partying, especially if it leads to sex) and that he delights in foiling his adversaries who
would deny him those pleasures, especially corrupt sheriffs, pious preachers, watchful mothers, and deceitful girls. Harris's crotchety trickster is a
truth-teller. He must operate, like Simon Suggs, in a world of flimflam;
unlike Hooper's crafty captain, however, Sut scorns impersonation, the
tack of joining the ranks of the deceivers in order to get what he wants.
Lacking deference and pretense, he indulges in behavior that is often excessive and sometimes borders on the mad.

i.

Though he is too eccentric to fit a category, Sut resembles the *jouisseur,*
the pleasure-loving trickster who skitters through European literature
but is never quite at home in American writing. The *jouisseur*-inspired text
entails loss, discomfort, and unsettled values, challenging the reader's
cultural and psychological assumptions. Roland Barthes notes that it also

1. Edmund Wilson, "The Myth of the Old South; Sidney Lanier; The Poetry of the
Civil War; *Sut Lovingood,*" in *Patriotic Gore: Studies in the Literature of the American Civil
War* (New York: Oxford University Press, 1962), 509.
2. Milton Rickels characterizes Sut—with his flow of words, his cruel and witty
repartee—as a descendant of the Renaissance fool, who sometimes acts the jester,
sometimes the scapegoat, and often "the bitter seer." *George Washington Harris* (New
York: Twayne, 1969), 105. For the groundbreaking work on Harris in the 1930s, see
Walter Blair, *Native American Humor, 1800–1900* (New York: Knopf, 1937), 96–101; and
Franklin J. Meine, ed., *Tall Tales of the Southwest: An Anthology of Southern and Southwestern Humor, 1830–1860* (New York: Knopf, 1930), xxiii–xxiv.

"brings to a crisis [the reader's] relation with language."[3] *Jouissance* takes its pleasure in disruption, and there is no American text in the entire nineteenth century that does this so aggressively as *Sut Lovingood's Yarns.*

George Washington Harris remains controversial because of the unfashionable biases he gives to his irreverent hero. Although his racism, sexism, and xenophobia reflect the general spirit of his age, Sut's scorn of African Americans, Jews, Yankees, Irishmen, and Dutchmen, and his slurs against most religious groups are more intense than those of his contemporaries. The beneficiaries of compassion vary from age to age, but within the *Yarns* they are rare enough to be numbered on one hand. Harris's brush slathers the tar in such full measure that the man wielding the brush may be nearly irredeemable—an unhappy state, since Harris is the one utterly unique author in our literature.[4] Quite aside from his unacceptable civic attitudes, he is unlikely to be rehabilitated in any widespread way. To most readers, Sut Lovingood's arcane dialect is a sufficient barrier. For a few others, the gusto with which his creator plumbs an embarrassing social class is itself too gross for appreciation.[5]

In a curious turn, however, it is Harris's use of farce that sets up much of the troubling resistance of readers who otherwise fancy comic modes. Like certain kinds of standup comedy, farce as a comic mode has never earned much respect. Unlike puns and other wordplay, in which whimsicality is joined by linguistic sophistication, farce comes across as mere slapdash physicality. When farce does sport with language to reinforce action, it still invites condescension because, until Samuel Beckett, dramatists who clowned around with words were barely more acceptable than Henny Youngman.[6] A widespread literary bias that privileges message, meaning, and significance in whatever genre generally rules out the farceur's specialty: horseplay on the most innocent (and perhaps tasteless) level of human activity.

3. Roland Barthes, *The Pleasure of the Text,* trans. Richard Miller (New York: Hill & Wang, 1975), 14.

4. "In all of nineteenth-century American literature," writes Hershel Parker, "there is no politically correct meal that remotely compares to the riches of Harris's banquet." "A Tribute to Harris's Sheriff Doltin Sequence," in *Sut Lovingood's Nat'ral Born Yarnspinner: Essays on George Washington Harris,* ed. James E. Caron and M. Thomas Inge (Tuscaloosa: University of Alabama Press, 1996), 220.

5. In reviewing *Patriotic Gore* (1962) for the *London Observer,* D. W. Brogan approved of Edmund Wilson's distaste for "such sub-Calibans as 'Sut Lovingood,' the horrible hero of odious Southern humour, perhaps the most dreadful of the specimens dredged up recently by over-industrious professors." *Lovingood Papers* (1964): 49.

6. See Robert J. Williams, *Comic Practice/Comic Response* (Newark: University of Delaware Press, 1993), 95.

Farce is everywhere in the Lovingood tales. A bull breaks up china at a wedding and takes its owner on a tumultuous ride; lizards stimulate a clerical striptease in the pulpit; humans brawl with beasts, insects, and other humans. The fecund acts of revenge, the intricate plotting of traps and surprises, the merging of frenetic physical action in a circumscribed space, the aggressive succession of self-conscious wordplay and rhetorical excess, the gratuitous social disruption: all these are the spoors of Sut Lovingood's trail. They also identify the generic reaches of farce. But farce in the *Yarns* is something more than horseplay. It is true that most of Harris's plots are enacted in a general context of bad taste and the taunting of taboo; what makes Harris disturbing as a comic writer, however, is his surprising and improper manipulation of the formal principles of farce. The horseplay of traditional farce often turns into violence—the real thing—in Sut's storytelling. Some would dismiss the cruelty to animals and human beings as simply the flourishes of narrative imagination; but even if they are "tales told rather than actions performed," they bespeak a dark complexity of character almost alien to farcical comedy.[7] In the midst of Sut's over-orchestrated schemes we suspect that both their frenetic spirit and their verbal clowning are meant to serve something other than farce, that they are not simply rebellious acts, the habit of insubordination gone mad.

That uneasiness is justified. Whether we like it or not, Sut Lovingood's role in his community is played out under the banner of principle. It is not too much, I think, to refer to this principle as a moral vision. And further, if Sut wages war against a society that is morally fundamentalist, he uses the same kind of weapon: a vision as fierce as his enemy's but—from his perspective—purified of moral corruption. Sut's ethic is informed by a profoundly Calvinistic sensibility, but one that is necessarily stripped of its ultimate theological burden. In Sut's world human depravity is rampant, just as the circuit riders charged, and the people stand in obvious need of regeneration. The agent of change, however, is Sut himself: relentless and, like grace, irresistible.[8] Harris so secularizes this spiritual process that the final goal of such doctrinal realism—the saving of souls—

7. Carolyn S. Brown, *The Tall Tale in American Folklore and Literature* (Knoxville: University of Tennessee Press, 1987), 80.

8. For the Calvinistic strand of southern religion, see Russel B. Nye, *The Cultural Life of the New Nation, 1776–1830* (New York: Harper, 1960), 216–21. In one view, Sut acts as "divine scourge" but "unintentional reformer." M. Thomas Inge, "Sut Lovingood: An Examination of the Nature of a 'Nat'ral Born Durn'd Fool,'" *Tennessee Historical Quarterly* 19 (1960): 245–46.

is conspicuously absent. Sut acts not in the name of God, Providence, or some abstract justice. He is the agent-at-large of redress, performing his role with determination, skill, and a little luck. Sut's ethic is a realism of the here and now whose system echoes something fiercely primitive and pre-Christian even as it anticipates the harsh naturalistic doctrines of Herbert Spencer and other scientific popularizers of the latter part of his century.

Unlike Simon Suggs, who views camp-meeting preachers merely as rivals in scam, Sut sees the circuit riders as out-and-out enemies. Squire Haney appears on the scene as a militant foe, "armed wif a hyme book, an' loaded tu the muzzil wif brimstone, bilin pitch, forkid flames, an' sich uther nicitys es makes up the devil's brekfus" (*SL*, 286). Sut's mother reminds the preacher that her family stands in no need of "wallin up ove eyes, nur groanin, nur secon han low-quartered pray'rs" (*SL*, 289). As an ethical realist Sut resists the measures of such men for correcting human depravity. He candidly enjoys what the preachers hate: drinking, dancing, courting, and all fleshly delights. At their best, says Sut, prayer meetings cannot serve the needs of the whole person; at their worst, they are pious covers for preacherly gluttony and lust. His description of Parson John Bullen can serve as his opinion of preachers generally: "infunel, hiperkritikal, pot-bellied, scaley-hided, whisky-wastin, stinkin ole groun'-hog" (*SL*, 51). On the other hand, Sut endorses quilting parties, his alternative to camp meetings, because they answer to a wider variety of needs. There is a "fur-seein wisdum in quiltins," he tells his friend George (Harris's stand-in), because they are "good fur free drinkin, good fur free eatin, good fur free huggin, good fur free dancin, good fur free fitin, an' goodest ove all fur poperlatin a country fas'. . . . One holesum quiltin am wuf three old pray'r meetins on the poperlashun pint" (*SL*, 139).

Sut is not being wholly ironic when he tells George that he is "es soun' a belever es they is." In contrast to the preacher who marries Sicily Burns, he insists that he is "ten times more ove a Cristshun than Clapshaw" (*SL*, 49, 105). His own rhetoric makes promiscuous use of scriptural diction and the sermonic practice of dividing the Word. Harris even devotes a sketch to "Sut's Sermon," his version of the mock sermon so popular with nineteenth-century audiences.[9] Sut declares his right to preach based on

---

9. For this subgenre of antebellum southern humor, see George Kummer, "Who Wrote 'The Harp of a Thousand Strings'?" in *The Frontier Humorists: Critical Views*, ed. M. Thomas Inge (Hamden, CT: Archon, 1975), 219–29; James L. W. West III, "A New Mock Sermon," in *Gyascutus: Studies in Antebellum Southern Humorous and Sporting Writing*, ed. James L. W. West III (Atlantic Highlands, NJ: Humanities Press, 1978), 209–14; and A. S. Wendel, "Another New Mock Sermon," in *Gyascutus*, 215–18.

five "strong pints ove karactar": he has a gizzard for a soul; he is too much the fool to come "even onder millertary lor"; he has the longest, most efficient legs that "ever hung tu eny cackus"; he can drink more "kill-devil whisky, an' stay on aind" than anyone else; and he gets into more "misfortnit skeery scrapes"—and out again, thanks to his legs— than other people (*SL*, 172). These cheerfully bumptious attributes are invoked in derisive defiance of the circuit riders and the validity of their calling ("I wud like tu know whar sum preachers got *thar* papers frum"), but they are primarily a claim for *Sut's* validity. Self-knowledge is *his* "papers." His mode of address is not the righteous attack on "you" gullible sinners but "Feller suffrers, he an' she" (*SL*, 173).

Consistent with his character, the concern in "Sut's Sermon" is for the material ills of a hostile world. One target is the generic "Perpyriters" of taverns and inns, who deceive, cheat, and abuse customers. Because they traffic in "dirt, sloth, swindle, sufferin, stealin, an' starvashun," the owners of taverns and "rail-road feed troffs" are "hell's recruitin ossifers." Hanging over them is "brimstone retribushun es big es a car shed." Concludes Brother Lovingood: "I'd jis' ruther du wifout the instertushun intirely." Armed with touching examples and explicating his "text" in familiar homiletic rhythms, Sut gives no comfort—only warning—to fellow sufferers about gouging proprietors: "Keep the dus' ove the dinin room ofen yer foot, an' the smell ove the bed-room ofen yer close, that yer days may be longer in the lan' what yer daddy's tuck frum the Injuns" (*SL*, 179–80).

The antics of Sut as a mock preacher have been defined as "clownish presentations of evangelical Christianity." His mocking, however, should not obscure a deeply felt vision that is, if anything, more sobering than that of rival preachers with their "papers." His wrath is not against Christian morality, but its perversions.[10] The substance of this vision is preacherly. Generic farce in the world of Sut Lovingood operates under the aegis of a moralist who evaluates human nature with a sharp appreciation for unregenerate humanity. Most theological truths may be much too hifalutin to apply to Sut, yet his perspective incorporates the grim truths of human finitude and the appalling contingency of human affairs.

In the *Yarns*, Sut is a spokesman for desire, the urgency behind his demand for an irrepressible autonomy uncurbed by community restraints.

10. James E. Caron, "Playin' Hell: Sut Lovingood as Durn'd Fool Preacher," in Caron and Inge, *Nat'ral Born Yarnspinner*, 274; Elmo Howell, "Timon in Tennessee: The Moral Fervor of George Washington Harris," in Caron and Inge, *Nat'ral Born Yarnspinner*, 145. See also David C. Estes, "Sut Lovingood at the Camp Meeting: A Practical Joker among the Backwoods Believers," *Southern Quarterly* 25 (1987): 53–65.

That urgency announces itself in Sut's very body. What makes this creative transaction interesting is how Harris makes pursuit of physical pleasure the motive of the most malformed character in all of Southwest humor. Sut is not the ugliest—Simon Suggs, the Andrew Jackson look-alike, has that honor—but with his entrance at Pat Nash's grocery, riding a sorrel horse that is equally ill-favored, Sut Lovingood enters our literature as its most grotesque fictional creation. He is "a queer looking, long legged, short bodied, small headed, white haired, hog eyed, funny sort of a genius"; and as his tales unfold, our attention is repeatedly drawn to his legs, most often by Sut himself. He reminds George how "these yere legs," his "only pendence for life," have always "toted me . . . safe an' soun" out of "the durndest wust sort ove scrapes" (*SL*, 171; *HT*, 255). Sut visually encapsulates the old mountain saying "a good run is often better than a bad stand," a local variant of Falstaffian wisdom. As his chief weapon of defense, his legs give him the means to outrun all dangers, but they also come to symbolize the whole man: his legs are the incarnated essence of Suthood.

His body, to which he refers with each assault against the respectables, is both a substantive reminder of the transgressive act and an ongoing burden of flesh that compels him to transgress. The body makes him do it. Sut's sensuality finds outlets throughout his community, and Harris's joke is that this misshapen rebel appropriates all the erotic energy mostly hidden in his respectable neighbors. Those who in their ordinariness follow the social codes must repress that energy, relegating it to opportune bouts and hushed assignations, while Sut uses it openly (if unsuccessfully in most cases), without shame or guise. Libidinal nature makes animals of all humans, but for him, in his reality-based creed for living, it is deliberately assaultive, raising his own transparent Suthood as an erotic flag to neighbors unwilling to admit the kinship.

What we expect as the norm in most writing—human beings depicted as human beings—is itself marginal in the Lovingood world. Grotesquerie, beginning with Sut himself, radiates as a material condition throughout the communal context. Whether created out of revenge or ingrained devilment, Sut's doings are the transgressions of the number-one, self-confessed exhibit of fallen man. His ingenious trickeries tend toward plots that accelerate the distortion of his enemies. Self-destruction may be the conventional expectation for those enemies (a Christian revision of the old eye-for-an-eye formula), but Sut needs to see their fate as a process in action. His mission to the fallen is to expedite the retribution. Leaving them to heaven is too slow, too passive. Although the instruments of acceleration are usually homely objects—a feeding basket, lampblack, red pepper, and varmints such as bees or lizards—Sut discriminates, almost with the precision of an ancient church father, such trifling immediate causes of disorder from the real cause: human nature. Disaster inevitably follows his schemes, but thrusting to the heart of the problem (the victim's lust, pride, or greed) allows Sut to deflect from himself the mere "material" causes. It also allows him, in the parlance of late-twentieth-century statecraft, "deniability."

Calling Sut "grotesque" comes easily to modern sensibilities, but Harris's *Yarns* answers to at least one definition of *grotesque:* the confusion in which "ontological, generic, or logical categories are illegitimately jumbled together"—or, in Sut-speak, "all mix'd dam permiskusly."[11] On a narrative level, the action of a Sut sketch consists of calculated chaos. In an otherwise stable setting, a clatter of energy from unsuspecting agents devolves into a triumph of disorder. Objects once fixed in their own integrity are shattered into component bits that project new and startling incongruities. Enraged bees chase an eviscerated clock's "running geer" when the "littil wheels [start] a-trundlin over the floor"; a little girl, "doll baby an' all," is found on the top shelf of a cupboard, "amung the delf, a-screamin like a littil steam whistil" (*SL*, 92, 72).

In one sketch, a runaway horse, carrying a Yankee trader tethered to a clock and a dog, collides with a miller on horseback carrying a keg of honey, a woman with a spinning wheel, and several sacks of cornmeal. The predestined "deserlashun an' sorrer" come to pass in a memorably disgusting scene: the woman hangs by one foot from a blackjack tree, the dead dog's intestines are "tangled up amung the mar's hine laigs," and the mare has a broken neck and a "spinin-wheel spoke a-stickin atween her ribs." Sut completes this study in composition with a final flourish by pouring honey and cornmeal over the head of the unconscious Yankee. When a neighbor down the road asks the fleeing Sut about the commotion, he responds, with a splendid indifference to the carnage, that it was all "the advance gard ove a big sarkis purclaimin hits cummin, ur the merlennium, an' durn'd ef I know'd which" (*SL*, 47). The choice would seem to be between the sacred and the secular, but in Sut's theology one is just as satisfying as the other. Spectacles are his delight; they are most satisfying when the animate and inanimate jostle and interchange their

11. Geoffrey Galt Harphan, *On the Grotesque: Strategies of Contradiction in Art and Literature* (Princeton, NJ: Princeton University Press, 1982), xxi.

natures to offer stunning new creations.[12] While the interwoven incongruities of animate and inanimate objects echo the origins of *grotesque,* the fusion of man-mare-dog-clock in nature is Sut-specific: not a decoration but an actual force in which dismemberment satisfies the aesthetic of a communal transgressor.

Modern readers understandably recoil at the insensitivity of Sut's casual attitude toward dumb animals because the cruelty is not cartoonish, as in the Roadrunner and Coyote adventures. The dog in this sketch suffers a drawn-out demise, entrails fluttering like ribbons, and he does not bounce back and trot away; the mare does not survive to pace again, but is buried by the Yankee. Yet the book is not an example of Howellsian realism, and first-time readers of the *Yarns* sometimes remark on the way the characters appear almost like cartoons, anticipating, say, Snuffy Smith. Like most of his fellow humorists, Harris was certainly not shy in his use of stereotypes, but the calculation with which he created his distortions does not primarily belong to the cartoonist's art. Except for Sut himself, the focus is not on exaggerations of a few human features, but on the momentary exchange of the human and nonhuman. Although some of the other authors use incongruity as a comic device, Harris makes it a compositional principle. A randy mountain Ichabod discourses on theology and laws of human nature; men and animals find common cause in interchangeable traits, while both assume the functions of machines; and machines perversely perform with human will and desire. Even nonmechanical objects in Sut's world are not merely things. They are compressed, miniature events, flowings of chaotic energy, pulsations, explosions, throbbing always at the edge of apocalyptic transformation. Further, Sut's creator is fond of allowing human figures that are only marginal to sink to an even lower state.

Like a hillbilly Hogarth, Harris paints with puritanical zeal the frailties of his fellows, taking pleasure in layering the excesses of their foolishness and delusion. In ridding himself of the "Hell-sarpints" planted in his clothes, Parson Bullen is forced to strip and leap over the pulpit into "the mos' pius part ove the congregashun," but it remains for Sut the initiator to describe both the literal and spiritual change in the brimstone-spouting preacher:

> Ole Bullin's eyes wer a-stickin out like ontu two buckeyes flung agin a
> mud wall, an' he wer a-cuttin up more shines nor a cockroach in a hot skil-

---

12. Milton Rickels in 1959 was the first to study the animal-machine imagery in the *Yarns.* See "The Imagery of George Washington Harris," in Inge, *Frontier Humorists,* 155–69.

let. . . . When he jumpt a bainch he shook the yeath. . . . He weighed ni
ontu three hundred, hed a black stripe down his back, like ontu a ole bridil
rein, an' his belly wer 'bout the size an' color ove a beef paunch, an' hit a-
swingin out frum side tu side; he leand back frum hit, like a littil feller a-
totin a big drum, at a muster, an' I hearn hit plum tu whar I wer. . . . [T]akin
him all over, he minded ove a durnd crazy ole elephant, pussessed ove the
devil, rared up on hits hind aind, an' jis' *gittin* frum sum imijut danger ur
tribulashun. (*SL*, 55–57)

Bullen is at once a lumbering bear and a dead cow, a child playing his
own belly as drum, and an elephant in heat. First, however, the reduction
to nakedness serves as a reminder of basic creaturehood. The parson,
known after his embarrassment as Ole Barbelly Bullin, in fact chooses to
preach his next sermon on the text "Nakid I cum intu the world, an'
nakid I'm gwine outen hit, ef I'm spard ontil then." Sut's retaliation is
specifically directed—Bullen, finding Sut and a young woman in the
bushes, has assaulted them with a hickory stick and preached about their
wickedness from the pulpit—but it is really a general reactive strike
against hypocrisy. If, in his code, reputation breeds moral arrogance, it
proceeds from the basic premise that reputation is closely tied to impersonation, which helps to disguise the fragile human commonality of
whatever station and calling.[13]

Sut's moral drama, restricted as it is to the here and now, is understandably body-centered. When he tries to shed a confining, over-
starched shirt, pulling skin and hair from his body, he describes himself
as looking "like a map ove Mexico, arter one ove the wurst battils." Dr.
Gus Fabin, known by impudent boys as Gut Fatty, is "four foot fourteen
inches high," with eyes "like ontu two huckelberrys . . . stuck deep inter
a big ball ove red putty." After being dragged behind a horse, that natural grotesquerie is enhanced: "He wer orfully swell'd, he'd a rolled wun
way es well es tuther, an he wer every color ever invented." Like his fellow character Mrs. Yardley, Sut is ever a noticer of little things:

His shut wer stuck es tite tu him es my pasted one, an he wer peppered all
over with broken aig shells, nara piece es big es a grain ove corn. . . . [A] little blood [was] oozing thru a sunflour calliker pattern on his belly ur his
laigs, an his har looked like hit had been dipped in thunder an litenin and

13. Although most of the humorists share their age's fear of the exposed human
body, only Harris makes nudity a trope for the "obscenity of the fallen world." Di-
vestment is the final confirmation of man as brute animal. Hennig Cohen, "Mark
Twain's Sut Lovingood," *Lovingood Papers* (1962): 23.

sky blue; he was no more like human than dad were like a hoss when he acted hit. (*HT,* 124)

An even stronger naturalistic dimension in the Lovingood tales is Harris's zealous insistence that humans are ever and always animals. As we have seen, the linkage of man and beast is a chord sounded frequently in Southwest humor, but what is insight in Lewis, Thorpe, or Robb is programmatic in Harris.[14] The point is made when we first glimpse the "queer looking" genius riding on a "nick tailed, low necked, long, poor, pale sorrel horse, half dandy, half devil" (*SL,* 19). In this welter of grotesquerie, man and beast, rider and ridden, are infused with each other's properties. Squire Haney, the "engineer ove the sin squelshin mersheen," comes calling on the Lovingoods, riding "his pius ole hoss [that] show'd a grieved spirit frum foretop tu lip" (*SL,* 286). The opening and closing sketches of the *Yarns* feature "the patriark ove this depraved famerly," the only person on earth who can vie with Sut for being the biggest "infunel nat'ral born" fool (*SL,* 288). In both sketches, Dad transforms himself into an animal: a plow horse in the first, a bull in the last. If both roles demand appropriate grunts and gestures on all fours, Harris suggests that the enactment involves no great stretch for the performer.[15]

In "Sut Lovingood's Daddy, Acting Horse," the link is genetic. After the family's only plow horse dies, and despairing that no "stray hoss mout cum along" in time for spring planting, the old man decides *he* will be the horse, pulling the plow while Sut drives him. To prove that his father is a greater fool than he, Sut stresses the fact that the "patriark" is not content to *play* hoss but, at least temporarily, to *become* hoss: he chomps on the bridle, tries to bite Sut on the arm, whinnies on all fours, and slings his legs at his wife (who wryly observes, "Yu plays hoss better nur yu dus husban'"). To "keep up his karacter es a hoss" the old man lopes into a sassafras bush, but in doing so he dislodges a hornet's nest. Fending off the furious varmints, he leaps off a high bank into the creek below, by now wearing only his bridle. Sut accommodates his father's playacting. As he would for any "uther skeer'd hoss," he lets go the reins ("Wo!

14. In the four-part "Sut Lovingood's Love Feast ove Varmints" (*HT,* 237–60), Harris concocts a virtual bestiary (inspired by his political enemies) of skunks, moles, groundhogs, wolves, and other creatures equally unattractive.

15. Though he plays an active role in only two of the sketches in the *Yarns,* Dad is a pivotal figure. He serves, Noel Polk observes, as "the touchstone" for Harris's dominant theme: unregenerate human nature. "The Blind Bull, Human Nature: Sut Lovingood and the Damned Human Race," in Caron and Inge, *Nat'ral Born Yarnspinner,* 158.

dad, wo!"), offers advice from the sidelines about the attacking hornets ("switch em wif yure tail, dad . . . an' arter they goes tu roos' yu cum home"), and promises appropriate rewards ("I'll hev yer feed in the troft redy; yu won't need eny curyin tu-nite will yu?") (*SL*, 23–27).

In "Dad's Dog-School," Harris raises the hazard level of interspecies conflict. To train Sugar, a new "bull pup," to "hole on" to the "varmint he's a-contendin' wif," Dad has himself sewn up in the skin of a recently slaughtered yearling bull. Sugar is a quick learner, taking eagerly to his quarry with a "steel-trap holt" on the bull-man's snout. Sut narrates the furiously kinetic animal-on-animal episode with his customary attention to relevant imagery: Dad is "es tetchy . . . es a sore-back hoss is 'bout green flies," and he is "quick es a fox" when Sut growls "like ontu a dorg"; little Sugar is as ugly as a "she-ho'net, an' brave es a trap't rat" (*SL*, 277–78). But the training exercise ends badly, as a blow from the ax-wielding Sister Sal is required to separate the bloodied contenders. Dad is knocked senseless; Sugar, now successfully trained, is dead.

Squire Haney, the religious interventionist, brings a conventional perspective to the scene. His outrage at the pup-training spectacle imposes a civilized ethic upon a naturalistic pattern of behavior. What the pious squire witnesses is a bestial conflict between a domestic animal and a theatricalized bull-man whose head, horns, and nose are pinned back along the neck, exposing a human face "smeer'd wif the blood an' fat" of the dead yearling. Dad "cudn't be beat," says Sut, "fur a big, ruff, skeery thing outen hell, ur a mad-hous'." What from a familial perspective is a fully predictable, if stupid, training exercise is from the perspective of civilization's agent a horrifying descent into primitive instincts. To Mam, Dad's scheme is "nat'rally foolish"; to an outsider, the entire family is a bunch of "depraved onregenerits." What for the family is a "privit soshul famerly 'musement" is recast by the community's regenerate branch—in Sut-speak, "sturgeon-backed, sandy-heeled ole maids, devarsed wives, ur wimen what orter been wun ur tuther." The major aim of these "thin minded pussons" is, says Sut, "the mindin giner'lly ove everybody else's bisness." While a residual hellfire and brimstone mark the language of the preachers, it is Sut's position that their rage for social control ensures their corruption in the most commonplace ways: lust and greed. And hovering over that appetitive mode is the exercise of power over others, particularly women among the faithful: "Passuns ginerly hev a pow'ful strong holt on wimen" (*SL*, 282–89).

If biblical and homiletic phrasing laces Sut's language, as it dominates the rhetoric of his enemies in the pulpit, it is because this rectifying agent has accommodated himself to the truth of man's condition. Like the old-style Puritan, whose skinflint charities and petty deceptions he skewers whenever he has the chance, Sut accepts the harsher realities of human nature according to the selective application in America of Calvin's tenets of Reformed Protestantism.[16] In Sut's theology, the human animal need not apologize for bracketing love and hate, intellectual perceptions and emotional responses. Had he been a student of religion, Sut would have found ironic nourishment in the Yankee theologian Jonathan Edwards and his conviction that an idea in the mind was both perception and the generative engine of love and hate.[17] He even makes room for belief in portents and signs and the possibility of ghosts, spirits, and devils. That he denies having a soul and that he sees no working of grace in the fallen world does not mean he takes his theology lightly. A materialist Calvinism forces him to take seriously the visible effects of hypocrisy, greed, and pride in the here and now.

While cynicism is his most pronounced mood in matters religious, Sut adopts it primarily to combat the preachers' aggressive onslaught on him. He is not indifferent to how he is defined by the social and moral standards of the community, nor to the fact that his family is excluded from that order. When he hears the sounds of Squire Haney's horse in the thicket around his yard, he says he was "sorter 'spectin a retribushun ove sum nater" for defiling the Lord's Day by dog training. And while his language generally bears a heavy freight of sarcasm, irony, and wry understatement, he so consistently betrays such unease that we may take him at his word when he says that he felt his face "a-swellin wif shame" over Dad's animal posture and Mam's "bar laigs an' open collar," a confession that shows how thoroughly aware he is of respectability as the measure of religion and of his family's lapse from it. Only Mam's determined resistance steels his wavering courage: "I made up my mine ef she cud stan the storm, I cud, an' so I didn't run that time—nara durn'd step" (*SL*, 286).

Sut's candor has little enough to do with class envy. Haney represents the best elements of a community from which the Lovingoods are ex-

16. The doctrines that had the greatest impact in the antebellum South were that of the "total depravity" of man, "double" predestination (in which an elected few are saved and all others damned), and the political and social status quo (accepting power structures as the will of God). Most denominations, not merely Presbyterians, were touched by Calvinistic tenets; but the Arminian influence of the camp meeting from 1800 to 1840, with its offer of "free grace," emotionalism, and the promise of promiscuous salvation, weakened doctrinal rigor in some sects while strengthening it in others. See *Encyclopedia of Religion in the South,* ed. Samuel S. Hill (Macon, GA: Mercer University Press, 1997), 125–27.

17. Perry Miller, *Errand into the Wilderness* (New York: Harper & Row, 1964), 178–82.

cluded, the dominant values that make no distinction between social respectability and religious piety. Sut the realist acknowledges the squire's denunciation of his "depraved famerly." He is untouched, however, by the social snobbery that spurns the pathetic Lovingoods. Fancy dress, pretentious airs, doctored genealogies, stilted modes of address, and planned marriages rankle Sut not because they are the superficial signs of a favored social class but because, in his experience at least, they are signs of crude impersonation—masks that he wants to strip away. Sut's values, for all his mischief-making and visceral immersion in social upheaval, do not constitute a laissez-faire moral system. His attitude toward conventional breaches of behavior—adultery or petty conning—is not detached, not live-and-let-live. Like some arbiters of morality, Sut seeks to punish the guilty and reestablish the situation prior to the violation. More intensely than the circuit riders, preachers, and guardian squires—almost all of them guilty of sexual peccadilloes themselves—he seeks to expose moral cheating, to embarrass the wrongdoers. He acknowledges community moral standards as they are inscribed in model behavior. When *he* departs from such norms, he expects "retribushun," and he is systematic in his scheme to make other trespassers aware of retribution even if they do not expect to get caught.

Like all his humorist contemporaries, Harris understood that *moral* and *social* were defined by the leaders, those who busied themselves with progress and promise in their ambitious century—the educated, the professionally expert, the genteel movers and shakers. Sut knows precisely which individuals possess the heft of leadership, and he accepts without much rancor his exclusion from that group. Indeed, underneath his self-centered pleasure-seeking lurks one kind of idealism, a respect for *appropriate* leadership that quietly motivates the watchdog in him. Accordingly, he holds judges, lawyers, and Christian missionaries to a higher standard of behavior than unrespectable people like himself; when they betray the same instincts as those he regularly acts upon, they must be exposed to public view.

For all his tonic evaluations of human nature, Sut occasionally shows grudging admiration for the skill of an adversary, and he is not exempt from romantic idealization. Saint John Chrysostom was convinced that woman—the generic descendant of Eve—was "a necessary evil, a natural temptation, a desirable calamity, a domestic danger, a delectable detriment, an evil of nature, painted with fair colors."[18] With a little less

---

18. J. W. C. Ward, *Doctors and Councils* (London: Faith Press, 1962), 74. See also C. Baur, *St. John Chrysostom and His Time* (London: Sands & Co. 1959).

gold in his tongue, Sut at one time or another runs through most of these variants in his bittersweet profiles of women. All the attributes listed by Chrysostom coincide in Sicily Burns, whom Sut holds up as a near-perfect specimen of womanhood. As he tells George, she "shows amung wimen like a sunflower amung dog fennil." Harris takes obvious pleasure in the kind of Renaissance "emblazoning" that signifies poetic praise of the loved one, transforming it into Sut-speak:

> Sich a buzzim! Jis' think ove two snow balls wif a strawberry stuck but-ainded intu bof on em. She takes adzactly fifteen inches ove garter clar ove the knot, stans sixteen an' a 'alf hans hi, an' weighs one hundred an' twenty-six in her petticoatail afore brekfus'. . . . [H]er skin wer es white es the inside ove a frogstool, an' her cheeks an' lips es rosey es a pearch's gills in dorgwood blossom time—an' sich a smile! (*SL*, 75–76)

Like much perennial country humor, this version comes from the clash of conventionalized romantic intent and its particularized rendering in the topography of mountain life. It does not diminish Sut's honest infatuation that Sicily Burns's measurements are those used for horses and oxen.

Like all flesh, comely or not, Sicily is still heir to *natur* and all its weaknesses. Adept at tricks of her own, she teases Sut with "a new sensashun," tempting him to drink two tumblers of concentrated soda powder that she implies are "luv-powders." The "fizilin" cocktails create "a-snortin, and scizzin" sound in his innards and an eruption "like a hi pressur steamboat." As he speeds away on his horse in search of the doctor, Sicily taunts him: "Hole hit down, Mister Lovingood! hole hit down! hits a cure fur puppy luv; hole hit *down!*" Meeting Sut on the road, Clapshaw, the circuit rider, takes the gurgling apparition for a "long-laiged shakin Quaker, fleein frum the rath tu cum" and making a sound "like ontu the rushin ove mitey warters" (*SL*, 81–83). Sut recovers. Since every physical act in Harris triggers a disproportionate reaction, Sicily's trick ensures an elaborate retaliation, a belated one especially timed to coincide with her wedding to Clapshaw.

Sicily's love powders affect one man; Sut's revenge involves an entire neighborhood, gathered at old Burns's place for the wedding celebration. Although the organizers pointedly exclude him from the festivities, Sut goes anyway, "slungin roun" outside the house, especially bitter at not being asked inside "when they sot down tu dinner." He finds his instrument of revenge in old Sock, Burns's prize bull. Remembering some barnyard lore (when bulls "git intu tribulashun, they . . . beller, an' back,

an' keep a-backin"), Sut upends a feed basket over Sock's head. The
backing bull, after upsetting a dozen hives of bees, crashes through the
house, smashing furniture, crockery, and the laden wedding table. Trying to halt his bull, Burns finds himself astraddle Sock, and "Burns, bas-
kit, an' bull, an' bees" scare off all the other livestock and wreak painful
havoc on the party (*SL*, 90–94).

The bull, a traditional symbol of untethered power and sexuality, is
also Harris's symbol of gross, appetitive human nature. If we find Sut
using a bull to further his schemes in several well-known sketches, we
also find him trying to control a bull in the service of order in the little-
known "Taurus in Lynchburg Market." Even when Sut clearly acts to
tame chaos, his role is unappreciated by those who enjoy the privileges of
order. What he gets for his trouble is not help from the interested by-
standers, but their laughter as he stands ankle-deep in bullshit. The
episode confirms Sut—at once a "monument ove enjurance, parsavar-
ance, an' dam fool"—in the truth of unregenerate humanity (*SL*, 131).[19]
Back home, in no mood for intervention, Sut allows bull nature its instincts. He summarizes the stinging chaos at Sicily's wedding: the guests
"loped outen windows, they rolled outen the doors in bunches, they clomb
the chimleys, they darted onder the house jis' tu dart out agin, they tuck
tu the thicket, they rolled in the wheat field, lay down in the krick, did
everything but stan still . . . livelyest folks I ever did see." Immersing herself in the waters of the family's spring, Sicily mourns that "these yere
'bominabil insex is jis' burnin me up!" Now it is Sut's turn to taunt her—
"Yu hes got anuther new sensashun. . . . 'Gin 'em a mess ove SODY.'" The
wedding, he tells George, "wer the worst fur noise, disappintment, skeer,
breakin things, hurtin, trubbil, vexashun ove spirrit, an' gineral swellin"
(*SL*, 95–96).

Sut is consistently compelled to deflate pride in all forms, and though
Mrs. Yardley's sin might seem to be innocuous, it is an aggressive example of communal values that he resists. The "old quilt-mersheen" is the
very symbol of neighborly competition, and the product of her hands is
the chief icon of domesticity. As usual, it is Sut's language that reveals the
man. While he thinks highly of quilting parties as scenes for sexual dal-
liance, Mrs. Yardley's affair is too visibly directed toward the conventional end of marriage and family for her daughter. The suffocating effect
of her handiwork extends from her house (where every drawer in every
chest is packed with quilts) to her yard: "All the plow-lines an' clothes-lines

19. See Polk, "Blind Bull," 166–67.

wer straiched tu every post an' tree. Quilts purvailed. Durn my gizzard ef two acres roun that ar house warn't jis' one solid quilt, all out a-sunnin, an' tu be seed. They dazzled the eyes, skeered the hosses, gin wimen the heart-burn, an' perdominated" (*SL*, 139–40). Moments before Mrs. Yardley finds herself enmeshed (literally) in Sut's disruptive scheme, she is standing in her doorway with another woman "a-holdin a nine-dimunt quilt spread out, a-zaminin hit an' a-praisin hits perfeckshuns." Sut has rigged up all the quilts on display with "bark strings" which he has attached to a "skeery" horse; when he whomps the horse, chaos ensues. In the midst of the general disorder, Mrs. Yardley ends her "operashuns on this yeath" by moaning, "Oh, my preshus nine dimunt quilt!" Readers are often distressed at Sut's callous attitude toward Mrs. Yardley, whose death results from a prank that cannot even be called revenge for previous actions. Unlike Parson Bullen, Sheriff Doltin, the encyclopedia salesman, or even Sicily Burns, Mrs. Yardley is an impersonal object of Sut's practical joking.

There is, however, always more to Sut's instigation of disorder than payback. He is a self-appointed communal disrupter. If Parson Bullen is his primary target in the hell-serpent episode, the "hard shells" in the congregation deserve their embarrassment at his exposure because they are followers of his mean-spirited brand of religion. Unable to abide Sut's gospel of freedom, they must suffer too. In Mrs. Yardley's case, even though Sut tells George at great length precisely how he managed his trick with the "skeery hoss," he refuses to take blame (or credit) for the ensuing chaos: "the hoss did hit hissef," but Mrs. Yardley would have survived it "ef a quilt hadn't been mix'd up in the catastrophy." That is, excessive pride of craft invites retribution. Being a disinterested agent, which means his "conshuns felt clar es a mountin spring," establishes for Sut "a frame ove mine tu obsarve things es they happen'd" (*SL*, 137, 144).

His attack on Parson Bullen's place in the social scheme and his response to Sicily Burns's wedding dramatize Sut's important difference from Simon Suggs. Though it seems hardly credible, that old con man's chief tactic is his knack for ingratiating himself in society. It is, of course, a trait selectively applied: his truckling is always momentary and his bonhomie is always target-specific. Both Simon and Sut are equally shrewd in analyzing the intricacies of human behavior, and its patterns of repetition provide them with a major weapon—predictability. But Sut's assessment of human nature, disinterested as it generally is, seems to have little to do with integrating him into a communal life. As a harsh and candid truth-teller, he sees no need to use his superior psychological insight into how people think and act as a social lubricant. Sut is unable to flatter, cajole, or seduce.[20] His payback schemes, hatched in scrupulous detail, rarely have the dimensions of communal intercourse. In social situations, whether he is out for sex or revenge, his single mode is attack, and his style ranges from insinuating dismissal and scornful sarcasm to taunts and broadside vituperation. Sut has his traps, but they are never honeyed. Even his storytelling, the one activity that would seem to grow out of his mastery of human weakness, is anti-communal. His propulsive stories are aggressively self-generated, one-man performances, with rarely a nod toward collaboration, even with George; and he withholds most solicitous gestures toward his audience.

Sut battles the standard-bearers of community justice, morality, and civilized manners because they refuse to acknowledge their own shortcomings. His neighbors are as deserving of punishment as their leaders because they are thoughtless, conformist pawns of the enforcers, mostly sheriffs (and other emissaries of the court) and preachers (fraudulent custodians of religion). Because Sut is so fearful of them and their power in the community, the enforcers are his most frequent targets: they must be not merely combated but humiliated and stripped of their symbolic power. As Sut confesses, "ef enybody sez 'sheriff,' I feels skeer, an' ef I hears constabil menshun'd, my laigs goes thru runnin moshuns, even ef I is asleep" (*SL,* 229). Sut's dark mind, swarming with demons, compels him to almost ritualistically demonize the enforcers at every turn. As fear and resentment trigger his obsessive schemes, he sees himself as the sole opponent worthy to counter these regulatory agents. Prone to licentiousness on the sly, institutional leaders are depicted as vindictive censors all too eager to deny others free-floating desire, the anarchic liberty fantasized by all radical individualists. Sut would have understood a fellow Tennessean's attack on an unworthy politician. In 1845 Andrew Johnson charged a congressional candidate of going about his district with "a bottle of whiskey in one hand, and his prick in the other."[21]

With retaliation as both motive and mode, Sut is satisfied only when he successfully executes his plans for appropriate retribution. Only rarely do others exact the kind of punishment on wrongdoers that Sut

20. Carolyn S. Brown argues that Sut's posture of outlawry is belied by his apparent popularity among the "loafers and hunters" in his community, and that even his social superiors solicit his company and "encourage his tales and pranks." *Tall Tale,* 76 ff. *Human nater* presumably makes them enjoy his disruptions.

21. *The Papers of Andrew Johnson,* ed. LeRoy P. Graf, Ralph W. Haskins, and Patricia P. Clark (Knoxville: University of Tennessee Press, 1967), 1:216–17.

prefers. In "Frustrating a Funeral," for example, a cuckolded husband, Old Shockly, exercises the right of "shot-gun ritribushun" against a circuit rider, Parson Bumpas, "fur onsantifyin his wife." Says Sut, "nobody name Bumpas hes been seed 'bout thar since, 'sceptin sum littil flax-headed fellers scattered thru the sarkit, wif no daddys, an' not much mammys tu speak ove" (*SL*, 222). A hard-shell preacher invades the merry-making in "Bart Davis's Dance" by "a-tchunin up his sighin an' groanin aperatus, a-shakin ove his head," and generally lamenting the transgressions of "a wicked an' a parvarse generashun ove vipurs." Undeterred, one enraged female mounts the old preacher and pulls out hanks of his hair. On the following Sunday, because of this "fust-rate flax-puller," a bald and battered hard-shell preaches "bout the orful konsekenses ove Absalom's hevin long har" (*SL*, 184, 192).

While he admires these few counter-attackers, Sut depends mostly on his own initiative. He can enjoy his detachment in observing things as they happen because his hatching of schemes is intense and calculated. Disrupting Parson Bullen's sermon or Sicily Burns's wedding is the fruition of cool planning and controlled rage. Though calculation sets such schemes in motion, he can never predict how they will play out. The chaos itself, however, in Sut's telling, is recast as motion elaborately choreographed. Sut earns high marks for his rhetoric of mayhem, but this cynical master of revels brings his calculated effects to quieter moments as well. Unfolding not only from his recital of eruptive acts but also from his meditative analyses of human conduct is linguistic art, the closest Sut comes to performing a redemptive act.

ii.

A contemporary once commented—it may have been Bret Harte—that Sam Clemens never forgave anyone he had injured. Sut Lovingood would have understood how that might have been true. In "Contempt of Court—Almost," Sut begins his tale by admitting that he hates one man "jis' caze he didn't seem tu like tu hear me narrate las' night," but he is cheerful enough in his hatred because "that's human nater the yeath over, an' yere's more univarsal onregenerit human nater: ef ever yu dus enything tu enybody wifout cause, yu hates em allers arterwards, an' sorter wants tu hurt em agin. . . . Yu may be shamed ove hit, but durn me ef hit ain't thar." This admission leads to more specific instances of how the Old Adam thinks and feels, though he does not always act on his impulses:

"[W]hen yu sees a littil long laiged lamb a-shakin hits tail, an' a-dancin staggerinly onder hits mam a-huntin fur the tit, ontu hits knees, yer fingers *will* itch tu seize that ar tail, an' fling the littil ankshus son ove a mutton over the fence amung the blackberry briars, not tu hurt hit, but jis' tu disapint hit. . . . Ur a baby even, rubbin hits heels apas' each uther, a-rootin an' a-snifflin arter the breas', an' the mam duin her bes' tu git hit out, over the hem ove her clothes, don't yu feel hungry tu gin jis' one 'cussion cap slap, rite ontu the place what sum day'll fit a saddil, ur a sowin cheer, tu show hit what's atwixt hit an' the grave; that hit stans a pow'ful chance not tu be fed every time hits hungry, ur in a hurry?" (*SL*, 245–46)

In Sut's moral realism, innocence and ignorance are no better than guilt and experience; seemingly undeserved punishment and arbitrary hostility are tonic reminders of *how things are* in a hard world. They serve as moral lessons for disabusing both children and "grown up babys" of their high self-regard: "Whar thar ain't enuf feed, big childer roots littil childer outen the troff, an' gobbils up thar part. Jis' so the yeath over: bishops eats elders, elders eats common peopil; they eats sich cattil es me, I eats possums, possums eats chickins, chickins swallers wums, an' wums am content tu eat dus, an' the dus am the aind ove hit all" (*SL*, 228).

Happily, this despairing vision of the here and now, in which residual Calvinism and nineteenth-century naturalism intersect, fails to crimp Sut's remediary duties. Since he neither labors nor is heavily laden, this moral realist is remarkably alert to the potential emotional satisfaction of simply watching "onregenerit" human nature in action. Sut enjoys moments of comeuppance because they give psychological pleasure, confirming the gap between desire and fulfillment, perception and actuality. His most comfortable area of operation is in that gap. This world may be "all 'rong enyhow," Sut tells George, but to paraphrase one of Flannery O'Connor's con men, "it don't hold him back none."

What remains undisguised in the *Yarns* is the power of misanthropy, much of it derived from the kind of debased religious fervor that fuels mountain culture. It is only fair to point out that Sut is an equal-opportunity scourge. Though in "Frustrating a Funeral" he tricks a Negro corn thief by pretending to be the devil, he elsewhere plays upon the superstitions of both whites and blacks, and his schemes result in a wide fallout: among his victims are a doctor, an adulterer, a sheriff, and a doggery proprietor. In each instance, playing the devil is, as he sees it, a "christshun juty."

What also remains undisguised is Sut's strong misogynistic strain. Yet in a trilogy of stories Harris dramatizes two different extremes of femininity. "Rare Ripe Garden-Seed," "Contempt of Court—Almost," and

"Trapping a Sheriff" form a continuous narrative about the deception and promiscuity of women. The objects of Sut's wrath are Mary Mastin and her mother, the widow McKildrin, a "vartus petticoatful ove widderhood." The widow abets her daughter's adultery by helping to persuade her cuckolded son-in-law, a "bullit-headed yung blacksmith," that he is the father of the baby born early in his marriage while he was off working in Atlanta. The cheating wife and her duplicitous mother are not, however, the primary target of Sut's plans; true to his priorities, that role is reserved for Sheriff Doltin, generically the source of Sut's fear and loathing, and genetically the father of Mary Mastin's baby.

Sut interjects himself in this domestic affair not because he himself has suffered at the hands of these women, but because he wants to help the slow-thinking husband rectify their wrongdoing. Sut is fond of punishing people for simply being what they are: in this case, an "ole relick" of a mother-in-law out to "plaster humbug over a feller"; a promiscuous woman ("I went tu school tu Sicily Burns, tu larn 'oman tricks, an' I tuck a dirplomer"); and a sheriff whose corrupt use of power allows him not only to cuckold married men but also "tu sell out widders' plunder, ur poor men's co'n." All three deserve their comeuppance according to the Lovingood moral code, and when even the dense Wat Mastin finally concludes that "the sheriff an' Mary wer doin thar weavin in the same loom," Sut, in the role of helpful bystander, is on hand to direct the revenge (*SL*, 229, 242).

In a curious counterpoint, however, Harris offsets his pair of wicked women with two women of unquestioned virtue. One is the wife of Wirt Staples, the blacksmith's cousin. If Mary Mastin is a lying cheat, this woman is pointedly praised for not being generic—that is, she is *not* "one ove yure she-cat wimmin, allers spittin an' groanin, an' swellin thar tails 'bout thar vartu." Unlike Mary, this is a wife with "es true a heart es ever beat agin a shiff hem, ur a husban's shut." She is not only as "purty es a hen canary"; she is also fun-loving, readily entering into the revenge scheme with her husband and Sut (*SL*, 260).

The second exemplar of female virtue is Sheriff Doltin's long-suffering wife. In the terminal stages of a wasting disease, she sits in a rocking chair, "a new moon ove indigo onder her eyes," where "two lights shin'd, saft, like the stars above 'jis 'afore thar settin." In this extended portrait of a dying woman, Harris taps into the romantic iconography of the nineteenth-century sentimental novel, translating the conventional imagery into a Tennessee mountain version. Sut describes Mrs. Doltin's pale hands "not like snow, but like paint, and the forkid blue veins made hit look like a new map ove the lan' ove death." Her coughing is no louder than "a cricket chirpin in a flute"; her smile "kiver'd her feeters, like a patch ove winter sunshine on the slope ove a mountin, an' hit staid thar es steddy an' bright es the culler dus tu the rose." Mrs. Doltin, "dealin wif death now," must once have been "temtin tu men tu look at," but now "she's loved by the angils, fur the seal ove thar king is stamp'd in gold on her forrid." Her shoulder blades resemble "wings a sproutin fur her flight tu that cumfort and peace she desarves so well" (*SL*, 257).

This is the surprising element in this trilogy of tales: an unembarrassed tribute to a worthy woman in language that, however inflected by its mountain context, echoes a popular genre otherwise alien to the sensibility of the trickster hero. And it is not only the diction that is surprising. The narrative situation is also the stuff of nineteenth-century romance: a forbearing wife is slowly dying even as her philandering husband carries on the surreptitious courtship of a married woman. In Sut's makeup, poignant empathy is a contraband emotion. This moral vigilante, however, recovers from his momentary lapse, not by denying such sentiment but by putting it to work as an added *incentive* to trap the sheriff. When he finds himself with the Doltins at home, he is offended. The spectacle of the morally mismatched pair in the same room nudges Sut into a musing that is more familiarly judgmental: "As I look fus' at him, an' then at her, I'd swore tu . . . *two* hiearters, by golly: one way up behint that ar black cloud wif the white bindin fur sich as her; the tuther hiearter needs no wings nor laigs ither tu reach: when you soaks yersef in sin till yer gits heavy enuf, yu jes' draps in" (*SL*, 257–58). What follows is Sut's extravagant fantasy, a whimsical mini-narrative of Sheriff Doltin's entrance into hell.[22]

The virtuous alternatives may not erase the images of sullied young wives and conspiring matrons, but their very presence in Sut's moral universe is a reassuring note in the *Yarns*. And there is another rarity in the Sheriff Doltin trilogy. Here we find the only instance in which Sut becomes a wholehearted collaborator, actually trusting others to aid him in his schemes of retribution. His co-conspirators are Wirt Staples and his spunky, loyal wife; and if Mrs. Staples represents a sterling alternative to Mary Mastin, her husband becomes something more than a clever alternative to his "bullit-headed" cousin Wat. To no other acquaintance does

22. This fantasy, brief and vivid, is a likely source for Ratliff's extensive fantasy of Flem Snopes's negotiations with the Prince of Darkness in book 2 of Faulkner's *The Hamlet* (1940). Indeed, Ratliff generally is drawn as a more humane Sut whose search for justice is less rough-hewn.

Sut grant such unconditional approval. Wirt Staples stands as Sut's masculine ideal. His portrait of Wirt derives from what we have seen as a familiar antebellum literary type: the half-horse half-alligator. "I'se jis' a mossel ove the bes' man what ever laid a shadder ontu this dirt," boasts the drunken Wirt; "my breff pizins skeeters, my yell breaks winders, an' my tromp gits yeathquakes." Unlike the generic ring-tailed roarer, Wirt finds no challenger among what he calls "siterzens, an' sojourners in this half-stock't town"; but like Sut himself he finds the judge a satisfactory target. His vituperation at Judge Smarty, sitting in session at the courthouse, reaches elegant heights: "Cum out yere, oh yu coward's skeer, yu widder's night-mar, yu poor man's heart ache, yu constabil's god, yu lawyer's king, yu treasury's tape-wum, yer wife's dam barril ove soap-grease, saften'd wif unbought whisky" (*SL*, 251). It is easy enough for Sut, a self-admitted coward, to acknowledge the fact that rhetorical bombast—what he calls the "hollerin stage ove the disease"—can conceal an aversion to physical combat. But Wirt Staples is a doer as well.

When the "hollerin stage" brings out Sheriff Doltin and his deputies to quiet Wirt down, the ruckus turns physical. After "a rushin tugether ove depertys an' humans," Wirt rides his horse through the courthouse, flinging a leg of venison at the judge's head ("Thar's a dried supeaner fur yu"). The episode leaves the sheriff on his back, "his belly pintin up like a big tater-hill, an' eight ur nine more in es many shapes," and Judge Smarty drenched in a "half pint ove ink" from a broken inkstand. As an agent of disorder, Wirt Staples is clearly close to Sut's heart. Even being fortified by whiskey damages neither his truth-telling nor the clarity of his focus in disrupting courthouse proceedings. Sut gives this specimen his highest accolade:

> I'll swar, tu look at him, yu cudn't think fur the life ove yu, that he hed over-bragged a single word. His britches wer buttoned tite roun his loins, an' stuffed 'bout half intu his boots, his shut bagg'd out abuv, an' wer es white es milk, his sleeves wer rolled up tu his arm-pits, an' his collar wer es wide open es a gate, the mussils on his arms moved about like rabbits onder the skin, an' ontu his hips an' thighs they play'd like the swell on the river, his skin wer clear red an' white, an' his eyes a deep, sparklin, wickid blue, while a smile fluttered like a hummin bird roun his mouf all the while.

Sut can be excessive in his praise of Wirt as mountain stud because he is now partnered with this champion in the plot to punish Sheriff Doltin;

but his encomium to Wirt's general worth goes beyond self-interest: "When the State-fair offers a premin fur *men* like they now dus fur jack-asses, I mean tu enter Wirt Staples, an' I'll git hit, ef thar's five thousand entrys" (*SL*, 253). Even for a storyteller of such verbal extravagance, this praise stands as unique in the Lovingood *Yarns*.

iii.

Verbal extravagance is of course the heart of Sut Lovingood as both character and storyteller. Harris conceives his most memorable creation as a linguistic outlaw whose moral transgressions are somehow insepa-rable from his storytelling mode—uncaged, permissive, wanton. Sut's practical jokes, as we have seen, are most often revenge schemes; and though he is sometimes entangled in them (he describes himself, after all, as a "durnder fool" than anybody "outside a Assalum, ur Kongriss"), he craves direct action: physical bouts of disorder to expose the bad charac-ter of others to public view. His language, on the other hand, is at once less direct and more subversive. It is his second-best weapon (his legs are his first), testily directed at casual individuals who cross him. Primarily, however, it is an accommodating armor that protects him from those few friends and many foes who would incorporate him into a functioning community. Like all deviant heroes of comedy, Sut must be either re-formed by society or ejected from it. In Sut's case, that resolution of for-mal comedy is perpetually deferred. Forever resisting the reforms that would make him respectable, he also resists the best efforts of society's custodians to oust him from their midst. His very language is the token of a face-off that is never resolved.

Once he invented Sut Lovingood, Harris ignored the cultural utility of respectable English, pouring all his energy into the creation of a dialect that is so ideolectal that it emerges almost as a new language.[23] This

23. One of his contemporaries placed Harris's mode of writing in what he called "the cacography school," but in a real sense that is a school of one. Quoted in M. Thomas Inge, "A Personal Encounter with George W. Harris," *Lovingood Papers* (1963): 12. As James M. Cox wrote of Sut: "His dialect is practically a new language, for it is a deviation so remarkable that a reader must literally reconstruct his own language as well as Sut's if he is to understand it." James M. Cox, "Humor of the Old Southwest," in *The Comic Imagination in American Literature*, ed. Louis D. Rubin, Jr. (New Bruns-wick, NJ: Rutgers University Press, 1973), 111. For a linguistic study, see Carol Boykin, "Sut's Speech: The Dialect of a 'Nat'ral Borned' Mountaineer," *Lovingood Papers* (1965): 36–42.

unique humorist was a native of Allegheny, Pennsylvania, near Pittsburgh, the birthplace a generation earlier of the rambunctious riverman Mike Fink. Brought to East Tennessee as a child, he enjoyed less than two years of formal schooling, but during his various apprenticeships he familiarized himself with the Bible, Dickens, Byron, Burns, Longfellow, and other authors of "many Standard works."[24] If his pre-Sut sketches read like Longstreet, it is because he followed the Georgian's literary credo to record the "manners, customs, amusements, wit, [and] dialect" of his specific region. Like most of the humorists, Harris began his writing career by describing the "odd specimens" he found in his area; he alluded several times to the humorous contributions in Porter's *Spirit of the Times*, sketches that he clearly used as models. But by 1854, in the first of the Lovingood pieces, he was writing like none of his predecessors. With a total of only twelve lines narrated by the author, "Sut Lovingood's Daddy, Acting Horse" is an oral *tour de force* recited by a fiercely original mountaineer who with his long legs has stepped beyond "specimen" status. Since he supports unsocialized pleasure as a primary human goal, he must concentrate his attacks on people of stature—judges, tavern proprietors, some widows—and especially on society's chief protectors—preachers, sheriffs, and some mothers. Some are more heinous than others, but custodial figures are all hypocrites because they represent the social institutions that would curb Sut's radical will. His battle plan is to flummox the oppressors, the toadies, and the conventional tagtails whenever they are roused to impose their constricting views on others.

Almost as vigorous is Sut's war against fancy language, particularly the exaggerated idioms of "perlite" society. Those who use the formulas of refined speech—and they may not necessarily be pretentious—can expect physical or verbal assaults: Stilyards, the Yankee schoolmaster turned lawyer; Parson John Bullen; even George. Sut heaps scorn on the text of a lecture that falls into his hands, a "complikated sort ove dockymint" that ranges freely among a variety of topics: "the commit, Niagray Falls, the merlennium, hatchin chickins, fallin frum grace, an' makin mush outen sawdust, an' generally . . . everything on the A'mitey's green yeath." Presumably, the multiple topics don't bother him—the lecture's rich variety resembles a Sut yarn—but he professes to be puzzled by the document's language. It all seems to have been written "in sum furrin tung,

---

24. Donald Day, "The Life of George Washington Harris," in Caron and Inge, *Nat'ral Born Yarnspinner*, 43. For Harris's early years, see Rickels, *George Washington Harris*, 95–98.

sorter like Cherokee, wif a sprinkil ove Irish" (*SL*, 62–63). On another occasion, when a pompous encyclopedia salesman interrupts Sut's story
with the announcement that he wishes "to repose," Sut snaps, "Yu mus
talk Inglish tu me, ur not git yersef onderstood" (*SL*, 244).

By that standard, Sut's friend George doesn't always get himself understood. Like most of his predecessors, Harris makes his narrator little
more than a generic straight man; indeed, "George" is the most recessive
of all the humorous narrators. He is literally a facilitator, providing occasion
for and supplying information about his yeoman friend's oral performances. George's own single attempt at storytelling follows a normaliz-
ing pattern, but Sut quickly intervenes, mocking the fashionable mode of
circumlocution, correctness, and formal order—another example of why
Sut Lovingood's Yarns radiates such an aura of belligerent self-sufficiency.
Seeking the untold story behind a told one, Sut challenges George to "tell
ur treat" (though, he adds, "I think yu orter du bof"). At the insistence of
his audience, George begins the story of "Eaves-Dropping a Lodge of
Free-Masons." At the core of his rhetoric of respectability is the poeti-
cized nostalgia of popular Victorian discourse: "Those who remember
Knoxville thirty-five years ago, must still almost see 'the old Stone Courthouse,' . . . 'College Hill,' . . . Scuffletown Crick, and its walnut-trees, 'the
Dardis lot, and its forbidden grapes,' . . . the 'old church,' and its graveyard. 'Tis strange how faithfully memory paints the paths and places belonging to our boyhood" (*SL*, 114–15). An impatient Sut breaks in with
"Oh, komplikated durnashun! that haint hit. . . . Yu's drunk, ur yure
sham'd tu tell hit, an' so yu tries tu put us all asleep wif a mess ove
durn'd nonsince, 'bout echo's, an' grapes, an' warnit trees; oh, yu be
durn'd!" (*SL*, 114–16).[25] Sut promises that if he can have a drink to refresh
his throat, "I'll talk hit all off in English, an' yu jis' watch an' see ef I say
'echo,' ur 'grapes,' ur 'graveyard' onst." "So," George comments, "Sut
told it *his* way." His refusal to naturalize the Sut texts leaves that deviant
style in undisputed command of the discourse. As Sut himself personi-
fies a cranky *non serviam*, so his style brooks no conciliation, no compromise with the mainstream policy of assimilation and interpretation.

25. If the narrator in Baldwin's "Justification after Verdict" is impatient with Paul
Beechim's reverence for Knoxville, Sut goes further here and in "A Razor-Grinder in
a Thunder-Storm," where he muses that a grinder "cudn't hev cum tu a better place"
than Knoxville "fur sweepin out the inside ove stuft up fellers' skulls clean ove all ole
rusty, cob-web, bigited idears, an' then a fillin it up fresh wif sumthin new an' activ."
He adds that after a while there he would likely say to himself, "*If* I gits away alive,
durn ef ever I cum *yere* agin" (*SL*, 61).

Sut's complaint is that George's fashionable sensibility ruins the narrative sense, but the narrator's inability to get on with his story is related to his weakness for a romantic idiom that has long since lost any hearable freshness. George speaks *nonsince;* Sut speaks *English.* In the George-Sut dynamic, the author-approved level of usage is smudged. By allowing his narrator to indulge in the degenerated romanticism of midcentury, Harris performs a speech action that is at once indulgent and self-mocking. Clearly, linguistic common sense lies not with his narrator but with his renegade hero. George's lugubrious nostalgia embodies both an appropriate attitude in Victorian America and the diction and syntax that honored it. From Sut's perspective, to follow the respectable course is "tu put us all asleep."[26]

I'll talk hit all off in English. Sut seems to offer unaffected bareness to counter what he sees as overrefined indulgence: his plain to George's fancy. Harris's great achievement with the speech of his yeoman hero, however, was to steer clear of yeomanlike simplicity. Sut is conceived outside nineteenth-century notions of primitivism, commonplaceness, spontaneity, and most of the other romantic categories that located virtue and linguistic innocence in the folk. When Sut tells George he has been "fixin" Mrs. Yardley "fur rotten cumfurtably, kiverin her up wif sile, tu keep the buzzards from cheatin the wurms," the narrator is forced to translate: "Oh, you have been helping to bury a woman." Here the plain speech is George's. Never mind Sut's professed admiration for George's mode: "Now why the devil can't I 'splain mysef like yu? I ladles out my words at random, like a calf kickin at yaller-jackids; yu jis' rolls em out tu the pint, like a feller a-layin bricks—every one fits" (*SL,* 134). If George rolls his words out to the point, his method is nevertheless crafted and mechanical, like bricklaying; Sut's own random ladling out of words is spontaneous and biological. The contrasting metaphors are resonant—as they always are in Sut-speak. For a moment Sut has us believing that his

26. Harris himself followed that course, as Walter Blair noted. In a late story, "Bill Ainsworth's Quarter-Race," he indulges (without self-mockery) his nostalgia for life before the war. Writing as a kind of mountain Stephen Foster, he summons up a montage of images stripped of wartime bitterness in a tone that suggests the resignation of a mind no longer able to eke out comfort in moral realism. It is the same mood that he gives Sut in a surprisingly mellow passage in which the lanky rebel remembers a horse race in 1833 at which "fat ole wimmen" offered cider, ginger cakes, and marriageable daughters to winking young men in short sleeves. In the sobering years of Reconstruction both the acerbic Sut and the respectable George came to sound alike. See Walter Blair, "Harris' Best: Bill Ainsworth's Quarter-Race," *Lovingood Papers* (1965): 16–25.

earthiness is simplicity itself (suggested by the animal imagery that constitutes the matrix of his world), that he does indeed talk like a "natural man." Sut's mode in fact is as adorned and embellished as pretentious high style. It is crafted, homespun posturing.

Sut's lingual ingenuousness can even be used as a tool for fomenting trouble. To avoid any misunderstanding between an Englishman and a Frenchman, Davy Crockett once turned himself into an unlikely explicator of the text. A more likely Sut Lovingood offers himself as an etymologist simply to stir up misunderstanding. The party in "Bart Davis's Dance" degenerates into a brawl fueled partly by wordplay. When the preacher, using flattery to cover his spoilsport function, tells the host that he is "hosspitabil," the thin-skinned Bart is insulted: being called "pitabil" is worse than being called a "hoss." Sut encourages the misinterpretation: *pitabil,* he argues, "is a sorter Latin tail stuck tu hit so yu moutn't onderstand; hit means pitiful hoss in Inglish" (*SL,* 186).

The prose generally is dense because Sut *likes* words. They tumble "permiskusly" over each other, agitating and altering expected meaning before they sort themselves out in a few recognizable patterns that any rhetorician can distinguish: aphorisms, catalogs, classifications, biblical phrases buried in erotic contexts, idiosyncratic metaphors, periodical clauses. Harris is a born-again Adam prodigally naming his world through his articulate spokesman, whose prose is in an idiom so rich it can afford to be squandered. The surfeit of Sut's style, stemming from metaphorical logic, is nurtured by a near-inexhaustible inventiveness. There is a dazzle in Sut's prodigal style, an exuberant abundance that belies the material poverty of his situation.

No Sut sampler can incorporate all the fervent creativeness of Harris's fictional hero. But almost any excerpt, randomly chosen, reveals Sut's favorite stylistic devices. His fondness for bold images and surprising analogies:

Jis' 'bout the time I wer ketchin my breff, I tho't I'd swaller'd a thrashin-meersheen in full blast, wif a cuppil ove bull-dorgs, an' they hed sot intu fitin; an' I felt sumthin cumin up my swaller, monstrus like a hi pressur steamboat. (*SL,* 81)

Hits widders, by golly, what am the rale sensibil, steady-goin, never-skeerin, never-kickin, willin, sperrited, smoof pacers. (*SL,* 141)

His rhetorical weakness for items in a series:

> Thar wer chickens cut up, an' fried in butter, brown, white, flakey, light, hot biskit, made wif cream, scrambil'd aigs, yaller butter, fried ham, in slices es big es yure han, pickil'd beets, an' cowcumbers, roas'in ears, shaved down an' fried, sweet taters, baked, a stack ove buckwheat cakes, as full ove holes es a sifter, an' a bowl ove strained honey, tu fill the holes. (*SL*, 261)

> [Sal Yardley] b'leved strong in married folk's ways, cradles, an' the remishun ove sins, an' didn't b'leve in corsets, fleas, peaners, nur the fashun plates. (*SL*, 137)

And his canny adaptation of country sayings:

> Oh dam ef ole muther-in-lors can't plaster humbug over a feller, jis' es saft an' easy es they spreads a camrick hanketcher over a three hour ole baby's face. (*SL*, 234)

> [Q]uick es an 'oman kin hide a strange hat. (*SL*, 239)

No trait, however, so individualizes Sut-speak as his inventive classifications. In a sketch from 1858, a remarkably detached Sut describes his fellow passengers waiting to change trains at a rain-drenched station house at Bull's Gap,

> sum a cussin tharsefs, sum a cussin Bull's Gap, sum a cussin wun another, sum a cussin the lake they stood in, sum a cussin that are shanty tavrin, sum a cussin fur supper, sum a cussin the strike nine snake whisky, an all a cussin thar levil best. One . . . feller frum Nashville endorsed all the cussin, an then sot in an cussed the world; sed hit wer all vanity an vexashun ove spirit—a dam onmitigated humbug frum the center all round tu the sea. (*HT*, 145)

When Parson Bullen strips himself in the pulpit to escape the lizards, Sut categorizes all the women in the congregation who witness the event. Some scream ("they wer the skeery ones"), some laugh ("they wer the wicked ones"), some cry ("they wer the fool ones"), some try to avert their blushing faces ("they wer the modest ones"), some seek out the naked preacher ("they wer the curious ones"), some cling closer to their sweethearts ("they wer the sweet ones"), some pray while their eyes follow the old parson ("they wer the 'saitful ones"), and the rest do nothing ("they wer the waitin ones; an' the mos' dangerus ove all ove em") (*SL*, 57–58). The uniqueness of Sut-speak is not its grounding in the vernacular—all Southwest humor has that strength—but in the aesthetic calculation of that linguistic base. Behind much of the vernacular is an adaptation of what has been called "high-spirited *enumeratio*," a device to which Sut is addicted.[27] Further, Harris does not simply recall and repeat folk wisdom, but extrapolates adages into startling modifications. Mountain imagery is filigreed with rococo conceits, puns, and homophones; sentences fall compulsively into homely rhetorical parallels enriched by scraps from earlier and statelier prose.

Most Sut admirers are surely right to single out Harris for his candor in treating sexual matters. It would be misleading, however, to associate that attitude with the liberation we now experience in the contemporary media, the kind that values frankness over reserve. Though Harris's achievement in such matters is substantial, the truth is that his attitude comes across largely through style. Sut-speak may be vernacular, but it is not plainspoken. It is a style that puts on airs, not to enforce propriety but to strip away its polite obliquenesses. Some of Harris's contemporaries—Crockett, Thompson, and Lewis, among others—also suggest the complexity, not the simplicity, of vernacular idioms. As we can see even in the arch self-parody of rural folk idioms on old television shows such as *Hee Haw* and *The Dukes of Hazzard*, metaphorical expressions in performance are neither economical nor succinct, but artful constructions in the service of country arcana, truths that can pass as country versions of the reality principle.[28] Harris fulfills his mission through the "realistic" modification of nineteenth-century vernacular metaphors and his canny instinct for double-entendre misspellings ("inexpressibles," "insex," "suckit-rider," "the wet seckshun ove an 'oman's constitushun"). These draw attention to the gap separating the euphemisms of respectable style from those of the backwoods, which, though artful, aggressively celebrate the most visceral of human functions.

There is yet another dimension of Harris's Sut-speak that merits praise. In most humorous sketches, the felt and heard presence of the narrator, whatever measure of empathy with the storyteller he reveals, is a significant psychological device as much as a technical one. This chief listener is always interposed between storyteller (whose idioms he hearkens to) and reader (whose interest he courts). In such classic sketches as Thorpe's

27. J. W. Smead, *The Theophrastan "Character": The History of a Literary Genre* (Oxford: Clarendon Press, 1985), 193.

28. As Ray B. Browne noted, Harris's pieces are not "*folk* humor or *folk* lore." The folk "cannot and do not stack double-jointed adjectives upon one another until they reach Glory," as Harris does in crafting Sut's style. "Marrying a Substitute," *Lovingood Papers* (1964): 22.

"The Big Bear of Arkansas" and Hooper's "The Captain Attends a Camp Meeting," the narrating voice as counterpoint to raw frontier speech is a comforting presence for the reader as well as a convenience for the author. But, as we have seen, Harris's narrator has only the slightest claim on our attention. He is neither authorial interpreter nor moral buffer. That structural difference, as Harris shrewdly knew, makes these pieces more immediately felt.

Sut Lovingood's Yarns is not a unique example of the recessive narrator. A few earlier pieces, which Harris probably knew, similarly reduce the narrator to function. Alexander McNutt's Jim and Chunkey stories (1845) open directly with backwoods speech, relegating the narrator (the "Captain") to the role of occasional questioner, a device that elicits just enough interchange to make the sketches dialogue rather than monologue. John S. Robb's "Nettle Bottom Ball" (1847) is pure monologue—opening, developing, and ending with the single colloquial voice of one Jim Sikes. Except for a concluding paragraph, Francis J. Robinson's "Rance Bore-'em" (1853) is a dramatic monologue by the title character, captured at an unspecified site where the contributions of others (presumably tall-tale tellers as well) are only implied, as are their exasperated exchanges with this "Loafer Bore." Each of Rance's topping tales begins with a verbal introduction such as "Gentlemen, speaking of hunting, when I was in Texas . . ." or "I can tell you, gentlemen, a better ice-cream story than that . . ." (Cohen, 384–85). As interposing agent, the narrator is well-nigh superfluous in all these pieces because the language needs so little glossing. The idioms in Robb and McNutt are unabashed but uncomplicated backwoods talk; Robinson's Rance speaks in the faux-elegant patterns of the frontier blowhard.

As we know from Edmund Wilson's famous revulsion, the omission of a buffer sensibility between Sut Lovingood and the reader is not an aesthetic decision that is universally admired. A number of readers who are otherwise well disposed toward the rambunctious crudities of Southwest humor draw the line at Harris, as the one author too permissive, with a shabby hero too morally degrading even for those who like backcountry louts. (These readers can find corroborating discomfort in Sut's virulent Lincoln-hating diatribes, which Harris penned during the Civil War.) Reading Sut-speak is not effortless, even for those who like the pungent immediacy of his voice. We may not fully understand Sut's peculiar language, just as we may not fully understand how it threatens, but by stripping away the carefully observed distance that the chief listener provides in the classic forms, Harris forces us into an in-your-face encounter with his figure of disorder. Sut's stories, that is, do not function as liberating agencies. They rather force teller and audience into a kind of yoking, a baleful enchainment to which the reader succumbs even while resisting. Who really wants to be yoked to such a creature as Sut Lovingood? In his preface to the *Yarns*, the calculating author-hero predicts accurately that his book will not "sit purfeckly quiet ontu the stumicks ove sum pussons" (*SL*, x). If he did not invent the recessive-narrator technique, Harris surely perfected it. Yet he aesthetically compensates for the undiluted impact of mountain vernacular with Sut's oracular artifice. Were Sut-speak not so arcane, so constructed an artifact in itself, the threat of vio-lation—the kind of contamination that Wilson railed about—would be even greater.

iv.

Most of Sut's neighbors unthinkingly subscribe to the hierarchical principle that makes them defer to preachers and sheriffs. Like most citi-zens of the republic everywhere, they indulge their appetites, even when that runs counter to the social codes of the enforcers, when jealousy, greed, or lust compels them. Yet they do it surreptitiously. Harris makes Sut not a representative figure but an exceptional one; his is a unique presence whose theology is uncomfortably excessive—a downward refinement as grotesque as his physical appearance. One of the marks of his uniqueness is the seamless continuity of his character and personality: his deeds stem directly from his beliefs. As the enemy of consensus, Sut neither in-gratiates himself with his neighbors nor dissembles in order to gratify his yen for revenge, sex, or amusement. His refusal to impersonate may not be high-minded morality, but his actions are conspicuous because of that jarring fact. Like many other humorous sketches, Harris's are sited in a nineteenth-century context in which donning disguises, assuming false identities, and playing theatrical roles for the purpose of conning others are accepted methods for undermining a society officially dedicated to order and moral progress. Sut's very presence in his community is a re-buke to those methods. Others' practical jokes, as we have seen, may be just as mean-spirited, but Sut's effrontery is in performing them by stand-ing before his fellows—and the reader—as himself, that rare creature whose deeds follow rigorously from his declared principles. He is a trick-ster, but the shock of his tricks is that they are engineered without guise.

The tendency of Southwest humor, even in Longstreet, is to disabuse the reader of the idea of a moderate, normative world interpreted by sentimentalism. It is not so much that this kind of humor strives toward some goal of realism—a materialistic or naturalistic bottom line, a Hobbesian representation, or even a claim to neutral authenticity in rendering things the way they are. It is rather, as Simon Suggs shrewdly perceives, a struggle against compassion, a resistance to the sympathy and fairness that a democracy entertains on a quasi-official level. Harris was the only one of his fellow humorists to systematize the instinct for denigrating sentimentality. By creating Sut Lovingood as a sustained character, he could attain the force of concentration that other authors were unable to achieve through fragments and occasional repetitions. Sut is profoundly troubling because he is fleshed out by internal principles and complementary external acts that are focused and consistent. Because of the nature of these principles—what I call his theology—he is our antagonist as much as he is Sheriff Doltin's.

Sut is unique among the comic figures because his creator conceived him as such. We know that, like Hooper's Simon Suggs, Sut was fashioned after a well-known local figure.[29] Having a real-life prototype, however, provides no surety that an author will achieve vivid and coherent characterization. Neither are the *Yarns* something found. Perhaps Harris's categorical assertion that his sketches "are all genuine folklore tales" was meant to ease the misgivings of the editors of the *London Folklore Journal* in 1867. We need not, however, believe that "not one" sketch was "cooked"—indeed, that no "part of one" was "an invention"—to understand the powerful role of Sut Lovingood and his *place*.[30] Whatever their sources, the two most accomplished creations in the antebellum South were the result of their authors' genius in conceiving characters and executing characterization.

What distinguishes Sut from Simon is his belligerent selfhood. Both figures share a choleric view of the world, not grim enough to be formally naturalistic (in the mode, say, of Frank Norris), but forlornly resigned to disappointment. They allow themselves to be ingeniously

29. That figure was Sut Miller, "an East Tennessee rascal whose obituary records that he 'died ignobly . . . after many conflicts with man and beast'" (Cohen, 194). See Ben Harris McClary, "The Real Sut," *American Literature* 27 (1955): 105–6; Jack P. Solomon, "Simon Suggs," in *Tallapoosa County: A History* (Alexander City, AL: Service Printing, 1976), 72–73.

30. Harris quoted in F. L. Pattee, "The Development of the American Short Story" (1925), in Andrew Levy, *The Culture and Commerce of the American Short Story* (Cambridge: Cambridge University Press, 1993), 42.

receptive to the opportunities that occasionally offer themselves, while knowing full well that such opportunities are surprising anomalies. Only Sut, however, leads the examined life; only he understands himself within an order of other selves, marshaling his energies to probe that order in all possible ways so that it might succumb, if only temporarily, to his own yearning will to pleasure. Only Sut has a selfhood sufficiently developed to demand recognition from a world, chary of such aggression, that dreads disruption. It is not merely preachers and sheriffs that want to lock Sut away; they are merely the most prominent representatives of a norm inimical to his imperious drive for autonomy. The anarchy that his aggressive interventions create is what a later generation would call collateral damage. His primary motive—unfettered autonomy—fuels the action in his untiring battle against the barriers that work to contain him.

George Washington Harris is the only obsessive among the humorists. His driving, repetitive quality emerges directly from the character of Sut Lovingood, who, once Harris created him, was similarly invested with obsessional energy to engage the demons of his world. It is not that other notable characters in the canon of antebellum humor are lacking in coherence and integrity—in addition to Hooper's Simon, Thorpe's Jim Doggett and Lewis's Madison Tensas stand out as figures whose typal consistency also suggests untapped depths in their creators. But only Sut is inscribed with a loopy rectitude that links his transgressive acts with a rigorous scale of values, an aesthetic quality that almost justifies his ethical single-mindedness.

In a curious way Sut's obsessional quirks seem to exist as eruptions of an abstract, fairy-tale code operating above and beyond human authority. Unlike the Suggsian narrative, Sut's has no practical chronology. Harris's priority, even in the sketches that place Sut in a family context, is neither progression nor development, but simply movement. Laws of physics are verbally photographed, as it were, often in a kind of predetermined slow motion, as repetitive cycles of action. The timeless effect of the narration also informs the ethics of the writing. Harris positions his cranky hero in a vaguely alternative order, as the emissary of some kind of atavistic moral system erupting in the comfortable fastness of the Tennessee mountains. Beyond its backwoods setting, there is nothing quaint about Sut's environing community. Its strong conformist group values and its weakness in dealing with their violations are found in all organized settlements, primitive and sophisticated alike. Search-and-destroy is an inevitable mission of any society emerging into civilization—

that is, it must do whatever is necessary to enforce herd morality and majority justice. In Harris's ethical standoff, Sut is the logical target of the mission, but he is protected by an alternative order that is at once divine and demonic.

In the eternal present of Sut's world, his libidinal desires will never abate. Sicily Burns, widows, and assorted wives will never cease to entice him, and his most fervent impulses will never be satisfied. A compensatory balance also governs his activities: preachers and sheriffs will never entrap Sut, whose role is to continue to prod, taunt, tease, and harass the petty regulators of ordinary, civilized, respectable society. If he can never realize his fantasy of sex shorn of artificial restraints, he can at least indulge his aggression against the social supervisors of those restraints. He will always frustrate the guardians of morality and justice; though he may often be tarred by the swipe of their brushes, he will use his natural-born instincts and long legs to escape their punishing feathers. A moral economy gives Sut license to play hob with the forces that would restrict his unencumbered desire while withholding satisfaction of his ultimate dream. Sut's festivals of transgression have his creator's blessing; but, even more, Harris suggests that Sut has the blessing of a primitive system that allows him to oppose a Christianity and a majority justice turned rotten by corruption. The agents of institutional society—preachers, sheriffs, parents of eligible girls, peddlers, mothers-in-law—therefore make it their job to neutralize Sut's disruptive energies. Unreliable, untrustworthy, unrepentant, Sut is the enemy among them.

Most of the humorists were occasionally subversive of the very order they submitted to. Even the Whiggiest among them understood that the pursuit of pleasure was a kind of rebellion against a society that, at whatever stage or however governed, had to be wary of those who put too much store in a freedom-loving body. Only Harris, however, confronted the stable order and sniped relentlessly at its enforcers. Even as a partisan Democrat, there was something more than an oppositional voice in Harris. His Sut Lovingood is a cultural outlaw who stoutly resists the coming of homogenized society—and the respectability that all the humorists foresaw (and mostly endorsed).

Afterword ✦

Historically, Southwest humor is a body of writing that was born in the breakdown of hierarchical social relations and the (perceived) triumph of egalitarian ideals. Vertical orders of authority never disappeared, of course, even as the horizontal dispersal of population strained traditional sources of power in the older east. Though they were privileged enough not to make too much of egalitarianism as a principle, the humorists, as we have seen, wrote with the assumption that the marginal geography (natural and human) they made their subject was fleeting, that it was destined to be assimilated into a future whole. They were thoughtful enough to appreciate a volatile society that opened opportunities for all men to secure both property and happiness, but as part of the "functional elite," they were also realistic about the tendency of class structures to hedge those opportunities and resume the hegemony of the already affluent and powerful.[1]

The social lesson behind much yeomanry humor is this: to enter the ranks of bourgeois civilization, backwater communities must forswear anarchic individualism, at least the kind that prospers outside the guises of cooperation and majority rule. Competition still dominates, and it is

1. The shift in national power structures in the expansionist antebellum years is one of the subjects in Daniel Walker Howe, *The Political Culture of the American Whigs* (Chicago: University of Chicago Press, 1979), and Major L. Wilson, *Space, Time, and Freedom: The Quest for Nationality and the Irrepressible Conflict, 1815–1861* (Westport, CT: Greenwood, 1974). Functional elites were merchants, professionals, and civil servants as well as planters.

expected to flourish within the institutions invented to nourish cooperation, but it operates under the banner of moral and social consensus. The
authors' careers coincided with a fluid economy, spurred largely by territorial expansion in which "rising" was both expected and praiseworthy.
That psychological climate encouraged all the usual signs of success that
mark changed conditions—new and improved homes, more fashionable
clothes, travel vacations. And attitudes. The predictable social price of
lording it over one's fellows was the recoil of resentment. In a pattern frequently recorded in antebellum personal histories, when success was followed by failure that resentment was so socially damaging that flight to
new places was often the only recourse.

By their very nature, American elites were always a minority, always
dependent upon the quiet acknowledgment of their status by a compliant majority. In the Flush Times era of settlement, elites were an even
more precarious minority, and the majority even less compliant. Social
ranks were as volatile as the economy which, more than ever before, determined them. Although the humorous writing of the time accepted the
middle-class view that rising from the ranks was a laudable ambition, it
also tapped the bittersweet fruits generated by that success: envy and resentment. If the quasi-literate commoners lent support to the new men
who bought land and slaves, lawyered and judged, lent money, preached,
doctored, and ran for public office, that support was always provisional.
Even in the face of the mutual benefits guaranteed by a deferential society, honoring community leaders was a rare expression fraught with
barely concealed suspicion. Gratitude was a scarce emotion, and loyalty
was both brief and shallow.

As historians point out, social demarcations among planter and yeoman classes were never rigid, in part because a planter could be expected
to have yeoman kin within his own extended family, and in part because
certain smart and lucky yeomen could be expected, over a decade of effort, to be transformed into planters themselves. On the other hand, such
success was not the rule. Even in the fluid economies of the migration period and beyond, and in the opening up of Anglo enterprise in the New
Southwest after the Mexican War, yeoman families tended to remain yeoman in both fact and outlook.[2]

Insofar as they claimed a place for themselves, the real elites were of
insufficient interest to attract the authors. The movers and shakers of the
Old Southwest are not players in the humorous writing. Except through

2. Avery O. Craven, *The Growth of Southern Nationalism, 1848–1861* (Baton Rouge:
Louisiana State University Press, 1953), 11–12, 23.

indirection, land speculators and their agents, political leaders, and gentleman planters in that found world do not exist in the world the humorists made. Their shadowy presence is suggested only by the recurrent appearance of frauds, make-do aspirants to the elite, reflecting both a belief in possibilities in the new country and a suspicion that, whoever asserts authority, *pretend* is the rule of the game. What both A. B. Longstreet and W. T. Thompson show in their writing about backwoods Georgians is the relativity of such categories as *quality, people of consequence, aristocracy.* Modest attainments in wealth and learning can earn reputations for wide and deep knowledge, political power, and psychological insight into human behavior. What is high profile in acts of veneration and respect, however, is also high profile in acts of retaliation and revenge. In a society that takes to heart egalitarian biases in all phases of life, the most cherished assumption is that all men must be equal in pursuit of a better life. Even though the humorous writing is the product of an (ambiguous) elite, some of the authors cannily adapt the dramatic structures of their sketches to accommodate the changed dynamics of actual social conditions. Like Mark Twain, who would later make it a vital ingredient in his work, Joseph G. Baldwin and Henry Clay Lewis use themselves as active participants, carefully casting their personas as would-be elites, tyro professionals who in their incompetence are sometimes humiliated by lesser humans. Most of the authors honor the egalitarian assumption of "the Democracy" even when some of them, as good Whigs, cannot approve its more strident manifestations.

Baldwin suggests that second-tier community leaders in the "hell-carnival" of Flush Times were often vulnerable to the sport of commoners, not only because their social and moral roles invited revenge, but also because their responses to being made objects of sport were so predictable. As the target of a shotgun blast, Tommy Peabody, a Yankee schoolmaster, feels a few pellets graze his buttocks as he flees danger, suffering, notes Baldwin, "in that particular region in which he had been the cause of much suffering in others." Not merely the perpetrators but the community at large are amused by the pedagogue's "clapping his hands behind" him and "bellowing out that the murderer had blown out his brains!" (*FT,* 64–65). A good Methodist, Burwell Shines is at once victim, witness, and performer at the trial of two ruffians who have attacked him—pursuing the "shadbelly with his praying clothes on!" Determined to use wit and ridicule to make "as light of the case as possible," the waggish defense attorney is preempted in his plans when Shines makes his appearance and inadvertently puts the courtroom in a comic uproar. For his testimony he has exchanged his praying clothes for attire befitting the "magnitude and dignity of the occasion": a bell-crowned hat of "nan-keen-colored nap an inch long," a single-breasted coat "with new brass buttons," a vest of "bluish calico," nankeen pants "that struggled to make both ends meet," and a cravat a little "smaller than a table-cloth." With his hair "roached up" and standing "as erect and upright as his body," Shines delivers a turgid oration in accents "modulated according to the camp-meeting standard of elocution." With the crowd having "laughed them-selves hoarse already," the witness in effect takes "all the wind out" of the witty counsel's sails (*FT,* 106–13).

Although the ignorant of a community are the likeliest targets for prac-tical jokes—the greenest are logically the most gullible—simple hood-winking brings only garden-variety satisfaction to the perpetrators and their audience. It takes a little learning and lots of unearned pride to in-spire amplified self-confidence. The comeuppance of affected schoolmas-ters and pious church types, no less than that of Mo Mercer and Dr. Peter Jones, is energetically welcomed, not passively appreciated—commu-nally approved, not merely tolerated. In the new country, aping one's betters, a time-honored comic device for deflating inferiors, begins with Longstreet and his skewering of pretentious village matrons, their ad-miring swains, and countrified dandies. The authors who follow him eagerly exploit the transition from backwoods to settlement culture, de-picting soirees with milling, awkward guests; musicales featuring lim-ited local talents; teas and dinners made to order for exposing both the ignorant and the know-it-alls; entertainment-hungry backwoodsmen who confuse theatrical conventions with reality; and cotillions in which imported forms are mangled by rural dancers still addicted to reels and pigeonwings.

Sensitive to manifestations of power, earnest readers a century and more later tend to see the taint of elitism behind such country satire more clearly than they do the "fun of the settlement." Though we may deplore it, nineteenth-century readers accepted as a matter of course the fact that culture on the margins is a subject inviting humorous exposure. Village pretenders are funny because their aping of cultural betters in estab-lished society is so transparently amateurish. The very act of exposure is necessarily elitist: there must be some prior notion of "betters" and "es-tablished" for the imitation to be seen as funny. Insofar as *Georgia Scenes, Streaks of Squatter Life,* and *The Drama in Pokerville* are self-conscious prod-ucts, their authors are elitist. But that term, with all its formidable mod-ern baggage of snobbish, magisterial pride of position, is finally not very relevant to Longstreet, Robb, or Field, or indeed to any of their peers.

Whoever the designated narrator may be in sketches of social exposure, the point of view always implies a democratic take on pretension. Tit-for-tat, the ancient tribal justice that civilization never quite eradicates, is common enough in all the humorous writing. Practical jokes generate other practical jokes, and one-upsmanship is expected in scenarios in which the bitten bites back. Yet such eruptions of *human natur* are usually contained by civilized codes monitored by the consensus of villagers. As we have seen, George Washington Harris's "repellent" hero is conceived outside the consensus of his social betters. As an oppositional figure with an integrity that nobody values, Sut Lovingood stays true to his counter-mission: to respond to the appetitive self-interest of the species without cover of respectability. Many of the inventive figures in the humor are mild subversives within a consensus compact, but their assaults are less brutal than Sut's. Yet even gentler modes of skewering, as we see in Baldwin's "Justification after Verdict," allow cultural custodians no honorable way out of the embarrassments they bring on themselves.

This interpretive predictability is another clue to the capacious, unideological humanity of the humorous authors. Their alert antennae are positioned to locate, amid the promiscuous mix of the population, the cultural squatters who are too quick with their claims of responsible possession. Even the historical leading men in *Flush Times* wear slightly corroded armor. Although the authors have a higher tolerance for illiterate backwoodsmen than for quasi-literate pretenders, their perspective is equable, restrained, even generous. Their acts of exposure are governed more by the indulgent leniency of Irving than by the derisory admonishment of the British travel writers. They can be genial and liberal about the gross pretenders in the cultural game because, at bottom, they themselves share something of that assertive need. The "new men"—doctors, lawyers, merchants, certain denominational ministers, and the occasional editor, banker, and forward-looking planter—provide an educated leadership in cultural networks. All are attracted to, even if they never join, literary clubs, library and thespian guilds, mechanics' associations, reform leagues, and lyceums. The humorists can be so authoritative in sketching out yeoman versions of such groups because of their attraction to similar groups. If pressed, they might readily admit that *they too* are leading men, but most of the time they only tactfully offer themselves as cultural spokesmen. The superior figure, however modestly he carries his superiority in the social mix, is *never* exempt from deflation.

Bibliographic Note ᚎᚎᚎ

For many years the most convenient source of references to humorous writing from the antebellum South has been the anthology *Humor of the Old Southwest*, edited by Hennig Cohen and William B. Dillingham. The third edition of this volume, which appeared first in 1964 as a Houghton Mifflin Riverside Edition, was published in 1994 by the University of Georgia Press. The editors' bibliography is still useful for both general studies of the humor and items on individual authors.

Although the antebellum newspaper humorists from the Old Southwest have fascinated literary historians for more than a century, critical appraisals of the writing are of more recent vintage. An important collection that samples both scholarship and criticism is M. Thomas Inge's *The Frontier Humorists: Critical Views* (Hamden, CT: Archon Books, 1975). Work by most of the names we still associate with this indigenous literature are represented—Walter Blair, Franklin J. Meine, John Donald Wade, Donald Day, Milton Rickels, and John Q. Anderson are among those who pioneered the Southwest humorists' legitimacy in the academy. A new generation of scholars and critics from assorted disciplines appears in a more recent collection edited by Inge and Edward J. Piacentino, *The Humor of the Old South* (Lexington: University Press of Kentucky, 2001)— these include J. A. Leo Lemay, William E. Lenz, David Rachels, Johanna Nicol Shields, David C. Estes, and others. The student of this humor could ask for no more fruitful place to begin than these two volumes. Both contain convenient bibliographies, but in the 2001 collection Piacentino incorporates the relevant data from the Cohen-Dillingham anthology and other checklists in "A Comprehensive Bibliography," a compilation of editions and reprints of anthologized collections since 1975, general books and articles on the humor, listings of pieces on individual authors, and a section on the impact of this writing on modern literature and popular culture. This 46-page bibliography is essential for any reader interested in antebellum southern humor. Continuing work in this field can be found in annual numbers of *Mississippi Quarterly, American Literary Scholarship: An Annual,* and the *MLA International Bibliography of Books and Articles on the Modern Languages and Literatures.*

As Mary Ann Wimsatt reminded us many years ago, the greatest need for students of this humor is reliable texts of the major humorists. Unlike our canonical American writers, the humorous authors wrote and published their pieces in a volatile and largely ephemeral newspaper environment; even the most popular humorists, who gathered their sketches for book publication, had to contend with a market of overlapping publishers, expedient editors, and notoriously sloppy typesetters. The more ambitious of these writers—Thomas Bangs Thorpe and Joseph Glover Baldwin, for example—were as concerned as Cooper or Hawthorne that their work be presented in accurate texts and attractive formats, but as "popular fare" even their work often suffered from inattention and dubious marketing strategies. Today those who are attracted to this field generally must still settle for corrupt texts. Over the past decade or so, there has been some movement to correct this gloomy situation. For example, David C. Estes's *A New Collection of Thomas Bangs Thorpe's Sketches of the Old Southwest* (Baton Rouge: Louisiana State University Press, 1989) is a superb edition produced with the kind of scholarly care normally expended on volumes by more familiar authors, and David Rachels's fine critical edition of Augustus Baldwin Longstreet's *Georgia Scenes* (Athens: University of Georgia Press, 1998), complete with sketches that never appeared in the various editions of this bellwether book, is indispensable. Interested readers and scholars alike must be grateful for modern editions of such figures as David Crockett, H. E. Taliaferro, C. F. M. Noland, Joseph G. Baldwin, Henry Clay Lewis, John S. Robb, and Johnson Jones Hooper; these are convenient and useful, but most are reprints with critical introductions and annotations. No final assessment of the value of the Southwest humorists can be made until we have better versions of what they actually wrote.

Since I conceived this book as a study of contexts—historical and cultural—that encompassed writing from the Old Southwest, the work of scholars specializing in nineteenth-century America has been invaluable, as my footnotes attest. These scholars' conclusions about relations between North and South, slavery, the status of women and minorities, migration patterns after the War of 1812, regional economies, and the politics of Whigs and Democrats often mesh but almost as often contradict the sentiments and attitudes found in the writing of the humorists.

Like everyone else in the field of nineteenth-century American culture, I have been rewarded and surprised countless times by Tocqueville's *Democracy in America* (1835). Almost as fascinating, however, is George Wilson Pierson's *Tocqueville in America* (Baltimore: Johns Hopkins University Press, 1996), a detailed account of places and informants in the French commissioner's itinerary. In *The Cotton Kingdom* (1861; reprint, New York: Da Capo Press, 1996), I found that Frederick Law Olmsted managed to surmount his obvious biases to supply valuable items on specific persons and sites that are available nowhere else. The most convenient overview of the region in its early years is *The Old Southwest, 1795–1830: Frontiers in Conflict*, the work of two seasoned historians, Thomas D. Clark and John D. W. Guice, published first in 1989 and in revised form in 1996 (Norman: University of Oklahoma Press). My footnotes indicate my indebtedness to this fine and readable book. The studies that I found to be most useful on specific topics were Lewis O. Saum's *The Popular Mood of Pre–Civil War America* (Westport, CT: Greenwood, 1980), a remarkable investigation of private forms—chiefly letters and diaries—penned by a wide spectrum of ordinary citizens from all regions of the country; Albert J. von Frank's *The Sacred Game: Provincialism and Frontier Consciousness in American Literature, 1630–1860* (Cambridge: Cambridge University Press, 1985); Michael Oriard's *Sporting with the Gods: The Rhetoric of Play and Game in American Culture* (Cambridge: Cambridge University Press, 1991); and Michael Allen, *Western Rivermen, 1763–1861: Ohio and Mississippi Boatmen and the Myth of the Alligator Horse* (Baton Rouge: Louisiana State University Press, 1990). One multidisciplinary work that transcends my chronology is David Hackett Fischer's brilliant *Albion's Seed: Four British Folkways in America* (New York: Oxford University Press, 1989).

In this rich welter of diverse methodologies and arguments I have of course found no consensus, but I have benefited enormously from consulting approaches and conclusions different from my own. If *Fetching the Old Southwest* fails to reconcile these disparities into a neater profile of the era, I hope it at least demonstrates the complexities of a period in American culture that is often reduced to its political contours. Several recent books have broken new ground in ways that my footnotes cannot fully suggest: Kenneth S. Greenberg's lively *Honor and Slavery* (Princeton,

NJ: Princeton University Press, 1996); Daniel Justin Herman's *Hunting and the American Imagination* (Washington: Smithsonian Institution Press, 2001); and Conevery Bolton Valenčius's *The Health of the Country: How American Settlers Understood Themselves and Their Land* (New York: Basic Books, 2002). Despite their differing methodologies, these volumes show in readable and imaginative ways what cultural studies can achieve. Finally, despite the humorists' lack of interest in the railroad (see Chapter 8), the national romance with antebellum technology suggests that a cultural survey of train travel would also be revealing of the era's social complexities. Such a work might serve as a prequel to Joseph R. Millichap's fine revisionist study of the railroad and its technology in the twentieth-century South, *Dixie Limited: Railroads, Culture, and the Southern Renaissance* (Lexington: University Press of Kentucky, 2002).

Index